Universal Design

Universal Design

Creating Inclusive Environments

Edward Steinfeld

Jordana L. Maisel

JOHN WILEY & SONS, INC.

This book is printed on acid-free paper. ♾

Copyright © 2012 by Edward Steinfeld and Jordana L. Maisel. All rights reserved.

Published by John Wiley & Sons, Inc., Hoboken, New Jersey.

Published simultaneously in Canada.

No part of this publication may be reproduced, stored in a retrieval system, or transmitted in any form or by any means, electronic, mechanical, photocopying, recording, scanning, or otherwise, except as permitted under Section 107 or 108 of the 1976 United States Copyright Act, without either the prior written permission of the Publisher, or authorization through payment of the appropriate per-copy fee to the Copyright Clearance Center, Inc., 222 Rosewood Drive, Danvers, MA 01923, 978-750-8400, fax 978-646-8600, or on the web at www.copyright.com. Requests to the Publisher for permission should be addressed to the Permissions Department, John Wiley & Sons, Inc., 111 River Street, Hoboken, NJ 07030, 201-748-6011, fax 201-748-6008, or online at http://www.wiley.com/go/permissions.

Limit of Liability/Disclaimer of Warranty: While the publisher and author have used their best efforts in preparing this book, they make no representations or warranties with respect to the accuracy or completeness of the contents of this book and specifically disclaim any implied warranties of merchantability or fitness for a particular purpose. No warranty may be created or extended by sales representatives or written sales materials. The advice and strategies contained herein may not be suitable for your situation. You should consult with a professional where appropriate. Neither the publisher nor the author shall be liable for damages arising herefrom.

Wiley publishes in a variety of print and electronic formats and by print-on-demand. Some material included with standard print versions of this book may not be included in e-books or in print-on-demand. If this book refers to media such as a CD or DVD that is not included in the version you purchased, you may download this material at http://booksupport.wiley.com. For more information about Wiley products, visit www.wiley.com.

Library of Congress Cataloging-in-Publication Data:

Steinfeld, Edward.
  Universal design : creating inclusive environments / Edward Steinfeld, Jordana L. Maisel
      p. cm.
  Includes bibliographical references and index.
  ISBN 978-0-470-39913-2 (cloth); 978-1-118-16680-2 (ebk.); 978-1-118-16681-9 (ebk.); 978-1-118-16845-5 (ebk.); 978-1-118-16846-2 (ebk.); 978-1-118-16847-9 (ebk.)
 1. Universal design.   I. Maisel, Jordana L..   II. Title.
NA2547.S74 2012
729—dc23
                                                              2011028935

Printed in the United States of America

10 9 8 7 6 5 4 3 2

Contents

Foreword xi
Preface xiii
Acknowledgements xvii

CHAPTER 1: Barriers and their Social Meaning 1
    Design as Evolution 1
    Barriers as a Universal Experience 3
    Barriers in Intellectual Life 4
    Social Functions of Space 8
    Socio-spatial Order 12
    Origins of Universal Design 15
    Summary 24
    Review Topics 24
    References 24

CHAPTER 2: Defining Universal Design 27
    Introduction 27
    Emergence of Universal Design 27
    Definition 28
    Origins 30

Modernism and the Modernist Style 31
Critiques of Modernist Style 33
Return to Human-Centered Design 34
Summary 42
Review Topics 42
References 42

CHAPTER 3: The New Demographics 45

Demography for Universal Design 45
Uses of Demography in Design 48
Beneficiaries of Universal Design 49
Demography: Points to Remember 60
Summary 62
Review Topics 63
References 63

CHAPTER 4: Practicing Universal Design 67

Introduction 67
Universal Design as Innovation 67
Tools for Increasing Adoption 70
Introducing Universal Design to Practice 82
Improving Practice 86
Summary 91
Review Topics 91
References 92

CHAPTER 5: Design for Human Performance 95

Introduction 95
Anthropometry 96
Biomechanics 103
Perception 108
Cognition 119
Summary 129
Review Topics 132
References 132

CHAPTER 6: Design For Health and Wellness 137
Introduction 137
What are Health and Wellness? 139
Injury Protection 140
Disease Prevention 142
Low-Resource Settings 147
Mental Health 149
Health Impact Assessments 152
Designing for Health and Wellness Guidelines 152
Summary 153
Review Topics 153
References 153

CHAPTER 7: Design for Social Participation 159
Introduction 159
Social Construction Theory 160
Interpersonal Interaction 163
Access to Resources 167
Segregation and Clustering 172
Design Participation 177
Summary 181
Review Topics 185
References 185

CHAPTER 8: Public Accommodations 187
Introduction 187
The Purpose of Accessible Design 188
Universal Design Strategies 197
The Future 213
Summary 214
Review Topics 220
References 220

CHAPTER 9: Housing 223
    Evolution of Accessible Housing Policy 223
    Community-Based Rehabilitation and Special-Purpose Housing 236
    Neighborhood Context 238
    Summary 242
    Review Topics 243
    References 244

CHAPTER 10: Home Modifications 245
Danise Levine

    Introduction 245
    Target Populations 246
    Purpose of Home Modifications 248
    Common Needs and Solutions 253
    Home Assessments 261
    Barriers to Service Delivery 263
    Policy 265
    Knowledge Needs 268
    Summary 269
    Review Topics 270
    References 271

CHAPTER 11: Universal Design and the Interior Environment 275
Mary Jane Carroll

    Introduction 275
    Wayfinding 276
    Acoustics 279
    Lighting 282
    Color 287
    Furnishings 292
    Floor Coverings 299
    Summary 302
    Review Topics 304
    References 304

CHAPTER 12: Product Design 307
Heamchand Subryan

    Introduction 307
    Assistive Technology 310
    Knowledge Translation Problem 312
    Changing Marketplace 316
    Smarter Products 321
    Case Studies 327
    Summary 334
    Review Topics 335
    References 335

CHAPTER 13: Public Transportation and Universal Design 339

    Introduction 339
    Background 339
    Access to Public Transportation 340
    Components of Public Transportation Systems 342
    Progress around the World 362
    Summary 363
    Review Topics 364
    References 365

INDEX 369

Foreword

This superb and well-illustrated book is intended not only for design students but for all who care about how we access, use, and enjoy the environment. Universal design differs significantly from what we have known in the United States through the language and litigation on accessibility in that it sets a paradigm of design excellence benefitting all users. The authors observe that barriers are part of our lives and deeply rooted in our artistic and social consciousness. Although usability, in a general sense, has been a part of design since the origins of civilization, crafting the built environment to reduce the undesirable impact of real and metaphorical barriers in order to facilitate social participation is a relatively new field of study, with roots in the civil rights movement and efforts to achieve social justice. Its impact is directly proportional to the degree we experience limitations in independence and social participation. Thus it is no wonder that this movement started among people with disabilities, whose engagement in society was restricted by artificial barriers in every aspect of their lives. But, attentiveness to civil rights drives design to benefit the many, not just the few. The lessons learned apply to design at a much broader level where achieving these goals for all is much more complex than simply complying with accessibility laws. The fundamental importance of the field is demonstrated by the fact that creative designers have thought about these ideas for a long time although they may not have articulated them. The authors note the example of the Guggenheim Museum in New York City, constructed before there were accessibility codes. Frank Lloyd Wright's vision for the building was nothing less than making art itself easier to access and more enjoyable for all museum visitors.

We have moved beyond the historical base and original delineation of universal design, which Ron Mace originally defined as the design of products and environments usable by all without the need for special accommodations. The authors propose a new definition, "a process that enables and empowers a diverse population by improving human performance, health and wellness and social participation." This new perspective supports an explicit relationship to sustainable design and active living, two more established progressive design initiatives. The emphasis on these two issues is a recurrent theme in the book and their importance is reflected in emerging design practices. For example, conferences held by the AIA New York Chapter under the banners of Fit-City and Fit-Nation have stressed the adoption of universal design to insure that sustainable and walkable cities and communities enable all to benefit from a healthier lifestyle and more physical activity. This new definition also eschews an overly utopian perspective by putting the emphasis on the process rather than an idealistic but long-range goal.

Of paramount importance are the ethical and pragmatic responsibilities design professionals share when designing towns, urban centers, buildings, and products for increasingly diverse social communities. Making the necessary adjustments to address demography and the cultural possibilities of a pluralist society is not a question of tweaking existing formulations, but starting fresh, recognizing that the stress of contemporary life can be mitigated by design that places a high priority on meeting the physical, psychological, and social needs of all citizens. The authors, an architect and an urban planner, identify a clear need for an interdisciplinary and evidence-based perspective that goes beyond traditional silo-oriented education and professional practice. Design that is "human-centered" transcends this segmentation by focusing attention on the needs that are common to us all. In fact, economic and demographic factors intersect in ways that require multidisciplinary initiatives, universal in outlook and inclusive in intent. In particular, the aging of our societies demands that the current economic downturn should not be used as an excuse for poor design and indifference. In fact, if we do not implement universal design now, the economic burden of an aging society will be even greater in the future.

The authors and contributors to the book are colleagues at the Center for Inclusive Design and Environmental Access (IDeA Center), which is a leading center for research and development in universal design in North America. They stress the importance of developing a "community of practice" in universal design that will educate, enhance, and empower a new generation of thought leaders in both academia and practice. They also argue for improved communications and pedagogy, illustrating efforts in this country and abroad, to make universal design a more central focus of design education, both in professional schools and through continuing education. Universal design education must focus on innovation and creative problem-solving. It can be clearly demonstrated that the incorporation of universal design attributes makes projects more sustainable, more durable, and more valuable. But, to accomplish these objectives, it is not merely a question of enhancing prior definitions of accessibility, but re-thinking how design can be beneficial for the long term.

The book builds upon the foundation formed by seven well-established Principles of Universal Design through the formulation of the Goals of Universal Design. These Goals clarify outcomes for practice and tie those outcomes to existing knowledge bases. The authors review the literature on human performance, health and wellness, and social participation to identify key evidence-based guidelines for design practice. They also provide hundreds of examples of universal design from all the design disciplines. One of the most interesting current efforts described in the book is the initiative to develop voluntary performance standards and a certification system for universal design modeled after similar successful efforts in the field of sustainable design. This effort can serve as the focus for the development of a community of practice, creating connections across design disciplines, between researchers and practitioners, and between the professional community and academia.

Whether in product design, building systems or public infrastructure, to advance the field of universal design it is crucial to both identify best practices and, as the authors put it "document the benefits of universal design solutions." This extraordinary book does both well in language accessible to both student and seasoned professional.

RICK BELL, FAIA

Preface

The field of universal design represents a convergence of several threads of design practice with a focus on usefulness. Since the origins of the design professions, theorists have acknowledged that usefulness is a critical factor in the success of any design, be it a city plan, a building or a sign. But, in the history of design, usefulness is rarely the central focus of attention in the design professions. Even during the early twentieth century when the phrase "form follows function" was uttered frequently by leading architects, there was more attention given to "form" than "function." Most architects who adopted that credo were concerned more with the concept of "integrity" of form, e.g. expressing function, than they were with actually making buildings more useful for the people who lived in them.

What about the people who did not live in them? People without decent housing, people with disabilities who could not enter most buildings, people isolated in institutions, factory workers, middle class housewives, children, refugees, etc.? Few design professionals thought about them unless they got a good commission to design a large institutional building or housing project for the "poor or unfortunate." Even then, the focus was more on pleasing the client or glorifying themselves than on the welfare of the inhabitants. Remember Howard Roark, the prototype for the late twentieth century architect?

The new century demands that we start thinking differently. For the last twenty years, we have witnessed the transformation of sustainable or "green" design, re-invented by a few "idealists" in the late 1950s, into a mainstream endeavor. This movement is the first example of design for all of us because it puts the focus on protecting the natural world in which we all have a stake. Notwithstanding the importance of protecting the environment, we have to ask whether protecting people is not just as important. If protection of people had been the focus of design from the origins of the discipline, we believe we would naturally have practiced sustainable design early on, simply because it was good for species survival.

There are three major trends that are operating together to change design culture. First, a diverse, consumer oriented culture on a global scale is emerging, starting with the high-income countries but spreading rapidly everywhere. This culture puts greater value on personal development and values difference rather than avoiding it. Those who participate in this culture are much better informed about their options and willing to change and be changed, in other words, to engage in transformative processes. Second, due to biomedical science and public health the world is aging rapidly. In the developing world, the older population is increasing even more rapidly than in the developed world. An interest in preserving quality of life during old age is increasingly driving decisions of all kinds. Third, economic forces are demanding higher standards of usefulness. Sustainability (eliminating waste) and better information are making performance more important in purchasing decisions by individuals and organizations.

The concept of universal design emerged through the disability rights movement, an example of the first trend above. Early experience with the concept has led leaders in the field to expand beyond those origins and to identify connections with design for aging, social sustainability and user centered design. At the same time, other proponents of design to improve people's lives are recognizing the value of the universal design paradigm. Thus, in writing this book we decided to avoid looking backward and look forward instead. We investigated how universal design could evolve and become more central to design thinking in the mainstream, with an admiring eye to how that happened with sustainable design. There are differences, of course. One can easily measure and quantify the benefits of sustainable design but we do not yet have all the tools we need to do the same with universal design. The cost of not paying attention to the environment is demonstrated clearly every day all around us—more pollution, less fish, higher fuel costs, etc. The cost of not practicing universal design is not as easy to perceive right now. One has to parse through statistics and learn how to look at things from the perspective of others. However, as with sustainable design, once we change our perspective and learn how to see the evidence, the future becomes clear.

We believe we are close to a watershed moment. Whether they know the term or not, the work of leading architects and design firms reflects the adoption of universal design concepts. Innovation in design practices occurs because good designers pay attention to what is going on around them. They may not necessarily label what they do, but they do it nevertheless. While writing this book, we also were completing an educational project that involved visits to other design schools and discussions with their faculty about how to bring universal design ideas to their curricula. One of the faculty members we consulted with listened a while and a look of awakening appeared on her face. She said, "We are already doing this! We just don't call it that." And it was true. As we speak the world is changing and we change to adapt to it, some faster than others. This book provides a cohesive yet open-ended view of the field with a futures perspective. It is said that good education is subversive; one of our major goals is to provide a tool for change.

The book is organized into three basic parts. The first part establishes a foundation and rationale for the universal design paradigm. This includes an essay on the concept of barrier, a chapter defining universal design as we see it evolving and one on the practice of universal design. The third chapter in the first section utilizes demography to demonstrate the trends that will drive the adoption of the concept. The second part of the book gives a summary of the three underlying knowledge bases for universal design practice. These are design for human performance, design for health and wellness, and design for social participation. The last part of the book provides summaries of practices in universal design across a broad range of topics. There are chapters on public accommodations, housing, home modifications, interior design, product design, and transportation. This structure is amenable for use as a textbook in a course on universal design, or, across several courses. It is also amenable for use in courses focusing on different disciplines using the first two parts in their entirety as the core material and one or more from the last part as an introduction to a more in depth examination of the discipline. For the instructor, we have prepared review topics in each chapter but there is also an instructor's guide available online from the publisher with supplementary materials, including quiz questions, sample assignments, and suggested media.

In summary, this book was developed to lead the way rather than reflect back upon what has already happened. We hope it will inspire others to bring their own wisdom and insights to the developing community of practice in this field because, as the reader will see, the development of this design paradigm will lead in many new directions and there is room for everyone. In particular, we hope it will lead to the evolution of universal design as an inclusive paradigm where all proponents of design to improve the quality of life for every citizen of the planet can find an intellectual home. Universal design is a search for design strategies that bring benefits for all.

—THE AUTHORS

Acknowledgements

The authors are indebted to several colleagues who contributed significantly to the production of this book. Danise Levine, Heamchand Subryan, and Mary Jane Carroll each wrote a chapter in the book. Jonathan White and Heamchand Subryan found, compiled, created, and managed the figures and graphics. Susan Hunter conducted much of the demographic research and developed many of the insights included in Chapter 3. We are also grateful to Victor Paquet for critically reviewing a preliminary draft of Chapter 5. Beth Tauke and Scott Danford have engaged with us in constant and creative dialogue on the definition of universal design, strategies for teaching, and examples of practice.

We must acknowledge all the leaders of the universal design movement throughout the world. Our interaction with them over the last 20 years was instrumental in forming the ideas presented in this book and we are indebted to this band of committed individuals for embracing an idea well before it was mainstream and investing their time and energy in building the foundation of a global initiative.

The development of this book was partly supported by the Rehabilitation Engineering Research Center on Universal Design in the Built Environment, a center of excellence grant provided by the National Institute on Disability and Rehabilitation Research (NIDRR). We thank NIDRR for funding the Center for Inclusive Design and Environmental Access (IDeA Center) generously for the last 12 years and recognizing the importance of dissemination and education as a critically important adjunct to research and development activities.

Barriers and Their Social Meaning

Design as Evolution

Much of life is about overcoming barriers. Every organism, from lowly one-celled animals to human beings, exists by interacting with its environment. This interaction includes moving from one place to another, creating a space for the self, lifting a load, or learning how to use a tool. Our ability to interact with the environment is, to a great degree, determined by our characteristics and abilities, such as height, strength, and intelligence, but also by the degree of resistance and its corollary, the support the environment provides in reaching our goals. The relationships humans have with the environment are much more complex than those of other organisms. We have reasoning abilities and tools that give us more freedom of interaction and a wider range of adaptive responses. Ants, for example, use instinctual foraging behaviors to find food and bring it back to their nests. If an ant encounters an obstacle in its path back to its nest, it may climb over or around it. If an observer drops more obstacles in its path, the ant continues to use the same limited set of behaviors to overcome the barrier. Humans, however, have a much larger range of adaptive behaviors. Faced with a situation similar to that of an ant, a person might remove the obstacle, use a map to find an alternative route, or find another source of food. People also can psychologically adapt to the presence of a barrier. A good example is the prisoner who overcomes physical confinement by exploring an interior intellectual world.

Human social groups have developed sophisticated methods of adaptation to overcome the resistance of environments. Design is an active, purposeful adaptation method that people use to adjust their world to their needs. Through design, humans both remove barriers and develop supportive environments, products, and systems to facilitate achievement of their goals. Design interventions have evolved with human experience and the development of technology. For example, one of the first tools early humans learned to use was a sharp-edged rock. Over time, some people discovered that such a rock could be enhanced by fashioning a sharper edge. Later humans discovered that fashioning a handle on part of the rock increased the comfort of using such a tool. To hunt larger game that would provide more food to support a growing community, others discovered that adding a long handle to the rock added leverage and reduced effort. This was the first prototype of the modern ax (Williams 1981). Figure 1–1 shows this evolution.

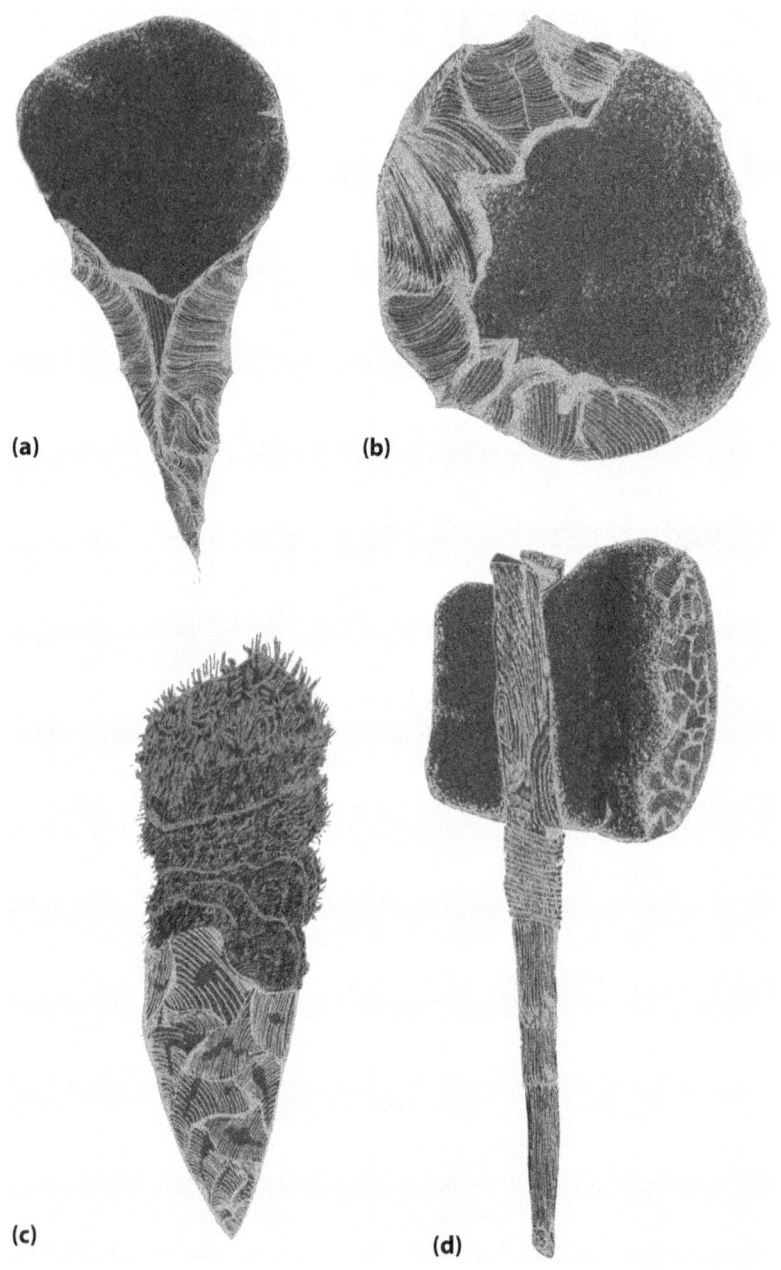

Figure 1–1: Evolution of the ax. Four examples of axes including (a) a rock fragment with sharpened edges, (b) a rock with a sharpened edge and a smooth area for easy grip, (c) a rock with sharpened edges partially covered with hide for a handle, and (d) a club with long wooden handle for leverage.
Source: Adapted from Williams (1981)

Technology can be a barrier as well as a facilitator for usability. For example, the flat-bottomed skiff is a traditional boat design that is ideally suited for use by shell fishers in shallow tidal water. The invention of the outboard engine offered opportunities for fishermen to be more productive, but mounting outboard engines on flat-bottomed skiffs made them unstable (Williams 1981). A new type of boat needed to be designed to overcome this problem. The Boston Whaler is an example of a modern design that works well in shallow water with an engine.

Adaptation is not always successful from an individual and/or community perspective. It can put an individual at risk, lead to maladaptive behavior, or put other people at risk. For example, if residents of a neighborhood adapt to violence by isolating themselves in their homes, afraid to go out in public, both the residents' quality of life and the health of the community suffer. Design interventions can also lead to negative consequences. Large residential institutions, such as poor houses, mental hospitals, and penitentiaries, were a late nineteenth-century adaptation to urbanization and the resulting increase in crime, poverty, and disability concentrated in cities. But these facilities created enormous barriers to independence and mental health, stigmatized their residents, and corrupted their caretakers (Foucault 1973; Rothman 1971; Sommer 1969). As knowledge about these problems developed in Europe and North America, most of these institutions were dismantled, and new policies of community living and short-term treatment emerged.

Within the context of human evolution, the purpose of design is to help the species increase its survival potential. Design is more than aesthetics, which is primarily a surface effect. Its fundamental purpose is to change the form and organization of our material world and even change how we interact with it. For example, changing the size of schools or developing a gestural language to control computers are both design decisions, even more important than the decision about what color, material, or shape to make the building or computer enclosure. Design is a "soft" tool that extends the effectiveness of human adaptive behaviors.

An environment can provide different degrees of support. Often people are satisfied with lower levels of performance than what could be achieved. Sometimes they accept barriers for some people but not for others. They may even intentionally create barriers to separate certain people from the larger community or one group from another, as in the case of the residential institution. Other goals, such as aesthetics or cost, sometimes may take precedence over the degree of enablement a built environment, product, or system provides.

Universal design, at its most elemental level, seeks to make our built environment, products, and systems as enabling as possible; in other words, it seeks both to avoid creating barriers in the first place and, through intelligent use of resources, to provide as much facilitation as possible to reach human goals. Social and technological trends have converged to put more value on enabling design. We discuss the underlying reasons for these trends in Chapter 3.

Barriers as a Universal Experience

Because the elimination of barriers is so central to the universal design philosophy, it is important to begin this book with an examination of barriers as an experiential and intellectual phenomenon. Doing this will help the reader to understand the potential scope of universal design and the reasons why it is so important in contemporary design thinking.

Any obstacle we encounter can be a barrier to reaching our goals. Barriers may not be complete obstacles but simply resistance of some sort. For example, although a narrow doorway may not entirely prohibit a crowd of people from exiting, it could increase the total time it takes to exit. In an emergency, this can be fatal for some occupants. Other types of barriers are less severe; nevertheless, if many, many minor barriers are encountered in a relatively short period of time, they can be annoying, deter people from reaching goals, and result in the behavioral adaptation of avoidance. For example, driving a car in a congested area for a business appointment may result in many small inconveniences that add up to missing the appointment. A few experiences like that in the same area could result in a decision to seek opportunities elsewhere.

In everything we do, there are barriers: barriers to movement, barriers to space and time, barriers to access, barriers to communication, to perception, or to expression. Although blockades such as walls or locked gates that totally preclude access are obvious, other barriers are not always that easy to perceive. Less obvious examples are steep slopes and inclines, channeling that forces choices and limits spontaneity, discontinuity in flows, distances separating people or things, shortages of space that require people to take turns, noisy places that limit conversation, and cultural markers with little physical substance but high prohibitions on entry. In the world of products, we encounter such barriers as complex operating procedures, excessive forces of operation, ill-fitting equipment and furniture, and things that make us look awkward and out of place in the eyes of others.

A barrier does not always totally exclude use. It can make use difficult, or it can also be a selective barrier that allows use by one group of people and not another or that regulates access by schedule. Moreover, a barrier may be supportive in one sense and restrictive in another. Crime scene tape is an interesting example. It is a very flimsy barrier but one that is very powerful because of its cultural significance and legal implications that force people to avoid an area without significant physical means. Some law enforcement authorities can pass through the marked-off scene while others can enter only with permission. Cubicle farms are another, less obvious type of barrier. They support increased communication among workers on one hand because there are no full-height walls or doors, but they limit our ability to communicate our unique personality, thus creating fodder for a genre of humor about cubicle culture.

If we reflect about encounters with barriers as a general class of experiences faced in daily life, we can conclude that they all impede or restrict the flow of action, information, and communication. Barriers are significant to us in many ways. They can block us out, slow us down, divert us from our goals, cause fatigue, limit our opportunities, or restrict our ability to express ourselves. Barriers can even be used to control people to make them follow a predetermined course of action determined by others, reducing their ability to make choices. Consider, for example, a voicemail menu system or a security checkpoint that forces us to complete a series of meaningless or even degrading tasks to obtain services or benefits.

Barriers in Intellectual Life

While we normally think about barriers as part of our everyday life, they play an important role in our intellectual life as well. The sculptures of Richard Serra are some of the most powerful examples of barriers in art. He constructs huge planes of steel to divide space. When experiencing these sculptures in person, the walls of crude steel are overwhelming. They heighten our perception of barriers and demonstrate the power to separate and divide. Serra's *Tilted Arc* was originally installed as a site-specific work in Federal Plaza, New York City (Figure 1–2).

Figure 1–2: *Tilted Arc*, a sculpture by Richard Serra. Constructed in 1981, this sculpture is a 120-foot- (36.6-m-) long slab of curved steel, 12 feet (3.66 m) tall and 2.5 inches (6.35 cm) thick. It was designed to bisect a public plaza in front of the Jacob Javits Federal Building in Manhattan.

The office workers who regularly used the space complained that the work ruined the plaza, cut off views, created an obstacle to pedestrians, and was a hiding place for criminals. After a long, protracted legal battle, eventually *Tilted Arc* was removed, even though the public had paid for it through a percent-for-the-arts program (Senie 2002). The reaction that this sculpture provoked illustrates the power that barriers have to affect our lives and the anger that people can feel when restrictions are imposed on them. Even though Serra's work was critically acclaimed, the regular users of the space experienced its direct impact, which overshadowed any value it had to them as art. New Yorkers put a high value on accessibility to public places. It is possible that *Tilted Arc* would not have provoked such a reaction in other locations. The story of *Tilted Arc* demonstrates the interpretive component of barriers. One person's art can be another person's symbol of government interference in his or her life.

By its very nature, two-dimensional art creates barriers to perception. That is the source of its power. A two-dimensional image cannot be explored; the artist presents only one perspective to us, and it communicates only a specific intent. The frame of a painting and the bounded edge of a photograph limit the viewer's access to information. We cannot see what is happening outside the frame. Moreover, the static image prevents us from seeing, exploring, and knowing what is beyond the forms within the frame of the art piece. A good example is *Melancholy and Mystery of a Street* by Giorgio de Chirico (Figure 1–3). In this painting, the shadow on the ground is a strong clue to the presence of something outside the frame, something quite foreboding. So much detail is left out of the representation of buildings and space that the painting creates the feeling of the city as an enigma, an unknown place where potentially dangerous events may occur. The fragile image of the child projects a sense of vulnerability that we often feel in some urban streetscapes.

Figure 1-3: *Melancholy and Mystery of a Street* by Giorgio de Chirico, 1914. The painting depicts an urban streetscape with a silhouette of a young girl pushing a hoop along a street. Out of view is a mysterious and ominous figure depicted only by a shadow falling across the street.
Source: Image redrawn by authors.

Physical restrictions are often used as metaphors in literature. One of the most interesting examples is the metaphor of overcoming resistance as a transformation in understanding. In the novel *Snow Falling on Cedars* by David Guterson, a relentless snowstorm serves as a metaphor for the gradual shift in the perception of history and fact surrounding a murder trial. As the snowstorm advances, the world of the island on which the story takes place presents more and more resistance to the activities of daily life. The chief protagonist, Ishmael (undoubtedly a reference to the narrator in Melville's *Moby-Dick*), the town's newspaper publisher and its only reporter and photographer, doggedly pursues facts about the case as the trial proceeds in the courthouse. As he does so, his perceptions of the case are altered. Here is a quote from the book:

> Outside the wind blew steadily from the north driving snow against the courthouse. By noon three inches had settled on the town. A snow so ethereal it could hardly be said to have settled at all. Instead it swirled like some icy fog, like the breath of ghosts. Up and down Amity Harbor's streets. Powdery dust devils frosted puffs of ivory cloud, spiraling tendrils of white smoke. By noon the smell of the sea was eviscerated. The site of it mistily depleted too. One feels the vision narrowed in close. Burned in the nostrils of those who ventured out-of-doors. The snow flew up from their rubbery boots as they struggled. Heads down towards Peterson's Groceries. When they looked out into the whiteness of the world, the wind flung it sharply at their narrowed eyes and foreshortened their view of everything. (p. 170)

The familiar world of the island was obscured. The snow created both physical obstacles and obstacles to perception where none had been before. The storm unfolds as the testimony in the trial makes the first and most obvious explanation of the death harder and harder to understand. But the true facts are not easy to uncover due to the complexity of the human relations leading up to the incident. Later, as Ishmael starts to solve the mystery, the weather changes:

> Outside he found the snow had stopped. Only a few scattered flakes fell. A hard winter sunlight seeped through the clouds. A north wind blew hard and fast. It seemed colder now than it had been that morning. The air burned in his nostrils. The wind and snow had scoured everything clean. There was the sound of snow crunching under his feet. The whine of the wind and nothing else. The eye of the storm he knew had passed. The worst of it was behind them. It occurred to Ishmael for the first time of his life that such destruction could be beautiful. (p. 427)

As the storm clears up, in the clarity of the bright sunny day framed by the virgin snow, barriers disappear, the murder mystery is solved, and the townspeople's perception is altered. They see things in a new light.

The barrier of disorientation has been used heavily as a metaphor in literature. In the famous existentialist novel *The Castle* by Kafka, a surveyor named K arrives at a town to which he has been summoned by a government official to do some work. K spends much of the story trying to contact the official who works and lives in the castle on the hill above the town. He does not know what is required of him and is unable to get a clear idea of whether he will even begin his work. Throughout the story, he is never able to make contact with the official or anyone else in the castle except through a messenger and other second- and third-hand sources. K suffers bouts of disorientation, disillusionment, and distraction. The most enduring image is of K trying to get closer to the castle, becoming confused by the labyrinth of streets in the town and never finding it. In fact, the closer he seems to move toward the castle, the farther it seems to recede in the distance.

The castle could be a symbol for life as a search for purpose. The inability to obtain clear "instructions" for life leads to a feeling of unease. This gap of understanding creates the psychological feeling of being lost and adrift, disoriented without purpose. This is a universal feeling that we have all experienced at one time or another as we try to understand the mystery of life.

Barriers as metaphors in film are also common. Consider all the *Die Hard* and *Lethal Weapon* films in which the heroes encounter incredible adversity and, of course, overcome it all by cleverness and toughness. But communication and emotional barriers are also fertile subjects for film. In Wim Wenders's movie *Paris, Texas*, space is used as a metaphor for psychological distance between people. The protagonist seeks to reconstruct his family after his wife has left him and their child. The empty barren Texas plains that he travels through on his quest to find her symbolize the emotional distance between them. When he does find his wife, she is working in an adult entertainment shop. He can only see her by buying time and talking through the glass of a peep show booth. This scene uses barriers in space and access to information as a powerful comment on the gulf between estranged partners. The movie highlights the role of negotiations, power, and desire in the relationships between men and women.

Barriers play an important intellectual role in scientific endeavor. Much like the fictional K, real scientists are forever running up against barriers to knowledge and understanding. In fact, it could be argued that the desire to uncover knowledge and overcome those barriers is a prime motivator behind the scientific endeavor. One good example is the limitation on our powers of perception to observe the workings of the universe. Even using telescopes, microscopes, and scanning devices, we cannot uncover or record phenomena beyond certain levels.

Beyond the physical, there are intellectual barriers in science as well. Science evolves through systematic research. Observations that do not fit within the established theories are identified. As these unexplained phenomena add up, they precipitate critical periods in the history of science when shifts in thinking, or new paradigms, occur (Kuhn 1962). Old theories are replaced by new or improved theories. The scientific "breakthrough" removes artificial restrictions on thinking within a limited frame of ideas and provides a new intellectual perspective to conduct further research. The two most obvious examples in the history of scientific paradigm shifts are the change in the conception of the world as a flat surface to a sphere and the shift from the belief that the sun and planets revolve around the earth to the understanding that the earth and other planets all revolve around the sun.

The experience of barriers in both everyday human life and intellectual life clearly is a central phenomenon of human existence. Not only do barriers serve to limit our everyday actions, they also can alter our perceptions and our understanding of the world, our place in it, and our sense of purpose. It is no accident that barriers play an important role in the life of the intellect as well as in the more ordinary aspects of human experience. The common shared experience of barriers in daily life makes them a ripe subject for intellectual curiosity and useful as metaphors to communicate universal truths.

Social Functions of Space

Barriers clearly play a major role in design at all scales. It is important to note that the same physical features can both facilitate and impede the achievement of goals. The most obvious example is how a door can simultaneously protect a home from unwanted entries (prevent people from coming in) while also providing privacy for the household (prevent information from going out). Another example is a toll road that both facilitates social interaction and excludes those who cannot afford the toll. A third is the mobile phone, which facilitates communications but also may increase interruptions. Thus, the barrier, as used here, is a psychosocial construct, not the physical feature itself. This psychological nature of barriers is always open to interpretation by individuals and groups. Understanding those interpretations is a major focus of universal design.

Figure 1–4: Public marketplace. This market is located in a public square in Stockholm, Sweden. Each vendor has a stand with a tent-like structure providing weather protection. All the stands are the same size and arranged in rows.

The relationship between the social order and spatial order of society is one of the most important topics in universal design. Ordering space is achieved by claiming space through protective or legal boundaries that control access to the resources within. This activity is called territorial behavior. Some territories are private and used exclusively by one person; some are shared by a few, and some are public in that a large number of people share them. Figure 1–4 shows two examples of territories in one space, a public marketplace with stalls that are owned, at least temporarily, by individual vendors. Objects can be part of territorial behavior; some objects, such as automobiles and camping tents, are territories themselves, although mobile rather than static. Claiming space is an innate behavior exhibited by all animals, not a behavior unique to humans. All animals defend and control access to places and things for their own benefit. Territorial behavior has survival value. It ensures predictable access to resources. It protects assets from being taken by another animal, helps organize social relationships, and communicates important rules of behavior within a group or species. Literal examples of territorial behavior among humans include the building of fences and walls to demarcate one's property, separating it from a neighbor's; protected national borders; and no-trespassing signs. The spatial distance that we normally keep between us and others, or the body buffer zone, is an example of a portable territory that is not tied to one particular set of spatial features but is a short-term claim on space (Hall 1969; Sommer 1974).

The resources that generate claims on space and objects are quite diverse. Territoriality may involve claiming strategic locations for commerce or defense. A good example in contemporary culture is how Starbucks attempts to dominate a coffee market in certain neighborhoods by claiming the most exposed locations on every street corner. Physical attributes of an environment or an object can be resources for their own sake. Thus, a home site with a good view of an ocean is a very desirable property; a comfortable chair may become a regular visitor's favorite seating location in the shared space of a library reading room. Proximity to other people can be one of the resources that people seek in claiming territory—for example, living in a high-status neighborhood or an arts district. Information can also be a desirable resource—an office located close to the leader of a work group is desirable for an aspiring executive, providing opportunities to share information (Steele 1986). Finally, sometimes it is the absence of something that makes a place desirable as a territory, as in a quiet neighborhood or distance from neighbors.

People, like many other animals, mark territorial boundaries to identify owners and communicate information about their social status. Shared understandings about these markings develop within a culture, including precise legal definitions. Social relations are reflected in both the pattern of territory and the markings used. These patterns and markings denote and connote many aspects of social relations, including social dominance and roles, such as gatekeeper or boss, and class. As an example in architecture, during the Renaissance in Italy, each urban estate house, or palazzo, was divided vertically into a servant floor, a *piano nobile* ("noble floor" or "noble level," the main floor in a Renaissance building), and living quarters. The spatial organization of a palazzo reflected the degree of access that different classes of outsiders might have to the inhabitants and the social status of different types of inhabitants as well. Stable hands did not get access to the *piano nobile*; family friends were entertained there but did not necessarily get access to the living quarters.

Privacy is the process of adjusting control over information about the self to desirable levels. It is a second function of barriers, often used in conjunction with territorial behavior. In privacy behavior, the physical and virtual environments are organized to control information flows between people. We need such control for many reasons, such as preventing negative information about the self from being known, maintaining security of financial information, or simply to provide an opportunity for self-reflection, free from the need to be "on stage" in social relations. The design of space, through physical boundaries, distance, and spatial organization, is a method used extensively to control the flow of information. Many boundaries created to maintain privacy are purposely adjustable because the desired state of information control varies over time. Closing and opening doors, gates, and curtains and other flexible boundaries help us achieve the state of privacy we desire. The desired level of control is based on the social interaction goals, emotional state, or activities of individuals and groups. Clearly, privacy behavior also can erect barriers to communication. The teenager who locks himself in his room to avoid his parents is a good example. Designing for privacy is also evident in the virtual world. The best examples are social networking Web sites through which individuals communicate their online identity but also restrict access to classes of people, such as friends, relatives, and colleagues.

Identity behavior is the third key function of barriers. People communicate important information to each other during social relations, which include friendships, work, education, politics, love, and rituals, such as religious activities. For example, we need some means to identify who is the teacher and who are the students, we need to know who is qualified to build a house or prescribe medication, we need to know how to recognize a police officer, and we need to know who our potential partners, friends, and enemies might be. If we are a teacher, a doctor, or a police officer, we use identity behavior to convey our status and obtain respect. If we are looking for a relationship, we use identity behavior to advertise who we are in order to attract a compatible person.

Territoriality and privacy are both two spatial practices that we use to manage identity. For example, territorial markers are often used to convey information about the owner of the territory, and the degree of privacy sanctioned for an individual is often an indication of rank in an organization's power structure. These spatial practices involve the use of products and information to convey status messages to others and evaluate the status of other people. However, identity behavior extends much further than claims on space or regulation of spatial boundaries. It encompasses a wide range of behaviors, including diet, clothing, hairstyles, language, posture, and mannerisms. It can be argued that there is nothing an individual does that does not somehow convey information about the self.

People manage their identity in many ways. We tell people things about ourselves and we withhold other information. We wear clothes and adornments that indicate our status, group membership, and personality characteristics. Obvious examples are military and public safety uniforms, religious emblems, and gang tattoos or colors. The style, material, and color of clothing, jewelry, and accessories and even their brands convey information about the self. We adopt certain mannerisms, rules of etiquette, vocabulary, and other elements of spoken language to make a specific impression. We even use gestures or body language, such as bowing, shaking hands, and conversation postures, to communicate personal information. We select and decorate our homes and personal vehicles to communicate economic status, group membership, or lifestyle interests. It is important to note that neglect of certain aspects of identity behavior, such as home décor or clothing, also communicates important information about an individual's identity. For example, a person who values spiritual things above material ones may choose to live a very ascetic lifestyle rather than accumulate possessions, even if he or she can afford them. In addition, people are adept at conveying false messages to trick others into believing they are someone very different from who they really are.

The ability to manage identity depends a great deal on the resources available and within an individual's or group's control. People with low incomes clearly have less autonomy than people with higher incomes because their resources are more limited. They often have to accept less autonomy to obtain the resources they need for survival. For example, to qualify for publicly assisted housing, individuals usually have to disclose details about their personal finances and may not be able to prevent managers from entering their apartment without permission. Thus, it can be more difficult for them to manage privacy or prevent territorial encroachment; consequently, they appear more vulnerable. In comparison, affluent people can afford to purchase a home in a neighborhood of their choice and fill it with objects that carefully communicate an identity that they fashion. They can also keep out neighbors and even the government, all of which reduces their vulnerability. But even high-income individuals may be subject to restrictions in autonomy. For example, a patient in a hospital has to abide by the hospital's rules, including wearing hospital gowns and eating prescribed foods. Hospitals, in fact, are uniformly disliked due to their active discouragement of identity behavior.

Individual or group characteristics can create a spoiled identity, or stigma (Goffman 1963). Stigma can originate with one characteristic but, through the interpretations of others (often due to misconceptions), spread to the whole person. Thus, people without money, homes, or possessions are often perceived to be "incompetent" due to their apparent inability to take care of themselves. The potential to have a spoiled identity is greater if negative characteristics of individuals are obvious and especially if these characteristics are associated with the body or mind. Some examples are physical disability or disfigurement, obesity, speech impediments, behavior associated with mental health conditions (e.g., talking to oneself), evidence of disease, or a criminal record. These characteristics can even overshadow the ability to control resources, such as high income or high status in an organization. Even a high government official, such as the president or a wealthy financier, can be stigmatized by illegal activity or disclosure of unusual sexual practices. Spaces and objects are often associated with high-status groups; consider McMansions and luxury automobiles. Likewise, spaces and objects associated with devalued or stigmatized groups can also carry stigma. Examples are decoration schemes associated with institutional life or grab bars, associated with healthcare facilities.

Sociospatial Order

When there is more than one person involved, spatial boundaries and organization are negotiated. Social order, spatial order, and information flows are intertwined. The social order determines the spatial order and communication channels, which, in turn, tend to reproduce the social order. But the patterns can be broken. The institutions described earlier are examples of attempts to change the social order by teaching poor people marketable skills, curing people with mental health conditions, and reforming criminals by using spatial practices. (They did not work.) Modernist designers sought to reform the established social order using design as a tool. There are many examples, but one in particular illustrates this goal in a way that has contemporary relevance.

The Schindler house (Figure 1–5) was designed and built in the 1920s by Rudolf Schindler, an architect, and his partner, Clyde Chase, for them and their wives, Pauline and Marion (Hayden

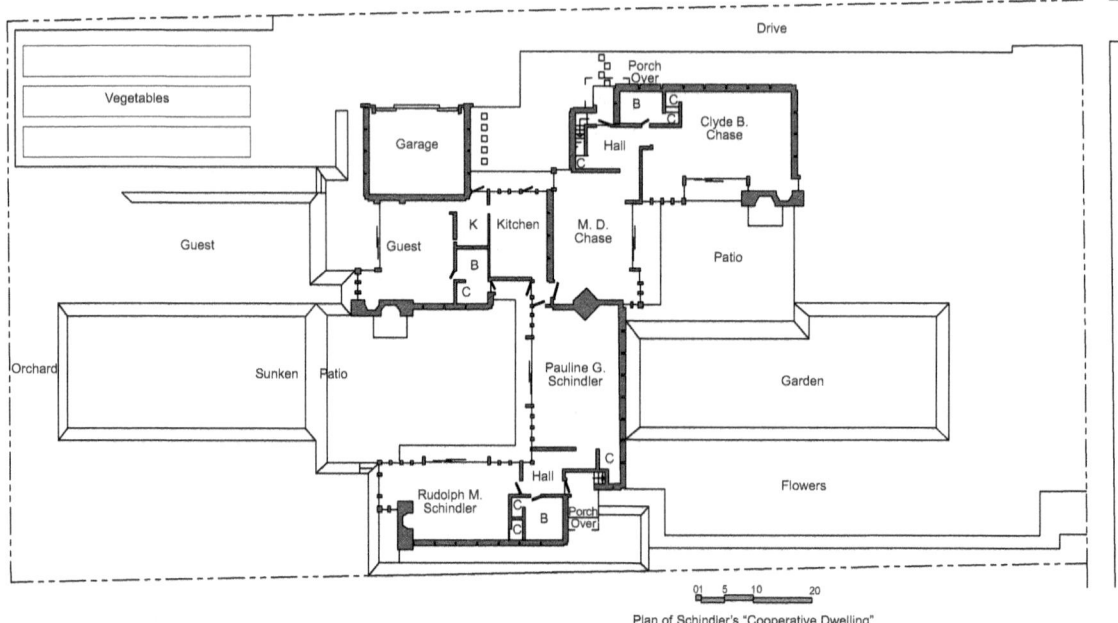

Plan of Schindler's "Cooperative Dwelling"

Figure 1–5: Plan of the Schindler House. The house has two interlocking L-shaped wings, one occupied by Rudolf and Pauline Schindler and the other by Clyde and Marian Chase. Each L-shaped unit defines an outdoor courtyard, and each wing of the L is a studio. The L's intersect at the kitchen and garage.

Source: Images redrawn based on that in Hayden (1982)

1982). The couples evidently had very egalitarian relationships for the time since each of the four individuals occupied similar spaces for work and personal territory. Rudolf and Pauline Schindler lived in one wing and their friends Clyde and Marion Chase lived in the other. Each couple had a great deal of privacy inside and outside, since each wing only had windows onto its own yard. However, the spatial organization of the home conveys a mixed message about gender equity. Each of the four people had similar access to the resources of the home—kitchen, garage, bathroom, and so on—but the women's studios are located next to the kitchen. What does this signify? Presumably, the spatial order of this household was negotiated between couples and between the men and the women; thus, the floor plan should represent the relative power of the couples and genders. Due to lack of information, we have no clear way to understand the dynamics of the negotiations. Did the women want more control over the kitchen and have the power to claim it? Were they delegated responsibilities for domestic duties the men did not have? Did the men claim the space with more privacy (and therefore less access) and less domestic responsibility? Whatever the reason, the floor plan demonstrates a very different use of space from a gender perspective than even most houses built today; it represents a social order leaning toward more communality and equality than that of typical American households.

The need for boundaries between people, control over traffic flows, and use of objects to communicate identity cannot be denied. Determining what those relationships should be is, in fact, a major responsibility of designers. But a major question for all of us is what barriers are created in the process and what they represent for society. Negotiated spatial orders define the differences between individuals: Who is in, who is out, who has access to resources, who is denied access, who wins, who loses, who is empowered, and who is neglected? The experience of barriers is universal, but not everyone has the same ability to overcome barriers that may restrict independence, social engagement, and the communication of a positive identity. Therefore, designers, their clients, officials, and others should understand the impact of their decisions, particularly on disadvantaged groups.

People with little power rarely have a voice in the negotiations over space, and thus their interests are often ignored, which makes it even more difficult for them to achieve functional independence and social participation. It is no coincidence that civil rights activists recognize the relationship between dominance and space and seek to alter both oppressive spatial and social practices. The term "breaking down barriers" is often a metaphor for achieving civil rights at the broadest level. Perhaps the best example of the relationship of powerlessness and space is homeless people, who essentially have no place of their own and have to carve out a territory in public space, a territory on which their hold is tenuous and that is subject to invasion at any time.

If a group is perceived to be a threat by the community or powerful elite, very drastic measures may be used to cut it off from access to community resources. For example, the Panopticon was a prototype design for prisons (Figure 1–6) based on the belief that the social environment was the cause of criminal behavior. The goal of the Panopticon was to separate criminals, keeping them from communicating with other criminals and to keep them under constant surveillance as a way to ensure that they would "behave." Enforcing cultural norms would reduce the chances that inmates would return to criminal life when they were released (Strub 1989). Thus, the prison actually was designed as a sort of machine for changing behavior. In a similar way, asylums were designed to regularize behavior and calm persons with mental illnesses. It was believed that living in a very regular (and understimulating) environment would be therapeutic (Shorter 1997).

Figure 1–6: The Panopticon. Developed by Jeremy Bentham, an English natural philosopher, the Panopticon is a design concept for prisons that, in its purest form, allows the guards, stationed in the middle of a circular plan, to have direct surveillance of all prisoners, whose cells are arrayed around the perimeter of the circular plan and stacked on multiple floors. Due to the configuration, prisoners cannot see into nearby cells.
Source: Image courtesy of Friman

Breaking down barriers can allow people who are disadvantaged or oppressed, in a literal sense, to gain access to resources. Elimination of barriers symbolically also marks progress toward the ultimate goal of social justice, even if it is not yet fully attained. In some cases, breaking down a barrier can become a symbol that liberation has finally been achieved, even though the removal of the barrier has no significant impact anymore. Unification of Germany and freedom of movement across the old border between East and West occurred prior to tearing down the Berlin Wall. But when people were allowed to begin physically tearing it down themselves, the symbolism of the act sparked a huge celebration.

It should be noted, of course, that restrictions on access sometimes are warranted. For example, the quarantining of people with contagious diseases makes sense because it helps to reduce the spread of the disease. And incarceration may be the only viable solution for very violent people who are a threat to the safety of other citizens. Finally, controlling borders to prevent terrorist infiltration and other aggressive actions is certainly understandable for the welfare of society. We are concerned here with the removal of *unnecessary* barriers that restrict individual and social development and ultimately social justice for all citizens.

Origins of Universal Design

Equality of access to the environment has always been an issue in civil rights. In the United States, prior to the Civil Rights Act of 1964, some states and municipalities had laws that banned African Americans from using the same building entries and hygiene facilities as whites, required them to attend racially segregated schools and public facilities, and to sit in the back of public transit vehicles. Segregated facilities were usually of inferior quality. Discrimination when renting and purchasing housing was also common, even in communities where there were no segregation laws. The apartheid policies in South Africa are another example of how spatial practices can result in discrimination and oppression by denying a class or classes of people access to such community resources as education, housing, healthcare, and recreation opportunities. These practices have been directed not only at racial groups but also at groups defined by many other characteristics, such as religion, ethnicity, class, gender, sexual orientation, and disability. Such practices need to be eliminated to ensure civil rights and provide social justice.

Universal design emerged out of the disability rights movement, which began in the late 1960s, although there are earlier precedents. Its goal is to bring people with disabilities into the mainstream of society by ensuring equal opportunity and eliminating discrimination based on disability. The movement is worldwide in scope and is evolving on all inhabited continents. A central activity in reaching the goal of equal rights for people with disabilities is removing barriers to access and use in the built and virtual (digital information) environment. In 1968, when the first U.S. federal law mandated accessibility of federally financed buildings to people with disabilities took effect, a struggle to change the physical character of our communities began—a struggle that is not yet over. Unlike other targets of discrimination, for people with disabilities, the details of environmental design are critical. For racial minorities, removing discrimination in access to public places means changing the rules of how a building or facility is used. In the case of religious minorities, it may mean removing restrictions on the construction of places of worship. To achieve civil rights for the citizenry in a dictatorship, it may mean open access to the Internet and freedom of assembly in public places. However, for people with disabilities, the actual design of built environments and information technologies is a part of the discriminatory practice.

Through the disability rights movement, people with disabilities have redefined themselves. The symbols used in the movement provide a good indicator of how far that change has come. The International Symbol of Accessibility (ISA) (Figure 1–7) denotes the availability of accessible facilities. The symbol was developed by a Danish design student who won a competition sponsored by Rehabilitation International, an international organization of rehabilitation professionals, in 1968. However, by the 1980s, disability rights advocates had started reinterpreting the ISA. Advocacy groups such as the Paralyzed Veterans of America felt that it was too passive and clinical looking. They developed alternative symbols to convey a more active, forceful image. The National Endowment for the Arts followed through with this approach in modifying the ISA (Figure 1–8).

Using the precedent of other civil rights laws, disability rights advocates in the United States were successful in obtaining passage of many laws that prohibit discrimination based on disability. Similar movements in other countries followed. The scope initially focused on public accommodations, but it has expanded to include housing, places of employment, public transportation infrastructure and vehicles, and communication systems, including the Internet.

16   Barriers and Their Social Meaning

Figure 1-7: International Symbol of Accessibility (ISA). Developed through a competition, the symbol is an abstract profile of a wheelchair user. It is static and passive looking because it portrays the wheelchair user reclining slightly to the rear.

Figure 1-8: Active Symbol of Accessibility. This symbol is similar in profile to the ISA, but it portrays the user in a more active posture, leaning forward.

Initially, accessibility was achieved in a haphazard manner. Figure 1–9 shows an early attempt to make the Everson Museum in Syracuse, New York, accessible. Accessible design like this was actually much like the conditions faced by African Americans in segregated public facilities in the United States, a separate-but-equal kind of status. This ramp is located at a little-used side entrance, not where most visitors would enter. Visitors who could not use stairs had to go out of their way to enter. Figure 1–10 shows another good example of "back-door access." The building shown is a library at Delft University in the Netherlands. The only accessible entry is through a service door near the rear of the building. To gain access at this entry, a visitor must ring a bell, and a librarian will come to let the person in. However, entry depends on the availability of a librarian and poses security problems for the library. In both these cases, the solution to accessibility was considered legal at the time. In other words, it was not defined as discrimination. Although there is legal access, there are clearly still barriers.

Many well-meaning people are motivated to help disadvantaged people because they view them as objects of pity rather than to ensure social justice. For example, most religions espouse the virtue of helping the poor. While charity is a good value, it may have negative consequences if it is expressed in a way that continues to foster dependence rather than self-reliance and autonomy. Western civilizations have historically used charitable institutions to care for people with disabilities. However, when people with disabilities are confined to institutions, they are rarely found in public spaces or living in residential neighborhoods; thus, it appears that it is unnecessary to provide accessibility to the community outside the institutions. Not only is the inmates' spoiled identity reinforced by the message that they cannot take care of themselves or participate productively in society, but the lack of accessible environments in the outside community also reinforces the belief that they are "incompetent" and cannot live like everyone else.

In the 1970s, much research documented the negative impact of institutional life (Sommer 1974). In the United States and northern Europe, advocacy led to moving people with disabilities

Figure 1–9: An early and unsuccessful attempt to make the Everson Museum in Syracuse, New York, accessible.

Figure 1-10: Central Library service entrance at Delft University, the Netherlands. The accessible entry is through this service door and requires a visitor to ring a bell.

out of institutions and into community housing (Lifchez and Winslow 1979). People with disabilities who lived with their families in a similar dependent state sought more independence as well. These two developments led to the Independent Living Movement, which began grassroots efforts to make communities and independent housing accessible. This movement has spread throughout the world. However, note that in some cultures, the obligation to care for a family member with a disability can be so strong that the idea that people with disabilities should live on their own is viewed negatively because it reflects badly on the family. Attempts in these countries to introduce initiatives to support self-reliance and alternatives, such as group living arrangements or independent living training programs, may be resisted.

It is important to realize that barriers to self-expression, especially barriers to the presentation of a positive social identity, still exist, even in countries that have pioneered in the advancement of disability rights. Figure 1–11a is a photograph of the Hall of Remembrance at the Holocaust Memorial in Washington, DC, constructed in 1993. The hall has stairs ringing the central space. Originally there was no way to get onto the lower level without using the stairs. This room is a holy place, where important events are commemorated—for example, memorial ceremonies for people who died in the Holocaust. Since the original design did not comply with accessibility laws, changes had to be made. Figure 1–11b shows the lift that was installed. Imagine being a wheelchair user coming to an event in the Hall of Remembrance. There is a good chance you would arrive late because you could not find an accessible parking place near the building. If

Figure 1–11: Hall of Remembrance at the Holocaust Memorial in Washington, DC. (a) Stairs surround the main floor level of the Hall. (b) A mechanical lift is installed on the stairs to provide access to the lower level.

you enter during a quiet part of the ceremony, all eyes would be on you as you use this lift, and its noise would ruin the spirituality of the event. You would become an unwanted spectacle, the object of pity and/or annoyance.

Figure 1–12 shows a picnic area. The sign reads: "Picnic area for handicapped only." Why is the sign here? This picnic area is in a parking lot. The other picnic benches are scattered over the banks of the nearby river. None was accessible. However, the area pictured evidently turned out to be very desirable for all picnickers because it is conveniently located next to the parking spaces and on a stable, hard surface, which is good for children's play. Therefore, many people who probably did not need an accessible table used it. When people with disabilities arrived, they had no place to picnic and perhaps complained. The authorities had to ensure that there would always be an accessible space for a person with a disability to picnic, so they passed a law and put up this sign to accomplish that goal. But if the entire picnic area had been accessible, there would have been no need for the sign because people with disabilities could go to any other of the picnic sites. Having even half of the sites accessible probably would have met the demand. Thus, in this example, the goal of nondiscrimination was subverted by well-meaning people to create an absurd situation where people with a disability are overly protected and privileged. This situation also reinforces the identity of being dependent and needing charity, in this case through the special protection of government.

Conditions in poor countries around the world are the most desperate for people with disabilities. In informal communities (shanty towns), they are often confined to their immediate living environment. Many people who cannot walk are forced to use a corner of their home for personal hygiene. If they have no family to help them, some may have no alternative than to beg on the street, using their disability to elicit charity. Since schools are inaccessible, they have no opportunity to improve their lives, even if they do have supportive family and friends (Tipple and

Figure 1-12: Sign at a picnic area. The sign reads: "Picnic area for handicap only. Local ordinance prohibits use by others!"

Coulson 2009). Needless to say, these conditions do not provide an opportunity to lead a healthy and dignified life.

Despite all the antidiscrimination laws and changes in public policy, examples of significant barriers exist in high-income communities, and the barriers to independence and autonomy in low-income settings are very severe. Social integration, acceptance, and understanding of disability have not yet been achieved in human civilization. There is a typical trajectory in architecture as societies develop more advanced perspectives on disability. The first stage is the architecture of exclusion, usually by neglect. The second is one of dependence through the development of institutions. The third stage is independence through the development of a legal framework and physical environment that eliminates discrimination and removes barriers to independence. We are now moving toward a new stage in many societies: the architecture of social participation, with the goal of equality in opportunity through universal design.

The result of the effort to eliminate discrimination, to make the world accessible and usable for all, is that unintended consequences are becoming evident. The picnic area described is a good example. A local law had to be passed to reserve the picnic area for people with disabilities. Why? Accessibility was desirable for all visitors. When we start to introduce accessibility into the community, even at a minimal level, we introduce conditions that seem to be good for everyone.

Figure 1–13 shows an underground subway station with an elevator. Even though the provision of elevators in subways was originally intended to make public transportation accessible to people with disabilities, it has proven to be a boon for many others—for example, parents with children in strollers and carriages, bicycle users, and travelers with luggage. In this station in Copenhagen, Denmark, the loading platform provides ample space for rush-hour crowds. The elevator has a very prominent location in the station. The glass enclosure provides a view and reduces entrapment by criminals. Note also the glass security barriers along the platform. Many new subway systems are adopting this design strategy. It protects visually impaired individuals from falling off the platform, but it also prevents people from committing suicide, prevents accidents during crowded conditions, and reduces the noise level in the station. All these are unintended consequences of providing accessibility. Two other good features of this underground station are the high ceiling and natural light, which reduce the negative feeling of being underground and improve visibility.

Another example is the unisex accessible restroom. This idea was originally developed to reduce the cost of making both men's and women's restrooms accessible in existing buildings. However, it was soon recognized that such restrooms were also very beneficial to many other people. For example, a mother can assist her son, a father can assist his daughter, or older people can assist their partners without embarrassment in these restrooms. Now we call these rooms family restrooms or companion restrooms, terms that symbolize the fact that the benefit to all has been clearly understood.

A final example of unintended consequences is the handicap parking permit. In many communities, a black market in these parking permits exists (Shoup 2005). Public officials have been exposed for influence pedaling in issuing permits. Permits have even been stolen and sold to people seeking more convenient parking (Shoup 2005). The value of convenient parking is so great that people are willing to risk arrest to obtain a permit. In response to this demand, business practices are emerging to provide convenient parking for other groups, such as older people, pregnant women, and parents with small children.

Figure 1–13: Subway station in Copenhagen, Denmark. (a) View showing one entry and the skylight, which, in conjunction with light from the two stairways, floods the underground station with light. The sign provides real-time arrival information. (b) View showing the glazed elevator, woman with baby stroller, and the other entry with escalator and stairs.

More and more people are starting to find accessibility touching their lives. Automatic doors are very convenient if you are carrying a package. Ramps and curb ramps are magnets for skateboarders. Elevators are a blessing when we are sick or injured. The disability rights movement has moved society in a direction that has broad implications for everyone, not just people with disabilities and their families. It led to the development of universal design, also known as design for all in Europe or inclusive design in the United Kingdom. Ron Mace, an architect with a disability, is often credited with the invention of the concept (Mace 1985). This new paradigm for removing barriers is radically different from the old access model.

Today, many writers use the term "universal design" as a substitute for "accessible design" without understanding its significance or how the terms differ. The goal of universal design extends beyond eliminating discrimination toward people with disabilities. A universal design benefits everyone or, at least, a large majority. Moreover, to avoid stigma, it engages the aesthetic realm as well as the pragmatic because it has to appeal to everyone. Universal design is about dealing with barriers as artists or scientists would. It demands creative thinking and a change in perspective. It is not sufficient merely to apply design criteria in accessibility regulations in a mechanistic way. Often a change in perspective is needed.

There have always been designers thinking creatively about removing barriers. The Guggenheim Museum in New York City is an early example of universal design (Figure 1–14). We usually think of building ramps to connect two levels, but Frank Lloyd Wright had a new

Figure 1–14: Guggenheim Museum, New York, NY. Designed by Frank Lloyd Wright, the museum is an early example of universal design. The museum's interior contains one continuous ramp from the top level to the lobby.

perspective on ramps. He ramped the building itself. Reportedly, he was inspired by his dislike of museums that took a great deal of effort to visit. He thought every museum visitor could benefit by taking the elevator to the top of the building and then effortlessly gliding down the ramp to observe the artwork along the way (Pfeiffer 1991).

Summary

Barriers are a part of everyone's lives. Artists use barriers as a subject for their work in extremely creative ways. Scientists also focus a great deal of creative effort on barriers, either by finding a breakthrough that advances knowledge to new levels of understanding or by learning the limits of technology. The work of artists and scientists can be a source of design inspiration. Designers cannot avoid dealing with barriers because they are an essential part of the built environment and virtual spaces. Thus, thinking about barriers creatively should be an important part of design, as it is in art and science.

Creating enabling environments is an important ethical goal of designers. Creating unnecessary barriers to independence and social participation should be avoided for the benefit of all. Spatial orders that result in limiting the potential of human beings can damage social identity, stifle the quest for autonomy, and increase dependency at great cost to society. Barriers are encountered at many levels of human experience, including the physical, the sensory, the cognitive, and the communicative dimensions. Throughout this book, we explore how universal design can address these complex issues. In the process, we show how the universal design philosophy can be as much of a creative challenge as other aspects of design, such as sustainability and affordability.

Although the idea emerged from the disability rights movement, this philosophy has implications for many other groups; in fact, it has universal benefits. It is perhaps one of the most profound ideas in the contemporary history of design. Many precedents, such as the Guggenheim Museum, are well known but have not been identified as precursors to universal design thinking. Through examples and case studies, we look to the past to demonstrate the power of universal design, but we study the present and future to imagine where this design philosophy can lead.

Review Topics

1. What is a barrier? Describe a barrier in your everyday environment in detail using a concrete descriptor, such as "barrier to perception." Describe why it is a barrier.
2. Define "privacy" and "territoriality." Identify and describe how they relate to sociospatial order.
3. What are the origins of universal design? Explain how universal design differs from accessible design.

References

Foucault, M. 1973. *The Birth of the Clinic: An Archaeology of Medical Perception.* London: Tavistock.
Goffman, E. 1963. *Stigma: Notes on the Management of Spoiled Identity.* Upper Saddle River, NJ: Prentice-Hall.
Guterson, D. 1995. *Snow Falling on Cedars.* New York: Vintage.
Hall, E. T. 1969. *The Hidden Dimension.* Garden City, NY: Anchor Books.

Hayden, D. 1982. *The Grand Domestic Revolution: A History of Feminist Designs for American Homes, Neighborhoods and Cities.* Cambridge, MA: MIT Press.

Kuhn, T. S. 1962. *The Structure of Scientific Revolutions.* Chicago: University of Chicago Press.

Lifchez, R. and B. Winslow. 1979. *Design for Independent Living: The Environment and Physically Disabled People.* Berkeley: University of California Press.

Mace, R. 1985. *Universal Design: Barrier Free Environments for Everyone.* Los Angeles: Designers West.

Pfeiffer, B. B. 1991. *Frank Lloyd Wright.* Cologne, Germany: Taschen Books.

Rothman, D. J. 1971. *The Discovery of the Asylum: Social Order and Disorder in the New Republic.* Boston: Little, Brown.

Senie, H. 2002. *The Tilted Arc Controversy: Dangerous Precedent?* Minneapolis: Regents of the University of Minnesota.

Shorter, E. 1997. *From the Era of the Asylum to the Age of Prozac.* New York: John Wiley & Sons.

Shoup, D. 2005. "Parking on a Smart Campus." In D. Mitchell (ed.), *California Policy Options.* 117–149). Los Angeles: UCLA School of Public Affairs.

Sommer, R. 1969. *Personal Space: The Behavioral Basis of Design.* Englewood Cliffs, NJ: Prentice-Hall.

Sommer, R. 1974. *Tight Spaces: Hard Architecture and How to Humanize It.* Englewood Cliffs, NJ: Prentice-Hall.

Steele, F. 1986. "The Dynamics of Power and Influence in Workplace Design and Management." In J. D. Wineman (ed.), *Behavioral Issues in Office Design* (pp. 43–63). New York: Van Nostrand Reinhold.

Strub, H. 1989. "The Theory of Panoptical Control: Bentham's Panopticon and Orwell's *Nineteen Eighty-Four.*" *Journal of the History of the Behavioral Sciences* 25 (1): 40–59.

Tipple, G., and J. Coulson. 2009. *Enabling Environments: Reducing Barriers for Low-Income Disabled People.* Newcastle, UK: Global Urban Research Unit.

Williams, C. 1981. *Origins of Form.* New York: Architectural Book Publishing.

2

Defining Universal Design

Introduction

All new ideas are born and develop in a historic and cultural context. In Chapter 1, we described how universal design emerged from the disability rights movement. Here we examine the cultural context surrounding the birth of the idea. Doing so will help to put universal design into perspective with respect to the history of design. By identifying current design issues related to universal design, we can also speculate intelligently on how universal design will evolve as it becomes more mainstream and intersects with other design initiatives and contemporary cultural trends.

Although this book is targeted at the design professions, the concepts underlying universal design are of value to other professionals as well. In fact, at the time of this writing, two books have been published on universal design in education and public health professionals in different parts of the world have started to adopt the universal design philosophy. Just as sustainability extends beyond the world of design professionals, universal design also has a broader constituency. The range of interest groups that see value in universal design will be very important for increasing adoption of the philosophy.

Emergence of Universal Design

Over the last 40-plus years, a great deal of effort has been devoted to making the built environment accessible. Accessibility laws, such as the Architectural Barriers Act (1968), Section 504 of the Rehabilitation Act of 1973, the Fair Housing Act Amendments (1988), and the Americans with Disabilities Act (1990) specify minimum requirements to ensure that the built environment does not discriminate against people with disabilities. Experience with accessibility laws led Ron Mace, Ruth Hall Lusher, and others (Bednar 1977; Lusher and Mace 1989; Welch 1995) to recognize the need for a different approach to design of the built environment, which they termed "universal design." The premise for this new approach was that the environment could be much more accessible than laws could realistically mandate on the basis of nondiscrimination. If more attention was given to improving function for a broad range of people, they argued, a usable world for people with disabilities would become the norm.

Universal design increases the potential for developing a better quality of life for a wide range of individuals (Russell 1999; Stineman et al. 2003). However, it does not eliminate the need for standards that define the legal baseline for minimum accessibility. It creates products, places, and systems that reduce the need for special accommodations and many expensive, hard-to-find assistive devices. It also reduces stigma by putting people with disabilities on an equal playing field with the able bodied population. It provides benefits not only to people with functional limitations but also to society as a whole (Danford and Maurer 2005). Universal design supports people in being more self-reliant and socially engaged. It does not substitute for assistive technology, but it makes such technology easier to use by providing appropriate support. For businesses and government, it reduces the economic burden of special programs and services designed to assist individual citizens, clients, and customers. Although we should not forget the origins of this design philosophy, as we shall see throughout this book, it no longer should be identified solely with disability.

Definition

The most common definition of universal design is:

> The design of products and environments to be usable by all people, to the greatest extent possible, without the need for adaptation or specialized design.
>
> —Mace (1985)

Experts and those with experience in the field understand this definition, but it leaves something to be desired in terms of explaining the concept to the uninitiated. What do the terms "all people," "greatest extent possible," and "without the need for adaptation and specialized design" really mean in practice? Imrie and Hall (2001), for example, argue that the definition, by the lack of explicit attention to disability, seems to promote the abandonment of special accommodations for people with disabilities. Moreover, if taken literally, the definition seems unrealistic. Everyone knows, for example, that there will always be someone who will not be able to use a particular product or environment.

Other terms have been used for the same concept. For example, the term "design for all" is used in Europe:

> . . . design for human diversity, social inclusion, and equality.
>
> —Design for All Europe (2008)

> [T]he intervention on environments, products, and services with the aim that everyone, including future generations, regardless of age, gender, capabilities, or cultural background, can enjoy participating in the construction of our society, with equal opportunities participating in economic,

social, cultural, recreational, and entertainment activities while also being able to access, use, and understand whatever part of the environment with as much independence as possible.

—*Design for All Foundation (n.d.)*

In the United Kingdom, the term "inclusive design" is popular:

The design of mainstream products and/or services that is accessible to, and usable by, as many people as reasonably possible . . . without the need for special adaptation or specialized design.

—*British Standards Institute (2005)*

Clearly, we are still in a time of transition regarding the definition of universal design, but there seems to be a developing consensus. The similarity in concepts is clear from the definitions. Some definitions are explicit about the outcomes for universal design practice that helps to clarify its purpose: social inclusion, equality, and independence. Others explicitly mention the concept of diversity beyond design for disability. An essential idea incorporated in all the definitions is that it will benefit a broader population than conventional practices—inclusion is the ultimate goal and design for inclusion results in benefits for all.

But there are still problems with all the definitions. Most also include a caveat on the need to be reasonable in pursuing that goal. This seems contradictory, a sort of cop-out. Imrie and Hall (2001), in criticizing the Mace definition of universal design, argue that the concept is too utopian and does not reflect the political nature of the process of inclusion. They point out that presenting design for inclusion in this way raises false hopes with an emphasis on technical solutions rather than process and leads to solutions that, in practice, do not really address all the needs of the population, particularly people with disabilities. Steinfeld and Tauke (2003) also reflect on the pitfalls of utopian thinking, particularly with respect to encouraging adoption by contemporary design educators who dismiss utopian and reformist ideas as a vestige of modernist thought that misled people into thinking that design alone could change the world. They point out, however, that idealism is not necessarily a bad thing and is attractive to both students and educators alike. According to Steinfeld and Tauke, the term "universal designing" may characterize the concept better than the noun form, as it reflects a constant evolutionary process leading to more and more inclusion over time.

In light of these critiques, we propose this improved definition:

Universal design is a process that enables and empowers a diverse population by improving human performance, health and wellness, and social participation.

In short, universal design makes life easier, healthier, and friendlier. This process involves continuous improvement, based on the resources available, toward the ultimate goal of full inclusion. Thus, universal design should recognize the context in which design takes place rather than imposing an absolute standard to every situation. The definition frames universal design as both an idealistic approach in the long term and a realistic approach in the short term. It specifically addresses the outcomes of the process, including the often neglected outcomes of improved health and social participation. In addition, it recognizes that inclusion must address the full diversity of the population. Finally, it does not focus design on the physical environment alone, recognizing that the concept is equally useful in the virtual world of information and in delivery of services.

Some critics have objected to the word "universal" because it implies that there is one design solution for everyone, but we believe that this word is essential to communicate the ultimate goal of design for inclusion. The word "universal" should be understood as it is used in terms like "universal suffrage" or "universal healthcare." The goal is universal access to the resources and benefits provided by civilized societies.

Origins

To put universal design into historical context, we need to go back to the origins of the design professions. In the first century BCE, Vitruvius, a Roman architect and engineer, wrote a treatise on architecture, *De Architectura* (*Ten Books on Architecture*, as it is known in English). This is the only book on architecture from the classical era of Western architecture that survives today. Vitruvius advanced the idea that good architecture must have three qualities: "firmness, commodity, and delight." In modern terms, we would call these qualities (structural) strength, usefulness, and character. This same credo can be applied to other design domains. Usefulness is the quality that underlies the concept of universal design. Clearly, it has been a recognized aspect of good design since the origins of the profession. However, the emphasis placed on usefulness has varied with the times and, with respect to this goal, the results often have left much to be desired. It is important to realize that there are many aspects to usefulness, from ease of construction to comfort, pleasure, and public benefit.

Vernacular buildings and products are usually constructed by the people who use them. Sometimes local craftspeople do some or all of the work, but they are still part of the same social world as their clients. Vernacular buildings and products are designed according to traditional patterns that change very little over time. In some societies, their forms have stayed pretty much the same for thousands of years. Usefulness plays a major role in the design of vernacular buildings and products (Williams and Williams 1974). Over time and through lived experience, vernacular building forms and tools were developed that closely fit the patterns of the inhabitants' lives, the availability of materials and knowledge, the local environment (e.g., climate and topography), and societal goals and values, the latter of which usually were derived from religion (Rapoport 1969). Some scholars have argued that vernacular designs are better than the work of professionals because of this close "fit" (Alexander 1964).

Most of the written histories of Western architecture and design, from the Renaissance on, have focused on the work of professional designers and ignored the vernacular. Since design professionals need to be paid for their work, only the upper classes and large institutions, such as governments and religious organizations, can usually afford to hire them. Although usefulness was important in architecture and urban design, between the Renaissance and the Industrial Revolution, it generally took a backseat to character in the professional ranks.

"Character" refers to the meaning of a place or object—its significance. It is important to note that character is not solely about aesthetics. Very practical things and ugly things have character as well as beautiful things designed primarily for aesthetic value. For the most part, professional designers were hired to create works that would enhance the positive meaning of places and objects to their clients or to the public. For example, a Gothic cathedral and the objects in it provide a place of enormous religious and cultural significance to the citizens of a city, particularly since its construction might span several lifetimes and involve the congregants in fundraising, daily appreciation, and even volunteer effort.

Aesthetic expression uses formal manipulations to elicit emotional response. In design, aesthetic expression contributes to character, but it also has many useful purposes. It can be used to personalize a territory by distinguishing it from neighbors or to attract or repel people to or from a place or an object. It is often used to connote status. In a landmark book called *Theory of the Leisure Class*, the American sociologist and economist Thorstein Veblen (1994 [1899]) demonstrated how the process of consumption involves identity behavior. "Good taste" and fashion cycles can be understood as a means through which people communicate their superiority and power by demonstrating their ability to spend large amounts of money on "useless" things, meaning things of no practical value; in other words, if you can afford to buy useless things, you demonstrate wealth by doing so. The result of this "conspicuous consumption" is that prestigious homes are much larger in scale than the households really need, and luxury automobiles use more gasoline than necessary in order to provide more power to propel a larger vehicle at greater speeds than a neighbor's car. Wearing rare jewels, which are just rare rocks, is a great way to demonstrate wealth. Veblen's most intriguing example is the manicured lawn, which not only has no intrinsic value but is created by essentially pouring money into the ground, something only really wealthy people could afford to do. Although none of these things have any practical purpose, if one wishes to communicate superiority, then they are useful in a social sense, such as signs and labels. Thus, before we label certain features "useless," we have to define what we mean by the term. Often, usefulness is defined by the culture and changes over time.

Modernism and the Modernist Style

After the Industrial Revolution, and especially after World War I, usefulness in architecture became more important in the architectural profession. The advances of technology, science, and social justice that emerged during the 100 years spanning the middle of the nineteenth century to the middle of the twentieth century brought "function" to the foreground of design. After World War I, avant-garde designers who created what came to be known as the modernist style, in particular, put great emphasis on usefulness, although their success in reaching their goals is debatable. In discussing the "modern era," it is important to distinguish between modernism as a worldview, in which science and technology are viewed as the means toward progress in human civilization, and the modernist style, which is a formal language associated with modernism, but not necessarily the only manifestation of modernism in architecture.

Many other design professionals, building owners, and land developers were also motivated by modernist thinking as a worldview but did not necessarily adopt the same style in their products. For example, the phrase "form follows function," coined by Louis Sullivan, an architect who practiced in Chicago at the turn of the twentieth century and considered by some to be the "father of modernism," is often quoted as a maxim of modernist architecture. However, Sullivan never abandoned ornament, and the character of his work owed a debt to neoclassical traditions. Yet he did adopt new building technologies and incorporated a new way of thinking about building interiors and form as well as program in response to the mercantile society of his era. Over the course of twentieth century, the modernist worldview led to the widespread adoption of many new technologies, including indoor plumbing, central heating, steel frame and reinforced concrete construction, elevators, electricity, telecommunications, air conditioning labor-saving appliances, and high-strength glass. These advances radically changed the built environment. Further, the use of new space planning concepts more suited to the nature of work and domestic life in an industrialized society improved productivity, comfort, and health.

The new approaches to architecture of the early twentieth century emerged at a time when social reformers and politicians viewed industrialization as an opportunity to eliminate the oppression of ruling elites and improve the welfare of the lower classes. Some architects in Europe, who were often overtly political in their goals, viewed industrialization as a means for social reform. They sought to develop housing types that would provide decent homes for the middle and lower classes and inspiring for all citizens of the new industrial states (Le Corbusier [1923] 1985). However, completed projects that addressed these goals were rare since, as mentioned, only wealthy individuals and large organizations could afford to pay architects to design their homes, and commercial and government clients tended to have conservative views about building design.

Modernist urban designers and planners needed to solve the problem of congestion, water distribution, and waste removal, which was impeding the utility of the city as a commercial and business tool, but they were also interested in solving the social problems of cities such as poverty, alcoholism, and communicable diseases, which were attributed to slums and substandard housing. They believed that their work should serve all citizens by providing affordable housing, efficient transportation, and healthy environments for all. This egalitarian idea led to experiments in social responsibility, such as Le Corbusier's housing for workers in Pessac, France, and his highly influential concept for a new urban paradigm, Ville Radieuse, a city of skyscrapers tied together with high-speed motorways that left vast areas of landscape open for use as recreation space (Le Corbusier 1985 [1923]).

After World War II, these ideas were put into practice on a grand scale to rebuild the devastated cities of Europe and accommodate the expanding populations of the postwar baby boom. Throughout Europe, the bombed-out cities and new suburban districts were planned using variations of the Ville Radieuse model. It was also used to replace inner city "slum" housing in North America under the rubric of "urban renewal." This could theoretically increase overall density and result in more economical construction than traditional low-rise, high-density housing, such as row houses and walk-ups as long as parking could be located underground or in garages. In practice, the modernists' concept for high-rise, high-density housing resulted in worse conditions than in earlier low-rise high-density neighborhoods. High-rise living proved to be dangerous and difficult to police, not suitable for low-income families with many children (see, e.g., Rainwater 1966).

In industrial design, modernist ideas were applied extensively in many different ways. One early trend of practice was the celebration of industrial materials and form. A second trend, which started in the early twentieth century but accelerated after World War II, incorporated rapidly emerging new technology, especially mechanization and electronics. New features were continuously introduced into manufactured products as each producer vied to attract market share. A third trend, which fueled the transition toward a consumer-oriented society, was the adoption of advanced technology and management practices to increase productivity in manufacturing itself. Intense competition on price inevitably led to the adoption of simple basic forms with limited variety, easy to manufacture in vast quantities at extremely low prices.

The consumption-driven marketplace is seen most significantly in the mass marketing of low-cost goods with short design-production cycles that introduce a dizzying array of innovative features every year. Today the product development cycle is, in some industries, less than six months. This practice gives the average citizen of industrialized countries access to a wide range of inexpensive products and tools that improve the quality of their lives immensely. Thus, from the perspective of affordability, product design after World War II has certainly benefited the average person in highly developed countries through the introduction of labor-saving devices, prepared foods, and other time-savers. However, these products are often poorly designed for comfort, health, and convenience, are prone to failure, and have a short useful life due to the emphasis on competitive pricing, fashion cycles, and planned obsolescence.

In Europe, America, and Asia, housing is now constructed just like mass-marketed products, with the goal of providing decent housing for the masses of middle- and working-class people. American builders, in particular, developed an economical method after World War II to build affordable single-family dwellings for the middle classes in the growing suburbs. They did this by adapting a vernacular form of wood construction based on the inexpensive lumber available in the huge American forests. They also used rapid construction techniques to build community infrastructure, such as roads, bridges, and civic and commercial buildings. In the United States, federal policy stimulated new home construction. The building of homes was viewed as an economic stimulus because new housing had to be furnished and equipped, which drove the development of markets for furniture, appliances, and other manufactured goods (Hayden 2003).

In the public sphere, as the modern era advanced, buildings were stripped of expensive ornaments and money was invested in air conditioning, larger windows, electric lighting, signs, parking lots, and other features. Larger stores, often owned by corporate interests, emerged, enabled by the automobile-oriented transportation system, which increased the catchment area for each business. The workplace was transformed into large sprawling factories and corporate offices in efficient high-rise buildings and corporate office parks. The modernist style included design practices that were well suited to corporate clients once the construction technology was up to speed: efficiency, mass production, and application of technological know-how. Thus, elements of the new style were used to manage the public identity of corporate entities, a form of branding. Leading architects and designers such as Albert Kahn, Skidmore Owens and Merrill, Victor Gruen, Raymond Loewy, and Henry Dreyfus adopted formal principles from the modernist style in service of corporate clients. Eventually, the style became associated with corporate power.

The significance of late-twentieth-century commercial architecture in North America can be understood in its close relationship to mass-marketed consumer products (Gottdiener 1997). Large suburban shopping centers and big-box stores are efficient delivery systems that feed desire stoked by marketing through mass media. The sprawling economy of the suburbs is dependent on the ability of residents to get from place to place inexpensively and quickly. American innovations in merchandizing were imported by other wealthy countries. Today the global design culture is driven mostly by consumerism. This theme is evident in all of material culture, including agriculture, manufactured goods, housing, and settlement patterns. It reflects the social transition from an industrial economy to a consumer-oriented economy and the emergence, within 50 short years, of a huge urbanized population that does not have the means or the time to sustain a vernacular crafts-based design tradition.

Critiques of Modernist Style

Contemporary critics of post–World War II development argue that modernism threw the baby out with the bathwater (Duany, Plater-Zyberk, and Speck 2001). They argue that post–World War II suburban architecture and town planning rejected principles of design that had been developed over centuries. New buildings, settlements, and products lost the good qualities of traditional urban development and artistry. It has become obvious that the material culture of the late twentieth century will not be sustainable for long due to its impact on the environment. Ironically, some of the blame for this situation can be assigned to the practitioners of the modernist style who were so sanctimonious in their missionary efforts, who controlled the leading design schools, and who had the ear of design critics.

Despite the claims of its adherents, the modernist style often was not very functional at all and not very inclusive in its perspective. For example, the residents of Pessac, the prototypical housing project designed by Le Corbusier, reacted to the difficulties of living in modernist-style buildings by radically transforming the original flat-roofed, unadorned houses into a quaint pastiche of traditionally inspired cottages with peaked roofs, decorative trim, and shutters (Boudon 1972). Social scientists studying social housing built using the principles of the modernist style discovered that, when urban redevelopment schemes and affordable housing concepts inspired by modernist ideas were applied to house low-income populations, they dislocated families, bred crime and alienation, and perpetuated the stigma of being poor (Gans 1962; Rainwater 1966).

Commercial interests and government policy makers produced architecture and urban development that was a successful adaptation to the social transition occurring, but, like early mass-manufactured products, also had some serious flaws. Such critics as Jane Jacobs (1961), Andres Duany (Duany et al. 2001) and Ellen Dunham-Jones and June Williamson (2009) argue that features of suburban development, such as single-use zoning and automobile-oriented traffic engineering practices, led to the construction of communities that are dysfunctional and perhaps antisocial. More recent research demonstrates that the low-density sprawl that makes up most urban areas in North America is even unhealthy due to air pollution and automobile dependency (Frumkin 2006; Marshall, Brauer, and Frank 2009; Schweitzer and Zhou, 2010).

Return to Human-Centered Design

The problems with modernism in architecture and urban development became evident as early as the late 1960s. At that time, architects, planners, and social scientists, often laboring in obscurity, began advancing the idea that design could be human-centered and truly dedicated to usefulness. This refocus on usefulness was motivated by a deep sense of social responsibility.

These designers were dedicated to advancing the cause of people who had been underserved by mainstream professionals, and often needed strong advocates with technical knowledge to ensure that building and community development projects were more consistent with the priorities, expectations, and values of end users. These designers sought to change professional practices by incorporating methods of practice that involve the end users and knowledge from the social sciences of psychology, anthropology, and sociology. In particular, they adopted the new social priorities that emerged in the 1960s and 1970s: affordable housing, urban revitalization, mental health, aging, and early childhood education. Several threads of human-centered design thinking were started during those years and continue today, often in separate communities of practice, all of which are now converging to frame the project of universal design.

One group of design professionals, the Community Design Center movement, focuses on changing the methods used in design practice to give more power to end users. These professionals found ways to provide free design services on a not-for-profit basis (Sanoff 2000). Another group developed methodologies for citizen participation in mass housing design like the SAR group in the Netherlands that developed methods for designing housing to enable participation of end users (Habraken 1973) and the cohousing movement in Denmark, which is based on forming a community prior to construction that then takes control of the design and development process from private firms and government (McCamant and Durrett 1994). The neighborhood preservation movement, inspired by Jane Jacobs, sought to relearn and update approaches to urban planning and architecture that had proven successful in the past and had been abandoned as modernism took hold (Gratz 2010).

Another group of design professionals, often in collaboration with research scientists, focused on changing the utilization of knowledge in design practice. Working with human factors and ergonomics (HFE) researchers, they started applying to building design problems scientific research on human performance that had been developed to improve productivity and safety in the workplace and in transportation (Wolski, Dembsey, and Meacham 2000). This thread of work continues to this day within the HFE field. The human factors researcher and design critic Donald Norman, a psychologist (2004) has been extremely influential in promoting a human-centered approach to product design, especially by demonstrating the role of the emotional aspect of design (aesthetics) in usability.

Another group of design professionals began working with social scientists to understand more about the relationship between the physical environment and human behavior and translating that knowledge into design tools (Hall 1969; Sommer 1969, 1974). In the late 1960s, this group formed the Environmental Design Research Association (EDRA), which still serves as an interdisciplinary forum for human-centered design. Still another research-oriented group, often overlapping with the EDRA group, emerged within the field of gerontology (the study of aging) through the Gerontological Society. These researchers focused on the importance of the physical environment to quality-of-life issues in old age (Lawton and Nahemow 1973). Today, design for aging, which used to be an exclusive concern of researchers and a few practitioners, has emerged as a major community of practice within mainline design professional organizations such as the American Institute of Architects.

The research community has embraced the development of evidence-based design guidelines as an efficient way to bridge the gap between research and practice. Guidelines can have a broader impact than discrete knowledge transfer activities within the context of a design project. In the United States during the 1970s, three government agencies were influential in sponsoring the development of such guidelines: the Center for Building Technology (CBT) at the National Bureau of Standards, the National Institute for Mental Health, and the Department of Defense. The Ford Foundation's Educational Facilities Laboratory also played an important role in sponsoring research related to educational environments (Marks 2009). CBT's influence was significant because most of its projects supported government-sponsored construction programs, and CBT leaders were key theorists in the study of "building performance" (Eberhard 2009). The performance concept for building design extended beyond user requirements to the full range of design issues. The performance concept was implemented through the "systems approach" that had been developed during wartime and the space race by operations researchers (Churchman 1968).

Even before these developments in the design professions, however, advocacy organizations for people with disabilities were organizing campaigns to make the public, the government, and the building industry aware of environmental barriers to independence and social participation. The barrier-free design movement actually began in the late 1950s in the United States as advocacy groups found that universities were not accessible to returning war veterans and young adults who had contracted polio during the postwar epidemic. These advocacy groups developed consensus standards, began public awareness campaigns, wrote white papers, and worked with the government to develop legislation and regulations. The Easter Seals Society and the President's Committee for Employment of the Handicapped were leaders in this effort. The civil rights movement of the 1950s and 1960s was used as a model to ensure that civil rights were extended to people with disabilities. The barrier-free design movement eventually intersected the other threads of human-centered design.

Today, design culture is changing once again. Many new issues have captured the attention of design professionals and their colleagues in related professions. Those issues with a close relationship to universal design include sustainability, design for healthcare, aging in place, health promotion, homelessness, and social justice. Universal design has much to contribute to solving any social problem in which usability, health and wellness, and social participation play a major role in design response. Some examples for each of these problems are listed next.

Examples of Fields Related to Universal Design

Sustainability

Sustainable products used in buildings need to be designed to be operable by people with limited function in order to comply with accessibility laws, but they also have to be usable for the broader population or they will not be effective in practice. Due to their novelty, they often present usability issues for end users. Take the example of a waterless urinal. Every men's restroom requires at least one lower urinal. Most urinals are designed for the higher, traditional position. Although they can be installed at a lower height, the shape of the bowl is not designed to accommodate the lower position. The arc of a flow of liquid expands with distance from the source; thus, the bowl of a low urinal should be wider and protrude out farther. Conventional applications overlook this, and the maintenance problems that can result could negatively affect the acceptance of waterless urinals (see Figure 2–1) since the odor from spray on the floor and walls may be attributed to the urinal technology. Furthermore, some waterless urinals require use of special products to maintain a seal over the water in the drain and have traps that need to be replaced periodically. Some require special cleansers to protect the finish and special tools and procedures to change the trap filter. If not properly maintained, the urinals will cease to function, start smelling, and anger building occupants and owners. Bad experiences like this can result in replacing the product and even abandoning the goal of sustainability. Acceptance of innovative sustainable products can be enhanced through universal design.

Design for Healthcare

The adoption of evidence-based design has become an important trend in the design of healthcare facilities. For example, research has demonstrated that spread of infection is a primary factor in length of stay at acute care facilities. Creating products and design strategies that can reduce infection in such facilities requires a universal design approach that recognizes the diversity of healthcare professional staff, including language, size, physical ability, and other factors. The strategies used to control infection also reduce employee fatigue and

Figure 2–1: Waterless urinal. This is a waterless urinal at the EPA Region 8 Headquarters. While such urinals have benefits for the environment, they can present maintenance problems when not properly designed to make them easy to use and service.

increase their ability to pay attention to infection control procedures. For example, designing nursing units in hospitals to reduce trips from one place to another is an important method for reducing the spread of infection. In addition, some successful strategies, such as providing only single rooms in acute care facilities, improve the overall environment of healthcare facilities for the patients (Figure 2–2).

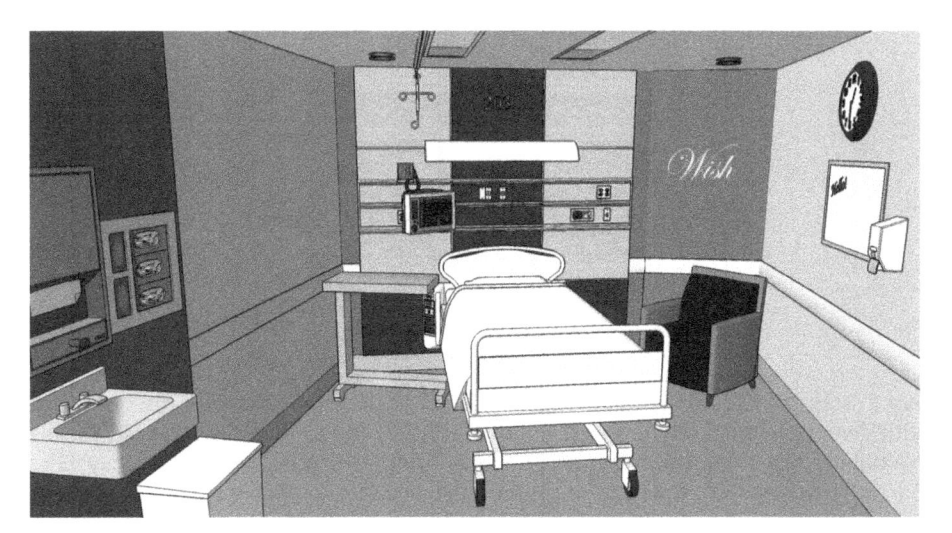

Figure 2–2: Single-patient recovery room. Single-patient rooms in healthcare facilities provide privacy without curtains and help prevent the spread of infections.

Source: Image courtesy of Smith + Associates Architects

Aging in Place

A large majority of individuals want to age where they currently live. However, at this time, only age-restricted housing for elderly persons can usually accommodate the health and social problems typically associated with aging. To remain in their own homes while aging, people need housing designs that can be adapted to a wider range of health conditions than traditional designs allow. Encouraging housing producers to adopt universal design features is a key aspect of design for aging in place. This includes a no-step entry, bathrooms on an accessible floor level, potential for a sleeping space on an accessible level, good lighting, efficient space planning, and other features that reduce effort and accommodate short-term and chronic disabilities (Figure 2–3).

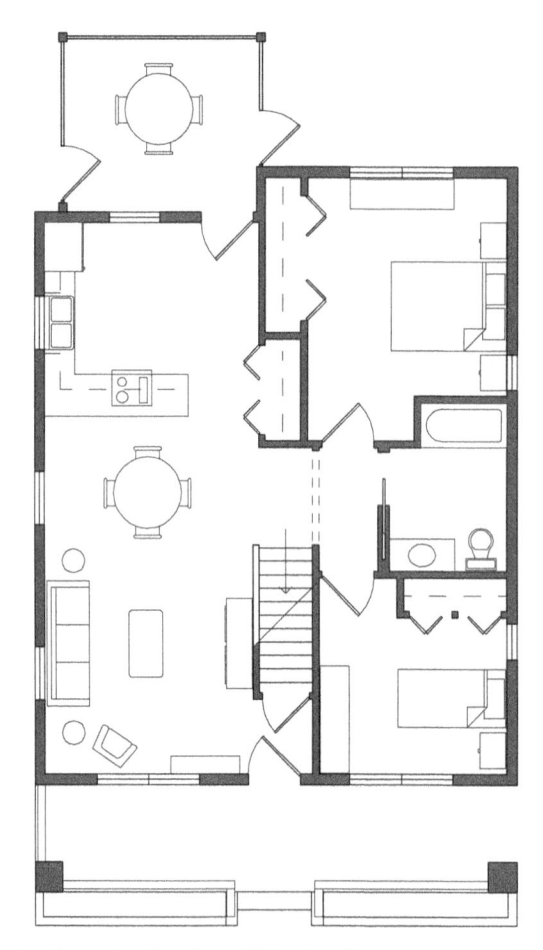

Figure 2–3: Home plan for aging in place. This plan has no-step entries at the front and rear. It has first-floor bedrooms, kitchen, and laundry facilities, and the tub can be easily replaced with a roll-in shower if needed. This home has a first-floor interior footprint of only 930 square feet, which demonstrates that homes can be small and affordable while still allowing aging in place.

Source: From Inclusive Housing: A Pattern Book Design for Diversity and Equality by The Center for Inclusive Design and Environmental Access. Copyright © 2010 by Edward Steinfeld and Jonathan White. Used by permission of W.W. Norton & Company, Inc.

Health Promotion

Environmental design is now recognized as a major component of health promotion. Nowhere is this more evident than in supporting active living to reduce obesity. Older people and those with disabilities have higher rates of obesity than the population at large. Thus, they are a major target group for such interventions. In addition, reducing obesity and inactivity in children is an important step in reducing disability rates in the future. Locating services within a half-mile radius of all residences is known to increase walking rates significantly. However, older adults, people with disabilities, and young children need a shorter distance to services to make them usable. Older persons and individuals with disabilities may also need additional public transportation options to maintain active lifestyles. Moreover, safe and accessible street crossings and good security are particularly important to encourage walking for all three groups. Active living interventions can benefit from applying universal design to land use planning, zoning, and accessible housing policy to increase choices of housing types and provide mixed-use centers that reduce travel distances and encourage walking (Figure 2–4).

Figure 2–4: Mizner Park, Boca Raton, FL. This mixed-use center in a popular retirement area includes residential, retail, entertainment, civic, and outdoor recreation facilities. Some on-street parking is provided. Additional parking is located in garages behind the commercial and residential buildings. Mixed uses promote active living because walking destinations are close to residences

Homelessness

Displacement from one's home is a frequent occurrence throughout the world. Lately it seems that each season brings another natural disaster or political upheaval with mass dislocations, even in highly developed countries. In low-income countries, chronic homelessness is a major social problem. Homeless people have disproportionately high rates of disability, especially mental health conditions. Women and children are particularly vulnerable to violence and exploitation when they are displaced, as in refugee camps. Applying universal design to this severe problem should be an important goal of humanitarian efforts. Such an initiative would involve rethinking everything from emergency response policy to product design. One example is the development of policy initiatives in emergency camps to protect vulnerable groups at shared sanitary facilities. Another is the design of water containers that reduce the number of trips members of a household have to make to obtain water for a day (Figure 2–5).

Social Justice

Throughout the world, designers with a sense of social responsibility are concerned that good design, like many other resources of society, is a commodity that many cannot afford. Although initially focused on disability rights, universal design can focus on any civil rights issue because ultimately design for diversity is concerned with social justice for all. Thus, universal design should give attention to supporting access to housing, education, healthcare,

Figure 2–5: Hippo Water Roller. This design, inspired by a lawn roller, reduces the need for lifting and carrying and allows an individual to carry more water at one time (hipporoller.org).

Source: Image courtesy of Grant Gibbs

transportation, and other resources in society for all those groups that have been excluded from full participation. Universal design is particularly appropriate in the context of design for low-income minority groups, which often have higher rates of disability than the general population (Figure 2–6).

Figure 2–6: Musician's Village, New Orleans, LA. Habitat for Humanity is building a village for low-income musicians complete with a music school where residents can give lessons and concerts. (a) Street view of houses. (b) Accessible home.

The examples just presented demonstrate the potential of universal design to solve contemporary social problems and the range of applications that are possible. Although universal design emerged as a response to the needs of people with disabilities, it is clear that the philosophy has much to contribute at an even broader scale. Increasing adoption of universal design in these other fields will provide greater resources to help practitioners, including more publications, design tools, and research. Thus, it is mutually beneficial for universal designers to develop alliances to advance policy, articulate the intersections to practice, and develop joint initiatives to address these social problems.

Summary

Usefulness has been an important part of design practice since the first principles of design practice were written. It was an important aspect of modernism, and it continues to have significance. Critics of both the modernist style and our contemporary consumer-oriented urban culture often focus on the need for more human-centered design, in everything from consumer electronics to urban planning.

The concept of human-centered design was formulated over 50 years ago, in the 1960s. Since that time, it has taken many forms. Many disciplines are involved in the various threads of human-centered design practice, including design professionals, industrial and biomedical engineers, behavioral scientists, rehabilitation scientists and therapists, physicians, nurses, and public health professionals.

Universal design married the ideals of human-centered design with the social goals of the civil rights movements. It has an important role to play in advancing human-centered design across a wide range of scales, from hand-held products to design of new cities, as well as many different social problems. We expect that, as the decade advances, more attention will be paid to a broader range of issues than disability rights. Developing initiatives that apply knowledge from universal design to these other issues is a particularly important direction for the continued evolution of the field.

Review Topics

1. Describe the history of "usefulness" in design and explain why it is becoming more important.
2. What are some critiques of modernism? How is universal design related to yet different from modernism?
3. What other contemporary design issues have a relationship to universal design? Explain the relationships using examples.

References

Alexander, C. 1964. *Notes on the Synthesis of Form.* Cambridge, MA: Harvard University Press.
Bednar, M. 1977. *Barrier Free Environments.* Stroudsburg, PA: Dowden, Hutchinson, and Ross.
Boudon, P. 1972. *Lived-in Architecture: Le Corbusier's Pessac Revisited.* Cambridge, MA: MIT Press.
British Standards Institute. 2005. "Design Management Systems," *Managing Inclusive Design* BS 7000–6.
Churchman, C. W. 1968. *The Systems Approach.* New York: Delacorte Press.
Danford, G. S. and J. Maurer 2005. "Empirical Tests of the Claimed Benefits of Universal Design." Paper presented at the Proceedings of the Thirty-sixth Annual International Conference of

the Environment Design Research Association. Edmond, OK: Environment Design Research Association, 123–128.
Design for All Europe. 2008, February 12. "Design for All." www.designforalleurope.org/Design-for-All/.
Design for All Foundation. n.d. "What Is Design for All?" www.designforall.org/en/dfa/dfa.php.
Duany, A., E. Plater-Zyberk, and J. Speck. 2001. *Suburban Nation: The Rise of Sprawl and the Decline of the American Dream.* New York: North Point Press.
Dunham-Jones, E. and J. Williamson. 2009. *Retrofitting Suburbia: Urban Design Solutions for Redesigning Suburbs.* Hoboken, NJ: John Wiley & Sons.
Eberhard, J. P. 2009. *Brain Landscape: The Coexistence of Neuroscience and Architecture.* New York: Oxford University Press.
Frumkin, H. 2006. "Cities, Suburbs, and Urban Sprawl." In N. Freudenberg, S. Galea, and D. Vlahov (eds.), *Cities and the Health of the Public* (pp. 143–175). Nashville, TN: Vanderbilt University Press.
Gans, H. J. 1962. *The Urban Villagers.* New York: Free Press.
Gottdiener, M. 1997. *The Theming of America.* Boulder, CO: Westview Press.
Gratz, R. B. 2010. *The Battle for Gotham: New York in the Shadow of Robert Moses and Jane Jacobs.* New York: Nation Books.
Habraken, N. J. 1973. "SAR Design Method for Housing: Seven Years of Development in the Real World." *DMG-DRS Journal for Design Research Methods* 7 (3). (July/Sept.).
Hall, E. T. 1969. *The Hidden Dimension.* Garden City, NY: Anchor Books.
Hayden, D. 2003. *Building Suburbia: Green Fields and Urban Growth, 1820–2000.* New York: Vintage Books.
Imrie, R. and P. Hall 2001. *Inclusive Design: Designing and Developing Accessible Environments.* London: Spon Press.
Jacobs, J. 1961. *The Death and Life of Great American Cities.* New York: Random House.
Lawton, M. P. and L. Nahemow. 1973. "Ecology and the Aging Process." In C. Eisdorfer and M. P. Lawton (eds.), *Psychology of Adult Development and Aging* (pp. 619–674). Washington, DC: American Psychological Association.
Le Corbusier. [1923] 1985. *Towards a New Architecture.* New York: Dover Publications.
Lusher, R. H. and R. Mace. 1989. "Design for Physical and Mental Disabilities." In J. A.Wilkes and R. T. Packard (eds.), *Encyclopedia of Architecture: Design Engineering and Construction* (pp. 748-763). New York: John Wiley & Sons.
Mace, R. 1985. *Universal Design, Barrier Free Environments for Everyone.* Los Angeles: Designers West.
Marks, J. 2009. "A History of Educational Facilities Laboratories (EFL)." www.edfacilities.org/pubs/efl2.pdf.
Marshall, J. D., M. Brauer, and L. D. Frank. 2009. "Healthy Neighborhoods: Walkability and Air Pollution." *Environmental Health Perspectives* 117 (11): 1,752–1,759.
McCamant, K. and C. Durrett. 1994. *Cohousing: A Contemporary Approach to Housing Ourselves.* Oakland, CA: New Village Press.
Norman, D. 2004. *Emotional Design: Why We Love (or Hate) Everyday Things.* New York: Basic Books.
Rainwater, L. 1966. "Fear and the House-as-Haven in the Lower Class." *Journal of the American Planning Association* 32 (1): 23–31.
Rapoport, A. 1969. *House Form and Culture.* Englewood Cliffs NJ: Prentice-Hall.
Russell, L. 1999. *The Future of the Built Environment. The Millennium Papers.* London: Age Concern England.
Sanoff, H. 2000. *Community Participation Methods in Design and Planning.* New York: John Wiley & Sons.
Schweitzer, L. and J. Zhou. 2010. "Neighborhood Air Quality, Respiratory Health, and Vulnerable Populations in Compact and Sprawled Regions." *Journal of the American Planning Association* 76 (3): 363–371.
Sommer, R. 1969. *Personal Space: The Behavioral Basis of Design.* Englewood Cliffs, NJ: Prentice-Hall.

Sommer, R. 1974. *Tight Spaces: Hard Architecture and How to Humanize It.* Englewood Cliffs, NJ: Prentice-Hall.

Steinfeld, E., and B. Tauke. 2003. "Reflection and Critique on Universal Design." Paper presented at the Proceedings of the American Collegiate Schools of Architecture Annual Meeting. Louisville, KY.

Stineman, M. G., R. N. Ross, R. Fiedler, C. V. Granger, and G. Maislin. 2003. "Functional Independence Staging: Conceptual Foundation, Face Validity, and Empirical Derivation." *Archives of Physical Medicine Rehabilitation* 84 (1): 29–37.

Veblen, T. 1994. *The Theory of the Leisure Class.* New York: Penguin Books. Originally published 1899.

Welch, P. 1995. "What 'Is Universal Design?'" In P. Welch (ed.), *Strategies for Teaching Universal Design,* Ch. 1, pp. 1–4. Boston: Adaptive Environments Center and MIG Communications.

Williams, C. and C. Williams. 1974. *Craftsmen of Necessity.* New York: Random House.

Wolski, A., N. A. Dembsey, and B. J. Meacham. 2000. "Accommodating Perceptions of Risk in Performance-based Building Fire Safety Code Development." *Fire Safety Journal* 34 (3): 297–309.

3

The New Demographics

Demography for Universal Design

Demography is a branch of sociology that studies population statistics. These statistics can include many different types of data, such as income levels, sex distributions, age distributions, living arrangements, educational levels, and others. The data are usually expressed in tabular or graphic format. Demographers also analyze the relationships among variables. For example, they might look at the percentage of married people of different ages and compare that percentage to the percentage of people who live in single-family homes across age groups. Few designers, planners, and policy makers are trained to review, understand, and interpret demographics. Although they do not necessarily have to become experts in demography, by understanding demographic trends, they can better understand the scope of universal design, be able to make a business case for universal design features, and even plan a career. In short, by understanding demography, we can learn about the issues that are important for universal design and gain a better understanding of priorities for design.

The founder of universal design, Ron Mace, and his colleagues observed: "Changing demographics, perceptions, and attitudes are fueling the demand for more sophisticated products, housing, and business environments that are accessible for people of all ages, sizes, and abilities. These changes signal a wide array of opportunities for designers to apply their creative energies to the solution of practical social and psychological problems" (Mace, Hardie, and Place 1991, p. 3). However, Mace also warned that designers "may also fall into a chasm of uncharted territory without the benefit of appropriate training or technical assistance" (p. 3). This chapter builds one bridge across that chasm by elucidating the demographic trends that provide a rationale for universal design and demonstrating how the designer can use and benefit from demography.

A basic understanding of demography is so important to modern life that it has become part of popular culture. For example, we like to label the generations using nicknames, such as the Baby Boomers or Generation X, Y or Z,* and are fascinated with understanding the

---

*Baby Boom (born 1946–1964); X (born 1965–1976); Y (born 1977–1994); Z (born after 1994) (Williams and Page 2010).

cultural differences among them. Thus, many designers already have some understanding of the importance of demography. This chapter takes a closer look at the subject to demonstrate how demography can support universal design practice.

The prevalence of disability is used most often to provide a rationale for adoption of universal design. When publications about universal design address demography at all, most report population statistics on the frequency of different disabilities, such as the number of people who have vision impairments due to chronic diseases and conditions. However, this is a limited perspective on the issue. In the study of demography, there are many other ways to define disability. For example, disability can be defined as a *functional limitation*, an inability to complete an activity independently, such as not being able to read print or recognize a person from across a room. Defined the first way, the number of people with a vision limitation in the United States is estimated to be 8.2 million; defined the second way, it is estimated that 13.5 million in the nation have limited visual abilities (Waldrop and Stern 2003). Furthermore, there are many types of demographic data in addition to the prevalence of disability that are relevant for universal design practice; for example, age.

A life span perspective enables us to understand how design priorities change as people pass through the life span. This perspective frames demographic trends in terms of changing abilities over time. Design for aging is often cited as a major issue in universal design since there is a strong relationship between aging and disability. One rationale for adopting universal design practices is the fact that many populations worldwide are aging. This argument reflects the fact that everyone eventually will benefit from universal design as they age. But a life span perspective should not ignore the needs of people at other stages of life, which are just as significant. For example, universal design can provide increased safety and security for children, reduce stress for parents, and support independence in old age. Demographic data, such as the extent of victimization of children or the percentage of single-parent families, is useful to demonstrate that older people are not the only age group to benefit from universal design.

Economic factors are very important in universal design practice. One of the arguments against adoption of universal design in developing countries is that it costs too much. However, demographic data on projected economic growth and household income can demonstrate where new markets are emerging for convenience goods and services. Demographic data on household expenditures can also identify trends toward new spending patterns that universal design can address. For example, the rising percentage of income devoted to transportation for U.S. households due to energy cost increases is useful to make a case for universal design applications in public transit. If new riders seeking to lower their transportation costs find that public transportation is pleasant and convenient, they are more likely to continue to use the service and less likely to switch back to automobiles when fuel costs decline.

Demographic factors interact in complex ways. For example, loss of income usually accompanies retirement. Thus, manufacturers used to believe that older people did not have the money to purchase goods and services and that targeting that market was counterproductive. However, data on expendable income show that a universal design industry could be supported by the aging population alone. On average, older households have substantially more assets than younger households do, and despite reduced income, they have more money to spend because their expenses are lower. In fact, the Boomer generation is expected to have even a higher disposable income than the current generation of seniors (McKinsey Global Institute 2008).

Disposable income is the amount of money one has to spend freely, that is, not committed to housing, food, healthcare, or transportation. The older generation has considerable assets and income at their disposal, and they have more freedom to spend it than younger groups because they do not have as many other obligations. A cohort is a group of people bracketed by a specific set of years, e.g., 45–50 years old. Figure 3–1 shows incomes and projected incomes of four generation cohorts as they aged and will age. The chart shows that each successive cohort has had higher and higher incomes (adjusted for inflation) and is projected to have higher and higher incomes during old age. Barring economic catastrophe, as the population ages, the youngest cohorts will enter retirement with substantially higher annual incomes than the current generation of older people, about $25,000 more on average. The point at which income starts to drop sharply reflects retirement. The chart also shows that the younger cohorts will postpone retirement about five years, thereby maintaining higher incomes for a longer period than the current generation. Thus, as the Boomers get older, there will be many more retirees with much higher disposable income. They will have a significant economic impact. Of course, prolonged recessions can alter the economic picture of the "golden years" significantly.

Note that not all older people are well off financially. There are, in fact, two marketplaces for universal design: the free market and the public sector. A relationship exists between independence among low-income older people and the burden on the public services. Obviously, providing services to large numbers of low-income people will have an economic impact on the public who supports those services by paying taxes and by charitable giving. In a caring society, if a growing older population needs many services, both government and not-for-profit public service agencies would provide them. As the population of older people grows, agency budgets are going to have to increase to meet the demand. If, however, their clients become more independent and rely less on the government services, the impact on the government and not-for-profit sector will be lower, and there will be less need to raise taxes or charitable donations.

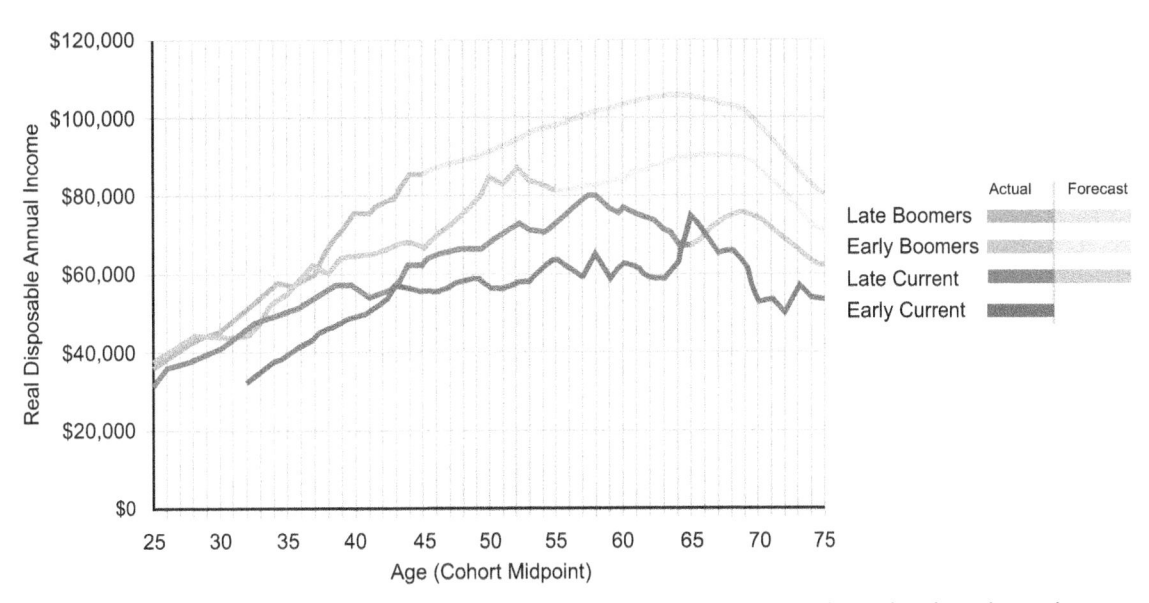

Figure 3–1: Disposable annual income per household by age and generation cohort. This chart shows that the Baby Boomer generation has more disposable annual income than younger people do and more than the current generation of older people. It demonstrates that older people today have significant purchasing power.

Therefore, universal design makes economic sense in the public sector as well as the free market. And, from the perspective of the public good, investing in universal design right now would also be a sensible political agenda item, given that the burden of services provided to the older generation is a major political issue.

Uses of Demography in Design

Demography is not just about compiling numbers; it is also about understanding what those numbers suggest about the target population, the groups that will be served by any project, their needs, and future social developments that must be anticipated. Assembling information on multiple demographic characteristics, or variables, such as age, gender, education, health, and disability, and learning about the relationships among these characteristics can provide insight for any design project. A universal designer who understands demography is analogous to a designer who knows a client well, only in this case the "client" is the population of people expected to use a design rather than an individual. A designer who understands demography well should have insights to produce a product that is more suitable for a wide range of end users.

Demography can help designers in many ways. These include:

1. *Predicting future demand and need for products, building types, or even urban design strategies.* For example, the rapid increase in the number of children born after World War II led to a huge increase in school construction, a major factor in community planning and suburban land development in the postwar years.
2. *Identifying features that are desirable in products or buildings.* As women entered the workforce in increasingly larger numbers, workplaces that were exclusively male had to be adjusted to address the implications of having women present. This included providing restrooms for women and allowances for pregnancy. But, the drop in the number of full time homemakers also drove a huge increase in the demand for child care settings, full-day kindergarten classes, disposable diapers, and prepared meals, among other products and spaces, changing the face of education and supermarket businesses.
3. *Career development.* Young professionals, in particular, can help their careers by anticipating and serving needs of population groups that more established professionals have neglected. Architects who understood the importance of the increasing size of the older population were able to learn the basics of design for aging and become leaders in that field before the rest of the profession even noticed.
4. *Knowledge translation.* New trends can identify the needs for knowledge. For example, increasing rates of asthma and other respiratory diseases suggest that interior designers and architects should learn more about indoor air pollution. Designers can apply knowledge about the factors affecting respiratory illnesses to address this issue.
5. *Networking and advocacy.* Establishing expertise in demographic analysis can increase exposure to government agencies, professional associations, and the business community, which can lead to jobs, referrals, and recommendations. In addition to a competitive edge, it can also help build a constituency for good design. Groups that have special needs, in particular, understand the necessity to promote their interests and influence both client decisions and public response. For example, representatives of advocacy groups can help to support a

project that has some community resistance (e.g., a plan to build additional senior housing that requires a zoning variance).

It is important to note that demography is not the only justification for design decisions. Sometimes demographic data can be misleading, and data are not always available to answer designers' questions. We need to learn to interpret demographic data, make judgments based on imperfect data, and determine when additional data may be needed to make a decision. To do this, we need to understand more about the beneficiaries of universal design. Who is universal design for, and whom does it benefit the most?

Beneficiaries of Universal Design

In most texts about universal design, people with disabilities are viewed as the target population, the primary beneficiaries of universal design practices. The aging of the population is often identified as an important demographic trend that will affect the market for universal design since aging is directly associated with disability; the longer one lives, the more likely one is to have a disability of some type. In the 1970s, lever-handled door openers and curb ramps were introduced into mandated accessibility codes and standards. At the time, they were viewed as special features that would benefit only a small group of people. However, experience has shown that the entire population finds these features much easier to use. Recognizing that the target population might be much larger, leaders in the field of accessibility began to study demographic data to demonstrate that the target population for accessible design was much larger than originally thought.

First, they started studying how disability was defined and found that there actually are many possible definitions. Most definitions of disability are developed to identify the extent of a public health problem, the need for services provided by government, business trends, or economic implications of a policy that provides benefits for people with disabilities. Thus, the prevalence of disability is often estimated by asking survey respondents the extent to which they are limited in activities of daily living (ADLs), which include toileting, walking, eating, reading, and so on. Such data can define the population that would benefit from a disability rights law or from eligibility policies for special housing or training programs. Many government policies need an even more focused definition. So, for example, a definition used to evaluate ability to work is needed to establish eligibility for disability benefits. For policy development in public health or healthcare, governments often obtain prevalence data on chronic conditions or impairments, such as heart conditions, hearing loss, vision loss, or dementia. They might also collect data on specific diseases, such as cancer, diabetes, or Alzheimer's disease. Governments may also want to know the number of people who use various assistive devices, such as wheelchairs or walkers, in order to budget properly for health programs that pay for such equipment. Note that while chronic condition, impairment, or disease data identifies the population at risk of functional disability, it also includes people who may not necessarily have a significant functional limitation at present. This is particularly true if they are in the early stages of a progressive disease or if their limitation is not severe. But, an at risk population has a high probability to benefit from accessibility during their lifetime.

Demographic data can be cross-tabulated with other variables, such as age and income. Usually surveyed respondents' location of residence is available, and data often are reported in aggregate form arranged by census tract, a method that is particularly useful to obtain local estimates. For planners, developers, architects, and interior designers, knowing whether a local population is different from that of the country as a whole is very useful. However, it is also important to understand the interaction of such variables as age and income in order to make more informed conclusions and predictions. For example, designers who recognize that both advanced age and low income are associated with higher disability rates will understand that product affordability is as important as good design for aging consumers.

In 1979, Steinfeld et al. devised the Enabler concept (Figure 3–2). The Enabler provides, in a simple ideogram, a representation of the population categories served by *accessible* design that can be used to make population estimates. The categories describe this target population in terms of functional limitation, such as inability to walk, total blindness, difficulty grasping, and extremes of size and weight. Data on the extent of functional limitations are extremely useful for designers because these problems can be related to specific parts of the environment. Unfortunately, although some demographic data is available on functional ability, there are many gaps, even 30 years later. This is due to the fact that the policy missions of government agencies often do not address the needs of the design professions for information. Thus, obtaining and interpreting demographic information on functional limitations that meets the specific needs of designers

THE ENABLER

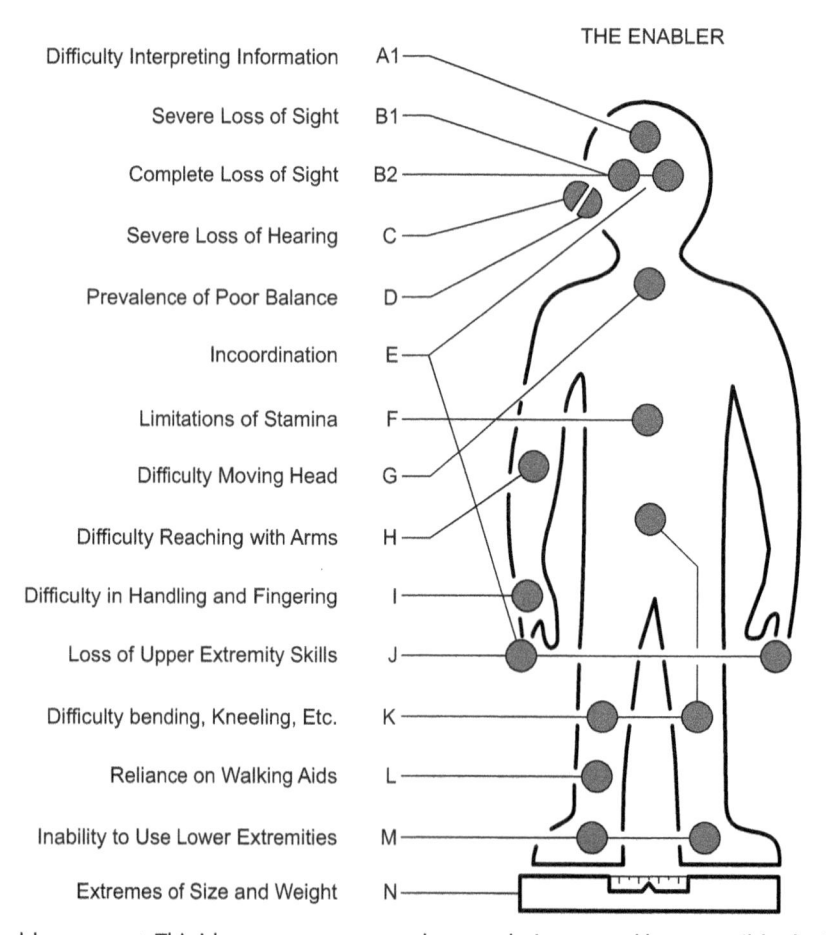

A1	Difficulty Interpreting Information
B1	Severe Loss of Sight
B2	Complete Loss of Sight
C	Severe Loss of Hearing
D	Prevalence of Poor Balance
E	Incoordination
F	Limitations of Stamina
G	Difficulty Moving Head
H	Difficulty Reaching with Arms
I	Difficulty in Handling and Fingering
J	Loss of Upper Extremity Skills
K	Difficulty bending, Kneeling, Etc.
L	Reliance on Walking Aids
M	Inability to Use Lower Extremities
N	Extremes of Size and Weight

Figure 3–2: Enabler concept. This ideogram represents the population served by accessible design.

may require some ingenuity and perseverance (see Steinfeld et al. 1979). In the case of estimates generated with the Enabler concept, the authors identified "at risk" populations when they could not obtain the appropriate data. Thus, for example, the prevalence of hearing losses in advanced age puts all people over the age of 75 in the "at risk" category for severe loss of hearing.

In general, the literature on universal design has focused on the same target population as the literature on accessible design: people with mobility, sensory, and cognitive impairments, including the older population as one at risk for these types of disabilities. This focus is limited for five reasons.

1. It assumes that only people in these groups can experience a temporary or permanent loss of function. However, other demographic groups have significant functional limitations as well.
2. Many social and economic characteristics can amplify the impact of barriers in life by creating limitations on access to resources, for example, dependence on inadequate public transportation systems.
3. Geographic location can cause barriers due to topography, lack of services, and exposure to extreme climatic or social threats. A good example is living in a neighborhood without convenient access to a supermarket.
4. This definition of the target population gives the false impression that young people without disabilities do not benefit from universal design, which limits the application of universal design principles in practice.
5. It creates an impression that universal design can be practiced simply by complying with accessibility codes, relegating the concept to a legal concern within the design professions and to technical specialists who are code experts.

Although universal design does have strong roots in the disability rights and design for aging movements, it is important to look beyond traditional disability and aging statistics when studying the target population, especially if we wish to consider the dynamic nature of modern societies that are experiencing vast socioeconomic shifts and rapid technological and economic changes. Universal design goals are better realized if designers understand the needs and preferences of a wide range of groups. Other demographic groups have needs that are as serious as those of people with mobility, vision, and hearing limitations. Some of these groups are likely to encounter many more barriers in their daily lives. A broader view of the target population for universal design would include, but not be limited to, eight groups:

1. People who are not typically defined as having a functional limitation but have temporary and permanent limitations in function due to body shape or stature. These include pregnant women, single mothers, children, and "outliers" in typical population distributions of human characteristics (e.g., very short, very tall, very light, or very heavy people).
2. Caregivers who have people dependent on them and benefit directly through an environment that supports their care activities and indirectly through reduced caregiver burden when those they care for are more independent. This group includes families with small children, families with members with disabilities, spouses of older people who serve as informal caregivers, and even professional caregivers, such as nannies.
3. People with psychosocial conditions, such as autism, Alzheimer's, and chronic depression, who encounter social barriers but also may have limitations in motor activities, perception, and cognition.

4. People with behavioral and/or functional limitations due to alcohol and/or drug dependency (both legal and illegal) or medications that alter perception or cognition.
5. Minority ethnic groups or foreign visitors with culturally based traditions, preferences, and expectations that are different from those of the majority population or host country, including differences in language, diet, social interaction norms, and related spatial behaviors.
6. Low- and even middle-income populations who often experience lack of access to services and resources due to residential location and limited mobility.
7. People who are displaced from culturally normal living environments and find themselves in temporary living situations or in vulnerable or exposed conditions due to extreme events, such as political unrest, war, or natural disasters.
8. Abused spouses, children, or homeless people who need protected environments with specialized services that can artificially restrict their freedom of movement and their access to community resources.

This broader approach to defining the target population for universal design changes our perspective significantly. Rather than viewing the target population as the less able, to whom we owe a charitable effort, it demonstrates that respecting everyone's right to an environment free of unnecessary barriers facilitates the development of products and environments that work equally well for all. To the designer, it emphasizes the importance of practicing universal design all the time, not just for certain projects and to meet legal requirements. Table 3-1 gives some selected demographics of traditional target groups for universal design.

Understanding the relationships among different demographic variables is just as important as knowing about independent populations. For example, people with disabilities are seven to ten times more likely than people without disabilities to report worse health than one year previously (Hendershot 2006). There may be many reasons for this finding; for example, chronic conditions

Table 3–1: Some Target Groups for Universal Design

Group	Percentage of U.S. Population
People age 65 and over	12.5[a]
People with some type of disability	19.3[b]
Ambulatory disability	6.9[c]
Cognitive impairment	4.8[c]
Hearing impairment	3.5[c]
Visual impairment	2.6[c]
People unemployed with a disability	2.9[b]
People using wheeled mobility devices	1.0[c]

Please note that some categories may overlap.

[a] U.S. Census Bureau, Current Population Survey, Annual Social and Economic Supplement (2009a).

[b] U.S. Census Bureau (2000).

[c] American Community Survey (2009b).

[d] LaPlante and Kaye (2010).

[e] Flegal et al. (2010).

get worse as a progressive disease advances, lack of accessible healthcare facilities, inadequacies in healthcare services for people with disabilities, and conditions associated with chronic disability that increase susceptibility to health threats. But the bottom line is that companies that make healthcare equipment and products or operators of healthcare facilities should make people with disabilities a major target population for design because they are likely to make up a significant user population. The relationship between health and disability also demonstrates that designers who work in the healthcare field need to pay attention to a broader range of demographic characteristics than just health status in order to identify the specific needs of the end user population.

Staying alert to changing demographic trends is particularly important to advance practice in any design field. Some trends are more important than others because they have wide-ranging impacts. However, it is important to avoid focusing on a single demographic trend to the exclusion of others. As noted, universal designers often argue that the most important demographic trend is population aging because of its relationship to disability. During the twentieth century, the number of elderly (people age 65 and older) in the United States increased tenfold (Figure 3–3). Since 1960, it has increased by 107 percent, while the overall population has increased only 50 percent (Friedland and Summer 2005). In 2009, the U.S. median age reached 36.7 years, its highest level ever, increasing 2.5 years between 1990 and 2000 and 1.4 years between 2000 and 2009. The increased numbers of older people indirectly increases the number of disabilities in a population because so many disabling conditions are age related.

However, another very important trend is society's increasing heterogeneity. In 2007, minorities constituted one-third of the U.S. population and totaled 100.7 million people, larger than the total U.S. population in 1910 and larger than the total population of all but 11 countries (U.S. Census Bureau 2007). By 2042, white people of European descent will no longer be a majority of the U.S. population, a trend also seen in many other highly developed societies

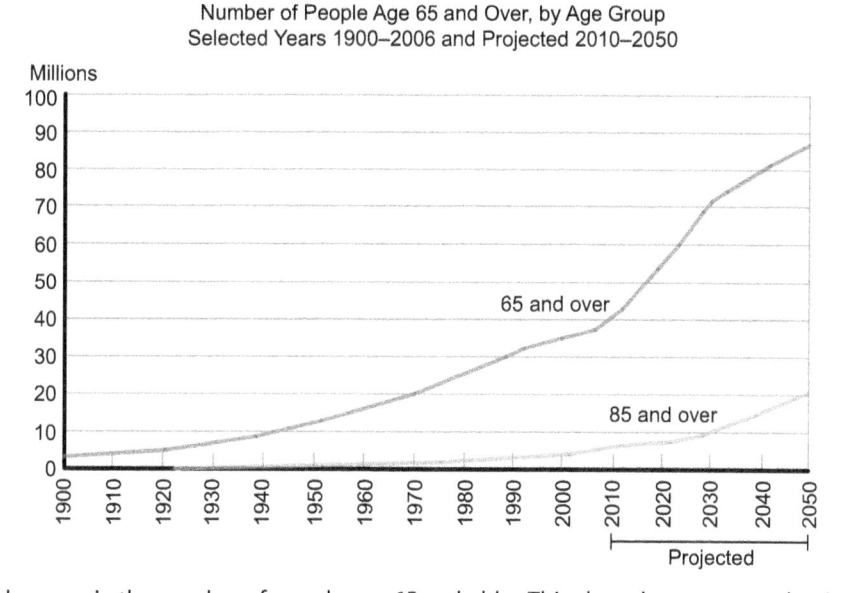

Figure 3–3: Increase in the number of people age 65 and older. This chart demonstrates the sizable population of older people in the United States.

(e.g., Canada, Europe, Australia, and New Zealand). At that time, the white population will be older as a whole than minority groups (U.S. Census Bureau 2008) (Figure 3–4). The next generation is truly a melting pot, with different values, needs, and aspirations from those of their parents and older white majorities. In 2009, children from minority groups became the majority in enrollment in southern U.S. public schools, a trend that is eight to ten years ahead of the country as a whole (Southern Education Foundation 2007; Viadero 2010). Minority status is closely related to many other demographic characteristics, such as language, family size, income, education, lifestyle choices, and health status. This increase in diversity is another good reason to practice universal design in general; it also demonstrates the importance of learning how to find, analyze, and interpret demographic data to avoid the misconception that disability and aging alone are the only drivers for universal design.

Despite the importance of disability, aging, and diversity, the demographic trend with the most impact on use of the environment might well turn out to be related to lifestyle. Most of us know that there is an obesity epidemic spreading around the world. The increase in obesity among U.S. adults is linked to diet and sedentary lifestyles (Sallis and Glanz 2006). This trend leveled off between 2005 and 2010, peaking at 34 percent, more than double the rate of 30 years ago (Flegal et al. 2010). Obesity is associated with a large number of chronic conditions that affect physical, sensory, and cognitive function, including diabetes, high blood pressure, cancer, severe liver damage, osteoarthritis, joint damage, and mobility impairments. Obesity and disability are

US Populatuion Projections to 2050
Percentage by race and Hispanic Origin

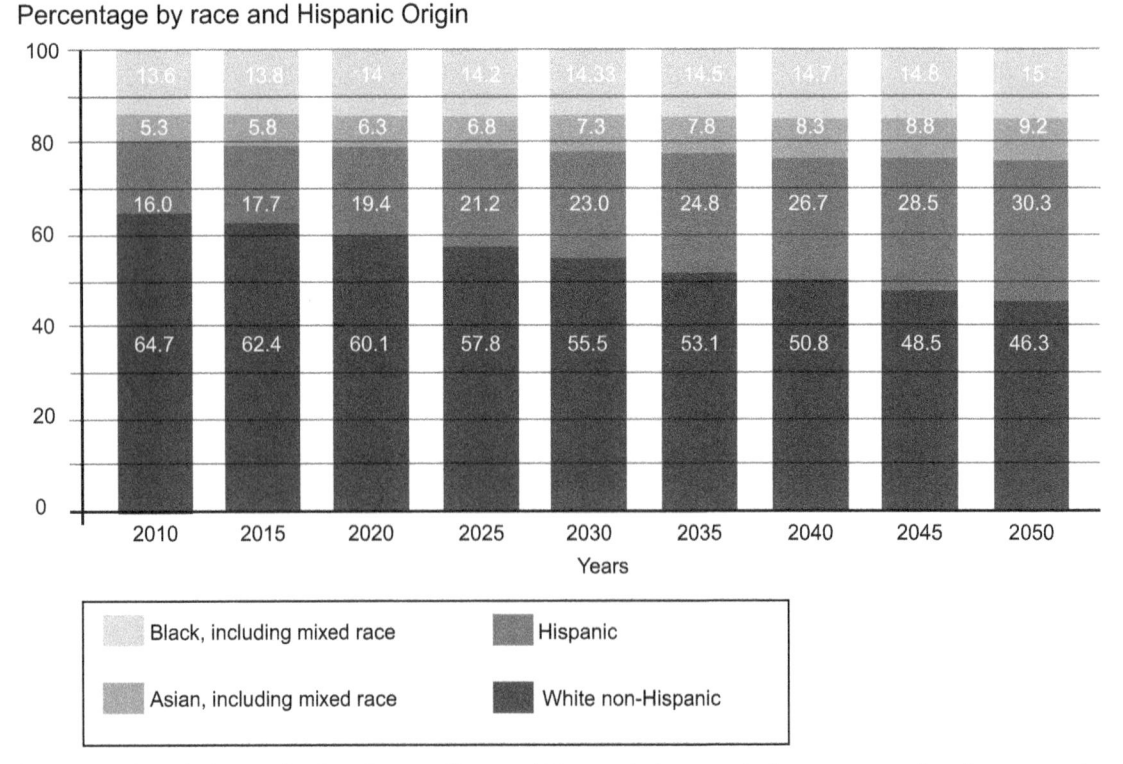

Year	Black, including mixed race	Asian, including mixed race	Hispanic	White non-Hispanic
2010	13.6	5.3	16.0	64.7
2015	13.8	5.8	17.7	62.4
2020	14	6.3	19.4	60.1
2025	14.2	6.8	21.2	57.8
2030	14.33	7.3	23.0	55.5
2035	14.5	7.8	24.8	53.1
2040	14.7	8.3	26.7	50.8
2045	14.8	8.8	28.5	48.5
2050	15	9.2	30.3	46.3

Figure 3–4: Population projections by race. Data on U.S. population trends demonstrates that the country is becoming even more diverse.

related; almost 33 percent of adults with disability and activity limitations are obese, compared with 19 percent of adults with no reported disability (Altman and Bernstein 2008). Although obesity is increasing in many countries worldwide, the United States has by far the highest rate (Figure 3–5).

Certain design issues are directly relevant for people with obesity. For example, universal design ideas could be adopted to accommodate people who are too wide to fit in a typical theater seat or too heavy to use certain devices. The increasing prevalence of obesity is already driving innovation in business practices, product design, and urban planning. It clearly results in a need for larger products that are structurally stronger (Weingarten 2010). For example, recently, a supersized and super-strong toilet seat was introduced on the market to accommodate people with extreme obesity. A 2010 study found that men with obesity are at higher risk not only of heart disease and diabetes but also of being seriously injured in car crashes because of differences in body shape, fat distribution, and center of gravity from men with healthy body weight (Zhu et al. 2010). Not only will car safety systems need to be redesigned, but even the crash test dummy is being altered (Sears 2007). The City of Trenton, New Jersey, made national headlines in 2010 when a Rutgers University study revealed that almost half of its children are overweight or obese (Ohri-Vachaspati et al. 2010). Thus, increasing obesity rates can create local priorities for planning, design, and services, for example, in the case of Trenton, improving the pedestrian and recreational environment to encourage greater activity by children, or, improving access to nutritional food. Obesity can lead to a variety of psychosocial problems, including depression, which can reduce work productivity and diminish quality of life. Obesity is age related as well, but if unchecked, the alarming increase in childhood obesity will lead to major changes in disability trends as the younger people with obesity age.

Which of these trends, then, is most important to universal design: Disability? Cultural diversity? Aging? Obesity? It should be clear by now that no one, two, or even three groups

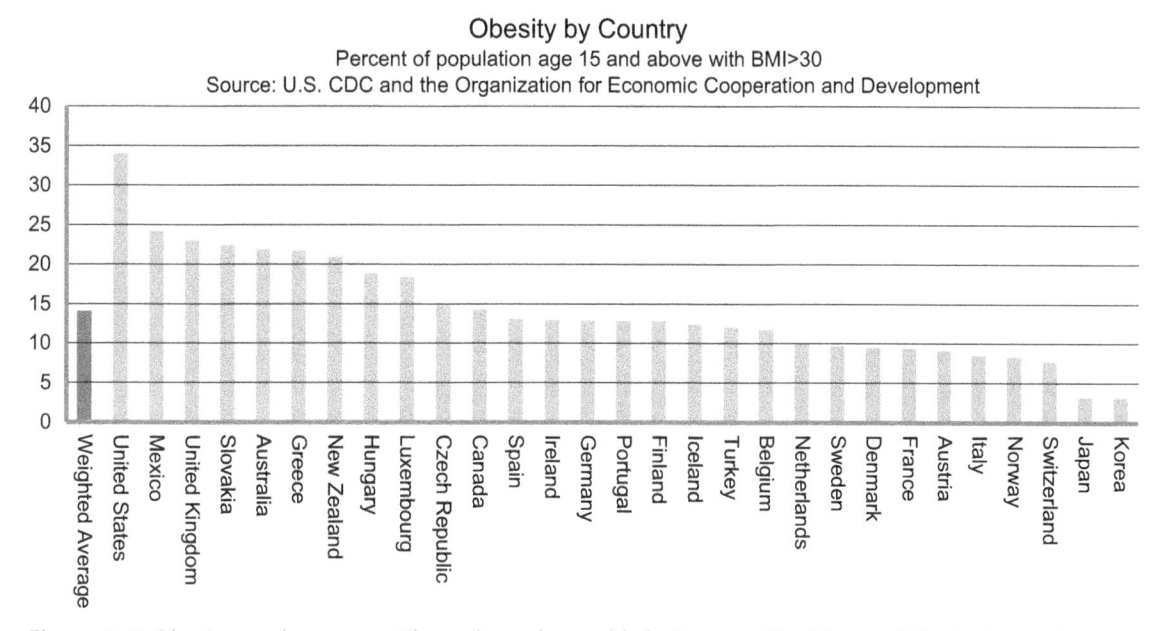

Figure 3–5: Obesity rate by country. Throughout the world, the increased incidence of obesity is creating health problems.

are the most important to universal design. The word "universal" implies just what it means. Universal design is about searching for design strategies that have *universal* benefits. We need to understand all the demographic trends that might be important and identify their intersections and implications as best we can. Then, as designers, we will have evidence to explain the benefits of universal design for a broader target population. We also need to use local demographic data to identify priorities for specific projects and policies in neighborhoods and regions.

The many design implications related to these demographic trends suggests that we need to take a closer look at the relationship between universal design and public health. For example, a safe, inclusively designed community makes it possible for elders and people with disabilities who cannot drive to maintain independence and engage in community life and local friendships. However, it also benefits many more groups. Walking is a great form of exercise and can contribute to long-term health for younger adults. For children, a safe, walkable community can reduce dependence on automobile transportation and encourage healthier behaviors (Frank, Andresen, and Schmid 2004; Sallis and Glanz 2006). Better nutrition for low-income people can be supported by improving accessibility of food markets (Larson, Story, and Nelson 2009). Demography can provide specific data to demonstrate the universal benefits of walkability—data on mobility of older and young people, crime statistics, and health statistics. The more diverse and extensive the need that can be documented, the stronger the rationale for implementing a walkable and/or inclusive environment.

Some of the questions that designers can ask when studying population demographics include:

- What sources of data are available to learn about a particular population?
- What demographic variables are useful for a particular project: age, occupation, health variables, and others?
- How big is a particular group or subgroup?
- How large is it relative to other groups?
- What are the future trends of growth or change in the group?
- Are trends inevitable and permanent or changeable?
- What are the interactions among different demographic variables?
- What are the differences among communities, states, or regions of a country?
- How do trends in one geographic area compare with those in other countries? What are the reasons for the differences?
- What are the implications of specific data for the design of environments and services?

Figure 3–6 dramatically illustrates the size of the target populations for universal design based on those groups at risk for activity limitation and for which we were able to find comparable data. The chart includes families as well as individuals because a family also benefits from an environment that supports increased independence and reduces caregiver burden. In 2010, while 55 million (18 percent) Americans had some disabilities and 37 million (12 percent) had severe disabilities, more than 87 million people (29 percent) were living in families with one or more members with disabilities. People living with obesity topped 89 million, and half of all adults (133 million people) had at least one chronic condition that limited ADLs (Centers for Disease Control and Prevention 2009).

Demographic data do not always exist to help make the full argument for universal design. In that case, it is important to think about demography creatively. The population served is not always represented by a neat demographic group. For example, people who are ill or fatigued can

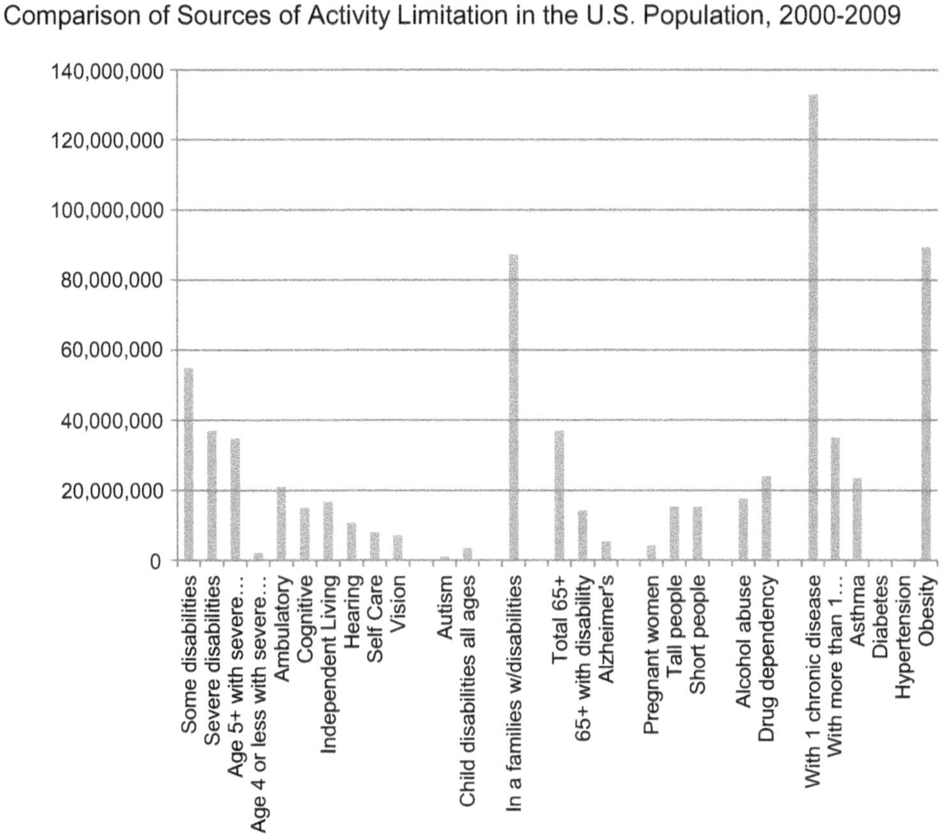

Comparison of Sources of Activity Limitation in the U.S. Population, 2000-2009

Figure 3–6: Target populations for universal design. This chart demonstrates the large population served by universal design.

benefit from shorter walking distances, lower forces to operate equipment, and other universal design features. Children can benefit a great deal and become more independent if they have more access to the environment and can use it safely without adult supervision. A person carrying a package with one hand is often limited as much as an individual with functional use of only one arm. The situation of parents pushing children in strollers is similar to someone accompanying a friend who uses a wheelchair. Both have difficulty using stairs. People with cognitive limitations often have a great deal of difficulty finding their way around. But anyone in an unfamiliar place can become disoriented, especially if he or she does not speak the local language. Population size for many potential beneficiaries of universal design may have to be estimated using unusual sources of data or adjustments to existing data; for example, the total population of people of childrearing age can be adjusted by pregnancy rates to estimate the number of pregnant women in a population. Alternatively, data can be obtained from observational surveys on how many people carry packages onto a transit system.

In summary, universal design benefits everyone. Obtaining specific estimates about key beneficiaries is important for making a business case for universal design features and establishing policy. The selected groups discussed in some depth in this chapter are only part of a much bigger picture. Local demographics can indicate the need for different priorities from place to place. And, it may be necessary to supplement demographic data with estimates obtained from other sources such as observational and survey research studies. The "In-Depth Focus" example that follows provides examples of how demographic data on one issue, aging, can be used to support universal design initiatives.

Example of In-Depth Focus on Aging

Analysis of the design implications related to aging has been limited. This in-depth focus illustrates how demography can be used to support universal design practice and uncover surprising and often-overlooked issues. Note that the design implications presented are not comprehensive. They are provided here only to illustrate the value of demographic data to universal design practice.

In 2006, 37 million Americans were age 65 and over—12 percent of the population (U.S. Census Bureau 2009). Baby Boomers born between 1946 and 1964 will start turning 65 in 2011, initiating a dramatic increase in the proportion of the population over 65. This increase will stabilize in 2030, when those 65 and over will compose 20 percent of the total U.S. population. Despite these statistics, the United States is relatively young for a developed country. Many other developed countries have larger aging populations because the United States has larger immigrant populations and a higher birth rate, which reduces the proportion of elders in the country, despite the expansion in size of older population cohorts. Today, more than 17 percent of Europeans and over 20 percent of Italians and Japanese are age 65 or older (Central Intelligence Agency n.d.). In many parts of the less developed world, the percentage of older people is rising even faster than in the developed world as public health improves. Aging populations present major social and political problems. Countries have to find the resources to support an older population. Increased numbers of older people mean significantly greater costs for Social Security, social services, and healthcare. These costs have to be borne by a proportionately smaller population of working adults to generate the tax revenue, particularly in a country like the United States, where Social Security benefits come from general tax revenue rather than from invested pension funds. From a political perspective, the increasing burden of the older population leads to an increased potential for political conflict between younger and older generations.

The size of the 65-plus population is increasing significantly. The overall rates of age-related disabilities will rise, but older people are staying healthier longer than at any time in the past. Although disability rates increase with age, the proportion of older adults with disabilities is declining (Friedland and Summer 2005). Disability rates among people over 65 declined by 1.4 percent per year from 1982 to 1999, (Friedland and Summer 2005). Treatments for such chronic conditions as heart disease, cancer, pain management, and osteopathic conditions have improved (Friedland and Summer 2005). Typical older citizens of the United States will spend most of their older years without disability. The World Health Organization projects that for the average 60-year-old in the United States, the healthy life expectancy is more than 15 years for men and almost 18 years for females (He and et al. 2005). Maintaining activity levels is a good way to prevent many disabilities, particularly those related to obesity. Thus, although design to support aging must account for eventual disability, there should also be a focus on providing support for maintaining activity as well as removing barriers.

As noted, in the United States, the next generation of older adults is expected to have higher incomes. It is also anticipated that they will continue to participate in the workforce to a greater degree than previous generations. They have relatively higher levels of education, fewer children, and a greater likelihood of having a living spouse than previous older populations. However, most elders are not rich, and those who are retired are more likely to have fixed incomes that are lower than during their working years. Thus, they are especially vulnerable to increases in housing costs, out-of-pocket healthcare costs, unanticipated expenses, and financial crises that affect retirement savings and investments.

Old age is a social phenomenon as well as an individual experience. While family members provide 85 percent of informal care for elders who need it, only 35 percent of older people report that their children live within ten miles (National Academy on an Aging Society 1999). Almost three-quarters of informal caregivers are female, more than half are employed full time, and almost half have children under the age of 18 at home. Twelve percent of caregivers are over age 65 themselves, typically caring for a spouse. In addition, almost 26 percent of grandparents 65 and older are providing care for grandchildren who live with them (U.S. Census Bureau 2004). Special services being provided in some localities for full-time caregivers include support groups, counseling, and respite services, in addition to other economic and social support services.

Gerontologists point out that older African American women are subject to a triple threat in quality of life. Each demographic category—gender, minority status, and age—increases the likelihood that a person will have lower disposable income, worse health, and other low quality of life outcomes (Bowen, Tomoyasu, and Cauce 1991; Washington, Moxley, and Taylor 2009). However, members of all three groups have an even greater chance of encountering those same problems than if they belonged to only one of those categories. The triple threat demonstrates that different groups within the aging population are much more vulnerable than other groups. In design practice, this knowledge has significant implications. For example, a program providing services to women from a minority population is likely to attract a group with many more disabilities and with lower incomes and unmet quality of life needs. This triple threat should inform both the design of the building and business practices of the organization that operates it.

This review of additional demographic issues related to aging suggests six important implications for universal design. They include:

1. *A growing older population will increase the importance of design to eliminate barriers.* The large older population and resulting increase in overall disability rates will make support for independent function a social and political imperative, not just a moral obligation.
2. *Design of workplaces and the design of work itself should provide support for older workers to lengthen their participation in work, increase tax revenue, and reduce their economic dependency on the rest of the population.* Strategies to adopt include improved ergonomics, flexible hours, and opportunities to work part time so that older workers can attend to caregiver responsibilities.
3. *Urban design and transportation planning should support a healthy lifestyle,* which can help reduce disability among the current older population but also among generations of people to come. Strategies to adopt include support for commuting by walking

and bicycling, support for maintaining a good diet, reduction of pollution and other environmental sources of health threats, and the provision of active recreational opportunities.
4. *Design for aging makes good business sense.* For their own benefit, commercial, public service, and cultural facilities need to implement efforts to attract older patrons and address their varied needs. In the future, competition for the disposable income of the older population will be fierce.
5. *Many housing choices for older people are needed to address the diversity of this population.* There must be solutions to accommodate the needs of low-income elders as well as the more affluent, elders who are in good health as well as those who have significant health problems, and elders who are caregivers themselves as well as those who are being cared for by spouses and families.
6. *There is not one aging population.* Vast differences exist in the needs and resources from one subgroup to another.

Demography: Points to Remember

Demographic data provide a business and moral case for adopting universal design. To build such a case effectively, designers need to understand basic approaches to using demographic data. There are seven key points to remember:

1. *Demography defines groups with distinct design needs and social relationships.* Demographic data are about groups that share characteristics, such as age, gender, race, ability, income, education, and psychosocial characteristics. Demographic groups are often depicted as being in conflict with other such groups. For example, many times generational groups are described as competing for social resources. Aging Baby Boomers are described as a group that will consume an unfair share of resources. As a population changes, demography describes the shifts in social composition, relationships, and tensions among different groups, and it describes the potential and/or need for resource redistribution. Universal design, in contrast, seeks to recognize that society is inherently diverse and to identify the largest target population for design by uncovering shared benefits.
2. *Demography is political.* Demography as a social science was created to help governments and businesses understand the beneficiaries of social programs and the markets for business products and services. Demographic data are often politicized because of their use in government policy. Documenting the size and characteristics of groups is critical in determining funding needs, setting eligibility requirements, and developing program responses to problems. Debates over what resources should be given to programs like Disability Assistance, Temporary Assistance for Needy Families, Social Security, Medicare, and veteran's programs often focus on demographic data. Thus, politics often defines demographic variables. For example, "old age" is typically defined as age 65 and over in the United States because this is the definition settled on when the Social Security program was established. Today, increasing life spans and the increased economic burden of retirement mean the retirement age—and hence the age of "dependency"—may rise. The change in eligibility

for full Social Security benefits from 65 to 66 is an example of this redefinition. In fact, every individual has a different rate of aging. Gerontologists talk about four types of aging: chronological (used by most social policies), biological, psychological, and social. Thus, the actual experience of aging is much different from what policy might suggest.

3. *Demography uncovers myths.* As awareness of certain groups enters popular consciousness, myths and misconceptions are inevitable. For example, people age 65 and over compose 12 percent of the U.S. population—about 40 million people. This group is often characterized as needy and dependent. The data presented in this chapter show that they are actually wealthier, better educated, and more active than previous generations of older adults and even younger age groups, which according to popular wisdom are more independent and capable. In fact, one-third of people over age 65 still work full- or part-time jobs, and another third volunteer. Forty percent are still supporting their children and grandchildren. The poorest people in our society are actually children, teens, and people in their early twenties. They are also a much more sizable group than aging Boomers. In 2009, people under the age of 20 made up more than a quarter of the U.S. population (27.3 percent) (U.S. Census Bureau 2009b).

4. *Lack of data or limited analysis of existing data often obscure important factors.* Facts about aging Baby Boomers became well known only because groups combating ageism (negative attitudes toward aging) were motivated to develop more accurate portraits of older Americans. Until recently, lack of demographic analysis has obscured disparities in health and disability statistics by income or class, racial groups, and urban/rural location. As obesity increases in our society and is better studied, its connection with poverty, race, and location of residence is being clarified. For example, the vulnerability of black and Hispanic people to obesity is now known to be "much more the result of societal inequalities than of any character flaw. For all the attention paid to obesity's economic costs, the epidemic's toll on children is a stark reminder of its moral dimension" (Ambinder 2010).

5. *Data often have limitations.* U.S. government agencies, such as the Census Bureau, the Centers for Disease Control and Prevention (CDC), and the National Institutes of Health, are often the best sources of demographic data. However, their point of view is determined by the government's interests and can be influenced by politics. Statistics from different sources often are not comparable without an understanding of the differences in the definitions used and the methods of data collection. Some demographic surveys collect data from a huge population; for that reason, they must limit the number of questions asked and the level of detail explored. Others are designed to get in-depth information on specific groups, and they may collect richer data on those groups. Universal designers have to learn how to use the data available most effectively, understand the limitations of the data available, and supplement it with other sources of information.

6. *Methods change.* Researchers may change or improve their methods. A comparison of the impact of changes in the disability-related questions from the 2007 to the 2008 American Community Survey illustrates this point. Because of the way in which the questions were asked, the number of people over age five with sensory disabilities "increased" by more than 3 million in one year, from 11.6 to 14.8 million. In reality, the questions were changed so the results were different. In 2008, the Census Bureau included new questions to define different disabilities. The result was that the percentage of people with cognitive, ambulatory, and self-care difficulties declined by 9.9 percent between 2007 and 2008, from 50.3 million to 39.8 million (Brault 2009).

7. *Trends are important.* Demographic trends can tell us a lot about future social changes that need to be considered beyond current conditions. Demographic data can provide an understanding of experiences by age cohorts . Cohort experiences may lead to future trends. For example, the experiences of the Depression-era generation had implications for their future purchasing patterns and lifestyles. When that generation passes from the population, these experiences lose their impact. In contrast, widespread trends across many cohorts in the population, such as obesity, will take longer to change. Another example is marital status. The year 2008 was not only a record year for births in the United States, 4.2 million, but also a record in that 40 percent of these were births to unmarried mothers. Perhaps in response to this demographic trend, the home improvement store Lowe's has begun to run ads targeting products for the young female handyperson, appealing to women who are buying houses and fixing apartments on their own.
8. *Understand differences.* Demographic patterns help us to understand regional and local differences. The prevalence of Hispanics in the Southwest may be common knowledge, but extrapolating the actual trends in their population growth demonstrates the influence the group will have in the future. Exceptions to the rule are often important. For example, extremely high rates of a particular illness in one region of the country or a community may help to identify environmental issues that need to be addressed. An example is the use of "cancer clusters" to identify public health risks. It is always good to put demographic trends in a broader perspective by comparing trends in the United States to other countries or comparing regions of the nation. For example, a research team in Arkansas demonstrated the unique nature of accessible housing needs in the state by studying data on poverty, education, health, and disability in the state in comparison to national data (Smith, Webb, and Williams 2010).

Summary

In this chapter, we have demonstrated that contemporary end user populations are exceedingly diverse. Demographic data of interest to designers includes chronic conditions related to functional limitations, health, and social participation, related social characteristics such as age and income, and health conditions such as obesity. These data can be used not only to identify target populations but also to suggest specific interventions. Demographic trends are as important as prevalence data that provides a snapshot of populations at one point in time. Moreover, the relationships among demographic variables need to be given as much attention as data on the population group as a whole.

A universal designer can employ demography to provide services that are more effective by:

- Understanding basic population composition and trends
- Reconsidering perspectives that are often established by common myths in popular culture
- Obtaining expertise on the needs of different groups that are not available through demography through supplemental research and observation
- Being more alert to the growing importance of cultural differences
- Avoiding unnecessarily limiting the target population for products and services

Universal design cannot be practiced effectively without a basic understanding of diversity. Responding to diversity is the basis of the field. In fact, diversity is the underlying rationale for universal design. Demography can support the business case for adoption of universal design by illustrating cultural shifts toward diversity, demonstrating the size of the beneficiary population, and identifying related policy issues. In any project, demographic research is the first step in making sure that end user populations are understood. To address their needs properly, populations must be identified accurately. Demography helps to address the needs of groups previously underserved, which may turn out to be critical for successfully introducing a new product or service. Demographic research can generate new design insights and even innovative ideas for new products, environments, and services. Such research can help design and development teams to envision what a successful output might be like and identify populations that can provide experiential input in the development process.

Studying demographic trends, in particular, helps to anticipate emerging end user needs which can help designers, developers, and manufacturers to position themselves to serve markets that currently are underserved (i.e., find new business opportunities or policy goals). Broadening the market for products, environments, and services is an essential aspect of competitiveness in a global marketplace. It is particularly important in designing environments and products that have a long useful life because anticipating trends can significantly reduce obsolescence of products and the need for renovation of environments.

Review Topics

1. Name at least three ways the study of demography can help designers.
2. Name at least two other target populations of universal design besides the aging population and people with disabilities. Describe how each can benefit from universal design.
3. What are some myths associated with the aging population? Describe how demographic data can help dispel some of these myths.

References

Altman, B. and A. Bernstein. 2008. *Disability and Health in the United States, 2001–2005.* Hyattsville, MD: National Center for Health Statistics.

Ambinder, M. 2010. "Beating Obesity." *Atlantic Magazine,* May 10. Available at www.theatlantic.com/magazine/archive/2010/05/beating-obesity/8017/ (accessed October 2011).

Bowen, D. J., N. Tomoyasu, and A. M. Cauce. 1991. "The Triple Threat: A Discussion of Gender, Class and Race Differences in Weight." *Women and Health* 17 (4): 123–143.

Brault, M. 2009. "Review of Changes to the Measurement of Disability in the 2008 American Community Survey." www.census.gov/hhes/www/disability/2008ACS_disability.pdf.

Centers for Disease Control and Prevention. 2009. "Basic Actions Difficulty and Complex Activity Limitation among Adults 18 years of Age and over, by Selected Characteristics: United States, Selected Years 1997–2009." www.cdc.gov/nchs/data/hus/hus2009tables/Table055.pdf.

Central Intelligence Agency. n.d. *The World Factbook.* https://www.cia.gov/library/publications/the-world-factbook/fields/2010.html?countryName=&countryCode=&regionCode=&.

Flegal, K., et al. 2010. "Prevalence and Trends in Obesity among U.S. Adults, 1999–2008." *Journal of the American Medical Association* 303 (3): 235–241.

Frank, L. D., M. A. Andresen, and T. L. Schmid. 2004. "Obesity Relationships with Community Design, Physical Activity, and Time Spent in Cars." *American Journal of Preventive Medicine* 27: 87–96.

Friedland, R., and L. Summer. 2005, March. *Demography Is Not Destiny, Revisited.* Center on Aging, Georgetown University. www.agingsociety.org/agingsociety/publications/demography/demographydestiny.pdf.

He, W., M. Sengupta, V. A. Velkoff, and K. DeBarros. 2005. *65+ in the United States: 2005.* U.S. Census Bureau Current Population Reports. www.census.gov/prod/2006pubs/p23–209.pdf.

Hendershot, G. 2006. "Health and Functional Status of Working Age People with Disabilities in the United States." Presented at the 2006 StatsRRTC State-of-the-Science Conference, *The Future of Disability Statistics: What We Know and Need to Know,* October 5–6, 2006, Cornell University, Ithaca, NY. Available at http://linux01.crystalgraphics.com/view/808ff-ZWNiY/Health_and_Functional_Status_of_Working_Age_People_with_Disabilities_in_the_United_States.

LaPlante, M. P. and H. S. Kaye. 2010. "Demographics and Trends in Wheeled Mobility Equipment Use and Accessibility in the Community." *Assistive Technology* 22 (1): 3–17.

Larson, N. I., M. T. Story, and M. Nelson. 2009. "Neighborhood Environments: Disparities in Access to Healthy Foods in the U.S." *American Journal of Preventive Medicine* 36 (1): 74–81.

Mace, R., G. Hardie, and J. Place. 1991. "Accessible Environments: Toward Universal Design." In J. V. W. Preiser, J. C. Vischer, and E.T. White (eds.), *Design Intervention: Toward a More Humane Architecture,* pp. 155–176. New York: Van Nostrand Reinhold.

McKinsey Global Institute. 2008, June. "Talkin' 'Bout My Generation: The Economic Impact of Aging US Baby Boomers." www.mckinsey.com/mgi/reports/pdfs/Impact_Aging_Baby_Boomers/MGI_Impact_Aging_Baby_Boomers_executive_summary.pdf

National Academy on an Aging Society. 1999. *Demography Is Not Destiny.* www.agingsociety.org/agingsociety/pdf/destiny1.pdf.

Ohri-Vachaspati, P., K. Lloyd, J. Chou, N. Petlick, S. Brownlee, and M. Yedidia. 2010. *The New Jersey Childhood Obesity Study: Trenton.* New Brunswick, NJ: Rutgers Center for State Health Policy.

Sallis, J. F. and K. Glanz. 2006. "The Role of Built Environments in Physical Activity, Eating, and Obesity In childhood." *Future of Children* 16 (1): 89–108.

Sears, N. (2007, August 23). "Crash Test Fatties: Dummies Getting Larger to Match Expanding Waistlines." *Daily Mail* (London). www.dailymail.co.uk/news/article-477101/Crash-test-fatties-dummies-getting-larger-match-expanding-waistlines.html#ixzz168eBgigd.

Smith, K., J. Webb, and B. T. Williams. 2010. *Just Below the Line: Disability, Housing, and Equity in the South.* Fayetteville: University of Arkansas Press.

Southern Education Foundation. (2007). *A New Diverse Majority: Students of Color in the South's Public Schools.* www.sefatl.org/pdf/New%20Diverse%20Majority.pdf.

Steinfeld, E., et al. 1979. *Access to the Built Environment: A Review of Literature.* Washington, DC: U.S. Department of Housing and Urban Development Office of Policy Development and Research.

U.S. Census Bureau. (2004). "We the People: Aging in the United States. Census 2000 Special Reports." www.census.gov/prod/2004pubs/censr-19.pdf.

U.S. Census Bureau. 2007. "Minority Population Tops 100 Million." *U.S. Census Bureau News.* www.census.gov/newsroom/releases/archives/population/cb07-70.html.

U.S. Census Bureau. 2008. "An Older and More Diverse Nation by Midcentury." U.S. Census Bureau News. /www.census.gov/newsroom/releases/archives/population/cb08-123.html.

U.S. Census Bureau. 2009. "Aging Statistics." www.agingstats.gov/agingstatsdotnet/main_site/default.aspx.

U.S. Census Bureau. 2009a. Current Population Survey, Annual Social and Economic Supplement. Table 1. Population by Age and Sex: 2009. Internet Release Date December 2010. United States Census Bureau.

———. 2009b. "United States — Age and Sex". 2009 American Community Survey 1-Year Estimates. United States Census Bureau.

Viadero, D. 2010. "Poor, Minority Pupils Are Now a Majority in the South." *Education Week,* January 19. www.edweek.org/ew/articles/2010/01/20/18south.h29.html.

Waldrop, J. and S. Stern. 2003. *Disability Status: 2000.* Washington, DC: U.S. Census Bureau.

Waller, P. F. and P. A. Green. 1997. "Human Factors in Transportation." In G. Salvendy (ed.), *Handbook of Human Factors and Ergonomics* (pp. 1,972–2,009). New York: John Wiley & Sons.

Washington, O.G.M., D. P. Moxley, and J. Y. Taylor. 2009. "Enabling Older Homeless Minority Women to Overcome Homelessness by Using a Life Management Enhancement Group Intervention." *Issues in Mental Health Nursing* 30: 86–97.

Weingarten, G. (2010, November 16). "Below the Beltway." *Buffalo News.* www.buffalonews.com/editorial-page/columns/national-views/article252511.ece.

Williams, K. C. and R. A. Page. 2010. "Marketing to the Generations." *Journal of Behavioral Studies in Business* 3: 1–17.

Zhu, S., et al. 2010. "BMI and Risk of Serious Upper Body Injury Following Motor Vehicle Crashes: Concordance of Real-World and Computer-Simulated Observations." *Public Library of Science Medicine (PLoS Med)* 7, no. 3.

4

Practicing Universal Design

Introduction

In this chapter, we explore the emergence of universal design practices in a range of professions, including educational, manufacturing, design, and service delivery fields. We present universal design as an example of innovation. We use research and knowledge on the diffusion of innovation as a point of departure for a critical analysis of current practices and to identify directions for advancing the field with a view toward increasing adoption of the concept. Based on this analysis, we then present a new conceptual framework, more compatible with the realities of professional practice, which we think can help advance the field. The main theme of this chapter is that increasing adoption of universal design requires a different approach from what has been used in the fields of accessibility, safety, and public health, where the focus has been primarily on compliance with regulations. In universal design, which has no legal mandate and should be viewed as a continuous improvement process rather than a compliance process, educational and dissemination activities are much more important than regulatory action. But, it is important not to view universal design as unrelated to regulatory compliance. Whatever we do to improve the adoption of universal design should also improve regulatory compliance since universal design practice has much more ambitious goals than regulatory action.

Universal Design as Innovation

The concept of universal design represents an innovative way of thinking about the built environment. This new perspective is catching on with the general public. Advertising campaigns featuring universal design ideas, such as usability, social sustainability, choice, and personalization, are evidence that the broad spectrum of society is thinking about similar ideas, although they might not be called the same things. These companies see that universal design ideas are marketable. Most professionals working in the field of accessibility are aware of the concept, as are many design professionals. Many business and nongovernmental executives and government officials, particularly those who have been advocates for disability rights, know the term also. The interest of a major publisher like Wiley in producing a textbook like this demonstrates that interest in universal design is growing. But, if one were to poll a large gathering of design professionals, as the authors have done frequently, usually only a few acknowledge a previous understanding of the term, even in continuing education programs that target accessibility. In other words, while interest is growing, universal design still has not become a mainstream idea.

Problems with understanding the difference between universal design and its precursors are still evident. Even some design and rehabilitation professionals still view universal design as a new buzzword for accessible design or assistive technology. In fact, many books and articles that include the words "universal design" in the title are primarily about compliance with accessibility laws or design for wheelchair use, not universal design (see, for example, Null 1998). Yet, there is evidence that the level of understanding is improving. For example, in the first edition of the *Universal Design Handbook* (Preiser and Ostroff 2001), a book of readings, 90 percent of the chapters were about accessibility and only 10 percent about universal design. In contrast, the second edition contained about 80 percent universal design content (Preiser and Smith 2010).

Even today, however, many experts believe that universal design simply means improving regulations. Although necessary, accessible design regulations create the illusion that only people with disabilities need increased usability and safety. This belief has two consequences:

1. Designers perceive that the demand for accessible products and environments is in "niche markets."
2. Providing better access is seen primarily as a regulatory or clinical matter. Thus, designers and producers (manufacturers of products, purveyors of services, or developers of buildings) believe that it is a problem for a small group of specialists to solve rather than an opportunity for creative design.

Practicing universal design, then, requires changing attitudes and perceptions on many levels. Producers need to understand that to be successful in the broader marketplace, universally designed products, environments, and services must be easier to use, healthier, and friendlier for people who do not have disabilities as well as those who do, and they must provide value worth the cost compared to the competition. Not only should universally designed products, environments, and services be affordable, but they should also be as attractive, durable, and reliable as their competition. Universal design features do not *need* to be more expensive, but they *can* be more expensive if they deliver increased value for the additional cost. OXO is a company that pioneered in the introduction of universal design features. Some of the OXO Good Grips products, such as the peeler and paring knife, cost nearly double what lowest-cost competitors were charging, but because they are inexpensive, the additional cost is only a dollar or two. This amount is still affordable for most consumers.

To illustrate how universal design means thinking differently, Table 4–1 provides some examples of the differences between universal design and accessible design.

Table 4–1: Differences between Universal and Accessible Design

Universal	Accessible
A universally designed home plan costs the same as any other plan to build that anyone can purchase	A custom-designed home based on an existing plan but requires additional costs for the redesign and custom construction details
Home improvement services that incorporate universal design as a basic service	Home modifications services by a contractor who charges more for specialized knowledge of design for disability and aging
Automobile instruments and controls customizable to accommodate differences in perceptual abilities, stature, motor abilities, and preferences	Assistive technology used to adapt an automobile display for people with special needs
A no-step building entry that everyone can use easily and together	A building entry with a ramp at the side that is out of the way for all visitors but is accessible by code
A hotel that has 100 percent universally designed rooms in a variety of types	A hotel that has only the code-required percentage of accessible rooms

Proponents of universal design must recognize that products and environments can never be fully usable by every person in the world. As described in Chapter 2, universal design is a process rather than an end state. There is never any end to the quest for improved usability, health or social participation. Viewed this way, practicing universal design means advancing beyond currently accepted norms, not simply addressing an initial goal. It also implies that it is important to help consumers and clients *recognize* universally designed products; the differences may not always be easy to perceive. However, practicing universal design is not about only incremental change. It requires constant innovation in form, technology, and marketing. Although it certainly requires creative design activities, practicing universal design also extends to marketing, education, policy making, and other non-design activities.

Looking beyond disability and aging, universal design ideas can be applied to address the evolving diversity of populations and consumer markets as globalization and urbanization trends advance. Recognizing that universal design is part of a general evolutionary and cultural process demystifies the idea, making it more familiar, but it also demands that we think about design as an innovation process, not just form making.

Everett Rogers (1995) defines an innovation as anything "perceived to be new." Thinking of universal design in this way suggests that we can gain insight into the best way to advance its adoption by applying general knowledge about innovation. Based on an exhaustive survey of research on the diffusion of innovations, Rogers proposes that innovation is diffused through a sequence of five activities:

1. *Knowledge.* Exposure to an innovation's existence and some understanding of how it functions.
2. *Persuasion.* Forming "a favorable or unfavorable attitude toward the innovation."
3. *Decision.* "[A]ctivities that lead to a choice to adopt or reject the innovation."
4. *Implementation.* "[P]ut[ting] an innovation into use."
5. *Confirmation.* "[R]einforcement of an innovation-decision already made or reversal of a previous decision to adopt or reject the innovation. (p. 169)

Knowledge is obtained through an established pattern of information collection. "Change agents" put a spin on that knowledge through their persuasive power. However, channels of communication already established through social networks and social worlds limit exposure to those agents. The confirmation or lack of it will affect further decision making one way or another. If a consumer product with universal design features does not sell, for example, the manufacturer may not be inclined to continue offering such features.

Utterback (1974) argues that the rate of diffusion depends on six attributes of the innovation:

1. *Relative advantage.* Diffusion is enhanced if there is a clear relative advantage for the new idea in financial, social, or other terms.
2. *Communicability.* Diffusion is enhanced when the innovation can be explained easily and separated or identified easily.
3. *Compatibility.* If the innovation is congruent with current norms, values, or structures, it is likely to be accepted more readily.
4. *Nonpervasiveness.* The greater the number of aspects of the organization or society that are potentially influenced by a change, the less likely it is that the change will take place.
5. *Reversibility.* Any innovation diffuses more quickly if it can be experimented with at relatively low cost of time, money, and commitment, making it easy to back out of the decision.
6. *Small number of gatekeepers.* The fewer people involved with "keeping the gates," the greater the chance of having the innovation adopted.

Knowledge about adoption of innovation, therefore, suggests that two important activities play a major role in adopting universal design in practice.

1. *Decisions to adopt universal design will be heavily influenced by communications* (both information in media and face-to-face contact) within and between organizations, industries, professions, and individuals. It is through these communications that awareness is raised (increased knowledge) and persuasion takes place.
2. *Decision-making strategies within an organization and by consumers heavily influence the rate of diffusion.* Within organizations, decisions to adopt a new idea are affected by compatibility with company and industry norms, established modes of operation, risks, benefits, and the complexity of implementation. Three factors affect consumer decision making:
   a. The way the innovation is communicated
   b. Consumer knowledge of product features
   c. Consumer assessment of perceived benefits and risks.

Thus, to assess progress in the diffusion of universal design as a new idea, we can review and evaluate these two activities. But first it will be useful to contrast practices that promote accessibility with those that promote universal design.

Tools for Increasing Adoption

The basic practice in the field of accessible design is regulatory action and related compliance procedures. Regulations can never demand more accessibility than that defined by their enabling legislation, in this case removing barriers that could be interpreted as discriminatory. Regulations do not address many important issues for accessibility beyond this because there is no way to regulate the solutions, the cost impact would be too great or the result would be too far a departure from conventional building practices to be accepted by the industry. For example, few requirements of regulations directly benefit people with mental health conditions or those with cognitive impairments. Adjustable devices, logical controls, easy-to-read instructions or easy to understand building circulation systems are not required. In addition, many designers interpret regulations to prescribe all that is needed to accommodate people with disabilities. Thus, the resulting benefits are often very limited.

Take the case of lavatory sinks found in most public restrooms. The regulations require that at least one sink in a restroom be "accessible" and define the features that sink must have. One such feature is that an accessible sink must be mounted a bit higher than lavatory sinks are typically mounted. So, in most public restrooms, there is one sink higher than the rest. It is often a "wheelchair" or "handicapped" sink that has been selected from a catalog because it is "ADA compliant." These sinks are modeled after surgical sinks used in hospitals and cost much more than the typical lavatory sink. It is ironic that the other lavatory sinks are actually too low for a large proportion of the ambulatory population. Many ambulatory people could benefit from a sink that is even higher than the "accessible" sink. One universal design strategy would be to make all the sinks meet the regulatory requirements rather than just one, which would not cost anymore because the more expensive sink is not really needed to meet the rules. A second strategy would be to include some high and some low sinks. In fact, a manufacturer developed a product that incorporated both high and low sinks in a single attractive unit. Another strategy is to add more choices, e.g., a sink at a third, lower height — one designed for children. Some museums that cater to families are providing lower sinks or steps at the lavatories to make their facilities more child-friendly. Universal design, then, addresses the issue of differences in body stature with creative solutions, not a simple regulatory response.

Similar examples can be found in the safety and health codes. Safety codes govern the minimum requirements for safe exit stairways or elevators, but they are not up to date on the latest knowledge about safe stairway design or contemporary emergency egress issues. Likewise, public health codes include rules that ensure habitability in buildings (e.g., the minimum amount of floor area in a bedroom, the amount of natural light required in a sleeping or living room, and room ventilation requirements), but they do not address how much space is needed for any particular activity, the best proportions for rooms, the location of windows, the impact on readability of computer screens, or even methods to reduce the spread of infection. These issues are in the domain of universal design.

Another example demonstrates the limitations of regulations very dramatically. Accessibility codes require that the highest operable part of a public telephone be within 48 inches (1,220 mm) of the finished floor. The typical solution is to lower the phone. However, this solution does not produce a usable telephone for tall people, who cannot see the keys without bending; people with vision limitations, who have trouble using the phone in difficult lighting conditions; or individuals who speak a foreign language. They also do not address such issues as preferences for payment or inability to speak. Solving these problems requires much more than simply lowering the existing unit. Universal design strategies might include a display and keypad that are adjustable for people of different statures and for different ambient illumination levels, instructions in different languages, error messages with instructions for correcting mistakes, or payment in several modes, including credit cards.

The usability limitations are only one set of the problem the public has with public telephones. Other problems are the lack of phones where they are needed and vandalism that often makes them inoperative. It is not too far-fetched to argue that a major factor contributing to the rapid adoption of mobile telephones was the poor accessibility and usability of the public telephone system as a whole. It was so hard to use and provided so few benefits to the population that people were willing to pay much more for the convenience of a mobile phone than they ever would to use public telephones. This is the attribute of "relative advantage" that is critical for increasing the adoption of an innovative idea. In fact, the demise of the public telephone is a demonstration that universal design works. Despite the fact that mobile phones still have usability issues, especially for people with hearing impairments, the increase in usability, safety, and convenience they provide has radically changed not only our telephone system but also our culture in a very short time period.

It should be noted that some regulations encourage universal design practices to a degree. Accessible housing requirements that apply to all dwelling units, such as Part M of the United Kingdom building code (Office of the Prime Minister 2010), promote a universal design perspective because they apply to all housing projects. The Fair Housing Amendments Act in the United States is another example because it incorporates the concept of adaptability to accommodate people with different needs (Toran 2000). If regulations are the key tool for implementing accessibility, is there a comparable tool for universal design? The most important tool for the practice of universal design developed to date is a document titled "The Principles of Universal Design" (Connell et al. 1997; Story 1998). A multidisciplinary group of experts* (including one of the authors of this book, Edward Steinfeld) wrote these Principles to clarify the scope of universal design, as it was perceived in the mid-1990s, and to provide guidance in both design and evaluation activities. In other words, the Principles were developed to communicate the concept more widely, in the hopes of making universal design easier to implement.

The Principles of Universal Design define seven basic universal design attributes:

1. *Equitable use.* The design does not disadvantage or stigmatize any group of users.
2. *Flexibility in use.* The design accommodates a wide range of individual preferences and abilities.
3. *Simple and intuitive use.* Use of the design is easy to understand, regardless of the user's experience, knowledge, language skills, or current concentration level.
4. *Perceptible information.* The design communicates necessary information effectively to the user, regardless of ambient conditions or the user's sensory abilities.
5. *Tolerance for error.* The design minimizes hazards and the adverse consequences of accidental or unintended actions.
6. *Low physical effort.* The design can be used efficiently and comfortably, and with a minimum of fatigue.
7. *Size and space for approach and use.* Appropriate size and space is provided for approach, reach, manipulation, and use, regardless of the user's body size, posture, or mobility (Center for Universal Design 1997; Connell et al. 1997).

The Principles helped to increase the "communicability" of universal design. By avoiding the development of a competitive regulatory effort, they also allowed the new concept to be introduced in a way that is compatible with accessible design practice. Compatibility is an attribute that contributes to the diffusion of innovation.

---

*The Committee was convened by the Center on Universal Design at North Carolina State University and included Bettye Rose Connell, Mike Jones, Ron Mace, Jim Mueller, Abir Mullick, Elaine Ostroff, Jon Sanford, Ed Steinfeld, Molly Story and Gregg Vanderheiden. The product of their work is cited in Connell et al. 1997.

Communicating the Idea

Many dissemination activities promote the idea of universal design. These include conferences, exhibits, publications, media, educational programs, and consumer information. Many websites provides information on key resources, such as conferences, a bibliography of publications, electronic media, consumer information, educational programs, and documented exhibitions. (See www.ap.buffalo.edu/idea, which also has links to other websites on this subject.)

Print media (newspapers and popular and trade periodicals) and websites contain many articles about universal design. Some advertising campaigns, although they do not emphasize universal design explicitly, certainly highlight the experiences that universal design creates or specific features of products that we would characterize as having universal design attributes. The media have covered universal design much less in comparison to sustainable design and even design for aging and accessible design. In particular, there has been virtually no television coverage either in the news or in entertainment sources like sitcoms. Although broadcast television is decreasing in importance as a media compared to Internet-based sources of information, it is still the primary media source for most citizens in developed and emerging economies. Accessible design, on the other hand, has received coverage in major television networks, particularly in sitcoms and public broadcasting.

National conferences, exhibitions, and educational programs with live instructors are very useful to help increase awareness and help professionals interested in universal design meet, share information, and discuss ideas. The personal relationships established through conferences are often more important than the information transmitted. Research on the diffusion of innovation demonstrates that knowledge transmitted through local professional meetings and informal networks is more likely to persuade professionals to adopt innovative ideas. There have been an increasing number of universal design conferences in the United States. There have also been conferences in countries as far flung as Korea, Brazil, Toronto, and Singapore. And, Japan has a well organized and large community of practice in universal design, including the International Association of Universal Design, which hosts international conferences periodically and is supported by many major global manufacturers.

Research on innovation demonstrates that media are the most effective method to increase awareness of an innovation, but existing social networks are more effective for persuading people to adopt them (Rogers 1995). Research also has identified different roles that people play in the diffusion process through their social networks. "Innovators" are the people to first develop and champion new ideas (about 2.5 percent of all adopters). These individuals usually have global or national social networks and look outward to the world at large for ideas rather than to their local peers. They attend national conferences and bring back ideas to their organizations and local peer networks. "Early adopters" are among the next 13.5 percent of all adopters and are locally based (Rogers 1995). They are usually persuaded by the innovators to adopt new ideas. The rest of the adopters come on board only after they obtain enough knowledge and confirmation from their peers, the important opinion leaders who are local early adopters. Thus, this group should be a major target of diffusion activities.

The typical way to illustrate diffusion rates is an adoption curve, such as the ones shown in Figure 4–1, which plots adoption rates over time. Adoption rates usually start out shallow, but most times each trend curve has a distinct take-off point. This point is where adoption rates start getting much steeper, indicating much more rapid adoption. It is safe to say that the curve for adoption of universal design by both consumers and producers (including the design

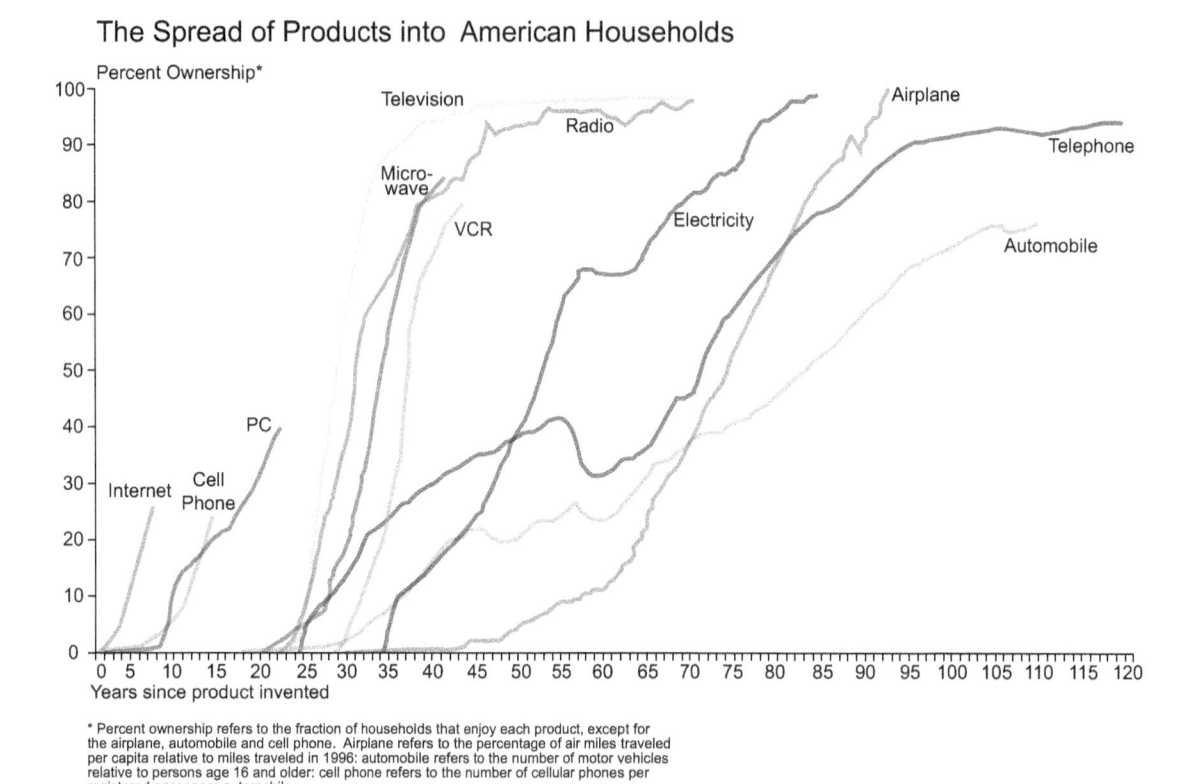

Figure 4–1: Innovation diffusion curves. This chart shows the changes in adoption rates in U.S. homes over time for 11 different products. It demonstrate how different products have very different rates of adoption.

Source: Image adapted from Federal Reserve Bank of Dallas 1996 Annual Report.

professionals) is still shallow but increasing steadily. It will take some years before the take-off point is reached. Likely the curve will track but lag a bit behind the aging of the population. The demographic shift will lead to more and more media attention to aging and growing diffusion through professional networks until the take-off point is finally reached. If there was a successful sitcom about an architect who practices universal design, the take-off point might come much sooner.

An important factor in increasing the rate of adoption will be the degree to which university professional education programs and continuing education programs embrace universal design. Professional education increases awareness and prepares graduates to be receptive to new initiatives in the future. Universal design advocates recognize the importance of education. Many educational efforts have targeted professional design students and designers in practice. In the field of interior design, for example, the accreditation body already requires each school to ensure that student work demonstrates the ability to apply universal design concepts. None of the other design disciplines in the United States has such requirements, although the National Architectural Accrediting Board has requirements to provide students with a working knowledge of accessible design and understanding of diversity issues.

Only a handful of architecture program websites in the United States mention a specific course in accessibility or universal design. Most seem to address these criteria through their design studio programs. The Architecture Department at the University at Buffalo, State University of New York, currently offers the only formal concentration in universal design in architecture programs worldwide, the Inclusive Design Research Group. The Royal College of Art's Helen Hamlyn Centre for Design has an Age and Ability Laboratory that focuses on universal design and offers a graduate degree. Design educators, professionals, and businesses in the Nordic countries have evidenced a greater general awareness of universal design than in other regions of the world. The Nordic School of Public Health has even developed a graduate-level "diploma" program in universal design, which attracts professionals of many disciplines from all the Nordic countries, the Baltic region, Poland, and Russia.

Educators with an interest in universal design have initiated several organized efforts to improve universal design education in design schools. Many of the efforts in the United States have been sponsored by the National Endowment for the Arts (NEA), the federal agency with the strongest commitment to professional education in this field. The first of these was the Universal Design Education Project (UDEP), sponsored by the NEA and led by Elaine Ostroff at Adaptive Environments (now the Institute of Human Centered Design) (Welch 1995). The UDEP project inspired similar projects in Norway, Sweden, Belgium, and Japan (Christophersen 2002). A website with educational resources for educators and students was established through a collaboration of the Center on Universal Design, the IDeA Center, and the Global Universal Design Educators Network. This website, called Universal Design Education Online (www.udeducation.org), was recently revised under the leadership of the IDeA Center. The Global Universal Design Educator's Network has been managing a program called "Access to the Design Professions," also funded by the NEA. Ostroff has recruited a group of professionals in practice and education who act as mentors for aspiring designers with disabilities.

In Europe, educational initiatives have been spearheaded and act as a forum for development of ideas and model programs (European Institute for Design and Disability 2004). The Malaysian government developed an interesting universal design initiative in the country's architecture schools (Whybrow et al. 2010). The country has few experts in this field, so this effort used a train-the-trainers' approach to build capacity in each school.

In general, these global educational efforts emphasize the development of communities of practice, informal or formal organizations through which professionals and educators interested in universal design can establish and maintain social networks. A community of practice is a good vehicle for diffusing innovations because it is grounded in direct social contact, either in person or through telecommunications, including the Internet. At the global and national level, such communities tend to attract the innovators. This leads to the phenomenon of preaching to the choir. To reach the early adopters, communities of practice have to be established through existing professional and educational organizations.

To help expand the community of practice in universal design beyond the innovators, the IDeA Center organized the University Educators Consortium in 2006. The Consortium provides a means to organize mentoring, assistance in curriculum development, and information sharing to member schools and outreach to other schools to develop a new generation of academic leaders in this interdisciplinary field. The focus initially is on schools in the United States.

In 2009, the IDeA Center received a grant from the NEA to initiate a program called "Bridging the Gap: Increasing Access to Universal Design to Meet the Needs of America's Black Communities." This project linked universal design with other initiatives related to design for inclusion, diversity, and social sustainability. Representatives from seven architecture programs from the historic black colleges and universities (HBCU) joined with the IDeA Center to discuss how universal design could benefit the missions of these schools. All of the HBCU schools of architecture have a strong background in inclusion and diversity education. They identified strategic curriculum development activities that could demonstrate the potential of universal design and shared examples of related educational projects already under way (www.udeworld.com/hbcuwelcome.html). A key collaborating organization was the National Association of Minority Architects, which is closely allied to the HBCU schools of architecture. With the involvement of the seven HBCU schools, there are now 13 members of the IDeA Center's Consortium. The Center hopes to help the member schools obtain resources to improve their own efforts, expand the Consortium to other design programs within the United States, and make alliances with similar groups, such as the European Institute for Design and Disability (EIDD), in other regions of the world.

Many experts on universal design routinely offer continuing education programs in several fields, usually as part of local and national professional conferences. The IDeA Center established an online continuing education program with courses designed for a range of professional interests. Advocates, builders/contractors, planners, architects, occupational and physical therapists, and policy makers have enrolled in these online courses. The program is designed for anyone interested in learning about the universal design of places, products, and systems with a particular focus on the knowledge bases relevant to many design problems, methods for obtaining information, and best practice examples.

Another form of dissemination and education occurs through exhibits. Exhibitions are good ways to reach the general public. There have been two major exhibits on universal design in North America. The first was at the Museum of Modern Art in New York in 1988. The second was at the Cooper Hewitt Design Museum in New York from 1989 to 1999. The second, called "Unlimited by Design," was reconstructed in three other locations, Toronto, Milwaukee, and Buffalo. The IDeA Center organized the exhibits in Milwaukee and Buffalo, each with over 300 products featuring universal design (Figure 4–2). Our experience demonstrated that small art and design museums are probably not the best venues in which to communicate universal design. Unless they are nationally recognized museums, such as the Museum of Modern Art and the Cooper Hewitt Design Museum, they have much lower attendance than family-oriented venues, such as children's museums and science museums. For example, only 3,000 visitors attended each of the two exhibits organized by the IDeA Center. Yet mounting a large professional exhibit can cost over $250,000. In addition, art and design museums generally discourage hands-on interaction with objects. Universally designed objects should be touched and manipulated to communicate their features better. Children's museums and science museums would be more appropriate exhibition venues.

Exhibits at trade shows (e.g., kitchen and bathroom showss) are another good method for educating the public on universal design. Exhibits like these can reach professionals, producers, retailers, contractors, distributors, and others involved in the building industry. Similar exhibits can be included in local home shows that target consumers. One of the most widely promoted exhibits like this was the "Real Life Kitchen" built by GE for the National Association of Home Builders convention in 1995. It then was exhibited around the United States at local home shows. Trade shows attract large numbers of industry people; if done well, exhibits create a lot of attention for manufacturers. These shows expose professionals from all parts of the country and industry sectors to universal design, thus helping spread the knowledge and awareness to the early adopter group. They also attract local and national media attention. Some local product distributors have featured universally designed products in their showrooms on a permanent

Figure 4–2: Unlimited by Design exhibit. People interacting with universally designed products at the exhibit when it was staged at the Center for the Arts, University at Buffalo, State University of New York.
Source: Image courtesy of Rhona Vogt.

basis, but doing this is difficult since, for business purposes, they must constantly rotate the products on display, and universal design is not the only issue they want to address. The Institute on Human Centered Design has a demonstration center on universal design in its offices, where it also sells products and offers continuing education programs to local professionals (www.adaptenv.org).

Demonstration homes educate individuals on changing homebuilding practices and are a good vehicle for encouraging a wide range of buyers to demand more universal design features. They introduce the general public to the concept of universal design and allow potential home buyers to see and experience the benefits of universal design firsthand. By showing how universal design concepts and products can be implemented in real-life design, they can eliminate stigma and counter preconceived notions that universal design only helps people with disabilities. For builders and other design professionals, demonstration homes provide an opportunity to highlight skills, abilities, new design concepts, construction methods, technology, and decorating ideas. Another important benefit is that they provide the opportunity for researchers to gather data on costs, consumer perceptions, and successful and unsuccessful applications of inclusive design.

Many universally designed demonstration homes have been included in local home expositions (Figure 4–3), a common annual community event in the United States organized by local homebuilder organizations. Builders who belong to the associations each construct a model home in the exposition, which is usually located on a new street or scattered sites within a neighborhood. Builders individually recruit landscaping and interior design professionals and product distributors to design the landscaping so that the homes have the latest models and

Figure 4–3: Exterior of a Universal Design demonstration home in Amherst, NY. This home was part of a local home exposition.

design trends. Each builder then stations a salesperson in the home during the exposition period. An admission fee covers the cost of organizing and managing the exposition. A typical exposition of this sort can attract 30,000 people over a month. Including a universal design home in such an exposition is particularly valuable because visitors can compare its features directly with those of the other homes.

Decision-Making Strategies

There is great variability in the degree to which organizations have adopted universal design in practice. Each company and organization has a different knowledge base for making decisions. Furthermore, the characteristics of organizations that contribute to the rate of diffusion, relative advantage, compatibility, pervasiveness, reversibility, and gatekeeping can be radically different for each industry or organization. Two examples illustrate these points.

Sam Farber, a retired executive who had a successful career in the kitchen utensil industry, developed the OXO Good Grips product line described earlier. He started the new product line when he and his wife could not find any utensils that were usable with arthritic hands. The initial line of Good Grips products all utilize a standard handle on which a variety of utensil types can be mounted (Figure 4–4). The handle is made of a plastic core with a large, soft, and easy-to-grip surface wrapped around it. The products utilize a high-contrast color scheme of white and/ or black with some color coding. The utensils are modestly priced although more expensive than the lowest-price competition. Establishing a completely new line of products in a new start-up

Goals of Universal Design

1 Body Fit
Accommodating a wide a range of body sizes and abilities

Dryers in a water play area of the Pittsburgh Children's Museum

The dryers are arranged on the wall in three rows of 6 to provide room for several people of all sizes the opportunity to dry off after water play. They can also be used to dry different parts of the body like heads and feet.

This illustration is discussed further in Chapter 5

Goals of Universal Design

2 Comfort
Keeping demands within desirable limits of body function

Aeron Chair

The design features of the Aeron Chair provide a supportive and comfortable chair that helps to reduce back injuries caused by the stress on the back due to prolong periods of seated work. The Aeron Chair includes an innovative mesh seat and back to keep the body cool, which reduces the risk of muscle injury. It has extensive adjustability and easy to use controls so that the user can vary their position periodically. It also comes in three sizes, small, medium, and large, to better accommodate the needs of people with different statures.

This illustration is discussed further in Chapter 4

Goals of Universal Design

3 Awareness
Ensuring that critical information for use is easily perceived

Tactile tiles in the Barcelona subway

The tactile guide tiles on the floor of this hotel lobby guide people from the entry, as well as other areas of the hotel, to the reception area. A different type of tile is used to mark the location of the pathways and waiting areas. These tiles help people with visual impairments find their way in the lobby and avoid getting too close to the reception area. They also assist the sighted traveler and serve as an affordance to help everyone remember to stay back and wait their turn.

This illustration is discussed further in Chapter 8

Goals of Universal Design

4 Understanding
Making methods of operation and use intuitive, clear, and unambiguous

Progress display in New York City subway cars

In the newest subway cars in New York City, electronic displays are mounted above the door that illustrate, with color and illumination, the progress of the train along its route. The next and last stops are also displayed at the respective ends of the display. These displays help all travelers understand their location and anticipate when the train will reach their station. They are particularly useful for people with hearing and communication impairments. Audible announcements are also provided.

This illustration is discussed further in Chapter 11

Goals of Universal Design

5 Wellness

Contributing to health promotion, avoidance of disease, and prevention of injury

Street improvements in Manhattan, New York City

The City of New York has an extensive initiative focused on improving pedestrian and bicycle travel. Using simple and inexpensive strategies like painting and planters, hundreds of streets are being transformed to provide safer bicycling opportunities and passive recreation sites. The photograph shows an improvement on the West Side in midtown with a bike lane, enlarged sidewalk, and planters. The initiative is designed to encourage walking and bicycling and outdoor recreation by improving both safety of the environment and streetscape amenities.

This illustration is discussed further in Chapter 6

Goals of Universal Design

6 Social Integration
Treating all groups with dignity and respect

Waterfront redevelopment in Malmo, Sweden

The photograph shows a waterfront redevelopment project in Malmo that creates a sustainable community with mixed uses. A pedestrian promenade has sitting and socializing spaces all along the waterfront side. On the other side of the promenade, mid-rise residential buildings are located with stores, restaurants, and offices on the ground floor, giving residents and visitors many reasons to frequent the promenade. Housing in the district includes residential opportunities for many different types of households and mixed incomes.

This illustration is discussed further in Chapter 9

Goals of Universal Design

7 Personalization
Incorporating opportunities for choice and the expression of individual preferences

The iStore, iPhone and iPad by Apple computer

The iStore introduced a new dimension to personal computing. By developing a simple and intuitive way to find, purchase, and install applications, individuals can easily personalize their devices with the tools, entertainment, and communication systems that they value. The screen grid and colorful icon interface features use familiar models of the candy box and bento box to organize one's applications in a manner that makes sense to the individual. The form of the iPhone and iPad readily accept a wide range of third party cases for personalization of the outside, and to address both function and presentation of self.

This illustration is discussed further in Chapter 12

Goals of Universal Design

8 Cultural Appropriateness
Respecting and reinforcing cultural values and the social and environmental context of any design project

The Hippo Water Carrier

The Hippo Water Carrier was designed to address the needs of low income people in developing regions and displaced persons in temporary camps. Supplying a household with water often requires a substantial investment in time to travel to and from the water supply location and wait for one's turn. The Hippo Water Carrier is a fat hollow plastic wheel that has a long U-shaped handle fastened at the axle. Individuals can pull the carrier behind them while it rolls on the ground. The photo shows the carrier in use juxtaposed with a woman carrying a bucket on her head. The carrier reduces the effort required to carry water significantly, and, as the photo illustrates, allows an individual to carry much more water at one time which also reduces the number of trips needed to maintain a household on a weekly basis.

This illustration is discussed further in Chapter 2

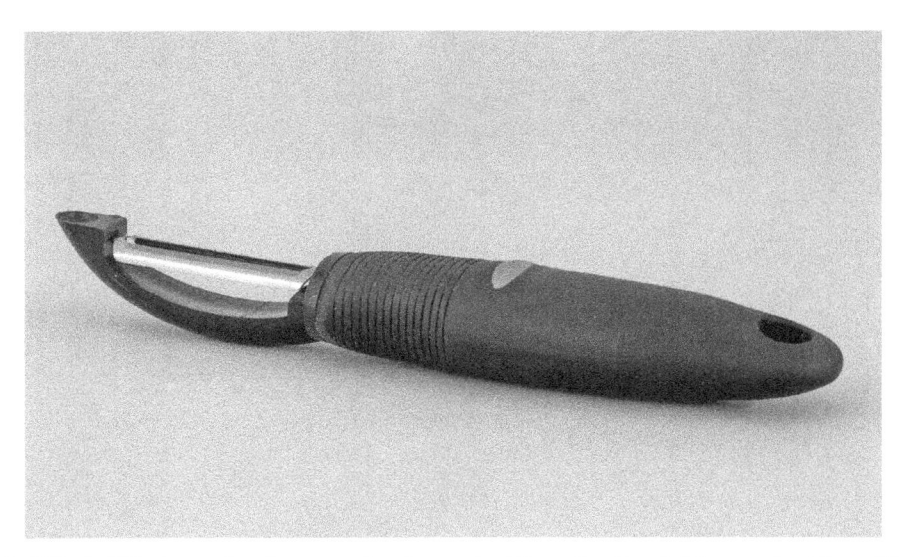

Figure 4–4 : OXO SoftWorks peeler. An example of a product from the Good Grips product line with the comfort-grip handle.

venture had its advantages. There were no gatekeepers, and Farber could use innovative materials without conflicting with existing practices since he was starting a company from scratch. Since the utensils are inexpensive, consumers can easily afford to experiment with the innovative product with little risk (reversibility). Furthermore, cutlery is sold directly to consumers. In a retail outlet, consumers can clearly see the relative advantage of the universal design for themselves. Good Grips have been widely distributed and are very popular with consumers. Within a very short time after Farber's products were introduced, products were on the market from competing companies that imitated the Good Grip concepts.

International Cushion Products (ICP) developed an innovative material—a tough plastic skin covering a soft inside core. The material was first used for water slides, where it provides increased safety, infection control, and ease of maintenance. ICP introduced the material into the plumbing fixture industry through a product called the "Soft Bathtub." This product provides a definite safety improvement over conventional tub materials because the risk of injury from a fall is much lower. Unlike the Good Grips example, the Soft Bathtub (Figure 4–5) had to overcome some serious barriers to adoption. It proved difficult to convince consumers of the relative advantage of the new material. Consumers associate soft surfaces with porosity (infection) and punctures. Unlike an inexpensive utensil, tubs are very expensive to buy and install so the reversibility of a consumer decision is much lower. It is also difficult for a small company to break into the existing distribution network for plumbing products in the United States (gatekeeping). Despite being available for many years, the Soft Bathtub has not yet been successful in the marketplace. ICP was sold to a large Korean plumbing fixture manufacturer, and the Soft Bathtub is now being marketed under the Whitespa brand name with a focus on safety and comfort. Although the cushioned material is a good example of a universal design feature, the company has not explicitly embraced universal design in other ways. For example, the product line does not feature tubs that are easy to use by older people, and its marketing material does not address usability. A more extensive commitment to universal design would increase the relative advantage of the products to consumers.

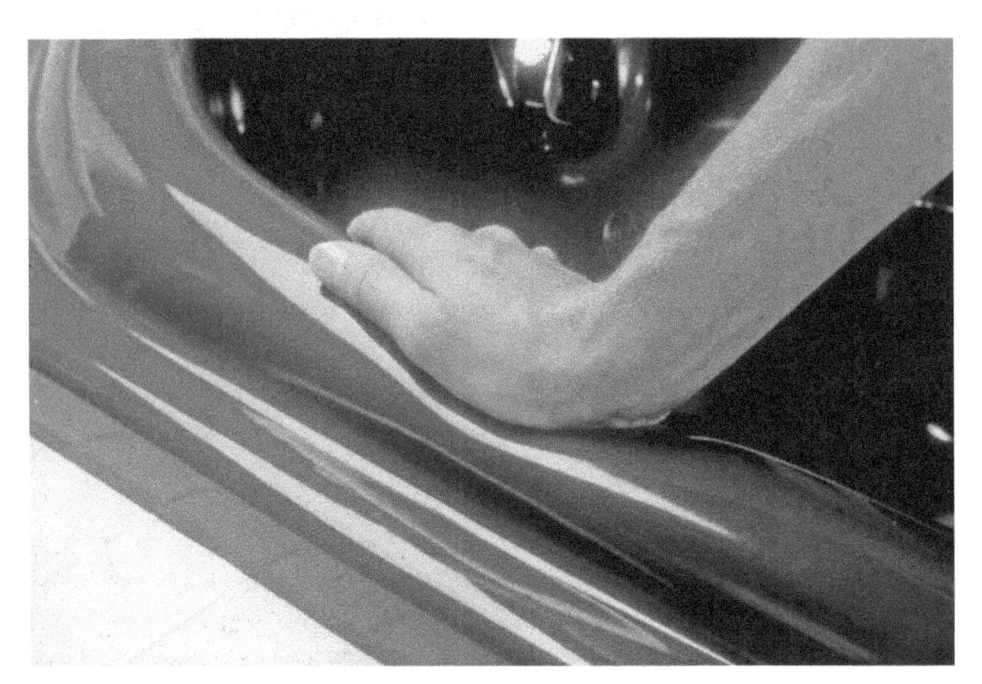

Figure 4–5: Soft bathtub. This soft bathtub material is a good universal design feature but the manufacturer does not include other universal design features in its products.

These two examples illustrate that there can be significant differences in the adoption of the universal design idea from producer to producer. OXO products were designed around the universal design idea from the start. The main goal was to introduce a product that people could use more effectively. With the Soft Bathtub, the goal was to introduce a new material. Although the material has universal design features, the tub designs themselves are no different from other bathtubs on the market. ICP/Whitespa did not conceive of the product from a universal design perspective from the start. It markets the products as "safer and healthier," but it has not embraced the full range of issues that would make the products true universal designs. In fact, its product line shows sunken tubs and tubs with very high rims. The company could easily offer some designs and installation concepts that would facilitate easy entry and egress, as well as more usable controls.

The examples also demonstrate that each industry sector presents different challenges for introducing universal design. Consumer demand is likely to be the most potent factor influencing the adoption of universal design in an industry. Where producers can directly affect consumer demand by introducing a new product in retail outlets, as in the kitchen utensil industry (OXO), usability will play a more important role in product innovation. Consumers can directly compare the products in the stores and decide which they prefer. Resistance to innovation will not be as pervasive as in an industry like the plumbing fixture industry in which marketing and distribution practices make it difficult to affect consumer demand directly. The plumbing products industry has two basic sales and distribution channels. The first channel is direct sales to consumers at home improvement retail stores. However, large home improvement stores carry only a limited number of brands, usually only from high-volume producers at very competitive prices. The second channel is indirect sales through builders and developers of new homes, where a third party (builder or design professional) makes decisions on product selection. Even if a builder provides some choices to a consumer, they are usually from a limited number of product lines and companies. Thus, although the soft material is very good from a usability and safety perspective, ICP/Whitespa has to break into the home improvement and builder market, which is much more difficult for it than it was for OXO to enter the retail market, especially given Farber's previous business activities.

Public agencies can play an important role in advancing the practice of universal design. The city of New York has made universal design a facet of its efforts to improve the quality of architecture and interior design in its buildings. The Mayor's Office for People with Disabilities commissioned the IDeA Center to produce a book on universal design in 2001, called *Universal Design New York* (Danford and Tauke 2001), which presented a business case for voluntary adoption of universal design and included many illustrations of good practices. In 2003, the city's Department of Design and Construction commissioned a second book from the IDeA Center, *Universal Design New York 2* (Levine 2003), which gave guidance to designers by demonstrating how legally mandated accessibility could be augmented by universal design. In 2010, the mayor's office published a third document called *Inclusive Design Guidelines* (City of New York Mayor's Office for People with Disabilities 2010). This document casts universal design into a building standards framework, and it is meant to be a companion to the city's building code. However, other than distributing the publications, the city has not developed a mechanism to encourage adoption of universal design, and there has been no attempt to determine if any of these documents are being used.

The Norwegian government began to engage in comprehensive planning for accessibility and universal design in 1997. Under the directive "Accessibility for All," the Ministry of the Environment encouraged municipalities and counties to include universal design features in master plans and encourage dialogue with citizens early in the design process. Evaluation research on 20 pilot projects conducted between 1998 and 2002 revealed that the Accessibility for All program had a positive effect on increasing participation for people with disabilities. An additional action plan was undertaken between 2005 and 2008 to increase accessibility in buildings, outdoor environments, and products through more permanent channels such as policies and laws. In 2009, universal design became a statutory requirement for regional and local planning and building. Today, Norway has one of the most progressive action plans for universal design with the goal of "Norway universally designed by 2025" (Bringa, Lund, and Ringard 2010).

In Australia, leaders of the residential building and housing industry and the disability and aging communities have recently joined to develop livable housing guidelines. A product of the federal government's National Dialogue on Universal Design, the 2010 livable housing guideline establishes three levels of standards—silver, gold, and platinum—and sets a target to make all new homes compliant with the Principles of Universal Design by 2020. The federal government has also agreed to contribute $1 million toward the establishment of an organization that will promote the new voluntary guidelines (Australian Government, FaHCSIA 2009).

The decision to adopt universal design is clearly influenced by the subculture in which decision makers operate: producer organization, industry sector, government, and others. Thus, improved awareness of successful universal design practices within each industry and government sector and across industry sectors can help to persuade decision makers that adopting universal design is a good business practice. Developing methods to educate consumers is critical. Consumer demand promotes adoption of innovations most effectively in retail businesses.

If a company demonstrates that its product is more convenient and usable to the broad population and the product achieves success in the marketplace, other companies in the same industry are more likely to adopt universal design in order to maintain a competitive position. It is also important to understand why products fail. Is it the result of poor design, poor marketing, undercapitalization, unfortunate timing of product introduction, changing executive priorities, or other reasons? It would be especially valuable to know why companies like GE Appliances abandoned universal design initiatives (see below).

The study of innovation diffusion demonstrates that, until an innovation is clarified, organizations and groups that adopt new ideas often reinterpret and reinvent them from their own perspective. As we have seen, the concept of universal design is still not clearly differentiated from accessible design. Although it can serve as a focus of many threads of human centered design practice, that role has not been clearly defined either. During the initial adoption period, as we are currently experiencing with universal design, we can expect to find a wide range of different approaches due to the unique nature of each adopting organization and its cultural context and the lack of good information on best practices. However, after a period of experimentation, we can expect that the concept will be clarified and that best practices will emerge.

Two strategies used with other innovations have not been adopted but offer promise in improving adoption rates significantly. The first is the development of a way to benchmark universal design practices. Benchmarking would be beneficial in providing information to both businesses and consumers. The success of consumer evaluation publications and websites demonstrates that such information is extremely important in consumer decision making and thus indirectly to producers . The second is exploring the relationship of universal design to other innovations. Research on innovation diffusion demonstrates that combining innovations (bundling) can increase adoption rates faster than separate initiatives. For example, a homebuilder can bundle universal design with sustainability, new materials, and wireless communication technologies. Bundling broadens the market for all by attracting customers with different interests and exposing them to many innovations at once.

Introducing Universal Design to Practice

There are three ways to introduce universal design in practice: (1) marketing, (2) product design, and (3) integration. The first method is concerned with the degree to which an organization views universal design as part of its effort to attract consumer or client attention. The second is concerned with the degree to which a company seeks to improve product and service effectiveness through universal design. The third method is concerned with the degree to which universal design can be integrated with the company's product lines and services.

Some organizations perceive of universal design primarily as a marketing strategy. This may indeed be a good approach to introducing universal design. If a company already has products that provide usability, safety, or health benefits, it can use marketing strategies to emphasize these features and the benefits to consumers. GE Appliances did this with its Real Life Design campaign. The heart of the campaign was the design and construction of a universal design kitchen for trade shows. This demonstration kitchen included GE products but also products from business partners, such as cabinetmakers and plumbing fixture manufacturers. By bringing the best of universal design products together with its own products, GE was able to demonstrate their combined impact in the kitchen. However, GE also had to reeducate its sales and customer service personnel to know the universal design features of the company's own products and to understand how to address requests for more information properly. For example, prior to introducing this program, a consumer might call the customer service line and ask if the company made "refrigerators for wheelchair users." The representative would often answer no. Part of the Real Life Design program educated the representatives to identify the model of appliance that would be most likely to address the customer's needs, such as a side-by-side model.

Others companies view universal design as a design philosophy that will improve quality. It may require investment in research and development to produce new products that will serve as exemplars in the industry. A good example is the Herman Miller Aeron Chair (Figure 4–6). Research on the causes of back injuries identified increased temperature as a factor in these injuries among office workers. Foam-based chair upholstery leads to overheating. This led to a search for new materials. The designers found an innovative material, a flexible plastic mesh that could eliminate the need for cushions and provide good air circulation for the back and seat. They incorporated a high level of flexibility in the adjustments possible, including the height of the seat, armrest and lumbar support, and several different types of tilt. In addition, they developed three different sizes for the chair—small, medium, and large—to provide a closer fit with the user's body size. It is important to note that the new design did not have just one new feature. By addressing usability and health concerns as much as possible with every feature of the chair, the company produced a design that was clearly an improvement on the state of the art. The new material also provided an opportunity to introduce an entirely new aesthetic to ergonomic office chairs.

Some companies, such as Herman Miller and OXO, are able to introduce major innovations, while others must take a series of baby steps before making a giant step. The baby-step approach lowers risk by increasing the ability to back out (reversibility) and by maintaining compatibility

Figure 4–6: The Aeron chair. Herman Miller addressed key usability and health concerns in the design of the Aeron Chair.

Source: Image courtesy of Herman Miller

with current practices. If a product does not succeed initially, the problems can be identified and addressed in a second venture. One way to take a small step is to create a "universal design line" separate from other product lines, while other companies might adopt universal design for all their product lines. The Aeron chair is a good example of a company developing a new line of products. The adoption of universal design as a branding approach is a more integrated approach. The OXO Good Grips utensil line is a good example of this approach. Fiskars (Figure 4–7), which produces hand tools, is another company that has been successful in the integrated approach. Perceived risks and opportunities form the basis for choosing strategies. To advance universal design practice, we must recognize the differences in each of these opportunities and collect information on which practices are most effective under which conditions.

Researchers have begun studying the practice of universal design in product development organizations (Dong, Clarkson, and Ahmed 2004; Dong, Keates, and Clarkson 2003; Goodman, Langdon, and Clarkson 2006; Keates, Lebbon, and Clarkson 2000; Vanderheiden and Tobias 2000). These studies indicate that designers who are resistant to adopt universal design are reluctant for three reasons:

1. It is perceived as design for special interest groups.
2. They believe it will lead to increased design time and cost.
3. They think it is difficult to market.

These studies found that designers do not understand the importance of universal design and are not familiar with enough good examples of universally designed products to serve as precedents. These research results indicate that perceptions play a major role in limiting adoption. More education and clarification are clearly needed to inform design professionals about the concept of universal design. However, businesses also need to understand that they must commit

Figure 4–7: Fiskars garden utensils. These tools are an example of using universal design as a branding approach to distinguish a company's products from the competition.

some resources to begin practicing universal design, just as with sustainable design. There is definitely a learning curve to do it well. With regard to marketing, there are many success stories to use as examples, where attention to usability, safety, and health has been an important factor in successful product designs. Besides the ones already mentioned, these include the Apple iPhone and the iPad, which are discussed in Chapter 12.

Some research has explored how end user issues are addressed during the design process. It was found that designers do not focus on end user responses until the design is near completion (Gyi, Porter, and Case 2000; Paquet, Nasarwanji, Lenker, and Feathers 2008). Even when users are involved in the design process, only a few are recruited, and they may not reflect the diversity of the actual user population (Gyi et al. 2000; Paquet et al. 2008). Recent information suggests, however, that 85 percent of companies believe it is important to consider the increased older adult population, although only 29 percent have started such initiatives (Gassmann and Reepmeyer 2008). Several of the nation's largest and most influential corporations were recruited to explore universal design through a project conceived by the Rehabilitation Engineering Research Center on Technology Transfer. The "Fortune 500 Project" helped these companies involve consumers with disabilities in all phases of product design and development (T2RERC, n.d.). Some of these initiatives led to successful products, but, when the initiative ended, the companies did not incorporate this approach as a standard practice.*

There is a need to identify best practices for implementing universal design within an organization's culture. Law (2010) investigated how ten mainstream businesses are responding to accessibility issues that affect customers. He studied the factors that contribute to the success of an organization in meeting the needs of customers with disabilities in the design, development, and delivery of products and services. Although his research is focused more on accessibility for people with disabilities, his findings are valuable in understanding how universal design can be introduced more effectively in business practices. The next seven points summarize the successful strategies he identified with their implications for universal design.

1. *Adopting a social model of function and ability.* The social model views disability as one aspect of diversity rather than as a medical condition. If the organization truly commits itself to design for diversity, it must recognize that every aspect of its operations and its products and services needs to accommodate differences in function and ability as well as gender, race, sexual orientation, religion, ethnic background—all the factors that lead to differences in needs, abilities, and perceptions.
2. *Establishing executive-level backing.* Leaders of the organization should measure performance on indicators that include achievement of universal design goals and insist that those who report to them take those indicators seriously. The identification of the need to address universal design could come from lower levels in management, but executive backing is critical to ensure that universal design will become part of the organization's culture.
3. *Establishing inclusiveness as a priority.* Often priorities are explicit but not necessarily supported by executive-level staff. In universal design, this can be a problem because the target population is so broad. For example, Law found that other diversity goals, such as gender equity, could take precedence over accessibility. In the practice of universal design, it is important that inclusiveness becomes the overriding goal and that it is addressed equitably.

---

*Joe Lane, conversation with the author, fall of 2010.

4. *Taking a planned, proactive approach.* Accessibility often is adopted only after a lawsuit, complaint, or other adverse event. Organizations that consciously plan are more successful in avoiding these events. Practicing universal design, in fact, is a proactive strategy that will reduce the probability of future problems with response to diversity of all types.
5. *Making accessibility a shared task.* It is not sufficient to give only designated people responsibility to implement accessibility. The same is true with universal design. Everyone in the organization must take responsibility and be held accountable. For universal design to be integrated into the culture of the organization, responsibility must be shared.
6. *Providing enabling resources.* Tangible resources, including money, tools, training, and guidance, are necessary for implementation. Innovation requires an investment at first. If done well, it has a payoff with interest down the road.
7. *Providing sources of accessibility expertise.* Initially, external resources (e.g., consultants or contractors) may have to be hired to provide knowledge about universal design. Over time, however, a source of knowledge should be developed within the organization itself, although external resources may still be utilized. Different types of expertise may be needed for external affairs, training, and implementation.

One of the major obstacles to increasing adoption of universal design is the perception of consumers. When demand is strong for a product or service, businesses usually respond. The aging of the Baby Boomer generation is creating many opportunities for development of new products and services. As discussed in Chapter 3, this is not the only demographic shift that will drive universal design, but, because of the purchasing power of the Boomer generation, it presents some significant business opportunities. Yet the needs of aging Americans do not necessarily predict purchasing decisions. Wylde and Hunter (2010) argue that aging consumers will not necessarily buy what is good for them even if they understand why. Products still must appeal to them in many other ways. The relationship between universal design and emotional responses to design, as described by Norman (2004) and discussed in Chapter 5, will play a major role in the success of new products and services.

Improving Practice

To combat the public's poor understanding and lack of awareness about universal design, some way to identify universal designs is needed. Many experts believe that the most helpful strategy to improve adoption rates would be a labeling and certification program, administered by an independent organization. The Good Housekeeping Seal of Approval, the AAA travel rating system, and UL safety labels are all examples of voluntary labeling combined with testing or certification practices that have advanced the design of products and environments in many industries. These labels help consumers to recognize products of quality and encourage the development of higher standards within industries through their role in consumer decision making. Furthermore, labeling and certification can be effective as part of a marketing campaign because third-party certification builds consumer confidence. Thus, these strategies encourage producers both to adopt improved practices and to communicate usability features to consumers, thereby educating them in the process and fueling further demand.

A certification program should have a good symbol, and, in the field of universal design, the symbol should represent its purpose and be a universal design itself. The Universal Design Identity Program (UD-id), another project of the IDeA Center sponsored by the NEA, developed

Figure 4–8: Proposed symbol for universal design. This symbol, an equal sign superimposed on a blue and green representation of a globe, is designed for use as a multisensory symbol to identify universal design products, facilities, and services.
Source: Image courtesy of Beth Tauke, copyright 2010.

a multisensory symbol and a public communications program to advance its recognition (Figure 4–8) (Tauke 2006). Guidelines for design of the symbol were developed through a review of the graphic design literature and online consumer surveys. The symbol incorporates universal design attributes with simple recognizable forms that are not based on a particular language. It can be produced in both visual and tactile forms and is flexible enough to be adapted for different applications, including a very small product certification mark. The center is making the symbol available for use with a "terms of use" agreement. By controlling the use of the symbol and establishing criteria for its display, we hope that companies and service organizations will have a tool to advance the recognition of universal design features.

Improving the "communicability" of universal design would be desirable to enhance diffusion (Utterback 1974). There has not yet been a consensus on what constitutes a universal design philosophy and, on the global scale, even the best term to describe it. The Principles of Universal Design were a valuable attempt to describe the scope of universal design and provide guidelines for practice. However, experience has proven that there is a need to clarify the concept further and provide more extensive information resources for all the design disciplines. Nine criticisms of the Principles have developed over the years.

1. *Fit with needs in the field.* Even as the Principles were being developed, several of the authors argued that they were more suited for product design than other design disciplines and that they were not readily applicable to specific design problems because the guidelines lack detail. Since the Principles were published, many variants have appeared in the literature, suggesting that they do not quite fit all stakeholders' needs.
2. *The issue of appearance.* Universal design requires more than just functional benefits. It extends the concept of inclusion to consumer "appeal" and benefits to people beyond those who have disabilities. A universal design would not be successful if other users found its appearance to be stigmatizing, if it made the user look awkward, or if it attracted undesirable attention.
3. *Language.* The Principles should be clear and translate well into other languages. The principle called "Tolerance for Error" seems to imply that errors should be tolerated; the intent of this principle was to reduce errors in the use of a product and environment. The "Equitable in Use" principle translates literally in at least one language (Japanese) to "equal opportunity," which is a legal term and thus confuses a voluntary design practice with legal mandates. The "Flexibility in Use" principle seems to imply that objects should bend during use.
4. *Goals.* The Principles and guidelines lack clarity of purpose. The "Equitable in Use" principle focuses on a social justice goal, "Flexibility in Use" is a design strategy, and the rest focus on human performance goals. Some principles overlap in objectives.
5. *Scope.* The Principles do not explicitly address several important issues, such as health promotion and disease prevention. The "Equitable Use" principle addresses only two social participation issues in a limited way—segregation and stigma. Other social participation issues, such as social interaction and friendship formation, support for social role engagement, and accommodation of cultural differences, are missing.
6. *Fit with context.* The Principles do not address the constraints imposed by context. There is a need to address contextual issues, such as historic preservation, sustainability, and urbanism, and constraints, such as available finances, human resources, and construction technology.
7. *Narrow focus on personal empowerment.* The Principles focus on human performance and ignore personalization and customization, which address broader diversity issues and social identity in a more inclusive manner.
8. *Difficulty for benchmarking.* The Principles and guidelines do not provide metrics or standards against which one can measure whether an environment, product, or service is indeed a good example of universal design. The terminology is not amenable to benchmarking. Thus, it is difficult to compare a universal design to one that is not and to establish best practices other than by professional judgment.
9. *Lack of an evidence base.* The lack of a body of evidence tied to the Principles is a serious barrier to their use in practice. Terminology related to established domains of knowledge would overcome this gap. The problem becomes apparent when trying to do an Internet search for information on "Flexibility in Use," "Tolerance for Error," or "Equitable Use."

To develop a good conceptual framework for universal design, it is useful to keep the ultimate goal in sight. Increasingly, professionals are being held accountable for their actions and are being asked to provide evidence for their decisions, which often involve spending large amounts of other people's money and putting lives at risk. Clients are no longer content to accept a professional's judgment without some justification. This trend is driving the development of evidence-based practice in which decisions are based on the best available knowledge about the problems that they address. Design viewed this way can be understood as a "knowledge translation" activity. Knowledge translation is any activity that transforms a discovery, from science or practice, to an innovation like that described in the Aeron chair or OXO examples above. To meet the challenges of the future, tools like the Principles should be evidence-based and tied to a body of knowledge and consensus on best practices. This practice will legitimize the information provided and make universal design a more powerful force for improving design quality overall. The success of evidence-based practice is already apparent in the design fields through the efforts of the Green Building Council, the Green Globes Program, and other sustainability initiatives. Evidence-based practice is also becoming a force in healthcare design, design for aging, and security planning and design as well.

To develop an evidence-based design approach in universal design, we need to start with an understanding of the type of information that designers will find useful. The producers of knowledge treat information differently than do the consumers of knowledge. Scientists are the prototypical knowledge producers, and professional practitioners are the prototypical knowledge consumers (Schon 1984). Those who generate knowledge for design are interested in understanding patterns and developing principles from specific cases. However, designers historically have sought useful information that provides a concise definition of design problems, clear directives to generate solutions, and precedents to use as models for new design solutions. As Schon observed, scientists work from the particular to the general; designers work from the general to the particular. Designers need information that can help them address very specific problems within a wide range of contexts. Good professionals know that every design challenge is different. Thus, while they find precedents useful, slavishly copying those precedents will not address the unique nature of every case. Designers also do not want to read lengthy scientific articles; they want their information in bits that are both easy to find and easy to use. The historic success of the Architectural Graphic Standards (Ramsey and Hoke Jr. 2000) and Time Savers Standards (Watson and Crosbie 2004), Neufert, Neufert, Bousmaha, and Wallman's Architects' Data (2002), and the Measure of Man and Woman (Tilley and Henry Dreyfuss Associates 2001) is evidence of the kind of information they find useful.

Four types of information—goals, guidelines, strategies, and best practices—are needed to provide a comprehensive knowledge base for professionals. Goals define the total scope of the concept; guidelines provide specific criteria for the design of places, products, and policies; strategies suggest potential approaches to meeting guidelines; and best practices provide precedents of practical applications (i.e., concrete solutions, ideally with graphic information). By developing a comprehensive set of goals, guidelines, strategies, and identifying related precedents, a useful body of knowledge for practice can be assembled. Ideally, these different types of information would be available in a knowledge base and linked to research sources in the scientific literature that a professional could search to address any universal design issue. However, achieving such a goal is a long way off. At this point in the history of universal design, we are still developing the conceptual framework to serve as a foundation for such a knowledge base.

Clarifying the specific goals for universal design is a useful first step. As described in Chapter 2, the purpose of universal design is to improve human performance, health, and social participation. From this point of departure and reflecting the critique of the Principles discussed previously, we developed eight Goals of Universal Design:

1. *Body fit.* Accommodating a wide a range of body sizes and abilities
2. *Comfort.* Keeping demands within desirable limits of body function
3. *Awareness.* Ensuring that critical information for use is easily perceived
4. *Understanding.* Making methods of operation and use intuitive, clear, and unambiguous
5. *Wellness.* Contributing to health promotion, avoidance of disease, and prevention of injury
6. *Social integration.* Treating all groups with dignity and respect
7. *Personalization.* Incorporating opportunities for choice and the expression of individual preferences
8. *Cultural appropriateness.* Respecting and reinforcing cultural values and the social and environmental context of any design project

The eight goals are stated very concisely in terms of measurable outcomes. They include four goals (Goals 1–4) that are oriented to human performance, each of which is focused on one of the four general areas of knowledge in this field: anthropometry (measurement of body size and characteristics), biomechanics, perception, and cognition. Three other goals (Goals 5–8) address social participation outcomes, including cultural appropriateness, which is a reflection of customs, social values toward resources, and physical context. Wellness (Goal 5) is a bridge goal that addresses both human performance and social participation. The crosswalk in Figure 4–9 shows how the Goals align with the Principles. Although it is possible to generate more goals from this list—for example, by breaking up any of the eight—we believe that, as with the Principles, limiting the number of goals will help people remember them easily and think consciously about them. Eight is pushing the limit of how many items people can easily remember. The Goals are illustrated at the end of this chapter.

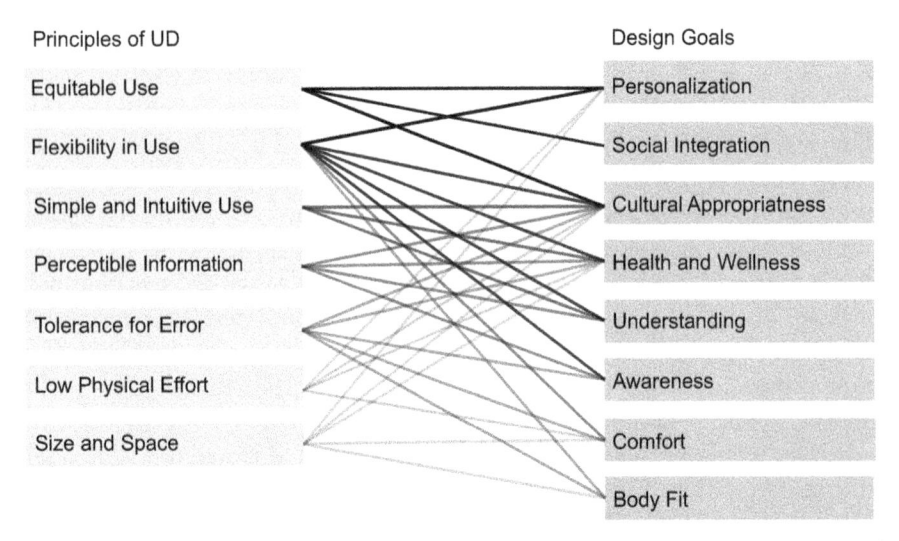

Figure 4–9: Crosswalk between the Principles and Goals of Universal Design. This diagram shows how the Goals of Universal Design are related to the Principles of Universal Design.

Summary

The concept of universal design is coming of age. More and more professionals and consumers are becoming familiar with it every day. Despite the variation in terminology used around the world, the concepts behind the various terms are the same. We believe that "universal design" is the best term to use because it reflects the ideal of providing universal benefits, captures the imagination of people who understand it, and has a distinctive identity. In the early 1990s, professionals and the public alike were scratching their heads when they heard the terms "sustainability," "virtual reality," and "cyberspace," but today these terms have entered the general vocabulary. We believe that the same will occur with universal design as adoption advances.

Encouraging adoption requires paying attention to the mechanisms through which innovation is diffused. The most direct way to make the public at large more aware of universal design is through widely used media, such as television and the Internet. To reach professionals, professional education and the development of communities of practice, especially among educators, is a priority. At this stage in the evolution of universal design, it is important not to limit models of practice to a "one best way" so that each sector of industry and professional practice can have a selection of practices to fit with its needs. Successful innovation requires compatibility with existing contexts of practice.

Innovators participating in the global community of practice also need to work within their local social networks to find and persuade early adopters of universal design. Doing this means developing local initiatives in professional societies, educational institutions, corporations, local government, and advocacy organizations. Activities that increase consumer awareness are critically important to advance adoption at the local level. To be successful in the implementation of universal design, businesses, service providers, and professional firms need to create an organizational culture of universal design. To help implement universal design in practice, there is a need to organize the knowledge available and facilitate evidence-based practice.

The ultimate test of how swiftly universal design will be adopted will be how the public responds. One of the most promising methods to promote consumer demand is certification and labeling with a rigorous review and approval process, because it supports marketing efforts on the producer's side while at the same time assuring real performance for the consumer. Currently, any business can claim that it is offering universal design products and services. An effective labeling and certification program could ensure that producers, building owners, and service businesses deliver good results when they make that claim. Developments in this area are discussed in Chapter 8.

Review Topics

1. What are the stages in Rogers's concept of innovation diffusion? How does innovation diffusion relate to universal design?
2. What are some critiques of the Principles of Universal Design, and how does the author's response address those critiques?
3. Describe at least three ways to improve adoption of universal design in practice.

References

Australian Government, Department of Families, Housing, Community Services and Indegenous Affairs. 2009. Livable Housing Design Guidelines. http://www.fahcsia.gov.au/sa/disability/pubs/general/Pages/LivableHousingDesignGuidelines.aspx

Bringa, O. R., E. Lund, and K. Ringard. 2010. "Norway's Planning Approach to Implement Universal Design." In W. Preiser and K. Smith (eds.), *Universal Design Handbook* (2nd ed.), pp. 10.13–10.10. New York: McGraw-Hill.

Center for Universal Design. 1997. *The Principles of Universal Design*, Version 2.0. Raleigh: North Carolina State University.

City of New York Mayor's Office for People with Disabilities. 2010. *Inclusive Design Guidelines: New York City*. Washington, DC: International Code Council.

Connell, B. R., et al. 1997, April 1. "The Principles of Universal Design." www.ncsu.edu/www/ncsu/design/sod5/cud/about_ud/udprinciplestext.htm.

Danford, G. S. and B. Tauke. 2001. *Universal Design New York*. New York: Mayor's Office for People with Disabilities.

Dong, H., J. Clarkson, and S. Ahmed. 2004. "Investigating Preceptions of Manufacturers and Retailers to Inclusive Design." *Design Journal* 7 (3): 3–15.

Dong, H., S. Keates, and P. Clarkson. 2003. "Designers' and Manufacturers' Perspectives on Inclusive/Universal Design." Paper presented at the the 14th International Conference on Engineering Design, August 19–21, 2003, Stockholm, Sweden.

European Institute for Design and Disability. 2004. "The EIDD Stockholm Declaration 2004." www.designforalleurope.org/Design-for-All/EIDD-Documents/Stockholm-Declaration/.

Gassmann, O. and G. Reepmeyer. 2008. "Universal Design—Innovations for All Ages." In F. Kohlbacher and C. Herstatt (eds.), *The Silver Market Phenomenon: Business Opportunities in an Era of Demographic Change*, pp. 125–140. Berlin: Springer-Verlag.

Goodman, J., P. M. Langdon, and P. J. Clarkson. 2006." Factors Involved in Industry's Response to Inclusive Design." In J. Clarkson, P. Langdon, and P. Robinson (eds.), *Designing Accessible Technology* (pp. 31–39). London: Springer-Verlag .

Gyi, D. E., J. M. Porter, and K. Case. 2000. "Design Practice and Designing for All." *Human Factors and Ergonomics Society Annual Meeting Proceedings* 44: 913–916.

Keates, S., C. Lebbon, and J. Clarkson. 2000. "Investigating Industry Attitudes to Universal Design." Paper presented at the 2000 Rehabilitation Engineering and Assistive Technology Society of North America Conference. June 28–July 2, 2000, Orlando, FL.

Law, C. 2010. *Responding to Accessibility Issues in Business*. Royal Melbourne Institute of Technoloy (RMIT) PhD. dissertation, University, Melbourne, Australia. Available at http://udprojects.com/Thesis/Responding_to_accessibility_issues_in_business_%28Summary%29.html.

Levine, D. (ed.). 2003. *Universal Design New York 2*. New York: City of New York Department of Design and Construction in partnership with the Mayor's Office for People with Disabilities.

Neufert, E., P. Neufert, B. Bousmaha, and N. Walliman. 2002. *Architects' Data* (3rd ed.). London: Wiley-Blackwell.

Norman. D. 2004. *Emotional Design: Why We Love (or Hate) Everyday Things*. New York: Basic Books.

Null, R. L. 1998. *Universal Design*. Belmont, CA: Professional Publications.

Office of the Prime Minister. Part M, UK Building Regulations. 2010. London: dowload from Mhttp://www.planningportal.gov.uk/buildingregulations/approveddocuments/partm/

Paquet, V., M. F. Nasarwanji, J. A. Lenker, and D. Feathers. 2008. "Incorporation of Universal Design into Mainstream Consumer Product Design Processes." Paper presented at the the International Conference of Aging, Disability and Independence. February 21–23, 2008, St. Petersburg, FL.

Preiser, W. and E. Ostroff (eds.). 2001. *Universal Design Handbook*. New York: McGraw-Hill Design.

Preiser, W. and K. Smith (eds.). 2010. *Universal Design Handbook* (2nd ed.). New York: McGraw-Hill Professional.

Ramsey, C. G. and J. R. Hoke Jr. 2000. *Architectural Graphic Standards* (10th ed.). New York: John Wiley & Sons.

Rehabilitation Engineering Research on Technology Transfer (T2RERC). n.d. "DP3. Fortune 500 Project: 'Improving Utility of Mainstream Products through Participatory Development'. http://t2rerc.buffalo.edu/development/fortune500/index.htm.

Rogers, E. M. 1995. *Diffusion of Innovations*. New York: Free Press.

Schon, D. A. 1984. *The Reflective Practitioner: How Professionals Think in Action*. New York: Basic Books.

Story, M. F. 1998. "Maximizing Usability: The Principles of Universal Design." *Assistive Technology 10*: 4–12.

Tauke, B. 2006. *UDid Universal Design Identity Project: Final Report*. Prepared for the National Endowment for the Arts. Buffalo, NY: IDeA Center. http://udeworld.com/udid/NEA_UDid_Final_Report.pdf.

Tilley, A. R., and Henry Dreyfuss Associates. 2001. *The Measure of Man and Woman: Human Factors in Design*. New York: John Wiley & Sons.

Toran, K. 2000. "Accessible Housing Database and Manual". Berkeley, CA: World Institute on Disability. http://www.wid.org/publications/accessible-housing-database-and-manual

Utterback, J. M. 1974. "Innovation in Industry and the Diffusion of Technology." *Science* 183 (183), pp. 620–626.

Vanderheiden, G. C., and Tobias, J. 2000. "Universal Design of Consumer Products: Current Industry Practice and Perceptions." Human Factors and Ergonomics Society Annual Meeting Proceedings, pp. 19–22. July 30-August 4, 2000, San Diego, CA.

Watson, D. and M. J. Crosbie. 2004. *Time Saver Standards for Architectural Design: Technical Data for Professional Practice*, 8th ed. New York: McGraw-Hill Professional.

Welch, P. (ed.). 1995. *Strategies for Teaching Universal Design*. Boston: Adaptive Environments Center and MIG Communications.

Whybrow, S., A. A. Rahim, V. Sharma, S. Gupta, L. Millikan, and C. Bridge. 2010. "Legislation, Anthropometry, and Education: The Southeast Asian Experience." In J. Maisel (ed.), *The State of the Science in Universal Design: Emerging Research and Developments*, pp. 144–152. Oak Park, IL: Bentham Sciences Publishers.

Wylde, M. A. and S. Hunter. 2010. "Emerging Markets for Great Design." In J. L. Maisel (ed.), *The State of the Science in Universal Design: Emerging Research and Developments*, pp. 20–30. Oak Park, IL: Bentham Sciences Publishers.

5

Design for Human Performance

Introduction

Human performance is the ability of people to complete activities and tasks. In universal design, we need to know how best to support human performance through the design of the environment and products. Four of the Goals of Universal Design are directly related to human performance: Body Fit, Comfort, Awareness, and Understanding. However, there is a strong relationship between these four Goals and the other four, Wellness, Social Integration, Personalization, and Cultural Appropriateness. For example, if a product or environment is not designed to fit the body or be easy to understand, it cannot support the social participation goals. Imagine a suit of clothes that is too big and makes the wearer look awkward and bizarre in social situations, or a music player with an extremely complex method of operation that makes its owner seem not smart enough to comprehend how it works. Poor design for human performance can also subvert achievement of Wellness. For example, a neighborhood filled with dangerous street crossings, bad lighting, and broken pavement can reduce physical activity and contribute to obesity and loss of bone density.

Each of the human performance goals represents a class of activities and tasks, but each also represents a distinct body of scientific knowledge that can be applied in design. Together, these bodies of knowledge are produced in the multidisciplinary field of human factors and ergonomics (HFE). Contributing fields include anatomy, physiology, rehabilitation science, exercise science, psychology, and anthropology. Needless to say, the amount of knowledge related to each of these activities and tasks is vast and constantly changing. There are four key bodies of knowledge that come into play:

1. *Anthropometry.* The characteristics and abilities of the human body at rest and in motion (Body Fit)
2. *Biomechanics.* The forces on the body at rest and in motion (Comfort)

3. *Perception.* The reception and interpretation of information from the world around the body (Awareness)
4. *Cognition.* Thinking, memory, and learning processes, including the mental representations we construct of the world and objects (Understanding)

Some designers argue that practicing universal design is really just practicing good ergonomic design, best practices that are already well known. However, the application of best practices in ergonomic design will not necessarily achieve universal design. In fact, one of the best-known general ergonomic principles—design for the largest part of the bell curve of characteristics and abilities (from the 5th to the 95th percentile)—excludes many people (Vanderheiden 1990). Rarely does an individual fit within this range for every characteristic or ability. A person with a long trunk may have short arms, or a person with short stature may have large hands. More significantly, circumstances of everyday life reduce human abilities all the time. Unfamiliar with a product or place, distracted by personal troubles, fatigued from too little sleep, or victim of a sudden storm or power blackout, people can suddenly find themselves "disabled" and functioning outside the 5th to 95th percentile range, particularly with respect to mental processes. Universal design requires a readjustment of typical HFE priorities. However, most basic principles of HFE can be applied to universal design.

In this chapter, we provide an overview of how each of these knowledge areas is important in universal design and outline selected design guidelines that can be derived from that knowledge and implemented for supporting human performance. At the end of the chapter, we present an example that demonstrates the relationships among these four knowledge areas. Here we focus on general human tasks rather than specific environments. In later chapters, we identify other key design issues that are related to specific environments, building on this basic knowledge base in human performance.

Human performance is related to both personal factors and environmental factors. We know from our personal experience that there are vast differences in performance among individuals and groups. The bodies of marathon runners from Kenya and Ethiopia are more suited genetically, and through conditioning, to long-distance running than are those of other groups of runners; thus, people with this heritage routinely place high in the major races. The bodies of men and women are more suited to different activities. Small, lightweight women have an advantage compared to larger, heavier women in ballet since men need to lift them. Men have stronger upper body strength and thus, as a group, outperform women in any activities that rely on that type of strength. Age plays an important role in human performance. There is a reason why professional athletes usually end their careers before age 40. Social and cultural differences play a major role in the design of space for even common, everyday activities. For example, cultures in which eating takes place on the floor versus tables require different environments to support eating and socializing, and written instructions can only be understood if they are written in a form that users of products can read and understand. Basic information on human performance needs to be modified to address these personal, social, and cultural differences. Space does not allow us to address these details in a comprehensive way, but they should be kept in mind while reading the chapter.

Anthropometry

Anthropometry is the measurement of body size, abilities, and other characteristics. Structural anthropometry includes measurements of the body at rest, including the size of body parts such as hands and hips, overall stature, and weight. It includes measurements taken in different postures, such as standing, sitting, and bending. Functional anthropometry measures the body in motion. This motion includes reach range, grasping ability, wheelchair clearances, and the space envelope required for different body movements, such as turning around or reaching. Any object with which a person physically interacts needs to be designed to accommodate the size and shape of the human body and the functional movements that a person may have to complete to use it (e.g., hand grips). Any space designed for human habitation or access must also accommodate the intended occupants and the movements that they may have to make within that space.

Body measurements can be made with manual instruments, photography or digital tools by measuring dimensions on the body using well-defined anatomical landmarks. There are specially designed tools for taking structural measurements of the body. Photography can be used to obtain a visual record of people's bodies from which measurements can be taken, correcting for distortions due to the photographic process. Increasingly, there is an interest in obtaining three-dimensional body measurements. Three-dimensional body scanners can be used for this purpose. The data from three-dimensional anthropometry can be used to construct a digital human model. These models can be used in computer-aided design to test the fit between body and designed object or environment. Since body scanners cannot obtain data on landmarks obscured to the scanning process, other methods may need to be devised. For example, in a three-dimensional study of wheelchair users, a digital probe was used to record the locations of body landmarks (Paquet and Feathers 2004).

Functional measurements can be obtained by measuring the space, or movement envelope, of a person. So, for example, Steinfeld et al. (2010) devised methods to measure the smallest space for wheelchair maneuvers. Video and digital recording methods can be used to capture movement data. The data collected can then be analyzed to identify the actual positions of body parts in space and how they change over time. Characteristics of the movement patterns, such as acceleration and deceleration in response to environmental features can also be studied (Chaffin et al. 2004).

Some applications of structural anthropometry include designing the handles of tools or utensils for a comfortable grip, deciding on how wide or high seating surfaces should be, determining how much space to allocate for wheelchair users, and determining how much range of adjustment a seat in an automobile requires for drivers to reach the controls. Anthropometry is also important in the design of information, or "virtual environments." For example, the size of a virtual "button" on a touch screen needs to accommodate the size of an operator's finger and be spaced far enough from other virtual buttons to avoid errors due to inaccurate movements. Anthropometry is also important for service providers, who need to know whether their facilities and equipment can accommodate the people who use them every day and also those who visit for short periods. For example, they may need to know how many occupants a meeting room can hold comfortably, whether young children will be able reach faucets in a bathroom, or whether tools provided to volunteers will be easy for them to grasp.

Some applications of functional anthropometry include identifying the size of a railing that can be grasped quickly when needed, planning the amount of space needed for circulation and serving in a restaurant dining area, determining where a switch or outlet should be placed to be within convenient reach, and identifying how much clear space is needed in a doorway to accommodate wheelchair users. Examples in design of virtual environments include determining the best shape and size of input devices like mice and locating display screens in a transportation terminal within a comfortable range of vision as people are walking toward them. Service providers can benefit from knowledge of functional anthropometry in purchasing products, planning furniture arrangements, and locating signs in their facilities.

Good body fit is essential to ensure safe operation of tools and equipment. If a tool or an operable equipment part does not accommodate the grip of the individuals who might use it, serious safety problems can occur. Prior to World War II, practically all truck drivers were large men because good strength was needed to steer the truck and use the brakes (Waller and Green 1997). In addition, drivers usually unloaded the trucks, so they had to be strong and, thus, usually large. The seats were fixed into position, and the distance to controls for hands and feet was planned accordingly. When these men went off to fight in World War II, women started driving trucks. Among other problems, they found that they could not reach the pedals while in the driver's seat; the pedals had to be built up to accommodate them. Eventually, manufacturers put adjustable seats in trucks to address the large range of differences in stature in the population. This feature increased the inclusiveness of vehicle design by making it much easier and safer for people of smaller stature to drive. However, these problems have not entirely disappeared from the automotive industry. For example, older drivers and passengers find it difficult to get up into vehicles built on truck bodies, and tall people find it difficult to be comfortable in smaller cars, which they may desire to purchase for economic or sustainability reasons.

In building design, anthropometry is very important for safety and convenience. Building regulations specify the minimum widths of emergency egress routes, including hallways and doors. These regulations are based on body size, including adjustments for the way people move in groups and the width of exit openings needed to ensure a fast flow of people. If enough space is not provided, all the occupants of a building may not be able to escape a burning building in time. Research demonstrates that current regulations may not be adequate for safe emergency egress in high-rise buildings. Existing code requirements for exit stairs do not provide enough room to accommodate opposing flows of traffic. For example, during the evacuation of the World Trade Center on September 11, 2001, people carrying wheelchair users and injured occupants down the emergency stairways got in the way of first responders climbing up (National Council on Disability 2005). Thus, new codes are being developed to provide other ways to evacuate buildings. For example, codes have been revised to make it safe to use elevators during emergencies to evacuate people who cannot walk the stairs. This example demonstrates that designing for body fit, as prosaic as it seems, may generate radically new ideas about building design.

Anthropometry is important for improving consumer acceptance and response to both products and environments. A good way to understand the importance of body fit is to try on a pair of shoes that are two sizes too small or large and walk around a bit. Poor fit leads to a negative consumer response, which often is very visceral because it causes pain. Good fit, however, is associated with the highest quality, such as custom tailoring. Products as diverse as door handles and automobile seating will be more successful in the marketplace if they fit properly. In environmental design, poor body fit can lead to the construction of environments in which we are always banging our heads, scraping our knuckles, or squeezing around obstacles. In poorly fitting spaces, people feel uncomfortable and annoyed, especially if they are paying a lot for service. This situation usually leads to an avoidance response. The value placed on good body fit is evident in the association of luxury with large spaces. In a large space, there is plenty of room to complete all the activities desired. Thus, the higher the price of services, the more space usually is provided to enjoy them. Hotel rooms demonstrate this relationship dramatically. Not only do designers need to know what dimensions are adequate to eliminate discomfort; they

Table 5-1: Data for Key Anthropometric Dimensions

Dimension (cm)	Wheeled Mobility Users			Adult Males (19–65 Years)		
	5th%	50th%	95th%	5th%	50th%	95th%
Standing Height	113.9	125.8	134.3	164	175.5	187
Eye Height	103.0	115.0	125.5	152.9	164.4	175.9
Breadth (bideltoid)	39.2	49.9	63.2	42.5	47.0	51.5
Sitting Height	62.1	74.1	83.3	85.5	91.5	97.5
Knee Height	54.6	62.3	71.5	49.5	55.0	60.5
Buttock–Knee Length	54.8	62.5	74.4	55.0	60.0	65.0
Waist/Hip Breadth	36.6	43.0	51.9	31.0	36.0	41.0

This table is a selection of only a few of the many typical dimensions used in anthropometric research. It compares the 5th, 50th, and 95th percentile of wheeled mobility users to U.S. males ages 19 to 65 years. Data in the table is taken from two recent research studies.

Source: Wheeled mobility user data from Paquet (2004); U.S. adult male general population data from Pheasant and Haslegrave (2006).

also need to know what dimensions contribute to a positive emotional response. Anthropometry reference books provide extensive information on body measurements and abilities. Table 5–1 gives some examples that are useful for designers.

Clearly, there is a close relationship between body fit and cost. The more space provided, the more a building will cost. The bigger the car, the more it will cost, all things being equal. Thus, in architecture and interior design, it is very important to know how much space is really necessary to complete an activity or task in order to avoid wasting space and money. In product design, larger is clearly not always better. It is no accident that high-performance clothing, such as that worn by athletes or dancers, is designed to fit as perfectly as possible and optimize freedom of movement. Likewise, products have to fit well to be efficient and safe in use. For example, if a hand tool has too large a grip clearance or grip shape, it may not be easy to grasp or control.

Research in human factors and ergonomics has identified four general guidelines for the application of anthropometric data:

1. Design for the extremes.
2. Design for choice.
3. Design for the average with accommodations.
4. Break with precedent.

Next we describe each principle and provide examples of applications in universal design.

Design for the Extremes

Anthropometric dimensions taken from a large enough population will distribute themselves in the normal distribution or bell curve. Most people will fall in the middle part of the curve (within two standard deviations from the mean) and very few at either of the extremes. As noted above, designing for the extremes generally has been interpreted to accommodate 95% of the population. This means designing to accommodate everyone above the 5th percentile in size and ability, if the parameter is concerned with a maximum value like the mounting height a control, or the 95th percentile in size and ability if the parameter is concerned with a minimum value, like the height of a doorway. If both extremes need to be addressed, for example, as in the grip diameter of a handle, the objective becomes designing to accommodate everyone between the 5th and 95th percentile. Since two different dimensions taken from the same person may be very different in percentile terms, a 5th or 95th percentile "person" alone cannot be used as the model for design. Each dimension has to be addressed separately using research data taken from as representative a sample as possible.

The rationale for not accommodating everyone is that it is not cost effective to do so since only a very few individuals will be at the extremes of the bell curve. But it is clear that the general rule will not address the Goals of Universal Design. For example, the space needed to turn around by a person who can walk, no matter how large they are, will be much smaller than the space needed by a wheelchair user or scooter user. Thus, in universal design, this principle needs to be reinterpreted. The first objective would be to try to accommodate everyone. However, when it is clear that some people will have to be excluded, the 5th–95th rule can be applied to the *population group that is the least common denominator.* For example, one can allocate enough space to accommodate the 95th percentile of maneuvering abilities for *wheeled mobility device users*. If their needs are met, it is likely that all ambulant individuals will have enough space as well (Steinfeld, Maisel, Feathers, and D'Souza, 2010).

Design for Choice

Designing for the extreme only can result in spaces and equipment that are not effective for some users. For example, designing a water fountain to accommodate people of very small stature will make it impossible for people of very large stature to use it without great difficulty and uncomfortable for a great many others. In these cases, a good strategy is to provide adjustability, as in modern automobile seating and steering wheels. Advances in technology are making it possible to introduce adjustability in more and more applications. In fact, once the basic technology is available, a wide range of adjustability often follows. For example, rather than simple lateral adjustments, automobile seats often provide six-way adjustability to improve comfort during long drives and to accommodate people of widely different sizes.

Sometimes, there are technological, social, or economic constraints to the provision of adjustable systems. For example, adjustable-height water fountains have yet to be introduced to the market. As an alternative, however, there are "hi-low" water fountains. These provide two spouts using the same plumbing fixture. One can serve people of short stature, including children, and one can serve the general adult population. Where multiple units are going to be provided anyway to meet demand, even more than two choices may be useful. Figure 5–1 shows dryers in a water play area of a children's museum. Since both adults and kids get wet in this area, and many people need to dry their hair, their clothes, and their shoes, providing many hand dryers made sense.

A third way to provide choice is to redefine the design constraints, which are often based on tradition rather than logic. In the United States, as in many other countries, separate restrooms for men and women are usually provided in public buildings. If the building is large enough, there are several toilet compartments in each restroom, one of which must be accessible to wheelchair users. This routine practice has several limitations. First, larger wheelchairs and scooters cannot be

Figure 5–1: Dryers in a water play area. By providing three rows of dryers at different heights, the Pittsburgh Children's Museum not only addressed differences in stature but also made it possible for people to dry off their entire bodies.

accommodated in the minimum sized code-mandated stall of 60 × 59 inches (1,525 × 1,500 mm), which is usually all that is provided in each restroom. Second, sex-segregation prevents couples of mixed sex from helping each other or adults from helping their children of the opposite sex. Third, women require more time to use a restroom and use more space (toilet versus urinal). Even if the number of stalls in a women's restroom equals the total of stalls and urinals in the men's restroom, there is usually a long line of women waiting when demand is high although the toilet compartments in the men's room may be empty. Some building owners have been including a unisex "companion" restroom as well as men's and women's rooms. These toilet rooms usually are larger than the standard accessible stall in order to accommodate two people, strollers for young children, and larger individuals and scooters. They also have a sink and a changing table and often a safety seat for children. Some even include a child-size toilet along with the adult toilet. Women can use the companion restroom for an extra toilet at peak times. In Scandinavia, toilet compartments are often unisex. A group of compartments is provided, each with full acoustic control and privacy and a lavatory as well as a toilet or urinal. A large companion restroom is provided as one of the compartments. The compartments all open up to a public circulation space. This strategy provides more flexibility with less space and even eliminates gender disparity.

Design for the Average with Accommodations

When design for the extremes or choice is not feasible, design for the average, or midrange, is a common fallback strategy in ergonomic design. A good example is the height of a kitchen countertop. The standard U.S. height of 36 inches (915 mm) is not ideal for many people and certainly not for many tasks. Although adjustable counters are recommended for kitchen counters (Grandjean 1973), that solution is generally infeasible when storage is located below. In universal design, we recognize that design for the average is likely to create significant barriers for many people. Thus, we need to be more creative about finding solutions. If every individual's needs cannot be met, we should strive to address priority needs at the expense of less important ones. For example, the Goals of Universal Design suggest that providing enough clearance in front of fixtures and appliances for a side approach by wheelchair users ensures that kitchens can be at least minimally accessible, despite the fact that clearance alone does not guarantee full usability.

It is important that the majority do not have to make sacrifices to address the needs of small minorities. That sometimes can lead to a negative reaction by the public toward universal design. When this may happen, a solution that includes options may be appropriate. But options do not always work well either. A good example is toilet height in hotels. Although some people with disabilities need higher toilets, if even 50 percent of toilets in a hotel were higher, many people would have to sacrifice comfort for the sake of those few people who need the higher seats. Adjustable-height toilets are on the market, but, at present, they are very expensive and hard to find. Another solution is an accessory device. Toilet seat "risers" are available to raise the toilet seat height. They are devices that are inserted into the toilet bowl and raise the seat height and could be used instead as an accommodation for those who need them.

Design for the average with special accommodations for those who will be inconvenienced, such as the toilet seat riser, should be used only when: (1) the solution does not pose a risk to safety, health, or social participation, (2) the solution is needed infrequently in the course of daily life, and (3) the task or activity requires only a short time and minimal effort to complete. For example, paying a cashier has virtually no potential risk and requires little effort. Thus at a cashier's station, designing for average introduces little discomfort and no health or safety risk. The needs of those who will be inconvenienced can be addressed by a special accommodation, for example, an auxiliary counter . In contrast, bending over to drink from a water fountain may require a significant effort and even cause severe chronic pain. A kitchen counter is not a good place to base a design on the average because it is used frequently, often for long periods of time, and for essential activities of daily living. In the toilet seat example, a riser may not be a good solution for a hotel where an individual may fall because of an unstable device. The provision of higher seats in a limited number of rooms is a better strategy, if there is some way to identify which rooms have this feature. Even though it may inconvenience some guests, most hotel guests only stay for a short time. This is why accessibility codes require higher toilets in designated accessible rooms, even though it is not the ideal solution because they are uncomfortable for shorter people. If toilets were designed to be adjustable in height, this problem would disappear.

Break with Precedent

Often, by breaking with precedent, it is possible to provide a solution that benefits everyone. Sales counters and cashier stations need to be designed for the safety and comfort of employees, but a design that is comfortable only for standing employees can make it impossible for customers who use wheelchairs to complete transactions independently, particularly when a high countertop must be used to transfer money, sign sales slips, swipe a credit card, or enter a personal identification number (PIN). Employee workstations can be designed for standing with a lower section of counter for the transfer of purchases to customers. This method actually benefits everyone by reducing lifting, but a problem arises with the use of swipe card devices that are located for the convenience of standing customers and employees. Often they are out of the reach and vision range for seated customers. Installing swipe card devices at both high and low counters or providing a wireless swipe card device or one with a long cable can solve this problem. Another solution, depending on the job requirements, would be to install a seated workstation for employees and provide only the lower counter, with a standing podium for most customers to use and one of the three options just mentioned for the swipe card device. All of these solutions would benefit employees as well as customers, particularly the seated workstation option, which could reduce back pain and provide a healthier working environment. Where there are many checkout counters, providing a mix of seated and standing stations would give employees an opportunity to change their working posture periodically.

Biomechanics

Biomechanics is effort produced by the human body while moving or resisting force. Research in this field studies the stresses on parts of the body, shoulders, or wrists while moving or on whole body systems, such as fatigue from heavy work. One goal of design for biomechanical fit is to adjust the level of effort required to use the environment to accommodate end users' abilities, tolerances, and preferences. A second goal is to reduce effort to increase efficiency and productivity in task performance.

Biomechanics, like anthropometry, is an interdisciplinary field. Industrial engineers have studied biomechanics to identify strategies for reducing workplace injuries due to lifting heavy objects and cumulative trauma. They also study the parameters of comfortable seating, how tasks can be simplified to reduce effort, and the biomechanical causes of injury from accidents. Psychologists involved in this field develop instruments to measure comfort, which is a psychological construct. Physicians and biomedical engineers study biomechanics to develop new surgical procedures and develop better artificial joints. Rehabilitation therapists traditionally have studied biomechanics to develop improved therapies, assistive technologies, and environmental interventions that improve independence for people with disabilities. Exercise therapists and physiologists study stamina and strength under different conditions. Architects, interior designers, and product designers have studied how to reduce effort and increase efficiency in space layouts and use of equipment. Several professions have studied falling, including stairway falls and floor slips. Recently, urban planners and geographers have started to study related issues, such as the effect of walking distance on utilization of community services. Each focus of biomechanics research tends to have its own community of practice with a corresponding social network of organizations.

Direct measurement of biomechanical effort may be completed with instruments that obtain information about muscle activity and body motion (Godfrey, Conway, Meagher, and OLaighin 2008; Marras et al. 1995). Perceptions of discomfort, pain, and effort are observed using self-report psychophysical scales—for example, scales that identify localized discomfort (Jung et al. 2010; Kyung, Nussbaum, and Babski-Reeves 2008). Ratings by trained observers may also be used to evaluate effort in completing tasks (James, Mackenzie, and Capra

2011). Epidemiological research is often used to identify the severity of problems that need biomechanical research attention (Kongsted et al. 2008; Pintar, Yoganandan, and Maiman 2010). For example, researchers may use accident reports and statistics to identify trends and frequencies of different accident types. Such research can lead to simulation studies, such as crash testing or studies that "reconstruct" accidents to identify methods to prevent or reduce injuries (Siegel et al. 2001).

Although there are many possible applications of biomechanical research in design, compared to anthropometry, design professionals use much less information from this field regularly. One exception is workplace design and rehabilitation, where ergonomists and occupational therapists are regularly involved. Another is product design, where safety and comfort are critical design goals, and ergonomists are often consulted. In architecture and interior design, many building regulations are based on assumptions about biomechanics. For example, building regulations for accessibility have requirements limiting the force of opening doors and the force required to operate devices in buildings, such as door handles. However, the codes tend to lag behind advances in research both in terms of the scope of issues covered and design criteria. Other codes are sometimes in direct conflict. For example, life safety codes mandate minimum forces for closing doors in emergency egress routes that result in higher opening forces than the maximum forces allowed by accessibility codes. In the building regulatory field, safety codes always prevail over accessibility codes, but this conflict signifies that more research and some technological innovation may be needed. If there is no change, people who cannot open exit doors are compromised during building evacuation. Another example is the relative lack of research information on slipping and falling on walking surfaces. Slips and falls are a major source of lawsuits in architecture. Although there is a basic understanding of why slips and falls occur, much more research is needed (Lockhart 2008).

The benefits of research and knowledge translation in biomechanics are best illustrated by research on materials handling. Back injuries from lifting heavy objects are major occupational safety and health issues (Nelson and Hughes 2009). To workers, back injuries can cause severe chronic pain, make it impossible to maintain employment, and lead to permanent disability. To employers, back injuries are a major cause of lost productivity due to absence from work and contribute to high insurance costs. Through research, biomechanics experts have developed several mathematical models that predict the forces produced by lifting on various joints in the body. Tasks can be analyzed using these models to estimate the risk of back injuries (Marras et al. 1995). For lifting that is determined to be dangerous, tasks can be redesigned to keep the stress on the body within safe limits. Approaches to reducing the stress include reducing the weight of the objects that need to be lifted, improved packaging that reduces the forces on the joints by placement of handholds, and devising equipment that can be used to lift heavy loads or reduce the need for lifting.

Applications of biomechanics research methods related to universal design in the fields of architecture and interior design include studying the efficiency of different circulation layouts. One group of researchers compared the efficiency of floor plans for hospital wards (Thompson and Goldin 1975) with respect to the time and effort required by nurses to complete their work activities. This study led to recommendations on how to design hospitals to optimize efficiency in circulation. A recent pilot study examined how long it takes to cross a street using a scooter or wheelchair (Schoon 2011). Another research team, through realistic simulation, studied responses to critical incidents in coronary care hospital units. The team identified the most efficient layout for utilities, furniture, and emergency equipment and was able to show how that layout would significantly reduce response times (Clipson and Wehrer 1973). Recent research in urban planning and geography has focused on how far individuals will walk to neighborhood services before they decide to drive (Agrawal, Schlossberg, and Irvin 2008; Ewing, Clement, Handy, Brownson, and Winston 2005; Rodríguez and Joo 2004). This research identified the impact of neighborhood planning on activity levels of residents, an issue in promoting healthy living. Research on ramp use examines the abilities of people with and without mobility impairments to manage different ramp slopes and lengths (Sanford 1996; Steinfeld et al. 1979). This research was used to develop standards for building accessibility. Research on the impact of different surface conditions on walking and wheeling is useful for developing recommendations for design and standards to ensure accessibility and safety for wheeled mobility users and other pedestrians (Axelson, Yamada, Kirschbaum, Longmuir, and Wong 1997; Koontz, Brindle, Kankipati, Feathers, and Cooper 2010).

Applications of biomechanics related to universal design in product design include studies on gripping ability and cumulative stress injuries on the hands (Huysmansa, Hoozemansa, Vissera, and van Dieën 2008). This research is useful for designing improved handles that reduce cumulative stress disorders. Research has led to the now widespread design practice of increasing the size of the gripping area and using nonslip materials for handheld tools, utensils, and writing implements. A similar example is research on hand and arm position while typing. Positions in which the wrist resting point is significantly lower or higher than the keyboard leads to excessive stress on the wrist joint, a major cause of cumulative trauma (e.g., carpal tunnel syndrome). Computer equipment manufacturers have responded by integrating wrist rests with their keyboards. Superthin and compact keyboards are now being introduced to eliminate the need for wrist rests entirely (Figure 5–2). Another related problem with keyboarding is ulnar flexion, bending the hands out toward the little finger as one taps the keys. This movement stresses the ulnar nerve, which runs along the outside of the hand and up the arm (Thomsen, Gerr, and Astroshi 2008). One way to reduce ulnar flexion is to break the keyboard into two parts that angle a bit toward the center (Figure 5–2). These examples demonstrate how putting biomechanics research into practice can benefit the entire population by reducing pain, disability, and discomfort in everyday activities.

Research in biomechanics has produced several general guidelines that are applicable at all scales of design activity. These include:

- Reducing unnecessary and potentially harmful movement
- Reducing unnecessary operating forces
- Reducing effort required for lifting
- Designing to maintain balance

Reduce Unnecessary and Potentially Harmful Movement

By reducing movement, human energy is conserved and stress on the body is reduced. However, a sedentary, inactive existence also reduces strength and stamina, causing a downward spiral in abilities. Thus, applying this guideline requires some careful analysis. In general, where productivity (speed in completing a task), injury prevention, and avoiding errors are critical, reducing movement is a good thing (e.g., reducing unnecessary keystrokes). Nonetheless, even in work settings, it also may be desirable to encourage more exercise through design. For example, providing stairways to connect work groups on different floors could be better than frequent use

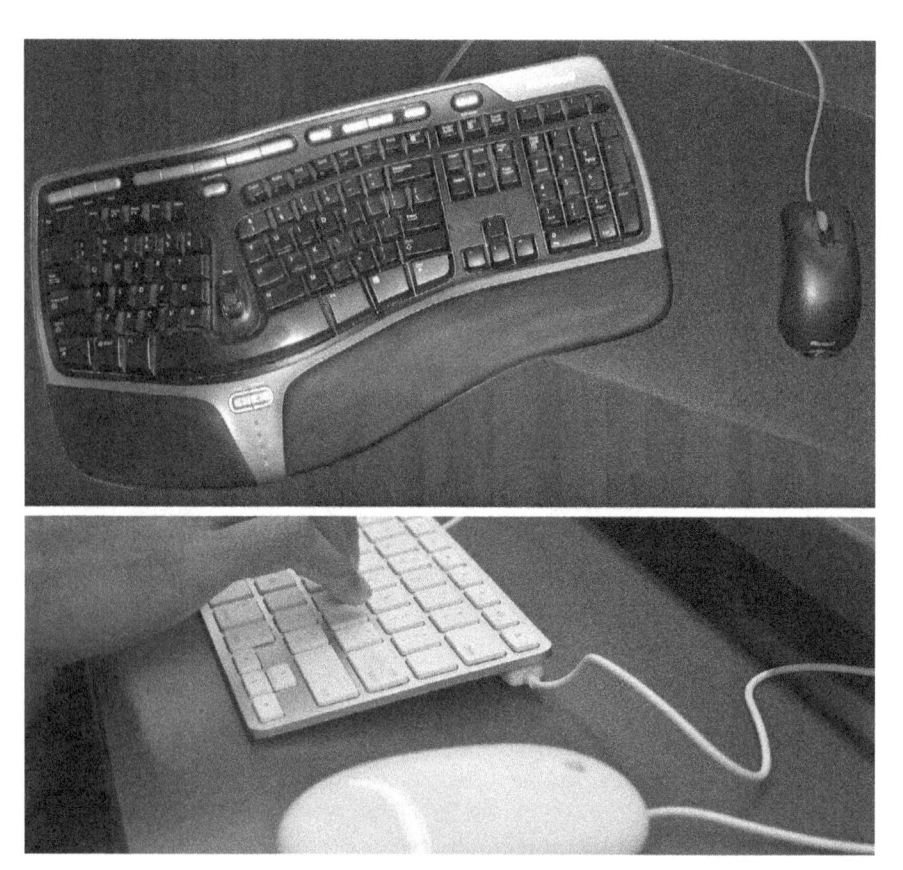

Figure 5-2: Ergonomic keyboard and thin Apple keyboard. The ergonomic keyboard (top) has an integrated wrist rest and a split keyboard to reduce stress on the wrist. The Apple keyboard (below) is so thin, that a wrist rest is not required.
Source: Image for ergonomic keyboard courtesy of Nick Skitch

of elevators, particularly if using the stairs is generally faster. However, this does not mean that elevators and escalators should not be available; some people cannot use stairs at all and, for others, using stairways may be dangerous.

Movement reduction strategies in community planning and campus design can focus on design to keep people active by providing local services, workplaces, and recreation settings within walking distance of residences (Cervero and Gorham 1995; Cervero and Kockelman 1997; Greenwald and Boarnet 2001). This reduces the number of automobile trips and increases activity levels.

In interior design, this principle can be applied by organizing workstations to reduce the need to move hands, arms, and legs and to reduce bending, twisting, and lifting. Keeping storage and equipment within the comfort zones of reach and in places close to the work surface are key design strategies (Grandjean 1973; Steidl and Bratton 1968). In product design, the aim to reduce movement should focus on reducing the number of hand movements needed to operate a product, such as the number of mouse clicks required to navigate a website or file directory.

Reduce Unnecessary Operating Forces

All tasks completed in the environment require exertion of force. As discussed earlier, eliminating all energy expenditure from human life is not a good idea. However, excessive energy expenditure can pose barriers to use, cause people pain, and result in accidents that should be avoided. Good examples of designs requiring excessive energy expenditure are ramps that are too steep, stairways that are too long, and doors that require a high degree of force to open. All of these are known to be barriers to people with disabilities and frail older people.

Handles and other gripping surfaces, such as grab bars and handrails, should be large enough to grip easily and not too large to allow small hands to grasp them. Ideally, gripping surfaces should keep arms and hands in the position where stress is least, often called the "neutral position" (Conlon, Krause, and Rempel 2009). Built-up handles and slip-proof grips help to reduce the need to grasp a small product, such as a screwdriver or pen, tightly, thus reducing the biomechanical load. Another strategy is to design the shape of objects to reduce the potential for slipping; for example, an hourglass shape for glassware requires a less firm grip. Handles should be designed to allow a power grip, one where the entire palm of the hand is engaged rather than just a finger and thumb (pinch grip), and be usable with alternative grips, such as a flat hand or two flat hands. One-handed use should be incorporated wherever possible. With computer use, eliminating mousing entirely by using voice recognition and gesture-based interfaces can reduce the stress on upper extremities when using virtual environments.

Designing to accommodate alternative methods for applying forces, such as pushing with a forearm, using either left or right hands, gripping with two hands, using either lower or upper extremities, or using elbows, accommodates a wider population and helps people use devices when they are holding something. Electrical controls and small hardware should have a shape and size that allows use by a flat hand, clenched fist, or knuckles. All devices and controls designed for physical interaction should be slip resistant and sized and spaced to allow use by people with limited gripping ability and coordination.

Reduce the Effort Required for Lifting

As discussed, there are well-developed methods for analyzing work tasks and identifying ways to eliminate lifting or reduce the resulting stress on the body. Key strategies include:

- Reduce the weight of the object that has to be lifted.
- Bring the work close to the person.
- Eliminate unbalanced loads.
- Support powerful grips.
- Provide protective devices.

These strategies can be applied to consumer product design and environmental design as well. A good example is the provision of wheels for garbage receptacles, which also allows the provision of a larger receptacle and thereby reduces overflow, a major cause of rat infestation (a health threat). Standardization of these receptacles also facilitates automated emptying and thus reduces lifting for garbage haulers. Many other possible applications of these strategies are possible. Consider these:

- Design handles into appliance boxes that are large enough for a power grip, positioned to balance the load and reduce the need for extending arms when lifting.
- Package consumables in smaller quantities and provide larger handles to allow power grips using the whole hand rather than finger grips.
- Include shoulder harnesses with leaf blowers or small vacuum cleaners.
- Make dishes, pots, and pans from lighter materials, and provide two handles instead of only one on the heavier items.

In work and home settings, interior design can also reduce the stress of lifting tasks by incorporating these strategies. For example:

- Locate counters adjacent to storage units for easy unloading.
- Install storage units on the back of cabinet doors or provide sliding shelves to bring the stored objects closer to the user.
- Provide "garages" for infrequently used small appliances at the rear of counters so they can be slid out without lifting.
- Incorporate rolling carts into cabinetry in laundries and kitchens to transfer loads with a minimum of lifting.

Design to Maintain Balance

Falls occur when people lose balance. The etiology of falls is not entirely understood. In general, design to prevent falls has focused on biomechanical issues. However, there is also evidence that the visual and acoustic environment may contribute to the onset of falls (Palm, Strobel, Achatz, von Luebken, and Friemert 2009). Physical causes of falls include walking surfaces that are uneven or irregular, stair treads that are not deep enough to support the foot, and surfaces that do not provide sufficient friction. Lack of adequate supports for maintaining balance or interrupting a fall, such as grab bars or railings, are contributors to injuries from falls. In homes, stairways and bathrooms are the locations where the greatest incidence of falling occurs (Carter, Campbell, Sanson-Fisher, Redman, and Gillespie 1997; Feldman and Chaudhury 2008). Thus, special attention should be given to safe design in these locations.

Perception

Perception is the process of interpreting information received from the senses (Goldstein 2010). Contemporary theory in this field views perception as an information processing activity (Fuster 2006). Conventional wisdom tends to equate perception with sensory reception—we perceive what information is "absorbed" by our senses. But that is far from the case. There is just too much information in the world to process. Thus, perception is as much of a mental process as it is a sensory process. Without some guidance from the brain, our senses would collect a lot of unnecessary information. And without interpreting and organizing data received by the senses, all we would notice is a lot of unconnected stimuli. The process of determining which information needs our attention, collecting the relevant information and making sense of it, is called situational awareness and is guided by motivation and previous experience. Situational awareness is a particularly important aspect of safety and usability. Awareness alone is not sufficient to use for making decisions; we have to interpret and organize the information we collect to decide how to act on it. Thus, the perceived world is actually "constructed" by our perception system, and we are active participants in seeking the information we need and organizing it in a way that is useful for taking action.

Our previous experience is the most critical factor in determining what stimuli we will attend to and what we make of the stimuli (Chun and Turk-Browne 2007; Summerfield et al. 2006). Our ability to recognize an object in poor viewing conditions demonstrates this. We may see parts of the object but not the whole; some of it may be in shadow, some may be obscured by glare, and some may simply be out of our field of view or hidden by other objects. But if we see enough of it, we can recognize it. For example, let us say we are searching for a bicycle in a storage shed. All we may need to see is a little piece of the front wheel and maybe part of the handlebars. How can we be successful in perceiving the whole from a few of the parts? Our perceptual system uses previous experience to help us recognize the object. The importance of this ability, in the evolutionary context, is clear if we can imagine how important it was for early humans to avoid predators and find food in hostile natural environments. At the same time, our ability to perceive things with little information can also work against us; we can easily make mistakes based on false assumptions when we have too little information.

In human performance, perception is critical for supporting task performance, safety, and productivity. To maintain awareness of our surroundings, we use a multisensory strategy. Ryhl (2010) found that, even when people do not articulate their use of multisensory perception, in-depth interviews demonstrate its importance to them. Individuals with limitations in one sense, or modality, need compensatory information from another sense. Since 70 percent of our sensory information comes from vision (Lefton and Brannon 2002), those who have no functional vision can be at an extreme disadvantage when it comes to awareness of the world around them unless adequate information is provided through sound, touch, and smell. For people who have limitations in hearing, the lack of audible information has a significant impact on their awareness of conditions in the surroundings that need immediate attention, such as a crying baby or a fire alarm. It also presents limitations in face-to-face communications, which has a great impact on education, employment, and social life.

Touch provides information on texture, vibrations, and thermal differences that are important for situational awareness. For example, driving requires feedback, such as vibrations from the roadway, that provides information to help understand the status of the vehicle and condition of the roadway. Drivers feel these vibrations through the steering wheel and control pedals. Reducing these vibrations too much reduces situational awareness and can affect driving ability (Morrell and Wasilewski 2010). The sense of touch is part of a larger perceptual system called the haptic system. This system includes sensory information derived from both skin sensors and active limb movements. Impairments to this system, often caused by diabetes, can lead to injuries and performance reductions due to limitations in situational awareness.

Like challenging topography or spaces that are too small for an activity, the sensory environment can be disabling too, for everyone, not just people with sensory impairments. There is a reciprocal relationship between the geographic world and the perceived world (Danford and Steinfeld 1999). On one hand, features of an environment or product that are difficult to perceive create barriers to access and usability. On the other hand, the inability to utilize and explore environments or products limits perception of the resources available to a person. Thus, a physically inaccessible environment or product can hamper perception just as much as limitations in sensory modalities, albeit only in that particular circumstance. Recognizing this relationship demonstrates why accessibility should be defined broadly. We tend to think of inaccessibility in physical terms. It clearly includes perception too, but it also may include affordability or availability. For example, lack of access to media can severely limit a person's perception of civic events and thus civic engagement. This observation reinforces the importance of thinking broadly about universal design.

There is a close relationship between perception and understanding. If we cannot perceive our environment well, we cannot use the information we retrieve from our senses effectively. This relationship becomes obvious in the use of office productivity software. Few people utilize all the features of word processing, e-mail, or presentation software. In fact, few even know about the shortcuts and tools that could help them in improving the efficiency of their work. The reason is that it these features are particularly difficult to perceive and the benefit of investing the time to learn about them is even more difficult to perceive. Poor awareness, in effect, hampers learning and understanding and, thus, restricts effective use.

Perception involves several processes (Goldstein 2010):

- Search for information from the environment
- Interpretation and organization of that information
- Evaluation of the information
- Decision making on the need to take action
- Directed action on the social and physical environment
- Feedback on the result of that action

The search process is guided by previous experience, which we use to identify the specific stimuli to which we should pay attention. Because our capacity to process information is limited, the greater the demand to process information in a fixed time period, the less we actually can use and the more we have to focus on perceiving critical stimuli, or cues (Proctor and Van Zandt 2008). We are conditioned to complete these processes through long experience, and often we are not even aware of our perception in action until something unusual occurs. Early perception of these unusual events is particularly important for safety and security. For example, if we hear a loud crash up ahead, even if we cannot see anything unusual, the sound alerts us to potentially dangerous events so that we can be more cautious and search for additional signs of danger.

Our ability to perceive important information (target) is directly related to the relationship between the strength of the stimuli we need to make us aware of it (signal) and strength of other, unimportant stimuli (noise). This type of task is called a signal detection task (SDT) (Wickens, Gordon, and Liu 1998). When the noise in a perceived field of perception makes it difficult to distinguish the target, error can occur. There are two types of error in SDT: false perceptions and misses. If an instrument panel has many different lights that turn off and on periodically, it is less likely that we will notice one particular light that goes on. Similarly, if there is a lot of background noise, it will be difficult to hear another person talking to us, particularly if he or she has a soft voice. The recognition of important cues, or attributes of information sources, is also a very important part of perception. Cues are learned from experience and can include all kinds of stimuli, including colors, shapes, and symbols. In addition to lack of awareness, we also make mistakes due to incompleteness, confusion, or ambiguity in the perceived signals. In the earlier bicycle example, it is possible that the pieces in sight might only be parts of a bicycle thrown in a junk pile. Incomplete information could cause the mistaking of the parts for a whole bicycle. Examples of confusion would be thinking the green light on a traffic light is on when it is off because glare is reflecting off the lens or misinterpreting a public address announcement due to high background noise. An example of ambiguity of form is a number "2" that looks like a letter "Z" or an alarm that sounds like a malfunction in a sound system.

The built environment and products can be designed to improve our perception. Doing this can help people identify important information faster, reduce errors or misperceptions, and thus reduce accidents and errors. Understanding how our perception system works can help us to enhance perception and improve stimulation. A group of experimental psychologists, starting in the early twentieth century, gave extensive attention to understanding perception of the sensory world (Kohler 1959). This group, called the gestalt psychologists, conducted many experimental studies and were able to develop an understanding of how people perceived the world around them. One of their important discoveries was the importance of the figure–ground relationship (Rubin 2001). In perceiving the world, in all senses, people tend to distinguish a "figure" from its surroundings, or "ground." Thus, we can distinguish a tune from random background noise or see a snake hanging from a forest tree with similar colors. We use a variety of perceptual cues to do this, although sometimes conditions can make it difficult to distinguish the figure. In general, design for good perception is primarily about reinforcing the ease of perceiving a designated "target," or figure, from the background. For example, we use color, shape, texture, and the like to make a door handle easy to perceive on a door. Signal detection theory translates the figure–ground relationship into a quantifiable and measurable relationship.

Gestalt psychology is important to designers because of its impact on twentieth-century design. The gestalt psychologists developed the gestalt laws, or principles of perception, to communicate their key findings. The members of the influential Bauhaus school of design in Germany between the world wars were influenced greatly by gestalt psychology, and their style of design was based on many of these principles. Essentially, they based their style on the principles of "good form" identified by the gestalt psychologists — forms that are clear, cohesive, and understandable (Behrens 1998).

The next example illustrates the more important gestalt laws with some examples of their application to design.

Gestalt Laws and Example Applications

Gestalt Laws

Law of Similarity (or Grouping)
Elements that are similar in characteristics tend to be perceived as a group. This law can be used to help find things in complex displays (e.g., color-coding the routes of specific lines on a transit map or grouping all express lanes to one side in a retail checkout area). The graphic (Figure 5-3a) demonstrates this law by depicting several identically spaced colored triangles and squares that the viewer perceives as separate groups.

Figure 5–3a

Law of Proximity

Elements that are located closer together in space or time tend to be perceived together. Thus, allocating a boundary zone between groups of cubicles in an open office will help people understand where a department's territory begins and ends by creating spatial clusters. Narrower spaces between groups of buttons or menu items will associate their functions. The graphic (Figure 5–3b) demonstrates this law with four columns, each with four equally sized and spaced squares. The second two columns are separated from the first two columns by a wider vertical space. The viewer perceives two separate groups of squares, rather than four groups, because a wider space separates the first two columns from the other two.

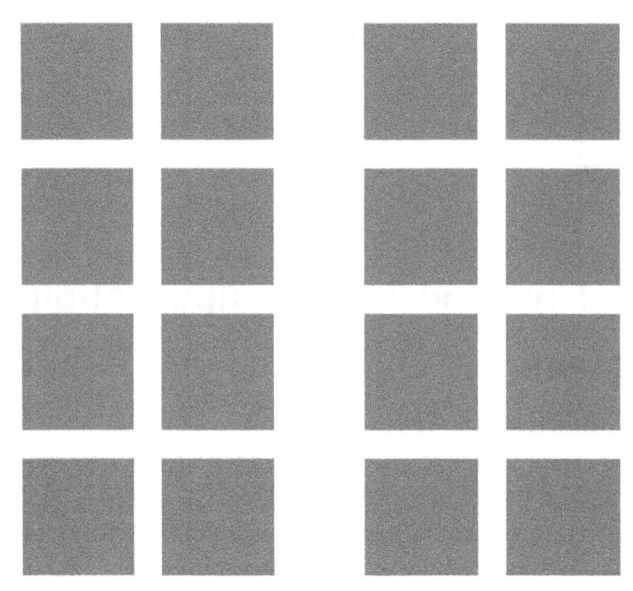

Figure 5–3b

Law of Symmetry

Symmetrical arrangements tend to stand out from the background. Thus, symmetry enhances perception and helps people to remember relationships. A symmetrical organization is easier to remember than an asymmetrical organization. Conversely, items that are out of place in an otherwise symmetrical arrangement will stand out more easily. The graphic (Figure 5-3c) demonstrates this law by depicting a line of three sets of brackets. The symmetry of the brackets visually frames the blank space between each pair.

Figure 5-3c

Law of Continuity

A group of similar elements is perceived as a line in the smoothest path. An example is a dashed white line on a road. Exploiting this law can help to organize a series of objects in a way that helps people perceive them together, such as a colonnade or a wilderness path marked periodically by piles of rocks. The graphic (Figure 5-3d) demonstrates this law by depicting a horizontal straight dashed line beneath a wavy dashed line. The viewer perceives both as lines despite the incompleteness of each line.

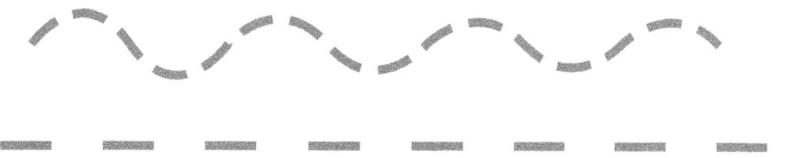

Figure 5-3d

Law of Closure

Open curves (including angles as a special case) tend to be perceived as complete forms. An example is a concave wall or courtyard between wings of a building. This law can be used to create feelings of enclosure with forms that maintain their individual distinctiveness. Uninterrupted boundaries around the edges are not needed to create this feeling. The graphic (Figure 5-3e) demonstrates this law by depicting four curved lines arranged so that the viewer infers a circular shape. The viewer perceives a closed circle despite the discontinuity of the curved lines.

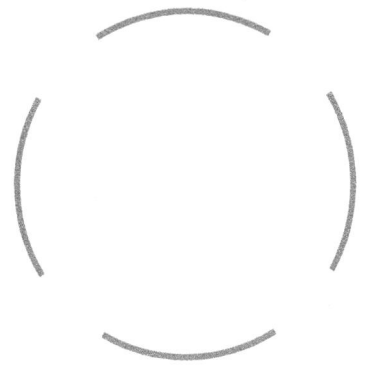

Figure 5-3e

Application of the Gestalt Laws in Design

Figure 5–4 shows a remote control for a television set that utilizes both principles of signal detection and the gestalt laws to make the controls easier to perceive and understand. Contrast with the background is used to increase the "target value" of the controls. Color and proximity are used to distinguish the different sets of controls (e.g., entering channel numbers, the key controls of volume and channel advance, cursor controls, and miscellaneous). Note the cursor control design that exploits the laws of symmetry, closure and continuity to group the cursor controls into a more meaningful circular shape and thereby set them apart from the rest. Size differences are also used to provide a subtle hierarchy of controls used most often and those used less often.

Figure 5–5 shows the gestalt laws at work in a much larger context, the Sydney Harbor in Australia. The law of continuity is demonstrated by how the building to the left is perceived as one large mass due to the continuity of horizontal lines and repetitive columns in its elevation, even though the towers are constructed of elements that are vertical and

Figure 5–4: Example of the gestalt laws in product design. A television remote control illustrates the use of the gestalt laws for improving usability.

Figure 5–5: Example of the gestalt laws in architecture. A building at Sydney Harbor demonstrates the application of the Gestalt Laws in building design, increasing the understanding of the building form, improving wayfinding, and supporting a positive emotional response.

Source: Based on Proctor and Van Zandt (2008).

interrupt the strong horizontals. The towers are key landmarks in this complex and clearly identify the main entries because they are taller than the rest of the building, their main elements are vertical instead of horizontal, and each has a distinctly different top, while all are generally cylindrical. Thus, the law of similarity makes the entries easier to find. The pavement pattern and lighting fixtures are organized using the laws of proximity and continuity to mark the promenade. The canopies and lower roof projections exploit the law of closure to break the scale of the building down and perceptually make the first-floor open spaces into more comfortable places.

It is important to note that the gestalt laws work in all sensory modalities. For instance, the timing (spacing) of a repetitive string of notes in music produces a recognizable rhythm because of the law of proximity and a melody because of the law of continuity. Some notes are closer together than others and thus perceived as pairs; a string of notes (arpeggio) is perceived as an audible "line." A wide variety of audible information can be produced using this law, as in Morse code. Braille is a great example of the use of the law of proximity to produce letters and numbers with different patterns of six dots. While environmental designers are used to applying these laws in visual terms, we still have a long way to go to exploit them in the other senses, but efforts are underway to do so.

Several writers have addressed the multisensory experience of architecture and provided many insights and ideas (Blesser and Salter 2006; Pallasmaa 2005; Prochnik 2010; Rasmussen 1959). In the realm of architectural practice, there are several examples of buildings designed for visually impaired or deaf residents (National Technical Institute for the Deaf, Charles Moore's House near New York, Tigerman, Illinois Regional Library for the Blind). These pioneering examples provide good opportunities to learn what works and what does not and introduce the good ideas into buildings for broader populations. Mobility and Orientation instructors have developed methods to convey information about the environment to visually impaired people using tactile and verbal means. An architect turned product designer has been using that knowledge base to develop learning and wayfinding products using tactile and audible information (www.touchgraphics.com). Another architect and his students at Gallaudet University, which is dedicated to educating people who are deaf, has been exploring how architecture can be conceived from the perspective of deafness and applying insights from the deaf community to Gallaudet's campus plan and buildings (Byrd 2007).

Given the highly mobile nature of contemporary life in developed countries, the impact of mechanized motion on the perception of one's surrounding has become an important field of research. Lessons learned from human factors research on driving are particularly useful in the design of circulation systems where automobiles, pedestrians, bicyclists, and wheeled mobility device users may come into contact. For example, researchers studying driver safety have discovered that drivers can easily develop the belief that they can perceive as much as night as during the day. Steering at night does not deteriorate and the main cues drivers need to perceive the road and follow the route are usually well lit or highly reflective, e.g., signs, traffic lights, road markings, other vehicles (Proctor and Van Zandt 2008). Thus, they come to believe that there is no deterioration in their ability to drive in darkness. However, animals on the roadway, people who are not wearing reflective clothing, bicyclists, and obstacles like those caused by landslides or floods, will not be as easy to perceive, so this is a false belief that reduces situational awareness.

Although the basic principles of perception apply to the use of all senses, there are differences between perception using vision, sound, and touch. For example, while we can close our eyes, we cannot close our ears. Thus, sound is a particularly useful method to attract attention in emergencies. People who cannot perceive audible emergency warnings, therefore, have to be provided with alternative messages that attract their attention and provide the same information without a serious delay. For example, stroboscopic visual signals can be provided to augment audible fire alarms for people who are deaf or hard of hearing. Sometimes the typical audible cues that are used by people with vision are not operable. Most nonvisual travelers can ascertain when traffic has stopped at street crossings. However, if it is particularly noisy in the vicinity or if there are complex patterns of turns, accurate perception of traffic flows may not be possible. In these situations, audible beacons affixed to pedestrian traffic controls with distinctive sounds that can be heard easily above the noise can be provided. There are two different types of tactile perception. Passive touch is when something or someone touches you. Active touch is when you touch something or someone else. These are perceived very differently (Gibson 1950). In both cases, however, the perception of touch requires movement across the skin for accurate perception, and, touch is not as sensitive to spatial detail as sight (Proctor and Van Zandt 2008). Thus, Braille and other objects we want to be perceived by touch must be much larger than those designed to be perceived by vision and clarity of presentation with good orientation cues is particularly important.

There are many detailed recommendations for designing for perception in the research literature but most apply to very specific applications, such as the design of control panels or highway signs. In later chapters, we will address some specific applications. There are several general design principles that are valuable for universal design practice that can guide designers even where specific knowledge is lacking:

- Clarify important information sources (target value).
- Reduce the impact of noise.
- Provide a rich multisensory experience.
- Provide appropriate stimulation for the setting.

Clarify Important Information Sources (Target Value)

Separating a target or signal source from its background enhances clarity. For example, the text on a sign is more readily perceived if it is presented in a simple field around the letters that visually isolates the text from the background visual scenes. Increasing contrast of information targets with their grounds is another effective way to clarify targets (e.g., white-on-black or black-on-white letters). Use attributes that are very easy to perceive for targets and signals that provide critical information (e.g., bright yellow and red). Illumination is needed to perceive signs in the dark. Higher frequencies are easier to perceive over most background noise. However, distinctive sounds such as bird calls or musical tunes (in a building or city street) can be noticed more easily than other high-frequency sounds. Avoid conditions that can lead to confusing illusions; these include decorative floor surfaces that create the illusion of depth or misinterpretations.

Providing good acoustical conditions for the perception of human speech is particularly important to support communications. Meeting rooms, lecture halls, and classrooms have to be isolated from background noise that can impede speech perception. This is even more critical in performing spaces. Acoustics should also enhance the most important signals (e.g., conversation). Many ordinary spaces are often not given proper acoustical treatment to support conversation, restaurants in particular. Transportation terminals often have such high levels of uncontrolled sounds that announcements are unintelligible; they can be very stressful for even short periods, but unfortunately, passengers often have to wait for a long time. Public address systems may be needed, which should include provisions for people who have difficulty hearing.

Reduce the Impact of Noise

Eliminate or control distractions. For example, computer displays in areas with large amounts of natural illumination should have shading devices (e.g., visors) to reduce glare off screens. Information displays should emphasize the most important information. Isolate spaces from background noise where it can disrupt activities such as performing arts events, meetings, lectures, and studying.

Signals or targets should be significantly stronger where background stimuli cannot be controlled. Adjustable signals and targets, preferably automatically controlled, are preferred to avoid overstimulation when not needed. For example, a sound beacon could automatically adjust to background noise levels. Tactile information needs to contrast significantly with its background texture to be perceivable. Thus, it is most useful where general textures and backgrounds are smooth. Since change is more easily perceived, blinking lights, musical sounds, or other dynamic displays can bring attention to a signal or an information target when noise levels are high, but they have to be used carefully to avoid being a source of noise themselves.

Make a special effort to attract attention to the important targets in a complex environment. Use more than one of the gestalt laws to enhance perception and account for different modalities. For example, emergency controls can be color-coded in bright colors, have a distinctive shape, or have different textures than other controls. Group services in buildings in one place to enhance exposure. One of the most effective methods to enhance awareness is to locate important targets of perception in highly visible locations. For example, directional signs should hang overhead rather than along walls.

Provide a Rich Multisensory Experience

The provision of information through more than one modality is an essential aspect of universal design. Pastalan, Mautz, and Merrill (1973) called this redundant cueing, or providing more than one "channel" of information. Multisensory information (e.g., larger size *plus* distinctive shape *plus* high contrast) supports awareness for everyone, but it is essential for those whose perceptual abilities are limited. Audible and tactile information are the primary sources of information about the world used by people who do not have functional vision, and they are are critical for people whose vision is severely limited. Thus, while improving perception for those with limitations in vision and hearing, we are enhancing perception for everyone. Redundant cueing does not mean repetition; it means enhancing perception by using several modalities. Figure 5–6 shows a sign for the third floor at a housing project for senior citizens. The interior designer may have sought to provide multiple stimuli, perhaps following a recommendation he or she read somewhere about redundant cueing. Imagine visitors' shock at arriving at floor 333. They may think that they have arrived in the Twilight Zone or are having triple vision!

Figure 5–6: Floor sign in a seniors' housing project. This is an example of poor signage, one that misinterprets the concept of redundant cueing and therefore causes confusion.

Vision is the source of most information used by the human species to perceive the world, but hearing plays an important role because it can detect evidence of events outside the field of view. Sound provides a 360-degree awareness of the world around us, even when we are focusing our vision in one direction. People who do not have functional hearing rely more on vision for situational awareness and interpersonal communications, but many have some residual hearing that can help with situational awareness (e.g., hearing a siren or loud noise behind them).

Touch provides a more intimate relationship with the environment than vision or hearing but is especially valuable when vision demands attention. For example, while driving, tactile and shape cues for adjusting controls reduces the diversion of attention from the roadway ahead. It is important to note that smell plays a role in perception, particularly by people with visual impairments who use smell as a landmark, but we do not yet have the technology available to manipulate smell as we do the other senses. Current deodorizing technologies are little more than masking strategies and might actually reduce the usefulness of smell as an orientation cue. Smell, nevertheless, is a useful source of information about the location of specific activities and certain events, such as gardens and cooking. Locations that have high olfactory content can provide strong landmarks for orientation. Some materials, such as odiferous wood, can also reinforce awareness of surroundings.

Provide Appropriate Stimulation for the Setting

Both architects and building management often have trouble providing appropriate levels of stimulation for specific settings. For example, in an effort to communicate as much information as possible to occupants through public address systems, hospitals and transportation terminals often create excessive levels of stimulation, defeating the original purpose by creating confusion and high noise levels rather than high levels of awareness. The result is that occupants reduce their conscious processing of sound. Where levels of stimulation become excessive, alternative systems should be explored for communications. For example, visual displays can disseminate less critical information, such as the end of visiting hours or flights boarding. Another approach is the use of more selective channels. Headsets and pagers can be used to communicate with hospital staff so that patients and visitors do not receive information that is not relevant to them.

Masking can be useful when noise sources cannot be isolated. For example, running water can mask annoying and distracting sounds in a workplace. White noise can also be effective if care is taken to ensure that the sounds are not particularly annoying to people with hearing disorders, hearing aids, or special sensitivities. Where low levels of stimulation create boredom, as in a waiting room of a healthcare facility, staff and management tend to add stimulation through television, radio, or recorded music to keep people who are waiting aroused. These sources of stimulation are often very unsatisfactory over a long period and contribute to high background noise levels. Adding other sources of stimulation to waiting rooms, such as plants, birds, cats, fish tanks, water features, artwork, or other more variable stimuli can be much more satisfying to those waiting. Music or television-based stimulation can be satisfactory too, if it is varied and appropriate for the audience (e.g., avoid rap music in a place where occupants or visitors are mostly elders).

Cognition

As with approaches to perception, contemporary approaches to environmental cognition utilize an information-processing model. Cognition is the process of understanding and using the information obtained through perception. It involves learning, interpreting, evaluating, decision making, memory, and recall (Sharp, Rogers, and Preece 2007). As indicated earlier in this chapter, the relationship between perception and cognition is very close, and the boundaries between the two processes are hard to define. In fact, many authors treat them as part of the same process; other authors consider some mental activities to be part of perception and others consider the same activities to be part of cognition. People with cognitive impairments, especially those who have disabilities that affect learning and memory, will have more difficulty understanding the environment. However, people whose ability to explore is limited due to mobility limitations and those who are limited in sensory reception abilities may also have a limited understanding of their world. In general, any design strategies that help people understand the environment will help everyone, as long as they address all sensory modalities.

Some research in this field focuses on how people learn about their surroundings, studying such topics as the role that personal factors (e.g., age, gender, or disability) play on environmental learning. Other research focuses on measuring the "cognitive load" of a task (the demands on the use of working memory) and the capacity for people to perform activities under conditions of varying demands. Still others study the accuracy of memory and recall. Others study subjective experience and how that is related to usability of products and environments. There are many other threads of research in this field, and thus a great deal of information and knowledge from the fields of human factors, psychology, geography, and cognitive science is available that has relevance to design. The most valuable information for design comes from research on the design qualities that lead to improving usability of environments and products. Research on cognition has provided four key concepts that are particularly important for designers to understand: affordances, conceptual models, mental maps, and emotional design.

Affordances are properties of objects and systems that convey information about the way they work (Gibson 1977; Norman 2002). An example is a lever-handled door opener, as shown in Figure 5–7. The lever is the same size as a hand. It is oriented in a direction that makes it easy to grasp using a power grip. In addition, it works by pushing down, conforming to the direction a person would expect to use to retract the latch on the door since, whatever the door location, that motion is moving away from the latch side. Another good example is the D-shaped cabinet pull. These handles have spaces between handle and cabinets that are large enough for fingers to be inserted. The size and shape of the space indicates exactly where the fingers should be placed to open a cabinet door or drawer. A third example is a running board on a vehicle. This device is located in such a way that it provides a feature we can exploit as we enter the passenger compartment, much like an outcropping or ledge we would grab while climbing a rock face. The rungs of a ladder are a similar example. No instructions or even previous experience is needed to utilize an affordance.

Affordances are useful only if the end user perceives them as such. For example, links on a web page that are difficult to distinguish from other text or a button that is flush with a control panel and looks like a label are examples of affordances that end users may not perceive. Likewise, false affordances are design features that look as if they are to be used for certain functions but that actually have no functional value. A constraint is a corollary to an affordance—a design feature that reduces choice and channels behavior very specifically. Examples include crowd control stanchions linked by ropes or belts, a pistol-grip-style handle with a trigger, or a username and password entry box on a website with controlled access.

A conceptual model (also called a "mental model") is a memory of how something works, developed through experience (Norman 2002). Unlike an affordance, we may even need instructions and training to establish a conceptual model. Usually this concept is discussed in

Figure 5–7: Lever-style door handle. This is an example of the use of affordances in design.
Source: Image courtesy of schnaars.

relationship to products, including information technology and telecommunications. Through interaction with products, we learn that there are a limited number of possible methods of operation. For example, to operate a faucet, we know that there will be a flow control and usually a temperature control. But the controls may take several forms, dual knobs, dual levers, single-lever, push knobs, presence sensor, etc. Each one is stored in memory as a conceptual model. To operate any faucet, we recall the models we have encountered and use the one that seems to fit. For some systems, there is only one basic model, often standardized by an industry to reduce complexity. For example, water faucets are generally standardized such that hot water controls are on the left or require turning a single control to the left while cold water is to the right. ATMs have been standardized to the extent that we know to insert a card to start, enter our PIN, select operations from a menu, complete the transaction, extract money, and a receipt, etc. Even though the exact features of each ATM may differ, the basic model of operation is the same.

Conceptual models are also operative at the building and city scale. For example, a double-loaded corridor plan is a common circulation type in buildings. From experience, we know that when we find this plan, rooms will very likely be located along both sides of the corridor, the elevator in the middle, and emergency exits at the two ends. As an example at the urban scale, we know that in traditional cities, the "central business district," or CBD, is the densest part. In the CBD, we will find the main railroad inter-urban station and a major regional transit hub. As we proceed away from the center, we will find lower densities and more local neighborhood services rather than regional services.

A mental map is more specific than a conceptual model. Affordances work because they exploit knowledge of our own bodies. Conceptual models are generalized memories of experience with a class of products or environments. Mental maps, however, are very specific memories of how the world is organized based on personal experience. In the research literature, mental maps are associated with cities and buildings (Lynch 1960; Weisman 1992), but we can also have mental maps of products and systems, for example, the menu of our own office voicemail system.

Research on mental maps demonstrates that people have a well-developed ability to construct a memory of places, but the accuracy of these maps varies by both person and environment. Some people are better at developing and recalling mental maps and some places are easier to map. People also change their mental map as they learn more about a place and as the place changes. Thus, we should distinguish these very specific memories from conceptual models, which are more generalized and more stable. The importance of this distinction is demonstrated by the effect of radical departures from conceptual models. Figure 5–8 shows a water faucet that reverses the conceptual model described earlier. The lever is pulled *forward* for cold and pushed *back* for hot. It is pulled to the *right* to open and to the *left* to close. The impact of this departure is that very few people can operate it without instruction, except for those who use it regularly. It should be noted that sometimes it might be useful to depart from common mental models. For example, if we are trying to limit access to a place or use of a product, we may want to include a deliberately complex access method, such as those used on child safety locks and child-safe bottles.

Figure 5–8: Faucet. This design reverses the typical conceptual model used for this product.

So far the discussion has illustrated the value of strong affordances and conceptual models. Products or environments that utilize affordances and common models will be much easier to use. Attributes of any specific environment and product that make them more memorable improve usability and help people understand "local" or "unique" features. These attributes help the individual to develop an accurate and memorable mental map of a place or product. The attributes that contribute to memorability include those that were discussed earlier in the section on perception: target value, clarity of signal, symmetry, rich multisensory experience, and so on.

New conceptual models can be introduced successfully, especially if they are intuitive and make use of older models. For example, the "click wheel" incorporates many controls on most versions of the Apple iPod music player. The click wheel was based on a type of cursor control common on remote controls, although it added a new function, the touch-sensitive circular gesture for navigation and volume. This new function fit with prior models for media systems, notably radio knobs. Thus its operation was relatively easy for people to understand and remember.

Information "in the world," such as labels, is sometimes preferable to information "in the head" because it requires fewer memory resources, reduces the time to understand operations, and improves accuracy (as long as the labels are clear and understandable). With complex systems and small products, it may be impossible to provide enough information "in the world." There is just too much to learn, and often not enough "real estate" to make it available. In fact, too many labels can defeat their purpose, creating visual noise that makes it difficult to perceive the information needed at any one time. Since the beginning of personal computing, many design concepts have been introduced to make more information available "in the world." The "tabs" on computer program interfaces are one of the latest examples. When all else fails, standardization, even if arbitrary, such as "hot equals left" and "cold equals right" for faucets, reduces uncertainty and improves our understanding (Norman 2002).

Manuals and illustrations often are still needed to explain how something works, especially when the item does not work the way it should; unfortunately, often manuals and illustrations are too detailed and poorly written to be helpful. The result is that usually they are not read thoroughly or they are thrown away or stashed somewhere and forgotten. Increasingly, as the boundaries between the physical world and virtual world are coming down, we have access to detailed instructions and assistance directly through links to Internet-based information or to a "help menu" that includes instructional videos with step-by-step instructions for using software or equipment. These aides can become intrusive however, such as pop-up boxes that continuously appear on a computer screen asking if we are trying to do a particular task and if we want help.

Perhaps one of the most difficult things to understand is a city. Although we do not perceive it as a tool in everyday use, it is probably the most complex technology that people have invented, incorporating and integrating both "hardware," such as buildings and street grids, and "software," such as traffic rules, social networks, etc. Although we can retain general knowledge about the nature of a city and maintain very accurate and detailed mental maps of the places we utilize regularly, we need to rely on more extensive information resources to access and use unfamiliar places. Two examples are street signs and addresses, which are both types of labels. A third is the conventional street map, which can be installed in a location (e.g., a you-are-here map) or provided in a portable form. A fourth is step-by-step route instructions, which often are conveyed verbally by local "experts" to strangers.

Today, we can have detailed and complex real-time instructions available both audibly and visually. Global Positioning System (GPS) navigational devices provide both maps and route instructions, but they also provide you-are-here map updates in real time. Many have voice output of instructions as well as text and graphics. The popularity of these devices clearly demonstrates the need for knowledge "in the world," or at least "in the hand." The introduction of GPS-based applications for smart phones has increased our available information about cities exponentially. Using a phone that we would carry anyway, we can search and find local resources, identify accessible buildings, reserve tables in restaurants, and learn about local landmarks.

Our understanding of the world around us applies to time as well as spatial features and product functions. Most environments are very stable over time, but often they do change in regular patterns related to the time of day, day of the week, or season. Researchers who study "ecological psychology" link time and space together using a concept known as a "behavior setting" (Barker 1978). They developed research techniques that can be used to identify patterns of behavior that occur regularly in space and time. These may be formal events, such as classes, or informal events, such as meetings of old friends at a coffee shop. Cognitive maps can incorporate these activities but may not include events that are unfamiliar to the user, which can lead to surprising discoveries. One of the authors once checked into a hotel near the theater district in New York City in the early evening. He noticed nothing unusual in the neighborhood. But when he went out for a late-night snack, he was surprised to find that prostitutes with hordes of hovering customers staked out the entire street outside the hotel. The "johns" knew that this was a pickup spot and when the prostitutes would arrive on the scene, but the unsuspecting guest had no idea. By the morning, all evidence of this activity had vanished.

We discussed situational awareness earlier as a perceptual issue, but it is also related to cognition. Because unusual and unexpected events are difficult to perceive, we have little understanding of them. Since they do not seem to affect our daily activities, we do not seek out the knowledge we need to understand them effectively when they do occur. One example is the presence of pickpockets in tourist locations. Other events can create unpredictability, such as an unreliable car, erratic public transportation, or unreliable mobile phone service. People with mobility impairments encounter this problem regularly. They are never certain that an unfamiliar building will have an accessible entry or restroom or that they will find an accessible parking space. Natural disasters, riots, terrorist acts, power failures, and other emergencies produce extreme uncertainty with little warning. People tend to avoid unpredictable environments if possible because in such situations, they cannot ensure their personal safety and security. Preparedness training through handbooks, drills and simulations is often provided to help people deal with the unusual circumstances of an emergency. But, even with such preparation, when they find themselves in an unusual situation, individuals often need direct assistance from public safety personnel, trained employees, or trained volunteers to cope.

Emergencies can transform a familiar environment into something very strange. Archea (1990) describes an emergency event in terms of "figure–ground reversal." What is important in daily life becomes unimportant in terms of survival and what is usually unimportant becomes important. When an earthquake begins, for example, a man sitting in his living room watching television may run toward his entertainment system and try to prevent it from falling. But during a tremor, items that normally sit on shelves become deadly missiles that are launched into the space of a room. The heavy entertainment system, propelled by the lateral force of the quake, could become impossible for one person to hold in place and trying to stop it from falling could be fatal. In a tall building, most people enter and leave through the elevators, but in a fire emergency, running toward the elevator may be exactly the wrong thing to do. Visitors to a building may not even know where the emergency exits are because these exits often are remote from the elevators and visitors have never seen or used them. Since these events are so difficult to understand, we may need special sources of information to provide the situational awareness necessary to manage successfully when the world becomes unstable. Thus, in emergencies, it becomes important to provide alarms that are perceivable and understandable, life jackets or evacuation chairs in key locations, communication systems that reach all occupants, real-time information on the status of events, and special accommodations to help people who cannot manage on their own. This is particularly important for people with disabilities and those without the adaptive capacity to respond independently, such as people injured in the event (National Council on Disability 2005).

Evaluation and emotional response is part of cognition. Research on Emotional Design and Kansei (Affective Engineering) demonstrates how we can design products and environments to be appealing to people (Desmet 2005; Nagamachi 2011; Norman 2004). Nagamachi (2011) cites the value of Kansei Engineering to, the practice of universal design. He argues that by focusing on the affective aspects of product design, designers take more of a human-centered approach to design, addressing the end users' needs, wants, and desires. Although the impact of emotions on the appreciation of a product or environment is part of conventional design wisdom, designers do not always think about its relationship to usability, nor do they know about the growing knowledge base on this topic. Norman (2004) reviewed the literature on emotions and their relationship to usability. There is evidence that a good emotional response contributes to usability. A positive emotional evaluation will mean that a user is more likely to invest the time necessary to learn about a product's features, whereas a negative evaluation discourages such learning. A positive response also encourages a user to overlook the faults of a product and learn how to cope with its limitations. Conversely, frustration and other negative experiences with products elicit negative emotions that can lead to frustration, abandonment, and avoidance behavior.

As we interact with a place or product, we evaluate the features and products. These evaluations are stored in our memory and have an impact on the content of mental maps. Stanley Milgram (1974) demonstrates how evaluative maps can be constructed of cities to identify places people like to avoid, what he called a "fear map," and how people remember places they value highly. Research on mental or cognitive maps demonstrates that people tend to exaggerate the size of features they view positively when they draw their mental maps of a place (Passini 1984). Researchers studying the emotional components of products have developed emotion-mapping techniques to elicit and analyze the range of emotional responses that any product might have (Desmet 2005). Less than a decade ago, designers, and researchers interested in this field formed the Design & Emotion Society (www.designandemotion.org).

Norman (2004) proposes that there are three dimensions to the emotions that products elicit:

1. *Visceral*. Unconscious, automatic, instinctual response based on our evolutionary experience
2. *Behavioral*. Unconscious, experience-based and goal-oriented, developed through practice (e.g., accomplishment in skill development, harmony with expectations, good fit)
3. *Reflective*. Conscious, personal significance, social meaning, self-reflective

The visceral dimension includes the responses that are hardwired into our brains. For example, humans generally prefer round, soft shapes compared to pointy and jagged shapes. Norman (2004) attributes this to a conditioned avoidance response to things that can puncture our skin and cause pain. The behavioral dimension is the usual province of ergonomic design.

When we encounter features of products and environments that do not support our goals and activities, such as very high noise levels in a restaurant or a complex video recording device, it generates a negative emotional reaction, such as frustration and anger. When a product or place facilitates the achievement of our goals with a minimum of difficulty in use, however, we are likely to have a strong positive emotion about it, such as satisfaction and accomplishment. The reflective dimension is about interpretation and meaning. Negative emotions may be provoked by attributes of products and environments that negatively affect our presentation of self. For example, a parent may resent the gift of a large-button telephone from an adult child because it reflects the fact that the giver thinks the receiver may be declining in abilities. Young people may not purchase a car that is marketed explicitly as "age friendly" because they do not want to be perceived as old.

These dimensions explain why a lot of assistive technology is rejected or abandoned by people who could benefit from using it. Assistive technology provides support by compensating for limited abilities, but often it does not address less instrumental goals, aesthetic concerns, and self-image issues. Good examples are walking aids and hearing aids. Many older people dislike walking aids because they are difficult to store in a vehicle and get in the way in crowded spaces. Canes fall down, and users cannot pick them up because cane users generally have difficulty with bending and balance. Hearing aids often pick up too much background noise to be useful. In all cases, people interpret these devices as symbols of declining ability.

To be successful, universal design has to address all the emotional design dimensions. It cannot be purely functional, and, in function, it has to address the full range of needs of an individual, in particular, support for social participation (e.g., avoidance of stigma) as well as human performance. From an aesthetic perspective, universal design cannot ignore visceral emotional responses, but it also has to address cultural differences that are part of the reflective dimension. For example, in the United States, the color red is often associated with danger, death, and injury. Conversely, in China, it is strongly associated with life and happiness. Red is a color that is very easy to see and attracts our visual attention; thus, it can be used to enhance perception of different design features, places, and objects. However, its emotional impact must be understood within a cultural context. This example illustrates the importance of personalization and flexibility in aesthetics as well as function. The personalization of personal electronics through sleeves, cases, and a range of color options is a good example.

These are four general universal design guidelines based on research in cognition:

1. Incorporate perceivable affordances.
2. Utilize well-known conceptual models.
3. Support the construction of accurate mental maps.
4. Incorporate features that lead to positive emotional responses.

Incorporate Perceivable Affordances

Handles should have a size and shape that fits the hand and conveys the nature of the grip and direction of applied force to be used. Designing for a full hand grip helps end users grip the shape and exert force most easily. Shapes that are perceived as more comfortable and inviting will be perceived more readily and used more frequently. Design interactive features for convenient use in relation to the tasks that they support. Examples of good physical affordances are controls and devices that can be operated with a flat hand in a neutral position, devices shaped to comfortably receive a powerful grip, interaction surfaces that provide a nonslip grip, and opportunities to recover strength, such as seating surfaces at stairway landings, or shelves to place packages where two hands may be needed.

In design of virtual interfaces, distinguish interaction targets from other objects in displays and organize information to communicate relationships among tasks. Utilize shape, color, shadows, and spatial organization to clearly distinguish buttons and links from ordinary text. Providing feedback, such as changes in cursor symbol or highlighting to signify actions needed, is another approach that reduces visual clutter. Using analogs of physical buttons helps to convey their purpose. Targets should be large enough to select even if movements are not highly accurate. For critical tasks, use constraints to force people to do things in sequence, but the use of too many constraints often causes frustration. A good example is a voicemail menu with many layers that have to be navigated to reach the destination mailbox or number.

Utilize Well-Known Conceptual Models

Many well-known conceptual models for user interfaces can be adopted for both physical and virtual products. They include motions, such as clockwise and counterclockwise, up and down, and left and right, which are associated with different types of operations in specific contexts. For example, clockwise is usually associated with increasing amplitude and up is usually associated with "on." Pressing a button down is associated with turning a device on; pressing it again to release is associated with turning it off. When many controls are provided for a set of devices, such as burner controls on a stove, using natural mappings in which individual controls are organized in the same relationships as the objects being controlled is quite effective. In virtual environments, use of physical analogs, such as file folder tabs, is helpful in reducing complexity.

Touch screens can pose a barrier for people who are blind or have severe visual impairments. However, the introduction of gestural interfaces has increased the range of options for universal design. Rather than a click or tap, it is now possible, using gesture recognition, to mimic many conceptual models in the physical world. The best example is the gesture for page turning. Such gestures are much easier to remember than arbitrary codes, such as tapping a different number of times for different functions. Gesture-based interfaces also provide opportunities to make touch screens easier to use without functional vision. For example, a gesture can be reserved for activating programs that read the icons and text on the screen as people touch them.

Where technological innovations are introduced, using conceptual models from earlier technologies helps to make unfamiliar technology understandable. For example, touch pad control panels can utilize well-known conceptual models, such as slider switches and calendars, along with swipe gestures to make their use intuitive. Adoption of familiar conceptual models can facilitate usability not only directly but also indirectly, as in the case of the click wheel example discussed earlier, because it can reduce the number of controls to increase legibility and reduce clutter.

In architecture and interior design, the use of common circulation plans, such as the ring plan, double-loaded corridors, single-loaded corridors, hollow square, central space, and the like provides a recognizable and easy-to-understand structure for the visitor. There are only a limited number of circulation plans that can really work in terms of efficiency and access to the spaces in a building. The best plan is usually related to the building's purpose and scale. Through experience people learn to understand these models and the associations. When a building is designed to expose the circulation plan clearly, visitors can more easily create an accurate mental map and use it effectively without relying on others. This reduces the feeling of loss of control and dependency, and leads to a positive emotional response.

Support the Construction of Accurate Mental Maps

Our mental maps of cities include landmarks, the paths that tie them together, definable boundaries, and distinct areas (Downs and Stea 1973; Lynch 1960). The mental map is "information in the head" that is mapped onto information in the world as we navigate through geographic space. The correspondence between the two improves with experience. Large buildings with unique features or natural features are often used as landmarks. Frequently used paths—streets, highways, and transit lines—link the landmarks together in a network. Nodes, or intersections of paths, are also memorable points in the network. Easy-to-remember street networks, such as New York's grid or Amsterdam's network of radial and concentric canals and streets, make it easier to develop accurate mental maps because they provide a strong framework for spatial orientation. Strong edges, such as mountain ranges, a river, or an ocean, serve as boundaries that help in orientation. Districts or streets with a definable visual identity, such as the Gothic Quarter in Barcelona or the Champs-Elysée in Paris reinforce the overall map. Our mental maps will be more accurate if key landmarks, edges, and paths are visible from a distance.

Research on how mental maps of buildings are constructed provides insight into how buildings can be designed to be more understandable. Building users find it easier to remember circulation systems that are generally symmetrical and have a coherent and clear form (Weisman 1992). Our mental maps of building interiors will be enhanced if there are recognizable landmarks, paths (e.g., corridors, hallways, elevator cores), and districts (e.g., floors, departments, etc.). Visual access to key parts of the building improves our awareness of the activities in the building and where different activities are located (Benedikt 1979).

In architecture, designers often strive to emphasize architectural features, such as wall planes and presentation spaces, and hide the utilities and services because they believe that the utilities and services are "noise" that obscures the architectural features. Interactive building elements should be rethought as targets rather than background noise. Controls, such as light switches and dimmers, public address volume controls, and thermostats, can be organized as control panels, as in a vehicle. Likewise, service spaces can be organized and positioned so that they are highly visible and have a distinctive appearance. That way they can serve as meaningful spatial landmarks for wayfinding. For example, restrooms, water fountains, vending areas, telephones, janitors' closets, and other service spaces can be grouped together as a block designed to contrast with the surrounding spaces. They can even have a distinctive color and shape that contrasts to the surrounding architecture.

The same strategies can be used, on a smaller scale, in product design. For example, colors and textures can be used to define important controls or features that are used often. Dyson, a company that manufactures vacuum cleaners, and Fiskars, a tool manufacturer, have both used this method effectively. Coding features with colors and materials can help users understand their function, especially if there is an understandable logic to the coding method (e.g., all controls are green). The creation of memorable product images not only improves recall of features but also contributes to branding and thus product recognition in a field of competitors.

Coding can be very effective in making locations in virtual environments, which tend to be very similar to one another, more understandable. Navigation in virtual environments can also be enhanced by applying knowledge of the mental mapping process. In virtual environments, such as websites and menus, screens are destinations and links are paths. Developing a coherent and easily understood network for navigation will help users remember how to use a Web site. For example, a "ring" organization for organizing a menu on a camera or a relatively shallow "tree" organization for a business website can help people understand the overall organization and thus reduce the time for searches. Graphical interfaces can be designed to facilitate navigation in a logical sequence. Symbols, such as arrows and icons, can be used much like landmarks to communicate the steps of navigation. Real-time locational information like that provided by street signs and addresses helps users know where they are within the system.

Incorporate Features That Lead to Positive Emotional Responses

The three dimensions of emotional design described by Norman are good starting points for developing strategies that will lead to positive responses by end users. Precedent designs, or designs that have been used in the past, can be analyzed using this framework to assess the limitations of previous design strategies. The research literature on Emotional Design and Kansei Engineering is also a valuable source of information. It is always useful to conduct a contextual inquiry to learn about the end users' perspectives and to frame their information needs (Beyer and Holtzblatt 1998; Holtzblatt, Wendell, and Wood 2005). Where resources allow it, targeted research on critical emotional response issues should be an important priority, especially when end users are very unfamiliar to the designers (e.g., a product that is intended for international markets or an unfamiliar population subgroup, such as an older demographic).

In product design, when thousands or even millions of units are going to be produced, in-depth research is crucial and cost effective. Companies that construct many buildings over a period of years or projects that are very large in scope, such as a major hospital, would benefit from research on emotions. But, in most environmental design activities that lead to only one constructed building, interior, or landscape, there is not enough time or money to conduct extensive research. In these situations, design participation is an alternative way to obtain information about emotional responses without extensive research. Through focus groups, using representatives of the target population for a design, potential end users can have a voice in the design process. Focus groups are also very valuable to validate assumptions of the design team and findings from empirical research. Universal design advocates recommend incorporating input from focus groups or representatives of the end user population throughout the design process and on an ongoing basis after the design is deployed.

Often design goals conflict with consumer preferences. Thus, design teams need to explore the many dimensions of emotions together, not simply compare preferences on independent design parameters. For example, fuel efficiency is an important design goal in automobile design. Reducing fuel consumption requires reducing the weight of the vehicle. But if consumers have a more positive emotional response to large vehicles compared to small, there is a conflict that needs to be addressed. The underlying emotional reasons for consumer preferences need to be understood: safety, powerful presentation of self, more comfort, or others. Armed with that information, creative designers can search for innovative solutions that resolve such conflicts.

Summary

This chapter demonstrates the extensive knowledge base available on human performance that can be used in the practice of universal design. The literature is very specialized and deep on each topic. We addressed the four major areas of human performance knowledge—anthropometry, biomechanics, perception, and cognition. For each of these areas, we provided an overview of the major topics with relevance to universal design covering all scale levels and both physical and virtual environments. We concluded each section with a set of general guidelines for design. In other chapters, we will return to these issues within the context of specific built environments. There are many handbooks in the fields of human factors and ergonomics that summarize this literature in more detail, several of which are cited in this chapter. However, they do not usually address building or product design in an integrative manner. Thus, we will conclude this chapter with an example ("Stairways in Apple Stores") to demonstrate the importance of an integrative approach.

Stairways in Apple Stores

At first glance, using a stairway appears to be a physical task, but mental activities play a very important role in using stairways safely. If we cannot perceive and understand a stairway properly, it can be impossible to negotiate safely. When we perceive it, we obtain information about the shape, size, and features of the stairs from our senses. We compare the specific stairway to our conceptual models of stairways and make assumptions to guide our actions. For example, we decide whether the treads are stable and we can trust them to hold our weight. As we proceed to use the stairway, we scan for features to help us create a mental map of it that we use to make decisions about action as we proceed. When we encounter a stairway and it looks like one of our conceptual models for a safe stairway, we are likely to pay less careful attention to it, but if we see broken treads, notice that it is extremely steep, or that the lighting is very poor, we may take more time to assess its safety and even conclude that we will not use it. As we proceed on the stairway, we obtain feedback and adjust our mental map to increase its accuracy. We see the edge of the next tread; we judge the distance we have to step to avoid stepping over the edge, we position our foot to land, and we activate our muscles to propel our foot to the target on the next tread. Although we do many activities like using a stairway or walking along a walkway without consciously thinking about them, our mind is at work, doing the information processing and making the decisions on autopilot, usually guided by our previous experience.

The photos in Figure 5–9 show a stairway in an Apple retail store in New York City. The design is common to many large Apple Stores around the world. It is a winding stairway surrounding a cylindrical tube made of glass in which the elevator is located. The stairway leads down to a large open retail space with a high ceiling, which often has hundreds of customers milling about and using the products on display. As people walk down the stairway, they are often searching for their companions or trying to understand the store layout. The stairway is made entirely of glass, including the supporting structure, providing total visual exposure to the retail floor below and the elevator as it moves up and down. These conditions are likely to create distractions as people divert their attention to the retail floor or the moving elevator. The winding configuration means that the view below is continually changing as the user proceeds, increasing the distraction potential even more.

Winding stairways are inherently more dangerous than straight stairways because the stair treads are tapered so that the left foot is using a different tread depth than the right and users must twist their bodies as they move up or down. The result is that the stair user

Figure 5-9: Glass stairway. At a retail store in New York, NY, a stairway made of glass treads is shown (a) during good weather, and (b) covered with carpet during rainy weather.

is forced into an unusual gait, which increases the potential for a misstep. Moreover, the "effective tread depth" is different in ascent and descent because the user cannot easily place their heel on the very back part of the tread when descending. Thus, the effective tread depth descending a winding stairway on the inside of the curve is often too small for good foot placement. People tend to stay to the right on stairways in the United States. As the photo in Figure 5–9a demonstrates, on a crowded stairway, they would naturally move to the outside, the safer part of the stairway in descent when the stairway winds counterclockwise. In Figure 5–9b the stairway winds clockwise. The individual is using the stairway alone and purposely went to the left to avoid the steeper slope and narrower treads on the right. But, if there were a crowd coming up the stairway, she would have been forced to stay to the inside, the more dangerous side.

The glass stair treads on both stairs have a nonslip coating, but when it is rainy or snowy in New York, customers track in water since each stairway is immediately inside the entries to the stores, which also have glass floors inside and outside. The water creates slippery conditions by pooling on the glass tread surfaces. When it rains or snows, the staff installs carpeting at the entry and on the stair treads to counter this problem, as shown in Figure 5–9b. However, this temporary surface may actually create additional problems if it is not securely fastened or if it starts to curl with repeated use.

While it appears to be just like many other stairways, this stairway, due to its context and materials, has some unusual conditions that may increase the risk of accidents. It dramatically demonstrates the importance of all four aspects of human performance and the attention to detail needed to insure a safe environment. Note that due to the elevator, this store is accessible to people with disabilities who cannot walk stairs, but from a universal design perspective, it may present conditions that could put other visitors at risk.

Review Topics

1. Explain the four key areas of human performance knowledge: anthropometrics, biomechanics, perception, and cognition.
2. Describe how each field of study specifically relates to universal design, and give an example of each.
3. How does the case study of the stairway highlight each of the human performance areas?

References

Agrawal, A. W., M. Schlossberg, and K. Irvin. 2008. "How Far, by Which Route and Why? A Spatial Analysis of Pedestrian Preference." *Journal of Urban Design* 13 (1): 81–98.

Archea, J. 1990. "Immediate Reactions of People in Houses." In R. Bolin (ed.), *The Loma Prieta Earthquake: Studies of Short-Term Impacts*, Monograph 50, pp. 56–64. Boulder: Program on Environment and Behavior, Institute of Behavioral Science, University of Colorado.

Axelson, P., D. Yamada, J. Kirschbaum, P. Longmuir, and K. Wong. 1997. *Accessible Exterior Surfaces: A Review of Existing Test Methods for Surface Firmness and Stability*. U.S. Architectural and Transportation Compliance Board, Washington, DC Contract No. QA96005001 to Beneficial Designs.

Barker, R. G. 1978. "Theory of Behavior Settings. In R. G. Barker (ed.), *Habitats, Environments and Human Behavior: Studies in Eco-Behavioral Science from the Midwest Psychological Field Station,* pp. 213–228. Stanford, CA: Stanford University Press.

Behrens, R. R. 1998. "Art, Design and Gestalt Theory. *Leonardo* 31 (4): 299–303.

Benedikt, M. L. 1979. "To Take Hold of Space: Isovists and Isovists Fields." *Environment and Planning B* 6: 47–65.

Beyer, H. and K. Holtzblatt. 1998. *Contextual Design: Defining Customer-Centered Systems.* San Francisco: Morgan Kaufmann.

Blesser, B. and L.-R. Salter. 2006. *Spaces Speak, Are You Listening? Experiencing Aural Architecture.* Cambridge, MA: MIT Press.

Byrd, T. 2007. "Deaf Space." www.gallaudet.edu/deaf_space_spring2007.xml.

Carter, S. E., E. M.Campbell, R. W. Sanson-Fisher, S. Redman, and W. J. Gillespie. 1997. "Environmental Hazards in the Homes of Older People." *Age and Ageing* 26: 195–202.

Cervero, R. and R. Gorham. 1995. "Commuting in Transit versus Automobile Neighborhoods." *Journal of the American Planning Association* 61 (2): 199–219.

Cervero, R. and K. Kockelman. 1997. "Travel Demand and the 3Ds: Density, Diversity, and Design." *Transportation Research Part D.* 2 (3): 199–219.

Chaffin, D. B., C. Woolley, C. Dickerson, and M. Parkinson. 2004. "Modeling of Object Movement Capability in the Spinal Cord Injured Population." *International Journal of Industrial Ergonomics* 33 (3): 229–236.

Chun, M. M. and N. B. Turk-Browne. 2007. "Interactions between Attention and Memory." *Current Opinion in Neurobiology* 17 (2): 177–184.

Clipson, C. W. and J. J. Wehrer. 1973. *Planning for Cardiac Care: A Guide to the Planning and Design of Cardiac Care Facilities.* Ann Arbor, MI: Health Administration Press.

Conlon, C. F., N. Krause, and D. M. Rempel. 2009. "A Randomized Controlled Trial Evaluating an Alternative Mouse or Forearm Support on Change in Median and Ulnar Nerve Motor Latency at the Wrist." *American Journal of Industrial Medicine* 52 (4): 304–310.

Danford, G. S. and E. Steinfeld. 1999. "Measuring the Influences of Physical Environments on the Behaviors of People with Impairments." In E. Steinfeld and G. S. Danford (eds.), *Measuring Enabling Environments,* pp. 111–137. New York: Kluwer Academic/Plenum.

Desmet, P. 2005. "Measuring Emotion: Development and Application of an Instrument to Measure Emotional Responses to Products." *Funology: Human-Computer Interaction Series* 3: 111–123.

Downs, R. M. and D. Stea (eds.). 1973. *Image and Environment: Cognitive Mapping and Spatial Behavior.* Chicago: Aldine.

Ewing, R., O. Clement, S. Handy, R. C. Brownson, and E. Winston. 2005, July. "Identifying and Measuring Urban Design Qualities Related to Walkability." Final report prepared for the Active Living Research Program of the Robert Wood Johnson Foundation.

Feldman, F. and H. Chaudhury. 2008. "Falls and the Physical Environment: A Review and a New Multifactorial Falls-Risk Conceptual Framework." *Canadian Journal of Occupational Therapy* 75 (2): 82–95.

Fuster, J. M. 2006. "The Cognit: A Network Model of Cortical Representation." *International Journal of Psychophysiology* 60 (2): 125–132.

Gibson, J. J. 1950. *The Perception of the Visual World.* Boston: Houghton Mifflin.

———1977. "The Theory of Affordances." In R. Shaw and J. Bransford (eds.), *Perceiving, Acting and Knowing: Toward an Ecological Psychology* (pp. 67–82). Hillsdale, NJ: Lawrence Erlbaum.

Godfrey, A., R. Conway, D. Meagher, and G. O'Laighin. 2008. "Direct Measurement of Human Movement by Accelerometry." *Medical Engineering and Physics* 30 (10): 1364–1386.

Goldstein, E. B. 2010. *Sensation and Perception*. Belmont, CA: Wadsworth, Cengage Learning.

Grandjean, E. 1973. *Ergonomics of the Home*. London: Taylor and Francis.

Greenwald, M. J. and M. G. Boarnet. 2001. *The Built Environment as a Determinant of Walking Behaviour: Analyzing Non-Work Pedestrian Travel in Portland, Oregon*. Paper UCI-ITS-AS-WP-01-4. Center for Activity Systems Analysis, University of California at Irvine.

Holtzblatt, K., J. B. Wendell, and S. Wood. 2005. *Rapid Contextual Design: A How-to Guide to Key Techniques for User-Centered Design*. San Francisco: Morgan Kaufmann.

Huysmansa, M. A., M.J.M. Hoozemansa, B. Vissera, and J. H. van Dieën. 2008. "Grip Force Control in Patients with Neck and Upper Extremity Pain and Healthy Controls." *Clinical Neurophysiology* 119 (8): 1840–1848.

James, C., L. Mackenzie, and M. Capra. 2011. "Inter- and Intra-Rater Reliability of the Manual Handling Component of the WorkHab Functional Capacity Evaluation." *Disability and Rehabilitation*, 33 (19–20): 1,797–1,804.

Jung, M.-C., D. Park, S.-J. Lee, K.-S. Lee, D.-M. Kim, and Y.-K. Kong. 2010. "The Effects of Knee Angles on Subjective Discomfort Ratings, Heart Rates, and Muscle Fatigue of Lower Extremities in Static-Sustaining Tasks." *Applied Ergonomics* 42 (1): 184–192.

Kohler, W. 1959. "Gestalt Psychology Today." *American Psychologist* 14: 727–734.

Kongsted, A., et al. 2008. "Acute Stress Response and Recovery after Whiplash Injuries. A One-Year Prospective Study." *European Journal of Pain* 12 (4): 455–463.

Koontz, A. M., E. D. Brindle, P. Kankipati, D. Feathers, and R. A. Cooper. 2010. "Design Features that Affect the Maneuverability of Wheelchairs and Scooters." *Archives of Physical and Medical Rehabilitation* 91: 759–764.

Kyung, G., M. A. Nussbaum, and K. Babski-Reeves. 2008. "Driver Sitting Comfort and Discomfort (Part I): Use of Subjective Ratings in Discriminating Car Seats and Correspondence Among Ratings." *International Journal of Industrial Ergonomics* 38 (5–6): 516–525.

Lefton, L., and L. Brannon. 2002. *Psychology*. Boston: Allyn and Bacon.

Lockhart, T. 2008. "An Integrated Approach towards Identifying Age-Related Mechanisms of Slip-Initiated Falls." *Journal of Electromyography and Kinesiology* 18 (2): 205–217.

Lynch, K. 1960. *The Image of the City*. Boston: MIT and the President and Fellows of Harvard College.

Marras, W. S., et al. 1995. "Biomechanical Risk Factors for Occupationally Related Low Back Disorders." *Ergonomics* 38: 377–410.

Milgram, S. 1974. "The Experience of Living in Cities." In C. M. Loo (ed.), *Crowding and Behavior* (pp. 41–54). New York, NY: MSS Information Corporation.

Morrell, J. and K. Wasilewski. 2010. "Design and Evaluation of a Vibrotactile Seat to Improve Spatial Awareness while Driving." Paper presented at the Institute of Electrical and Electronics Engineers (IEEE) Haptics Symposium, 2010, March 20–26, 2010, Waltham, MA.

Nagamachi, M. (ed.). 2011. *Kansei/Affective Engineering*. Boca Raton, FL: Taylor and Francis.

National Council on Disability. 2005. *Saving Lives: Including People with Disabilities in Emergency Planning*. Washington, DC: National Council on Disability.

Nelson, N. A. and R. E. Hughes. 2009. "Quantifying Relationships between Selected Work-Related Risk Factors and Back Pain: A Systematic Review of Objective Biomechanical Measures and Cost-Related Health Outcomes." *International Journal of Industrial Ergonomics* 39 (1): 202–210.

Norman, D. 2002. *The Design of Everyday Things*. New York: Basic Books.

———2004. *Emotional Design: Why We Love (or Hate) Everyday Things*. New York: Basic Books.

Pallasmaa, J. 2005. *The Eyes of the Skin: Architecture and the Senses.* Chichester, West Sussex: John Wiley & Sons Ltd.

Palm, H.-G., J. Strobel, G. Achatz, F. von Luebken, and B. Friemert. 2009. "The Role and Interaction of Visual and Auditory Afferents in Postural Stability." *Gait and Posture* 30 (3): 328–333.

Paquet, V. and D. Feathers. 2004. "An Anthropometric Study of Manual and Powered Wheelchair Users." *International Journal of Industrial Ergonomics* 33: 191–204.

Passini, R. 1984. *Wayfinding in Architecture.* New York: Van Nostrand Reinhold.

Pastalan, L. A., R. K. Mautz, and T. Merrill. 1973. "The Simulation of Age Related Sensory Losses: A New Approach to the Study of Environmental Barriers." In W.F.E. Preiser (ed.), *Environmental Design Research*, Vol. 1 (pp. 383–391). Stroudsburg, PA: Dowden, Hutchinson and Ross.

Pheasant, S. and C. Haslegrave. 2006. *Bodyspace: Anthropometry, Ergonomics, and the Design of Work* (3rd ed.). Boca Raton, FL: Taylor and Francis.

Pintar, F. A., N. Yoganandan, and D. J. Maiman. 2010. *Lower Cervical Spine Loading in Frontal Sled Tests Using Inverse Dynamics: Potential Applications for Lower Neck Injury Criteria.* Technical Paper 2010-22-0008. Warrendale, PA: Society of Automotive Engineers (SAE) International.

Prochnik, G. 2010. *In Pursuit of Silence: Listening for Meaning in a World of Noise.* New York: Doubleday.

Proctor, R. W. and T. Van Zandt. 2008. *Human Factors in Simple and Complex Systems* (2nd ed.). Boca Raton, FL: Taylor and Francis.

Rasmussen, S. E. 1959. *Experiencing Architecture.* Cambridge, MA: MIT Press.

Rodríguez, D. A. and J. Joo. 2004. "The Relationship between Non-Motorized Mode Choice and the Local Physical Environment." *Transportation Research Part D* 9 (2): 151–173.

Rubin, E. 2001. "Figure and Ground." In S. Yantis (ed.), *Visual Perception*, pp. 225–229. Philadelphia: Psychology Press.

Ryhl, C. 2010. "Accessibility and Sensory Experiences: Designing Dwellings for Visually and Hearing Impaired." *Nordisk Arkitekturforskning* 22 (1/2): 109–122.

Sanford, J. A. 1996. *A Review of Technical Requirements for Ramps.* Washington, DC: U.S. Access Board.

Schoon, J. G. 2011. "Crossing Times and Trajectory Characteristics for Wheelchairs and Mobility Scooters Based on GPS Data." Paper presented at the 90th Transportation Research Board (TRB) Annual Meeting (session number P11-1193), January 23–27, 2011, Washington, DC.

Sharp, H., Y. Rogers, and J. Preece. 2007. *Interaction Design: Beyond Human–Computer Interaction* (2nd ed.). Hoboken, NJ: John Wiley & Sons.

Siegel, J. H., G. Loo, P.C. Dischinger, A.R. Burgess, S.C. Wang, L.W. Schneider, D. Grossman, F. Rivara, C. Mock, C.A. Natarajan, K.D. Hutchins, F.D. Bents, L. McCammon, E. Leibovich, and N. Tenenbaum 2001. "Factors Influencing the Patterns of Injuries and Outcomes in Car versus Car Crashes Compared to Sport Utility, Van, or Pick-up Truck versus Car Crashes: Crash Injury Research Engineering Network Study." *Journal of Trauma* 51 (5): 975–990.

Steidl, R. E., and E. C. Bratton. 1968. *Work in the Home.* New York: John Wiley & Sons.

Steinfeld, E., et al. 1979. *Barrier-Free Access to the Man-Made Environment—A Review of Literature.* Washington, DC: U.S. Department of Housing and Urban Development.

Steinfeld, E., J. Maisel, D. Feathers, and C. D'Souza. 2010. "Anthropometry and Standards for Wheeled Mobility: An International Comparison." *Assistive Technology* 22 (1): 51–67.

Summerfield, J. J., J. Lepsien, D. R. Gitelman, M. M. Mesulam, and A. C. Nobre. 2006. "Orienting Attention Based on Long-Term Memory Experience." *Neuron* 49 (6): 905–916.

Thompson, J. D. and G. Goldin. 1975. *The Hospital: A Social and Architectural History.* New Haven, CT: Yale University Press.

Thomsen, J. F., F. Gerr, and I. Astroshi. 2008. "Carpal Tunnel Syndrome and the Use of Computer Mouse and Keyboard: A Systematic Review." *BMC Musculoskeletal Disorders* 9: 134.

Vanderheiden, G. C. 1990. "Thirty-Something Million: Should They Be Exceptions?" *Human Factors* 32 (4): 383–396.

Waller, P. F. and P. A. Green. 1997. "Human Factors in Transportation." In G. Salvendy (ed.), *Handbook of Human Factors and Ergonomics,* pp. 1,972–2,009. New York: John Wiley & Sons.

Weisman, L. K. 1992. *Discrimination by Design: A Feminist Critique of the Man-made Environment.* Chicago: University of Illinois Press.

Wickens, C. D., S. E. Gordon, and Y. Liu. 1998. *An Introduction to Human Factors Engineering.* New York: Addison-Wesley.

6

Design for Health and Wellness

Introduction

Universal design seeks to address the needs of the entire population. Health and wellness are generally accepted indicators of quality of life and well-being. Within the field of public health, there is a growing realization that design of the environment has significant health impacts. Moreover, there is a strong relationship of health to issues of diversity because of ongoing health disparities related to socioeconomic status, race, and gender. Public health professionals already see this connection, and they are starting to embrace the universal design agenda. In Chapter 2, therefore, we proposed a new definition for universal design that explicitly identifies health and wellness as a *universal benefit* of universal design practices. Including design for health and wellness as part of the universal design mission expands and solidifies its focus to a set of issues that clearly have an impact on the entire population. Due to rising healthcare costs, seeking design solutions to health issues is not only a socially responsible goal but also a financial necessity.

The International Classification of Functioning, Disability, and Health (ICF) model of the World Health Organization (WHO) incorporates the idea that disablement is socially defined. The "treatment" for disablement must take into account not only personal factors but environmental factors as well. Likewise, in understanding health and wellness, it is not sufficient to focus only on treatments, personal characteristics (e.g., genetic background, age, etc.) and personal behaviors (e.g., diet and exercise). The environment deserves careful attention as well. Good examples of health issues related to environmental design are environmental factors in falls, contributors to obesity such as inactive lifestyles and "food deserts" (neighborhoods with limited food retail options), the health impacts of secondhand smoke in buildings, other indoor air quality issues, and reactions to chemicals in building products. Health problems, if severe, often result in disablement. Thus, rather than viewing design narrowly as a reaction to disablement by removing barriers, universal design can also support health and wellness through positive action to reduce the incidence of disablement and improving quality of life. This is why Wellness is included as one of the Goals of Universal Design.

Improved health outcomes require attention to social, political, and economic factors (e.g., poverty and political unrest), living and working conditions (e.g., housing, work environment, access to food and air quality), and public service infrastructure (e.g., clean water, transportation, healthcare, etc.). The universal design concept is an ideal way to conceptualize the environmental perspective within the discourse on public health issues. Universal design can be enlisted to help reduce the injuries from accidents, prevent the spread of disease and infection, optimize human potential, improve mental health, and support healthy lifestyles.

Unfortunately, very limited research exists to guide designers as they strive to practice universal design with the goal of improving health and wellness. More evidence-based research and practice is needed to address the diverse needs for information in this field. Health and wellness are issues for the entire population, but priorities vary with the population of concern. Abraham Maslow proposed a hierarchy of needs as part of his theory of self-actualization (Figure 6–1). People have both deficiency needs (e.g., physiological hunger and thirst, safety/security, love/acceptance, and esteem) and growth needs (e.g., self-actualization). Individuals are ready to fulfill their growth needs only once all of their deficiency needs are met (Maslow 1954). Satisfaction of basic needs for safe and sanitary housing does not address all the health issues of concern to an individual. For those living in conditions that cause basic health problems, such as squatter settlements or refugee camps, the most important priority, or even the only affordable focus of design intervention, may be preventing the spread of disease from poor hygiene facilities, unsanitary water, and insect infestation. In a more affluent community, where such deficiency needs are already addressed, the focus may be on higher-order needs like eliminating isolation preventing obesity, overcoming depression, and achieving personal challenges.

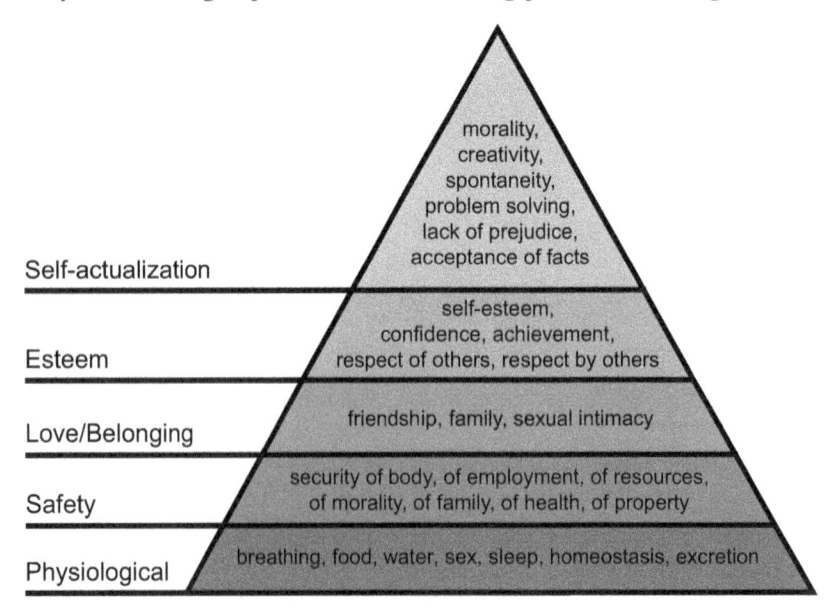

Figure 6–1: Maslow's Hierarchy of Needs. This graphic representation displays the most basic needs at the bottom of a pyramid. Listed from the bottom of the pyramid to the top, those needs are: physiological (e.g., breathing, food, water, sex, sleep, etc.), safety (of self, family, possessions, etc.), love/belonging (friendship, family, intimacy), esteem (confidence, respect, etc.), and self-actualization (morality, creativity, lack of prejudice, acceptance of facts, etc.).

While universal design alone cannot help everyone achieve self-actualization, designing to improve human performance (see Chapter 5) through environmental interventions, service practices, and policy can improve many current health problems and situations. This area of universal design is very new, and only a limited number of examples have been identified to demonstrate good practices. Therefore, this chapter focuses more on identifying the issues of concern and the priorities for action and describing how universal design can be used as a tool in public health than on strategies and solutions. Some specific research needs and examples are also provided.

What Are Health and Wellness?

The terms "health promotion" and "wellness" are often used interchangeably, but they do not necessarily mean the same thing. The *American Journal of Health Promotion* defines health promotion as the science and art of helping people change their lifestyle to move toward a state of optimal health, which is a balance of physical, emotional, social, spiritual, and intellectual health (O'Donnell 1989). Although this approach focuses on the physical dimension of health, including exercise, weight control, and injury prevention, a growing field of research now focuses on emotional health (e.g., reducing stress, overcoming depression, etc.). Wellness means different things to different people. The *Merriam-Webster Dictionary* defines wellness as "the quality or state of being in good health especially as an actively sought goal,"[1] which sounds very similar to health promotion. However, to others, wellness focuses more on an individual's psychological health, social engagement, and spirituality (Maley, Costanza-Smith, and Tangeman 1998; Nosek 1997). The National Wellness Institute (NWI) defines wellness "as an active process of becoming aware and making choices toward a more successful existence."[2]

Not surprisingly, many theoretical models for wellness exist to help explain its complexity. Dr. Bill Hettler, cofounder of the NWI, developed one of the most widely used contemporary models. His "Six Dimensions of Wellness" include:

1. *Physical dimension.* Recognizes the need for regular physical activity
2. *Intellectual dimension.* Recognizes one's creative, stimulating mental activities
3. *Occupational dimension.* Recognizes personal satisfaction and enrichment in life through work
4. *Emotional dimension.* Recognizes awareness and acceptance of one's feelings
5. *Social dimension.* Encourages contributing to the environment and community and emphasizes the need for people and nature to live in harmony rather than in conflict. In other words, "It is better to live in harmony with others and our environment than to live in conflict with them."
6. *Spiritual dimension.* Recognizes the search for meaning and purpose in human existence (NWI n.d.)

Examining both health promotion and wellness reveals the similarities and differences between the two concepts and ultimately the need to focus on both. Whereas health promotion is more research based in its pursuit to prevent diseases, reduce injuries, improve productivity, and optimize health, wellness emphasizes experiential factors and societal goals.[3]

---

[1] *Merriam-Webster's Collegiate Dictionary* (10th ed.), s.v. "wellness."
[2] See www.nationalwellness.org/index.php?id_tier=2&id_c=26.
[3] See Health Promotion Advocates, www.healthpromotionadvocates.org/resources/definitions.htm.

Injury Protection

Injury protection has always been recognized as an aspect of universal design, but the focus has been solely on the design of safe products. Universal design also protects against injuries through interventions in both building and streetscape design. Moreover, it can include business practices like training programs for improving safety in the workplace. These interventions create safer systems that reduce the potential for accidents. "An accident is an undesired and unplanned (but not necessarily unexpected) event that results in (at least) a specified level of loss" (Leveson 1995, p. 175). Accidents are the fourth leading cause of death in the United States after heart disease, cancer, and strokes. This ranking includes all types of accidents, such as motor vehicle accidents, drowning, fires, falls, natural disasters, and work-related accidents. Collectively, accidents cost the nation $150 billion yearly, as a result of lost wages, medical expenses, insurance administration, property damage, and indirect costs (Goetsch 2011). Preventing accidents therefore has financial benefits as well as health benefits.

What causes accidents? Whereas human error can certainly lead to mishaps, poor design and maintenance are also important causes. Stairways and streetscapes provide two examples of how universal design can strive to address current design problems and eliminate disabling injuries.

Stairway Safety

People of all ages fall on stairs; however, falling in general is most prevalent among older adults (Chi, Chang, and Tsou 2006; Templer 1995). In a study of problematic activities, people with leg and foot impairments reported stairs as a problematic activity more often than other groups (Danford, Grimble, and Maisel 2009). However, groups with perceptual and balance limitations are also vulnerable to stairway falls; these include people who wear bifocals, those who have amputated limbs, and people who have excess body mass (Alimusaj et al. 2009; Reeves et al. 2008). Use of stairways is clearly a cross-disability issue (Archea, Collins, and Stahl 1979; Pauls 1982; Templer 1995). The challenge of stair walking leads many older adults and individuals with disabilities to limit their activities, restricting participation in family, social, and community life (Brechter and Powers 2002; Kassi et al. 2005).

Stair design is particularly important as we expand the definition of universal design to address health promotion because walking stairs is often endorsed as a means to be more physically active. However, without improving stair design, increased utilization of stairs will increase accidents. In 2008, unintentional falls took the lives of 24,000 people in the United States. More than 82 percent of these people were 65 years old or older (CDC 2010). Stair-related falls typically make up more than half of these deaths (Elliot et al. 2009). Statistical trends over a three-decade period in the United States indicate that the problem is getting worse. Stair-related injuries are increasing by about 2 percent per year, in contrast with annual decreases over the same period of approximately 3 percent per year for fire-related injuries to civilians[4] (Stevens 2006). The estimated total cost of stair-related injuries in the United States in 1995 was approximately $50 billion (Lawrence et al. 1999).

In the late 1970s, it was estimated that 54 percent of the stair falls in the United States were a result of inadequacies with stair geometry (Alessi, Brill, and Associates 1978). According to Templer (1995), a study conducted by the National Institute for Occupational Safety and

---

[4] J. Pauls, personal communication with the author, June, 2010.

Health provides the strongest evidence that step dimensions affect accident rates. "Geometry" here refers to the size and shape of stair elements. A "riser" is the vertical distance from one stair to the next; a "nosing" is the projection of the tread over the riser. The "tread run" is the horizontal distance from the end of one nosing to an adjacent nosing. "Tread depth" can be defined as the sum of the run and nosing, although there are different terms for this dimension. Research has demonstrated that the tread run, riser height, and the shape and projection of the nosing have important influences on stair safety (Carson et al. 1978; Templer 1992). Despite a long history of research on stair accidents, the evidence underlying some existing design criteria is still very limited. As a result, it is difficult to identify best practices and improve design guidelines. In particular, there is an ongoing controversy in the safety community on stair nosing sizes and the degree of variation that should be allowable in the size of stair elements, such as riser height.

The lack of consensus on best practices for stair geometry has led to difficulties in enforcement of existing codes and standards and is often the subject of litigation. Human performance research, in addition to improving stairway design, would provide a better understanding of the risks associated with using stairways, clarify the economic impact of stair-related accidents, and demonstrate the benefit to society of providing accessible entries and elevators by reducing exposure of vulnerable people to the risk of falling.

Pedestrian Safety

At the community infrastructure scale, streetscape design causes both accidents and a fear of accidents, which leads to avoidance behavior. In a national poll of people over 50, 47 percent said it was unsafe to cross the street near their home. Almost 40 percent said their neighborhood lacks adequate sidewalks (Lynott et al. 2009), creating a disincentive to walking. The oldest pedestrians (75-plus years) suffered fatality rates of 2.69 per 100,000 people, a rate nearly twice the national average for those less than 65 years of age (Ernst and Shoup 2009). From a universal design perspective, streetscapes present important design challenges, including excessive cross-slopes (the slope of a walking surface measured perpendicular to the path of travel), rough and slippery surface materials, breaks in sidewalks, and lack of curb ramps (Axelson et al. 1997, Kockelman et al. 2000). Figure 6–2 illustrates a common problem with street crossings. Poorly designed street crossings like this can be found in most communities, often at dangerous, high-volume intersections. Although Americans make fewer than 8.6 percent of their trips on foot, 11.4 percent of all traffic fatalities occur among pedestrians; of the pedestrian deaths for which information is recorded, almost 60 percent occurred in places where no crosswalk was available or where crosswalk availability was not known (Ernst 2004).

Other streetscape features also present safety risks. In public rights-of-way, walking surfaces often have a combination of incongruous grades and cross-slopes that require people to alter their gait (Redfern and DiPasquale 1997; Sun et al. 1996). They are less likely to recover from slips on sloping surfaces (Cham and Redfern 2002b). Although researchers have investigated the parameters of slipping and strategies to ensure stable traverse of sloped surfaces (Al-Yahya et al. 2009; Arendt-Nielson et al. 1991; Grönqvist, Hirvonen, and Tuusa 1993; McIntosh et al. 2006), research is still needed to understand how wheeled mobility users and ambulant people with mobility impairments are affected by subtle changes in grades, cross-slopes, transitions, and other dangerous surface conditions found in real-world environments. These results benefit not only people with disabilities but also parents with strollers, travelers with luggage, and delivery people

Figure 6-2: Unsafe intersection. This crosswalk has an island without an accessible path through it, which forces wheelchair users, parents with strollers, and bicyclists to move out into the traffic zone when crossing.

using dollies and hand trucks. Slip resistance is an important factor in safety and usability of ramps and streetscapes; it is affected by shoe materials, characteristics of the surface material, and properties of surface contaminants (Cham and Redfern 2002a; Hanson, Redfern, and Mazumdar 1999). Slip resistance is particularly important in cold-weather climates, where ramps can be contaminated by rain, mud, ice, and snow. Icy surfaces in general are a concern, even when they are level.

Although research in all of these areas is still not conclusive on specific design criteria, supportive physical and social environments contribute to healthier communities and a higher quality of life (U.S. Department of Health and Human Services 2000). Therefore, introducing recommendations based on current human performance research in stair and streetscape design can help reduce the potential for accidents and increase convenience for everyone.

Disease Prevention

Preventing diseases also has both financial and health implications. Total medical expenditures are expected to rise as health risk factors linked to lifestyle, including cholesterol, inactivity, and obesity, become increasingly prevalent (Leutzinger et al. 2000). Community planning and design have been identified as contributors to the obesity epidemic as well as to rising asthma rates. Universal design practices can both reduce these threats to health and support healthier behaviors. Recognizing this connection, the fields of public health and urban planning are becoming interested in the adoption of universal design as a means to foster safe, livable, and healthier communities. In addition to health outcomes linked to lifestyle choices, applying universal design principles can help reduce the spread of disease and control infection for vulnerable populations in both developed and less developed countries. The threat of infections has increased due to the increasing globalization of world culture and widespread unsanitary conditions found in the developing world, particularly the persistence of informal (squatter) settlements in response to poverty and rapid urbanization and the creation of large emergency settlements in response to natural disasters, political unrest, war, and violence.

Active Transportation

The prevalence of U.S. adults who were overweight or obese doubled between 1980 and 2008 to over 72 million people. During the same time, rates for children tripled (CDC 2011). Beyond the United States, higher prevalence rates have been found regardless of the nation, ethnicity, or sex. For example, in Australia, one study revealed a rise from 7.1 percent in 1980 to 18.4 percent in 2000 of individuals with obesity (Cameron et al. 2003). More disturbing, however, was the fact that the prevalence of overweight children and adolescents almost doubled during this same period. As obesity increases, the risk for secondary diseases, including type 2 diabetes, cardiovascular disease, and breast cancer, also increases. If untreated, as many as 300,000 premature deaths each year can occur due to obesity. This is a critical burden on the healthcare system. In the United States, it is estimated that more than $100 billion is spent as a result of obesity each year (Flegal et al. 2010).

Exercise is commonly recognized as a key to maintaining a healthy weight. However, several barriers prevent people from exercising regularly during their normal daily activities. These include sedentary jobs, lack of public transportation, and a built environment that is not conducive to active living. The impact of the built environment on public health has received substantial attention in the design and urban planning professions (Frank and Kavage 2008; Jackson 2003; Kochtitzky et al. 2006). The environment both creates and restricts opportunities that influence whether people exercise and whether they eat nutritious foods as opposed to junk foods. For example, low-density suburban developments and parking surrounding retail outlets discourage walking. Not only does a low-density development pattern with large parking lots make walking from home to store, from store to store, and to and from bus stops excessive for convenient walking, but it also makes walking dangerous and unappealing, especially when sidewalks and pedestrian traffic controls are not provided everywhere, or at all.

The lack of funding for improving pedestrian and bicycling opportunities, called planning for "active transportation," makes the problem difficult to solve. According to the Alliance for Biking and Walking, funding allocated to biking and walking is not commensurate with current bike trip levels and traffic fatality rates, and it is not at a level that would encourage more utilization of active transportation modes. Despite the need for increased physical activity, only 1.2 percent of federal transportation funding goes toward biking and walking, even though 13.1 percent of all traffic fatalities are biking and walking related (Alliance for Biking and Walking 2010). Figure 6–3 shows a street that accommodates many modes of transportation and socialization opportunities as well. It was modified simply by painting the pavement, adding street furniture, and reducing the area devoted to automotive vehicles.

Figure 6–3: New York City streetscape. Streets that allow active transportation provide accommodations for pedestrians and bicyclists as well as the automobile. They attract pedestrians and increase public social interaction opportunities in addition to supporting a more active lifestyle.

Design interventions on a community scale can increase activity levels and help reduce the increasing prevalence of obesity (Saelens et al. 2003). Well-connected sidewalks, designated bike paths and parking, streetlights, and aesthetically pleasing streetscapes encourage children to walk to school, employees to bike to work, and families to take afternoon strolls. While bike paths and sidewalks encourage physical activity and usually are accessible for people with mobility impairments, they may pose dangers as well. Street rights-of-way pose many problems for pedestrians with gait limitations and for wheelchair users. Often existing street rights-of-way are not well maintained and include broken and uneven pavement, dangerous curb ramps and street crossings, lack of adequate pedestrian crossing controls, and traffic signal timing that does not support safe crossing. Increased bicycle use, if not controlled properly, can be a serious barrier for older people and people with vision impairments, among others. As new concepts are introduced to provide safe bicycling environments, it is important that new barriers to people with disabilities and elders are not created.

The need to support more active lifestyles is reinforced by the growing number of federal initiatives (e.g., the Partnership for Sustainable Communities by the Department of Housing and Urban Development, the Environmental Protection Agency, and the Department of Transportation, and the United States National Physical Activity Plan), high-profile class action lawsuits against municipalities (e.g., *Barden v. Sacramento* and *Californians for Disability Rights, Inc., v. California Department of Transportation*), and public policies (e.g., Complete Streets) that stress the importance of safe and accessible pedestrian environments. Complete Streets initiatives actually extend beyond the pedestrian realm. These initiatives are "designed for the safety and comfort of all road users, regardless of age and ability" (Lynott et al. 2009, vii). The Complete Streets movement has grown rapidly over the past ten years, with more than 300 initiatives. Complete Streets encourages local, regional, and state planning agencies to change right-of-way policies and procedures so that multimodal accommodations are a routine part of development projects.

Food Security

Access to healthy food is critical to preventing disease and encouraging a healthy lifestyle. Food sustains our existence and accompanies our celebrations. It also defines the communities in which we live. When the supply and quality of food is poor, our neighborhoods are threatened (SUNY-Buffalo 2003). Unhealthy eating leads to obesity, secondary diseases, and ultimately a greater strain on community resources. The lack of affordable and nutritious food in some neighborhoods even creates barriers to developing healthy eating habits. Residents, especially those who do not drive or cannot afford a car, often have to rely on junk foods from local convenience stores.

According to the United Nations' Food and Agriculture Organization: "Food security means that food is available at all times; that all persons have means of access to it; that it is nutritionally adequate in terms of quantity, quality, and variety; and that it is acceptable within the given culture. Only when all these conditions are in place can a population be considered food secure" (Koc et al. 1999, p. 1). Becoming food secure requires proactive steps to create a community food system that enhances citizens' access to nutritious and affordable food at all times. Some communities are at a greater disadvantage in obtaining food security than others. Although few empirical studies exist on neighborhood food environments (Raja, Ma, and Yadav 2008), previous studies have shown racial disparities, even when controlling for income, in access to healthful food sources (Helling and Sawicki 2003). Neighborhoods with limited food retail options are referred to as food deserts (Cummins and Macintyre 2002). Using a more functional definition, only areas with limited *healthy* food options are classified as food deserts (Wrigley, Warm, Margetts, and Whelan 2002). Regardless of how a food desert is defined, planners and public health workers agree that increasing access to affordable, healthy, convenient, and culturally appropriate food is essential to healthy eating.

A variety of innovative strategies to combat food deserts exist. Cooperative grocery stores (co-ops) are retail outlets that are owned and operated by members in order to provide affordable, healthy food to both members and to the public. Members have a say in decision making related to these voluntary organizations. Other strategies seek to support existing food businesses. Community-supported agriculture (CSA) works on the basic premise that people buy "shares" in a farm up front, often for a season but sometimes from month to month, and then receive a portion of the crop in return periodically throughout the growing season (Rayasam 2007). Unlike the more traditional farmers' market system, CSA shareholders do not choose the produce they receive but instead receive whatever is ripe and in season. This system benefits both farmers and shareholders, in that farmers do not need to take out loans to cover up-front business costs and shareholders get a steady supply of fresh, local produce throughout the season. Many farms that participate in CSAs raise organic foods and, therefore, tend to attract people interested in their own health as well as the health of the environment. With the increasing interest in organic, natural foods, CSAs are a good way to help people connect with the food they are eating and the farmers who produce it. Despite their benefits, memberships in CSAs can be expensive. Recent efforts have striven to make them more affordable. In the United States, food stamps, a form of food subsidy, can be applied toward farm shares as long as they are paid weekly or monthly, although most are not (Guthman, Morris, and Allen 2006). The federal government has seen the benefit of the CSA system by allowing CSAs to serve as a nutritional option for some older low-income people who receive food subsidies (Brown 2006). These solutions, although a step in the right direction, do not completely address the problem of food security for all low-income people, particularly older citizens and those with disabilities who may have trouble traveling to the locations where the best food is available.

Other solutions attempt to bring healthier food options closer to residents. Community gardens not only provide a source of food but gardeners also report feelings of relaxation, and healing, and a sense of community pride, as a result of their efforts (SUNY-Buffalo 2003). In addition to the previously mentioned innovative and alternative food strategies, local, small grocery stores should strive to offer healthy food options, so residents without transportation can have access to affordable and healthy food within their own communities.

Although planning, activism, and CSAs are all good examples of universal design practice, the design of actual gardens is an excellent focus of universal design, particularly for reducing the effort needed to raise crops. The "Keyhole Garden" is a design concept, developed by CSA advocates in Africa. These compact gardens make it easier for people to plant and care for their crops. By raising the beds, less bending is required and the keyhole shape puts all plants within reach of the perimeter. This makes the garden more accessible to older and disabled gardeners. Raised beds also reduce contamination by lead and other dangerous elements that can often be found in urban soil and lining the beds with masonry, stones, sandbags, or other dense materials helps to retain the heat in the soil and increase the growing season. A composting bin in the center continually adds nutrients to the soil, another effort reducing strategy.

Reducing Pollution

Increasing sprawl and low-density community growth not only contributes to obesity but also directly contributes to a greater number of vehicle miles traveled and, consequently, more pollutant emissions. As people live farther away from cities, they have to travel greater distances to reach places of employment, retail outlets, restaurants, and services. Results from the 2009 National Household Travel Survey show that daily travel in the United States totaled about 3.7 trillion person miles, with an average of 36.13 daily miles per person annually (Santos et al. 2009). Between 1960 and 2000, the use of a private vehicle as a means of travel to work increased from 69 percent of all commuters to 88 percent (McGuckin and Srinivasan 2003). This trend has contributed to an increase in the number of person trips in private vehicles to/from work—an increase of more than 22 percent (ten billion trips) from 1990 to 2009 (Santos et al. 2009).

With more miles traveled, individuals risk exposure to greater vehicle pollution emissions. Motor vehicle traffic is the main source of ground-level air pollutants with recognized hazardous properties (WHO 1999). Exposure to air pollution exacerbates symptoms of asthma and causes asthma attacks. In the United States in 2009, asthma prevalence was 8.2 percent, affecting 24.6 million people (17.5 million adults and 7.1 million children ages 0 to 17 years) (Akinbami and Moorman 2011). Children with asthma are believed to be particularly sensitive to air pollution (President's Task Force on Environmental Health Risks and Safety Risks to Children 2000). Reducing children's exposure to environmental pollutants such as traffic emissions will reduce the frequency and severity of their asthma attacks (Jackson and Kochtitzky 2001).

Controlling Infections

Disease prevention strategies are also triggered in response to infections. According to the Centers for Disease Control and Prevention (CDC), as many as 1.7 million people acquire a new infection during a hospital visit, and of those, nearly 100,000 die annually (Klevens et al. 2007). These hospital-acquired infections occur for three reasons: (1) Infected patients come to the hospital to seek health care because they have symptoms of sickness, but it can take several days for staff to detect the presence of infection, during which time contamination spreads to other patients; (2) people in hospitals often have suppressed immune systems and are more easily infected than healthy individuals; and (3) multiple bedroom designs and the need for staff to treat many people at once create conditions that are ideal for infectious bacterial growth and transmission. Today's healthcare facilities need to be designed with this problem in mind.

Most surfaces are capable of harboring, sustaining, and transmitting disease-causing organisms. Many bacteria are becoming resistant to common antibiotics, which makes infections even more difficult to prevent and treat. The most commonly known infections are staph infections. One such infection, methicillin-resistant *Staphylococcus aureus* (MRSA), has received a lot of attention due to recent outbreaks. In fact, MRSA is responsible for 63 percent of hospital-acquired staph infections (Calfee et al. 2008). It can live for more than 12 days on a laminated countertop, 11 days on a plastic patient chart, and 9 days on a cloth curtain. Studies have shown that MRSA also is often found on door hardware; one study, in particular, found that 27 percent of door handles were contaminated with MRSA (Hosokawa, Ole, and Kamiya 2002; Huang et al. 2006).

According to the CDC, the 1.7 million healthcare-associated infections (HAIs) add an estimated $5 billion to the nation's annual healthcare bill. In an effort to reduce HAIs and enhance patient safety, Medicare has stopped reimbursing healthcare facilities for the increased costs of treating certain preventable infections. Many private insurers have expressed their intentions of following suit (Connovich 2009). Since hospitals are now responsible for absorbing the added cost of treating patients who contract infections on their premises, it is in their best interest to reduce HAIs. Here are some strategies for infection control through design:

- Consider how infectious agents, such as bacteria and viruses, are transmitted when planning healthcare facilities.
- Standardize use of single-bed inpatient rooms to help decrease infection rates through cross-contamination (see Figure 2–2).
- Antimicrobial surfaces should be used as a method for infection control.
- Install electronic faucets with LEDs (light-emitting diodes) that illuminate for the duration of the recommended hand-washing cycle. This will help healthcare workers become aware of the time they spend washing their hands (Connovich 2009).

Low-Resource Settings

Evidence suggests that it is difficult to meet advanced building standards in very low-income settings, including rural areas with traditional forms of construction, informal settlements, and refugee camps, and when reconstructing areas damaged by natural disasters. Relief workers in developing countries report that contemporary accessibility standards, in particular, are too complex and inappropriate for the problems found in refugee camps and reconstruction projects (Whybrow et al. 2010). Studies of informal settlements in India and South Africa demonstrate that the conditions in such communities require a different approach from solutions used in high-income countries. One example is the need to provide accessibility and privacy in mass latrines that are rapidly constructed in refugee camps. Western-style accessible bathroom standards are simply not useful for such an application. Serious security, privacy, and financial barriers exist in these communities that demand as much attention as issues related to accessibility (Tipple and Coulson 2009). For example, public toilets are locations that everyone needs to use; thus, they become frequent sites of criminal activity. This safety concern leads to avoidance behavior, with health consequences, such as urinary tract infections, or it contributes to unsanitary conditions elsewhere.

Even in high-income countries, providing emergency housing in the aftermath of a major natural disaster presents some major challenges to implementing the technical standards intended for more conventional construction. Standards distributed throughout the world for use in economic development programs, refugee camps, and disaster recovery projects do not address the issues raised in these differing contexts. For example, one handbook produced for use in "post-conflict and developing countries" included copies of illustrations from the Americans with Disabilities Act Accessibility Guidelines for bathrooms (Dilli 1997), and guidelines produced by U.S. and U.K. aid agencies *require* all their projects to comply with their respective standards, even though doing so may be both costly and inappropriate for the context.

Access to water and sanitation is a problem for everyone living in informal settlements but is more serious for people with mobility limitations (Tipple and Coulson 2009). The problems include:

- *Lack of access to communal toilets.* Where access is lacking, residents with disabilities are forced to use spaces in their dwellings, nearby open fields, or rubbish dumps for toilet needs.
- *Obstacles to carrying water* from communal pumps or water trucks to individual dwellings. Often there are long waiting times for water. In addition, the containers are often too heavy for many people, who are thus dependent on the assistance of families and neighbors.
- *Obstacles to mobility.* Narrow, congested, unpaved, and cluttered paths are significant barriers to moving around the neighborhood (Tipple and Coulson 2009).

Access to water and sanitation services remains an enormous challenge to people with disabilities who live in low-income communities, yet very little has been published on this topic (Jones and Reed 2005). Researchers and practitioners have learned that universal design is a practical and affordable strategy to address these problems even in developing countries (Jones and Reed 2005; Raheja 2008). If improvements are designed to help a broad population, their value will be obvious, and community members will be more supportive and willing to invest the effort to increase accessibility of their communities further. For example, a seating platform next to a communal hand pump can provide rest opportunity for everyone while pumping water, and it enables small children to reach the pump (Jones and Reed 2005). Ramped access and a wide concrete apron at the pump stanchion not only allows access by people in wheelchairs but also makes it possible to bring larger wheeled water containers to the village pump and reduce the number of trips a household has to make (Raheja 2008). Fitting a bench over a pit latrine can make the latrine easier for everyone to use (Jones and Reed 2005). Building a raised pad at a bus stop with ramp access, even where there are no sidewalks, makes it easier for people with mobility impairments to access the bus, helps people with visual and cognitive impairments find the stop, and improves safety and usability for everyone while waiting for a bus, especially during rainy seasons (Rickert 2007).

Universal design not only improves independence for people with disabilities in low-income communities, it also reduces the burden on family caregivers by supporting more independence among people with disabilities (Jones and Reed 2006). Often one member of a low-income family must devote most of his or her time to a caregiving role, forsaking income production, because the person with a disability cannot take care of him- or herself in an inaccessible environment. The burden of caring for a family member is a major source of mental health problems for caregivers.

Mental Health

A growing proportion of older adults have a cognitive disability such as dementia. Based on the Aging, Demographics, and Memory Study (ADAMS), 13.9 percent of people 71 years and older in the United States have dementia (Plassman et al. 2007). More than 5.2 million Americans 65 and older had Alzheimer's disease, the most prevalent type of dementia, in 2011(Hebert et al. 2003).[5] A reduction in capacity due to aging magnifies the needs of this population, so that many of the accommodations and compensations that are effective at a relatively young age become ineffective later in life. Homes and everyday products can provide solutions that address these limitations in capacity, ability, and daily living needs (Demirbilek and Demirkan 2004). Universal design of housing can help ensure that the specific needs of this user group are satisfied and makes it easier to add enhancements as people have more significant needs. The universal design features will likely improve usability for all end users, such as caregivers and staff in care facilities.

Although older adults with dementia have impairments in short-term memory and planning capabilities, often their long-term memory is still intact. Therefore, any new product or space designed for this population must support functional ability by incorporating features that are recognizable or familiar to users based on previous experiences. This concept of *familiarity* and its impact in helping older adults learn how to use a new product effectively has not received much attention within the field of universal design. Research on architectural design for dementia, however, has identified familiarity as a key design goal for preserving independent functioning (Cohen and Weisman 1991), and maintaining familiarity of the environment is a key design goal for frail older people in general (Regnier 2002). Norman (2002) demonstrated how dramatic the effect of unusual affordances and methods of operation can be for the ease of usability of products for the general population. In fact, one of the Principles of Universal Design is "Simple and Intuitive Use" (Connell et al. 1997). Thus, it is surprising that there has not been a sustained focus of research on this design strategy.

The purposeful introduction of familiar features is not uncommon in design practice. A well-designed product or space often takes advantage of a user's familiarity with the product (or similar products) through the incorporation of well-known conceptual models (see Chapter 5). Difficulty in using a novel product is often directly related to the adoption of novel conceptual models

---

[5]Number of Americans over age 65 with Alzheimer's disease for 2011 is based on linear extrapolation. Data given in Alzheimer's Association 2011.

(Norman 2002). For example, graphical user interfaces for computers made use of personal computers possible for the masses by the adoption of icons and organizational concepts that were familiar, e.g., file folders, menus, stop signs. Design scenarios become more complex when users are completely unfamiliar with a product, and even more so when they have a cognitive impairment. People with cognitive impairments may have a drastically increased learning curve, which may lead to frustration on the part of users, and eventual abandonment of a device. A good example is a patient-lifting system for transferring immobile people from a bed to a wheelchair or a wheelchair to a toilet or bath. Most people do not have any need for using a patient lift until they become a caregiver. Thus, the first hurdle a caregiver has to overcome is learning how the unfamiliar device works. If the person they are caring for has a cognitive impairment, the caregiver may have a much more difficult task on their hands caused by of fear of the new device on the part of their charge. In such a situation, the risk of injury to caregiver or care recipient is great, which adds stress and reduces the threshold of tolerance.

Research suggests that, besides familiarity, lighting and minimizing complexity can play an integral role in affecting behavior of older adults with dementia. Approximately 90 percent of institutionalized patients with dementia suffer from nocturnal restlessness and wandering (Hoof, Aarts, and Schoutens 2009). The safety of people with mild dementia is a particular concern since they are likely to have lowered *situational awareness*, the perception and understanding of their surroundings and environment (Smith and Hancock 1995; see Chapter 5). Although the literature typically uses the term "situational awareness" in reference to work environments or high-performance settings, it may also be relevant to cognitive aging, when older adults' lessening perception and understanding of their environment becomes critical to everyday functioning and physical activities. By facilitating older adults' situational awareness, it may be possible to reduce the impact of age-related cognitive declines, such as dementia (Caserta and Abrams 2007). For example, as a substitute for pharmacologic interventions, which tend to reduce situational awareness, high-intensity bluish light (6500 K) was shown to play a role in managing restless behavior in a study population (Hoof et al. 2009). Designers should also strive to minimize complexities and provide an environment that allows older adults with dementia to participate safely in dynamic situations.

Another issue, depression, is one of the most prevalent mental health conditions in the United States, with rates ranging from approximately 10 percent to 22 percent for men and women, respectively (Kessler et al. 2003; Un 2004; WHO 2005). The widespread use of antidepressant pharmaceuticals may alleviate the symptoms of depression, but it does not address the causes, some of which may be environmental. For example, media exposure among teenagers (Primack et al. 2009), less dense settlement patterns (Frumkin, Frank, and Jackson 2004), and poor living conditions (Galea et al. 2005) are all known contributors to depression. Additional research is needed to explore how design can serve as a useful tool for combating these causes and curtailing symptoms.

Other Issues

Many other health-related issues require more research and exploration. This need for knowledge extends to diseases and safety risks in both developed and less developed countries. One area receiving a great deal of attention is the application of universal design for emergency evacuations from buildings. Experience from major disasters has shown that people with disabilities and older people are often either left behind during such evacuations or experience injuries and hardships at a higher rate (Steinfeld 2006). Other problems can also arise, such as when first responders to an emergency are unprepared for evacuees who are dependent on ventilators or other medical equipment. Attempts are being made by designers, policy makers, and first responders to find better management approaches for emergencies by improving building design, providing training, and conducting preparedness exercises. Universal design can also help in enabling communications and assistance during evacuations, with new technologies ensuring that people with sensory and cognitive impairments are kept informed about the emergency and are not left behind (Escape Rescue Systems Ltd. n.d.). Better communications during evacuations, using a universal design approach, will benefit all occupants of a building, as well as first responders.

The design of public accommodations is placing increasing attention on environmental irritants. Indoor air quality is particularly important because most Americans spend up to 90 percent of their time indoors, and indoor air quality affects the comfort and productivity of building occupants (Office of Air and Radiation 1997). Common environmental irritants include biological contaminants (e.g., bacteria, mold, etc.), chemical pollutants (e.g., cleaning products, gases, etc.), and particles (e.g., dust, drywall, etc.). Maintaining good indoor air quality requires attention to the building's heating, ventilation, and air conditioning (HVAC) system; simple strategies for design and layout of furniture and equipment can ensure that air circulation is not blocked (Office of Air and Radiation 1997).

Multiple chemical sensitivity (MCS) is a term used to describe severe sensitivity or a reaction to different pollutants including solvents, volatile organic compounds (VOCs), perfumes, building materials, smoke, and other "chemicals." Whereas allergies are well understood and can be treated, MCS is only partly understood. In addition to a lack of information on its causation, the difficulty in treating MCS is compounded by its variability between individuals.[6] Aside from avoidance and increased exposure to fresh air and specialized products, very few design solutions are available to assist the growing number of people with MCS. According to Alison Johnson, chair of the Chemical Sensitivity Foundation, approximately 7 million Americans may suffer from MCS (Johnson 2010). Although attempts to accommodate chemically sensitive people are often futile, and additional research is needed, awareness of chemical sensitivities and workplace air quality can create more efficient and productive work environments. At present, design participation activities with people who have MCS may be a very worthwhile approach for designers since individuals are aware of the specific irritants that bother them and often have devised coping strategies that can be implemented beyond the home environment. One example of a universal design strategy in this field is the Pure Room program for providing hotel rooms free of known allergens (see www.pureroom.com).

In less developed countries, water-related and waterborne diseases pose a greater threat to wellness than air pollutants. In these countries, access to water and sanitation does not guarantee access to *safe* drinking water. Over 3.5 million people die each year from water-related diseases (e.g., diarrhea, malaria, polio), where diseases are passed because individuals do not wash their hands or cooking utensils are not cleaned properly. Children make up more than 1.5 million of these deaths (Pruss-Ustun et al 2008; UNICEF/WHO 2009). Contaminated water sources lead to waterborne diseases (e.g., cholera, hepatitis A, tuberculosis, and trachoma). The WHO estimates that tuberculosis causes nearly 2 million deaths per year and will infect nearly 1 billion more people by 2020.[7] More research and funding are needed to solve this international health crisis. Universal design can be applied to the development of new methods for filtering water

---

[6]See "Multiple Chemical Sensitivity? What Is It?" www.multiplechemicalsensitivity.org/index.php.
[7]See "Tuberculosis" on the WHO website (http://apps.who.int/tdr/svc/diseases/tuberculosis); see also WHO 2010.

that are easy to use and effective in low-income settings. One example of an effort like this is the TAMU Water Project (see www.tamuwaterproject.wordpress.com). This R&D team developed very inexpensive ceramic filters that are now used in Africa and Southeast Asia as well as in the Colonias settlements along the Texas border with Mexico to provide access to safe drinking water.

Health Impact Assessments

As an increasing amount of attention focuses on environmental impacts on health and wellness, a new field of research has emerged that seeks to quantify the relationship between the built environment and health and wellness. Health impact assessments are "a combination of procedures, methods, and tools by which a policy, program, or project may be judged as to its potential effects on the health of a population, and the distribution of those effects within the population" (WHO n.d.). These systematic assessments are needed because they help determine the health impact of policies, plans, and projects in order to raise awareness, inform design decisions, and develop new policy. Based on assessment results, decision and policy makers make recommendations so future initiatives minimize health risks and maximize health opportunities.

Designing for Health and Wellness Guidelines

1. *Support policy efforts related to health and wellness issues.* As the built environment continues to prove its critical relationship to health and wellness, planners, public officials, and end users must embrace policies and regulations that support inclusive design interventions. For example, recent movements such as Complete Streets allow a greater number of individuals to participate in the community. Streetscapes that support alternative modes of transportation ultimately lead to more walkable communities, less reliance on automobiles, and healthier communities.
2. *Identify appropriate access solutions based on affordability.* Universal design recognizes that a one-size-fits-all solution will not resolve most accessibility problems; individuals' needs are far too diverse and complex. This is particularly true when addressing accessibility needs in low-income settings. The priorities in higher-income settings may not be as relevant in less developed regions. For example, whereas some individuals with mobility impairments in higher-income settings might have multiple wheeled devices for various terrains and/or hobbies, people with the same impairments in lower-income settings might be concerned with gaining access to at least one wheeled device. Similarly, individuals with disabilities in higher-income communities might focus on the latest technology, while individuals with the same impairments in low-income communities might concentrate on basic necessities, such as accessible bathrooms. Therefore, proposed accessibility solutions to a built environment, product, or any other system must address and be sensitive to the financial resources of the region.
3. *Plan for short and long term.* Expectations for wellness opportunities increase as deficiency needs are addressed. Some low-resource environments are only temporary; others, although intended as temporary, wind up being permanent. Planners and designers of short-term solutions such as refugee camps and emergency housing should take a long-range view and begin planning for the future as soon as conditions are stabilized. Planning should involve residents and engage them in developing creative solutions. Even in higher-resource settings, recognition of health needs often is not sufficient to gain popular support for new projects,

such as building sidewalks or bicycle paths. One of the primary barriers to acceptance is difficulty understanding the benefits of design for health and wellness. Knowledgeable professionals and policy makers can work together to develop a road map and visions of what the future would be like, including projections of health benefits.
4. *Practice evidence-based design.* There is a growing body of research on design for health, including strategies for controlling infection, reducing recuperation time, and the physiological impact of illumination and air quality. Universal designers should participate in the growing community of practice in evidence-based design of health facilities to learn about current research and identify opportunities for knowledge translation to other fields of design.
5. *Identify solutions that are culturally appropriate.* Just as recognition of local financial conditions is necessary, access solutions must be sensitive to local issues, cultures and traditions, and the local physical environment. To achieve this sensitivity, planners and public health officials should work with local experts and advocates in the field who understand the local context and traditions.

Summary

Health and wellness serve as the foundations to positive living. With good health comes the ability to engage in the community, to interact with family and friends, and to fulfill one's own potential. Universal design practices and policies can help facilitate and promote all of these by eliminating barriers and offering innovative solutions. Issues that can be addressed by known approaches in universal design include injury protection, disease prevention, informal settlements, and mental health. Other areas still require additional evidence-based research and exploration. As the challenges facing our communities become more complex and interdisciplinary, a collaborative effort that includes planners, architects, public health officials, policy makers, and end users is needed to effect positive change and to ensure that improvements to health and wellness are sustained. But as Maslow (1954) noted, not everyone has the same needs. While some individuals are more focused on satisfying basic needs, others are striving to reach more growth-oriented goals. Professionals need to remain mindful of these differences and the external constraints that they present, including the affordability of solutions, competing priorities, the availability of technology and knowledge, and differences in cultures and languages.

Review Topics

1. Describe the difference between health and wellness.
2. Describe how known approaches in universal design can address a health and wellness issue such as injury protection, disease prevention, low-resource settings, or mental health.
3. Name at least three guidelines to keep in mind while designing for health and wellness.

References

Akinbami, L. J. and Moorman, J. E. 2011. *Asthma Prevalence, Health Care Use, and Mortality: United States, 2005–2009.* Washington, DC: U.S. Department of Health and Human Services, Centers for Disease Control and Prevention.

Al-Yahya, E., H. Dawes, J. Collett, K. Howells, H. Izadi, D.T. Wade, and J. Cockburn. 2009. "Gait Adaptations to Simultaneous Cognitive and Mechanical Constraints." *Experimental Brain Research* 1 (October): 39–48.

Alessi, D., M. Brill, and Associates. 1978. *Home Safety Guidelines for Architects and Builders. NBS-GCR 78–156*. Gaithersburg, MD: National Bureau of Standards.

Alimusaj, M., et al. 2009. "Kinematics and Kinetics with an Adaptive Ankle Foot System during Stair Ambulation of Transtibial Amputees." *Gait and Posture* 30 (3): 356–363.

Alliance for Biking and Walking. 2010. Bicycling and Walking in the United States 2010: Benchmarking Report. Washington, DC: PeoplePoweredMovement.org.

Alzheimer's Association. 2011. "2011 Alzheimer's Disease Facts and Figures." *Alzheimer's & Dementia* 7 (2): 1–63.

Archea, J. C., B. L. Collins, and F. I. Stahl. 1979. *Guidelines for Stair Safety. NBS-BSS 120*. Gaithersburg, MD: National Bureau of Standards.

Arendt-Nielson, L. A., T. Sinkjær, J. Nielsen, and K. Kallesøe. 1991. "Electromyographic Patterns and Knee Joint Kinematics during Walking at Various Speeds." *Journal of Electromyography and Kinesiology* 1 (2): 89–95.

Axelson, P., D. Yamada, J. Kirschbaum, P. Longmuir, and K. Wong. 1997. *Accessible Exterior Surfaces: A Review of Existing Test Methods for Surface Firmness and Stability*. Minden, NV: Beneficial Designs.

Brechter, J. H. and C. M. Powers. 2002." Patellofemoral Joint Stress during Stair Ascent and Descent in Persons with and without Patellofemoral Pain." *Gait and Posture* 16 (2): 115–123.

Brown, B. 2006. "The New Marketeers: Why Growing and Selling Food Locally Is a Hot Second Career." *AARP Bulletin* (June 13), www-static-w2-md.aarp.org/leisure/food/articles/farmers_market.html.

Calfee, D. P., C. D. Salgado, and D. Classen, et al. 2008. "SHEA/IDSA Practice Recommendation Strategies to Prevent Transmission of Methicillin-Resistant Staphylococcus aureus in Acute Care Hospitals." *Infection Control and Hospital Epidemiology* 29: S62–S80.

Cameron, A. J., T. A. Welborn, P. Z. Zimmet, D. W. Dunstan, N. Owen, J. Salmon, M. Dalton, D. Jolley, and J. E. Shaw. "Overweight and Obesity in Australia: The 1999–2000 Australian Diabetes, Obesity, and Lifestyle Study." *The Medical Journal of Australia* 178: 427–432.

Carson, D. H., J. Archea, S. T. Margulis, and F. E. Carson. 1978. Safety on Stairs. BSS 108. Gaithersburg, MD: National Bureau of Standards.

Caserta, R. J. and L. Abrams. 2007. "The Relevance of Situation Awareness in Older Adults' Cognitive Functioning: A Review." *European Review of Aging and Physical Activity* 4 (1): 3–13.

Centers for Disease Control and Prevention, National Center for Chronic Disease Prevention and Health Promotion. 2011. "Obesity: Halting the Epidemic by Making Health Easier." *At a Glance, 2011*. Washington, DC: CDC. www.cdc.gov/chronicdisease/resources/publications/aag/pdf/2011/Obesity_AAG_WEB_508.pdf.

Centers for Disease Control and Prevention, National Center for Injury Prevention and Control. 2010. Web–based Injury Statistics Query and Reporting System (WISQARS). www.cdc.gov/injury/wisqars/ (accessed July 30, 2011).

Cham, R. and M. S. Redfern. 2002a. "Changes in Gait when Anticipating Slippery Floors." *Gait and Posture* 15 (2): 159–171.

———. 2002b. "Heel Contact Dynamics during Slip Events on Level and Inclined Surfaces." Safety Science 40: 559–576.

Chi, C. F., T. C. Chang, and C. L. Tsou. 2006. "In-Depth Investigation of Escalator Riding Accidents in Heavy Capacity MRT Stations." *Accident Analysis and Prevention* 38: 663–670.

Cohen, U. and G. D. Weisman. 1991. *Holding on to Home: Designing Environments for People with Dementia*. Baltimore, MD: Johns Hopkins University Press.

Connell, B. R., et al. 1997, April 1. "The Principles of Universal Design." www.ncsu.edu/www/ncsu/design/sod5/cud/about_ud/udprinciplestext.htm.

Connovich, R. 2009. "Designing for Infection Prevention: Design Tips on Dealing with the One Problem that Doesn't Ever Seem to Go Away." *HealthCare Design* 9 (11): 46–54.

Cummins, S. and S. Macintyre. 2002. "A Systematic Study of an Urban Foodscape: The Price and Availability of Food in Greater Glasgow." *Urban Studies* 39 (11): 2115–2130.

Danford, G., M. Grimble, and J. Maisel. 2009. *Benchmarking the Effectiveness of Universal Design. Leadership in Architectural Research between Academia and the Profession*, Architectural Research Centers Consortium (ARCC) 2009, San Antonio, Texas, April 15-18, 2009.

Demirbilek, O. and H. Demirkan. 2004. "Universal Product Design Involving Elderly Users: A Participatory Design Model." *Applied Ergonomics* 35: 361–370.

Dilli, D. 1997. *Handbook: Accessibility and Tool Adaptations for Disabled Workers in Post-conflict and Developing Countries*. Geneva: International Labour Organization.

Elliot, D. B., A. Vale, D. Whitaker, and J. G. Buckley. 2009. "Does My Step Look Big in This? A Visual Illusion Leads to Safer Stepping Behaviour." *PLoS ONE* 4 (2): 1–6, www.plosone.org/article/info:doi/10.1371/journal.pone.0004577 .

Ernst, M. 2004. *Mean Streets 2004: How Far Have We Come? Pedestrian Safety, 1994–2003*. Washington, DC: Surface Transportation Policy Project.

Ernst, M. and Shoup, L. 2009. *Dangerous by Design: Solving the Epidemic of Preventable Deaths (and Making Great Neighborhoods)*. Washington, DC: Surface Transportation Policy Partnership and Transportation for America.

Escape Rescue Systems Ltd. Israeli Escape Rescue System. n.d. www.escaperescue.com/movie_window_wma_swat.htm.

Flegal, K., et al. 2010. "Prevalence and Trends in Obesity Among U.S. Adults, 1999–2008." *Journal of the American Medical Association* 303 (3): 235–241.

Frank, L. and S. Kavage. 2008. "Urban Planning and Public Health: A Story of Separation and Reconnection." *Journal of Public Health Management and Practice* 14 (3): 214–220.

Frumkin, H., L. Frank, and R. Jackson. 2004. *Urban Sprawl and Public Health*. Washington, DC: Island Press.

Galea, A., J. Ahern, S. Rudenstine, Z. Wallace, and D. Vlahov. 2005. "Urban Built Environment and Depression: A Multilevel Analysis." Journal of Epidemiology and Community Health 59 (10): 822–827.

Goetsch, D. L. 2011. *Occupational Safety and Health for Technologists, Engineers, and Managers* (7th ed.). Upper Saddle River, NJ: Prentice-Hall.

Grönqvist, R., M. Hirvonen, and A. Tuusa. 1993. "Slipperiness of the Shoe–Floor Interface: Comparison of Objective and Subjective Assessments." *Applied Ergonomics* 24 (4): 258–262.

Guthman, J., A. W. Morris, and P. Allen. 2006. "Squaring Farm Security and Food Security in Two Types of Alternative Food Institutions." Rural Sociology 71 (4): 662–684.

Hanson, J. P., M. S. Redfern, and M. Mazumdar. 1999. "Predicting Slips and Falls Considering Required and Available Friction." *Ergonomics* 42 (12): 1619–1633.

Helling, A. and D. S. Sawicki. 2003. "Race and Residential Accessibility to Shopping and Services." Housing Policy Debate 14 (2): 69–101.

Hebert, L. E., P. A. Scherr, J. L. Bienias, D. A. Bennett, and D. A. Evans. 2003. "Alzheimer's Disease in the U.S. Population: Prevalence Estimates Using 2000 Census." Archives of Neurology, 60 (8): 1119–1122.

Hoof, J. V., M. P. J. Aarts, and A.M.C. Schoutens. 2009. "Ambient Bright Light in Dementia: Effects on Behaviour and Circadian Rhythmicity." *Building and Environment* 44 (1): 146–155.

Hosokawa, S., I. Ole, and A. Kamiya. 2002. "Contamination of Room Door Handles by Methicillin-Sensitive/Methicillin-Resistant Staphylococcus aureus." *Journal of Hospital Infection* 51 (2): 140–143.

Huang, R., S. Mehta, D. Weed, and C. S. Price. 2006. "Methicillin-Resistant Staphylococcus aureus Survival on Hospital Fomites." *Infection Control and Hospital Epidemiology* 27 (11): 1,267–1,269.

Jackson, R. 2003. "The Impact of the Built Environment on Health: An Emerging Field." *American Journal of Public Health* 93 (9): 1,382–1,384.

Jackson, R. J. and C. Kochtitzky. 2001. "Creating a Healthy Environment: The Impact of the Built Environment on Public Health." *Sprawl Watch* 3 (41): 1–19.

Johnson, A. 2010. "Multiple Chemical Sensitivity: A Rapidly Growing Disorder." National Institute of Environmental Health Sciences. Presented at a seminar on October 27, 2010 at the NIEHS Keystone building as part of National Disability Employment Awareness Month.

Jones, H. and R. Reed. 2006. "Water and Sanitation for Disabled People and Other Vulnerable Groups: Designing Services to Improve Accessibility." Loughborough Water and Develeopment Center. Loughborough University, Leicestershire, UK. http://wedc.lboro.ac.uk/docs/research/WEJFK/Cambodia_WEDC_watsan_for_disabled_report.pdf.

Kassi, J., M. O. Heller, U. Stoeckle, C. Perka, and G. N. Duda. 2005. "Stair Climbing Is More Critical than Walking in pre-Clinical Assessment of Primary Stability in Cementless THA in Vitro." *Journal of Biomechanics* 38 (5): 1143–1154. www.ncbi.nlm.nih.gov/pubmed/15797595.

Kessler, R. C., P. Berglund, O. Demler, R. Jin, D. Koretz, K. R. Merikangas, A. J. Rush, E. E. Walters, and P. S. Wang. 2003. "The Epidemiology of Major Depressive Disorder: Results from the National Comorbidity Survey Replication (NCS-R)." *Journal of the American Medical Association* 289: 3,095–3,105.

Klevens, R. M., J. R. Edwards, C. L. Richards Jr., T. C. Horan, R. P. Gaynes, D. A. Pollock, and D. M. Cardo. 2007. "Estimating Health Care-Associated Infections and Deaths in U.S. Hospitals, 2002." *Health Care Reports* 122 (March-April): 160–166.

Koc, M., R. MacRae, L .J .A. Mougeot, and J. Welsh (eds.). 1999. *For Hunger Proof Cities: Sustainable Urban Food Systems*. Ontario, Canada: International Development Research Centre.

Kochtitzky, C., et al. 2006. *Urban Planning and Public Health at CDC*. Atlanta, GA: Centers for Disease Control and Prevention.

Kockelman, K., Y. Zhao, L. Heard, D. Taylor, and B. Taylor. 2000. Sidewalk Cross-Slopes Requirements of the Americans with Disabilities Act: Literature Review. *Transportation Review Board, 1705* (1), 53–60.

Lambert, G. 2006. "Rising Rates of Depression in Today's Society: Consideration of the Roles of Effort-based Rewards and Enhanced Resilience in Day-to-Day Functioning." *Neuroscience and Biobehavioral Reviews* 30: 497–510.

Lawrence, B. A., T. R. Miller, A. F. Jensen, D. A. Fisher, and W. Zamula. 1999. "Estimating the Costs of Nonfatal Consumer Product Injuries in the United States." *Injury Control and Safety Promotion* 7 (2): 97–113.

Leutzinger, J. A., R. J. Ozminkowski, R. L. Dunn, R. Z. Goetzel, D. E. Richling, M. Steward, and R. W. Whitmer. 2000. "Projecting Future Medical Care Costs Using Four Scenarios of Lifestyle Risk Rates." *American Journal of Health Promotion* 15 (1): 35–44.

Leveson, N. 1995. *Safeware: System Safety and Computers*. New York: Addison-Wesley.

Lynott, J., et al. 2009. *Planning Complete Streets for an Aging America*. Washington, DC: AARP Public Policy Institute.

Maley, S., A. Costanza-Smith, and P. Tangeman. 1998. *A Preliminary Pilot Investigation of the Wellness Definitions and Practices of Persons with Physical Disabilities*. Portland, OR: Oregon Health Sciences University.

Maslow, A. 1954. *Motivation and Personality*. New York: Harper.

McGuckin, N. and N. Srinivasan. 2003. *Journey to Work Trends in the United States and Its Major Metropolitan Areas, 1960–2000*. Publication No. FHWA-EP-03-058. Washington, DC: U.S. Department of Transportation.

McIntosh, A. S., K. T. Beatty, L. N. Dwan, and D. R. Vickers. 2006. "Gait Dynamics on an Inclined Walkway." *Journal of Biomechanics* 39 (13): 2,491–2,502.

National Wellness Institute. n.d. *The Six Dimensions of Wellness Model.* Stephens Point, WI: National Wellness Institute, www.nationalwellness.org/pdf/SixDimensionsFactSheet.pdf.

Norman, D. 2002. *The Design of Everyday Things.* New York: Basic Books.

Nosek, M. A. 1997. "Wellness Among Women with Physical Disabilities." In D.M. Krotoski, M.A. Nosek, and M.A. Turk (eds.), *Women with Physical Disabilities: Achieving and Maintaining Health and Well-Being,* pp. 17–33. Baltimore, MD: Paul H. Brookes.

O'Donnell, M. P. 1989. "Definition of Health Promotion: Part III: Expanding the Definition." *American Journal of Health Promotion* 3 (5): 5.

Office of Air and Radiation. 1997. "An Office Building Occupant's Guide to Indoor Air Quality." Washington, DC: EPA-402-K-97–003.

Pauls, J. 1982. *Recommendations for Improving the Safety of Stairs.* Ottawa: National Research Council Canada.

Plassman, B. L., K. M. Langa, G. G. Fisher, S. G. Heeringa, D. R. Weir, et al. 2007. "Prevalence of Dementia in the United States: The Aging, Demographics, and Memory Study." *Neuroepidemiology,* 29 (1-2): 125–132.

President's Task Force on Environmental Health Risks and Safety Risks to Children. 2000. "Asthma and the Environment: A Strategy to Protect Children." http://aspe.hhs.gov/sp/asthma/appxd.pdf.

Primack, B. A., B. Swanier, A. M. Georgiopoulos, S. R. Land, and M. J. Fine. 2009. "Association between Media Use in Adolescence and Depression in Young Adulthood." *Archives of General Psychiatry* 66 (2): 181–188.

Pruss-Ustun, A., R. Bos, F. Gore, and J. Bartram. 2008. *Safer Water, Better Health: Costs, Benefits, and Sustainability of Interventions to Protect and Promote Health.* Geneva: World Health Organization.

Raheja, G. 2008. *Enabling Environments for the Mobility Impaired in the Rural Areas.* Doctoral dissertation, Indian Institute of Technology, Roorkee, India.

Raja, S., C. Ma, and P. Yadav. 2008. "Beyond Food Deserts: Measuring and Mapping Racial Disparities in Neighborhood Food Environments." *Journal of Planning Education and Research* 27: 469–482.

Rayasam, R. 2007. "Growing Crops and Community Ties: Both Help Bind a Business." *U.S. News & World Report* 142 (23): 60–60.

Redfern, M. S. and J. DiPasquale. 1997. "Biomechanics of Descending Ramps." *Gait and Posture* 6 (2): 119–125.

Reeves, N. D., M. Spaanjard, A. A. Mohagheghi, V. Baltzopoulos, and C. N. Maganaris. 2008. "The Demands of Stair Descent Relative to Maximum Capacities in Elderly and Young Adults." *Journal of Electromyography and Kinesiology* 18 (2): 218–227.

Regnier, V. 2002. *Design for Assisted Living: Guidelines for Housing the Physically and Mentally Frail.* Hoboken, NJ: John Wiley & Sons.

Rickert, T. 2007. "Bus Rapid Transit Accessibility Guidelines," http://siteresources.worldbank.org/DISABILITY/Resources/280658-1172672474385/BusRapidEngRickert.pdf.

Saelens, B. E., J. F. Sallis, J. B. Black, and D. Chen. 2003. "Neighborhood-based Differences in Physical Activity: An Environment Scale Evaluation." *American Journal of Public Health* 93 (9): 1552–1558.

Santos, A., N. McGuckin, H. Y. Nakamoto, D. Gray, and S, Liss. 2009. "Summary of Travel Trends: 2009 National Household Travel Survey." Report No. FHWA-PL-11-022. Washington, DC: U.S. Department of Transportation Federal Highway Administration.

Smith, K. and P. A. Hancock. 1995. "Situation Awareness Is Adaptive, Externally Directed Consciousness." *Human Factors* 37 (1): 137–148.

Steinfeld, E. 2006. "Emergency Evacuation of People with Disabilities." *Journal of Security Education* 2 (1): 107–118.

Stevens, J. A. 2006. "Fatalities and Injuries from Falls among Older Adults — United States, 1993–2003 and 2001–2005." *Morbidity and Mortality Weekly Report (MMWR)* 55 (45): 1221–1224.

Sun, J., M. Walters, N. Svensson, and D. Lloyd. 1996. "Influence of Surface Slope on Human Gait Characteristics: A Study of Urban Pedestrians Walking on an Inclined Surface." *Ergonomics* 39 (4): 677–692.

SUNY-Buffalo. 2003. *Food for Growth: A Community Food System Plan for Buffalo's West Side*. Buffalo: University at Buffalo, State University of New York.

Templer, J. 1992. *Studies of Safer Stairs and Ramps. Educational Workshop on Building Safety.* Atlanta: Georgia Institute of Technology.

Templer, J. 1995. *The Staircase: Studies of Hazards, Falls, and Safer Design*. Cambridge, MA: MIT Press.

Tipple, G., and J. Coulson. 2009. *Enabling Environments: Reducing Barriers for Low-Income Disabled People*. Newcastle, UK: Global Urban Research Unit.

Un, H. 2004. "Current Trends for the Management and Treatment of Depression." *The American Journal of Managed Care* 10: S171–S172.

UNICEF/WHO. 2009. "Diarhhoea: Why Children Are Still Dying and What Can Be Done." http://whqlibdoc.who.int/publications/2009/9789241598415_eng.pdf.

U.S. Department of Health and Human Services. 2000. *Healthy People 2010*. Washington, DC: U.S. Government Printing Office.

Whybrow, S., A. A. Rahim, V. Sharma, S. Gupta, L. Millikan, and C. Bridge. 2010. "Legislation, Anthropometry, and Education: The Southeast Asian Experience." In J. Maisel (ed.), *The State of the Science in Universal Design: Emerging Research and Developments*, 144–153. Oak Park, IL: Bentham Science Publishers.

World Health Organization (WHO). 1999. *Third Ministerial Conference on Environment and Health*. London: World Health Organization, European Region.

———. 2005. "Depression." www.who.int/topics/depression/en/.

———. 2010. *2010/2011 Tuberculosis Global Facts*. www.who.int/tb/publications/2010/factsheet_tb_2010.pdf.

———. n.d. "Health Impact Assessment." www.euro.who.int/en/what-we-do/health-topics/environmental-health/health-impact-assessment.

Wrigley, N., D. Warm, B. Margetts, and A. Whelan. 2002. "Assessing the Impact of Improved Retail Access on Diet in a 'Food Desert': A Preliminary Report." *Urban Studies* 39 (11): 2,061–2,082.

7

Design for Social Participation

Introduction

The need for attention to social participation in universal design is evident from the history of civil rights movements. The doctrine of "separate but equal," legally applied in the U.S. South until the 1960s, resulted in severe restrictions on human rights for a racial minority. Similar policies can be found all over the world with regard to many different minority groups. There is not much point in providing support for human performance, health, and wellness if one's civil rights are restricted by government policy. However, even where government policy guarantees human rights for all citizens, regulations, traditions, business practices, and attitudes can affect the actual enjoyment of such rights.

Since it was founded in 1948, the United Nations (UN) has led the development of a series of Conventions on Human Rights (UN 1948). These conventions address human rights for women, children, and people with disabilities, among others. In their development stages, they serve as a focus for global dialogue on the definition of human rights and, after adoption by the UN, as a focus for national efforts toward ratification by each country. After ratification, they can serve as a framework for advocacy at the national and local level and for research on progress made toward achievement of rights. These conventions are not perfect. Notably absent are conventions related to race and sexual orientation. Many countries with poor human rights records have ratified the conventions with no intention of upholding the rights that should be guaranteed by the documents. The United States, although involved actively in the development of conventions, has lagged behind other highly developed countries in ratifying some of them, even though the United States has extensive legal guarantees for human rights and active regulatory and legal efforts to prohibit discrimination. The United States has not ratified the conventions on the rights of women and children. In 2009 President Obama signed the Convention on the Rights of People with Disabilities, but it has not been ratified by the Senate.

Many of the conventions specifically include statements that prohibit discrimination in political and public life, healthcare, education, housing, and other activities that are essential for social participation, but the Convention on the Rights of People with Disabilities specifically mentions the provision of *access* to public accommodations, transportation, housing, and information and communications technologies, and it includes a statement that countries should conduct research and education in universal design (UN 2006). The emphasis on accessibility as opposed to universal design reinforces the need to redefine universal design as we did in the early chapters of this book. Many leaders of disability rights movements in middle- and low-income countries view the concept of universal design as a luxury, an unaffordable add-on to basic accessibility. This is not an accurate perception since universal design can be practiced in a low-income context. Two initiatives are needed to change this perception: (1) the practice of universal design has to address affordability more often, and (2) good practice examples from low-income contexts need to be disseminated throughout the world. Nevertheless, the mandate for research and education on universal design is a good first step toward development of the field.

As the UN Conventions demonstrate, social participation is an important part of human rights. It is through social participation that the most important outcome of universal design, an inclusive society, is realized. Moreover, it is through a focus on this issue that the connection between universal design and design for diversity, inclusion, and social justice becomes evident. We focus on social participation for people with disabilities and elders in this chapter because these are the populations for which the evidence base for the benefits of universal design is strongest. However, as discussed in Chapter 3, there are close parallels and relationships with other human rights issues. We address some of them in the following pages. Note that this is one of the first attempts to delineate the scope of universal design for social participation. There is a need to identify further issues and concerns for different social groups in order to expand and define the scope of universal design practice.

Social Construction Theory

A bumper sticker promoting disability rights reads "Attitudes Are the Greatest Disability." In the quest for human rights, often attitudes of others are the most difficult barriers to overcome. Even well-meaning policies can have a negative effect on social life if underlying attitudes do not support social participation. In Chapter 1 (see Figure 1–12), we described a picnic area that was accessible according to law but that resulted in a segregated setting, exactly the opposite result of what accessibility laws are trying to achieve. Disadvantaged people are often the victims of such well-meaning social interventions, attempts by others to help them, usually motivated by pity, which can wind up doing as much harm as good. In universal design, the underlying goal should be to provide all social groups the opportunity to help themselves and achieve their full potential rather than create dependency on others.

Before exploring the specific ways that design can address these goals, it is important to lay a foundation through social theory. There are many theoretical perspectives on the relationship between the physical and social environment (Altman and Chemers 1984). We believe that the one that has the most relevance to universal design is symbolic interactionism (SI) (Blumer 1969; Steinfeld 1981). SI theory seeks to explain and predict human behavior by understanding the significance of human experience to individuals and groups, from their own perspective. Research and theory in this field put stress on identity, both from the perspective of the individual (self concept) and from the perspective of society (social idendity). A major subject of SI research has been the study of diversity and how individuals, groups, and societies deal with difference.

The central concept in SI theory is the "self." SI theorists argue that human beings can be distinguished from other animals by our advanced social interaction skills, intelligence, and powerful imaginations. Through the internalization of social interaction, we develop a "looking-glass self" (Cooley 1902). This means that we develop a sense of self through our interactions with other people in our *social network*, the people with whom we regularly interact, such as family, friends, classmates, and coworkers. Essentially, we pay attention to how others perceive our actions by creating an imaginary social interaction with ourselves. Our view of ourselves changes with experience. In fact, there are customary timetables for key status changes in the life of an individual; these include childhood, family formation, retirement, and widowhood (Sheehy 1995).

In homogeneous traditional societies, the rules of social interaction are prescribed and known to all. But, in diverse contemporary societies, social interaction patterns are fluid and complex because there are fewer rules that are shared in common and social pressures to conform is not as great. We can engage in several different *social worlds* at once (groups where beliefs, attitudes, and patterns of behavior are shared). Good examples are the "art world," the "underworld," and the "sports world." We participate in many *social roles*, such as parents, students, and employees. Cultures or *societies* are defined by shared values and beliefs, customs, and language, often tied to the geography of settlement and migration patterns. When people interact among themselves significantly more than with others, a *subculture* can emerge that is characterized by a unique set of behaviors and beliefs, including language, dialect, or vocabulary. This often occurs among immigrants who speak the same language, or share the same country of origin or ethnic background (e.g., Jewish Americans or Greek Canadians). Isolation within a larger culture, by choice, by discrimination, or by force, can lead to the development of a subculture (e.g., among convicts, soldiers, or residents of institutions).

In SI theory, social practices can be understood as products of interaction, or *social constructions*, which can be social, physical, or even systems of communication, such as language. Settlements, buildings, and products, including the virtual environment, are elements of material culture produced by human societies. As one form of social construction, they embody the values and attitudes of the society that makes them (Rapoport 1969). Just like social institutions, material culture acts as an agent to transmit values to future inhabitants by structuring social relations. This is particularly true of buildings and settlements because of their long lives and the great expense required to modify them (Hillier and Hanson 1984). For example, a hospital building is designed to fit a specific social organization. By its design, it creates constraints that limit the form and practices of social organizations that are housed within it, although there is a degree of slack that allows some variation.

Some artifacts, such as sake cups, chopsticks, baseball bats, or recycling containers, owe their existence to customs of a society. Due to the universal needs of the human body and child rearing, many similar products can be found across diverse human civilizations. The characteristics of these products, however, vary greatly from society to society. Thus, although human bodies are constructed of the same parts everywhere, clothing is very different from society to society due to differences in cultural attitudes toward presentation of self, comfort, modesty, and aesthetic preferences. In a globalizing world, the diversity of material culture across the globe is diminishing due to both the economics of large-scale production and the common aspirations of consumers.

From the perspective of SI theory, any social practices, including face-to-face interaction patterns and informal or formal organizations, reflect the values of the people who participate in them and who perpetuate them. Just as the self can be seen as a reflection of the person in the looking glass of society, social participation patterns can be viewed as reflections of the society that created them. Changes in these patterns likewise reflect the changes in a society. As an example, Duncan (1981) describes the transformation of a home as a "container of women" to a "status symbol" as a society shifts from a "collectivist" orientation to an "individualist" orientation.

As noted in Chapter 3, one of the most important social changes in the world today is the increase in size of the older population. Businesses tend to view "design for aging" as the way to address this population group's needs and desires. However, the cultural attitudes toward aging play an important role in how designs will be received. Design for aging is a very hard sell if it is not presented in a culturally appropriate manner (Burke 1981–82). Basic accessibility features, such as a one-story house plan or grab bars in showers, may be viewed negatively by the very people who need them the most. Later in life, changing abilities and social status require psychological adjustment. Nevertheless, in a culture that is youth oriented, not everyone will admit that their abilities and needs are different from what they were when they were younger. They attempt to avoid the stigma associated with old age by avoiding the outward appearance of decline. Thus, they resist using a cane, wearing a hearing aid, or installing bathroom grab bars. Purchasers of retirement housing seem to have no hesitation buying into expensive "active living" retirement communities designed with bedrooms on second floors served only by stairs, raised whirlpool tubs, or steps at all entries to the home. The most important features to them are the social clubhouse and the recreational facilities, symbolizing an active lifestyle.

Designers need to address these important emotional issues with creative solutions. How can environments and products that provide accessibility and health benefits also be attractive to the older generation? Universal design demands that this question be addressed. For example, can toilets come with arms like armchairs? Can hearing aids look like jewelry or be integrated into smart phones? Can canes be designed to be fashion accessories as well as providing additional functional benefits beyond support for balance? How can media help to overcome stigma? Manufacturers and developers have to give more attention to these questions and think about how their business practices can avoid the stigma associated with "design for aging" and appeal to the broader population.

Like health and wellness, achieving full social participation for all citizens is not possible without significant social changes in many countries and even within specific social organizations. How many countries, for example, have laws that protect people with mental illness from discrimination in housing, let alone provide appropriate accommodations? How many have laws that protect people who are transgendered from discrimination, let alone provisions to provide safe access to public bathrooms? Thus, social change may be required before universal design goals can be achieved at their highest level. However, in any particular social organization, such as a commercial establishment or a social housing project, it may be possible to meet these goals at a higher level than in the rest of society. Social participation as an overarching design goal particularly demonstrates the need for a broad perspective on universal design practice, one that incorporates policy, business practices and services, as well as design.

The three social participation Goals of Universal Design—Social Integration, Personalization, and Cultural Appropriateness—are highly related and are addressed in similar ways. Thus, it is more appropriate to discuss them together than apart and to demonstrate the interrelationships. However, it is useful to distinguish the aspects of environment that have a direct and indirect influence on achievement of social participation. The environment of *interpersonal interaction* is the most direct way that social participation is experienced. The environment supporting interpersonal interaction includes furniture arrangements and the space provided for interaction in the near environment of rooms, outdoor spaces, public transportation, and social media. *Access to resources* in the community and *clustering* are two key vehicles for supporting social participation. This includes use of policies and spatial practices, such as the organization of space, to reduce forced segregation of devalued groups and support communication. The *practice of design* itself needs to be structured so that diverse groups have a voice in the production of material culture. It is important to note that social participation is also influenced by social policies and programs that can constrain or facilitate the construction of settlements, buildings, products, and other artifacts.

Interpersonal Interaction

The quality of social interaction in the physical world is shaped by interpersonal interaction distances (Hall 1969). Thus, maintaining appropriate distances is crucial to ensuring social integration. The face-to-face distance individuals maintain between each other while interacting is strongly related to emotions. Comfortable social interaction distances are based on the type of interaction desired at any one time and cultural patterns (Cultural Appropriateness). By providing space and "props" that allow people to maintain appropriate distances, individuals feel more secure and stress is reduced. Where interaction is primarily unilateral, as in a lecture room, the speaker needs to speak loudly to communicate; the speaker cannot be too close, or the audience will be uncomfortable. At the other extreme, one-to-one interaction requires speaking softly and, in some cultures, touching; thus, furniture arrangements that space people too far apart can create barriers to friendship formation and intimacy, such as the comfort extended by friends and family at a time of grief. Note that the angle of face-to-face contact is also important. In some situations, direct face-to-face positions are confrontational. Angled positions may reduce conflict and increase informal interaction (Sommer 1969).

To ensure that the goal of Social Integration will be met, social distances and interpersonal relationships have to support good-quality communication in places where social interaction is a key activity (e.g., a restaurant or a hotel lobby). To ensure that the goal of Personalization is met, individuals should have opportunities to pursue the type of social interaction they desire (e.g., public or private, exposed or hidden, etc.). In other words, social interaction spaces should provide the support people need to adjust their relationships to each other and to the public at large. This applies to subcultural groups as well as individuals. For example, in public spaces, options for gathering and people-watching should be available for low-income individuals as well as those with the money to pay for more luxurious accommodations, or for people who cannot use stairs and for those who can. To ensure that the goal of Cultural Appropriateness is met, local customs and expectations should be addressed. For example, in some cultures, it is appropriate for men and women to share toilet rooms or unisex facilities, but in others, this would not be acceptable. And some places are designed for very public types of behavior. Providing conditions to support intimate interaction between couples in those places would be undesirable.

The most important factor in establishing supportive interpersonal interaction is culture. There are major differences in the interaction distances used by individuals based on whether a culture is a contact culture or a non-contact culture. Mediterranean, Middle Eastern, and Latin American countries, for example, are contact cultures whereas the United States and Japan are non-contact cultures. Moreover, cultural differences in patterns of behavior also have an impact on space design. In some cultures, dining on the floor is customary; in others, it is not. Thus, it may be desirable to have different types of seating where people of different cultures are likely to be visiting. For example, in a Japanese restaurant, both in Japan and abroad, it is not uncommon to find both traditional seating on floor mats and Western style seating at tables. In some cultures, everyone shares food from a common vessel, and in others they each have their own servings. Each approach to serving may require a different table type and size. Interaction distances vary with different types of relationships, and may be closer in contact cultures than in non-contact cultures. It is important to note that, in face-to-face interaction, being too far away is as bad as being too close. Each type of social interaction has its own appropriate distance zone. The box "Interpersonal Distances" provides a description of appropriate social interaction distances for different purposes, based on North American culture.

Interpersonal Distances

Have you ever felt uncomfortable when a relative stranger stands too close to you? Culture dictates the interpersonal distances people keep when they interact. People often keep these distances unconsciously. Misunderstandings about interpersonal distance are often used as a source of comedy—close proximity is misinterpreted as a desire for a more intimate relationship that leads to embarrassment or anger. Despite some rare mistakes, most people conform to the "appropriate" distance, learned from their surroundings and upbringing. Edward Hall (1969) identified four zones of comfortable interpersonal distances based on the nature of people's relationships: intimate, personal, social, and public. But the dimensions of these zones vary based on culture and other factors. Designers need to become aware of culturally appropriate interpersonal distances so they can support face-to-face interaction and avoid designing spaces that cause alienation. The following zone descriptions represent Hall's findings for American interpersonal distances.

Hall defines intimate space as closer than 18 inches (45 cm). The close phase (closer than 6 inches [15 cm] or touching) is often for love, comfort, and protection, but also can be for a passionate argument (think of a baseball manager yelling in an umpire's face). Often these distances are not seen in public between adults. Although crowded transit systems may force people closer than desired, even into contact, people will withdraw and tense their muscles to limit contact as a response to the lack of comfort in these situations. Hall defines personal space as ranging from 1.5 to 4 feet (45–123 cm). This is a "normal" contact distance for communications in public. The close personal zone (1.5–2.5 feet [45–76 cm]) would be acceptable, for instance, for domestic partners or lovers to maintain in public but not appropriate for other pairs. The outer limits of the personal zone would be acceptable for conversation about topics of personal interest. The social zone (4–12 feet [123–366 cm]) is acceptable for a wide range of contact types. It is typical in business settings and used when people need to communicate in a way that is not intimate or personal. The close phase of the social zone (4–7 feet [123–213 cm]) is typical among coworkers and at social gatherings. The far phase of this zone is often for

> communications considered more formal, such as those between an executive and his or her employee. The desk of an executive is often wider than that of a typical employee to hold visitors to the far phase of this zone. The public zone is greater than 12 feet (366 cm); people generally keep this distance on formal occasions and between high-status figures.
>
> When the design of spaces and furniture does not support the appropriate social interaction types for location, people are uncomfortable, either because they have to act inappropriately to maintain contact (e.g., shout) or because they get too much information about the other person (e.g., body heat, smell of breath, eye contact, etc.).

Sensory access to others is an important factor in social relations. For example, research on the influence of table shape and seating location on social interaction shows that individuals seated at the head of a rectangular table will more likely dominate conversation than those sitting in other seats because they have visual access to everyone. Likewise, round and square tables tend to foster more involvement of all participants in a conversation (Altman and Chemers 1984). "Sociopetal" furniture arrangements are those that facilitate social interaction; "sociofugal" arrangements are those that discourage interaction (Hall 1969).

Spaces are sociopetal when they enhance communication in all the senses in an appropriate way for the specific interaction. Arranging chairs, for example, very close and at angles allows participants to see facial expressions clearly, touch, and hear each other at intimate conversation levels. This facilitates "personal" interaction between individuals because they get the feedback they need to ensure that the other person is paying close attention and to gauge the other's emotional response to the conversation. Where interaction among a group is desired, seating around a circle will increase face-to-face interaction and lead to more participation, while auditorium seating arrangements, where the audience can only see the speaker, will reduce interaction but maximize access between each audience member and the speaker and avoid distraction by irrelevant information. This distance also allows a degree of freedom for the "audience" to let attention lapse periodically. Spacing between people determines the character of a conversation; the farther away people sit from each other, the louder the participants have to speak and the more difficulty they will have perceiving nonverbal cues, such as facial expression and body language. Lighting and acoustics are important influences on communications, although they often are overlooked by designers, because they support or create barriers to interpersonal communications. Posture also plays an important role in social interaction both in terms of helping with communications, for example, leaning close to hear a whisper, and in terms of how the other party interprets body language, for example, threatening or friendly.

People with partial hearing and sight limitations need to have better support for maintaining interpersonal communications. High noise levels, glare, and low light levels can all affect the quantity and quality of the information they obtain during interpersonal relations. People who are hard of hearing may need alternative listening systems to provide an amplified signal. Those with no functional hearing or sight need compensatory sources of information. For example, people who are deaf or hearing-impaired need to be able to see their companions well to lip-read or sign; so, in a group, they need to have a direct line of sight to all the people involved in the conversation. Blind individuals depend more on hearing, so they require a higher-quality acoustic environment to maintain good conversations. It is difficult for a person sitting and one standing to have a good conversation for very long because maintaining eye contact will cause fatigue for both, and the seated person will feel subordinate to the standing individual.

There is evidence that advanced age may lead to a "physiological screen" due to reductions in the quantity of sensory stimuli a person can receive, which results in a compensatory behavior by the older person during social interaction (Pastalan, Mautz, and Merrill 1973). Elders may reduce distances to hear and see better and may increase the use of touch to maintain contact during social interaction. Some older people even hold on to the arm of those with whom they are conversing. One researcher, observing this in an American context, explained this as a way to prevent the younger person from pulling away because a very close interaction distance (within 18 inches [45 mm]) with a stranger is uncomfortable for them (DeLong 1970). When older people cannot obtain the information they need for maintaining good interpersonal communications, they may withdraw and avoid contact. Thus, it is common for older people who have hearing limitations to avoid noisy places and events.

When designers give more attention to social interaction spaces, they not only provide a more inclusive environment that encourages participation by a larger number and variety of people, they also provide an environment that responds to individual differences. In many cases, providing choices and flexibility can avoid potential conflicts. For example, restaurants often have adjustable lighting controls, but only for large zones in the space such as an entire room. Different zones can accommodate people with different abilities and provide flexibility for different types of social interaction. Control of the lighting at each table allows customers to make choices appropriate to their needs. A single person eating alone may want to read while waiting to be served whereas a couple having a romantic dinner may want to eat by candlelight. Likewise, dining rooms that provide spaces with different levels of acoustic control can provide a choice to eat in either a festive, noisy environment or a quiet setting. Providing a variety of different table sizes and shapes or the ability to combine tables creates the flexibility to accommodate parties of different sizes. Seating arrangements can incorporate chairs that can be moved easily to address cultural differences, differences in the level of intimacy desired, or the needs of people who have hearing and vision limitations. Space for wheelchairs or flexible seating arrangements allows people who are ambulatory to sit down when talking with those who are using wheeled mobility devices, providing more equitable and comfortable face-to-face interaction. In general, having seating available wherever there is likely to be social interaction is a benefit for elders and others with limitations of stamina or who have pain from standing for long periods of time.

In the virtual environment, fewer factors determine the quality of interpersonal communications. These factors are mostly related to the quality of software and hardware and access to it. For example, low bandwidth can limit the quality of real-time video interaction. The rapid development of telecommunications and social media can be viewed as an important advance in interpersonal communications, the use of technology to overcome barriers of distance. Issues of privacy are clearly just as important, if not more important, than in the physical world since everything we do or say in cyberspace can be recorded. As the virtual environment develops in sophistication, particularly as technology allows continual contact with others, it is likely that software will provide us with the virtual equivalent of the social interaction zones. There are already signs of that they are emerging. Internet users often adopt different personas online for different types of interaction, such as business, family or work. Social media sites provide some adjustability such as blocking access to content and deciding who receives notifications of new content posted on a site. We can expect more sophistication in online social relations as this media is further developed, such as automated mediation of interaction between people based on the purpose (e.g., business or friendship) of the contact and who the parties are (e.g., close associates or clients).

The widespread use of personal communication devices has an important impact on social behavior. For example, when people need to have an intimate conversation on a mobile phone, they often leave a group to find somewhere with more privacy to talk. Thus, designers now have to consider the use of these devices in the design of public and shared spaces. If there are no places nearby to have an intimate conversation on a mobile phone, people may simply leave the area to find one. Doing this may disrupt group dynamics, particularly in a work or social setting. The opposite problem is an invasion of personal space, where individuals have intimate conversations in inappropriate places. Some people use electronic messages to avoid face-to-face social interaction (Sommer 2002). This behavior may not be conducive to the health of an organization, friendship, or individual mental health. Design of environments that reduce avoidance behavior by supporting privacy could be one solution to this problem, which is discussed in the next section.

Access to Resources

As the various UN conventions on human rights affirm, just societies should protect all their citizens from discrimination in politics, civic life, employment, education, healthcare, recreation, public transportation, and other public services. The Convention on the Rights of People with Disabilities supports the right of all individuals to "full and effective participation and inclusion in society" (United Nations 2006, Article 3). Accessibility regulations address this goal by ensuring that the design of the physical and virtual environments and some products do not create barriers, from a human performance perspective, but regulations do not dictate other aspects of the design that facilitate social integration and personalization. Examples include design of space to support friendship formation, privacy, territoriality, and control. Today, these issues are most relevant to the design of communities, buildings, and sites where people have face-to-face relationships rather than the virtual environment. However, as the latter evolves, we may see the same issues emerging in cyberspace.

Spatial proximity plays a major role in structuring social interaction patterns. Research has demonstrated that people who live close to each other are more likely to become friends (Michelson 1976). This is because there is a higher probability that "neighbors" will come into social contact with each other because they share more spaces with their neighbors than with those who live farther away. There are two types of proximity: physical and functional (Festinger, Schachter, and Back 1950). The former is the actual distance between one space and another measured as the crow flies. The latter is the distance measured along the path of travel between people based on the circulation path between two points.

In Figure 7–1, dwelling A is physically closer to dwelling B, but dwelling A and dwelling C are functionally closer because they share a circulation pathway and, thus, the inhabitants are more likely to have face-to-face contact. Other shared spaces cause functional proximity; these include clusters of mailboxes, laundry rooms, neighborhood services used by all residents, and water fountains and coffee stations in a work setting. Since people select their friends based mostly on shared interests, the influence of proximity is most powerful when all the occupants of a building or area are homogeneous (Michelson 1976). This homogeneity provides more opportunities

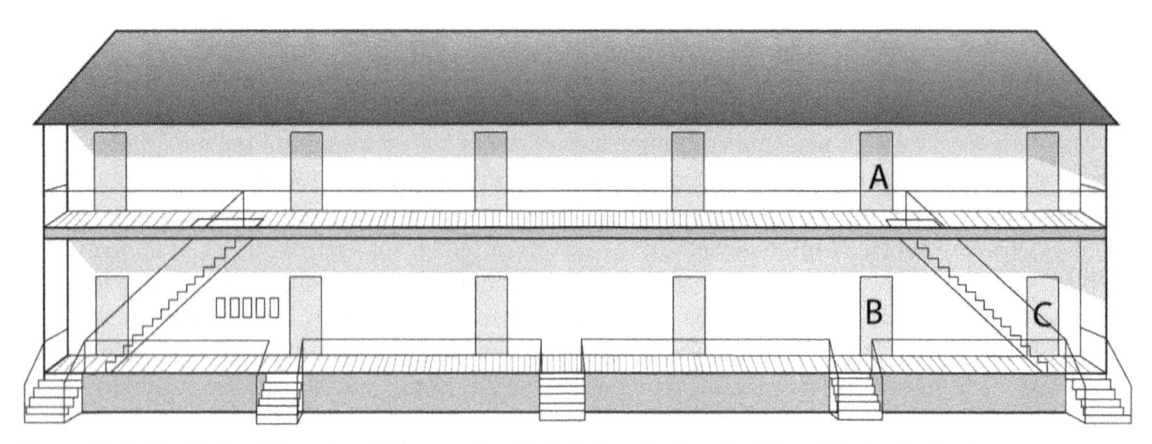

Figure 7–1: Physical and functional distance. In this building design, dwelling A is physically closer to dwelling B because they share a floor/ceiling. But, functionally, it is closer to dwelling C because the inhabitants of dwelling A will encounter those in dwelling C more often as they enter and leave their homes.
Source: Adapted from Festinger, Schacter, and Back (1950).

to make friends within the occupant population as compared to within a more heterogeneous group. Thus, proximity can be very effective in promoting friendship formation in housing where residents tend to be in the same socioeconomic group and stage of life, in places of employment, in educational facilities, and in many other settings.

Territorial control is a major goal of architectural design. For example, banks must control access to the money and information that they protect; public recreation programs cannot simply let people take equipment or use facilities without exerting some control; individual families have to protect their possessions and privacy. Territorial behavior establishes the ownership of space and determines who can access and who is excluded, and what behaviors are allowed (Altman and Chemers 1984). Territorial control essentially is a regulatory function that maintains stability in human settlements by ensuring both fair access to public facilities and maintenance of property rights for individuals.

Territorial control, as described in Chapter 1, can be used to isolate and abuse minorities, particularly those who are not able to protect themselves. In the movement for civil rights of racial minorities, fair and equal access to community resources is a focus of community action. Accessibility policies and regulations are a similar strategy to ensure that people with disabilities are treated fairly. However, unlike policies supporting civil rights of racial minorities, accessibility policies do not address community planning and development, only the individual land uses. Public space access is a primary locus for informal social contact and civic engagement. In early human settlements, public streets and gathering spaces, such as town squares, were the only sites of public gatherings and free association. Planners have criticized the tendency toward the privatization of public space (Kohn 2004; Mitchell 2003). The owners of private shopping centers, for example, can evict visitors from their property they don't like (e.g., teenagers who hang around and socialize in malls), as long as they are not practicing discrimination. Through site selection, design, and access control, they can limit access to social groups. For example, denying a public transit agency permission to locate a bus stop at a shopping mall can effectively limit access by low-income people who depend on public transit. It can also put transit users at greater risk of victimization by criminals because it forces them to traverse a large parking lot and public streets to reach a bus stop late at night. In the traditional street, however, private entities do not have a legal right to chase people off the sidewalk in front of their land, and they cannot prohibit the location of a bus stop on their block.

Universal designers should support planning and design that ensures access to public spaces for all citizens. For example, shopping centers and large recreational sites, even if privately owned, should have direct access by public transportation and pedestrian pathways. Development of private/public partnerships can be used to facilitate good accessibility. Many transit agencies that own land in prime retail locations are developing partnerships with real estate developers. The agencies grant air rights to build shopping, retail, and offices above terminals and parking facilities. In such partnerships, public agencies can ensure that financing from commercial developers provides a higher standard of accessibility, convenience, and safety for transportation facilities, housing opportunities for transit-dependent people, and other public benefits, while obtaining capital to improve transportation infrastructure.

Figure 7–2 is a photo of Mizner Park (see also Figure 2–4). This project was completed on the site of a bankrupt shopping mall in Boca Raton, Florida The city took over control of the property and prepared a development plan that included housing and civic buildings, as well as

Figure 7–2: Mizner Park in Boca Raton, FL. The street is bounded by buildings with shops below and apartments above. On-street parking is provided, and there is a recreation space with attractive landscaping in the middle of the divided street.

commercial facilities built around a public streetscape reminiscent of a Spanish *rambla*—a public pedestrian space in between vehicular traffic. The exclusive private nature of the original mall has been abandoned with the introduction of the central streetscape and civic buildings and the presence of housing above the commercial space, which gives a 24-hour life to the place. Public parking lots are set behind the mixed-use buildings with reserved access to spaces for residents.

Privacy behavior is used to control access to information about the self (Altman and Chemers 1984). People use many methods to obtain privacy, including personal reserve, clothing, environmental props, distance, and barriers to information flow. Buildings establish a structure through which inhabitants regulate the flow of information between themselves and others. Social interaction levels are related to the amount of privacy one has available. For example, people who live in shared rooms will interact less in public spaces to compensate for lack of privacy in their bedrooms (Lawton and Nahemow 1973). By paying close attention to privacy needs, universal designers can provide appropriate conditions for inhabitants that reinforce social engagement and maintain privacy.

People use spaces to modulate the degree of privacy and social interaction they desire at any one time. Archea (1984) demonstrated that social uses of space are related to visual access and exposure from point to point. For example, older people in a nursing home unit will congregate at points that have high levels of both visual access and exposure to the rest of the unit, such as a nurse's station, which, in traditional nursing home designs, is usually situated in a strategic location, so nurses can maintain visual surveillance of the entire unit. People seeking intimacy or solitude, however, will seek out places that have a low level of visual exposure.

Access to information provides situational knowledge and control, but exposure produces obligations to behave in certain ways and reduces freedom of action. Some places can be highly exposed and have high levels of access at the same time. Others can have high access but much lower exposure. These are ideal locations to scope out the social opportunities before deciding to make oneself available for contact. Furthermore, by moving in space, we can adjust our levels quite dramatically, even if we move just a few paces, such as around a corner. Architects and interior designers can ensure that levels of access and exposure are appropriate for the place and that they provide a range of choices that suit the needs of occupants. This design strategy is very important in group residential occupancies, places of employment, libraries, and other locations where there is a dynamic relationship between affiliation and privacy. At some times, individuals need privacy; at other times, they need opportunities for social interaction.

Privacy is also used for protection. Some activities put people at risk if done in public. For example, sleeping in a public place can result in victimization. Women, in particular, can become victims of assault simply by being alone in public places. In some societies, girls are not allowed to attend school because of concerns about modesty that prohibit them from using the outdoors for relieving themselves, even though there is no such prohibition for boys. Thus, the lack of private toilet facilities in schools restricts girls' access to education, which is a denial of human rights.

It is important to note that the use of information and communications technology can subvert the social functions of space. For example, violent or suicidal prisoners may be placed under constant surveillance, even in remote and hidden locations. Likewise, in public spaces under surveillance, the ability to escape exposure, and thus have freedom of action, has been reduced. On one hand, the use of technology can increase social control and reduce privacy, but on the other, it also can be used to increase situational awareness and knowledge of the world, a type of augmented perception. A good example is the ability to tap into webcams on highways to see the level of congestion prior to selecting a route. In the village culture of preindustrial societies, everyone knew everyone else's business, so social pressure to conform was high. The new "intrusiveness," if not abused, could actually herald a return to more civil behavior in public.

The organization of space plays an important role in access to resources. Hillier and Hanson (1984) proposed that there are two fundamental types of "spatial syntax": treelike and ringlike spatial organizations (Figure 7–3). Spatial syntax structures the interaction between inhabitants, between inhabitants and the outside world, and between parts of buildings. Hillier and Hanson

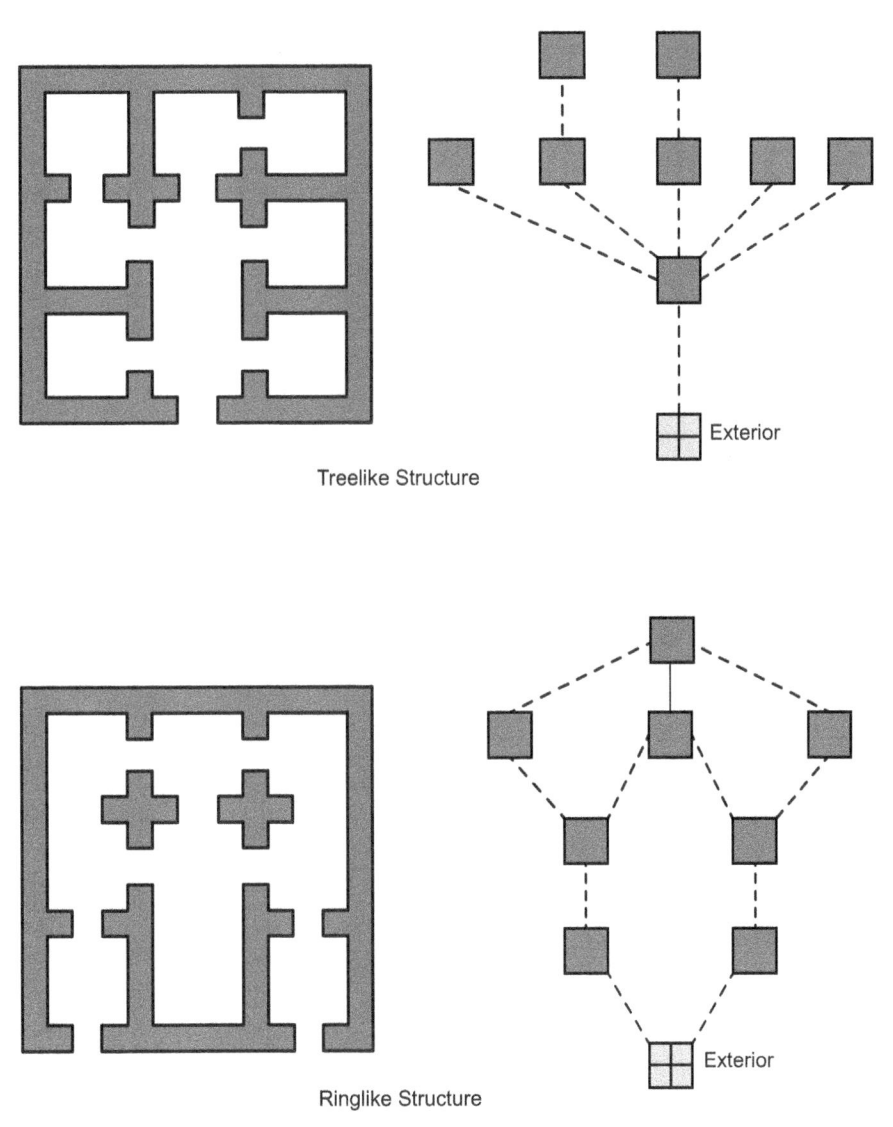

Figure 7–3: Two basic types of spatial syntax. The figures and related diagrams show two distinctly different spatial organizations. The first is a treelike organization in which each successive space leads to another and moving from those deeper into the building requires doubling back down the tree. The second is a ringlike organization in which one can proceed to make a circuit of spaces without doubling back.

Source: Adapted from Hiller and Hanson (1984).

demonstrated that treelike spatial organizations have a high degree of control over access from one space to another or to the outside. In ringlike buildings or settlements, there is less control because there are more alternative paths to the same destination. Treelike organizations are more likely to be found in types of buildings and settlements where control is the driving principle (e.g., prisons, institutions, military bases); ringlike organizations are more likely to be found in places where freedom of movement and communication is valued (e.g., workplaces, educational facilities, public parks).

Spatial syntax can also be characterized in terms of "depth," or the number of steps through distinct spaces that it takes to penetrate to the deepest location in a spatial organization. Deep buildings are less well integrated into the surrounding community than shallow buildings because they put more social distance between inhabitants and others. Individual homes and retail stores are generally shallow; hospitals or administrative headquarters are deep. These examples, however, are just generalizations. Each building may have sections that are treelike and others that are ringlike, some that are deep, and some that are shallow. The depth of spatial patterns also applies to neighborhoods. Figure 7–4 shows two street patterns for a neighborhood. In Figure 7–4a, the street pattern, a conventional grid, keeps the number of steps to reach a house to a minimum. In Figure 7–4b, a branching street pattern making heavy use of cul-de-sacs, each home is many steps in from the entry point.

Spatial syntax analysis can help to identify where the organization of space may be causing barriers to social interaction. Then, interventions can be planned to alter the syntax or develop compensatory features. For example, in the conversion of an old psychiatric facility to residential use, the facility's deep treelike spatial syntax might need to be addressed to ensure that residents are not isolated from one another. If office uses were contemplated, ensuring access to the public and communications between one department and another would be critical. In communities, a treelike spatial syntax can make travel from one point to another more difficult and increase congestion at certain points. In the plans shown in Figure 7–5, urban designers discovered that by adding a few missing links in the street pattern, they could create better circulation in the community, which would facilitate the utilization of public transportation, improve access to civic locations, and reduce congestion.

Hillier and Hanson (1984) also make a distinction between two types of building occupants: residents and visitors. Residents are those who control access to spaces; visitors are those who are given permission by residents to occupy spaces temporarily. In each building, residents have a higher social status than visitors do, which enables them to control the space. The territories of residents are more likely to be found in the "deepest" part of a building, but there are some buildings, which the authors call "reversed buildings," where visitors are found deep within the structure. A good example is a prison or hospital. In these buildings, the staff members are the residents, and the prisoners and patients are the visitors. In some cases, as in prisons, "visitors" might inhabit the building for very long periods of time, even longer than some residents.

Segregation and Clustering

There are many examples of forced segregation, through which groups are kept separated from others due to beliefs that the group is dangerous to society or less than human, or simply due to historical animosity and conflicts over territory. Forced segregation is obviously counter to the goals of universal design. Separation intended to reduce conflict between parties at war or

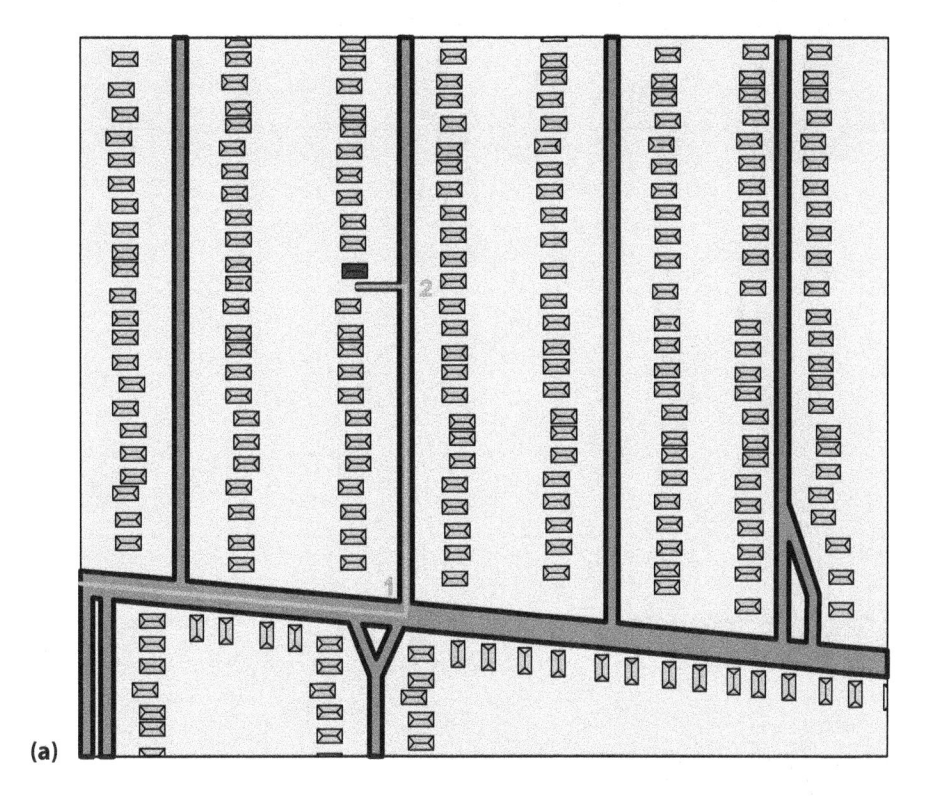

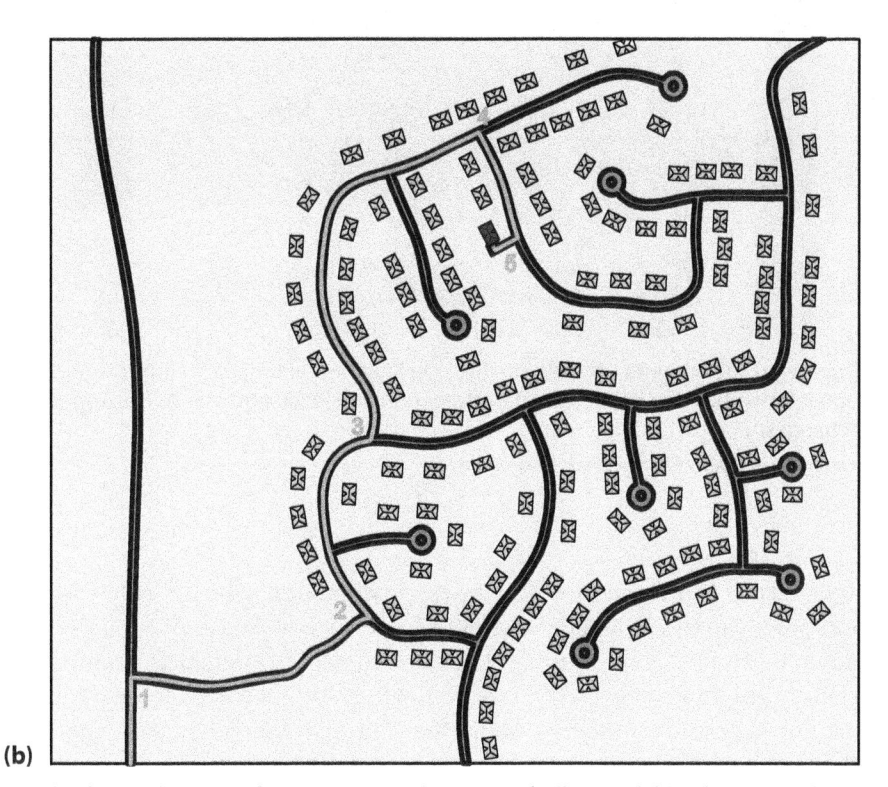

Figure 7-4: Depth of spatial syntax. The two images show (a) a shallow and (b) a deep spatial syntax.

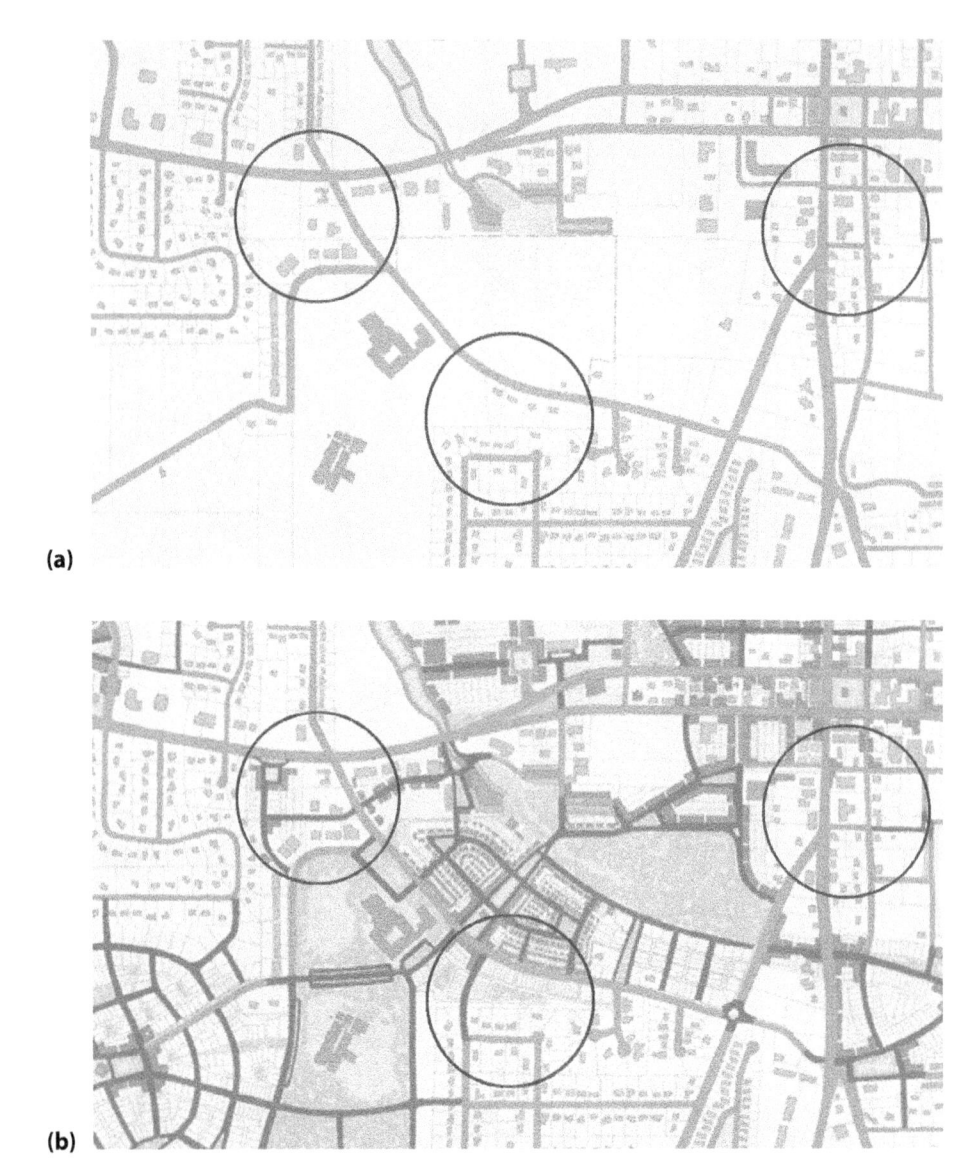

Figure 7-5: Improving spatial syntax. By adding "missing links" in the original neighborhood street pattern, an urban design intervention can improve social interaction and local mobility. (a) Existing street pattern. (b) Proposed changes.

Source: Images courtesy of Duany Plater-Zyberk & Company.

as a protective measure is different. In these cases, separation may be the only way to reduce loss of life and protect innocent and defenseless people from violence. As long as human rights are addressed on both sides of the boundary, separation may be needed as a temporary solution to reduce conflict, just as when two children are fighting and they need to be pulled apart. Segregation at this scale is obviously not under the control of individual designers. Broader issues must be addressed by diplomats, activists, politicians, and military forces. It is important for designers, however, to recognize these conditions and their causes.

Underprivileged groups often voluntarily cluster together to provide mutual support and protection in enclaves. *Voluntary* clustering like this can be beneficial to minority groups, especially immigrants, low-income individuals, homeless people, or victims of spousal abuse (Rapoport 1977). Such clustering, which may be at any scale from a small building to a large squatter settlement, allows group members to live in a supportive community of peers, learn a new language and new customs, obtain an education or job training, overcome substance dependencies, and build skills for future integration into the majority culture. Where there are no discriminatory barriers to prevent such integration, residents of enclaves (e.g., ethnic neighborhoods) usually integrate into the majority culture over time; in some cases, however, some groups prefer to remain to preserve deeply held religious and cultural values. Often enclaves of "devalued" people are viewed by a majority culture as slums that are both unhealthy for their occupants and generators of social pathology, but, in fact, research has demonstrated that such settlements support a rich social life (Fried 1972; Gans 1962). Methods can be used to upgrade substandard housing and public hygiene conditions without destroying the social fabric of such communities (Turner 1976; Turner and Fichter 1972).

Housing policy has a major impact on social integration. Through government policy, the most grievous practices that reinforce stigma can be prevented. In the United States, the Olmstead Law gives people with disabilities a legal right to living accommodations that provide the "least restrictive" environment and are integrated into the community (*Olmstead v. L.C.*, 98–536 C.F.R. 1999). However, in implementing policies like this, attention to the design of buildings and how they are managed is critical; otherwise, "mini-institutions" will simply take the place of larger institutions. Research demonstrates that design features of community residences for people with disabilities and other devalued groups can perpetuate negative and stereotypical attitudes if they are institutional in appearance (Butterfield 1984; Liu 1991; Robinson, Thompson, Emmons, Graff, and Franklin 1984; Thompson, Robinson, Dietrich, Farris, and Sinclair 1996; Vegso 1992). The buildings need to be the right scale to fit into the neighborhood's context, which means that a one-size-fits-all approach will not work. For example, a one-story, 5,000-square-foot (SF) (500 square meter [SM]) home on a street filled with two-story 2,000-SF (200-SM) houses will look awkward and out of place. A large parking area for staff, a tall carport to unload high-top vans, and long access ramps with railings will make the difference even worse. Residential details, including roof shape, windows, level of detail, materials, and landscaping are also important for a good fit.

Deinstitutionalization

In North America and Europe, people with developmental disabilities and mental health conditions were often incarcerated in large residential institutions (Rothman 1971; Wolfensberger 1975). These buildings were constructed with a deep treelike spatial syntax and protected perimeters to control access by the public and prevent "escape" by residents. Such facilities needed large parcels of land because the land was often farmed to provide food for the institution. They were isolated from the surrounding communities by distance and physical barriers. The interiors had an institutional atmosphere, characterized by high levels of visual access by staff, high levels of exposure of residents (little privacy), and sociofugal furniture arrangements, as well as institutional fixtures and materials. This atmosphere reduced social interaction, discouraged visitors, and increased control (and the potential for abuse) by the staff (Sommer 1974; Wolfensberger 1975).

The "community residence" concept was developed in the 1970s as an alternative to reduce the social isolation that such facilities create (Robinson et al. 1984; Thompson et al. 1996; Vegso 1992). Each residence houses 6 to 12 people in a family-style arrangement, with support staff and residential furniture arrangements. The spatial syntax of these residences is as close to a single-family home as possible, very shallow in depth and contains spaces with a rich range of access and exposure conditions, including privacy and intimacy in resident bedrooms. Because of their small scale, they can be located on residential streets, within apartment buildings, and near commercial districts. The concept is welcoming to visitors, including youth groups and religious organizations, as well as family and friends, and increases exposure to the public, reducing the potential for abuse.

Research on the benefits of community residences has demonstrated the great positive impact of this strategy for the residents, including improvements in independent functioning and social behavior (Vegso 1992). Community residences were initially intended to be homes for "higher-functioning residents," those who professionals believed, due to less severe disabilities, were capable of more independence and integration into the community. But success with this group and pressure from advocates of institutionalized people eventually led authorities to extend the use of group homes to house even residents with very severe impairments like those who have limited ability to communicate and very restricted mobility. Simply due to their small size, these residences improve the quality of life for individuals with severe disabilities because the residents have more personal relationships with a smaller staff and their peers. The staff can more easily bring residents outdoors and to community recreation sites, and it is also easier to engage residents in making decisions about their immediate living environment like decoration of the rooms. Moreover, the more residential atmosphere of the buildings provides a higher level of stimulation. Even if the residents have limited communication abilities, staff can notice the difference in emotional response to environmental stimulation and adjust the environment to fit the needs and limitations of specific residents. The provision of a more normative residential environment supports the development of a normative lifestyle and reduces symptoms of institutional care, helping to overcome stigma and prejudice toward severely disabled people.

To overcome entrenched interests, significant policy changes had to be implemented to dismantle large institutions and create an entirely new approach to housing people with developmental disabilities. Similar changes are occurring in the long-term care industry. Recently, groups in the United States have developed a small scale living concept, called The Green House® Project (www.thegreenhouseproject.org), to house frail older people as an alternative to large age-segregated care facilities (Rabig et al. 2006). The Green House model, and other competing "brands," can help to break down the spatial barriers to community engagement caused by larger-scale institutional buildings. These barriers include great functional distances between residents and friends and relatives who live elsewhere and a deep spatial syntax that discourages interaction with the "outside," even those who live in a different part of the same institution.

Design Participation

The social construction paradigm leads directly to a critique of professional design practices that exclude representation of end users in the design process. Since the social processes that produce the designed environment shape the environment, if elements of society are not well represented in the process, it is likely that their perspective will not be well represented in the final product. In the field of barrier-free design, this fact became quite obvious early on. The professionals who were developing the first codes and standards needed to understand the experiences of people with disabilities before they could identify the best way to eliminate barriers to independence in the buildings and outdoor environments. The best way to do that was to engage representatives of that group in identifying common barriers. This was accomplished by including advocates for different groups in the standards development process and in building design projects, particularly public buildings and facilities.

Designers have learned the value of citizen participation in many other contexts, especially in housing. Working in squatter settlements, design professionals have learned that low-income people not only are valuable partners in design but also can build better-quality housing for lower costs than when government tries to do it for them (Alexander 1985; Turner 1976). Architectural theorists in the 1970s developed several approaches to design that facilitate participation of end users (Alexander, Ishikawa, and Silverstein 1977; Habraken 1972). These approaches provide a social and procedural structure within which design takes place, increasing efficiency and reducing conflicts. Due to constraints of budgets or time, it is not always possible to involve end users in the design process, and not all end users want to be involved. In many building projects, the actual occupants of the building may not even be known prior to completion of the building. However, finding ways to obtain the perspective of building users is an essential part of universal design practice and is one way to ensure that the social participation goals of universal design will be met. Thus, in the development of universal design standards, the Global Universal Design Commission has included points for end user participation (Global Universal Design Commission 2010).

One of the most interesting examples of end user participation is the cohousing movement (McCamant and Durrett 1994). Denmark, where cohousing originated, has adopted a policy for development of all social housing projects that engages prospective residents from project conception through management. The process starts with the formation of a cohousing community by a few future residents. This group is expanded until almost all the future residents of the community are identified. Using professional facilitation, the group then finds property, selects an architect, and participates in the design of their community and individual homes. The government social housing program provides guidelines within which the group must work, such as maximum dwelling unit sizes, cost constraints, land development guidelines, and deliverables. Each cohousing community is autonomous within the constraints of government rules and the budget provided for development. In the design process, the community makes decisions about the site plan, dwelling unit design, and construction methods with the guidance of the team of professional consultants and a development facilitator provided by the government program. Designers usually present options to the community for discussion and selection, gradually working toward a resolution.

Once the project is completed, the cohousing community continues to manage the community property, which often includes volunteer work in maintenance, improvements, and construction of amenities. In some communities, residents participate in the construction of their own units

178   *Design for Social Participation*

as well. Residents of cohousing usually share several meals a week, preparing them cooperatively. Cooperative child care, gardening, and other activities are also often part of community life. In the United States and in Denmark, commitment to a sustainable lifestyle is often a major founding principle of cohousing communities. Figure 7–6 is a community facility of a cohousing project in Denmark. This building was built by the residents and was constructed using timber frame and straw bale construction. A related outdoor community space is visible to the left between the shed and the building. Figure 7–7 shows houses in a suburban cohousing community in Atlanta, Georgia Because two early members of the community used wheelchairs, this community decided that all the homes and all the common facilities should be accessible to ensure full social integration of all members. Figure 7–8 shows an urban cohousing community in Boston, Massachusetts. This community is also completely accessible and has some units for elders right in the community building, where they have enclosed access to the shared facilities and an elevator. Elder cohousing is a new trend. Most multigenerational communities give a high priority to child rearing. Thus, elders are establishing their own communities, either separate or affiliated with a larger multigenerational community, to focus on the priorities of aging. Chapter 9 features an example of an elder cohousing project in Denmark that incorporates a high level of universal design as a major feature.

Figure 7–6: Community building, Roskilde, Denmark. This small building provides a space for residents of a cohousing community to gather informally on a daily basis. The residents prepare and enjoy meals together here at least three days a week.

Figure 7-7: Suburban cohousing community, Atlanta, GA. All the housing in this multigenerational cohousing community is accessible.

Figure 7-8: Urban cohousing in Boston, MA. The units designed for elders in this urban multigenerational cohousing community are located in closest proximity to the community building.

The cohousing development process is not without its limitations. In the United States, the developments are privately owned and have little government involvement, but projects often take years to complete. There are also difficulties with financing since the ownership structure is not typical. Common facilities are usually owned by the community organization, while individual units are owned by each household. In Scandinavia, dwellings tend to be smaller than the equivalent conventional units since 10 percent of the cost of each dwelling is turned over to the community to build the common spaces, effectively reducing the size of the individual units by about 10 percent. Developing a new community and managing it after construction without a management company requires significant member participation. Many people are not willing to accept the responsibility and time required to participate or do not wish to belong to such a close-knit community. Thus, cohousing members are generally people who value community building, a consensus process, and a close-knit community.

Cohousing represents the highest level of design participation. However, participation can be accomplished in many simpler and less intensive ways. The methods used can be tailored to the constraints of time and money. In cases where the end users are known (e.g., in building replacement or renovation projects), representative inhabitants of the old building can be organized into an advisory committee to provide input for the project through periodic review sessions. A diverse set of representatives should be included to obtain a wide range of insights; for example, women, people with disabilities, and different employee categories should be included. A second useful technique is called the charrette. In this workshop format, led by a facilitator, interested parties and/or the public attend an intensive session designed to solicit user requirements, design strategies, and ideas. If there is no existing building, representatives of the groups who are part of the target population to be served can be recruited. Several successive charrettes can be held during the course of a project.

Technology for improving understanding of designs and their implications can support design participation. Advanced visualization techniques, such as realistic computer-generated simulations, can be used to give people a virtual experience that simulates use of the building. Virtual reality techniques can be used to create a highly immersive simulation. Online surveys can also be used to solicit ideas, especially when as much input as possible is desired. Surveys may be useful for preserving confidentiality when participants are asked about sensitive issues that may jeopardize their employment or embarrass others. They are also useful for creating interest in more intensive involvement and for obtaining reality checks on ideas developed by an advisory committee.

In product design, end users are usually involved in the new product development process. Initial focus groups and interviews are used to define user requirements, followed by further focus groups where actual prototypes are evaluated (Caplan 1990). Alternative designs using rapid prototypes (e.g., full-scale mockups, nonworking prototypes, computer simulations, etc.) can be tested to evaluate alternative features. Later, as the design is narrowed down, working prototypes can be tested by focus groups or a set of individual consumers. In universal design, the goal of such participation is to widen the range of end users who are recruited to participate than would be the case in conventional practice. The range of end users recruited should be as diverse as possible to ensure that the product will be fully vetted; groups of different age groups, people of different sizes and abilities, and people of different income and ethnic backgrounds, for example, should be consulted.

Full-scale prototype testing is not common in architecture and interior design; however, there are many projects where hundreds of spaces of the same type may be included, for example, hospital rooms, hotel rooms or office workstations. In such projects, design participation through focus groups and user testing can be extremely valuable to fine-tune a design for the repetitive spaces and avoid omissions or mistakes that could multiply in significance once constructed. Another reason to invest in full-scale modeling is that a very expensive design element with critical human performance issues will be included. Examples are laboratories for special research equipment and hospital operating rooms.

Summary

To summarize the ideas in this chapter, we include here three examples that demonstrate the importance of social participation issues in design. The first, an example of voluntary clustering of older people, demonstrates that if the broader culture does not make "space" to support the aspirations of a group, by coming together in a protected environment, the group members will find a way to make a community that suits their needs. The second example, participation of women in the workplace, illustrates how changes in social attitudes led to major shifts in culture, including spatial practices, to enable social participation. The third, the policy of institutionalization of people with disabilities, which contributed to the oppression of Native Americans, demonstrates the vulnerability of a minority group and how spatial practices contributed to their oppression.

The lack of universal design in most communities creates a market for communities that are safer, more accessible, and more convenient. Some older people respond to the declines in performance associated with aging by clustering together in places where there are fewer social and environmental barriers to independence. Business interests have responded by creating age-restricted "retirement" communities. Examples are the Century Village communities in South Florida, the Leisure World communities, and the Del Webb communities. A visit to one of these places will convince casual visitors that life is quite different inside their boundaries and has many of the characteristics of a subculture. For example, daily activities revolve around leisure-time pursuits, such as sports, performances, and visual arts rather than work and business. Thus, retirement communities often have extensive art studios, well-equipped theaters, and exceptional sports facilities that enable seniors to participate in their chosen pursuits in a high-quality setting, without competition from younger people. Studying these large communities and smaller versions provides excellent insight into how universal design can appeal to the older population. These insights can be applied directly to design of age-friendly communities that are not age-segregated.

The Villages, an unincorporated community of over 75,000 people in Florida, north of Orlando is one the most interesting experiments in retirement living. Unlike most retirement communities, there are no gates to control access. It straddles three counties and, although it is not technically age restricted, it has an abnormally low population of adults of child-rearing age and thus only a very small population of persons under 18 (less than 1 percent). Like other retirement communities, The Villages is leisure-oriented, with many golf courses and even polo fields. It has several town centers with commercial, entertainment, and civic buildings. Its most unusual feature is an entire network of roads dedicated to electrically powered golf carts. One can drive a cart on these roads without a driver's license, although the design of the vehicles is regulated and there are speed limits. Carts are everywhere, to the extent that there are traffic jams at intersections on the cart network (Figure 7–9). Cart decoration and styling have even become a popular art form.

Figure 7-9: Golf cart traffic jam. Golf carts lined up at an intersection of golf cart trails at The Villages, FL.

There are still traffic jams on the local roads, however, because most of The Villages has been constructed using the American suburban low-density, automobile-oriented, single-land-use model. The popularity of the electric carts demonstrates residents' desire to maintain continuity with past suburban lifestyles and autonomy in mobility, but it also demonstrates a willingness to explore innovations. The very popular and lively town centers suggest that high-density mixed-use centers are very desirable to the 50-plus generation.

Historically, there have been barriers preventing women from participation in the workforce on an equal basis with men because of beliefs that women were not as capable as men or due to the perceived disruption of childbirth and child rearing. Barriers to participation of women in the workforce can be removed through social policy. Laws can mandate that, if a woman wants to get a job as a firefighter and is physically and intellectually qualified to do the work, she should receive a chance to compete for the job on an equal basis with men. Another example is parental leave, a policy under which an employer removes a barrier to continued employment of women immediately after childbirth. Design serves policy by supporting workforce participation for women. For example, if firefighting equipment and protective gear is designed for people of smaller stature and smaller hands, it will make firefighting easier for women to do (and perhaps also for many men). For the parenting problem, urban design and transportation can reduce the time of the trip to work; workplaces can incorporate child care settings; residential design can support working at home; and improved communications technologies can make it easier to raise children and still continue working. These are all examples of universal design, at many different scales. In conjunction with social policy—or even in its absence—they help to remove social participation barriers, but they require changes in policies and business practices before design can follow through.

Scholars in the field of disability studies have been investigating the intersection of disability with race, gender, and poverty. It is clear that the potential for discrimination is amplified when a person belongs to several different groups, each of which is subject to discrimination. For example, until the late twentieth century in the United States, discrimination against Native Americans was compounded by policies on educational and health services that served to fragment and disrupt family life and the maintenance of vital communities (Burch 2011). Youth were forcibly sent to regional "Indian schools" operated by the Bureau of Indian Affairs (BIA), a government agency, where they were isolated from their families. Agents of the BIA could decide, without a medical examination, that a student was "mentally ill." Agents often did so to get rid of disruptive or recalcitrant students. Such individuals were not sent to local institutions, where they could be close to family. Rather, they were sent to a special BIA-operated psychiatric facility, of which there were only two in the entire country. Native Americans from tribes based as far away as Florida were sent to the facility in North Dakota. There is evidence that the location was chosen because a state politician wanted to bring federal jobs to his constituency and the BIA wanted to ensure that families could not cause the agency trouble. Once incarcerated, inmates would have had to be very lucky to gain their freedom or see their families again. Such treatment was possible only because of the lack of protection for Native American rights and people with mental health conditions at the time. Where policies protect one minority group, they can help prevent oppression of others as well.

Research on the issues discussed in this chapter leads to 11 important guidelines on design to support social participation:

1. *Provide support for the human performance issues in social interaction.* Designers need to think about the ergonomics of social interaction as they design spaces where it is desirable to foster face-to-face contact and friendship formation. This includes providing opportunities to sit as well as stand, furniture arrangements that encourage eye contact, and interaction distances (head to head) that will support good communication. In addition, the ambient environment must support communication through good signal detection for both hearing and vision. Further, furniture and space sizes should support appropriate social interaction distances based on culture, age, and other personal factors.
2. *Implement sociopetal furniture arrangements.* Furniture arrangements should suit the type of social interaction desired in any particular location. Cluster seating at angles encourages social interaction. Circular and square tables encourage more equitable interactions. Avoid side-by-side seating unless it is desirable to discourage interaction. Providing a variety of different interaction opportunities can allow people to select the seating location that is optimal for their needs. Space needs to be provided to accommodate wheeled mobility devices. Ideally, seating should be lightweight and movable to allow occupants to adjust the furniture arrangements to suit their needs.
3. *Use spatial proximity and syntax to maximize social interaction opportunities.* Clustering individual territories around shared spaces increases contact opportunities. Locating spaces for social interaction at strategic circulation nodes will increase functional proximity. Mailboxes, laundries, and food service locations, for example, are also ideal locations for informal social interaction settings.

4. *Ensure that individuals have access to personal territory.* Every individual needs a personal territory that he or she can control. This maximizes his or her privacy behavior, sense of security, and sense of autonomy. Personal territories also provide opportunities for managing presentation of self through furniture arrangements, decorations, and status symbols. Personalization opportunities should be available on the outside of personal territories as well as on the inside. An example is the ability to decorate windows and doors in multifamily housing. Even the ability to have a personal screen saver on a monitor or digital picture frame can be a personalization opportunity where shared workstations do not provide permanent opportunities for presentation of self.
5. *Provide a continuum from personal to semipublic to public territories.* Where space is organized so that personal space is contiguous to semipublic space and semipublic space contiguous to public space, social interaction levels will be higher and more privacy will be obtained than when semipublic space is absent or not connected to personal space. This continuum should allow individuals to have control over visual and physical access from one level of public engagement to another.
6. *Provide visual access to support interaction and presentation of self.* Visual access to social spaces—for example, through interior windows, views from a distance or screen walls with some degree of openness—is critical to ensure that individuals are aware of social interaction opportunities. In particular, because people do not like to be forced into social interaction, having visual access from a distance provides an opportunity to decide whether or not to engage without social pressure. In addition, by having advance information, individuals can make sure that they present themselves in the best possible way before being visible to the other party.
7. *Provide mechanisms to regulate privacy.* Privacy needs vary over time. Sometimes a person may want isolation (e.g., during personal hygiene tasks). At other times, the same person may want to encourage others in interactions. In a residential setting, at work, and even in public, opportunities need to be provided to adjust visual and acoustic exposure as needed. This can include providing semiprivate space and territorial markers, such as fences, walls, and doors with locks. In some settings, locked doors and full-height walls, which present barriers, may be undesirable; for example, in work settings where teamwork is a priority or in an intensive care unit where visual surveillance may be necessary. However, in these locations, alternatives can be provided: partial visual barriers that block visual exposure to seated occupants, arranging workstations to avoid direct eye contact, and flexible boundaries like curtains. Acoustic control to mask the sound of conversations and other noise from interaction may also be desirable.
8. *Utilize a ringlike and shallow spatial syntax to improve autonomy.* Buildings and zones within buildings that have all spaces within two "steps" from the entry reduce the feeling of control that "deeper" spatial syntax can cause. Where more depth is necessary, countermeasures such as increasing visual permeability through low walls and glass partitions can be beneficial to help improve access to information. A ringlike spatial syntax will increase choice in paths of travel, which not only contributes to autonomy but also increases efficiency in circulation. This layout can work at the community scale as well as the building scale.
9. *Support policies to reduce discrimination and increase social integration.* Designers, as citizens, can engage in their own organizations and communities to reduce discrimination and increase social integration wherever policies are limiting the enjoyment of human rights. They can also use their projects to demonstrate how eliminating discrimination and stigma will benefit communities.

10. *Reinforce positive presentation of self.* No one likes an environment or product that is associated with devalued status, not even people who themselves are the victims of stigma. To be accepted in the mainstream, products not only have to provide universal benefits, but they need to overcome, through strong emotional design, features that could be stigmatizing if they are associated with devalued status.
11. *Implement design participation strategies.* The more that people of diverse backgrounds are involved in the design process, the more likely that environments, products, and systems will reflect the needs of a wide range of end users. Some effort should be made to include representatives of end users in the design process of every design project. The wider the range of people involved, the better.

Review Topics

1. How is universal design related to the concept of social construction?
2. Describe three ways in which social relations have an impact on design. Give examples of how universal design could address each.
3. Describe at least three design guidelines to support social participation.

References

Alexander, C. 1985. *The Production of Houses.* New York: Oxford University Press.
Alexander, C., S. Ishikawa, and M. Silverstein. 1977. *A Pattern Language.* New York: Oxford University Press.
Altman, I. and M. M. Chemers. 1984. *Culture and Environment.* New York: Cambridge University Press.
Archea, J. 1984. *Visual Access and Exposure: An Architectural Basis for Interpersonal Behavior.* Unpublished doctoral dissertation, Pennsylvania State University.
Blumer, H. 1969. *Symbolic Interactionism: Perspective and Method.* Berkeley: University of California Press.
Burch, S. 2011. "Dis-remembered: Disability and Removal in U.S. History." Unpublished lecture at the Center for Disability Studies, University at Buffalo, Buffalo, NY, February 24, 2011.
Burke, J. 1981–82. "Young Children's Attitudes and Perceptions of Older Adults." *International Journal of Aging and Human Development* 14 (3): 205–222.
Butterfield, D. 1984. *Design Guidelines for Exterior Spaces of Group Homes.* Chicago: University of Illinois Press.
Caplan, S. 1990. "Using Focus Groups Methodology for Ergonomic Design." *Ergonomics* 33 (5): 527–533.
Cooley, C. H. 1902. *Human Nature and the Social Order.* New York: Charles Scribner's Sons.
DeLong, A. J. 1970. "The Micro-Spatial Structure of the Older Person: Some Implications of Planning the Social and Spatial Environment." In L. A. Pastalan and D. H. Carson (eds.), *Spatial Behavior of Older People,* pp. 68–87. Ann Arbor: University of Michigan Press.
Duncan, J. S. (ed.). 1981. *Housing and Identity.* London: Croom Helm.
Festinger, L., S. Schachter, and K. Back. 1950. *Social Pressures in Informal Groups: A Study of Human Factors in Housing.* New York: Rinehart and Winston.
Fried, M. 1972. "Grieving for a Lost Home." In R. Gutman (ed.), *People and Buildings,* 188–210. New York: Basic Books.
Gans, H. J. 1962. *The Urban Villagers.* New York: Free Press.
Global Universal Design Commission. 2010. "Universal Design Commercial Building Standards Version 1.0." Unpublished committee document. Syracuse, NY: GUDC, Inc.
Habraken, N. J. 1972. *Supports: An Alternative to Mass Housing.* New York: Praeger.
Hall, E. T. 1969. *The Hidden Dimension.* Garden City, NY: Anchor Books.

Hillier, B. and J. Hanson. 1984. *The Social Logic of Space.* New York: Cambridge University Press.
Kohn, M. 2004. *Brave New Neighborhoods: The Privatization of Public Space.* New York: Taylor and Francis.
Lawton, M. P. and L. Nahemow. 1973. "Ecology and the Aging Process." In C. Eisdorferand and M. P. Lawton (eds.), *Psychology of Adult Development and Aging,* pp. 619–674. Washington, DC: American Psychological Association.
Liu, S. 1991. *Searching for a Real Home.* Buffalo, NY: State University at Buffalo.
McCamant, K. and C. Durrett. 1994. *Cohousing: A Contemporary Approach to Housing Ourselves.* Oakland, CA: New Village Press.
Michelson, W. 1976. *Man and His Urban Environment: A Sociological Approach.* Reading, MA: Addison-Wesley.
Mitchell, D. 2003. *The Right to the City: Social Justice and the Fight for Public Space.* New York: Guilford Press.
Pastalan, L. A., R. K. Mautz, and T. Merrill. 1973. "The Simulation of Age Related Sensory Losses: A New Approach to the Study of Environmental Barriers." In W.F.E. (ed.), *Environmental Design Research,* Vol. 1 (pp. 383–390). Stroudsburg, PA: Dowden, Hutchinson and Ross.
Rabig, J., W. Thomas, R. A. Kane, L. J. Cutler, and S. McAlilly. 2006. "Radical Redesign of Nursing Homes: Applying the Green House Concept in Tupelo, Mississippi." *Gerontologist* 46 (4), 533–539.
Rapoport, A. 1969. *House Form and Culture.* Englewood Cliffs, NJ: Prentice-Hall.
Rapoport, A. 1977. *Human Aspects of Urban Form: Towards a Man–Environment Approach to Urban Form and Design.* New York: Pergamon Press.
Robinson, J., T. Thompson, P. Emmons, M. Graff, and E. Franklin. 1984. *Toward an Architectural Definition of Normalization: Design Principles for Housing Severely and Profoundly Retarded Adults.* Minneapolis: Center for Urban and Regional Affairs, University of Minnesota.
Rothman, D. J. 1971. *The Discovery of the Asylum: Social Order and Disorder in the New Republic.* Boston: Little, Brown.
Sheehy, G. 1995. *New Passages: Mapping Your Life across Time.* New York: Ballantine Books.
Sommer, R. 1969. *Personal Space: The Behavioral Basis of Design.* Englewood Cliffs, NJ: Prentice-Hall.
———. 1974. *Tight Spaces: Hard Architecture and How to Humanize It.* Englewood Cliffs, NJ: Prentice-Hall.
———. 2002. "Personal Space in a Digital Age." In R. B. Bechtel and A. Churchman (eds.), *Handbook of Environmental Psychology,* pp. 647–660. Hoboken, NJ: John Wiley & Sons.
Steinfeld, E. 1981. "The Place of Old Age: The Meaning of Housing for Old People." In J. S. Duncan (ed.), *Housing and Identity: Cross-Cultural Perspectives,* pp. 198–246. London: Croom Helm.
Thompson, T., et al. 1996. "Architectural Features and Perceptions of Community Residences for People with Mental Retardation." *American Journal on Mental Retardation* 101 (3): 292–313.
Thompson, T., J. Robinson, M., Dietrich, M. Farris, and V. Sinclair. 1996. "Architectural Features and Perceptions of Community Residences for People with Mental Retardation." *American Journal on Mental Retardation* 101 (3): 292–313.
Turner, J. F. C. 1976. *Housing by People: Towards Autonomy in Building Environments.* New York: Pantheon Books.
Turner, J. F. C. and R. Fichter (eds.). 1972. *Freedom to Build: Dwelling Control of the Housing Process.* New York: Macmillan.
United Nations. 1948. *The Universal Declaration of Human Rights,* www.un.org/en/documents/udhr/index.shtml.
———. 2006. *Convention on the Rights of Persons with Disabilities.* www.un.org/disabilities/default.asp?id=259.
Vegso, S. R. 1992. *Resisting Normalization: A Multi-Perspective Analysis of Four Group Homes for Developmentally Disabled People.* Buffalo, NY: State University at Buffalo.
Wolfensberger, W. 1975. *The Origin and Nature of Our Institutional Models.* Syracuse, NY: Human Policy Press.

8

Public Accommodations

Introduction

As described in Chapter 2, experience with the first accessibility laws led to the emergence of universal design. The first laws required all buildings and facilities *financed by public funds* to be accessible. Today, accessibility laws in many countries cover all "public accommodations," including privately owned buildings and facilities open to the public, such as stores, restaurants, amusement parks, parks and other recreation facilities, street rights-of-way, and transportation systems. Public accommodations are a critical domain for universal design because they are the location of key social participation activities, including engagement in civic affairs, employment, recreation, education, and community mobility. We have devoted Chapter 13 to public transportation because it is so important and has many unique issues related to system planning, vehicle design, and information resources. Nevertheless, the issues and recommendations in this chapter also apply to facilities that are part of transportation systems such as terminals and stops.

Early in its history, the scope of accessible design was very limited. Over time, the scope has broadened significantly to the point that there is very little in any new construction project that accessibility codes and standards do not address. To practice universal design, it is important to understand accessible design, including the history of the laws, codes, and standards. Beyond that, it is necessary to understand the practical differences between accessible design and universal design. Many other source materials are available for learning about accessible design, including many free publications produced by government agencies and available on the Internet. Thus, in this chapter, we do not describe the requirements of regulations or provide technical criteria. Rather, we begin with historical background on accessible design, summarize the state of the art of accessibility in public accommodations today, and demonstrate why there is a need for universal design as a supplement to meeting the accessibility codes and standards. We provide examples from practice to show the differences between universal design and accessible design. We conclude with a description of current efforts to develop a universal design standards, certification, and social branding program modeled after similar programs in the field of sustainable design.

The Purpose of Accessible Design

How would an able-bodied adult react to a public building in which the doors were all 16 inches (41 cm) wide, ladders were the only way to reach upper floors, light switches were mounted at 84 inches (213 cm) off the floor, and counters were a minimum of 48 inches (122 cm) high? A few tall, thin people passionate about fitness would feel comfortable in such a place, but most people would avoid using the building. Who would be blamed for the fact that no one wanted to come there? Would we shrug and blame the users for not being thin, tall, and able enough?

The basic goal of accessible design is to remove artificial restrictions to opportunities—access to resources for people with disabilities that other citizens enjoy. From the perspective of social theory, providing accessibility shifts the "blame" for lack of ability from the person to the environment. In an inaccessible environment, people with disabilities cannot function effectively, but in an accessible environment, they can. Accessible design allows people with disabilities to demonstrate that they have capabilities—to work, manage a household, marry and raise children, and play a vital role in the community. Not only does this benefit them, but it helps change social stereotypes of disability and aging. Accessible design, however, does not include specific strategies designed to improve broader aspects of human performance, health and wellness, or social participation; for example, it does not help to improve the visual environment of stairways, reduce the spread of infection in hospitals, facilitate social interaction, or provide secure public restrooms.

There are limits to the degree of accommodation that governments can mandate. The content of accessibility codes and standards is negotiated, since the public is never willing to provide expensive features for a small group of people, especially if it means that other groups will have to sacrifice. For example, accessibility codes cannot mandate automated faucets and toilets since there are lower-cost accessible solutions. In the case of the United States, the negotiations over minimum requirements take place through a committee that includes representatives of interested parties. This committee develops a voluntary consensus standard that can be adopted by building regulatory agencies throughout the country. The consensus standard is sometimes referenced and sometimes used as the basis for standards issued and enforced through building codes. Universal design does not require a regulatory process, and thus is less subject to formal negotiations.

Thus, universal design does not depend on regulatory control although it could be adopted in a regulatory framework. In some cases (e.g., a rural village in an undeveloped region, where there is no accessibility to start and perhaps not even any building regulations), universal design may be implemented by providing a lower level of accessibility than might be found in a highly developed region with accessibility laws in place and the capacity to reach a higher level. In other cases, a government agency may develop incentives for adoption of universal design in order to implement a higher level of usability and have an impact on a broader population than basic accessibility laws would provide. Government may even mandate universal design. For example, the State of Louisiana recently passed a bill, which is now signed into law,[1] that requires a percentage of funds for constructing or remodeling state buildings to be used for implementation of universal design principles ("RS 38:2318.2 Percent for universal design program" 2010).[2]

---

[1] Acts 2009, No. 368, §1, eff. Jan. 1, 2010.
[2] "RS 38:2318.2 Percent for universal design program; established." 2009 Louisiana Code Title 38 Public Contracts, Works and Improvements, http://law.justia.com/codes/louisiana/2009/rs/title38/rs38-2318.2.html.

Accessible design is intended to benefit only those with disabilities. Although the population-served argument is part of the debate about accessibility laws (Howard 1994), the size of the beneficiary population should not be an issue in public building design at this point in history, unless one rejects the idea that people with disabilities have the same rights to social participation as other citizens. The real debate should be about whether the regulations are achieving their goal in a cost-effective manner. We do know that the cost of meeting accessibility regulations in new public buildings is very low, usually adding less than one percent to the total construction cost (Schroeder et al. 1979). Further, a cost-benefit study on public buildings completed in the late 1970s demonstrated that there are huge benefits to society from making buildings accessible, justifying the application of accessibility standards in economic terms (Chollet 1979). Increasing the cost by raising the bar with mandatory regulations, however, could result in significant affordability issues for small businesses, government, and not-for-profit organizations.

Some argue that universal design also should be mandated by law or through government policy. In fact, many requirements of accessibility standards do incorporate universal design. One example is door handles that do not require tight grasp or twisting the wrist. Another is the curb ramp. These examples demonstrate that accessibility has beneficiaries beyond people with disabilities and is a part of universal design. Implementing universal design as a mandate could have a much higher cost impact than accessibility regulations. For example, automatic doors installed at every exterior and interior doorway would increase the cost of each doorway by $800 to $1,500. This is a cost burden that not every building owner can afford. However, many universal design features cost very little or have significant value. The issue of value is part of the business case for adoption of universal design. When the value to the public or building owner outweighs the cost, there is a good economic argument for adoption of universal design. Installing an automated door at the entry to a hotel, for example, is a case where the value exceeds the cost.

Danford and Steinfeld (1999) studied the relative impact of universal design and accessible design in bathrooms, for both people with disabilities and those without. They found that people with disabilities had a significant positive improvement in performance when only minimum compliance with accessibility codes was provided. However, people without disabilities required a much higher standard of usability before there was any difference in their performance. Over time, we can expect that more universal design features will find their way into accessibility codes, particularly those that have little or no cost impact and/or have obvious benefits to all building users.

Universal design, as defined in Chapter 2, includes goals beyond basic accessibility, such as health and wellness, social participation, and safety, and a much higher standard of performance than accessible design. Universal design is aspirational and evolutionary—continuous quality improvement. Accessibility laws do not have this purpose. Some experts, the authors included, argue that codifying universal design in a regulatory framework could slow adoption of better universal design practices. They believe it would raise the bar for accessibility codes but reduce aspirations on a project-by-project basis and limit flexibility, product innovation, and experimentation. Accessibility standards provide a minimum bottom line that legally defines what building owners and designers need to do in order to comply with antidiscrimination laws. Addressing the goals of universal design requires a different approach.

That is not to say that government policy should not support the adoption of universal design. The LEED Standards are a good model. LEED stands for Leadership in Energy and Environmental Design. The Green Building Council developed these voluntary standards to promote the adoption of sustainable design. They are implemented through a certification program. The LEED standards include a set of performance guidelines and a list of strategies that can be used to meet each guideline. Adopters can select which guidelines they want to address and which strategies they want to include in their buildings. They receive points for each one selected and depending on the point total achieved, receive a level of certification, e.g. silver, gold, platinum. This is very different than total compliance with a set of rules. But, government agencies often ask architects to achieve specific LEED ratings for their buildings. Doing so not only saves the public money in the end but also sets an example for the private sector and demonstrates the feasibility of innovative design approaches. The key difference between the LEED standards and conventional building standards, however, is that the LEED standards provide a flexible framework within which a level of overall building performance can be achieved. Another approach to government support for universal design is to provide incentives for adoption. For example, in competitions for contracts or grants, proposals that agree to adopt universal design standards could receive more points compared to competing proposals. This approach is used widely to increase minority and women-owned business participation in government contracts.

Accessibility in the United States

The United States was the first country to develop consensus standards on accessibility. The document was produced by the American National Standards Institute (ANSI) as a voluntary standard called ANSI A117.1 (1961), "Specifications for Making Buildings and Facilities Accessible to and Usable by the Physically Handicapped." Two organizations, the Easter Seals Society and the President's Committee for Employment of the Handicapped, led the initiative to develop these standards.

A voluntary standard is not a regulation, but it can be referenced by regulations or used as a basis for writing them. In 1968, the Federal Architectural Barriers Act (PL-90-480) (ABA)3 was passed, requiring new buildings financed in whole or in part with federal funds to be accessible.[3] ANSI A117.1 was referenced as the technical design criteria that would be used to implement the law. The second version of the ANSI A117.1 Standard (1971) was fewer than ten pages long. It focused on wheelchair access to public buildings in a very general manner. With no legislation mandating use of the voluntary standard from 1961–71, it was not adopted in the building industry. In fact, despite the ABA, a General Accounting Office study in 1975 found that out of 314 federal buildings surveyed, all built after 1968, not one fully met the ANSI A117.1 Standard.

After that study, the government became more serious about compliance. Several federal agencies that sponsored building construction issued numerous regulations and standards for accessible design for their own construction programs in order to implement the ABA. They addressed specific information needs not addressed in the ANSI A117.1 Standard, such as the design of hospital rooms or apartment buildings. Between 1975 and 1980, however, there was a dramatic increase in both the number of federal and state regulations and in the degree of their enforcement. This was due to the passage of a new law, the Rehabilitation Act of 1973–74 (PL-93-112).[4] Section 503 of this law mandated that employers who hold federal contracts could

---

[3]Architectural Barriers Act, PL-90-480, Amended through 1978 42 USC 4151 et. seq., www.usbr.gov/cro/pdfsplus/arcbarr.pdf.
[4]Rehabilitation Act of 1973–74, Public Law 93-112 93rd Congress, H. R. 8070 September 26, 1973, www.dotcr.ost.dot.gov/documents/ycr/REHABACT.HTM.

not deny employment solely based on disability; they had to make their employment offices accessible and make accommodations for new or existing employees with disabilities. Section 504 required that programs supported by federal funds providing services to the public could not exclude people from participation solely based on disability. The act also set up the Architectural and Transportation Barriers Compliance Board (United States Access Board) and gave it power to review and coordinate the regulatory activities of the federal agencies related to the act. The U.S. Access Board was charged with developing uniform guidelines for accessibility. The creation of an agency with this mission and a budget to carry it out made a significant impact on progress toward enforcing the existing laws.

Each of the states also passed accessibility laws. Although most of the states adopted the ANSI A117.1 Standard in their regulations, many modified it or adopted their own standards. In 1974, concern about multiplying and diverging standards led the Easter Seals Society and the President's Committee to approach a federal agency, the U.S. Department of Housing and Urban Development, to fund research and develop an improved standard (Aiello and Steinfeld 1979; Steinfeld 1977, 1986; Steinfeld, Schroeder, and Bishop 1979; Steinfeld et al. 1979). The revised standard was ANSI A117.1 (1980), "Making Buildings and Facilities Accessible to and Usable by Physically Handicapped People."

Sections 503 and 504 were not implemented until 1977, when regulations were finally issued, after an extensive advocacy effort on the part of people with disabilities (Shapiro 1993). This act introduced the concepts of *program accessibility* and *readily achievable*. Program accessibility extended the accessibility mandate to existing buildings, but allowed service providers to make just enough of their existing physical plant accessible so that people with disabilities could receive services on an equal basis with other participants. Program accessibility does not require *total* accessibility. Optional methods for service delivery are allowed if they are not discriminatory. Any modifications made to existing buildings had to comply with the standards. "Readily achievable" was defined as easy to accomplish without much difficulty or expense. This definition considered not only the expense and technical difficulty but also the resources of the covered entity—for example, the resources of a local library are very different from those of a federal courthouse. To implement their increased responsibilities under the new act and coordinate the standards used, in 1984 the federal agencies developed the Uniform Federal Accessibility Standards, which were based on the 1980 version of ANSI A117.1, but added scoping provisions.[5] "Scoping" refers to the parts of buildings and the types of buildings that need to be made accessible to comply with technical criteria in the standard.

The Americans with Disabilities Act (ADA) was passed in 1990. This landmark law extended the scope of accessible design to all public accommodations, not just those that have a connection to public funding. It also adopted the program accessibility and readily achievable concepts. The ADA has several titles, three of which address public accommodations in some way:

> Title I requires all employers with 15 or more employees to make existing facilities and equipment accessible for employees with disabilities who need them, including common use facilities and access to employment offices and the work site.
>
> Title II applies to state and local government. It reaffirms the provisions of Section 504 of the Rehabilitation Act on program accessibility as they apply to government agencies.

---

[5]Uniform Federal Accessibility Standards, 49 FR 31528, www.access-board.gov/ufas/ufas-html/ufas.htm#intro.

Title III requires commercial and business establishments to remove architectural barriers under certain conditions. New buildings and any renovations must be accessible from the start. Existing buildings must provide accessibility to the degree that it is readily achievable.

The ADA gave a mandate to the U.S. Access Board to develop guidelines for implementing the Act. In 1991, the Access Board issued the ADA Accessibility Guidelines (ADAAG). This document was based on the Uniform Federal Accessibility Standard and was adjusted to address the new initiatives of the ADA. The U.S. Department of Justice (DOJ) is the federal agency charged with enforcing the federal accessibility laws. DOJ approved the first major revision to the guidelines in 2010, which combined the rules for implementing the ABA with those for the ADA into the ADA-ABA Guidelines (U.S. Access Board 2005). The ADA-ABA Guidelines were "harmonized" with the technical provisions of ICC/ANSI A117.1 (2003), the latest edition of the ANSI Standard at the time. ("ICC" stands for International Codes Council, a model building code association in the United States that took over administration of the ANSI A117.1 Standard.) ICC/ANSI A117.1 (2009) is the newest version, published in early 2011. The two most important documents on accessibility in the United States are now out of phase in their evolutionary development because the latest revisions to the ICC/ANSI A117.1 was approved in 2009, whereas the ADA-ABA was developed in 2004 and based on the 2003 standards, although it was not approved by the Department of Justice until 2010. It is also important to note that from humble beginnings of fewer than 10 pages, the ICC/ANSI A117.1 Standard, after numerous revisions, now includes 122 pages of text and illustrations. The ADA-ABA Guidelines weighs in at over 400 pages.

The Access Board produces additional materials to address other mandates of the ADA and other federal legislation. For example, it has produced guidelines on design for children's facilities, recreation facilities, and public rights-of-way, although not all these guidelines are mandatory. DOJ also publishes and distributes extensive materials related to the existing statutes.

As noted previously, all of the U.S. states also have laws and/or regulations on accessible design. Some states include the actual design standards in the law; in others, sections of the state building codes address accessibility. Still others have special accessible design codes. A number of states have established accessible design boards or divisions of government that have power to issue standards, hold hearings, enforce compliance, and even certify plan examiners who review plans for the building regulatory agencies. A few municipalities also have incorporated accessible design laws or regulations in local building codes or other ordinances. This is more common in large urban areas, such as New York City, which maintain their own building codes rather than use a state or model code. Since the adoption of the ADA, many states have adopted the ADAAG in place of the ICC/ANSI Standard. Although this has reduced conflicts between state codes and federal rules, the differences across the country present a challenge to design professionals who work beyond their local area and also to businesses that operate nationally, such as chain stores and restaurants. Moreover, the burden on designers to assimilate and understand the huge amount of information is significant.

Transition to Universal Design

Although practical experience and consumer advocacy both have their place in the development of regulations, research on human performance issues and on the social and economic impact of regulations can provide a more reliable knowledge base (Maisel, Smith, and Steinfeld 2008).

Some early human performance research on accessible design did not fully document the participants, research methods used, or results. (For a review of early research, see Steinfeld et al. 1979.) Many design recommendations were derived from experiments using very small groups of individuals selected from clients of a rehabilitation center with little consideration given to how they compared to the broader population of people with disabilities. Most of the research prior to 1974 took place in other countries where construction methods, rehabilitation techniques, and equipment differ from those in the United States. Early research on the economic impact of regulations was limited to ballpark estimates of the cost to meet the ICC/ANSI A117.1 Standard in new construction. Even the research completed in the United States in the late 1970s that was used to update U.S. standards has limitations (Aiello and Steinfeld 1979; Schroeder et al. 1979; Steinfeld, Schroeder, and Bishop 1979; Steinfeld, Schroeder, Duncan, et al. 1979; Templer 1974).

Since the 1980s, there has been a significant increase in research on the human performance requirements. Most of this work has been better documented and carefully designed to produce reliable data. Although much research still needs to be done, there has been a substantial improvement in our knowledge (Steinfeld 2010). One exception is in the area of social impact. To give a few examples, we have no research-based data on the effectiveness[6] of accessible restroom requirements, accessible parking regulations, or tactile signs (raised characters). Where we do have effectiveness data, we do not have data on the ultimate goal: the impact on social inclusion.

Disability rights laws are modeled after earlier U.S. civil rights laws. Thus, they include mechanisms for citizens to file complaints and obtain legal recourse when building owners, including government agencies, do not comply with the regulations. In the United States, lack of compliance can result in financial penalties for the architect of record as well as the owner. One very important legal provision allows plaintiff's attorneys to obtain compensation for their fees from the defense when a case is decided in favor of the plaintiff. These legal remedies have resulted in many ADA lawsuits. Popular media have focused on what some refer to as "drive-by lawsuits," trivial lawsuits filed by unscrupulous lawyers and their clients simply to shake down targets through a quick settlement (Diament 2010). Many high-profile lawsuits, mostly on behalf of a class of individuals with disabilities (e.g., students of a university, residents of a city, customers of a business, etc.), have resulted in major settlements or decisions where the defense side has either agreed to make significant changes in their building stock or has been ordered to do so by the courts.[7]

Class action lawsuits have the effect of increasing compliance significantly, as similar organizations seek to avoid litigation, and raise awareness among design professionals. For example, if a major motion picture theater chain settles or loses a case, its competitors will start paying closer attention to the accessibility of their own building stock, and their architects will be more attentive to the requirements of the law. In fact, the initiation of a lawsuit alone often increases the effort that organizations devote to compliance. The litigation has elevated the importance of accessible design to a standard part of design practice and has created a market for specialists in this field, increasing capacity to practice accessible design. In the past, architects and

---

[6]*Effectiveness* refers to the actual impact of an intervention in use. For example, although we have research-based data on the human factors of tactile signs, we do not have data about whether they actually help people in the field.
[7]U.S. Department of Justice, "ADA Enforcement," www.ada.gov/enforce.htm#anchor201570.

building owners often simply ignored accessibility because no one was watching. It is important to note, however, that there are still notable lapses. A good example is the U.S. Holocaust Memorial Museum on the National Mall in Washington, DC, constructed in 1993, where there were many violations of the ADA that had to be fixed, including the Hall of Remembrance (see Figures 1–11a and 1–11b in Chapter 1).

The history of accessibility policy offers many lessons for other countries. In the 50 years since the first accessibility standard was developed in the United States, there has been enormous progress throughout the country. This progress can be attributed to a very active disability advocacy community and political support for disability rights, which have ensured that the laws and standards are comprehensive and that they contain effective enforcement procedures. Another important contribution has been the allocation of federal resources to stakeholder education and enforcement. One of the most important aspects of accessibility laws is that they cover existing buildings and are triggered whenever alterations or renovations are made. This ensures that, over time, the built environment eventually will reflect a minimum baseline level of accessibility. Nevertheless, there is a lot to be done to reach that point. Two particularly important areas in need of attention are public rights-of-way in older cities and recreational settings.

It is tempting for other countries to adopt the practices that have been effective elsewhere, but conditions are often different in each nation. In particular, differences exist in the legal and regulatory systems and in the resources available to all stakeholders. Other high-income countries have also made significant progress, and examples are available from middle- and low-income countries as well. A recent report provides an overview of the state of the art in accessibility from a global perspective (World Health Organization 2011).

As early as the late 1970s, experts in accessibility started to recognize that the achievement of a truly inclusive society was more complex than simply developing better standards. This awareness led to the development of the universal design philosophy. There are several benefits of universal design:

- *Reducing the complexity of compliance with accessibility laws by striving for a higher standard.* Implementing a higher level of accessibility reduces problems with noncompliance that occur when designers fail to meet minimum requirements. For example, mounting a dispenser with its controls at 40 in. (1020 mm) rather than the maximum allowed of 48 in. (1220 mm) will eliminate the possibility of noncompliance simply due to a slight installation error.
- *Reducing the knowledge gap between research and standards, which take a long time to update.* Practitioners and researchers are generating new information on a continuous basis. If practiced as evidence-based design, universal design will incorporate the latest scientific and practical knowledge.
- *Engaging the creative imagination of designers and other stakeholders rather than focusing on a rule-based approach.* Universal design seeks to overcome the idea that accessibility is a regulatory constraint and make designing for diversity a major focus of good design. This leads to creative and innovative solutions.
- *Increasing the scope of issues important for development of an inclusive society.* A greater impact can be achieved by including a broader range of human performance issues, social participation goals, and a concern for environmental health issues.

Thus, universal design, as a practice, has an expanded set of activities as well as scope. These activities span a wide range of domains:

- *Policy* – Introduction of universal design into policy initiatives (e.g., standards, purchasing regulations, housing subsidies, tax credits).
- *Education* – Increasing public awareness of universal design and increase adoption of universal design in professional education.
- *Business practices* – Integrating universal design concepts into corporate culture, including customer relations, workforce development, and marketing.
- *Broader focus on human performance* – Increasing the adoption of design strategies that eliminate stress, improve efficiency, and reduce injuries and errors.
- *Health and wellness* – Increasing attention to design issues that affect health (e.g., chemical sensitivity, medical device design, disease prevention, air pollution).
- *Social participation* – Designing for social integration, reduction of stigma, and fit with context.

One of the most important targets of universal design, from a global perspective, should be the development of strategies that make sense for low-income countries and regions. In particular, universal design ideas can provide the flexibility needed to address the differences in context within one country, such as a rural village where buildings are constructed using traditional hand-building methods and a luxury resort where multinational corporations and host governments may invest huge sums to attract affluent tourists. Using lower standards for the former can introduce some appropriate solutions that can improve quality of life greatly, while higher standards for the latter can help increase the knowledge of local design professionals in this field. As time goes on, that knowledge can be harnessed to improve accessibility countrywide. Standards and related implementation programs can include a focus on accessibility but make allowances for affordability issues and provide incentives to continuously improve buildings over time and to exceed basic accessibility goals where possible.

The box illustrates some universal design strategies developed by Raheja (2008) to improve accessibility in rural Indian villages. The strategies demonstrate the importance of universal design in a low-income context and the fact that universal design is still feasible when resources are limited. In fact, the impact of universal design is probably greater in a low-income context because people are more dependent on environmental resources and more exposed to health and injury risks. In higher-income settings, there is more money to provide services and assistance, and there is a well-developed public health infrastructure.

Universal Design in a Low-Income Context

Rural settlements in India often have open drainage ditches that make it impossible for people with mobility impairments to travel around the village without help. Water for cooking and drinking is obtained from a communal pump that is elevated on a concrete platform. Each household has to obtain its daily water supply by filling and carrying containers back to the home. Shower and bathing facilities are often a nearby natural water source and sometimes a communal bathhouse. Residents use the open fields for toilets, but people with mobility impairments often cannot reach them and have to use a corner of their homes for a toilet.

Raheja has developed a design for a concrete prefabricated bridge element to span the ditches (Figure 8–1a). He proposes that a shallow landscape ramp be used to provide access to the communal pump (Figure 8–1b). The sides of the ramp are walls that can be used to sit and socialize while waiting one's turn. The ramp and bridges not only provide accessibility but also allow the use of wheeled devices to transport water. Using wheels reduces the effort needed and allows larger containers to be used, reducing the number of trips to the pump. A communal hygiene facility that is also accessible would not only provide access for residents with disabilities but also reduce the danger of drowning by washing in rivers, improve sanitation for the whole village, and reduce the spread of communicable diseases (Figure 8–1c). All these designs can be constructed with methods already used in the villages and built by residents themselves.

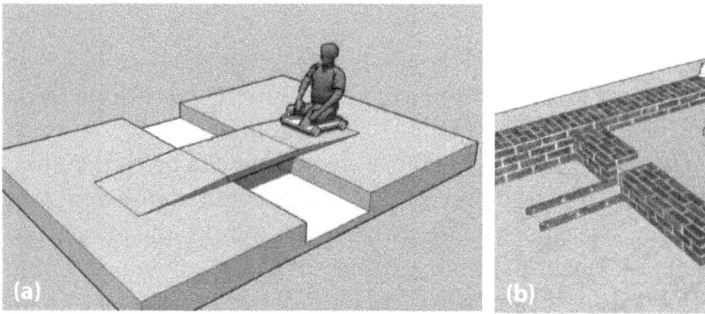

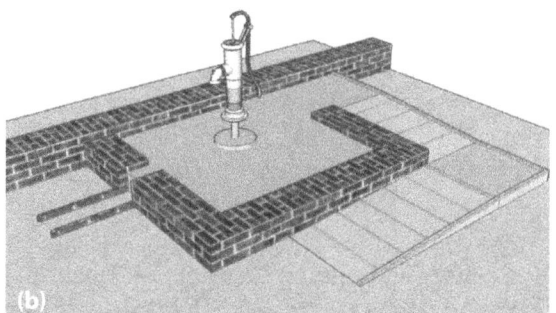

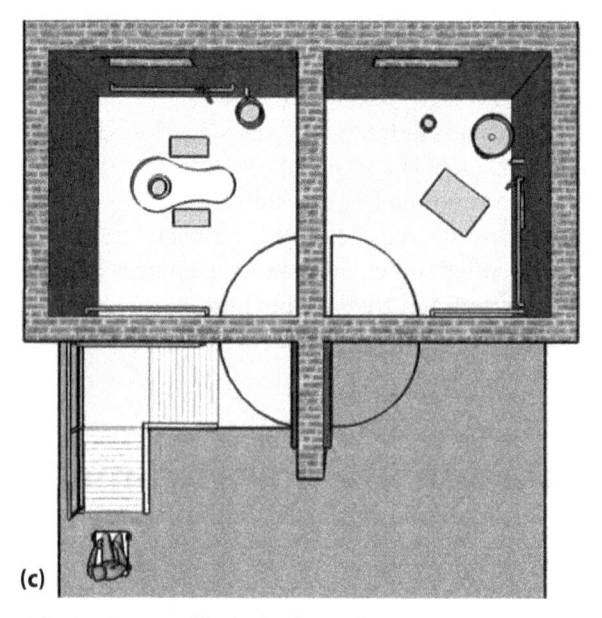

Figure 8–1: Universal design in a rural Indian village. These examples show (a) a prefabricated bridge for drainage ditches; (b) ramped access to a water pump with a sitting wall; (c) an accessible community toilet and bathing facility.

Source: Copyright 2008 Gaurav Raheja, "Enabling Environments for the Mobility Impaired in the Rural Areas," Unpublished PhD dissertation, Indian Institute of Technology, Roorkee.

One good rationale for the adoption of universal design is the limitations of the regulatory approach. However, as we have seen in other chapters, the rationale for adoption is much broader. It involves a business case and a moral case, and it applies to societies with all levels of resources. Most important, the population that benefits from universal design is not only people with disabilities. In the rest of this chapter, we illustrate the scope of universal design in public buildings in a selection of key design issues. For each one, we summarize the typical accessibility requirements and follow that with a list of complementary universal design strategies. Illustrations provide some examples of how selected strategies can be implemented. At the end of the chapter, we provide several more extensive examples.

Universal Design Strategies

Design Process

Accessibility regulations and standards are applied through a legal process, either through building code review or driven by complaints. The format of the guidelines and standards used is extremely complex; the objective is to eliminate loopholes, but the result is that they are also quite difficult to follow and very detailed. In practice, all the relevant requirements must be met for a project to be approved. Thus, effectively, each requirement has the same value. For example, the location of toilet paper is treated similarly to the slope of a ramp or width of an entry door. Any noncompliant item can lead to rejection by a regulatory official or a lawsuit. Regulations are also conceived as a set of rules for the design professional, builder, or owner to follow without any preconceptions about the experience or abilities of those people on one hand and without concern for whether the layperson can understand them on the other.

In a democratic system, antidiscrimination laws and regulations need to define a minimum threshold of compliance in order to establish the legal basis for government regulatory actions. But goals like those of universal design should not be conceived as a pass/fail proposition. That approach would lead to a regulatory mind-set and discourage innovation. Moreover, to ensure that the social participation goals are met, the process of implementing universal design should not be adversarial, as regulatory activity is; it should be a participatory activity in which representatives of all the stakeholders, including the end user groups, have a voice (Ostroff 1997). Thus, universal design standards should be written using a simple format and language that anyone can understand and follow. They should also respect differences in projects and contexts.

Public Rights-of-Way

Accessibility codes and standards require these features for the design of the walking surfaces in public rights-of-way:

- Stable, firm, and slip-resistant surfaces
- Maximum running slope (in the direction of travel) and cross slope (perpendicular to the path of travel) to facilitate wheelchair use

- Elimination of dangerous drop-offs at sides
- Minimum width, usually the space needed for one wheelchair user
- Prevention of accidents from protruding objects, such as overhead signs or tree branches to protect people with vision impairments

Universal design strategies could include many more provisions to increase safety and reduce congestion, such as:

- Finished topography that diverts water away from pedestrian pathways
- The use of permeable pavement to reduce water collection on surfaces
- Low-reflectivity surfaces
- Use of photoluminescent materials to mark edge conditions at night
- Width of a sidewalk based on expected capacity rather than the minimum space needed for wheelchair use

Accessibility codes do not address street crossing design other than the requirements for walking surfaces mentioned earlier and the provision of curb ramps at intersections.

Universal design strategies can address many additonal aspects of street crossings, including:

- Curb bulbs (widened sidewalk area at each end of the crosswalk that protrudes into the parking lane) to reduce the travel distance in the crossing
- Markings for the pedestrian crossing area
- Signal timing that provides sufficient time for slow-moving pedestrians to cross
- Pedestrian traffic controls, such as walk/don't walk signs with countdowns
- Audible beacons or talking signs to aid visually impaired pedestrians and increase situational awareness for all
- Measures to prevent water pooling at the bottom of curb ramps
- Strategies to eliminate curbs entirely, such as the use of bollards or pedestrian barriers
- Traffic-calming techniques, such as narrowed lanes and rumble strips

Accessibility regulations and standards do not address the potential conflicts among vehicular, bicycle, and pedestrian traffic.

Universal design guidelines should ensure safety of pedestrians, including separation where necessary, and provide methods to reduce conflicts at intersections.

Pedestrian Safety at Intersections

The street crossing in Figure 8–2 has been raised from the adjoining street level and is made out of brick paving units to mark the safe area. The crossing area is raised a few inches from the surrounding street elevation, and the street slopes up on both sides to meet it at the same level as the adjoining sidewalks. The raised crossing slows traffic due to the change in height. Cobblestone strips define the edges for pedestrians with visual impairments and create rumble strips to slow traffic even more. Bulb-outs reduce the street crossing distance.

Bollards and chains, in a historic style, prevent people from jaywalking outside the marked crossing area. Tactile warning strips mark the edge of the street in the crossing area in place of curbs.

Figure 8–2: Street crossing in Nelson, New Zealand. This crossing in a historic area incorporates design interventions to slow traffic, help pedestrians with visual impairments, and prevent jaywalking.

Site Circulation

Accessibility codes require specific pedestrian routes within a site to meet access code requirements but the rest of the paths on the site do not have to comply:

- At least one from accessible parking spaces and accessible passenger loading zones, public rights-of-way, and public transportation stops to each accessible building or facility
- At least one connecting each accessible building or facility

Universal design expands on these requirements to address usability, safety, and security in the entire pedestrian path system on a site. In fact, accessibility codes do not require any pedestrian paths on a site at all. For example, if a municipality does not require sidewalks, no accessible paths are required along an adjoining roadway or from the site boundary to buildings on the site. Universal design guidelines, on the other hand, address pedestrian safety as well as accessibility. For example, they can include guidelines for:

- Well-marked pedestrian, bicycle, and vehicular access points to the site
- Controlling the complexity of information and improving perception at site entry points for drivers, bicyclists, and pedestrians
- A continuous accessible pedestrian and bicycle path network on the site that protects pedestrians
- Pathways that are well lit and provide protection from extreme weather
- Design to increase visibility of accessible entries
- Wayfinding information to help find destinations

Site Topography

Accessibility codes do not address site topography; therefore, it is often overlooked. Careful attention to topography is an essential element of universal design to reduce the level of effort needed to access buildings and facilities. Some universal design strategies include:

- Entries with grade-level access to reduce the effort needed to enter and reduce the potential for falls created by stairs and ramps
- Grading the site to eliminate the need for ramps or reduce their length/height wherever possible
- Adjusting grades of a new site to facilitate access to buildings and facilities
- Planning the location of building entries where they can be made accessible more easily
- Integrating the interior and exterior circulation network so that pedestrians can use elevators in the building to overcome steep topography
- Ensuring that accessibility provisions do not harm the historic value of a site or building

Figure 8–3 shows two options for providing an accessible entry to an historic building. The first option (Figure 8–3a) is the architect's first proposal to provide access in accordance with the regulations. The second (Figure 8–3b) is the authors' proposal to provide a universal design approach to the entry. The original proposal included a long switch back ramp that would have been very visually intrusive. Although it uses more space, the second option includes some minor grading around the entry. The grading allowed part of the entry ramp to be replaced by a gently sloping walkway which does not require railings. Moreover, the remaining ramp section is much shorter than the one in the first option, reducing effort for use. The walls on either side of the sloped walkway can be used as a sitting area for people of different stature. An additional accessible sitting area is provided at the beginning of each ramp (the ramp shown is mirrored on the other side of the entrance) to encourage the entries to be used as gathering places. The authors' proposal was accepted, and construction will start soon.

The design of the Eileen Fisher Store in Manhattan demonstrates how to plan the location of entries to fit with the topography of a site (Figure 8–4). Rather than use the alley to provide an "alternative" accessible entry, the designers improved the alley to make it the access path for all customers. This solution not only reduces chances of stairway accidents for all but also provides more exposure to the merchandise inside the store, a good business practice.

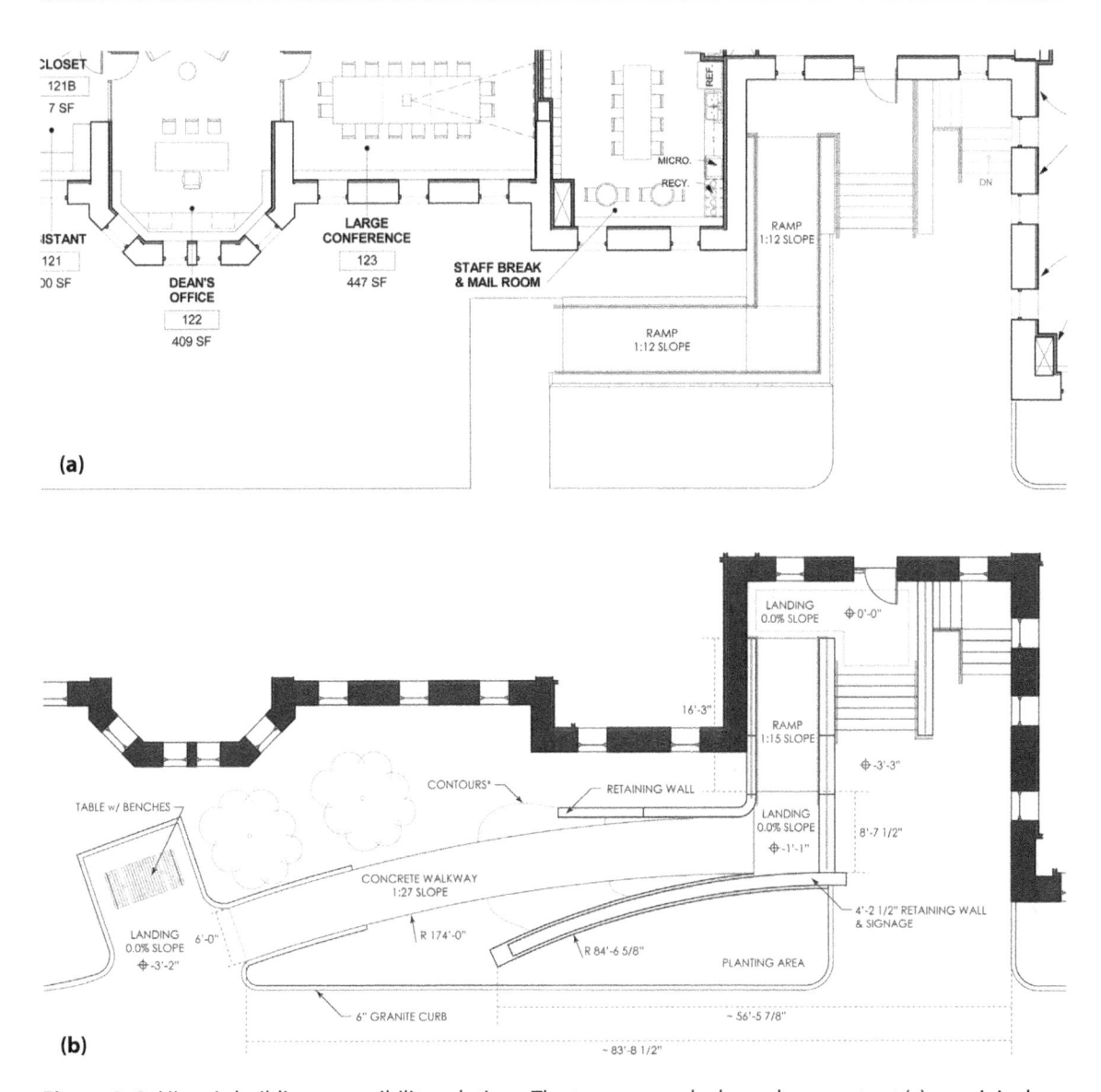

Figure 8-3: Historic building accessibility solutions. The two proposals shown here contrast (a) an original proposal with (b) the authors' proposal for making an aesthetically pleasing front entry that does not detract from the historic architecture.

Parking

Accessibility codes specify minimum requirements for accessible parking, including:

- A specified number of reserved parking spaces for people with disabilities, based on total spaces available
- Access aisles so that people who use wheeled mobility devices have room to transfer in and out of their cars

Figure 8–4: Entry to retail store, New York, NY. This entry demonstrates how adapting to the physical context of the environment can significantly improve accessibility and have other benefits as well.

- Signs marking the spaces
- Location of the reserved spaces in closest proximity to accessible entries served by the lot

It is noteworthy that parking is the major source of complaints related to accessibility laws in the United States (U.S. Access Board, personal communication, 2005). Access codes do not address paid parking at all except in terms of equipment design. Universal design guidelines address a wider range of human performance issues for parking and expand the idea of "priority parking" to a wider population. For example, universal design guidelines for parking include:

- Additional priority parking at convenient locations for older people, pregnant women, and parents with small children
- Simplified payment options for paid parking, such as smart tags and payment by credit card
- Dynamic information displays at the entry to lots and garages to indicate where parking is available, including available accessible parking spots
- Priority parking for people who wish to pay for the spaces closer to building entries with free use of the same spaces for people with disabilities

Entries

Accessibility regulations do not require all entries in new buildings to be accessible. For example, the ADA-ABA Guidelines require accessibility only to:

- 60 percent of entries to the building
- Specific types of entries, such as direct entries from parking garages

Moreover, accessibility codes do not require any particular design features at entries to make them easier to find or use, nor do they require coordinating the location and design of entries with other site elements. Finally, they do not address wayfinding information that may be useful to visitors planning a trip.

In universal design, as many entries as possible, including employee entries, should be accessible. Universal design features at entries might include:

- Landmarks at each primary entrance/exit, including building features, acoustic treatments, and lighting features
- Entrances that provide the shortest and most direct route to primary destinations in the building
- Weather protection to facilitate entry and exit in poor weather, waiting and social interaction
- Prominent signs to identify entrances/exits
- Similar but different graphics to identify each class of entrances/exits (e.g., number or color system)
- Information about entrance/exit locations available on the Internet, including construction conditions and alternate routes

The Smithsonian Institution in Washington, DC, provides extensive information on its website for visitors. Figure 8–5 shows a map of the Federal Mall, where most of the Institution's facilities are located. The map shows the location of subway (Metro) stops, buildings, and entries. It also shows curb ramp locations, accessible entries to the Institution's buildings, accessible parking spaces, and accessible entries to the Metro. Maps of other Smithsonian facilities in Washington are also available.

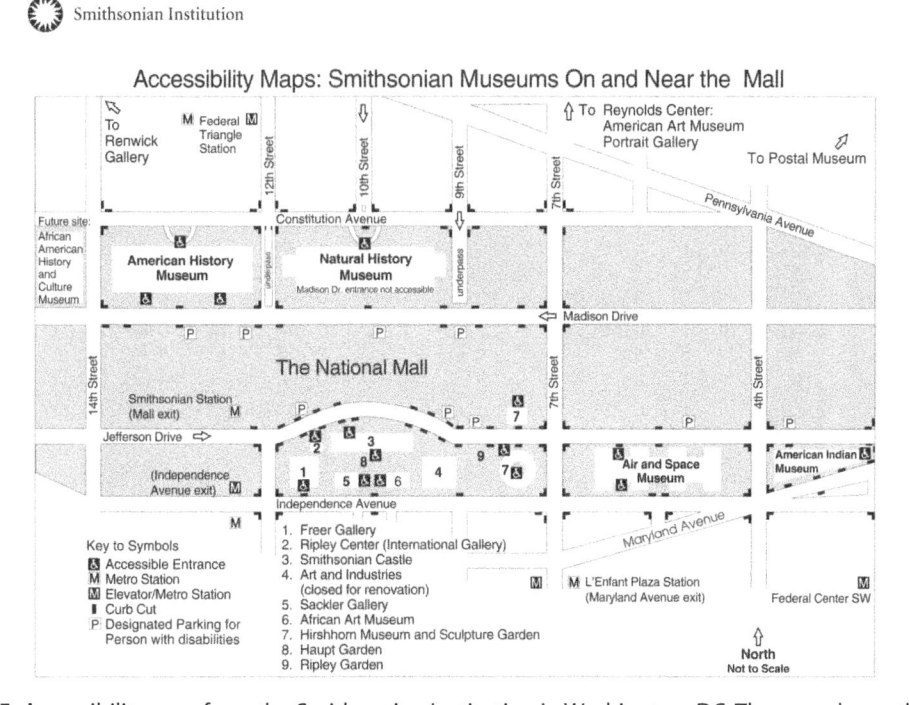

Figure 8–5: Accessibility map from the Smithsonian Institution in Washington, DC. The map shows the accessibility features near its facilities on the Federal Mall.

Figure 8–6 shows an entry and terrace to a pub in a historic area of Sydney, Australia. Stairs, ramps, and terraces are constructed of concrete with dynamic forms that contrast with the traditional building, providing a landmark for the pub and entry location. During busy times, the ramp and stairway serve as additional gathering and serving space, extending the activity of the pub into the immediate neighborhood and enlivening the streetscape. The canopy provides protection from the sun and rain to people waiting to get inside. The slope of the existing sidewalk was used to reduce the length of the ramp.

Figure 8–6: Pub terrace, Sydney, Australia. This restaurant exploited the need for accessibility to improve the immediate outdoor environment of its facility. (a) View from side. (b) View from front.

Space Planning

Accessibility standards address only a few design issues related to circulation inside buildings, including:

- The minimum widths of circulation pathways
- Clearances needed for turning wheeled mobility devices
- Door maneuvering clearances
- Removal of overhanging hazards that might injure people with vision impairments

Universal design should use more generous clearances to address the needs of contemporary wheeled mobility users. Universal design standards should also address a much broader set of issues, such as:

- Direct access to the primary spaces used by visitors to the building
- Building layouts that increase efficiency for employees during everyday work activities
- Locating rooms that have closely related activities in close proximity to each other
- Locating outdoor facilities adjacent to related indoor spaces
- Locating related services together, such as restrooms for men and women and drinking fountains
- Locating informal social interaction spaces at strategic positions

The Gates Building for the School of Computer Science at Carnegie Mellon University includes several types of informal gathering spaces scattered throughout the building that small groups of students, faculty, and staff can use for group work or simply for socialization. The work spaces all have features that attract people to them. One type has whiteboards (Figure 8–7a). Some are located at strategic locations in the circulation system (Figure 8–7b). Most have very comfortable furniture and good views to outdoors or interior activity zones (Figure 8–7c). Others have tables and small kitchenettes to prepare meals and snacks (Figure 8–7d). Note that lower tables are available.

Ramps and Stairs

Accessibility standards have requirements for these features of ramps:

- Maximum length
- Minimum width
- Edge protection
- Railing design
- Landing design

Accessibility regulations require only that accessible design requirements be applied to stairs that are part of a means of egress. Even then, the design requirements are limited to:

- Tread and nosing depth
- Riser height

206 *Public Accommodations*

- Tread surface
- Railing design
- Minimum widths for wheelchair use
- Minimum landing sizes to maneuver wheelchairs

In practice, ramps are often placed to the side of stairs, providing an alternative, less direct route. Moreover, these ramps usually use the maximum allowable slope, even though many

Figure 8–7: Informal work and gathering spaces in the Gates Building, Carnegie Mellon University: (a) work space with whiteboards; (b) comfortable furniture and view; (c) strategic location of spaces; (d) space adjacent to kitchen.

people may not be able to manage it (Sanford, Story, and Jones 1996; Steinfeld et al. 1979; Steinfeld, Schroeder, Duncan et al. 1979). Minimum landing sizes do not accommodate larger-wheeled mobility device users, especially scooter users.

Universal design should include some strategies that can improve usability and safety, such as:

- Planning ramps as the main circulation path with the width needed to accommodate the expected traffic
- Running the ramp in the direction of circulation to reduce extra effort
- Reducing the slope below the maximum allowed
- Designing landings to accommodate the largest wheeled mobility device users
- Providing seating along the ramp or on landings
- Using inclined moving walkways (if the slope for inclined moving walkways is low and constant)

Stairs should include additional safety features and features to support situational awareness for everyone, particularly those who have sensory impairments. Some universal design strategies for stairs include:

- Tactile walking surface indicators at the top of stair runs
- Riser and tread proportions that reduce falling and support comfortable gait
- Extra space on landings for resting
- Seating at landings
- Tactile, visual, and/or auditory cues to indicate changes of direction and the top and bottom of run
- Surfaces and edges made from slip-resistant material without excessive friction
- Surfaces free of glare
- Edges of stair treads that contrast well with the stair tread below
- Stair treads, ramp surfaces, and handrails evenly illuminated
- Lighting conditions that eliminate strong shadows on stair treads
- Photoluminescent striping used to help identify stair nosing and edges in dark locations (e.g., outdoors)

Circulation as a Metaphor

An addition to an historic library was built between a major street in Copenhagen and the main canal, a major path for recreational boating (Figure 8–8). The new building connects to the old building via a bridge over the street. The architects used the metaphor of circulation to create a memorable building concept in three dimensions. The first floor of the building houses functions that serve the public most directly, such as a café and exhibit spaces, and looks out onto the major vehicular artery on one side and the canal on the other. The circulation desk and public computer catalog is on the bridge, symbolizing the importance of circulation visually and the circulation area as a bridge between the old physically based information world and the new digital world. The dramatic inclined moving walkways in the atrium create a landmark in the center of the building and facilitate access to the library resources. Elevators and stairs are also available for those who prefer them. All the public circulation in the new building is on the edge of the atrium space or the street side. The dramatic view of the canal is visible from most of the circulation spaces in the new building. Thus, it is very easy to understand where everything is in relationship to the central circulation and in relationship to the major street.

Figure 8–8: The Royal Danish Library, Copenhagen. This library was designed using the metaphor of circulation. (a) View showing old and new buildings. (b) Main circulation space with inclined sliding walkway. (c) View of street and bridge. (d) View from bridge to canal.

Restrooms

The restroom is a particularly important site for the practice of accessibility and universal design. Being able to complete personal hygiene tasks and grooming effectively and with dignity is essential for maintaining health and is an important aspect of social participation because it supports social role participation and helps people avoid stigma. Accessibility standards have many requirements for restroom accessibility, most of which are based on providing access by wheelchair users. These include:

- Scoping provisions that specify how many toilet rooms must be accessible and how many toilet stalls and urinals within them
- Requirements for signs, including symbols showing whether the restroom is accessible
- The location and design of grab bars to assist in transferring to and from the toilet
- Minimum door clearances
- Minimum clearances for positioning wheelchairs at fixtures and equipment, including knee clearances
- Minimum clearances for maneuvering wheelchairs within the space
- Maximum mounting heights for fixtures, equipment controls, mirrors, and coat hooks
- Maximum forces of operation for controls
- Minimum sizes for accessible toilet stalls

Current accessibility standards in the United States and most other countries are based on data on the sizes and maneuvering abilities of wheeled mobility device users in the mid-1970s. Accommodating a full range of sizes and abilities requires increasing the sizes of space clearances and maneuvering clearances significantly, particularly if scooter users are to be accommodated. However, in small spaces such as restrooms and toilet stalls, doing so can have a significant impact on design. Therefore, new ideas need to be introduced to provide access to the individuals with the largest space needs. Other research demonstrates that older people who are ambulatory or semi-ambulatory need different types of grab bars from those currently required by accessibility codes.

Many other issues not addressed by accessibility codes fit within the scope of universal design. People often need to help others in restrooms. Having someone do so not only requires more space, but sometimes an adult of the opposite sex may be the caregiver. In some public restrooms, as in transportation terminals and performing arts spaces, there is a great deal of congestion at times. Women take longer to use a restroom, so they often find themselves waiting at such times while there is space available in the men's restroom. People often take things into restrooms, such as purchases or luggage that get in the way and are difficult to protect while using the facilities. Many people with severe disabilities have limitations in grip and reach, which makes operating equipment difficult, even if it is mounted and located in accordance with standards. Restrooms are also places where communicable diseases, such as influenza, can be transmitted easily. In addition, supplies of paper and soap often run out.

Universal design strategies for restrooms include:

- Making all restrooms accessible
- Extra-large entries
- Maze entries without doors

- A companion restroom that is large enough to provide assistance to companions and has enough space for large wheeled mobility devices to turn around
- Enhanced lighting and mirrors to support grooming
- Adjustable grab bars or alternative configurations to accommodate different needs
- Extra space in stalls and at lavatories to accommodate luggage, briefcases, and packages
- Shelves to rest personal items on temporarily
- Touchless control of fixtures and other equipment
- Smart fixtures and equipment that notify maintenance staff before supplies run out
- Receptacles designed to collect medical waste (e.g., used needles)
- Identification signs to make the nature of facilities understandable to all users

The Cincinnati, Ohio, airport has companion restrooms designated by the sign "Family Restroom." The sign has been printed in two languages, English and Chinese, and an ideogram showing an adult and child (Figure 8–9). The Companion Restroom is located between the women's and men's restrooms to make it highly visible.

Figure 8–9: Companion restroom. This restroom at the Cincinnati, OH, airport is highly visible and has a sign explaining its use in two languages plus an ideogram.

Business Practices

Many public buildings, such as museums, tourist destinations, restaurants, retail facilities, hotels, and recreation centers, attract a very diverse set of visitors. The program accessibility provisions of Title II of the ADA require covered organizations to offer services that are accessible to people with disabilities. For example, museums covered by Title II must provide alternative media for people who are deaf or have sight impairments.

The idea of program accessibility can be expanded through universal design practices that address diversity issues beyond disability. Doing this also can help private businesses not covered by the ADA to better serve people with disabilities, their friends, and families. Universal design strategies for business practices to address the diverse needs of visitors include:

- Receptionists trained to ask about special needs of visitors
- Information provided on websites to help people understand the environmental challenges they might encounter at the site or the features available to support their visit
- Information handouts in multiple languages, including floor plans that identify important features and amenities (e.g., accessible entries, food service, and restrooms)
- Equipment and supplies available to visitors, especially in hotels (e.g., umbrellas, bicycles, mobility devices, transfer benches, reachers, toilet seat risers, volume controlled telephones, assistive listening devices, etc.)
- Alternative experiences for visitors who cannot participate in the regular tours or activities (e.g., tactile and audible artwork in an art museum, or texts of tour guide presentations for people who are deaf)
- Virtual tours that can help people plan their visits
- Supervised child play areas where parents can leave their children while shopping, receiving medical care, waiting in lines, or doing other activities during which the presence of children would be distracting or disruptive
- Food options that address special diets

Business Practices

IKEA, the international home furnishings store, has pioneered in business practices that make shoppers feel comfortable and welcome (Figure 8–10). The company's dual emphasis on affordability and style attracts a wide range of income groups. Each store has a supervised child-care area. Furniture arrangements and displays are designed to let shoppers try out the products, which helps them understand their features and communicates home improvement and decorating ideas. The restaurant offers many healthy food choices in addition to special Scandinavian treats. The showroom merchandizing concept reduces the need to carry heavy purchases out to vehicles. Shoppers simply write down the items they want and pick them up at the in-store warehouse right before checkout. Every store is similar in layout, making it easy for shoppers to remember and understand. The circulation pattern allows choice but, for simplicity, has a default linear path that exposes customers to the full range of products available. Aisles are wide, and merchandise is not tightly crammed together, which facilitates the use of

Figure 8-10: IKEA store, Toronto, ON. The IKEA company has pioneered in providing customer-friendly environments. (a) Store entrance with designated family parking space and loading area. (b) A shopping cart being pushed along a main circulation path with wayfinding cues. (c) Kitchen appliances and cabinetry displayed in context.

shopping carts. IKEA was one of the first businesses to include changing tables in both men's and women's restrooms. For knock-down furniture, the company provides visual assembly instructions that are understandable without use of language. Assistance with assembly is available. A convenient loading zone allows shoppers to load their cars with a minimum of effort. This statement from the "IWAY Standard" sums up the company's business practices:

Our guiding principles when working with these issues are:

- What is in the best interest of the child?
- What is in the best interest of the worker?
- What is in the best interest of the environment?

These practices encourage loyalty by communicating the feeling that the firm cares about its customers and employees. Many of these practices have been adopted by other businesses.

Other Issues

Universal design in public accommodations can address many other issues. The topics discussed earlier give readers an understanding of the differences between accessible and universal design. The sections to follow provide additional examples. Several other sourcebooks of ideas and websites are listed in the references at the end of this chapter.

The Future

The universal design movement is just beginning to get legs. Up to now, there have been few tools to practice universal design and a limited community of practice. There are no credentialing systems and no objective methods to recognize achievement or identify best practices. Two noteworthy efforts are under way to advance universal design and address these gaps. They both hope to extend the adoption of universal design beyond knowledgeable practitioners to the mainstream.

Recently, a collaboration of organizations and professionals embarked on a mission to improve adoption of universal design. With support from the public and private sectors, the Global Universal Design Commission, Inc. (GUDC) was established as a not-for-profit corporation dedicated to increasing understanding and use of universal design to change the world in which we live (www.globaluniversaldesign.org). The first task of the GUDC was to develop voluntary consensus standards that can be adopted to incorporate universal design features into new and existing commercial buildings. Based on the Goals of Universal Design, the standards complement existing accessibility standards by identifying and encouraging the incorporation of features that increase usability, safety, health, and social participation for a diverse end user population.

The Universal Design Commercial Building Standards are organized and written to be understandable to all stakeholders. A set of performance guidelines describes the experience that users should have in a universally designed building. Each guideline has a list of approved strategies that can be implemented. A design team can decide to include all the strategies, none, or some for each guideline. Each strategy will be assigned points. Projects will be certified based on the total number of points obtained. Thus, each project may include very different features, based on the priorities of the project team and constraints of context. Priorities for universal design are addressed by weighting the points. Version 1.0 of the standard was approved by the committee in summer of 2010.

Adoption of the Standards will automatically mean higher levels of accessibility; for this reason, the Standards should also have the added effect of making compliance with regulatory mandates easier. Most important, the Standards include a process that will integrate design for human performance, health, and social participation into the culture of adopting organizations. The Standards will be flexible so that they can be easily improved to keep up with the state of knowledge. The aim is for the Standards to become the basis of a certification and accreditation program, modeled after the success of such programs in the field of sustainable design (e.g., U.S. Green Building Council's Leadership in Energy and Environmental Design [LEED], Green Globe Certification (www.greenglobes.com), and the Living Building Challenge (www.ilbi.org). Fees for certification, accreditation, and related educational activities will fund the operation of the GUDC. The guidelines and strategies presented earlier and elsewhere in this book were derived from the first draft of the Standards.

The second noteworthy effort to advance universal design is called The Flag of Towns and Cities for All Program. It is a social branding project of the Design for All Foundation in Europe (www.designforall.org/). Towns and cities that participate in the program commit to improving the quality of life for all citizens and visitors by adopting universal design. This commitment will be demonstrated by spending a portion of the municipality's investment budget on improving access to the physical environment and services. Cities that join the program must allow the Design for All Foundation to conduct periodic audits of the investment, the physical environment, and city services. If the municipality demonstrates continuous improvement, it will be allowed to exhibit a special flag demonstrating its achievement. Membership fees provide funding to support the program.

Summary

To conclude this chapter, we present several case studies of public buildings—museums, to be specific. These case studies graphically summarize how universal design of public buildings complements and extends accessibility. They also demonstrate how universal design incorporates design for human performance, health, and social participation to create exciting and interesting environments that engage the public. Several different types of museums are included to demonstrate a range of strategies.

Museums are a type of public accommodation where we can find many best practices in universal design. The reasons are easy to understand. Museums need to provide an emotional connection with their audience to attract repeat visitors and spread their reputations. They also need to accommodate very diverse visitor populations—individuals of all ages, including children, visitors who do not speak the local language, people of all backgrounds and lifestyles. They attract large crowds and therefore must make their facilities and services easy to use to avoid increasing the burden for staffing their facilities. Many museums want visitors to interact with the exhibits, and many try to find novel ways to entertain as well as educate. Visitors to museums often spend an entire day, which usually includes having a meal and shopping as well as attending formal presentations, experiencing exhibits, and learning about the collections. Thus, even without knowing the term, many creative thinkers in the museum world and their design professionals have developed extraordinary examples of universal design.

Robert Irwin, an artist, designed the central garden at the J. Paul Getty Museum in Los Angeles, California (Figure 8–11). Part of the garden is located on the side of a hill. To provide accessibility, the path through the garden had to wind back and forth along the slope of the hill. The artist installed steel slabs on either side of the zigzag path that are buried in the ground and protrude above to mark the edges of the path strongly. Additional railings improve awareness of the edge of the pathway and protect the garden. The path winds through intensive plantings of grasses, ornamentals, and two rows of mature trees organized along the slope to create a wonderful promenade through the garden. Seating areas are scattered throughout, and widened spaces at the changes in direction provide room for the large crowds, as well as wheeled mobility devices.

The Morris Arboretum in Philadelphia, Pennsylvania, has a Tree Adventure area that gives visitors an idea of what it is like to live up in the tree canopy like a bird (Figure 8–12). Entered from the top of a steeply sloping hill, a bridge projects out over the slope to a platform raised about 50 feet (15 m) over the ground and among the high branches of mature trees. The bridge has a very low slope. Small children, older adults with limited stamina, and wheelchair users can all easily get to the platform. The bridge and the platform are wide enough so that groups can

Figure 8–11: Sculpture garden at the J. Paul Getty Museum in Los Angeles, CA. This sculpture garden is designed as a meandering path through a multisensory landscape.

stay together. In the center of the platform, cargo netting allows children of all ages to lie down on their stomachs and feel suspended in the air over the ground below. The platform is an ideal place to watch birds. Visitors can place their heads between two megaphones so that they can also hear the birds at a distance. The device is mounted on a counterweighted pulley system so it can be adjusted to people of all statures. For small children, there is a giant nest with eggs at another platform. Children can imagine themselves as birds hatching babies in the nest.

The Pittsburgh Children's Museum in Pittsburgh, Pennsylvania, is an adaptive reuse of two older buildings united by a new addition placed in between. It is a highly interactive museum and incorporates many universal design ideas to create an enticing and exciting place for children and their families. The new central addition was used as a means to provide an accessible entry to the facility and to connect and integrate the two older buildings. The entry has ramps from the two main directions of approach (Figure 8–13a). Inside, a wide ramp provides access from the reception area to the café and auditorium area (Figure 8–13b). The ramp allows adults to accompany children easily and accommodates traffic in both directions. A screened-off climbing structure provides a safe place for children to climb high above floor level while adults follow them up along the stairway (Figure 8–13c). Very small children and children with mobility and sensory impairments can use this structure safely because of the protective screening and climbing ledges designed so that all the children using it have to crawl. The water play area is one of the most popular exhibits, offering many different alternative ways to play with water (Figure 8–13d). After play is over, a rack of dryers enables people of all statures to dry their clothes and shoes, as well as hands (see Figure 5–1). In an old planetarium hall, a high

Figure 8–12: Tree Adventure exhibit. This exhibit at the Morris Arboretum in Philadelphia, Pennsylvania, provides visitors the birds' perspective of living in the tree canopy. (a) Overview showing the oversized "nest." (b) Platform with children playing on cargo netting. (c) Image showing visitors of all ages using the platform. (d) An augmented hearing device.

platform served by both a stairway and a lift allows visitors to experiment with parachutes and pulleys (Figure 8–13e). Several spacious single-user restrooms are provided that allow adults to accompany children. The stairway has railings at both adult and toddler height.

The renovations to the Centraal Museum in Utrecht, the Netherlands, introduced an accessible circulation system into a meandering historic building complex to make it more understandable and reduce barriers of distance and weather exposure for museum visitors. The original complex included a large multistory main building with several outbuildings grouped around an open space (Figure 8-14a). The new additions elegantly inserted circulation elements that become powerful landmarks for constructing a strong mental image of the confusing building plan. The architects created these landmarks by exposing the technology used to build the elevator, stairs, and innovative folding stair lift to create a strong contrast with the existing historic stone building (Figures 8-14b, 8-14c). These glass-enclosed areas also provide views out and breaks from the closed in character of the historic building that become memorable landmarks in the building (Figure 8-14d). The finished complex includes an underground connection from the main building to the outbuildings. The most famous

Figure 8–13: Interactive children's museum. The Pittsburgh Children's Museum in Pennsylvania introduced many universal design features in its building. (a) Entry with ramp. (b) Interior ramp. (c) Climbing wall. (d) Water play area. (e) Parachute and pulley exhibit.

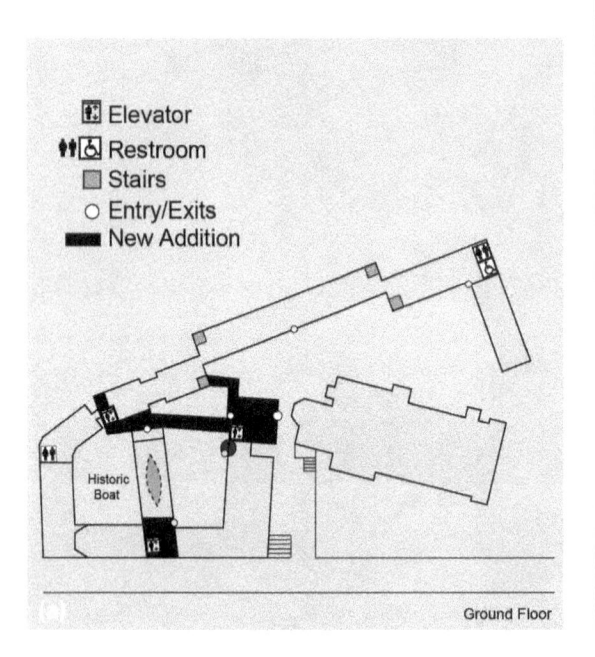

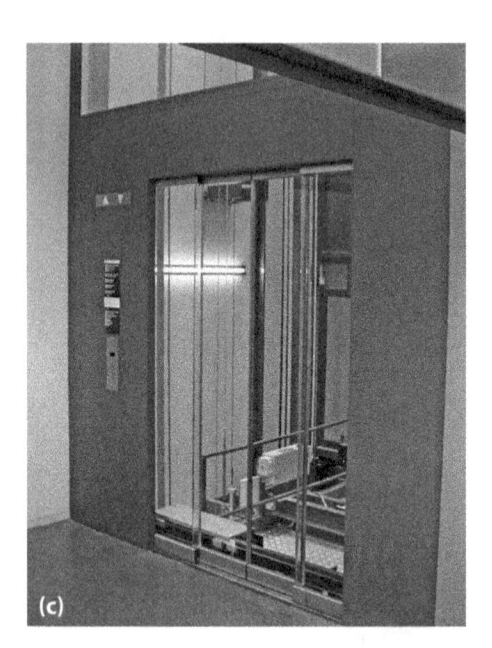

Figure 8–14: Rethinking a historic museum. The design of the renovation to the Centraal Museum of Utrecht, the Netherlands, focused on improving circulation, both vertically and horizontally. Key elements of the new circulation system were designed to be landmarks for visitors and help improve their orientation. (a) Floor plan diagrams. (b) Entry. (c) Elevator. (d) View from the courtyard.

exhibit is a Viking boat that was salvaged from a river where it had been preserved underwater for centuries. Since the boat is very fragile, it has to be maintained in a climate-controlled subterranean vault, which was built under the courtyard. The dramatic lighting, high humidity, and musty odor of the ship make visiting it a vivid multisensory experience that recalls the ship's original resting place in the river mud. The underground circulation link cleverly passes through the boat vault, marked at either end by "air locks" that keep the vault climate controlled but also define it as a landmark along the underground path. From a wayfinding perspective, this provides a special experiential and physical landmark in what could have been an uninteresting and difficult-to-remember space.

The MESI Museum in Tokyo, Japan, is a showplace of interactive exhibits for all ages, emphasizing the mysteries of technology and science. It has many universal design features. The two most striking features are a main entry hall that integrates mechanical circulation with stairs (Figure 8–15a) and a feature exhibit: a huge globe constructed of LED (light-emitting diode) panels surrounded by a gently spiraling suspended ramp that delights all museum visitors (Figure 8–15b). In the main circulation spaces, elegant stainless steel tactile guide strips

Figure 8-15: MESI Science Museum, Tokyo, Japan. The new museum used several universal design strategies to improve orientation and wayfinding. (a) Central stairs and escalators. (b) Digital globe exhibit with spiraling ramp. (c) Tactile guide path. (d) Ideograms on restroom door.

are installed in the dark grey terrazzo floor (Figure 8–15c). Not only do these guide strips help people with visual impairments; they also provide an affordance for other museum visitors to lead them through the museum. The designers devised ideograms for the restrooms that communicates the range of people who can find support inside (Fig 8-15d). These ideograms are not only functional but are cute and thus create a positive emotional response. All these universal design features provide memorable landmarks within the building that aid in wayfinding for all visitors. They are particularly useful because they do not rely on language. The museum has visitors from all over the world.

Review Topics

1. What is the basic goal of accessible design?
2. Explain what led to the universal design philosophy. What are some examples of universal design in accessibility codes?
3. Describe some examples of universal design in public accommodations.

References

Aiello, J. F., and Steinfeld, E. 1979. *Accessibility for People with Severe Visual Impairments.* Washington, DC: U.S. Department of Housing and Urban Development.

ANSI A117.1. 1961. "Specifications for Making Buildings and Facilities Accessible to, and Usable by, the Physically Handicapped." New York: American National Standards Institute, Inc.

———. 1971. "Specifications for Making Buildings and Facilities Accessible to, and Usable by, the Physically Handicapped." New York: American National Standards Institute, Inc.

———. 1980. "Specifications for Making Buildings and Facilities Accessible to and Usable by Physically Handicapped People." New York: American National Standards Institute, Inc.

Chollet, D. 1979. *A Cost-Benefit Analysis of Accessibility.* Washington, DC: U.S. Department of Housing and Urban Development.

Danford, G. S. and E. Steinfeld. 1999. "Measuring the Influences of Physical Environments on the Behaviors of People with Impairments." In E. Steinfeld and G. S. Danford (eds.), *Enabling Environments: Measuring the Impact of Environment on Disability and Rehabilitation,* 111–138. New York: Kluwer Academic/Plenum.

Diament, M. 2010. "'Drive-By' ADA Lawsuits Have Business Owners on Edge." (August 23) www.disabilityscoop.com/2010/08/23/ada-lawsuits/9881/.

General Accounting Office. 1975. "Report to the Congress: Further Action Needed to Make All Public Buildings Accessible to the Physically Handicapped" (July 15), http://archive.gao.gov/f0402/096968.pdf.

Howard, P. K. 1994. *The Death of Common Sense: How Law Is Suffocating America.* New York: Warner Books.

ICC/ANSI A117.1-2003. 2004. "Accessible and Usable Buildings and Facilities." New York, NY: International Code Council and American National Standards Institute, Inc.

ICC/ANSI A117.1-2009. 2011. "Accessible and Usable Buildings and Facilities." New York, NY: International Code Council and American National Standards Institute, Inc.

Maisel, J., E. Smith, and E. Steinfeld 2008. *Increasing Home Access: Designing for Visitability.* Washington, DC: AARP.

Ostroff, E. 1997. "The User as Expert." *Innovation* (Spring): 33–35.

Raheja, G. 2008. *Enabling Environments for the Mobility Impaired in the Rural Areas.* Roorkee, India: Indian Institute of Technology.

Sanford, J. A., M. F. Story, and M. L. Jones. 1996. "Accessibility Requirements for Ramp Slopes." Paper presented at the Rehabilitation Engineering and Assistive Technology Society of North America, Salt Lake City, Utah, June 7–12, 1996.

Schroeder, S. et al. 1979. *The Estimated Cost of Accessibility.* Washington DC: U.S. Department of Housing and Urban Development.

Shapiro, J. P. 1993. "No Pity: People with Disabilities Forging a New Civil Rights Movement." *Journal of Rehabilitation* 59 (July).

Steinfeld, E. 1977. "Developing Standards for Accessibility." In M. Bednars (ed.), *Barrier-Free Environments*, pp. 81–87. Stroudsburg, PA: Dowden, Hutchinson and Ross.

———. 1986. "ANSI A117.1: A Case Study in the Development of a Research Based Building Accessibility Standard; the Cost of Not Knowing." Paper presented at the Proceedings of the 17th Annual Conference of the Environmental Design Research Association, Atlanta, Georgia. April 9–13, 1986.

———. 2010. "Advancing Universal Design." In J. Maisel (ed.), *The State of the Science in Universal Design: Emerging Research and Developments*, pp. 1–19. Oak Park, IL: Bentham Science Publishers

Steinfeld, E., et al. 1979. *Barrier-Free Access to the Man-Made Environment—A Review of Literature.* Washington, DC: U.S. Department of Housing and Urban Development.

Steinfeld, E., S. Schroeder, and M. Bishop. 1979. *Accessible Buildings for People with Walking and Reaching Limitations.* Washington, DC: U.S. Department of Housing and Urban Development.

Steinfeld, E., S. Schroeder, J. S. Duncan, R. Faste, D. Chollet, M. Bishop et al. 1979. *Access to the Built Environment: A Review of Literature.* Washington, DC: U.S. Department of Housing and Urban Development Office of Policy Development and Research.

Templer, J. 1974. *Stair Shape and Human Movement.* Doctoral dissertation. New York: Columbia University.

U.S. Access Board. 2005. "ADA and ABA Accessibility Guidelines for Buildings and Facilities," www.access-board.gov/ada-aba/final.cfm.

World Health Organization (WHO). 2011. *World Report on Disability*. New York: WHO and The World Bank.

9

Housing

Evolution of Accessible Housing Policy

Set-Aside Approach

Government housing programs are generally called social housing programs, although in the United States they are called public housing or publicly assisted housing, depending on how the financing is provided. The U.S. Architectural Barriers Act (ABA), enacted in 1968, requires all buildings constructed, leased or financed with federal funding to be accessible. The government can finance housing in many ways, for example, direct subsidies and grants for construction, loan guarantees that stimulate lending by the private sector, rent subsidies to private developers, mortgage insurance for homeowners, or tax credits. The ABA covers social housing programs that directly subsidize housing production, provide loan guarantees for developers or rent subsidies. These programs were designed to serve low-income rental tenants. The ABA has not been applied to mortgage insurance programs, such as those run by the Federal Housing Administration (FHA) or the Department of Veterans Affairs, which are used widely to reduce the cost of single-family housing for middle-class home buyers. Housing that qualifies for tax credits is covered by Section 504 of the Rehabilitation Act.

The ABA requires that 5 percent of the units in all new construction to be accessible and, to an extent, set aside for occupancy by people with disabilities. Substantial renovation of an older building is treated as new construction. This percentage is roughly equal to the percentage of adults with *severe* disabilities in the population at large. The set-aside units must be designed to be fully accessible, including such features as accessible paths to and within the unit, wider doors, grab bars, roll-in showers, low counters and storage space, knee clearances, and higher toilets, among other features. Public and common spaces must also be accessible, as in public buildings. This policy prompted many states to pass laws similar to the federal laws or that added additional requirements for public and even some private housing (Steinfeld and White 2010). The accessible units are required to be first offered and rented to qualifying people with disabilities, unless there are no potential tenants with disabilities interested in the units, at which time they can be offered to other potential tenants. Similar state and local laws exist across the country for publicly sponsored housing built with local and state government funding.

The set-aside policy was a major breakthrough because it mandated that some accessible units actually would be constructed in all federal programs. However by the late 1970s, advocates for disability rights began to realize that there were some problems with the policy (Steinfeld and White 2010). One problem was the limited impact it had on the housing market. The total number of all accessible housing built under this policy was significantly lower than the number of people with disabilities who need accessible units since publicly funded housing construction is only a small part of total housing production in the United States. When the accessible units are occupied, they are no longer available until an occupant moves out, which could be years. Finally, since this policy applied only to new construction, it adds very few units to the total housing stock each year.

Other problems with the set-aside policy involve choice. Accessibility features are one of several factors people with a disability consider when choosing a place to live. For example, access to public transportation is important for those who do not have a motor vehicle. Many federally subsidized buildings are restricted to residents above a certain age, allowing younger individuals only if they have a disability. This restriction sometimes creates conflicts due to lifestyle and generational differences. Social housing often had only small apartments, especially in buildings reserved for senior citizens. In fact, a family with children under 18 years old cannot live in senior citizen buildings. Social housing is not available in all areas, and in the United States, most individuals do not qualify for it due to maximum income eligibility requirements. Finally, a person with a disability cannot choose which accessibility features are included because they are all built in, regardless of the occupant's actual needs. Some wheelchair users have limited ability to stand, while others do not. Some use the kitchen, while others do not. Some have sensory or cognitive rather than mobility impairments. The limitations of scope and choice inherent in the set-aside policy created a need for a new approach (Steinfeld and White 2010).

Example: Set-Aside Apartments

To demonstrate the restrictions that housing policy can inadvertently create, let us study a building in detail. The building shown in Figure 9-1 is a federally subsidized housing facility, owned by a nongovernmental organization (NGO). It was constructed in a suburb of Buffalo in the late 1970s. This project is typical of many built at the time and not much different from many built recently. Occupancy is restricted to people who are 62 years old and older with the exception that adults who are mobility impaired can also live in the accessible units. Only people whose incomes are below a certain level are eligible for residency. Public spaces are provided on the first floor, including a multipurpose room with a kitchen, large lobby, elevator lobby, laundry facilities, mailroom, and restrooms. All of the public spaces are accessible per public building requirements. No features are included to enhance perception and cognition other than typical lighting and acoustic treatment (e.g., a dropped ceiling and fluorescent lighting in the community spaces).

Figure 9-1: Apartment building, Williamsville, NY. This federally subsidized housing facility illustrates the restrictions housing policies can create.

The building is located on an access road to an office park and adjacent to a large supermarket. When the facility was constructed, there was no sidewalk or direct pathway to the supermarket. Residents had to drive, or they could walk to the main street and then to the supermarket parking lot. From there they had to walk across the lot to the entry. A walkway was soon constructed directly to the supermarket parking lot from the apartment building's property.

There are 150 units in the building, 15 of which are accessible. This is double the amount of accessible units usually required as a set-aside by building codes. This increase was planned because the building serves an older population. The number of residents needing accessible units is likely to be higher in such a facility. The accessible units are larger than the others are and have space clearances large enough for wheelchair use, as specified by the standards of the era. In these units, toilets are higher than those in the other units, and grab bars are provided next to the toilet and at the side of the bathtub. The closet rods are lower. There is an open space under the kitchen countertops rather than base cabinets as in the other units. The countertop is 2 inches lower than those in the other units. Upper cabinets are also lower, to make them easier to reach.

Government-subsidized housing is constructed to strict standards that limit the size of the units to control costs. One-bedroom units in buildings like this are generally between 525 and 600 square feet (53–60 square meters [sq m]). As in many projects like this in the United States, visitors to the apartment who need to use the bathroom have to pass through the bedroom. It is assumed that this provides more usable space in the bedroom, but that assumption is questionable since the path to the bathroom has to be kept clear of furniture even if it is inside the bedroom.

When buildings like this open up, they are often filled with residents who are relatively young and independent. Many are still driving, and some may even be working part time. At the time this building opened, they had difficulty renting out the accessible units even to people with disabilities. Part of the difficulty renting accessible units may be traced to the fact that a one-size fits all approach to accessibility does not accommodate everyone. One of the coauthors visited the building soon after it was built and found that a frail older woman was living in one of the accessible units. She was short in stature and complained that the toilet was too high for her. In contrast, the low closet rods, which were fixed in position, were too low to keep her long dresses off the floor. She also complained about the open space under the countertops that reduced her storage and was unattractive because of the visible plumbing underneath and because she had to store some items there. The lower countertop and wall cabinets were an advantage to her, however, because of her height.

Over time, the residents of buildings like this age in place, so the demand for accessible apartments increases over time. It is relatively common for such a building eventually to have residents with an *average* age in the mid-80s. Most tenants who experience advancing physical disability but do not have an accessible apartment must wait until such a unit is available or move to another building. Their physical condition may require them, in the meantime, to obtain assistance from social and health service agencies or personal care aides for cooking, bathing, and grooming. When they relocate, they may move to an assisted living facility or long-term care facility, which is much more expensive. When their resources are depleted, government programs pick up the cost, putting the burden for care on the public.

Sensory or cognitive limitations can also reduce tenants' ability to maintain themselves independently in a building like this. However, such buildings provide no support for sensory impairments beyond tactile signage and visual emergency alarms. The onset of dementia can force an individual out of the building because the law allows owners to evict a tenant who may be a danger to self or others by, for example, leaving stove burners on or forgetting to take out the garbage. These problems are not unique to social housing. One of the coauthors recently visited a privately owned "active living" retirement complex where many residents had private aides, often very low-income immigrants, who were living with them and sleeping on the living room sofas. For the elderly residents, paying an aide was a less expensive solution than assisted living or a nursing home, where the aides are provided as part of the rent.

Another reason that the accessible units may be difficult to rent is their location. Buildings like this are also often so isolated that social interaction opportunities beyond those among the residents themselves are limited to visits by family and friends. In this suburban location, public transportation service is very infrequent. Thus, if residents do not have their own automobiles, they have convenient access only to the supermarket. During the long, cold, and snowy Buffalo winter, even this may not be an option for three months of the year. This situation may be satisfactory to older residents because they have 149 other households to socialize with, but it can be very isolating for a younger resident with a disability, who would lack the opportunity to socialize with age peers.

There is a federal construction program targeted for people with disabilities. Aside from the possibility that more young people might be residents, it has similar limitations. In summary, the social housing policy in the United States restricts choices in dwelling unit size and social participation opportunities. Some states, NGOs, and private developers understand the problems with this type of accessibility and have developed options that adopt universal design thinking. Housing policies in other countries are more enlightened when it comes to age and disability. We describe some examples later in the chapter.

Adaptable Housing

Adaptable housing is a concept conceived in Sweden in the early 1970s by the Fokus Society. It spread to many countries in northern Europe and gained the attention of policy developers in the United States in the 1970s (Steinfeld, Schroeder, and Bishop 1979). This housing was built to promote social integration for people with severe disabilities. Nevertheless, Fokus units were built in all types of projects. Since many of the residents had family members or aides who were not disabled, the units had more extensive accessibility features, such as adjustable countertop heights, grab bars that swung away, whole-room shower floors, and movable storage units under countertops. The basic concept was to provide a unit that could be easily adapted to the specific needs of an individual and would support a household that was diverse in abilities.

Adaptable housing in the United States and other countries is intended for a much wider population than was Fokus housing. Typical adaptable housing includes fewer accessibility features from the start than required by the set-aside policy, but it is intended for application across a much broader range of units. The assumption is that all housing should include basic access features that support easy and inexpensive upgrades to full access if needed in the future. For example, adding reinforcement to walls where grab bars would need to be located means that walls do not need to be partially demolished and reconstructed in order to add grab bars. This reduces the cost of adaptations and eliminates the clinical appearance associated with grab bars. Another example is a kitchen cabinet that has a removable base to allow knee clearance for a wheelchair user.

Surveys of Americans with disabilities confirmed the assumptions supporting the adaptability concept (Bostrom, Mace, Long, and Corning 1987; Steinfeld et al. 1979). The 1980 ANSI A117.1 accessibility standard (see Chapter 8) included design criteria for adaptable housing, and the 1988 Fair Housing Act Amendments incorporate a version of the concept. The Fair Housing Act covers all apartment buildings with more than three units regardless of funding source or ownership. This means that all units in elevator-equipped buildings and all ground-floor units in buildings that are not elevator-equipped must be adaptable, even in privately financed buildings. Common areas of these buildings must be accessible as required in all public buildings by the Americans with Disabilities Act. Note that adaptable housing is not a substitute for, nor does it fulfill the set-aside policy requirements. Rather, the policies complement each other. The adaptable housing policy provides more choices and opportunities, while the set-aside policy provides people with severe disabilities many additional accessible features necessary to live independently (Steinfeld and White 2010). Since the set aside is usually only required in publicly financed construction, it does not cover most multifamily housing.

The multifamily housing laws in the United States have evolved over time, gradually improving access and equality for many. Some other countries, notably those in developing economies, have adopted set-aside laws similar to those in the United States (Steinfeld and Seelman 2011). Other countries, such as the Nordic nations, have not made any distinctions between housing and public accommodations in their laws; nor have they distinguished between single-family and multifamily building types. In these countries, one law covers all buildings, and accessibility is required to all dwelling units. These countries have included adaptable housing in their new construction for years, in both multifamily buildings and single-family buildings. In fact, even walk-up apartment buildings of three and four stories with only one stairway serving four to eight units have elevators to comply with the law. It is important to note that the largest segment of the American housing market is not covered by existing accessibility laws: single-family housing. Two new inclusive design concepts address the single-family portion of the market in the United States: visitability and life span design.

Example: Adaptable Walk-Up Housing

Let us look at another example to see the difference between adaptable housing and the set-aside approach. Figure 9–2 shows a building with four rental units on two levels served by a central stairway and entry. No public funding was provided for their construction, and they are designed to serve a varied resident population, including families with children. A set-aside of accessible units is not required in this type of housing since public funding was not included in the project. However, the Fair Housing Act and the state building code require that the units on the first floor be adaptable and all public/common spaces be accessible. According to the Fair Housing Act Accessibility Guidelines (FHAAG), the kitchens and bathrooms must have enough space to position a wheelchair at each fixture, an accessible path of travel within the unit must be provided to all rooms, and closets must have access. Outdoor terraces and balconies must be accessible also, although any balconies constructed of concrete can have one step down from the unit floor level. The wall next to and behind the water closet and the walls around the bathtub are reinforced to allow future installation of grab bars. In very small bathrooms, the door must open out to provide the necessary wheelchair clearances inside.

The photograph (Figure 9–2) demonstrates that this housing does not look any different from similar inaccessible housing. However, it also has only minimal adaptable features. The kitchen cabinets and work surfaces cannot be adjusted to address different needs, shelving is not adjustable, and there are no features to aid people with visual impairments, such as task lighting in the kitchen and contrasting edges for the countertops. In addition, there are no provisions to support people who have hearing or cognitive impairments. Thus, while the interiors provide a minimum level of adaptability, it is unclear whether these features would be sufficient to support aging in place or the onset of a severe disability. However, they would be usable for guests or tenants who had a temporary disability or less severe limitation. Additionally, because basic accessibility is provided, customizing the units to one's needs is relatively easy, with some exceptions. One major exception is that the Fair Housing Act does not require an accessible shower. Converting a bathtub to a shower would be costly and many people with severe disabilities need a roll-in shower.

Figure 9–2: Adaptable housing, Williamsville, NY. These apartments demonstrate that accessible housing does not need to be visually different from inaccessible housing.

This project is in the same suburban town as Figure 9–1. Unlike that project, this one is a complex of small walk-up buildings scattered on a large site with many different types of units, suitable for families as well as single individuals. Elevators are not generally required in the United States unless housing has more than three stories. Like the project in Figure 9–1, it is also isolated from community services and, unlike Figure 9–1, it is not within walking distance of a supermarket. The complex does have sidewalks and all pedestrian pathways are accessible, but public transit services are minimal. There are large parking lots, and accessible parking is provided close to all of the buildings. Like most housing in this suburban town, residents are dependent on private automobiles for mobility in the community, and the parking design reflects the importance of automobile access. In effect, the project is a self-contained island of accessibility. Projects like this may have accessibility features, but they still fall short of universal design as we have defined it. To achieve that, much more attention has to be paid to the site and neighborhood context. Ideally, all units would also be served by elevators.

Visitability (Basic Access)

Single-family housing is the dominant form of housing in the United States, and the vast majority of those homes are built in the private sector. In fact, about 69 percent of Americans live in a single-family dwelling (U.S. Census Bureau 2009). Canada, Australia, and New Zealand also have this pattern of housing construction and ownership. In predominantly rural areas all over the world, the single-family home is the norm. Thus, in the United States, existing accessibility regulations do not cover housing for the largest portion of the housing stock. Building a custom home or making major renovations to an existing home is the only option for people who want or need an accessible single-family home. Several factors often restrict this option. One is that accessibility features are usually perceived to be more expensive and difficult to build. Builders generally charge a high premium to add accessibility features to a new home. A second is that designers and builders who are knowledgeable enough to design and build accessible housing properly are difficult to find. Disability rights advocates argue that these restrictions amount to de facto housing discrimination. "Visitability" is a housing initiative that aims at addressing the situation and affecting a small change toward a more accessible housing stock (Maisel, Smith, and Steinfeld 2008; Steinfeld and White 2010).

Visitability is an approach for providing basic access features in single-family housing that originated in the United Kingdom. It is an affordable, sustainable, and accessible design approach introduced to the United States in 1987 by disability rights advocate Eleanor Smith and her advocacy organization, Concrete Change. The idea is to make a limited number of accessibility features standard in new home construction that is not covered by the Fair Housing Act (one- to three-family dwellings). The focus is on providing access to people with mobility impairments because most people with other disabilities can visit or live in a home without permanent accessibility features. In order for a person with mobility impairments to visit or temporarily live in a home, however, these features are essential (Steinfeld and White 2010):

- One no-step entrance
- Low thresholds
- Doorways that provide at least 32 inches (815 mm) of clearance
- Hallways with at least 36 inches (915 mm) clear width
- Basic access to at least a half bath on the main floor
- Reinforcement in walls next to toilets for future installation of grab bars
- Light switches and electrical outlets within comfortable reach for all

Currently over 50 state and local governments in the United States have either a voluntary or mandatory visitability program in place (Maisel et al. 2008). However, most of those programs apply only to single-family housing built with public support, but, unlike the set-aside policy, the visitability approach applies to 100 percent of publicly funded housing. The definition of "public support" varies, but it is much broader than the policy used in set-aside housing. Depending on the region, it may be defined as use of public land, waivers of building permit or utility hookup fees, cash grants, tax credits, and other forms of direct or indirect public support. Currently, only a few of the existing visitability ordinances apply to all publicly and privately funded single-family housing. Some cities have implemented voluntary incentive programs that have been quite successful in extending visibility beyond publicly supported housing. A federal law is in development that would apply to all single-family housing built with federal assistance in the United States (Maisel et al. 2008).

As local and state governments adopt visitability policies, several different interpretations of the requirements have emerged. Most do not provide detailed criteria for the visitable features, which leads to confusion. Many model-building codes such as the International Code Council (ICC) codes and state accessibility laws reference the consensus standard for accessibility in the United States, the ICC/ANSI A117.1 Standard. Until recently, the standard defined two types of units, Type A and Type B. Standards for Type A units are intended for the 5 percent set-aside rules. Standards for Type B units mirror the Fair Housing Act requirements. The latest version of the standard includes a new Type C unit that defines the technical requirements of visitability. Inclusion of this definition will help reduce confusion and create uniformity as new laws are passed (Maisel et al. 2008).

The new A117.1 Standard includes many provisions not included in all current visitability laws. Local governments can adopt the standards but should provide exceptions based on their specific needs. For example, in many urban neighborhoods, it is desirable to build walk-up dwelling units above a garage or store. Such units would be illegal if the standard was not modified before adoption because they would most likely not meet all the requirements. Exemptions would also be needed on flood plains, such as those along the Gulf Coast, where post–Hurricane Katrina federal standards now require that houses to be raised up to 12 feet (3.6 m) off the ground (Steinfeld and White 2010).

The cost of accessibility is often an issue in developing accessible housing policy. A study of nine existing housing developments found that all 30 dwelling unit designs in these projects could be redesigned to comply with the Fair Housing Act and ANSI standards without increasing size or decreasing marketability (Steven Winter Associates 1993). Developers estimated their own cost impact. It was estimated that accessibility to all units and the sites would result in only a marginal increase of less than 1 percent. Although this study focused on multifamily housing, it illustrates that even small homes can be made accessible without major effects on cost.

Since the cost of the limited set of visitability features is very low, the universal application of basic accessibility to all new single-family homes would have minimal cost impact. The estimated added cost of visitability, when incorporated intelligently, is even lower—about $100 for new homes built on a concrete slab, including 25 percent in overhead and profit. This estimate includes a zero-step entry, 30-inch (762 mm) clear interior doors, lever handles, and reinforcement in bathroom walls (Williams and Altaffer 2000). For homes with crawl spaces or basements, the cost is still only an extra $300 to $600 (Concrete Change 2008). In comparison, retrofitting for visitability would result in significantly higher costs. Very few house plans cannot be redesigned for visitability. Visitability adds value to a home because it benefits the entire population and can have a positive impact on safety, aesthetics, livability, long-term maintenance, resale, and other factors (Maisel et al. 2008).

Example: S.M.A.R.T. Program

The City of Austin, Texas, has pioneered in the provision of visitable housing through an incentive program called S.M.A.R.T.™ (Safe, Mixed-Income, Accessible, Reasonably-priced, and Transit-oriented). Housing developers who build housing that meets the city's requirements for the program receive four benefits from the city:

1. A density bonus that allows them to build more units in the same land area
2. Reduced permit fees
3. Fast-track approvals through different city agencies that must approve the design and construction
4. An ombudsman service that provides assistance if any problems arise with city approvals

The S.M.A.R.T. program is popular with builders because it increases profitability when the market for higher cost housing is not strong. Many types of housing have been constructed through the program, including detached single-family housing subdivisions (Figure 9–3a), individual units built on vacant lots within existing neighborhoods (Figure 9–3b), and mixed-use apartment buildings (Figure 9–3c). Note that the last example would have to be accessible anyway in the United States because of the Fair Housing Act. This building would require an elevator since the first floor of dwellings is not at grade. However, the density bonus allows the builder, if he desires, to build up to four stories instead of three, which makes an elevator more affordable. This program has not only resulted in thousands of accessible single-family homes but also has increased the number of adaptable multifamily units constructed. Furthermore, by linking accessibility to affordability, location along transit corridors, and sustainability, the program is improving the sustainability of housing in the city along several dimensions.

Figure 9–3: Housing in Austin, TX, constructed through the S.M.A.R.T.™ program: (a) detached single-family housing with accessible entry at rear from alley; (b) infill housing built on lots that had been abandoned; (c) mixed-use apartment buildings.

Life Span Design

The current generation of older people is more aware of their future needs. For example, 70 percent of home buyers over age 50 prefer single-story homes (Wylde 2002). Because many older Americans prefer aging in place, life span housing must include a broader range of features than adaptable or visitable housing. Life span housing designs include accommodations for sensory limitations, security, and the prevention of falls. Livable communities and neighborhoods with convenient services, recreation, jobs, street life, and informal gathering places are necessary for aging in place with a good quality of life. Despite the tendency to view it as only desirable for people over the age of 50, aging in place has features that are desirable for all age groups. Single-parent households, households where both parents need to work, demands of competitive work environments, the need to protect children, rising asthma rates, and increasingly sedentary lifestyles all suggest that a life span approach to provide safe, convenient, and healthy homes and neighborhoods would be desirable for all home buyers and renters.

Builders are marketing housing designed for aging in place in many countries. Unfortunately, the features included in these home designs often are not sufficient to support the needs of older home owners. Thus, there is a need to codify what features should be expected in such housing for the protection of consumers. The first attempt to do this is the Lifetime Homes (LTH) program in the United Kingdom (www.lifetimehomes.org.uk). The LTH standards emphasize accessibility for mobility impairments. A more inclusive approach is desirable for aging, particularly since there are significant age-related limitations in vision, hearing, and cognition. Two newer programs, the Lifemark Initiative in New Zealand and Livable Housing Design in Australia, have developed more expansive approaches.

The authors believe that a mix of essential and optional design features should be provided for aging in place. This mix will provide uniformity across a country, so consumers know what to expect, but also flexibility to address differences in the housing market and physical context of communities. The box "Life Span Design Features" describes examples of optional and essential features that could be included in life span housing (Steinfeld and White 2010).

Life Span Design Features

Essential
- No-step access to the home and all patios, balconies, and terraces
- Low-threshold doorways that provide at least 34 inches (865 mm) of clearance
- Lever-type door handles located 34 to 38 inches (865–956 mm) high
- Direct entry to home from off street parking area, if provided
- Hallways at least 42 inches (1065 mm) clear wide
- Access to at least one full bath on the main floor
- Reinforcement in walls next to toilets and tubs for future installation of grab bars
- A means to see and talk to visitors at the door without opening the door and usable for both ambulant people and wheelchair users
- Kitchen cabinetry that allows a person to work in a seated position with knees under the work counter
- Light switches and electrical outlets located 24 to 48 inches (610–1220 mm) high
- Stair treads at least 11 inches (280 mm) deep and risers no higher than 7 inches (180 mm)
- Good lighting throughout the house with task lighting in critical locations like stairs and kitchen counters
- Nonglare surfaces
- Contrasting colors at floor surface boundaries
- At least 30 by 48 inches (760 by 1220 mm) of clear space in front of all appliances, fixtures, and cabinetry
- Front-loading laundry equipment on an accessible path of travel
- Ample kitchen and closet storage within, or adjustable to be within, 28 to 48 inches (710–1220 mm)
- Comfortable reach zones throughout the home

Optional
- No steps on any entry path
- One-story plan, residential elevator, or planned space for future elevator
- Secure area for children's outdoor play

- If off-street parking is provided, shelter from extreme weather for at least one vehicle
- Storage for recreational and exterior maintenance equipment accessible from outside
- Open plan in living spaces providing visual access from each main living spaces to all the others
- Space for home office convenient to living spaces
- Mudroom to store outdoor clothing with space for seating
- Adjustable-height kitchen and bathroom sinks or two sink heights
- At least one roll in shower in an accessible bathroom
- Appliances and cabinets with built-in convenience features
- Intercom system
- Security system
- Laundry equipment mounted on podiums to reduce the need for bending
- Fall detection system that can notify caregivers automatically in case of a fall
- Programmable controls for electrical, heating, and air conditioning systems
- Controls that are easy to perceive and intuitive to use

The concept of aging in place has benefits at every stage of life. It provides safety and security for children, stress reduction for parents, and access features for older residents. Although life span housing benefits everyone, the key market is currently the older population. This market includes people who hope to move to a new home and age in place for the rest of their lives, such as early retirees and parents whose grown children have recently left home. As the Baby Boomer generation ages, the demand for age-restricted communities likely will increase simply because the population of Boomers will be far greater than that of previous older generations; however, few older people are interested in these communities. The majority of buyers over the age of 50 want to age in place, something best accomplished with housing designed for the life span (Mattimore et al. 1997).

Example: LIFEHouse™

The LIFEHouse™ is a concept home design and constructed by New American Homes in Newport Cove, a northern suburb of Chicago, Illinois. The authors, through the IDeA Center, provided assistance with the design of the first dwelling unit. New American Homes is developing a subdivision of 67 homes. The company studied the demography of the local market and concluded that residents who were over 50 years of age would be a prime target market for houses in their development, but it did not want to create the impression that younger households would not be welcome. Thus, they decided to develop a line of homes that would incorporate life span design features and be attractive to people at any stage of life. Using an existing model it had built before as a basis, it made modifications that introduce universal design throughout the home and built a new model home on the site.

The home is designed in the "Craftsman" style but has a double garage that is essential for marketability in this location. It is raised off the ground, but, by clever grading of the site, New American Homes was able to include a landscaped path with no stairs to the front entry. The model house has stairs to the second floor and lower level. An elevator is optional. Due to the site topography, the lower level also has on grade access to the outdoors. The LIFEHouse™ concept has many amenities and features beyond visitability. It includes all the features in the essential list for life span design presented earlier plus many of the optional features and introduces some unique twists to the concept. Key features include:

- First-floor master bedroom suite
- Open plan with generous circulation spaces for improved communications and circulation
- Good views out with low windowsills
- Three levels of lighting in each space: general illumination, accent lighting, and task lighting (Figure 9–4)
- Home office in central location on the main floor open to living spaces
- Stacked closets designed for future installation of an elevator to serve the top floor, basement, and garage level
- Accessible terrace on the ground floor
- Multiple work center levels in the kitchen and a food preparation island (Figure 9–4)
- Accessible storage features
- Fixtures and appliances with universal design features (Figure 9–4)

This home will be the first in a series contemplated by the company. Unlike other "accessible" or "universal design" home plans on the market, the LIFEHouse™ is a complete package with construction details worked out and a set of preselected products. A great deal of care was taken to select products and design details that provided strong contemporary aesthetic values married with the universal design attributes. Thus, the concept provides a positive visual identity to associate with life span living.

Figure 9–4: LIFEHouse™. This image shows many levels of lighting, multiple work center levels, food preparation island, and fixtures and appliances with universal design features.

Community-Based Rehabilitation and Special-Purpose Housing

The term "community-based rehabilitation (CBR)" refers to rehabilitation efforts that occur outside of medical and institutional contexts. CBR engages people with disabilities as active partners in decisions related to their quality of life, including medical care. It mandates that professionals tailor their practices according to the specific needs and backgrounds of the people they serve. Universal design seeks to ensure social participation in all aspects of life and, thus, is very compatible with the CBR philosophy. Planning and housing policies can support CBR by providing a range of housing choices and accessible community infrastructure.

Advocates of CBR argue that this participatory approach is far better than treatment-based (medical) approaches that promote isolation and stigmatization. Proponents of the latter may argue that some people have disabilities that are too severe to allow them to direct the course of their own treatment or that the services they need are not available except in institutional settings. CBR proponents counter that this leads to a dependence on others, reduces independence, and creates learned helplessness, isolation, and stigma. The principle of providing care in the least restrictive environment can be used to address limitations on available services and living environments or funding.

CBR can occur in many settings: private residences, group homes, service-supported housing, and assisted living facilities, among others. Many people with severe disabilities can live entirely independently if there are no barriers to access and can enjoy the same places, rights, and benefits as everyone else in the community. However, some people may not have the physical or cognitive ability to live entirely independently, even if all physical barriers are removed. They may require varying degrees of support services, ranging from occasional medical intervention and therapy to full-time personal care attendants. Where constraints prevent full community integration, the goal should be to provide a living setting that is the least restrictive for the individual.

Although group homes, service-supported housing, and assisted living facilities are examples of settings that support CBR, often they are designed and operated using a medical model. A universal design approach to both design and service delivery can integrate these facilities into neighborhoods and engage residents, family, and community members to foster the highest degree of social participation possible. The rest of this section discusses how the community-based approach to rehabilitation grew from the deinstitutionalization movement and the housing features that support this approach.

In the 1960s, disability rights advocates, families of people with severe disabilities, and professionals serving these populations became concerned about poor institutional conditions and ineffective treatments (Wisnewski and et al. 1981). In the United States, the care of people with severe disabilities is governed by state law and provided through state agencies. Building on models established in northern Europe, a campaign emerged during the early 1970s in the United States using legal action in the courts, legislation, and presidential directive to rethink the institutional model of care (O'Conner 1976). Some professionals had expressed concern over institutional practices as early as the 1920s. They believed that the complexity of cognitive impairments, in particular, demanded flexibility and individual care that cannot be achieved in large institutions (Scheerenberger 1983).

By the 1980s, many community living alternatives had been established throughout the country, usually in the form of group homes and supported apartments. Leaders in the mental health establishment, in particular, recognized that institutions do not increase competence and, in fact, can have a detrimental effect on skill development by retarding skill development and fostering "abnormal" behaviors (Sommer 1974). Community living arrangements, however, provide a normative residential environment with opportunities for skill development that encourage development of competence (Wisnewski and et al. 1981). Since that time, state governments have mandated that such community institutions provide the least restrictive environment to support the life of a person with a developmental disability. Deinstitutionalization and the development of CBR practices, which emerged from this movement, have their roots in the principle of "normalization."

"Normalization" is a "systematic formulation of how to maximize the likelihood that people who have been socially defined as deviant (devalued) become socially valued or revalued" (Wolfensberger 1977, p. 135). Wolfensberger defines the principle of normalization as "the utilization of culturally valued means in order to establish and/or maintain personal behaviors, experiences, and characteristics that are culturally normative or valued." He argued that functions of an environment are interpreted by both internal users (residents) of the place and the community at large. These functions have an impact on the social valuation of people with disabilities (Wolfensberger 1977).

Social valuation is the process within cultures that determines a person's value to the society. For example, within many cultures, the role of doctor has high value, but bus driver has low value. Historically, people who are "socially deviant" are given low value, while people whose actions and behavior are consistent with local culture are given higher value. A person is considered socially deviant if others attribute a negative value to some characteristic or attribute of the person that is different from the norm (Wolfensberger 1977). Since people with physical or cognitive disabilities are often considered socially deviant from the rest of society, they are often unconsciously devalued. Characteristics of a building, such as a large psychiatric hospital, can be associated with the devalued status of its residents, especially when outdated perceptions of mental illness contribute to this devaluation. Wolfensberger (1977) lists eight different perceptions of people who are considered socially deviant. These are:

1. Less than human
2. Menacing and/or dangerous
3. Sick
4. An object of ridicule
5. An object of pity
6. A burden of charity
7. Childlike
8. A holy being

The physical environment helps to overcome devaluation when it is equitable in terms of access to resources and it also facilitates growth and rehabilitation.

Outdated perceptions often lead to residential environments that are isolated, lacking in amenities, and institutional in appearance—that look like hospitals, schools, or even jails rather than homes. Much of how people act in society is dependent on their interactions with other people. Isolated residential environments and limited opportunities for social interaction only perpetuate the perception of deviancy. If a particular type of behavior is the predominant form of behavior in a person's everyday setting, then that behavior becomes the norm. If, however, the same person is exposed to typical daily interactions in the community, such as in a supermarket, park, or restaurant, the chance of skill development increases and behavior may become more normative based on community expectations.

Homes that are institutional in appearance also have a negative effect on occupants. If a home does not have the features of a typical home, individual growth of residents will be restricted, and they may not learn acceptable behaviors for home life. For example, a lack of personalization opportunities, individual possessions, and personal territory can lead to unacceptable behaviors, such as invasions of other individuals' spaces and disrespect of others' possessions. Fixed beds, seating, and chairs result in a very institutional appearance and limit the opportunities for residents to make decisions about socialization and comfort for themselves.

Normalization theory suggests that equipment and technology that is typical to a home environment should be available in community residences for people with disabilities. The ability to use common household objects, such as window shades, light switches, and kitchen appliances, will familiarize users with those objects and promote development. Research has demonstrated that there are certain qualities that make a home appear institutional (Thompson and et al. 1996). For example, the larger the lawn relative to the size of the house, the more institutional a home appears. Similarly, the percentage of the facade covered by vegetation is inversely related to institutional appearance. Finally, the smaller the percentage of roof visible in proportion to facade, the more institutional the building appears. To avoid an institutional appearance, housing should be located in residential neighborhoods and have live-in care. The research findings suggest that in planning alternatives to institutional care, policy makers and planners must address the environment and that it may even be as important as the service program itself.

As early as 1977, Wolfensberger concluded that environmental features should be based on values, ideology, and role perceptions that are developmental, normalizing, and status enhancing. Facility names, elements, locations, programs, and other items should be carefully planned. The design should be based on occupancy type (e.g., residential, educational), not the users' perceived level of functioning. Neighborhood location and scale are critical. Facilities must have access to integrative social opportunities, educational services, and recreational opportunities in order to provide successful community integration. Newly built facilities must be designed so that they can be adapted for different purposes if the service is no longer needed. Existing institutional structures that cannot be modified to be appropriate for the service they offer should be adapted to serve other purposes more appropriate for the type of building, such as government offices, classrooms, and civic meeting places. Further, laws and codes must be examined to remove roadblocks to siting and constructing appropriate human service buildings and locations. Finally, projects must raise the public's awareness that most devaluation is unconscious and is even more destructive than poor service quality.

Neighborhood Context

The neighborhood is an extremely important factor in achieving universal design in housing. Livable communities and neighborhoods are necessary for aging in place and social integration of people with severe disabilities. Features of a livable neighborhood include conveniently located services, recreation, and jobs as well as a healthy street life and informal gathering places. These features are essential for a good quality of life. Traditional urban neighborhoods and small villages have provided the kind of environment that is most conducive to social integration and aging in place. Unfortunately, widespread contemporary practices in land development have created barriers to these goals.

Following World War II, the automobile became the driving force behind land use policies in the United States. The Interstate Highway System made it easier to travel long distances. Combined with government subsidies for new single-family home construction, it led to the creation of automobile-oriented communities (Duany, Plater-Zyberk, and Speck 2001). Single land use planning separated communities into business zones and residential zones. These land use practices have become so commonplace that they are often used in the redevelopment of older cities besides being practically the only practices used in suburbs. The segregation of land uses creates barriers to accessibility for all. Not only does it reduce the chance of informal social interaction and neighborliness, it reduces access to services, recreation, and jobs. It discriminates against those who do not or cannot drive, such as children, low-income households, people with visual impairments, some older people, and some people with mobility and/or cognitive impairments (Steinfeld and White 2010).

The proliferation of suburban sprawl also leads to dangerous and unhealthy street patterns. Large-radius curbs, wide streets, a treelike circulation plan, and lack of sidewalks in local neighborhoods facilitate high-speed automobile travel and create hazardous conditions for all pedestrians (Duany et al. 2001). Neighborhood streets feed into collector streets and arterials with four to six lanes of traffic, creating barriers to street crossing, safety, street life, and social interaction. However, the most obvious impact of land use planning today is the uniformity of development. Population density is similar everywhere, and traffic congestion is uniform everywhere as well. Even housing type and character is relatively uniform, sometimes throughout entire municipalities. This means that neighborhoods lack unique aesthetic and social character that makes a place special to inhabitants. Instead of unique buildings and street details providing neighborhood character, cost, quality of schools, highway proximity, and local amenities define the neighborhoods. Choices are reduced to a minimum, which is certainly not consistent with an inclusive design philosophy or even an American ideology that respects and celebrates difference (Steinfeld and White 2010).

Supporters of Traditional Neighborhood Development (TND) aim to provide that unique aesthetic and social character to define diverse neighborhoods. TND refers to land use practices that mirror historically proven approaches to neighborhood planning, urban design, and housing design. Prior to World War II, neighborhoods either formed in an organic manner as settlements grew or were planned to ensure proximity to services, recreation, jobs, food, religious establishments, and schools. Proponents of TND argue for a return to these practices for social reasons, as well as for sustainability reasons. They also argue that we can learn from the most successful and enduring urban neighborhoods and apply their lessons to new development and city infill projects (Ellis 2002). However, one problem with returning to traditional practices is that traditional housing often did not accommodate people with disabilities or the aged. Traditionally, people with disabilities and the aged lived either with family or in institutions. Advancements in rehabilitation technology and civil rights changed our views on accessibility to public buildings, and we are now seeing the impact on housing as well. Just as TND proponents have found ways to accommodate the automobile, there are ways to accommodate accessibility (Steinfeld and White 2010).

Although current land development practices still make TND difficult, its proponents are exploring new ways to overcome these barriers, and there are many success stories all over the world. Many good practice examples exist of TND in a range of densities that provide accessible services and recreation within walking distance of all residences and transit-oriented planning. King Farm in Rockville, Maryland, is a popular and very desirable TND community served by transit that contrasts greatly with the surrounding suburban sprawl within which it was built. Habersham in Beaufort, South Carolina, is an example of a new development that provides an alternative to conventional suburban planning. Park DuValle in Louisville, Kentucky, is an example of a mixed-income urban neighborhood. In suburban Miami, the epitome of suburban sprawl is being transformed into a TND development around a regional mall to be called Downtown Kendall. Stapleton is another example in the outskirts of Denver. It is known for its emphasis on sustainable design and integration with the natural environment.

A recent study demonstrated the market value of TND. Housing resale appreciation is often greater in urban neighborhoods than for similar houses in conventional suburban locations. In fact, housing in smart growth developments sold for a higher average price per square foot in 80 percent of the comparisons conducted (Environmental Protection Agency 2011). The barriers to TND will become easier to overcome as the popularity of walkable neighborhoods increases due to the aging of populations and higher fuel costs. It is important to note that most TND developments are good examples of universal design in the neighborhood context but not in terms of accessible housing. In fact, the extensive use of multistory row houses and raised porches has resulted in a paradox. People who need accessible housing or are aging in place cannot find it in the most accessible neighborhoods available!

Despite the lifelong benefits of inclusive housing and neighborhoods, critics argue that accessibility laws have a negative effect on "neighborliness." However, these views are based on their own experience with home modifications rather than with houses designed to be accessible from the beginning (Steinfeld and White 2010). A very long ramp that fills the entire yard might be an ugly intrusion; if the home had been accessible from the beginning, there would be no need for any ramp at all.

Even people with disabilities do not like the unwanted attention that comes with a long, ugly, ramp or industrial-looking lift because such adaptations could make the owner a target for crime, create animosity with neighbors due to the awkward appearance, and reinforce the stigma of disability (Steinfeld and White 2010). Since most houses are not designed to support accessibility renovations, awkward designs are the obvious result. However, if accessibility features are part of the original design, they will contribute to sustainable and lifelong neighborhoods.

Books often illustrate suburban examples of accessibility. Suburban homes are easily adapted for accessibility because of their large lots and nondescript aesthetics. However, in urban housing, inclusive design must embrace and reinforce neighborliness (Steinfeld and White 2010). Designers cannot just copy details from technical manuals when accessibility is required; they must treat accessibility as an integral part of creating livable homes and neighborhoods. Designing inclusive housing from the beginning is one way of integrating accessibility with neighborhoods for the life span.

Example: Neptuna

Neptuna is a multifamily midrise building built in a new neighborhood on the outskirts of Malmo, Sweden (Figure 9–5). It was built by a company specializing in social housing for older people and serves residents who qualify for social housing due to low income as well as those who can afford to pay market-rate rents. All the apartments are accessible at a level similar to that in Figure 9.2. However, many universal design features provide a much more extensive level of adaptability in the bathroom. These feature include an adjustable-height shower spray; a shower area built into the floor, eliminating curbs; room-surrounding grab bars; and adjustable-height sinks. The kitchens are all accessible to a similar level as in Figure 9.2 with the addition of wall ovens and a full-height pantry, both of which reduce the need for bending in food preparation and storage access.

The public spaces in the building are fully accessible. A wide range of services is provided in the building, including personal care services, fitness activities, social services, and meals. Meals actually are provided in a commercial restaurant that rents space in the first floor. This restaurant accepts vouchers from residents but also serves a regular clientele. On the top floor of the building, there is a sauna and whirlpool bath for recreational and therapy use. These facilities have a magnificent view of the strait between Sweden and Denmark. On the first floor, the building has a winter garden, which provides a tropical garden accessible all year long. The winter garden is located in the middle of an outdoor courtyard for good-weather seating and recreation. The community room has a view and opens directly into this courtyard.

The site is part of a redevelopment project in a former industrial port area. It is on the coastline and is only one of many buildings constructed on the site using principles of sustainable design and TND. It is located on a block right on the ocean along the main pedestrian walkway, which is a large public promenade along the water with many recreational amenities that attract all ages. Many other apartment buildings that are not age restricted are also located along this promenade. The neighborhood includes a big-box shopping area with a supermarket and many other stores occupying first-floor spaces on the streets. Parking is provided on the vehicular streets and in remote lots and garages rather than right next to the units. There is also public transportation service available on-site.

This project provides good support for life span living. All the apartments are universally designed. The age-restricted setting increases peer-related social interaction opportunities and facilitates service delivery without isolating residents from the community. The neighborhood is also fully accessible and tied through transportation to the rest of the city of Malmo. The neighborhood context provides opportunities for social integration with all age levels. Services are provided on site to maintain health and nutrition. There are many recreational opportunities, both in the building and in the neighborhood, and the environment has many amenities and a high level of sensory stimulation. There are no restrictions with regard to income so it is not only affordable but also does not exclude those who are able to pay market rates. No stigma is attached to living in this building. In fact, residents feel a great deal of pride. This building will allow residents to age in place while obtaining the support they need. Thus, the project demonstrates how universal design extends beyond the bricks and mortar of housing to services provided and to the neighborhood context. Because of the amenities offered, this building is likely to prevent or at least postpone the need for higher levels of services that are not provided in buildings like those shown in Figures 9–1 and 9–2.

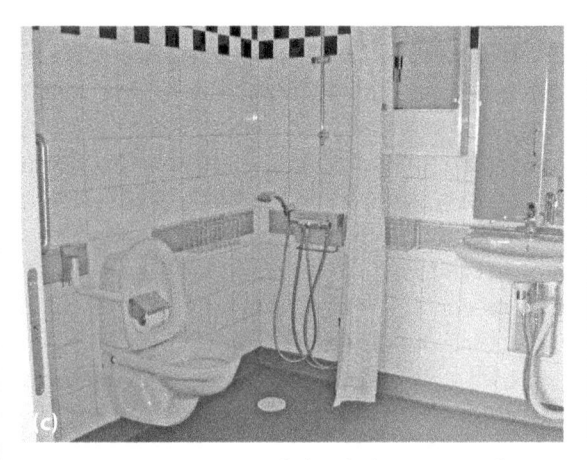

Figure 9-5: Neptuna multifamily housing, Malmo, Sweden. (a) View of the building from the seaside promenade showing the winter garden and courtyard. The restaurant is on the first floor on the corner of the building. (b) Resident lounge with direct access to the courtyard. (c) Typical bathroom showing the "in-floor" shower, adjustable grab bars and storage, and adjustable sink. (d) View of the mixed-use development along the waterfront including the use of the promenade for recreation and socialization.

Source: From *Inclusive Housing: A Pattern Book Design for Diversity and Equality* by The Center for Inclusive Design and Environmental Access. Copyright © 2010 by Edward Steinfeld and Jonathan White. Used by permission of W.W. Norton and Company, Inc.

Summary

Accessible housing policies and practices are evolving throughout the world and moving toward the adoption of universal design. In some places, policies and practices already include universal design characteristics.

The initial approach to providing accessible housing was the set-aside approach. This approach still has not been adopted in many countries but is well established in others. It has some significant limitations. The units are generally all the same in terms of features and often cannot be adapted easily for the specific needs of an individual. To ensure that people with disabilities are the ones that benefit from them, they have to be reserved for this segment of the population, which is often not feasible financially unless sufficient outreach is completed prior to construction to find qualified tenants. This type of housing also may not be in locations that are places that the people who need the units want to live, for example, close to accessible public transportation.

Adaptable housing is more of a universal design approach. It is easy to adapt to individual needs and can be applied on a much wider basis. In some countries, adaptable housing is required for all housing or for major segments of the housing market, e.g., multifamily housing. In the United States, the Fair Housing Act requires all multifamily housing to be accessible except for the above-ground floors of walk-up buildings.

In some countries, such as the UK and the Nordic countries, all housing units have to have at least basic accessibility provisions, even single-family homes. In North America, there is a trend to apply basic accessibility requirements, often called "visitability," to single-family homes, but most communities do not have any accessible single-family homes except those built or modified specifically for homeowners with disabilities.

In addition to policies focused on improving the accessible housing stock in general, the elimination of large-scale institutions for people with severe disabilities is another important development. Community-based rehabilitation practices have lead to the construction of small-scale residences for people with many types of disabilities who need assistance with daily life. These community residences are also being utilized to house other devalued populations, such as abused women and children, recovering substance abusers, and others. Universal design can be applied to housing specifically built for people in these groups to help integrate them into the community, reduce stigma, and eliminate harmful devaluation.

The aging of the population is driving the development of housing that can support aging in place, which, if implemented properly, has many more universal design features than the other types of accessible housing. These features include consideration of sensory and cognitive limitations in addition to mobility limitations. The authors call this type of housing "life span design," and argue that the features should accommodate people at all stages of life by providing safety and security for children, stress reduction features for working age adults, and support for independence and reducing caregiver burden in old age.

Perhaps the most neglected aspect of universal design in housing at this point in its evolution is the neighborhood context. Without a neighborhood that provides the features necessary for everyday life and access to employment sites or transportation to them, housing may support independence but not social participation. Moreover, health conditions that lead to disability, such as obesity and asthma, are related to lack of attention to neighborhood context. New initiatives underway concerned with environmental sustainability and social justice, such as the TND movement, offer great promise for finding common ground with advocates of universal design. Neighborhoods that provide safe, secure, and efficient pedestrian networks, provide access to public transportation and nutritious food, reduce pollution, and increase opportunities for active lifestyles also support improved social integration of disadvantaged groups.

Review Topics

1. What is the set-aside approach to accessibility, and what are its limitations?
2. Describe adaptable housing, visitability, and life span design. How do they differ?
3. What is "normalization," and why is it important when designing for people with disabilities and other socially devalued groups?

References

Bostrom, J. A., R. L. Mace, M. Long, and B. Corning. 1987. *Adaptable Housing: Marketable Accessible Housing for Everyone.* Raleigh, NC: Barrier Free Environments, Inc. for the United States Department of Housing and Urban Development Office of Policy Development and Research.

Concrete Change. 2008. "Construction Costs" http://concretechange.org/.

Duany, A., E. Plater-Zyberk, and J. Speck. 2001. *Suburban Nation: The Rise of Sprawl and the Decline of the American Dream.* New York: North Point Press.

Ellis, C. 2002. "The New Urbanism: Critiques and Rebuttals." *Journal of Urban Design* 7 (3): 261–291.

Environmental Protection Agency. 2011, Feb.. "Market Acceptance of Smart Growth." No. 231-R-10–001. www.epa.gov/smartgrowth/pdf/market_acceptance.pdf.

Maisel, J., E. Smith, and E. Steinfeld. 2008. *Increasing Home Access: Designing for Visitability.* Washington, DC: AARP.

Mattimore, R. J., et al. 1997. "Surrogate and Physician Understanding of Patients' Preferences for Living Permanently in a Nursing Home." *Journal of the American Geriatrics Society* 45(7): 818–824.

O'Conner, G. 1976. *Home Is a Good Place.* Washington, DC: American Association on Mental Deficiency.

Scheerenberger, R. C. 1983. *A History of Mental Retardation.* Baltimore, MD: Brookes.

Sommer, R. 1974. *Tight Spaces: Hard Architecture and How to Humanize It.* Englewood Cliffs, NJ: Prentice-Hall.

Steinfeld, E., S. Schroeder, and M. Bishop. 1979. *Accessible Buildings for People with Walking and Reaching Limitations.* Washington, DC: U.S. Department of Housing and Urban Development.

Steinfeld, E. and K. Seelman. 2011, June 10. "Enabling Environments." In *World Report on Disability*, pp. 167–195. Geneva: World Health Organization.

Steinfeld, E., and J. White. 2010. *Inclusive Housing: A Pattern Book.* New York: W. W. Norton.

Steven Winter Associates, Inc. 1993. *The Cost of Accessible Housing.* Washington: U.S. Department of Housing and Urban Development.

Steven Winter Associates, Inc. 2001. *A Basic Guide to Fair Housing Accessibility: Everything Architects and Builders Need to Know About the Fair Housing Act Accessibility Guidelines.* New York: John Wiley & Sons.

Thompson, T. et al. 1996. "Architectural Features and Perceptions of Community Residences for People with Mental Retardation." *American Journal on Mental Retardation* 101 (3): 292–313.

U.S. Census Bureau. 2004, Dec. 24. "We the People: Aging in the United States. Census 2000 Special Reports." Retrieved from www.census.gov/prod/2004pubs/censr-19.pdf.

U.S. Census Bureau. 2009. "Selected Housing Characteristics: 2005–2009." *American Community Survey 5-Year Estimates.* http://factfinder.census.gov/servlet/ADPTable?_bm=y&-geo_id=01000US&-qr_name=ACS_2009_5YR_G00_DP5YR4&-ds_name=&-_lang=en&-redoLog=false&-format=

Williams, T., and W. Altaffer. 2000. *Cost Analysis Review for Proposed Visitability Ordinance.* Tucson, AZ: Commission on Disability Issues.

Wisnewski, H. M., et al. 1981. *The Identification and Prescription of Environmental Conditions Affecting Growth in Personal Competence of Persons with Developmental Disabilities Phase One.* Staten Island, NY: New York State Department of Mental Hygiene. Inter-Office Coordinating Council Over-recovery Project..

Wolfensberger, W. 1977. "The Normalization Principle, and Some Major Implications to Architectural-Environmental Design." In M. J. Bednar (ed.), *Barrier-free Environments,* pp. 135–169. Stroudsburg, PA: Dowden, Hutchinson and Ross.

Wylde, M. 2002. *Boomers on the Horizon: Housing Preferences of the 55+ Market.* Washington, DC: National Association of Home Builders.

10

Home Modifications

Introduction

Many people reside in housing that is inadequate for their physical and social needs. For a variety of reasons, their homes are restrictive, inconvenient, or dangerous, and they or their visitors have difficulties performing simple daily tasks safely. These difficulties might include climbing up and down the stairs, getting on and off the toilet, getting in and out of the bathtub, and reaching for items in upper cabinets. Universal design has been conceived as a means to avoid the need for home modifications. However, new housing construction cannot entirely meet the need for accessible housing in a community. Many people simply do not have the finances to buy or rent a new accessible home. Relocation often results in the disruption of social networks and can be economically unfeasible for many. Not enough new housing can be constructed to meet future needs in every neighborhood. Thus, there is also a need to improve the accessibility of existing housing stock. Home modification services expand the supply of accessible, usable, and safer housing for people with disabilities in existing neighborhoods and strengthen social sustainability by providing additional opportunities to live in a neighborhood, whether they are moving in or are long-term residents. Home modification practices can also benefit greatly from the application of universal design to address the diversity of needs and contexts for services and to ensure that modifications give attention to issues beyond function.

In the field of rehabilitation, the International Classification of Function (ICF) has increased awareness of the role that context plays in preventing or creating excess disability (Üstun et al. 2003). The ICF acknowledges that environmental interventions have outcomes on health and function. This awareness has brought renewed attention to the need for home modifications to contribute to improving the quality of life and performance abilities of persons with disabilities. However, there is a need to increase awareness and improve home modification services for a broader population. For decades, scholars in the fields of sociology, behavioral psychology, and human factors engineering have sought to identify the problems with the fit between home environment and ability (Altman et al. 1992; Dovey 1985; Lawton 1982; Tanner 2011). However, knowledge transfer among these disciplines to design practice has proven difficult. The implementation of accessibility laws that address housing, such as the Fair Housing Act, and increased government funding for people with disabilities have served to raise awareness of the importance of this information, but these policy initiatives do not incorporate universal design perspectives or give guidance about strategies for modification of existing housing. Many professionals still view home modifications as an exercise in applying accessibility codes meant for new construction rather than focusing on the universal design goal of Personalization. In addition, many ignore the goal of Cultural Appropriateness, especially the importance of aesthetic norms in presentation of self.

Target Populations

Only 7.1 million U.S. residents, or about 2.3 percent of the total US population, have made modifications to their homes to improve their ability to perform activities safely and more independently (Kraus, Stoddard, and Gilmartin 1996). It is quite common for people with chronic or temporary limitations to adapt their behavior to their environment instead of adapting their environment to accommodate their needs (Pynoos et al. 1997). Whether a household has older adults who wish to remain in their own home as they age, younger people with physical and cognitive disabilities, or people whose environment simply does not support their activities properly, home modifications can improve quality of life.

As the population of a country ages, the need for programs to facilitate improvement of existing housing becomes even greater and the benefits to society become more significant, especially when public funding is used to provide expensive long-term care because a home environment full of barriers does not support independence in daily life for its residents. How do we ensure that we provide for people who need more usable home environments? Strategies include increasing consumer awareness, improving the capacity of the home improvement industry, developing new funding sources, and revising housing and healthcare policies to provide greater incentives and flexibility to rehabilitate older homes. All these strategies contribute significantly to the realization of socially sustainable housing for all.

Improved consumer awareness is needed in rental housing because tenants often are hesitant to make adaptations on their own. They believe property owners may penalize them for such changes. However, the Fair Housing Amendments Act of 1988 requires property owners to allow tenants with disabilities to make modifications to their individual living units or even public and common areas at their own expense to improve accessibility. This legislation has broad implications for both tenants and housing providers. It provides a legal basis for tenants to improve dwellings and an obligation for housing providers to support their actions (Steinfeld, Shea, and Levine 1996). A universal design approach should seek to increase the value of the property and not require removal when a tenant leaves. Good design is more desirable than simple compliance with the law to tenants since the Fair Housing Act requires them to bear the expense of removal of the adaptations to dwelling units if the property owner desires it. It is also desirable to property owners because it improves property values.

The benefits of home modifications are not limited to people with disabilities. Home modifications make environments supportive for diverse populations with varying abilities. For instance, when asked where they would prefer to spend their years after retirement, 90 percent of people over the age of 65 said that they would like to age in place in their own homes (AARP 2000). For many older adults, quality of life is associated with remaining independent. Living at home promotes a positive sense of self and normalcy in the face of the multiple personal losses associated with aging (Gitlin 2003). In 2005 in the United States, 79 percent of older adults, or approximately 29 million people, lived independently in single-family homes or apartments (U.S. Census Bureau 2006), but very few lived in homes that are designed to support aging in place. Approximately 80 percent of community-dwelling older adults are living in accommodations that require some type of home modification in order to match age-related cognitive and physiological changes (Gill et al. 1999; Yuen and Carter 2006).

Home modifications are necessary when the fit between individuals and their home environment is disrupted, compromised, or unsafe. The need for home modification can grow slowly over a period of time or emerge quickly because of accidental injury or the onset of a sudden medical condition. For instance, as we age, we lose strength in our lower limbs so that standing from a seated position can become more difficult. Tasks such as getting up from the toilet can pose a problem but can be made easier by installing a grab bar or some type of handhold to provide both stability and leverage. Although the addition of a grab bar is a simple inexpensive adaptation, far too many older adults opt to improvise a support system by using anything they might find around them, such as a towel bar, shower curtain, toilet paper holder, or the edge of a sink. Since many of these devices are not designed to support an adult's weight, this adaptive behavior can increase the risk of falls in the home.

Younger people with physical, sensory and cognitive disabilities also benefit from home modifications, but in different ways than the older population. Demographic data on this population suggest that more than half do not achieve their potential for performance because they are restricted by their environments (Stark 2004). For young adults, accessibility at home provides opportunities to be independent from family and develop a positive self-image. For middle-age adults, it means being able to maintain established roles as parent, wage earner, and/or homemaker. Children with disabilities living in the community are generally cared for by either a parent or a paid caregiver. They may learn skills to become independent and self-sufficient through physical and occupational therapy but come home to challenging circumstances that undermine that skill development. Although environmental support is needed for both them *and* their caregivers, most homes have not been modified for either. Home modifications can promote early childhood development and ease caregiver burden, reducing both financial and emotional stress (Mann 2005).

One group that is often overlooked but can benefit significantly from home modifications are people who vary so much in size and stature from the majority of the population, such as those who are very tall, very short, or very heavy, that they are not accommodated by conventional design standards. This group includes the 74 million Americans over the age of 25 who are overweight, obese, or extremely obese, as well as the over 2 million who are under 5 feet (1.52m) in height and the 9 million who are over 6 feet (1.83 m) tall.[1] The number of people who are oversized or undersized is far greater than the combined populations of older people and people with disabilities, and they have their own set of unique challenges. As noted in Chapter 3, obesity increases the risk of disability. Thus, increasing activity is very important for this population and home modifications are often necessary to create supportive environments for such people to become more active. Moreover, according to the Centers for Disease Control and Prevention, due primarily to inactivity, 36 percent of adults with disability and activity limitations are obese, compared with 23 percent of adults with no reported disability.[2]

---

[1] National Center for Chronic Disease Prevention and Health Promotion, "National Health Statistics Reports," www.cdc.gov/nchs/data/nhsr/nhsr010.pdf.
[2] Centers for Disease Control and Prevention, "Disability and Obesity," www.cdc.gov/ncbddd/disabilityandhealth/obesity.html.

Purpose of Home Modifications

"Home modification" is a term used to describe adaptations made to an already existing living environment. These adaptations are intended to increase ease of use, safety, security, and independence for residents. Experts have defined home modifications to include "any alteration, adjustment, or addition to the home environment . . . to improve functional capability of or to minimize environmental demands on individuals and their caregivers to meet the situational needs for promoting performance of daily activities as independently and safely as possible" (Sanford 2004).

Accessible and supportive environments improve the quality of life for older adults and younger persons with disabilities. Vergrugge and Jette (1994) propose that: "We are not disabled by accident or illness but rather by our surroundings," and "[d]isability is not a personal characteristic, but is instead a gap between personal capability and environmental demand." Home modifications target physical features of the home and are intended to eliminate that gap. Generally, these modifications serve five purposes:

1. Security
2. Fire safety
3. Risk reduction
4. Accessibility
5. Usability

Modifications might include structural changes (e.g., widening doorways and moving walls), installation of special equipment (e.g., smoke detectors, whirlpool therapy bathtubs and ceiling-mounted track lifts), assistive devices (e.g., shower chairs and toilet frames), and the rearrangement of items (e.g., moving furniture, removing loose rugs and clutter). Home modifications can range from relatively inexpensive additions (e.g., door hardware, hand-held showers, lighting, handrails, and grab bars) to complicated and expensive changes (e.g., remodeled kitchens and bathrooms, installation of powered lifts or elevators). Home modifications are different from assistive devices, such as bath benches and walkers, because home modifications generally are attached to the building and assistive technologies are portable. Home modifications serve a compensatory function—enhancing independence, efficiency, and safety for those who have diminished abilities—as well as a preventive function—reducing injury risk and improving efficiency for activities of daily living (ADLs) and instrumental activities of daily living (IADLs) (AARP 1999; Wahl et al. 2009).

It is commonly acknowledged that there are at least five primary goals of home modifications:

1. Reduce the likelihood of accidents
2. Support caregiving and healthcare
3. Make life simpler
4. Decrease environmental demands
5. Support social interaction and engagement

The overall goal of modifying home environments is to bring the support provided by the physical world into a closer fit with the capabilities of the resident. Home modifications are like custom tailoring for the home. Lawton and Nahemow (1973) developed a model to describe the relationship between individual capability, or what they called competence, and the demands of the environment, or *environmental press*. Research on environments for aging demonstrate that older people feel most comfortable in their environments when their capabilities match the demands of the environment so that they can be more self-sufficient. In general, people try to find a comfortable fit between what they can do and what they need to do to meet their daily needs. Home modifications help to neutralize the stress of a demanding environment by reducing barriers, giving people freedom of choice and action in their homes. Even the smallest adaptation can make a difference. For example, a burned-out light bulb that a person cannot replace can make stairs so dangerous that he or she may not leave the home after dark, which restricts social participation opportunities. However, it is also important to avoid creating an environment that is so understimulating that adaptive capacity, or the ability to deal with environmental demands, is reduced. Institutional care reduces adaptive capacity; that is why making modifications to homes is more desirable than relocation to a protected environment, where lack of stimulation and challenges leads to atrophied abilities and "learned helplessness," meaning a condition where a person feels they have lost control and feel helpless to change their situation.

Reduce the Likelihood of Accidents

Approximately 30 percent of older adults fall each year, and the majority of these falls occur in and around their homes (Clemson et al. 2004). Studies show that home modifications to both interior and exterior environments can have a significant impact on reducing falls (Cumming 2002). The most common tripping hazards include steps, stairs, floor coverings, and pathways (Clemson et al. 2004). Examples of interior home modifications related to fall prevention include removing furniture and obstructions from hallways to ensure a clear path of travel, taping scatter rugs to floors to prevent tripping over edges, and providing nonslip flooring in wet areas, such as bathrooms and front entryways. Exterior examples include motion-sensitive lighting, providing safer paths of travel by fixing uneven pavement and providing nonslip walking surfaces, and installing handrails on exterior stairs.

Support Caregiving and Healthcare

Providing care at home for people with disabilities is a demanding task, both emotionally and physically. Home modifications help to make the physical characteristics of the home environment as supportive as possible to ease both the physical tasks of caregiving, such as lifting, supporting, and transferring, and the emotional impact of stress associated with providing care to a loved one. Reducing caregiver burden can improve the performance of both paid and volunteer caregivers. In addition, it can even reduce the need for caregiving, perhaps to a few hours per day or even less.

Make Life Simpler

Home modifications are about usability, but they are also about making ADLs easier and more convenient. To date, there has been little research to quantify the role of simplifying the environment, although it is a proven technique in occupational ergonomics. Reducing clutter and improving visibility and reach to supplies and tools are design strategies that can be used to simplify home environments in bathrooms and kitchens.

Support Social Interaction and Engagement

Depression and isolation are common problems for many elders and people with physical disabilities. Participation in family and community life can have a major impact on psychological well-being because it helps people to maintain a sense of belonging and purpose. Home modifications, particularly those that facilitate entry and egress to the home and hosting visitors, help make this participation possible.

A supportive and accessible environment can make ADLs such as eating, cooking, cleaning and bathing easier to accomplish and can help to increase independence, self-confidence, and self-esteem (Ainsworth and de Jonge 2011). According to Drewnowski and Evans, older adults show more interest than any other age group in modifying their behavior to maintain healthy lifestyles through diet and exercise. Environmental factors, including physical activity and dietary habits, play a major role in the health and functioning of older adults (Drewnowski and Evans 2001). To date, limited research has been conducted in this area in part because the definition and measurement of "healthy" are no longer based on mortality and morbidity but rather on an absence of infirmity and disease as well as a state of physical, mental, and social well-being (Ware 1987).

Since resources for making modifications are often in short supply, an important question for service providers is: Which home modifications will have the greatest impact on users? One of the ongoing challenges in identifying the need for home modifications and their impact is the unique nature of every home, including residents' furnishings and equipment. Likewise, the needs of each individual for support are highly varied. Generally, we know that home modifications contributing to good person–environment fit fall into three categories:

1. Those that improve functional ability (e.g., lever handles on doors, walk-in bathtubs, higher toilets)
2. Those that reduce long-term care expenditures and other costs associated with institutional care (e.g., ceiling-mounted track lifts, roll-in showers, wheelchair ramps)
3. Those that improve safety and reduce the risk of falls (e.g., grab bars in the bathroom, handrails on both sides of stairways, nonslip flooring), which are the leading cause of injury in the home (Clemson et al. 2004)

Decrease Environmental Demands

Whether it is replacing doorknobs with lever handles or removing thick carpeting in hallways to make the use of mobility devices easier, adaptations that help to make environments easier to navigate and reduce environmental demands. Homes that match the demands of the environment with the needs of the user allow older adults to stay in place longer, help to the slow down the disablement process, and slow or reverse declines in health.

Universal Design through Home Improvement

Not many people would picture their dream house with a large ramp leading up to the front door and grab bars in the bathroom, as in Figure 10–1. These features are associated with medical, institutional, and temporary interventions, and their awkward appearance reinforces the stigma of disability. Even

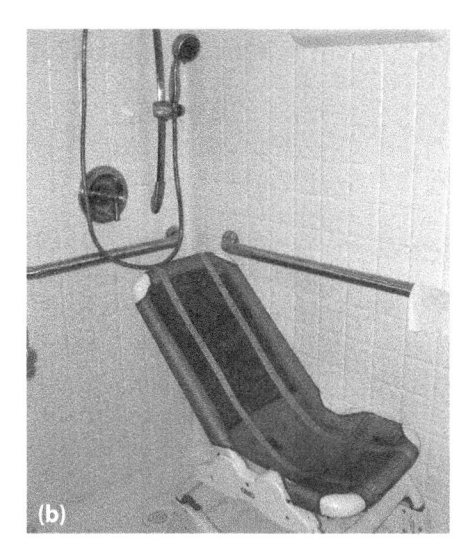

Figure 10–1: Common home modifications. (a) This wooden ramp and (b) these bathroom grab bars are obtrusive and give homes an institutional appearance.

though they can make an important contribution to maintaining independence for a person with a disability, they are seldom viewed as desirable or aesthetically appealing. A home that has been designed using universal design principles bridges the gap between practicality and aesthetics by providing solutions that are based on life span design. The convenience and safety features included in a universally designed home improve marketability rather than detract from it. Homes that are modified using universal design principles should provide support, safety, and convenience in creative, appealing ways. Universally designed home modifications are focused on improving quality of life for people and should be seamlessly integrated into the existing home design.

It is important to note that universally designed home modifications support intergenerational living as well as independent function. Older adults and people with disabilities often require additional assistance to accomplish ADLs. Family members or other caregivers often provide this assistance. As noted earlier, modifications can assist caregivers by reducing the stress and physical demands required when providing assistance. For example, roll-in showers eliminate the need for a caregiver to lift a person in and out of a bathtub. Adding grab bars on shower walls or adjacent to the toilet reduces the risk of caregiver falls when lifting or assisting a person on and off a shower chair or toilet seat.

Rather than detract from the marketability of an existing home, universal design home modifications can increase the value of the home and make it appeal to a broader market. It is important for people to see that there is value to incorporating universal design features and that they are not just for those with disabilities. For example, front-loading washers and dryers placed side by side that are raised off the ground are easier to use for someone in a seated position but are equally convenient for standing users. This layout allows people to transfer wet clothes easily from washer to dryer without having to bend. Regardless of who the user is, raising a dishwasher up off the floor will minimize bending and reaching. It also creates a higher countertop 42 to 45 inches (1067mm–1143mm), which would provide an alternative work surface height to the standard 36 inch (914mm) high countertop. This countertop serves taller users and provides a location for performing fine motor tasks that require good visibility.

Need for Capacity Building

Trade magazines on home improvements and publications on home modifications typically provide photographs of exemplary projects to illustrate solutions to common problems (e.g., stairs at the front entry). Very rarely do they provide poor examples, even though there are more of them than there are exemplars. Unfortunately, practices in the field are often less than satisfactory for many reasons, including lack of technical knowledge, poor quality control in construction, limited sources of funding, lack of effective credentialing in the field, and lack of consumer awareness and education. Too often, modifications to homes are made by family members and contractors without the involvement of professional designers. Professionals also often have limited understanding of the issues and many false preconceptions. Figures 10–2 and 10-3 provide two examples of projects that demonstrate the limitations of current practices. The problems could have been avoided easily with the involvement of a qualified, experienced home modification designer and contractor and an informed home owner.

Example: Slope Miscalculation

The ramp in Figure 10–2 was built by a contractor at the front of the house to provide a no-step entry for a person who used a wheelchair. The contractor was careful to provide a 1:12 slope that began at the front door but did not properly calculate the space needed in front of the house to accommodate a ramp. As the contractor built the ramp, he realized that there was not enough room to finish it so he added four stairs at the bottom of the ramp to meet the sidewalk. This rendered the ramp unusable; the client still could not leave her house. The railings on the ramp are unusable for someone with limited gripping ability. The ramp also was not properly constructed to avoid damage from moisture at ground level. It is important to take precise measurements of the site and to understand the purpose of ramps and the different ways that they can be designed to accommodate limited space. It is not enough to know the requirements of accessibility standards alone. Knowledge of good practices in construction is also important.

Figure 10–2: Slope miscalculation. Incorrect measurements by the contractor led to this ramp with stairs at the end.

Example: Lack of a Level Landing

Figure 10-3 shows a ramp constructed by the home owner to provide accessibility into and out of the front door of this house for an elderly person who used a wheelchair with assistance from a family member. The ramp is extremely dangerous for several reasons.

1. The surface is constructed with plywood, which is extremely slippery in wet weather.
2. The slope is extremely steep with no level landing at the top. Although there are 1-inch (2.54-cm) curbs, they are insufficient to prevent an accident on a ramp this steep. Because there is no landing, anyone exiting the building would be on the ramp's sloping surface without the benefit of a transition space.
3. Entering the building is problematic. As one opens the door, the wheelchair would roll backward.
4. The lack of handrails makes the ramp dangerous to negotiate even for a person without a disability.
5. Lack of concern for the appearance of the ramp means that it wound up looking like a gangplank at a dock, and not a very attractive one at that.

Figure 10-3: Plywood ramp. This homemade ramp is slippery and dangerous. Missing handrails add to the danger.

Common Needs and Solutions

In this section we present a summary of some common needs and home modifications that address them.

Exterior Access

One of the most common home modifications is remodeling an entry to provide a no-step access into the home. Many older people, people with low stamina, and people with mobility impairments experience difficulty getting in and out of their home mainly because most homes are raised off the ground. Access typically is gained by climbing a set of stairs to a landing or porch, or through a garage. While some would consider this desirable or even necessary based on the climate in which they live, houses built in this manner are problematic to anyone who cannot climb stairs or who has balance issues. In these conditions, there are a few strategies for providing a no-step entry. The first is to install a ramp. Ramps can be constructed of wood, concrete, or a composite decking material. These types of ramps are constructed on-site and typically are chosen when a more durable, permanent installation is preferred. An alternative solution is a modular ramp system made of prefabricated lightweight aluminum. These systems consist of components that can be easily assembled with ordinary hand tools and disassembled when it is necessary to move the ramp to a new location.

Most homeowners assume that a ramp needs to be in the front of the house, but ramps can be constructed at any entry where it is practical and where there is adequate space to build a ramp with the proper slope of 1:12. For example, often a site's topography provides an opportunity to access a home from the side or rear with a ramp that is much smaller than may be required from the front (Figure 10–4).

Building a ramp to a side or rear entrance can reduce the visual impact of the ramp while providing some privacy. Figure 10–5 shows a ramp providing access to a side entry of a house on a corner. In this example, the slope of the side street meant that the front entry of the home was much higher off grade compared to the side entry. Thus, the length of ramp needed was much shorter.

Figure 10–4: Ramp location based on topography. This ramp was located to take advantage of topography to reduce its length and visibility.

Figure 10-5: Ramp at side entry. This ramp is discreetly placed along the side of the house so that it appears to be a natural extension of the porch.

Figure 10–6 shows a ramp at the end of a gradually sloped driveway connecting to a rear deck. Cars can be backed into the driveway, providing a convenient way to get packages into the kitchen, which opens onto the deck. Children can also roll their bicycles and tricycles up the ramp to keep them out of sight on the back deck. The ramp needed to the deck was half the length of what it would have been at the front.

Figure 10-6: Ramp to rear deck. This ramp connects a driveway to a rear deck, allowing the ramp to be half the length that would be required if it were at the front entry.

A ramp can also be placed in a garage if it is large enough to support the length needed to accommodate the change in level from grade to the first floor. This is more convenient than an outdoor ramp because it is closer to a parked automobile, and it protects the potentially slippery inclined surface from inclement weather.

When installing any type of ramp, it is important to have a well-thought-out plan, for both usability and appearance. Ramps that are not well designed can be just as much of an obstacle to some people with disabilities as stairs, particularly if they are steep. Ramps can be designed to blend in with the overall aesthetic of the house, even if they have to be in the front. The ramp in Figure 10–7 was designed to be part of a new landscaping scheme. From the street, it looks like a series of garden walls. Note that the owners preferred not to add handrails. The ramp was designed to accommodate their daughter who uses a wheelchair but will never be able to propel herself. Handrails can be added later if the parents find they may need them in old age.

If a ramp is not feasible because limited space is available, a platform lift can be installed, as shown in Figure 10–8. Lifts occupy much less space than ramps and, because of their small footprint, can fit into places that safe ramps will not. To many people, ramps are preferred to lifts because lifts always have the potential for mechanical breakdowns, which result in both inconvenience and costly repair bills. A lift is the best choice, however, if a ramp is infeasible due to space limitations. Lifts should be protected from children and objects that might get

Figure 10–7: Landscape ramp. Ramps designed as part of the landscape plan blend with the overall aesthetic of the house.

Figure 10–8: Vertical lift. Lifts can improve accessibility in spaces that may be too small to accommodate a ramp.

underneath the platform and prevent their use. In cold climates, they can be constructed under a porch roof or with their own enclosures. Sometimes it is possible to locate a lift inside the home and provide a door directly from the outside to the lift platform.

Doors and Doorways

Some of the most common accessibility modifications are those involving interior and exterior doorways, particularly because many people have difficulties negotiating through narrow doorways. Many features can render a doorway unusable, but the biggest obstacle is often the width of the door opening. Where doors are too narrow for wheelchair use, it is quite common to see extensive damage to doorjambs and doors from repeated contact. To provide easy access, doorways should be widened, preferably to 36 inches (914mm) wide, so that any user, including a person who uses a wheelchair, a person using a cane or walker, or even someone moving furniture can easily navigate through them without difficulty.

The following list outlines some other common modification strategies for improving usability of doorways:

- Where doorways cannot be widened for structural, spatial, or economic reasons, an alternative solution is to install an expandable offset hinge that is designed to add 2 inches (51mm) of additional clearance to most doors by swinging the door clear of the opening.

- Remove standard round doorknobs that require grasping and twisting and replace them with lever handles will increase usability for people who have diminished strength and grasping ability. In situations where the doorknob cannot easily be replaced, doorknob grippers can be installed directly over a doorknob.
- Install delayed-action door closers to allow the door to remain open for a preset period of time before closing at a slow speed. This type of closer allows older persons, people in wheelchairs, children, and any other slow-moving person to pass through the door without having to close the door after they pass through.
- Install automated door openers in existing doorways that can open and close a door using a remote control, push pad, or voice activation. This benefits people who have difficulty reaching and grasping and anyone carrying packages.
- Install threshold ramps to eliminate raised thresholds or abrupt changes in level to avoid possible tripping hazards and create smooth transitions between rooms or from the ground to a doorway.
- Remove door latches, locks, and other operating devices that require a person to exert a significant amount of effort to operate and replace them with hardware that can be engaged with simple, one-handed operation or a keyless entry system.

Interior Vertical Circulation

Bedrooms and bathrooms are often located on the second floor or higher in residential settings. For people who have difficulty walking, climbing the steps to use the bathroom can become more and more difficult as they age. To remove this barrier, many home owners install a stair lift, an inclined stair platform lift, or an elevator so that vertical circulation is still possible. A residential stair lift is an assistive mechanical device that is installed in a stairwell to help people to go easily up and down stairs. Stair lifts are generally easy to install and the most economical way to provide access to other levels.

To use a stair lift properly, the user must first transfer onto and off the chair at the top and the bottom of the stairs. Once the person is seated, the chair rises or descends as it moves along a rail system that is fixed to the wall or stair. Users who need a wheelchair will need one at both top and bottom level or a stair lift that also can carry a folded wheelchair.

The most common problem in installing a stair lift is that stairways are often not wide enough or structurally sound enough to support them. In such cases, rebuilding the stairway and adding the lift are required. Another problem is that curved or switchback stairway configurations require a customize solution with a curved rail, which adds to the cost.

Another option is an inclined stair platform lift. This lift is a platform that travels the path of the stairs along a rail. It can carry a person in a wheelchair or on a foldout seat. In many models, the platform folds up when not in use to leave the stairway unobstructed. The advantage of this type of lift over the stair lift is that a person who uses a wheelchair can travel to many levels without having to transfer.

Residential elevators offer greater accessibility than a stair lift or inclined stair platform lift, but they are also the most expensive of the three options. A home elevator can cost $20,000 or more. Elevators are most commonly housed in a shaft about the size of a small half bath. In many homes, it is difficult to find open spaces on every floor within the house. A shaft can be added to the exterior of the house with minimal disruption to the interior space. This strategy should be used only where the shaft will not eliminate important views or needed daylight and where it will not detract from the overall appearance of a home, inside or out.

Residential elevators are available in a wide variety of cab sizes, entry configurations, fixtures, and finishes. When selecting an elevator for the greatest usability, these features should be considered:

- *Cab and size.* The elevator cab should be large enough to accommodate the needs of everyone living in the house. The cab should be sized to accommodate a person in a wheelchair, even if the individual may not need it immediately.
- *Door configuration.* Several door configurations are available. The most inexpensive configuration is to have one door, but it requires available space on each floor on that side of the shaft. This layout requires a person in a wheelchair to back in or out on one level. Doors can be included on adjacent sides, but turning in or out may be difficult for the individual. Doors on opposite sides allow a person to enter and exit the elevator facing forward.
- *Doors.* Elevators with automatic sliding doors provide the highest level of independent operation compared to swing or accordion-type doors. Doors should also be selected to provide the largest clear opening possible.
- *Safety features.* Elevators should have a telephone or two-way communication system in place in case of emergency. This device should be reachable to both standing and seated users. There should also be a backup battery system or manual system in the event of a power failure or a mechanical malfunction.

To keep elevators and lifts running properly, many elevator manufacturers and installers recommend purchasing an annual maintenance contract, which adds to the overall cost but provides more psychological security.

Bathrooms

Bathrooms are one of the most dangerous yet important rooms in the house. For older adults who wish to age in place, the bathroom is generally high on the list of possible home modifications. However, most people do not want a room that implies that they have lost abilities or anything remotely institutional. Designing a bathroom improvement using universal design principles puts the focus on added features that can both help promote safety and comfort in the future and at the same time enhance the room's beauty and elegance.

Bathrooms are dangerous because they are often very small, lack sufficient maneuvering clearances, have surfaces that can be slippery, and lack adequate storage for the placement of items. Here are eight subtle yet effective methods of incorporating accessibility features without compromising on style.

1. *Remove the existing bathtub and install a roll-in shower.* A roll-in shower that includes a flexible handheld, height-adjustable showerhead is a clever way to integrate life span design into a bathroom. This type of shower is both elegant and practical as it adapts easily to the needs of children, people in mobility devices, and those who prefer to sit while showering. Shower floors should slope slightly toward the drain and be waterproof to eliminate leakage. Home owners also often have concerns that without a threshold water will splash outside of the showering area and accumulate on the bathroom floor. In such instances, collapsible shower

dams can be installed. These flexible devices collapse when stepped on or rolled over and then return to their original shape.
2. *Remove the existing toilet and install a comfort-height toilet.* A slightly higher toilet reduces bending and takes less lower-limb strength to sit and stand.
3. *Remove an existing bathtub and install a walk-in bathtub, otherwise known as a bathtub with a door.* Many people prefer to bathe rather than shower, but one of the most challenging areas of a bathroom as we age is getting in and out of the tub without difficulty. Movements such as lifting ourselves over the tub edge or stepping into a deep tub without losing our balance can become increasing difficult without assistance. Walk-in bathtubs solve this issue. If removing the existing tub is not feasible, door insert kits are a low-cost solution. These kits convert existing bathtubs into walk-in baths by putting a door in the side wall of the tub.
4. *Install grab bars on shower and bathtub walls, near toilets, and at any other location in the bathroom where additional support is needed.* Grab bars are most commonly straight and mounted on the wall horizontally, but they come in a variety of shapes and sizes and can be installed in many different configurations. Vertical and diagonal grab bars help people pull themselves up to a standing position and maintain their balance. They also provide varying gripping heights for individuals who live in the same household but are of different statures and have different preferences. Fold-down grab bars, also referred to as hinged or flip-up grab bars, swing down from the wall and lock into place when needed. These are useful when a toilet cannot be located next to a wall, to provide support on the side of the toilet away from the wall, or to provide grab bars closer to a person and lower for use in pushing up as from an armchair. Grab bars should always be fastened securely to a wall by anchoring them into the studs.
5. *Remove the existing base cabinet below the sink and install an adjustable cabinet or one with knee clearance hidden behind cabinet doors.* This type of cabinet provides flexibility to hide a child's standing platform when not needed or afford space for a wheelchair user.
6. *Remove existing knob faucets and replace them with lever faucets.* Lever faucets are always the best option, whether they are single-lever models or have two handles. Knobs require more dexterity and greater strength. Knobs also become slippery when hands are wet or covered with soap. Levers have the additional benefit of being easier to clean.
7. *Remove existing floor covering and replace with a nonslip surface.* Flooring choice is particularly important in the bathroom as floor surfaces often get wet. Nonslip tile and linoleum are the best options as they are easy to maintain and are aesthetically pleasing.
8. *Add additional lighting fixtures in areas around sinks, mirrors, bathtubs, and toilets.* For added safety, it is important to ensure that there is sufficient lighting and color contrast for users with low vision.

Home Automation

A smart home is a home that incorporates advances in information technology and automation to assist occupants with their day-to-day lives. Installing advanced technology into homes makes residents' lives easier, and helps them to remain functionally independent and age in place longer. Technologies that are installed in smart homes may be as simple as remote-control lighting or as complex as a whole-house fall detection system. Until recently, smart home technologies have been marketed as luxury goods. Home automation is often included in high-end new construction as a marketing device. However, advances in technology have made these devices more affordable and, therefore, available to a wider range of users.

When considering the installation of a home automation system, the cost of both the hardware and service should be evaluated by considering the potential for savings in long-term home care or a nursing home. Other concerns for older users include the user-friendliness of the devices, potential invasions of privacy, and the need for training tailored to older learners. Studies indicate that areas where advanced technologies would realize the greatest return on investment for older adult residents include emergency help, prevention and detection of falls, and monitoring of physiological status. (Demiris et al. 2004). Many companies now offer stand-alone monitoring systems for older adults without the added features of whole-house home automation. These systems are much less costly to install but provide only security and safety benefits. Combined with other less expensive universal design products and design strategies, however, they may be all that an individual needs to remain living independently.

Home Assessments

Methods

Home modification services are provided by a variety of professionals with complementary expertise, including architects, physical and occupational therapists, design and construction professionals, home health teams, and case managers (Gitlin 1998; Siebert 2005). A collaborative framework for making assessments is needed to provide effective home modifications. The need for careful assessments is often overlooked in this field because immediate needs seem so obvious, e.g., a ramp to gain access to the home, but home modification projects can be deceptive. Projects often have a hidden complexity that require careful investigation and evaluation of strategies to address client needs, the constraints of the existing building construction, budget and contextual issues, such as climate, neighborhood character, and long-term maintenance.

Design professionals can work in a several different ways to help clients get the most from renovations. When working with older adults to improve a home for aging in place, designers usually work one on one with their clients to develop plans that will best fulfill both short-term and long-term goals. In cases that involve a client who has a disability, designers should coordinate their work with an occupational therapist or physical therapist to determine the most appropriate and effective adaptations to meet the needs of the individual, the caregiver (if there is one), and the rest of the household. Designers who are not knowledgeable about construction should work with a home improvement contractor or experienced licensed architect to ensure that the design is practical and structurally sound. A creative design professional often can provide assistance to identify innovative solutions that a contractor or therapist might not consider. Contractors should not assume that they know how to design home modifications for people with disabilities or older people without specific experience and knowledge needed to serve these populations effectively. They should consult with therapists or professional designers who have the experience they lack. It is important that plans address both immediate needs as well as projected needs to ensure that modifications support the client's current abilities but also anticipate potential changes in the abilities over time.

Purpose of Assessments

The assessment of person-environment fit is complicated. Many different assessment tools have been developed in the pursuit of simplification, and to address the relationship between the person and his or her ability to function in the environment (de Jonge and Cordiner 2011). No one tool can assess all aspects of environmental fit since each tool has a different focus (Cooper et al. 2005). Assessment tools are used by a variety of stakeholders, including occupational therapists, designers, and clients to help facilitate the information gathering process. For instance, designers working with older adults who wish to age in place use assessment tools to determine the most efficient and aesthetically pleasing solutions for their clients. Assessments that are completed with the participation of both a qualified designer and a rehabilitation specialist will help older adults to make the right choices to support their needs and at the same time will ensure marketability of their homes if they should need to relocate. A more thorough assessment is required when working with people who have disabilities. This type of assessment should identify the needs, capabilities, and preferences of the individual (ADLs and role of caregivers, if any), the constraints of the home (space availability and options, condition of structure, and structural limitations), and future possibilities related to health and environment.

Although each home modification assessment is different, there are some general areas that designers and therapists focus on when doing a home assessment. These are:

- Identification of fall risks, such as loose rugs, lack of grab bars, slippery flooring, or stairs without handrails
- Unobstructed pathways to bathrooms and living spaces
- Support for ADLs and IADLs
- Support for caregiver activities, including protection from injuries from lifting

When selecting an assessment tool, it is important to understand the purpose and focus of that particular tool before putting it to use. The tools described below provide a snapshot of those that are available to consumers and professionals at this time. Each focuses on a very different set of issues and uses different sources of information. For instance, the Housing Enabler uses a three-step process, including a personal component, an environmental component, and a resulting accessibility score; the Comprehensive Assessment and Solution Process for Aging Residents (CASPAR) tool is a self-administered tool directed at the consumer; and the Home Environmental Assessment Program (HEAP) was developed for use in homes of people with dementia.

Housing Enabler

Developed by Susan Iwarsson, an occupational therapist at Lund University in Sweden, and modeled on the earlier Enabler concept by Steinfeld (Steinfeld et al. 1979), the Housing Enabler (HE) is a computer-based tool that measures and assesses housing accessibility problems by comparing individual functional limitations with the physical environment (de Jonge and Cordiner 2011). This instrument covers a wide range of functional and mobility impairments, including blindness, low vision, and level of manual dexterity. It focuses on identifying barriers to independence in the environment. It can be used to quantify the degree of environmental accessibility of an environment for an individual client based on a scoring system that assigns predefined points for each environmental barrier identified. Because the HE is very detailed, it requires administration by a skilled professional to ensure the reliability of results (Iwarsson and Slaug 2001). Although developed initially for assessments of individual clients, the software has also been used successfully in municipal planning scenarios and in studying the relationship between housing and healthy aging in place for older adults (de Jonge and Cordiner 2011).

Comprehensive Assessment and Solution Process for Aging Residents (CASPAR)

Developed by Extended Home Living Services, a home modification contractor in Chicago, the Comprehensive Assessment and Solution Process for Aging Residents (CASPAR) focuses largely on the physical aspects of the environment. The purpose of this tool is to help make modifications available without requiring specialists for costly on-site assessments (Sanford et al. 2002). Information, such as ability to operate lighting and temperature controls, and complete activities for daily living is collected by an occupational therapist or other service provider. Descriptive information on the home is also obtained. "The protocol assesses an older adult's functional limitations and occupational difficulties; identifies task-related environmental features that are in need of modification; obtains detailed information about the physical environment (i.e., measurements, layout, design details) that are necessary to specify and/or design modifications" (Sanford et al. 2002, p.46). In addition, the client and family identify their highest priorities for interventions. Thus, the protocol incorporates client perspectives on their abilities and difficulties in functioning in the home (de Jonge and Cordiner 2011). Once this information has been gathered, it is sent to an architect who specializes in home modifications to make recommendations and to do the necessary drawings and technical work.

Home Environmental Assessment Protocol (HEAP)

The Home Environmental Assessment Protocol (HEAP) is designed to evaluate the safety of homes for persons with cognitive impairments, such as dementia. The HEAP is a research and clinical practice tool developed by Gitlin et al. to meet the urgent need for a specific dementia-focused assessment tool. Given that a poor environment-person match may result in negative behavioral responses and exacerbate functional limitations, the HEAP focuses mainly on environmental impact rather than considering a client's specific abilities or functional performance. For example, one environmental factor that may cause disorientation for people with cognitive impairment is visual overstimulation due to clutter. The HEAP considers four dimensions that may contribute to the well-being of dementia patients and their caregivers in the home environment: the removal of common home hazards to improve safety, home modifications to support activities for daily living, the use of orientation cues, and the presence of meaningful items. Information is gathered through structured observation and self-report from family members. Ratings are derived from the information gathered. Raters are provided with training prior to administration of the tool (Gitlin et al. 2002).

Barriers to Service Delivery

One of the most significant barriers to service delivery of home modifications is "homeowner denial." Even though we know that physical and cognitive changes will occur over our life span, and that modifications to our homes can make a difference in our ability to age in place, many people are reluctant to add features to their homes that will support this process. Researchers have identified three variables that influence whether or not people will choose to make environmental modifications: level of awareness, affordability, and adequacy of the service-delivery system (Pynoos et al. 1997).

Many people who are in need of modifications do not have the knowledge to identify what modifications would benefit them and to find qualified professionals knowledgeable about remodeling and accessibility to complete the job. Many elderly people do not make modifications to their homes because they are unaware of the risks involved in not making them or because they do not understand the benefits of having a safer and more livable home (Pynoos et al. 1997). Individuals have often lived in their homes for decades and have adjusted to inconveniences like very small bathrooms or stairs without handrails or good lighting. Thus, it is difficult for them to perceive potential changes. In addition, many older people are reluctant to seek and accept help because they fear a loss of privacy and independence, deny that they are growing older, or are embarrassed that they need help. In fact, because many older persons who experience functional limitation do not see themselves as having a disability, they resist making any changes to their environment (Faletti 1984). Older people fear the stigma attached to aging, disability, and the need for adaptations (Aminzadeh and Edwards 1998). For example, to many people, the image of a ramp or lift installed on the front of a house suggests that an older person or person with a disability lives there, and they would rather not present themselves to the world in that way.

One of largest barriers to the completion of home modifications is lack of funding. Physical interventions cost money and effort to implement. Approximately 80 percent of home modifications completed in the United States are self-financed by homeowners. The other 20 percent are supported by a variety of programs and service organizations (Fagan 2007). These include the U.S. Department of Housing and Urban Development, foundations and disability-specific organizations (such as centers for independent living), statewide home modification loan programs, state grants for specific populations and assistive technology projects, the U.S. Department of Veterans Affairs, and the Medicaid Home and Community Based Waiver Program, to name a few. Funding is complicated by eligibility requirements that vary from program to program. Other countries have better organized and comprehensive programs for both people with disabilities and older people. The differences in policies are discussed further in the next section.

If people can adapt to a barrier by changing their behavior, which usually means adjusting their expectations to a lower quality of life, no cost is involved (Steinfeld and Shea 1993). Thus, the perception of relative advantages to making changes can be a deciding factor in initiating a project, especially for older clients who will be financing the renovations themselves. It may take outside intervention by family or professional outreach worker to increase awareness enough for an individual to see the value of investing in a project. In some cases, adult children of older clients play a significant role in the financial decision. In the case of major renovations, their perception of the value is the deciding factor in the decision to start a home modification project. It is important to note that family can have a conflict of interest in the decision-making process. For example, if the renovations will be costly, they could reduce the value of an inheritance. Or, if the cost will be borne by a child, the project might mean that a personal goal or desire would have to be sacrificed to help the parent.

Many homeowners or family members can make minor adaptations themselves, such as replacing knobs on kitchen cabinets with inexpensive pulls that can be purchased from any hardware store. Once simple and low-cost improvements are identified and the benefits experienced, this can help to increase interest in more significant investments. More complicated modifications, such as removing a bathtub and replacing it with a roll-in shower, require skilled professionals. Some clients have the financial resources to pay for a project themselves, but many find the adaptations they need cost prohibitive, especially older people and people with disabilities who live on fixed incomes and have limited or no savings. An AARP study (2000) found that one-third of persons who need modifications do not make them because they are not affordable. For those who qualify for existing programs, increasing knowledge of available financial support is therefore a key strategy for overcoming financial barriers.

The mental burden of making changes to a home can be a barrier to making renovations, especially to households that are grappling with the impact of an accident, rehabilitation from a disabling illness or a progressive deteriorative disease such as Parkinson's or ALS. The process includes many complex tasks, such as identifying what changes are needed, determining whether the home environment can support the changes, finding and purchasing equipment and materials, and constructing the renovations or installing equipment. The complexity requires the participation of many different professionals and business entities. Even the coordination of tasks and individuals involved can be an overwhelming and arduous undertaking for many people and their families. The lack of qualified service providers is a major problem in the United States and many other countries. As Pynoos et al (2002) suggests, the ideal system for providing home modification services would include a group of professionals working collaboratively to meet consumer needs and facilitate the process of completing the home modifications. To address the mental burden, potential partners in service delivery should include caseworkers who can take on the burden of coordination.

Policy

The United States, like many other countries, does not have a national policy on home modifications. Home modification services are provided by a mix of professionals with complementary expertise (Gitlin 1998; Siebert 2005), but the roles of the various disciplines are not clearly delineated and there is no common system of service delivery that brings the knowledge of the different disciplines to bear in an efficient manner. Some limited examples of practice guidelines (Siebert 2005) and practitioner certifications exist (e.g., Certified Aging in Place Specialist; National Association of Home Builders 2010). A range of public and private financing sources is available with varying eligibility requirements that create confusion among consumers (Pynoos and Nishita 2003). Third-party payers do not routinely pay for home modification costs (Wahl et al. 2009), and, as mentioned, most home modifications are paid for out of pocket (Fagan 2007).

As in many other countries, there are no consensus standards for service delivery or design and construction of modifications in the United States. Unlike other aspects of the building industry, the field is largely fragmented and unregulated (Gitlin 1998). As a result, consumers experience considerable variation in practice patterns and quality of services. In addition, administrators of funding programs that do exist cannot determine if their funds are allocated and invested efficiently. Programmatic barriers include "inadequate assessment instruments, unavailability of skilled providers, and lack of knowledge about effective solutions that will meet the needs of clients" (Pynoos and Sanford 2002, p. 67).

Several other countries have significant initiatives in home modification service delivery that can serve as models for others. Here are some brief examples of noteworthy initiatives.

Australia. The Home Modification and Maintenance Services program was developed in 2002 to help frail older people, people with disabilities, and their caregivers to remain within their homes longer. Under this program, state governments operate many Home Modification and Maintenance Services outlets staffed by occupational therapists. The Home Modifications Information Clearinghouse, a university-based center for research and dissemination located at the University of New South Wales in Sydney, was created to support delivery of services in Australia by developing best practice information.

Germany. Each of the 16 federal states of Germany provides subsidy programs for home modifications. The size of the subsidy is tied to the type of housing and the urgency of need. Specifically targeted housing types include private homes and apartments that house those who are ill, elderly, or disabled. Special subsidies are also available to help people with severe disabilities to purchase existing homes (Piltner and Halbich 2001).

Sweden. Home modifications are provided through the national government, using a coordinated approach that involves both therapists and professional designers. There is no cap to the funding provided, which is need based. Professional assessments by occupational therapists and creative design solutions are used to control costs. All services are coordinated through case managers. Modifications to new homes are also provided during construction. This policy allows residents to live in any building that has an accessible entry. It supplements the construction of new housing with funding to provide universal design features, such as automated doors and adjustable-height kitchen counters (Lilja, Mansson, Jahlenius, and Sacco-Peterson 2003).

Canada. The Canada Mortgage and Housing Corporation offers financial assistance for renovation of existing homes, particularly for older adults, low-income households, and people with disabilities. In addition, it has developed a program for new construction that encourages the use of flexible housing plans so that houses may change as the needs of their occupants change. Called FlexHousing, this design concept is based on four principles: adaptability, affordability, accessibility, and healthy housing.[3] Plans can be changed easily to meet changing household needs; features of FlexHousing include stacked closets that can be converted into a lift, no-step entries, and two-story home designs that can be converted into two flats. Thus, this program removes barriers by making new housing easier to modify if needed.

In the Nordic countries and other countries in northern Europe, funding for home modifications is provided through mandatory long-term care insurance, part of the package of social welfare benefits. Like mandatory car insurance, this program ensures that funding will be available late in life or in the case of a catastrophic health incident to make the necessary renovations to homes and also to provide home care, both of which may be needed to support independent living and aging in place. Most Nordic countries have home modification service delivery systems similar to Sweden's, but the other countries have caps on expenditures as well as a needs-based eligibility policy. One advantage of a dedicated funding stream with large amounts of public money involved is the need to ensure cost effectiveness. This has lead to the development of coordinated service delivery and evidence-based practice. Another advantage is the ability to provide financing to provide universal design features in new housing. As new housing is being constructed, a caseworker coordinates the use of funding from the home modification program with the construction of an individual client's dwelling. This can even involve making renovations to a brand new unit if it makes sense.

---

[3]Canada Mortgage and Housing Corporation, "FlexHousing™." www.cmhc-schl.gc.ca/en/co/buho/flho/index.cfm.

An interesting example demonstrates how coordination of services can lead to significant benefits for both individual clients and the public. Figures 10–9 and 10–10 show examples of modifications in a suburb of Copenhagen that were made to a new apartment during its construction. The kitchen (Figure 10–9) is fully accessible, including an automatically adjustable kitchen countertop. A middle-aged couple owns the apartment. The husband, who uses a wheelchair, is a cook, and the fully accessible kitchen allows him to prepare meals for a fee at home to earn an income. Staff in a nursing home across the street, where his wife works, come to his apartment for a nutritious dinner after their shift, which they pay him to make. Thus, the extensive modifications provide him not only with access to the kitchen but also a means of employment. This example dramatically demonstrates the social participation benefits of universal design.

Figure 10–10 shows the openness of the apartment. In a cooperative building like this, residents own a percentage of their apartment and facilities are shared. Residents actively participate in decision making and work together to maintain the space. The family participated in design of the unit's interior and, working with design and rehabilitation professions, were able to ensure that their apartment met their accessibility needs. The addition of special features like the automated countertop did not require any major renovations to the new building, reducing

Figure 10-9: Flexible kitchen. The flexibility in the design of this kitchen allows the user to work out of his home as a cook even though his mobility is restricted.

Figure 10-10: Open floor plan. The resident of this unit designed this apartment specifically to meet his needs. The kitchen island provides access on both sides of the kitchen and a convenient storage location for serving.

the overall costs of making an accessible home. The additional features simply personalized the unit for the family a bit further. Note that the building has universal design features as well. Stairways serve six apartments each. Elevators at each stairway serve all the units in this three-story building, providing life span living opportunities. Note the large folding glazed doors that provide access to the outdoors and ample ventilation, even though there are no balconies.

Countries like Canada and Denmark have realized that there is a close relationship between home modification costs and the construction of new housing. The latter supports the efficient use of funding for home modification and long-term care. If housing has universal design features, it can reduce future renovation costs over the life of the building and facilitate the delivery of services in the home environment rather than through institutional care. This not only makes the new housing more sustainable from an environmental perspective, but it also has significant social benefits by allowing people to remain in their home and neighborhood even as their needs change over their life span. The FlexHousing program demonstrate how this relationship plays out in single-family housing and the example above demonstrates how it can also work in multifamily housing.

Knowledge Needs

Several reviews of the literature have concluded that home modifications support functional ability, reduce disability-related outcomes, and, to a lesser extent, reduce accident-related outcomes such as falls (Barras 2005; Lord, Menz, and Sherrington 2006; Tse 2005; Wahl et al.

2009). Although substantial public and private funds are spent on home modifications, little cost-effectiveness data are available to support current practices (Barras 2005). Wahl and colleagues (2009) recommended that future research should identify best practice guidelines and enhance the quality of research measures.

There are two interrelated needs for advancing the state of the art in research and practice in home modifications: (1) development of consensus-based practice standards and (2) development of valid, consumer-centered measurement tools that can be efficiently applied by researchers and practitioners in real-world settings. With respect to the former, research is needed to "determine best practices or combinations of strategies, the range of benefits evinced by older people, and who benefits, in what ways, and why from adjusting different attributes of home environments" (Gitlin 2003, p. 629). With respect to the latter, Gitlin (1998) pointed out that there is no uniform terminology or typology of home modification intervention strategies. This need remains and has substantial ramifications for research and practice. As Gitlin (1998) observes:

> Persistent inconsistencies in the definition and categorization of strategies and their measurement has made it difficult to draw meaningful conclusions across studies. Defining and grouping strategies that represent the scope of home modifications is critical for the design of interventions and making possible an evaluation of which strategies work best and for whom. (p. 190)

Lack of common metrics makes it difficult to develop cross-study comparisons of home environments and home modification interventions (Gitlin 2003). This point was reinforced in a recent review that concluded: "Given the fact that psychometrically sound instruments are essential for examining the role of home environments, . . . tool development should be one of the priorities of this area of inquiry" (Wahl et al. 2009, p. 364). Tool development includes creating an instrument to complete more efficient and accurate home modifications.

It is logical to conclude that modifications such as ramps or stair lifts give people the opportunity to engage in major life activities both inside and outside of the home and that other features, such as handrails on the stairs and grab bars in the bathroom, can help prevent accidents. But how do we know which modifications will have the greatest impact on improving quality of life for which individuals? How do we quantify the need for adequate space and access in order to facilitate informal caregiving by relatives and friends and minimize the need for costly personal care services delivered by paid caregivers? Further research is needed to evaluate current home modification practices, develop a research infrastructure to measure and evaluate interventions, and create guidelines based on best practices. This research is critical because the demand and need for home modifications will increase with the aging of the population.

Summary

The relationship between a person and the home environment is very important to health, safety, and emotional well-being. Environments that fit the characteristics and abilities of their users are more likely to meet the needs of their inhabitants. For aging older adults, people of atypical size and stature, and younger people with disabilities, person–environment fit often requires adjustments to existing housing due to the limitations of traditional home design concepts. Home modifications that improve fit for these special user groups require thoughtful planning to ensure that long- and short-term needs are met. If designed and constructed well, home modifications can not only help to support the occupants but also extend the useful life span of a home and improve its market value on resale. Modifications may range from the very simple, such as changing doorknobs to levers, to the very complicated, such as adding a lift or a ramp. Regardless of the scope, home modifications create supportive environments for diverse populations and encourage aging in place.

Although policy initiatives exist all over the world, particularly to address the long-term needs of households with people who have developmental disabilities and in response to the aging of the population, some countries, such as the Nordic countries, the Netherlands, and Germany, have extensive and well-coordinated policies and programs. Other countries need to learn from the experience of these existing programs. By studying existing practices, researchers can identify how to overcome barriers to implementation and policy and best practices for service delivery. It is noteworthy that Canada and the Nordic countries coordinate the provision of more expensive modifications with the design of new accessible housing. This policy removes barriers to making renovations in the future. Housing developers provide the basic features of architectural accessibility, and then the government program augments the design of specific units with more extensive equipment. However, this policy works only when housing incorporates universal design concepts from the start. Because housing has a long useful life span, the promotion of universal design in new housing is an important strategy that should be initiated as soon as possible to meet the needs of future generations.

Review Topics

1. What are the differences between home modifications and general home improvements?
2. Describe the scope of home modifications. What are the most common modifications? What are the most common mistakes?
3. Name three key barriers to increasing implementation of home modification practices.

References

AARP. 1999. Universal Design and Home Modifications. Washington, DC: AARP.

AARP. 2000. Fixing to Stay: A National Survey on Housing and Home Modification Issues—Executive Summary. Washington, DC: AARP Public Policy Institute.

Ainsworth, E., and D. de Jonge (eds.) 2011. *An Occupational Therapist's Guide to Home Modification Practice*. Thorofare, NJ: SLACK Inc.

Altman, I., B. B. Brown, B. Staples, and C. M. Werner. 1992. "A Transactional Approach to Close Relationships: Courtship, Weddings and Place Making." In W. B. Walsg, K. H. Craik, and R. H. Price (eds.), *Person–Environment Psychology: Models and Perspectives,* pp. 193–204. Hillsdale, NJ: Lawrence Erlbaum.

Aminzadeh, F., and N. Edwards. 1998. "Exploring Seniors' Views on the Use of Assistive Devices in Fall Prevention." *Public Health Nursing* 15 (4): 297–304.

Barras, S. 2005. "A Systematic and Critical Review of the Literature: The Effectiveness of Occupational Therapy Home Assessment on a Range of Outcome Measures." *Australian Occupational Therapy Journal* 52: 326–336.

Clemson, L., R. G. Cumming, H. Kendig, M. Swann, R. Heard, and K. Taylor. 2004. "The Effectiveness of a Community-based Program for Reducing the Incidence of Falls in the Elderly: A Randomized Trial." *Journal of the American Geriatrics Society* 52: 1487–1494.

Cooper, B., L. Letts, P. Rigby, D. Stewart, and S. Strong. 2005. "Measuring Environmental Factors." In M. Law, C. Baum, and W. Dunn (eds.), *Measuring Occupational Performance: Supporting Best Practice in Occupational Therapy*, pp. 316–344. Thorofare, NJ: SLACK Inc.

Cumming, R. G. 2002. "Intervention Strategies and Risk-Factor Modification for Falls Prevention. A Review of Recent Intervention Studies." *Clinics in Geriatric Medicine* 18: 175–189.

de Jonge, D. and R. Cordiner. 2011. "Evaluating Clients' Home Modification Needs and Priorities." In E. Ainsworth and D. de Jonge (eds.), *An Occupational Therapist's Guide to Home Modification Practice* (pp. 113–137). Thorofare, NJ: S LACK Inc.

Demiris, G. et al. 2004. "Older Adults' Attitudes towards and Perceptions of Smart Home Technologies: A Pilot Study." *Informatics for Health and Social Care* 29 (2): 87–94.

Dovey, K. 1985. "Home and Homelessness." In I. Altman and C. M. Werner (ed.), *Home Environments* (pp. 33–64). New York: Plenum Press.

Drewnowski, A. and W. J. Evans. 2001. "Nutrition, physical activity, and quality of life in older adults: Summary." *Journals of Gerontology*. Series A, Biological Sciences and Medical Sciences, 56 Spec No. 2, pp. 89–94.

Fagan, L. A. 2007. "Funding Sources for Home Modifications." *Home and Community Health Special Interest Section Quarterly* 14 (3): 1–3.

Faletti, M. V. 1984. "Using Technology to Adapt Environments." *Generations* 8: 35–38.

Fange, A. 2007. "Challenges in the Development of Strategies for Housing Adaptation Evaluations." *Scandinavian Journal of Occupational Therapy* 14 (3): 140–149.

Gill, T. M., C. S. Williams, J. T. Robison, and M. E. Tinetti. 1999. "A Population-based Study of Environmental Hazards in the Homes of Older Persons." *American Journal of Public Health* 89: 553–556.

Gitlin, L. N. 1998. "Testing Home Modification Interventions: Issues of Theory, Measurement, Design, and Implementation." *Annual Review of Gerontology and Geriatrics* 18: 190–246.

———. 2003. "Conducting Research on Home Environments: Lessons Learned and New Directions." *Gerontologist* 43 (5): 628–637.

Gitlin, L. N., S. Schinfeld, L. Winter, M. Corcoran, A. A. Boyce, and W. Hauck. 2002. "Evaluating Home Environments of Persons with Dementia: Interrater Reliability and Validity of the Home Environmental Assessment Protocol (HEAP)." *Disability and Rehabilitation* 24 (1): 59–71.

Iwarsson, S. and B. Slaug. 2001. *Housing Enabler. An Instrument for Assessing and Analysing Accessibility Problems in Housing*. Nävlinge, Sweden: Veten and Skapen HB, Slaug Data Management AB.

Kraus, L. E., S. Stoddard, and D. Gilmartin. 1996. *Chartbook on Disability in the United States*. Berkeley, CA: National Institute on Disability and Rehabilitation Research.

Lawton, M. P. 1982. "Competence, Environmental Press, and the Adaptation of Older People." In M. P. Lawton, P. Windley, and T. Byerts (eds.), *Aging and the Environment* (vol. 7, pp. 33–59). New York: Springer.

Lawton, M. P. and L. Nahemow. 1973. "Ecology and the Aging Process." In C. Eisdorfer and M. P. Lawton (eds.), *Psychology of Adult Development and Aging* (pp. 619–674). Washington, DC: American Psychological Association.

Lilja, M., I. Mansson, L. Jahlenius, and M. Sacco-Peterson. 2003. "Disability Policy in Sweden." *Journal of Disability Policy Studies,* 14(2):130–135.

Lord, S. R., H. B. Menz, and C. Sherrington. 2006. "Home Environment Risk Factors for Falls in Older People and the Efficacy of Home Modifications. *Age and Ageing* 35 (S2): ii55–59.

Mann, W. C. (ed.). 2005. *Smart Technology for Aging, Disability and Independence: The State of the Science.* Hoboken, NJ: John Wiley & Sons.

National Association of Home Builders. 2010. "What Is a Certified Aging-in-Place Specialist (CAPS)?" www.nahb.com/.

Piltner, K. and B. Halbich. 2001. "Housing Policy and Funding Mechansims for Elderly and Disabled People in Germany." *Universal Design Handbook* : 39.1–39.23.

Preiser, W. F. and E. Ostroff (ed.). 2001. *Universal Design Handbook.* New York, NY: McGraw-Hill.

Pynoos, J., P. Liebig, J. Overton, and E. Calvert. 1997. "The Delivery of Home Modification and Repair Services." In S. Lanspery and J. Hyde (eds.), *Staying Put: Adapting the Places Instead of the People,* p. 171 Amityville, NY: Baywood.

Pynoos, J. and C. M. Nishita. 2003. "The Cost and Financing of Home Modifications in the United States." *Journal of Disability Policy Studies* 14 (2): 68–73.

Pynoos, J. and J. Sanford. 2002. "New Tools for Better Home Modifications." *The Case Manager* (13)1: 67–70.

Sanford, J. A. 2004. "Definition of Home Modifications." Included in L. A. Fagan and J. A. Sanford, *Home modifications: Assessment, Implementation, and Innovation.* Presented at the 84th Annual Conference and Expo of the American Occupational Therapy Association (May 19), Minneapolis, MN.

Sanford, J., J. Pynoos, A. Tejral, and A. Browne. 2002. "Development of a Comprehensive Assessment for Delivery of Home Modifications." *Journal of Physical Therapy and Occupational Therapy in Geriatrics* 20 (2): 43–55.

Siebert, C. 2005. Occupational Therapy Practice Guidelines for Home Modifications. Bethesda, MD: AOTA Press.

Stark, S. 2004. "Removing Environmental Barriers in the Homes of Older Adults with Disabilities Improves Occupational Performance." *OTJR: Occupation, Participation and Health* (24): 32–39.

Steinfeld, E. et al. 1979. *Access to the Built Environment: A Review of Literature.* Washington, DC: U.S. Department of Housing and Urban Development Office of Policy Development and Research.

Steinfeld, E. and S. Shea. 1993. "Enabling Home Environments: Identifying Barriers to Independence." *Technology and Disability* 2 (4): 69–79.

Steinfeld, E., S. Shea, and D. Levine. 1996. *Technical Report: Home Modifications and the Fair Housing Law.* Buffalo, NY: Center for Inclusive Design and Environmental Access, School of Architecture and Planning SUNY/Buffalo.

Tanner, B. 2011. "The Home Environment." In E. Ainsworth and D. de Jonge (eds.), *An Occupational Therapist's Guide to Home Modification Practice* (pp. 3–16). Thorofare, NJ: SLACK Inc.

Tse, T. 2005. "The Environment and Falls Prevention: Do Environmental Modifications Make a Difference? *Australian Occupational Therapy Journal* 52: 271–281.

U.S. Census Bureau. 2006. *2006 American Community Survey,* www.census.gov/acs/.

Üstun, T. B., S. Chatterji, J. Bickenbach, N. Kostanjsek, and M. Schneider. 2003. "The International Classification of Functioning, Disability and Health: A New Tool for Understanding Disability and Health." *Disability and Rehabilitation* 25 (11–12): 565–571.

Verbrugge, L. M. and A. M. Jette. 1994. "The Disablement Process." *Social Science and Medicine* 38: 1–14.

Wahl, H. W., A. Fange, F. Oswald, L. N. Gitlin, and S. Iwarsson. 2009. "The Home Environment and Disability-Related Outcomes in Aging Individuals: What Is the Empirical Evidence?" *Gerontologist* 49 (3): 355–367.

Ware, J. E, 1987. "Standards for Validating Health Measures: Definition and Content." *Journal of Chronic Diseases,* 40 (6):473-80

Yuen, H. K. and R. E. Carter. 2006. "A Predictive Model for the Intention to Implement Home Modifications: A Pilot Study", *Journal of Applied Gerontology,* 25 (1): 3-16.

11

Universal Design and the Interior Environment

Introduction

Regardless of climate, North Americans spend about 90 percent of their time indoors (U.S. Environmental Protection Agency 2008). This is a sobering statistic, and one that reinforces the need for interior environments that function well for all users, regardless of size, age, cultural background, and/or physical or cognitive ability. In the design of buildings, interior designers or interior architects generally make the decisions concerning the planning of interior environments. Interior designers work collaboratively with architects to determine the spatial organization, needs of occupants, selection of finishes, furniture, wayfinding systems, and lighting in most public and some residential buildings. Research demonstrates that the decisions made by interior designers affect the quality of life of building users and contribute to health, inclusion in public life, personal safety, and psychological and emotional well-being. Universal design has become central to the design process because it combines function with aesthetics. This chapter describes the role of the interior designer in creating inclusive environments for both residential and public buildings. There are seven key elements of an interior—wayfinding, acoustics, lighting, color, furnishings, and floor coverings. Each of these elements is discussed. For each, evidence-based practical guidelines are provided that raise awareness of the need for inclusively designed interiors and objects and provide design professionals with a better understanding of how to apply universal design to interiors.

Although this chapter considers building design from the perspective of the interior designer, it is important to acknowledge that designing a building requires the input of many different design disciplines, including industrial design, graphic design, and textile design.

Wayfinding

In a sense, all first-time visitors to buildings are "disabled" by a lack of knowledge. However, in a complex building, many longtime "residents" also can become lost and disoriented at times, particularly if they tend to spend the majority of their time in one part of the building. Good design for wayfinding facilitates user access, increases satisfaction, and reduces stigma and isolation of users with disabilities. It reduces the confusion of visitors and mistakes by employees, saving time and money and preventing accidents. It also reduces stress, boosting health and productivity (Evans and McCoy 1998). "The ability to find one's way into, through, and out of a building is clearly a prerequisite for the satisfaction of higher goals" (Weisman 1981, p. 189).

Wayfinding design is integral to universal design because it fosters understanding and better utilization of buildings, and aids social integration. The design of interior features can assist users in orienting themselves in space, finding their destinations, and identifying their locations. "Cueing" is the technical term used to describe the set of prompts, either visual or non visual, that help users to navigate space. The most common form of cueing is visual cueing. For those with loss of or diminished sight, audible, tactile (haptic), or olfactory/aromatic cues can also provide the necessary information to negotiate space successfully. Cues help us to perceive and understand important things in our world such as where the edge of the table is located and how long a corridor might be. If the designer has used spatial cues effectively, all users should be able to navigate the environment successfully. Environments that provide strong architectural cueing complemented by a thoughtful signage system contribute substantially to participant satisfaction and future frequency of use. People will avoid places that are hard to understand and cause them to lose their way.

Interior design features are crucial for improving the awareness and understanding of the path system, establishing interior landmarks, and linking interior directions to a larger orientation system. Users with visual impairments may remember only the features necessary to prompt turns or mark distances along path segments (Golledge 1999). Thus, the design at decision points is particularly important, especially major intersections—"nodes" in Kevin Lynch's (1960) terminology.

Design features that can aid wayfinding include lighting effects that reinforce paths and distinguish them from one another and design schemes that create interior "districts" with a particular character. Landmarks can be created using all of the senses, not just sight. Color and distinctive artwork are probably the most frequently used methods to create landmarks, but other methods can be used effectively. Acoustic cues include differences in reverberation levels, water features, and background music; tactile cues include the location of floor surface changes, "shorelines" that mark the edges of paths or enclosed spaces, tracks made with floor materials that contrast with the general background flooring and wall materials that hands can feel while moving around a space; olfactory/atmospheric can be produced by odiferous plants and even humidity changes (see Utrecht Central Museum described in Chapter 8). Multisensory cues should be used as much as possible both to accommodate people with sensory limitations and also to create a stronger "signal." A good example is a player piano that provides not only a visual landmark but an acoustic and tactile landmark as well. Another is an aromatic planting, such as an orange tree or a regularly replenished cut flower display, providing a distinctive olfactory and visual landmark.

Texture and pattern provide sensory cues to all users and can be used to distinguish interior "districts." An interior without much variation in texture and pattern will be more difficult to remember and will be less aesthetically pleasing to the user. Texture and pattern add another sensory modality to landmarks. For example, a change of floor material combined with a player piano or feature planting enhances the landmark through four sensory modalities. But an interior with too much texture and pattern also can prove problematic and can cause overstimulation and sensory "noise." The use of pattern in interior design to meet all user needs is complicated because building inhabitants might perceive pattern in unexpected ways. For example, people with certain types of visual impairments and people who need to take psychotropic medications may misinterpret some cues and perceive illusions like a false sense of depth. Excessive use of pattern may also cause agitation and overstimulation for those with dementia.

Despite its demonstrated importance to building use, costs, and safety, wayfinding receives less attention than it should in planning, research, and building evaluation. Often the investment in wayfinding systems is less than that devoted to amenities such as art and furnishings. Planning for wayfinding systems begins at the earliest stage of design, and it should incorporate input from prospective residents and visitors to the building. In addition, a postoccupancy evaluation can identify further problems that can be corrected after the building is completed. Problems can become quite serious when not addressed prior to occupancy, and usually the response is ad hoc, such as taping up a cardboard sign. Too much of this can lead to even more confusion by introducing clutter in the environment.

Architectural wayfinding systems are supported by a well-planned signage system. Signs help us navigate the built environment and are an important tool in design for wayfinding. They help building users orient themselves in space, find their destinations, and identify their locations. Signs also provide valuable information about events and activities in buildings. A signage system that is readable and legible by all users is a fundamental part of environmental communication. The U.S. Census Bureau reported that 3.7 percent of U.S. citizens (7.8 million people) over 15 years of age "had difficulty seeing words/letters" and that "6.6 million people were unable to read printed signs at normal viewing distances" (Brault 2008, p. 3). This increases to 12.1 percent for individuals 65 years of age and older. The World Health Organization (2010) reported that worldwide there are approximately 185 million persons with vision disabilities. Signage systems designed without accommodating for this significant portion of the population leave people "lost in space."

Often, signage systems are intended to be permanent, which leads to lack of flexibility and can introduce some serious problems when room assignments are changed. When a signage system has too many accumulated errors, people will become suspicious of its usefulness. The most effective signage systems are those that can be changed easily and inexpensively, preferably by the building management (VanderKlipp 2006). To comply with accessibility standards, only room numbers, restroom signs, and signs pointing the way to accessible facilities need to be tactile as well as visual. This provides flexibility for changing the individual room name on the sign without changing the number, but only if the two parts of the sign are separate elements. The size of characters needed to read a tactile sign, with the room or occupant name, would often exceed the space available. Audible signs can provide even more information to more diverse groups than standard graphic signs. Interactive digital signs can provide extensive information on events in and contents of rooms. Content on interactive signs can be changed easily practically without cost and they can include audible information for participants who or blind or have low vision. With a menu to drill down for information, interactive signs can also be designed to provide the level of information necessary at any one time. For example, at the top level they might only provide the name of the room, but they could also provide details on the availability of a room shared by a work team through an interface with a shared work team calendar.

Designers should consider four key issues when designing or specifying graphic signs: font, arrangement, environmental factors (e.g., whether a sign is illuminated), and personal factors (e.g., the level of attention of the viewer). Table 11–1 summarizes important characteristics and recommendations to consider when designing a graphic signage system from a universal design perspective.

Table 11–1: Graphic Signage System Guidelines

Characteristic	Recommendation
Letter height	1" min. (2.54 cm) plus another 1" (2.54 cm) in height for every 35 ft. (10.68 m) in viewing distance. An increase of 1" (2.54 cm) in height is needed every 17 ft. (5.34 m) for people with vision impairments, including normal age-related deficits.
Width-to-height ratio	0.7:1.0 (w:h)
Stroke width-to-height ratio	1:5 (w:h)
Text Color	Green, yellow, or gray letters on high-contrast background
Font	5 x 7 for uppercase 7 x 9 for lowercase
Intercharacter spacing	25%–40% letter height
Interline spacing	75%–100% of letter height between lines of text
Case	Uppercase or title case for single words Lowercase or sentence case for longer messages
Contrast	70% min. contrast between letters and background Legibility is compromised when contrast approaches this threshold
Serifs	Serif or sans serif Sans serif only for tactile signage per the American with Disabilities Act

Wayfinding Design Guidelines

- Design wayfinding systems for first-time visitors because repeat visitors can rely on their experience for navigation.
- Organize information consistently and hierarchically, and provide multisensory landmarks at key decision points (VanderKlipp 2006).
- Carefully control circulation to limit confusing options and reduce congestion. Limiting vehicular or pedestrian traffic can have the additional benefit of increasing privacy for staff and clients and enhancing security (VanderKlipp 2006).
- Keep the visitors' mental state in mind (e.g., distracted, tired, jangled nerves; worried patients at a medical facility) when choosing colors and deciding on the size of fonts.
- Begin coordination among architects, interior designers, and graphic designers early in the design process.
- Provide information in ways that are easily updated.
- Design the size of text on signs to be legible from the intended viewing distance.
- Select a signage system that provides enough flexibility to accommodate the needs of building occupants for information and also over time as room uses change.

- Research issues prior to design, including obtaining the end user perspective (Brown, Wright, and Brown 1997; Garling, Book, and Lindberg 1988).
- Provide users with an ordered environment that has "a clear possibility of choice and a starting-point for the acquisition of further information" (Lynch 1960, p. 4).
- Provide a place where users can obtain a clear visual sweep of the building interior. The panoramic experience not only delights but helps the user obtain a view of the larger spatial configuration that enhances memory.
- Use design to reinforce existing social meanings by using appropriate styles and landmarks (e.g., historic photos of places in the neighborhood).

Acoustics

We experience our environments with all of our senses, not just our eyes. How we hear a building is as important as how we see a building, and hearing is an active process (Tauke and Schoell 2011). Environments provide acoustic cues and signals that define an area spatially and provide the information for those with sight impairments to create a mental map. Acoustics play multiple roles in the environment, including assistance with orientation, location identification, and situational awareness, and contributes to the overall experience of enjoyment by all users (Truax 1984). It is important for designers to provide soundscapes that include sound signals (e.g., alarms), keynotes (e.g., distinctive background sounds), and soundmarks (e.g., waterfalls, bell towers) to help users to navigate through the environment (Schafer 1977).

Over the course of our lifetimes, most of us will experience some form of hearing loss, even if only temporarily. This loss may occur when we are young children because of genetics, allergies, or infections; as adults from accident or extended exposure to loud noises; or as we age because of presbycusis, or lessening reduction of high tone hearing acuteness resulting from age-related changes in the ear ("Presbycusis" 2011). Hearing loss is a more common sensory deficit than vision loss, but often it goes undetected for long periods of time. This is because vision loss is more immediately apparent than hearing loss. We quickly realize when things and people appear to be fuzzy, but we can easily attribute diminished hearing to mumbled speech, low volume, or noisy environments.

Hearing loss can have a dramatic impact on quality of life. The primary outcome of hearing loss is the barrier it creates to communication. This barrier can lead to problems in personal relationships, jobs, socioeconomic status, and access to education (David 2008). Hearing loss is also linked to physiological problems, such as dizziness and imbalance, that can lead to injury. Fundamentally, independence and personal well-being can be adversely impacted, resulting in loneliness and isolation, particularly for older adults.

The 1990 International Standard (ISO) defines a "hearing handicap" as the disadvantage imposed by a hearing impairment sufficiently severe to affect one's personal efficiency in activities for daily living, usually expressed in the inability to understand speech in low levels of background noise (ISO 1990). Hearing loss may occur for many reasons, but it can generally be categorized as either conductive hearing loss or sensorineural (SNHL) hearing loss. Conductive hearing loss is usually a result of an illness, such as an ear infection or allergic reaction, or a genetic defect. People with this type of hearing loss usually experience a reduction in sound level and are unable to hear faint sounds. Medical or surgical interventions can often correct this type of hearing loss (American Speech-Language Hearing Association n.d.). SNHL hearing loss is the most common type of permanent hearing loss (presbycusis is a type of SNHL) and occurs when there is damage to the inner ear (cochlea) or to the nerve pathways from the inner ear to the brain (American Speech-Language Hearing Association n.d.). Unfortunately, medical or surgical interventions usually cannot correct SNHL.

The numbers of people impacted by a hearing impairment is significant. The National Institute of Deafness and other Communication Disorders (2011) estimates that 30 to 47 percent of people 65 and older have a hearing impairment and that, in total, about 17 percent of Americans, or 36 million people, have some degree of hearing loss. As the population ages, that number is expected to rise. Additionally, men are more likely to experience hearing loss than women. This may not be biological but may be attributed to environmental factors, such as their places of work, as traditionally more men than women have worked in heavy industry and construction.

It is also more difficult to correct hearing impairments than vision impairments, as our hearing mechanism is very delicate and difficult to replicate. New technology has improved the quality of hearing devices, and in some instances, surgery, such as cochlear implants, can help correct hearing impairments. Nevertheless, hearing aids receive the highest user dissatisfaction ratings of any assistive device (Bakker 1997).

Getting the acoustic plan right in a space depends on a number of contributing factors, including the room's purpose, the number of occupants, the length of time occupants spend in the room, the activities that take place in it, and the room's location within the building. The box provides some general guidelines for acoustics that should be considered in all universally designed spaces (Laszlo 1999).

Design Guidelines for Hearing Loss

1. Design for good acoustics and noise control.
2. Design for appropriate visual conditions, including placement of light sources, levels of illumination, and adequate signage.
3. Build in nonacoustic alerting and notification systems.
4. Include augmented telecommunication systems.
5. Include provisions for assistive communication technologies as part of the design.
6. Acknowledge the effect of design elements on people with hearing loss.

Source: Laszlo (1999).

Laszlo (1999) determined that the most supportive acoustic designs are those that:

- Endeavor to reduce or eliminate all extraneous sound from potential disruptors, such as waterfalls, fountains, piped-in music, fluorescent lights, and radios.
- Strategically use carpeting, ceiling height, wall surfaces, and chair pads to control sound attenuation and reverberation. (Designers should specify the quietest plumbing, heating, and air duct devices.)
- Locate rooms that are noisy as far away from quiet spaces as possible.

Residential Acoustics

Residential buildings are seldom designed with an acoustic plan, even though we spend much of our time in these environments. Designers working in long-term care and senior housing environments must pay particular attention to the acoustic quality of space because the majority of their population will have some form of hearing impairment. To create more supportive interior environments, designers should consider:

- Reducing background noise from outside the building and neighboring spaces by good acoustic separation and window selection.
- Reducing reverberation by carpeting and by lining draperies.
- Providing doorbells that ring in many rooms of a dwelling unit and that are connected to other devices, such as lamps to create a flashing signal when someone is at the door.
- Including smoke detectors with flashing light signals as well as sound signals.
- Providing sociopetal seating arrangements that provide good sight lines for conversation.
- Ensuring that heating and air conditioning systems are quiet (Bakker 1997).

Acoustics in Open Offices

Acoustics are particularly important in the design of open-plan office landscapes because nearby speech can be very intrusive to privacy and disrupt work flow. Here are some important factors to consider.

- The higher the sound absorption quality of the ceiling, the less sound will reflect into adjacent workstations.
- Barriers between workstations should be at least 5 foot 4 inches (162.6 cm) in height; barriers panels should be sound absorbing.
- Sound transmission class (how well a building barrier attenuates airborne sound) between barriers should be rated at least a 20.
- The floor should be carpeted (Warnock 2004).

Acoustics in Schools

Acoustic design is also very important in educational environments because traditional methods of learning are delivered through speaking and listening. "Speech produced in one place in a room should be clear and intelligible everywhere in the room" (Nabelek 1987, p. S44). Good acoustic design can improve learner focus and information retention. Noise and excessive reverberation in the space due to hard surfaces, noisy HVAC systems, hallway noise, and materials with poor sound absorption can have a direct negative impact on learning (U.S. Access Board 2003). This is especially true for students who have hearing impairments, have ear infections, or are listening to a nonnative language. Significant research has been completed on this topic. The Acoustical Society of America has produced a comprehensive hands-on resource for classroom design, "Acoustical Barriers to Learning" to help designers in educational settings (Nelson, Soli, and Seltz 2002).

Lighting

> Lighting for universal design is lighting that grows and shrinks as we do; it lives with us, and adapts to our needs.
>
> —*Patricia Rizzo, Lighting Research Center*

Light is essential to our physical and emotional health. We require light to regulate our inner circadian (24-hour) clock so that we know when we should sleep and when we should be awake, to prevent depression in the dark months of winter, and to provide essential nutrients for growth. Lighting is also essential to support safe movement through space, but it requires energy use, contributing to the operating cost of facilities. Thus, lighting plans need to consider a set of complex goals, including support for occupants' functional needs, the aesthetic qualities of a space, and energy efficiency.

The most successful lighting plans provide lighting solutions that meet the complex needs of diverse user groups, particularly in commercial and public spaces, where diversity of occupants is highest. Of particular importance are the needs of older adults because shifts in demography have made this portion of our population significant in size. As our physiology changes over our life span, so do our needs and requirements for light. A good lighting plan is concerned with both the quantity *and* the quality of light in a space and is flexible enough to adjust easily to change as we grow older.

Designers usually use lighting data schedules developed and distributed by the Illuminating Engineering Society of North America (IESNA) as guidelines when developing a lighting plan (Rea 2000). Until 2007, the IESNA schedules were based on the needs of a 23-year-old, so they were limited in scope. They did not adequately reflect current demographic trends. In an effort to address this problem, the newest IESNA data schedules, released in 2007 (DiLaura et al. 2007), incorporated a three-level range partially based on user age. Still, the oldest group considered is just 50—a number that does not accurately reflect the aging population.

To ensure that the lighting plan is both energy efficient and accommodates the needs of all users, it is important to address key lighting design decisions as early as possible in the planning process. This practice allows designers to maximize the use of both natural and artificial light sources. To ensure that lighting receives the attention that it deserves, interior designers or interior architects should be involved in the early phases of design, rather than after the architectural design is finalized, as is common in conventional practice.

Lighting is a very complex topic. The next sections provide a general overview of key lighting design issues as they relate to universal design. Lighting design must take into account changes in physiology, different types of light sources, how the body responds to light sources, and how to use light effectively in an inclusive way.

At some point as we age, all of us will experience a reduction in vision or a visual impairment leading to reduced clarity of sight (reduced visual acuity). "Visual impairment" is defined as a functional limitation of the eye(s) or visual system that may manifest as reduced visual acuity, reduced ability to see contrast, sensitivity to light (photophobia), visual field loss, double vision (diplopia), visual distortion, visual perceptual difficulties, or any combination of these (Garvey 2001). Some of the earliest signs of age-related vision loss include the reduction of depth perception and the inability to distinguish details. Accommodation, or adjusting to abrupt light level changes, and reading small text may become more difficult. In a complex and confusing environment, age-related vision loss might lead to disorientation and impede the ability to navigate space.

As the eye ages, much higher levels of illumination are required in order to accomplish the same tasks. The amount of light needed to maintain good visual performance doubles every 13 years after the age of 20 and relates directly to the reduction in pupil size as we age (Garvey 2001). A 60-year-old person may require two or three times as much light as a 20-year-old to perform the same task in the same room (Garvey 2001). Normal physiological aging will result in changes such as the thickening of the lens of the eye, the reduction of the sensitivity of the retina, or the eye's loss of transparency. Other age-related issues affecting vision include the effects of eye diseases common in old age, such as cataracts and glaucoma. The focus should not be on simply increasing light levels but on providing people the control occupants need to have good visual performance. Individual needs for illumination vary and too much illumination can produce disabling glare. Thus, inclusive lighting plans can compensate for these changes by providing flexibility in the amount, type, and placement of illumination available.

In planning an interior environment, designers have two types of light sources from which to choose: artificial light and natural sunlight. Each of these lighting types has its strengths and weaknesses, and the best lighting plans usually include balanced use of both.

Artificial Light

Traditional lighting plans relied heavily on natural light. With the advent of improved technology, subsequent generations of buildings were designed to be more dependent on artificial light to shape space, create atmosphere, and provide visual cues. Artificial light is more easily controlled and is more predictable and consistent than natural light. Until recently, this type of light was also promoted as "cleaner" and "healthier" for users. The most frequently used artificial light sources are incandescent (the common household light bulb), fluorescent, halogen, LED (light-emitting diode), and HID (high-intensity discharge) lamps. The quality of light in a space relates directly to the source of the light, and the advent of new lighting technologies has expanded the range of light sources available.

Not all light sources give off the same quality of light. To the layperson, most artificial light sources seem to give off white light. However, many light sources actually have a very restricted color range that affects the appearance of objects they illuminate. For example, the low-pressure sodium lamp, such as those commonly used in hockey arenas and in big-box stores, produces a monochromatic yellow light that appears white to the naked eye but has a very limited color spectrum. Colors, therefore, have a very different appearance under these lamps than they would in natural light.

The types of artificial light used most frequently by designers, including their pros and cons, from a design perspective, are listed below:

Incandescent lamps. For decades, the incandescent lamp was the most popular light source, particularly in residential settings. Some of the advantages of incandescent lighting include a warm color spectrum, low cost of lamps, wide variety of lamp sizes and types, and the ability to control light levels easily by dimming devices. Disadvantages include inefficient use of energy, generation of high levels of heat, short life of lamps, and the resulting need for frequent replacement. High-wattage incandescent lamps that are unprotected by shades often create excessive glare that is particularly difficult for users with vision loss. Incandescent lamps have fallen into disfavor due to their high energy utilization. Many countries have banned their use altogether. In the United States, incandescent lamps are no longer manufactured, and they will not be sold after 2012. For many designers and users, the warm quality of the ambient light these lamps cast outweighs the their negative features, and it has proven difficult to find a comparable replacement. However, new standards mandating the use of alternative energy-saving technologies are driving innovation in the industry. The desirable warm light of incandescent bulbs is now achievable with other bulb types. Life span of an incandescent bulb: 750 to 1,000 hours

Fluorescent lamps. In most commercial interiors, fluorescent lights have been the primary source of illumination due to their energy efficiency. The initial cost of a fluorescent lamp is greater but with a life span of up to six times that of an incandescent lamp, the overall costs are lower. Fluorescent lamps also generate less heat. The original fluorescent bulbs had a limited color spectrum, were slow to start, produced a flicker, and were often noisy. Improved fluorescent bulbs are now available that are appropriate for the residential sector. Compact fluorescent lamps (CFL) can be used in the same type of socket as incandescent lamps, simplifying replacement. New CFL bulbs are available with improved light quality similar to soft white incandescent. Thin fluorescents are also available for use under cabinets and for strip lighting to produce efficient indirect lighting effects. While better than their predecessors, these lights still have a slow warm-up time and cast a cool, diffuse light. Life span: 6,000 to 15,000 hours.

Halogen lamps: Halogen lamps produce whiter, brighter light than either incandescent or fluorescent lamps. Halogen lamps have a tungsten filament, like an incandescent lamp, but rely on a chemical reaction using a type of halogen gas within the lamp to create light. Halogen lamps are small but very powerful. They provide very good color rendition and can be used to provide focused lighting effects. Because they are so small, they can be hidden for added drama. However, the halogen lamp is very hot to the touch, so it is best when used in a pendant fixture or when wall or ceiling mounted outside the reach range of building occupants. Life span: 2,000 to 2,500 hours.

LED: LEDs are frequently used in commercial environments because they require less energy, have a longer life span, and produce a better color rendition than other types of lamps. LEDs are used less frequently in residential settings than in commercial settings due to their high cost and limited availability. However, they are becoming more available for residential applications, particularly in new forms. LEDs powerful enough for room lighting are relatively expensive and require more precise current and heat management than compact fluorescent lamp sources of comparable output. The most common use for LEDs at present is for small strip accent lights on railings, stairs, and under cabinets. LED bulbs with warm light similar to incandescent light are now available. Life span: Can be as high as 45,000 hours.

HID: HID lighting systems are generally used in applications where high light levels are desired for large areas, such as industrial and street lighting. They are used primarily to provide an efficient, low-cost form of light but are not desirable where good color rendition is needed. Life span: 3,000 hours.

Natural Light

Architects and designers have sought to harness the sun as a source of illumination and a source of power since the early history of architecture. Daylighting, the proper term for this practice, is defined as "architectural design solutions that gather, direct, and reflect natural light deep into single or multistory buildings" (Brawley 1997, p. 96). With the availability of cheap electricity, the practice of building design for daylighting almost disappeared. Illumination of interiors with natural light requires higher ceilings, interior courtyards, and light wells or narrow building forms. It was easier and more efficient to control interior environments through artificial means, especially in dense urban settings and high-rise construction. In recent years, sustainable design practices have led to renewed interest in the use of natural illumination. Daylighting has once again become an important form of energy efficiency in buildings.

Daylighting can also help to combat some of the psychological changes attributed to the changing seasons. Many people experience mood disorders, particularly in the winter months. These are commonly referred to as seasonal affective disorders (SAD). Although the exact cause of SAD is not yet fully understood, we do know that the production of body chemicals (serotonin, melatonin, etc.) that affect emotional states fluctuate with light exposure and that improved access to daylight within a building can help to neutralize these fluctuations. New research is uncovering surprising connections between lack of sunlight exposure and other health problems, for example, a link between reduced vitamin D3 levels and the prevalence of autoimmune diseases like multiple sclerosis (MS). MS is more prevalent in northern latitudes where lower levels of sunlight reduce vitamin D3 levels during winter months (see "How Sunlight May Reduce the Severity of Multiple Sclerosis" 2011).

The use of daylighting in a building is not costly. Methods of practice used to help keep construction costs low and to improve efficiencies over the life span of the building include high ceilings, large windows, and north-facing skylights to maximize light diffusion deep into building interiors. The key to making the most of a daylighting plan is to provide adequate daylight to the space without adverse side effects, such as uneven light distribution, glare (excessive brightness contrast within the field of view), excessive heat gain and loss, and excessive reflectance and absorption by interior finishes. If used properly, daylighting contributes to improved worker productivity and satisfaction, reduced energy costs, and a reduced carbon footprint (Worrell, Laitner, Ruth, and Finman 2011). When carefully coordinated with the architectural design, window treatments and other interior elements can reduce glare and reflections. Automated control systems may be required to account for the diurnal and seasonal changes in light quantity.

Recommended Lighting Design Guidelines

Currently there are no nationally recognized regulations for lighting. The nine guidelines here reflect both universal design practice and sustainable design practice. They are adapted and modified from those developed by Elizabeth Brawley to assist designers working with Alzheimer's patients (Brawley 1997) and those developed by the Lighting Research Institute.

1. *Distribute light evenly throughout a building to reduce distortion and disorientation.* Poorly distributed or uneven lighting levels most negatively impact people with impaired vision and older adults. People can have difficulty when the placement of light alters their perception of an environment, creating distractions that look like "pools" of light that are highly reflective spots on a floor surface. For older adults and those with cognitive difficulties, this effect can produce agitation and disorientation. When establishing lighting levels, it is valuable to work directly with end user groups to prevent unexpected results. Natural illumination is often highest at the window side of buildings but drops off quickly as the distance increases from the window. This uneven illumination can increase eyestrain and hot spots in the field of view. Light shelves, sloped ceilings, and other architectural design elements can help to distribute natural light more evenly in a space.

2. *Provide ambient light in each room.* The best sources of ambient or available light are natural daylight and dimmable fluorescent lamps. (Evenly distributed fluorescent illumination almost eliminates shadows.) Light can enter building interiors through atria and light wells. Light cannons and other devices can transmit natural light from exterior walls and roofs deep into building interiors. "Low-E" glazing allows a more complete range of light to pass through windows while at the same time reducing glare and heat. Manufacturers now make fluorescent lamps that very nearly replicate the light of the sun, providing good color rendition and a more pleasant work atmosphere.
3. *Use indirect light to improve illumination.* A plan that combines low overall ambient light levels using indirect lighting with controlled and flexible task lighting is another reliable method to provide general illumination. Making this combination successful requires the use of uplighting to create a uniform ceiling brightness and downlighting for balance to achieve the same luminance on the floor as on the ceiling. Indirect hanging fixtures, pedestals with hidden light sources, and cove lighting are excellent methods of up lighting. IESNA defines a uniformly bright ceiling as one that does not include areas four times brighter than the area between fixtures. However, because older adults are extremely sensitivite to glare, a 3:1 ratio is even better.
4. *Reduce reflective glare.* Glare, or strong steady bright light, can cause headaches and disorientation. People experience indirect glare when it becomes impossible to see a target due to reflected light—for example, when bright light from a window obstructs a computer screen or when a shiny desk reflects the lights from above into the eyes. Reducing glare increases visual comfort by reducing eyestrain, reduces falls due to disorientation, and increases attention spans. As we age, our sensitivity to glare increases. It affects both vision and balance for elderly persons and often is responsible for limiting mobility and activity. Reflective glare can add to eyestrain, headache, and lowered ability to accomplish tasks. Methods of controlling reflected glare include the careful location of light fixtures to avoid reflections off computer and television screens and the selection of matte finishes for walls, countertops, furniture, and signs. Designers should avoid positioning highly polished reflective surfaces and objects in places where they may affect visual performance.
5. *Prevent direct glare.* People experience direct glare when light shines directly from the source into their eyes from a light source without adequate shielding (e.g., a bright light source without a lampshade). Designers should avoid direct glare for all users, not just older adults. Direct glare may result from a number of sources. The most common is natural daylight streaming in from windows or a skylight. If the ambient light level is too dim compared to the daylight coming in through the window, glare will result. Designers should balance and control daylight whenever possible to prevent direct glare.
6. *Provide gradual changes in light levels.* When the lighting level change is extreme in transition spaces between outside daylight areas and indoor spaces, it may cause disorientation to users with sight impairments. This is particularly true for older adults. As we age, our eyes do not adjust quickly. Quick adjustment can be painful and can hasten the deterioration of the retina. Designers should provide transition so that sensitive eyes have time to adjust from bright daylight to lower ambient interior lighting levels. Moving from a dim corridor into a bright room or from daylight into a dark lobby can cause momentary blindness, and this temporary loss of vision may cause visual obstruction of the edge of a rug or a step. This is called disability glare, meaning that it is severe enough to inhibit an individual from performing a visual task. Seating areas can provide a place for older adults to allow their eyes to adjust.

Extra ambient illumination can reduce the impact of hot spots in the visual field by reducing the difference in illumination between the ambient light level and the hot light source. Stairs and ramps are particularly important locations to eliminate disability glare.
7. *Ensure access to natural daylight.* As described earlier, the benefits of natural daylight cannot be overemphasized. When windows are open, exposure to natural daylight can provides a good source of vitamin D, which combats depression and, in northern climates, may prevent or lessen the impact of diseases like MS. It is also a good source of energy efficiency, both as a power source and for illumination.
8. *Provide adequate task lighting.* Fixed sources such as undercabinet lighting or adjustable sources such as desk lamps provide specialized task lighting. Task lighting is generally adjustable in level and can be very bright to accommodate task performance where illumination is critical, as when reading small text. Local task lighting can be useful even when there is good general lighting, but if no local task light is available, the general lighting should provide illumination of about 30 footcandles (fc) to 75 footcandles at the work surface. A footcandle is defined by the Heritage online dictionary as "a unit of measure of the intensity of light falling on a surface, equal to one lumen per square foot and originally defined with reference to a standardized candle burning at one foot from a given surface." Undercabinet incandescent strips or low-voltage lights are excellent ways to balance lighting in task areas such as workstations or kitchens. Undercabinet task lighting should be located carefully so that it does not cause reflective glare from work surfaces.
9. *Specify high-CRI lamps.* The color rendering index (CRI) is a rating scale used to gauge the accuracy with which a light source renders color on a scale from 0 to 100 with 0 as the lowest and 100 as the highest. Full-spectrum light, which has a very high CRI, reflects more accurately the true color of skin tones and the surface of objects and is the closest match to sunlight available in commercial lighting. It also helps to reduce eye fatigue. Compact fluorescents with good color quality are an ideal way to utilize fluorescent lighting without losing the benefits of incandescent light. For indirect ambient light in areas without natural daylight, the color rendering index (CRI) should be 80 or above; full-spectrum fluorescent light 91 CRI out a possible 100 points. More information follows.

Color

Color is so much a part of our daily experience that we take it for granted and pay little attention to its physiological and psychological impact. Human beings use subtle color cues continuously to help us understand and move through space. These cues include the most obvious ones, such as traffic signals and team colors in sports. Designers need to understand the properties of color, how people perceive it, and how colors interact with one another. For instance, the advancing and receding properties of color can be used to create the impression that objects are heavier or lighter, that walls are closer or farther away, or that edges are defined or vague. Contrasting colors can emphasize elements in the visual field that need to stand out from their background, such as stair treads, furniture, or plumbing fixtures.

Very few spaces are perfect in size and appearance. Illusion is a common strategy used to mask these imperfections. Illusionary techniques can be used to make spaces appear to be bigger or smaller, to hide unsightly mechanical systems, or to make architectural flaws disappear. The strategic use of color in conjunction with lighting effects can accomplish this without making any structural changes

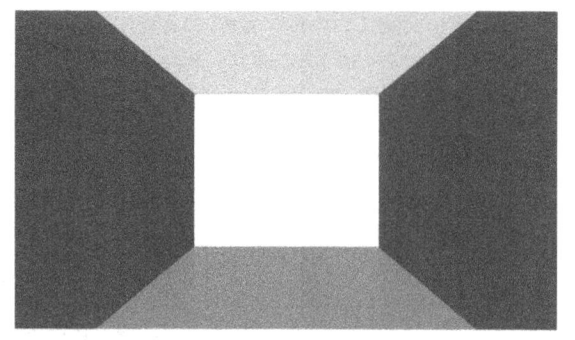

Figure 11-1: Color as an illusion technique. Although these two representations of spaces are identical in size, the one on the left seems smaller than the one on the right because it has darker colors on the side walls.

to the space. The boxes in Figure 11–1 provide a good example of this phenomenon. Both spaces are identical in all ways except for the use of color. The vertical surfaces in the box on the left are darker so they appear to be closer together, making the space between them appear smaller. Some colors, like red, are "advancing," and some are "receding." By using colors carefully, the illusion of more space can be created, even when conditions restrict options for actual changes. A well-lit perimeter of a room will make the room appear larger than the same room with uniform light distribution (Figure 11–2).

This use of illusion to manipulate space can help to hide spatial flaws or imperfections, but, if used inappropriately, it can create real problems for those with low vision or cognitive limitations, or people who are taking psychotropic medications. For instance, the use of highly contrasting color and lighting on floor surfaces, if not controlled properly (Figure 11–3), can cause illusions, especially for older people. Glare, light pools, or sharp shadows across a floor may appear to be holes or drop-offs, or potential falling hazards like slippery surfaces. Fear of falling may discourage residents from leaving their rooms and contribute to a sense of frustration, isolation, and depression.

Figure 11-2: Lighting as an illusion technique. Lighting the perimeter walls of this room creates the illusion that the space is larger than its actual dimensions.

Figure 11–3: Glare on floor surfaces. The textured pathway with good color contrast in the photo provides a wayfinding aid, but the reflected glare on the surface could present problems for occupants who have limited vision.

Legibility refers to clarifying the perception of space. For instance, a legible environment will have furniture that is clearly differentiated from walls, stairs that are readily differentiated from corridors or flat surfaces, and entrances and exits that are easy to find, regardless of cognitive ability or vision level. Legibility is also an important factor in design for wayfinding and signage systems. A legible environment has clearly discernible nodes, landmarks, pathways, edges, and districts (Lynch 1960). Figure 11–4 shows a room in a senior citizen housing facility with furniture that is highly legible due to its color and its contrast with the surrounding walls.

Figure 11–4: Example of legibility. For users with low vision, furniture that is clearly distinguishable from the wall is easier to find and to use.

Hue (the name that we give to a color), saturation (the lightness or darkness of a color), and value (how gray a color appears) contribute significantly to the emotional response, which people experience at an unconscious level in all spaces. Designers working on hospitality projects, such as nightclubs or theaters, will use color to create spectacle, just as designers working in health and wellness projects, such as mental health facilities or hospitals, will use color to create interiors that are soothing and support the healing process. However, even where color is not consciously used to create an impression in visitors, it will have an emotional impact. Colors with high value are deeply saturated, in a primary hue, and seem more dynamic than do those with low value and low saturation seem. Thus, high-value colors are more appropriate to use in active places, such as daycare centers and gyms or for accents to enliven other spaces.

Color has an impact on both usability and emotional response to building interiors. For example, color-coding is often used as an element in wayfinding systems. Signs and landmarks use color to provide users with important environmental cues. For those with vision impairments, such as color blindness, reliance solely on color-coding can result in unnecessary exclusion, disorientation, and frustration. Color-coding must be supplemented with another form of information to serve a broad population. And, research shows that color in our environment may influence involuntary bodily processes such as resting body temperature (Miller 1997). One study discovered that the recorded body temperatures of people in a room painted with warm colors were higher than the body temperatures of those in a room painted in cool colors although the physical temperature of each room was the same (Miller 1997).

Two tools are available to help designers understand the relationship of illumination and color perception. The CRI, described earlier, quantifies the ability of a light source to reproduce the colors of various objects faithfully when compared with a full spectrum (natural) light source. When selecting light sources, the CRI should be used in conjunction with the Correlated Color Temperature (CCT) chart, a standard method of describing colors expressed in Kelvin (K) units of measure. The CRI describes the color rendition of objects by a source. The CCT describes the color of the source itself. Both of these attributes are important. Figure 11–5 shows both charts with example values of specific light sources. It is important to note that the CRI reflects rendition of selected standard colors but not necessarily the color rendition preferred by building users, particularly for colors not represented in the standard set.

Color is the transmittance, reflectance, and/or absorption of light from the surface of an object (Miller 1997). We see color only because of the physiology of the human eye. Light exists as wavelengths of radiation. When the wavelengths meet a surface, the surface absorbs some and reflects others back to the eye. Those wavelengths that enter the eye are part of the visible spectrum, and sensors in the retina of the eye, called rods and cones, respond. The rods are sensitive to low light, and the cones, which require a greater intensity of light, are sensitive to color. Portions of light wavelengths pass to the optic nerve and then on to the brain (Espinda 1973). If a person experiences any disruption to this system, it may compromise his or her ability to see color. People who experience these disruptions have the most common form of color-related visual impairment and are commonly referred to as being color-blind.

As described in Chapter 5, when we do not have enough information about the world around us, we make assumptions about reality based on experience and create a "perceptual reality."

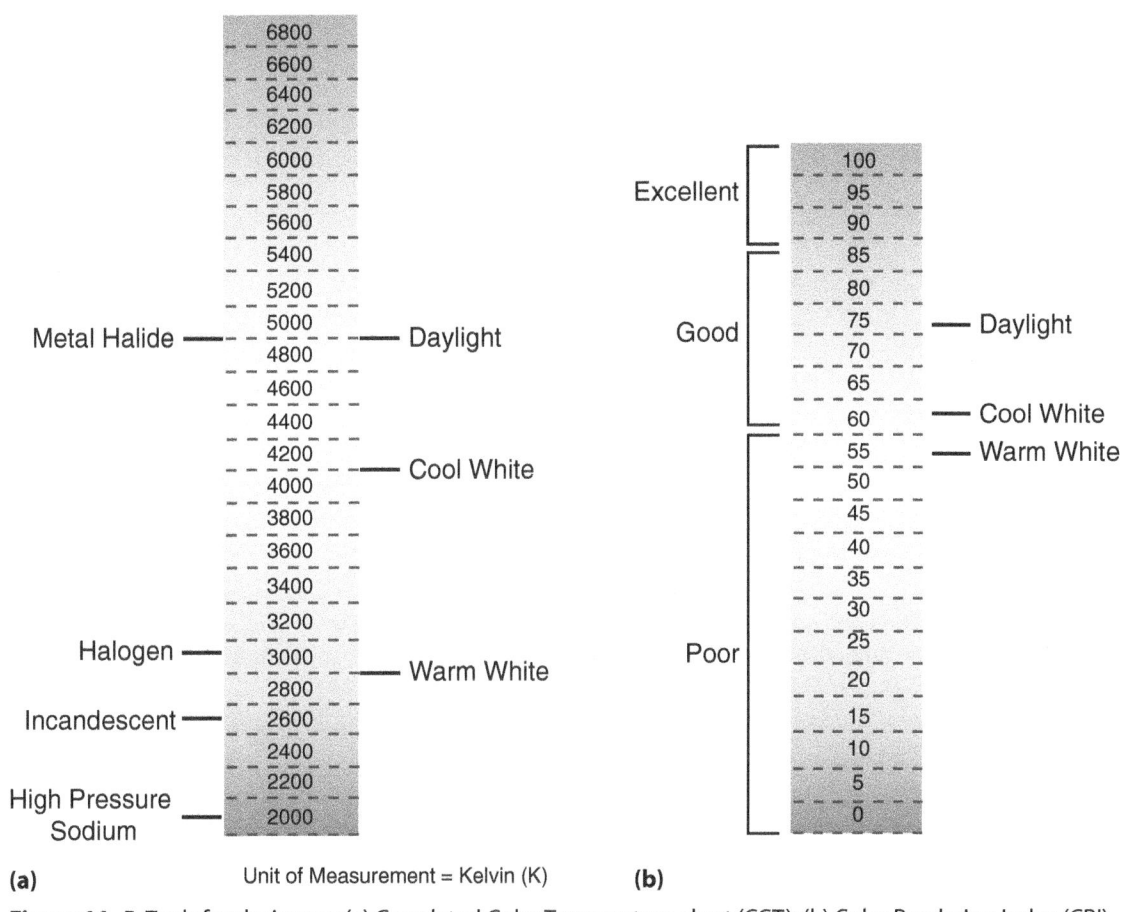

Figure 11–5: Tools for designers: (a) Correlated Color Temperature chart (CCT); (b) Color Rendering Index (CRI).

However, when our perceptions are not accurate, errors in decision making and disorientation may occur. Legible interiors are those that provide clear, easily understood color cues. The groups most impacted by an inability to read these color cues are people with color vision deficiency (CVD), or color blindness, and other color impairments and those with reduced vision. Figure 11–6 demonstrates how CVD affects visual perception.

A surprisingly large number of people are impacted by the inability to see true color. In the United States, about 7 percent of males and 0.4 percent of females experience some form of CVD (Montgomery 2008). Included within this group are those who experience protonopia (reduced vision of red, orange, and yellow) and deuteranopia (red-green color blindness). One out of every 10 to 12 males and 1 out of every 200 females in America is believed to be color-blind (Montgomery 2008), with over 10 million people in the United States experiencing some degree of CVD. Globally, more than 200 million people are believed to be color-blind. The rate of occurrence of CVD varies, depending on ethnic background and ancestry, differing from country to country (Espinda 1973). Color-blindness does not affect visual acuity. People who are color-blind have normal eyesight and can see small objects clearly. They have difficulty, however, differentiating colors from one another when viewed together. For instance, some people who have CVD will have difficulty differentiating between purple and blue when they are placed side by side. Others may have difficulty differentiating between red and green.

(a) **(b)**

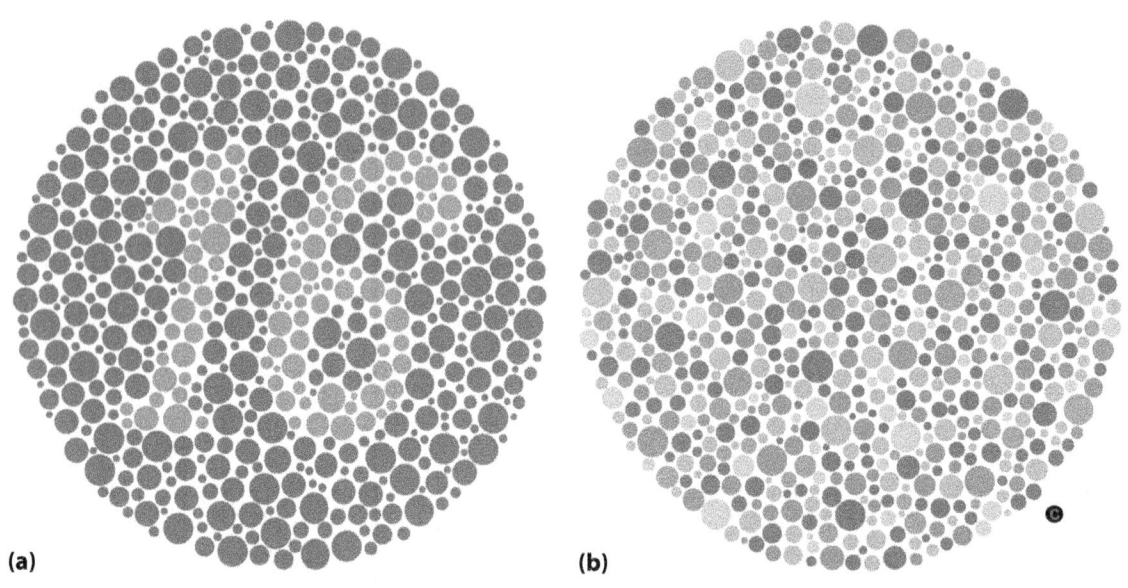

Figure 11–6: Contrast test used to determine color blindness. This illustration uses black and white images to demonstrate the difficulty people who have color blindness have understanding some color images. The image on the right is camouflaged by the lack of contrast between the color of the figure (numeral 5) and the background.

Source: Images courtesy of TestingColorVision.com and http://colorvisiontesting.com.

There are two different types of CVD. One type is genetic and inherited. The second is a form of vision reduction caused by age-related changes in the physiology of the eye. The lens of the eye thickens, loses transparency, and turns yellow-brown in color (Winn, Whitaker, Elliott, and Phillip 1994). As the eye thickens, the sensitivity of the retina also diminishes. The combined effect of the reduction in size of the pupil and thickening of the lens results in two-thirds less light reaching the retina for most people by the age of 65 (Winn et al. 1994). Since less light enters the eye, color is experienced differently. Colors that once appeared vibrant, such as forest green, may appear to be black or brown to the aging eye. This experience is particularly important to consider when working with older adults.

Furnishings

The wide diversity of shapes and sizes of the human form complicates the selection of furniture. In order to accommodate differences, designers have traditionally relied on anthropometric data that described the "average-size person," usually defined as the 50th percentile in height. As noted in Chapter 5, few, if any people are truly "average" in all respects. Moreover, cultural trends mean that the anthropometry of the population is in flux. The "average American" of the 1950s is now 20 percent heavier and 3 percent taller (Lethbridge-Cejku, Rose, and Vickerie 2006); a greater proportion of our population is older. One size does not fit all, as people with disabilities, especially those who use wheeled mobility devices, vary significantly in terms of body dimensions (Steinfeld et al. 2010; Steinfeld et al. 2011).

The result of this change is that furniture and case goods, such as bookcases, built-in cabinetry and display cases, do not fit many people well. We have become accustomed to adjusting to furnishings that require us to reach too far or bend too low and that put unnecessary strain on our bodies. One exception is the higher-end sector of the office furniture industry. The manufacturers of ergonomic desk chairs and office furniture systems serve a market where anthropometric fit is a major factor in purchasing decisions. Back injuries and repetitive stress injuries caused by long periods of work in poorly fitting chairs are a critical concern in office work. Some employers have learned that purchasing good-quality chairs pays for itself in reduced incidence of injury and increased productivity. Many manufacturers also offer office systems furniture with adjustable work surface heights, integrated accessories that support better posture for computer work, and adjustable storage that can be located within easy reach or positioned for optimum use by each individual.

Specifying furniture that is flexible, easy to manage for everyday tasks, easy to maintain, and accommodating to a wide range of sizes is of fundamental importance to an interior inclusive to all. In this section, we focus on those items of furniture that have the greatest impact on our physical comfort in a space: large items such as seating, beds, wall systems, and workstations, which require special consideration if they are to be universally usable.

Picking furniture that is flexible, adaptable, and easy to maintain is only part of the solution when designing furniture arrangements. It is also important that the space layout accommodate social interaction, traffic flow, and ease of movement. Space that functions well, providing the appropriate visual cues for easy navigation and maneuverability, is much more desirable space than a room that is aesthetically pleasing only.

Here are a few key factors to consider when planning a furniture layout:

- *Use sociopetal seating organizations.* Seating should provide 90-degree and direct visual contact between individuals. The distance between sitters should not exceed 8 feet (243.84 cm) for good communication. This distance may need to be closer for cultural reasons and for older people (see Chapter 7).
- *Plan the room to accommodate several different furniture arrangements where long term occupancy will occur.* Every room designed for long term stays, should provide options that work. People will routinely adjust rooms to meet their preferences and are frustrated when the result is not satisfactory. Thus, each option should provide some significant advantages like good views or more privacy.
- *Integrate space for wheelchair users into the seating arrangement.* Lightweight furniture that can easily be moved out of the way can be used, but where many wheeled mobility users are likely to be present (e.g., a long-term care facility), more space is required, so too much furniture should be avoided. Figure 11–4 shows the use of lightweight furniture in a sociopetal arrangement. A chair can be moved out of the way for wheelchair users if necessary.
- *Provide adequate task lighting in places where one may expect people to be reading for long periods.* Ensure that this lighting has three-way bulbs and movable arms to allow for customization.
- *Provide more than one path of travel through each room without disrupting the viability of conversation and room activities.* Major traffic paths should be 36 inches (91 cm) wide.
- *Ensure that coffee tables are high enough to prevent tripping.* A coffee table that is between 24 and 30 inches (61–76 cm) high is generally the most useful.
- *The distance between the seat and television screens should be three times the size of the screen* (i.e., for a 50-inch screen television, place seating 12.5 feet [3.8 m] away).

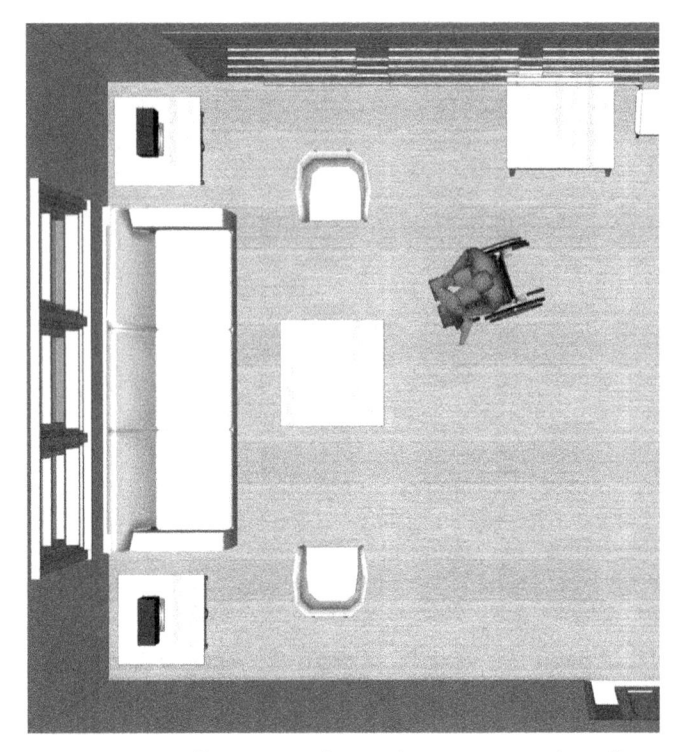

Figure 11–7: Furniture layout. Even small spaces can be made to accommodate all users, as shown in this layout. The sofa doubles as a pullout bed for even greater flexibility.

Seating

Chairs must be flexible and adaptable to accommodate a wide range of body shapes and sizes. This is particularly true in commercial and public settings, where individuals do not have the opportunity to choose what is most comfortable for them. A comfortable chair allows the sitter to place both feet flat on the ground and support the weight primarily on the buttocks, thighs parallel to the floor with space between the thighs and front edge of the seat (Null and Cherry 1996). Figure 11–8 illustrates some of the important factors to consider when specifying seat furniture:

- *Seat height.* Adjustable between 13 and 20 inches (33–51 cm) above the finished floor
- *Seat back height.* Adjustable 8 to 13 inches (20–33 cm) above seat
- *Armrest height.* Maximum 8½ inches (22 cm) above seat
- *Seat depth.* Greater than 15 inches (38 cm)
- *Seat width.* Greater than 16 inches (41 cm)
- *Back slant.* Increased depth of seat = increased slant to chair back
- *Removable or retractable armrest*
- *Seat cushions firm enough* so as not to depress more than 1 inch (2.54 cm)
- *No stretchers.* Stretchers interfere with movement when users push to rise. (Stretchers are reinforcing braces used at the base of furniture legs.)
- *Benches, loveseats, and sofas with armrests* for support while rising to a standing position

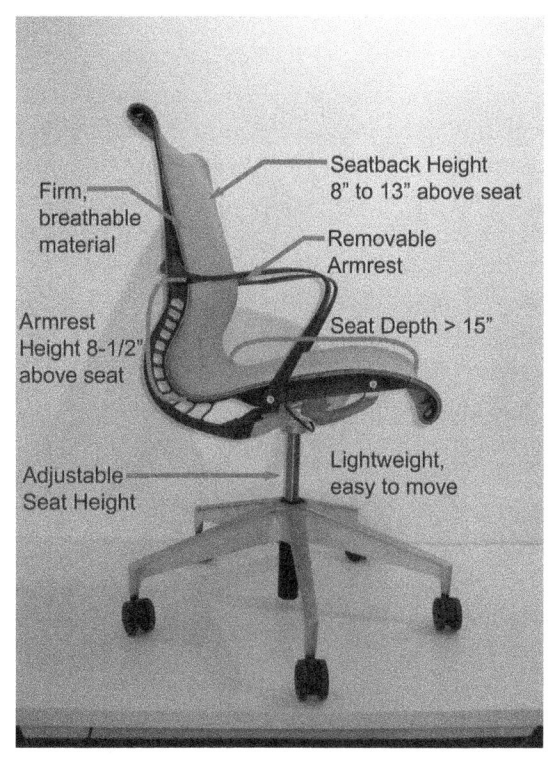

Figure 11-8: Important factors when specifying seat furniture. Ergonomic seating is particularly important in workplace settings.

Storage Systems

The most accessible and usable storage systems are adjustable to accommodate users of all heights and reaching ability. They also should be flexible enough to provide open space for knee clearances when needed. Integrated electrical supply and lighting improves flexibility even more, allowing users to plug in equipment and provide task lighting where needed. Kitchen cabinetry is particularly complicated because of the variety of activities performed and users who need accommodations and the need for compatibility with appliances made by different manufacturers. Kitchen cabinetry systems could be much more flexible than conventional designs. In particular, rather than being built-in, they could be designed for relocation and include mobile components, as workplace furniture systems do. The prototype Universal Kitchen, designed by Marc Harrison and his students at the Rhode Island School of Design (Mullick and Levine 2001; Rhode Island School of Design n.d.) demonstrated how universal design can lead to a radical rethinking in kitchen systems. Harrison and his students completed time and motion studies of how people actually prepare foods; they identified improvements to conventional cabinetry systems and appliances that reduced effort for everyone and provided accessibility at the same time. An important design innovation in this kitchen was the use of distributed refrigerated storage units integrated into the cabinet system. Another was the development of a very efficient corner unit, called the "Mini," for applications where meal preparation is focused mostly on prepared foods.

The following are some guidelines to consider for universal design of storage systems.

- *Counter height.* The ideal work surface height depends on the type of work involved and whether the worker is standing or sitting. To accommodate all types of work, including light assembly work, fine motor tasks, and heavy work, counters should be adjustable to between 28 and 42 inches (71–107 cm) above the finished floor. Where adjustability is not desirable or is cost prohibitive, a range of heights should be provided for different tasks.
- General recommendations for work surface height:
  - Fine motor skill tasks: just above elbow height
  - Light assembly work while standing: just below elbow height
  - Light assembly or writing work while seated: at elbow height when arms are dangling
  - Heavy work (pastry making, washing dishes, or packaging goods): 3 to 10 inches (8–25 cm) below the elbow
  - Legs should be parallel to the work surface.
  - Space and clearance for knees
- *Drawer height.* Drawers should begin 4 to 9 inches (4–23 cm) above the finished floor to allow for footrest clearance.
- *Drawer depth.* Drawers should be full-extension drawers for full access without reaching.
- *Work surface depth.* Depth should not exceed 25 inches (64 cm).
- *Under-counter storage units.* Knee and toe clearances should be provided for seated work. Full-extension drawers and shelving are particularly important in lower cabinets. Increasing the height of toe kick spaces and raised height of the lower shelf provides more maneuvering space for people in wheelchairs.
- *Above-counter storage units.* Shelves used frequently should be no more than 48 inches (122 cm) above the finished floor for forward reach and a knee space of at least 12 in. (122 cm) should be provided for wheelchair users. For storage where side reach is possible, the maximum reach to items on frequently used shelves should be no higher than 54 inches (137 cm) high. Shelves above this are more appropriate for longer-term storage because they are unusable by so many people. Adjustable heights are preferred.
- *Full-height storage units.* Full-height units, such as pantry cupboards and broom closets, are useful to store tall items. They can substitute for upper cabinets when users have limited reaching ability and for lower cabinets when knee clearances are needed for seated work.
- *Movable storage.* Turntables, sliding shelves and storage racks, and racks attached to the back of doors bring stored items within closer reach and improve access to stored goods. Adjustable shelving allows workers to arrange their workstations to fit their needs.
- *Floor clearances.* Each workstation should have a clear floor area to accommodate people using wheeled mobility devices on either a parallel approach or a front approach with knee clearance. The latter, which is much more desirable, can be provided by relocating under-counter storage. Work areas should also have access to a space where users of wheeled mobility devices can easily turn around, although it does not have to be a clear circular area. Space under counters and cabinets and space to make T or K type turns can be utilized effectively.

Note that following these recommendations for counter height would provide work surfaces that are above or below the standard 36-inch (91-cm) counter height. For example, tasks that require fine motor skills or reading while standing would require a much higher counter and workstation than doing the same while seated. In general, wherever a wide range of needs

Figure 11-9: Contemporary kitchen. This kitchen is both aesthetically pleasing and easy to use. Features include: ample circulation space, easy-to-reach storage wall elements, full extension drawers, front-mounted stovetop controls, knee space below both the stovetop and the sink, and an oven/microwave within reach while seated. Note: Front stovetop controls provide accessibility for adults and those with mobility issues, but are not ideal for families with small children.

must be accommodated in one space, such as a residential kitchen, these guidelines support the provision of adjustable workstations. The kitchen in Figure 11-9 demonstrates many of the guidelines above.

Beds and Mattresses

Of all the furniture in our homes, our beds are perhaps the most important. A good night's sleep is part of maintaining good health and so it is important that both bed and mattress be comfortable. For most of us, the bed performs a variety of functions beyond sleeping. It can be a place to spend leisure time watching television or reading a book, a place for intimacy between couples, or, for older adults and those with mobility impairments, a place to receive family and friends. The selection of a bed is a very subjective activity, and it is important for designers to consider how the client will use the bed when specifying a mattress and frame. Of particular importance is the height of the mattress from the finished floor. This height will determine how easy or difficult it is for the user to get into and out of the bed. If a bed fits its user well, his or her feet should be able to touch the ground when sitting on the edge. Whenever possible, bed height should be adjustable to accommodate any change to our abilities, particularly as we age. A good rule of thumb is that the top of the mattress should be 18 inches (46 cm) maximum above the finished floor, which supports transfer from a wheelchair. A few inches of adjustability below this would accommodate people of shorter stature as well. For older adults or those with mobility issues, designers should consider electric beds for their adjustability and customization.

The choice of mattress is perhaps even more important than the choice of frame. Consumers have a wide variety of options available from which to choose, and it is really an individual, personal choice. A common misconception is that a firm mattress is best for older adults, as it will provide the greatest amount of support. Actually, the opposite is true. Older adults are susceptible to hip and shoulder pain that can be aggravated by sleeping on an extremely hard surface. Designers should encourage clients to explore all options when choosing a mattress and foundation. Mattress choices include a spring mattress (the core of the mattress is made of steel coils or "inner springs"), the use of a mattress overlay pad, open-cell latex mattresses (foam-core mattress with more support than spring mattresses), or air beds (air chambers that provide the mattress core). Figure 11–10 shows a variety of mattress options. Box springs create further complexity, as these are available either as a rigid frame with coils inside, with traditional wood slats, or as a combination grid foundation. How the box spring and mattress combine depends on the individual user as well as on the type of bed.

Figure 11–10: Mattress options. The choice of mattress is very important for comfort when sleeping. A wide range of mattress types is available, including (top) an active pocket spring mattress, (middle) a latex foam mattress, and (bottom) a memory foam mattress.

Floor Coverings

Falling is the most common reason for injury for those who experience difficulty walking and for older people in general. About one-third of adults over the age of 65 fall each year, and the risk of falls increases proportionately with age. At 80 years, over half of seniors fall annually (Baker, Gottschalk, and Bianco 2007). Many falls go unreported by seniors or unrecognized by family members or caregivers. In addition, about half (53 percent) of older adults who are discharged for fall-related hip fractures will experience another fall within six months (Baker et al. 2007). Falling is one of the most common types of accidents in building interiors and a major source of lawsuits against building owners and designers.

Floor coverings are a critical factor in preventing slipping and tripping. Slipping can be prevented by using slip-resistant floor surfaces. It is important to consider where a surface is located, especially if the floor will be exposed to moisture. Although impermeable materials such as glass, stone, or concrete can be treated to be slip-resistant under dry conditions, they will not always be slip-resistant under wet conditions, when a thin film of moisture on the surface becomes a lubricant between the surface and the sole of the shoe. Any surface immediately inside an exterior entry door should be slip-resistant in all types of weather. Wherever spills are likely, as in a restaurant or supermarket, floor surfaces should allow easy and rapid maintenance. Liquids, such as soap, can build up on floor surfaces and become extremely slippery even when there is only a small amount of moisture present and the liquids might not be perceivable under dry conditions.

In both commercial and residential settings, it is important to minimize tripping hazards. Some examples of typical tripping hazards include unsecured area rugs or mats and abrupt changes in the height of floor surface materials between rooms. For people using walkers or for those who shuffle their feet, even the smallest difference can result in an accident. Carpeting can also be a barrier if the depth of the carpet pile is too high, thereby restricting movement for people using walkers or with canes. For older adults, navigating a deep-pile carpet can lead to complications beyond falling. The energy required to move down the hallway on a poor walking surface may become so great that residents may remain alone in their rooms. This can result in reliance on assistance to leave the room, with associated atrophy of walking ability as well as negative emotional and morale impacts.

Some floor coverings can create a hazardous and difficult environment for people with reduced vision. They are more vulnerable to unstable surfaces and abrupt edges because they cannot see them as easily as others can. They may also be more susceptible to illusions caused by bold patterns on flooring. Accessibility standards include maximum limits for abrupt edges (e.g., where floor surfaces change in level), threshold height, and carpet height and type. These requirements are helpful to reduce tripping hazards, but the visual environment is also critical. An appropriate lighting level for visibility without glare on walking surfaces, of course, is a key component of safety for people with vision limitations.

Despite the potential problems, floor coverings can have a positive impact on the acoustic quality of a space and provide insulation to reduce energy expenditures. When used skillfully, floor surface materials can provide highly effective sensory wayfinding cues. Thus, they have multiple benefits and are desirable in many locations for many reasons. In universal design, it is important to use materials for their positive benefits and learn how to avoid their negative impact.

Carpet

Carpet is one of the most commonly specified flooring materials for residential and commercial/institutional spaces. It is warm under foot, so it is comfortable, especially on bare feet. It can reduce reverberation times so it helps reduce uncontrolled background noise. However, carpeting masks movement, footsteps, and other noises that support situational awareness. Where noise is not a problem or is controlled in other ways, carpeting may reduce stimulation levels too much. Carpet is available in a wide range of patterns, textures, and depths, so it can be used effectively as a wayfinding cue.

One of the difficulties with carpeting as a flooring choice is that it can be hard to maintain. Wear marks and staining are the two primary maintenance concerns. To combat these problems, designers in commercial settings have begun to specify carpet tile rather than broadloom. Carpet tiles are more economical to replace and so are more cost efficient, extending the life of the carpet. (Note that when ordering carpet tiles, it is important to purchase a sufficient number of extra tiles of the same dye lot to avoid future color-matching difficulties.)

A common misconception about carpeting is that it encourages airborne allergens and that there is a link between carpet use, allergies, and asthma. A study done by the German Allergy and Asthma Association (Buttner, Cruz-Perez, Stetzenbach, Luedtke, and Luedtke 1985) found that carpeting is actually beneficial in an environment, as it naturally traps allergen-causing particles, such as dust, and keeps them from becoming airborne. Results found that fine dust is in much higher concentrations in indoor rooms that have smooth flooring materials than in indoor rooms covered with wall-to-wall carpets. Fine dust is particularly problematic for allergy sufferers, but dust causes irritation for all people. Airborne particles can become trapped in air passages and cause irritation. This experience is magnified for those who have bronchial conditions, so it is important to minimize the presence of dust in the environment. Note that maintenance and ventilation also play an important role in the presence of airborne allergens.

For those with mobility issues, soft or loose carpeting can be a real barrier to moving through space easily. Consider these factors in selecting carpet:

- *Height of carpet pile/tuft density.* Carpet pile, or the fibers that form the upper surface of a carpet, and tuft density, or the amount of yarn in a given area of carpet, are important factors to consider when specifying a carpet. The best choice of carpet to accommodate all user groups is carpet with low pile height and high tuft density, which make it firmer and more easily used by people with walking aids, for those who shuffle their feet, or for those who use wheeled mobility devices.
- *Recommended pile height.* The recommended height is ¼ to ½ inch (0.635 cm to 1.27 cm) with ¼-inch (0.635 cm) height being best for people with mobility issues. Carpet edges should have a beveled transition to adjacent floor surfaces, with a ratio no greater than 1:2.
- *Hypoallergenic carpet.* Carpert should incorporate bacteria guard, mildew guard, and nonallergenic fibers. All carpeting choices should also have low volatile organic compound ratings.
- *Carpet installation.* All carpet should have either a firm cushion, pad, or backing underneath it or no cushion or pad underneath it.
- *Area rugs.* They should be avoided or be fastened securely to avoid tripping hazards.
- *Fire resistance rating.* Carpeting should have a good fire resistance rating for the intended use. All carpets come with documentation regarding flammability and appropriate usage.

Wood

In the past two decades, the use of wood flooring has regained popularity because it is easy to maintain, warm to walk on, beautiful, and resilient. Wood is a renewable resource so it is also a sensible environmental choice. Whether refinishing an existing floor or installing a new wooden floor, it is important to ensure that the floor finish is neither too shiny nor too slippery. Shiny floors create reflection and can cause visual distractions. For those with vision loss, reflections from a flooring surface can create an illusion of instability. Wood is not be a good choice where a floor might get wet frequently. Finally, floors with wide beveled joints can cause vibrations for wheelchair users or hang up users of walking aids.

Bamboo is a popular choice for use in residential and low-traffic interiors because it is made from a sustainable material that is harder than oak or maple. Bamboo has the same warm look and feel of hardwood but is a rapidly replenished resource, so it is also one of the most eco-friendly choices. However, it expands and shrinks with large variations in heat and cold. It is also vulnerable to wear in heavy-traffic areas.

Ceramic Tile

Ceramic tile is a popular flooring choice because it is available in a wide range of styles, sizes, and finishes. The most frequently used tiles for flooring are ceramic and stone. Tile floors are very durable and easy to clean but can cause problems if the surface is too smooth and does not provide enough traction. This is especially important if the tiles are in an area that will get wet. Whenever possible, tiles with nonskid surfaces should be chosen where tile surfaces will get wet, or resilient materials should be considered as an option. Most tiles are hard and cold to stand on for long periods of time and can lead to back pain or fatigue. Dropped objects will break easily on tile floor, so this is not a good choice for anyone with reduced tactility. Other concerns include shiny surfaces (the reflection can create ambiguous space) and grouted joints that are too wide (wheels on mobility devices may become stuck). Joints between tiles should not exceed ¾ inch (1.9 cm). Tile floors should not have uneven surfaces because they can cause problems with balance, potentially leading to falls.

Resilient Materials

Resilient flooring is very popular in commercial settings because it is easy to clean, inexpensive, and durable. The term "resilient flooring" refers to flooring types such as cork, linoleum, and vinyl composite tiles (VCT), all of which are generally made from natural materials. Resilient flooring is sold either in sheets (linoleum) or in tiles (VCT). Resilient floors are easier to stand on for long periods than tile or stone and can withstand moisture. They also are mold and bacteria resistant. Resilient flooring is an excellent choice for healthcare settings, institutional settings, and retail settings due to its nonslip surface finish. As discussed, exercise caution when choosing patterns on any flooring surface that might be used by someone with low vision.

Of all the choices described, the most sustainable flooring material is cork (Figure 11–11). Cork flooring is made from the bark of the oak tree and is a renewable resource. Cork is naturally beautiful and is soft to the touch. It is even used for making textiles. When produced as flooring, cork has a density high enough to withstand heavy traffic and weight. One of the characteristics of cork is that it has a "memory" and therefore recovers well from compression even under the weight of heavy furniture. A polyurethane surface finish can further protect the cork and improve maintenance. Cork provides superior sound and temperature insulation and is a natural anti-allergen. The structure of the bark is comprised mainly of air, which makes cork an excellent sound reducer between rooms. It does not conduct heat or cold as other flooring materials do. A naturally occurring substance in cork called suberin repels mold, termites, and other pests, so it benefits people with allergies. Cork does not hold up well in high-traffic areas and will discolor in areas exposed to the sun.

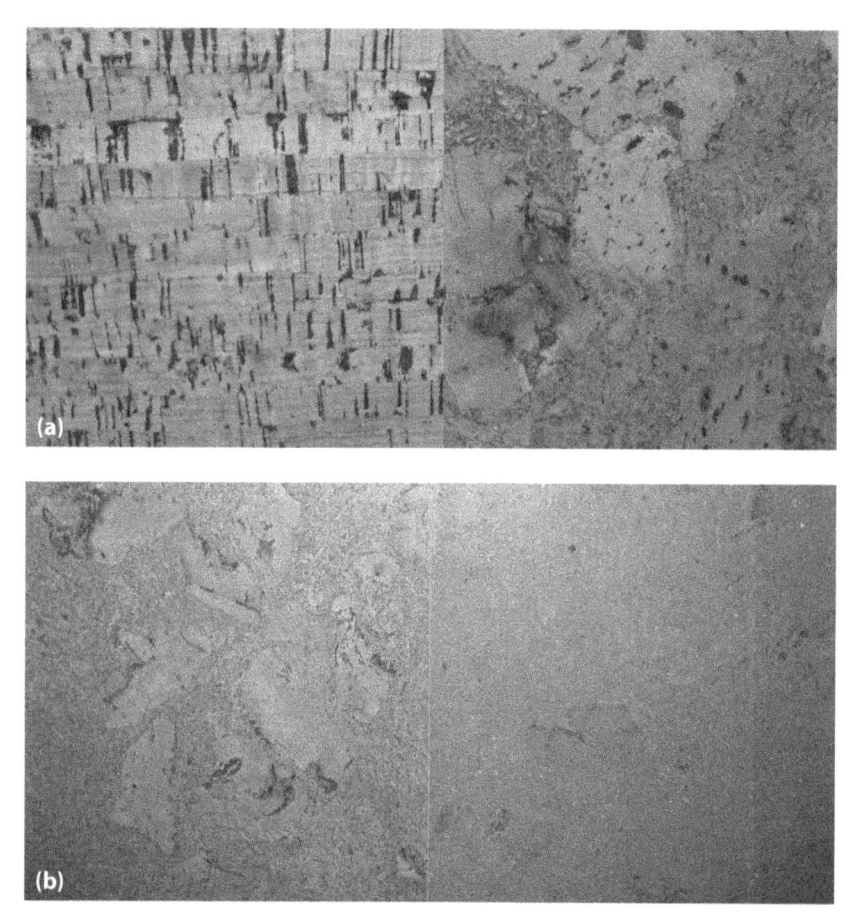

Figure 11–11: Cork flooring. One of the most sustainable flooring choices is cork. This flooring type is resilient, long wearing, and comes in a wide range of colors and patterns as shown.

Summary

Interior design is an important aspect of building design. From small spaces in the home to the large spaces of sports arenas, office buildings, and airports, interior design decisions support wayfinding, sedentary activities such as reading, and energy-intensive activities such as indoor sports. Each interior is different, and each has its own multiple design goals. Interior design brings life to buildings and provides richness to the architectural design. It is important that interior designers work with building architects closely to coordinate the design of interior surfaces, lighting, and furnishings to reach universal design goals. Otherwise, the full potential of buildings will not be realized.

This chapter focused predominantly on interior design, but other design disciplines, such as industrial design, graphic design, and even textile design, play significant roles in the level of comfort and support provided by interiors. The interior designer's role is to create interior environments that support all users. At the most basic level, design decisions should meet accessibility guidelines. More inclusive environments can be realized when interiors are designed from the start to fit all users and user activities comfortably. With careful consideration of wayfinding, lighting, acoustics, color, furnishings, and floor coverings, we can remove undesirable barriers to improve safety, diminish frustration, and improve the quality of life of all end users.

Example: New York City Subway

Signage

The New York City subway system is one of the most complicated underground transportation systems to navigate in the world. Adding to the complexity is the highly diverse population it serves. Getting the signage system right has been a top priority for the New York City Transit Authority (NYCTA) since the 1960s, when the agency first recognized a need to improve traffic flow, reduce confusion, and improve accessibility. The NYCTA commissioned the firm of Noorda and Vignelli to create a unified system of signs to replace the chaotic mismatched system that had evolved. Although the modular system has undergone many changes, including the adoption of Helvetica typeface on all signs in 1989 and the reversal of the color scheme to white letters on a black background, the foundation Noorda and Vignelli laid has proven very flexible and effective. Features of this wayfinding system include letter size that ranges from the smallest at 1½ inch to the largest at 3 inches (3.8 cm to 7.6 cm); the use of ten different hues for color coding for each of the lines for easy identification; diamonds to indicate part-time trains; symbols for the JFK "Train to the Plane"; and special signs to denote escalators, elevators, restrooms, and accessible features. Now controlled by the Metropolitan Transit Authority, the most recent innovations to the subway wayfinding system include dynamic LED displays in all trains to indicate "this stop," "next stop," and transfer stations (Figure 11–12). In addition, stops are announced, and a red icon designates station accessibility.

Figure 11–12: Dynamic signage in the New York subway. The signage system combines both light and sound to alert riders in real time of stops and transfer points.

Example: Erickson Retirement Living

Design for Wayfinding

Erickson Retirement Living builds and operates retirement communities (ERL). These communities cater to middle-income retirees. To make their facilities affordable, ERL relies on economies of scale and high density—high-rise campuses with about 2,000 residents on each. Studios, one- and two-bedroom independent living apartments, as well as assisted-living apartments and skilled nursing care are offered. The campuses are self-contained to meet most of the daily needs of seniors with public spaces, including medical facilities and an emergency ambulance service, a pharmacy, health club, pool, convenience store, banks, hair salons, and a variety of fine and casual dining options, distributed throughout the campus on the first two floors of the buildings and all connected internally. This complexity and scale could result in negative consequences if public spaces were not designed to be easy to understand. One of the hallmarks of ERL facilities are the well-designed public spaces with simple, easy-to-understand circulation systems and good use of landmarks, signs, texture, color, and lighting to support wayfinding. This encourages heavy utilization of public spaces, an active lifestyle, and high levels of social participation.

Review Topics

1. What interior design features support good wayfinding? Describe a universal design issue related to each interior design feature.
2. Why is acoustic design a critical universal design issue? Describe some universal design strategies related to acoustics.
3. What are the pros and cons of natural and artificial lighting? In your opinion, which is better, and why?

References

American Speech-Language Hearing Association. n.d. "Hearing Loss." www.asha.org/public/hearing/Hearing-Loss/.

Baker, D. I., M. Gottschalk, and L. M. Bianco. 2007. "Step by Step: Integrating Evidence-based Fall-Risk Management into Senior Centers." *Gerontologist* 47 (4): 548–554.

Bakker, R. 1997. *Elderdesign*. New York: Penguin.

Brault, M. 2008. Americans with Disabilities: 2005. *Current Population Reports (P70-117)*. Washington, DC: U.S. Census Bureau.

Brawley, E. 1997. *Designing for Alzheimer's Disease: Strategies for Creating Better Care Environments*. New York: John Wiley & Sons.

Brown, B., H. Wright, and C. Brown. 1997. "A Post-Occupancy Evaluation of Wayfinding in a Pediatric Hospital: Research, Findings and Implications for Instruction." *Journal of Architectural and Planning Research* 14 (1): 35–51.

Buttner, P., L. D. Cruz-Perez, P. J. Stetzenbach, G. Luedtke, and A. E. Luedtke. 1985. "Measurement of Airborne Fungal Spore Dispersal from Three Types of Flooring Materials." *Aerobiologia* 18 (1): 1–11.

David, M. 2008. *Universal Design and Barrier-Free Access: Guidelines for People with Hearing Loss*. Ottawa, Ontario: Canadian Hard of Hearing Association.

DiLaura, D., K. Houser, R. Mistrick, and G. Steffy. (eds.). 2007. 10th *Edition of the Illuminating Engineering Society Lighting Handbook*. New York, NY: IES.

Espinda, S. D. 1973. "Color Vision Deficiency: A Learning Disability?" *Journal of Learning Disabilities* 6 (3): 163–166.

Evans, G. and M. McCoy. 1998. "When Buildings Don't Work: The Role of Architecture in Human Health." *Journal of Environmental Psychology* 18: 85–94.

Garling, T., A. Book, and E. Lindberg. 1988. "Spatial Orientation and Wayfinding in the Designed Environment: A Conceptual Analysis and Some Suggestions for Postoccupancy Evaluation." *Journal of Architectural and Planning Research* 3: 55–64.

Garvey, P. M. 2001. *Synthesis of Legibility of Variable Message Signing (VMS) for Readers with Vision Loss. Final Report to the Public Rights-of-Way Access Advisory Committee.* Washington, DC: United States Access Board.

Golledge, R. G. (ed.). 1999. *Wayfinding Behavior: Cognitive Mapping and Other Spatial Processes.* Baltimore, MD: Johns Hopkins University Press.

"How Sunlight May Reduce the Severity of Multiple Sclerosis." 2011. *ScienceDaily* www.sciencedaily.com/releases/2011/03/110303065335.htm (March 3, 2011).

International Organization for Standardization (ISO). 1990. *Acoustics—Determination of Occupational Noise Exposure and Estimation of Noise-Induced Hearing Impairment.* International Standard ISO 1999. Geneva, Switzerland: International Organization for Standardization.

Laszlo, C. A. 1999. "It Is About Communication!" Paper presented at the October 18, 1999 Canadian Acoustical Association Annual Conference, Victoria, BC.

Lethbridge-Cejku, M., D. Rose, and J. Vickerie. 2006. *Summary Health Statistics for US Adults: National Health Interview Survey, 2004.* Washington, DC: Government Printing Office.

Lynch, K. 1960. *The Image of the City.* Boston: MIT Press and the President and Fellows of Harvard College.

Miller, M. C. 1997. *Color for Interior Architecture.* New York: John Wiley & Sons.

Montgomery, G. 2008. "Breaking the Code of Color: Color Blindness: More Prevalent Among Males." www.hhmi.org/senses/b130.html.

Mullick, A., and D. Levine. 2001. "Universal Kitchens and Appliances." In W. Preiser and E. Ostroff (eds.), *Universal Design Handbook* (pp. 41.1–41.10). New York: McGraw-Hill.

Nabelek, A. K. 1987. "Speech-Communication in Lecture Halls and Classrooms for Hearing-Impaired." *Journal of the Acoustical Society of America* 81: S44–S45.

National Institute of Deafness and Other Communication Disorders. 2011. "Quick Statistics." www.nidcd.nih.gov/health/statistics/quick.html.

Nelson, P. B., S. D. Soli, and A. Seltz. 2002. "Acoustical Barriers to Learning II." Melville, NY: Technical Committee on Speech Communication of the Acoustical Society of America, www.centerforgreenschools.org/docs/acoustical-barriers-to-learning.pdf.

Null, R. and K. Cherry. 1996. *Universal Design: Creative Solutions for ADA Compliance.* Belmont, CA: Professional Publications.

"Presbycusis." December 2010. "Age Related Hearing Loss" A.D.A.M. Medical Encyclopedia. http://www.ncbi.nlm.nih.gov/pubmedhealth/PMH0002040/

Rea, M. S. 2000. *The IESNA Lighting Handbook: Reference and Application*, 9th ed. New York: Illuminating Engineering Society of North America.

Rhode Island School of Design. n.d. "Designing the Ultimate User-Friendly Kitchen" www.risd.edu/Designing_Ultimate_User-Friendly_Kitchen/?dept=4294967928.

Schafer, R. M. 1977. *The Tuning of the World.* New York: Alfred A. Knopf.

Steinfeld, E., J. Maisel, D. Feathers, and C. D'Souza. 2010. "Anthropometry and Standards for Wheeled Mobility: An International Comparison." *Assistive Technology* 22(1): 51–67.

Steinfeld, E., V. Paquet, C. D'Souza, C. Joseph, and J. Maisel. 2011. *Anthropometry of Wheeled Mobility Project: Final Report*. Buffalo, NY: Prepared for U.S. Access Board by the IDeA Center.

Tauke, B. and D. Schoell. 2011. "The Sensory House." In W. Preiser and K. Smith (eds.), *Universal Design Handbook* (2nd ed.), pp. 27.1–27.9 New York: McGraw-Hill.

Truax, B. 1984. *Acoustic Communication*. Norwood, NJ: Ablex.

U.S. Access Board. 2003. "Listening for Learning 5: Retrofitting a Noisy Classroom". http://www.quietclassrooms.org/ada/adahandout5.htm.

U.S. Environmental Protection Agency. 2008. *EPA's 2008 Report on the Environment*. Washington, DC: National Center for Environmental Assessment.

VanderKlipp, M. 2006. "Develop a Successful Wayfinding System." *Buildings* 100 (4): 28.

Warnock, A.C.C. 2004. "Acoustical Design Guide for Open Office Plans." IRC-RR-163. National Research Council of Canada.

Weisman, J. 1981. "Evaluating Architectural Legibility: Way-Finding and the Built Environment." *Environment and Behavior* 13 (2): 189–204.

Winn, B., D. Whitaker, D. B. Elliott, and N. J. Phillip. 1994. "Factors Affecting Light-adapted Pupil Size in Normal Human Subjects." *Investigative Ophthalmology and Visual Science* 35 (3): 1132–37.

World Health Organization. 2010. "WHO Releases the New Global Estimates on Visual Impairment." from www.who.int/blindness/en/.

Worrell, E., J. A. Laitner, M. Ruth, and H. Finman. 2011. "Productivity Benefits of Industrial Energy Efficiency Measures." Paper LBNL-52727. Berkeley, CA: Lawrence Berkeley National Laboratory.

12

Product Design

Introduction

Industrial designers often criticize assistive technology products because they do not look appealing, are too expensive, and do not have the reliability and durability of good-quality consumer products. Likewise, designers of assistive technology bemoan the lack of concern for accessibility, and function in general, in consumer product design. In this chapter, we propose that more attention be given to the relationship of assistive technology and consumer product design. We believe that universal design can be a way to overcome the gulf between the two.

Throughout the history of industrial design, innovative products conceived for special populations have evolved into mainstream consumer products. When innovations are first designed and developed, often they are crude and expensive. However, once perfected through limited use by special populations, usually the broader benefits are recognized. The products or technologies are then transformed into mass-manufactured products for the general market. In many cases, inventors are motivated to address a particularly difficult problem for special populations and then wind up discovering something of more general value. The special markets can be viewed as proving grounds in which unique needs justify the higher cost of innovative products. Four special markets in which numerous products have been tested and then brought into the mainstream are the space program, the athletic equipment market, the field of medical technology, and assistive technology. Many examples of special-to-mainstream market transformations are in wide use, but their origins are not usually understood. In this chapter, we describe several well known examples from each of these markets with an emphasis on assistive technology.

The *Global Positioning System* (GPS) was initially conceived and developed by the National Aeronautics and Space Administration. It is now integrated into many facets of everyday life, including telecommunications, aviation, precision agriculture, geo-location, surveying and mapping, and weather forecasting. The largest use of GPS today is vehicle navigation and positioning ranging from large-scale infrastructures that monitor fleets of commercial trucks, trains, ships, and planes to personal vehicle navigation systems (Kumar and Moore 2002).

Athletic equipment is designed to support the highest level of performance to enhance competitiveness. High-tech *athletic shoes* have penetrated all sectors of mainstream footwear markets, covering the feet of both professionals and great-grandparents seeking comfortable walking shoes. They have also become a fashion statement in pop culture and are used for the everyday task of walking to work ("Athletic Shoes" 2008). They are perhaps the most widely applied innovations from the world of sports.

Velcro owes a debt to both the sport shoe industry and the space program. Created by Georges de Mestral, Velcro received its first wide usage in the space program by helping astronauts get into space suits easily, and served as a means to fasten equipment securely to walls on space shuttles (Reuters 1990). Today, applications of Velcro can be found in many industries, including equipment for sports and recreational activities, for luggage, and as a substitute for zippers and buttons in clothing (Stephens 2007).

Eyeglasses were once a special market product. In the 1930s, they were considered medical appliances, with wearers considered "patients" (Pullin 2009). Early eyeglasses, in fact, were never intended to be worn in public. In the late 1990s, eyewear became more than a medical appliance; today it is marketed as a mainstream fashion item (Pullin 2009). The fashion industry dominates eyewear design, and eyeglasses are a ubiquitous part of daily life. The stigma associated with eyewear is gone; now it is perceived to be both functional and fashionable for those who need it. Even people who do not need eyeglasses may use them as a fashion statement, especially sunglasses.

Assistive technology (AT) has the most relevance to universal design because of its emphasis on supporting everyday life. The roots of AT go back to prehistory. One of the main specialties in AT practice is prosthetics and orthotics, or artificial limbs and braces. Early evidence shows prostheses in the form of artificial legs and hands fitted the body crudely. It was not until the early sixteenth century that a higher level of craft and fit was achieved (Mihm 2002). War served to advance the development of AT significantly. Prosthetics, for example, were further improved during the U.S. Civil War period to accommodate the large number of injured war veterans (Crabb 2009). Later color and articulation were added to artificial limbs to make them look more natural and to allow a previously isolated group of individuals to blend in more with the "normal" population (Serlin 2010).

After World Wars I and II, the number of people with disabilities increased dramatically. Federal programs were established to provide funding for vocational rehabilitation for veterans with disabilities. Healthcare professionals recognized the need for improved prosthetic devices, such as artificial legs and wheelchairs, and developed their own ad hoc solutions when necessary. Similarly, therapists working in private homes and workplace settings devised aids and environmental modifications to help their clients increase independence and function. Examples include built-up handles for utensils, reaching devices, and adjustable work counters. Engineering expertise was recruited to bring advanced scientific knowledge to the field. To a more limited extent, industrial and interior designers have participated as well.

There is also a long history in development of aids for children who have disabilities, particularly children with hearing, vision, and cognitive impairments. The polio epidemic in the 1950s focused more attention on rehabilitation of children with disabilities. Federal legislation designed to improve long-term quality of life for children with disabilities, such as the Education for All Handicapped Children Act (1975), created opportunities for both service providers and businesses to provide AT that would help in education and childhood development. The advent of telecommunications and information technology has significantly changed the AT field. New specialties have developed, such as augmentative communications and adaptive computer interfaces. The aging of the population and the huge expenditures of public funds on care for older people are the latest social trends to affect the industry.

AT is now a well-established field for the development of products that compensate for lost function. The Technology Assistance for Individuals Act of 1988 (TECH Act of 1988) defined AT as "any item, piece of equipment or product system, whether acquired commercially off the shelf, modified or customized, that is used to increase, maintain or improve the functional capabilities of individuals with disabilities" (Morrissey and Silverstein 1989). The AT field comprises a wide range of products that offer distinct benefits to people with unique needs. Products vary from simple everyday tools that assist those with upper extremity disabilities to squeeze toothpaste from the tube to complex JAWS Screen Reading Software to help the blind and visually impaired to navigate the Web. Today, Abledata.org, the world largest AT database, has in its catalog nearly 40,000 devices in 20 specific areas of function. This number will continue to grow; however, the creation of new markets influenced by changing demographics and technological innovations is slowly erasing the line between what is assistive and what is mainstream (Morris, Mueller, and Jones 2010).

A personal interest in disability is often a motivation for inventors. A good example is Alexander Graham Bell, inventor of the telephone. Bell's wife and mother were both deaf. Like his father and brother, he became an educator of people with hearing impairments and, through that interest, became obsessed with developing artificial speech. This led to his experiments in transforming sound into an electrical signal and back again to sound and eventually to the invention of the telephone (Greenwald 2009). He also was one of the inventors of the audio recording player.

Digital sound synthesizers were originally developed in the hope of aiding people who are blind or who have visual impairments. Ray Kurzweil developed the first commercial application of optical character recognition and synthesized speech. He created a reading machine that transformed printed words to speech and helped visually impaired and blind individuals access many forms of print media. Working with a blind musician, Stevie Wonder, Kurzweil later designed a digital synthesizer (Figure 12–1). Although synthesizers had been around for many years, the Kurzweil 250 was the first to create sounds similar to those of a real piano (Byrd and Yavelow 1986).

Developed by the U.S. Department of Health, Education, and Welfare and the Public Broadcasting System, closed captioning allows people with hearing impairments to follow the content of television programs. The first captioning technologies included a coded signal sent over the air as part of the broadcast and a decoder device attached to the television that displayed the signal as words on the screen. The decoder devices were expensive, costing as much as a television itself, and were about the size of a DVD player. Beginning in 1993, all new television sets sold in the United States were required to incorporate a microchip to decode and display the signal. Since then, captioned text has become ubiquitous. Furthermore, the Telecommunications Act of 1996 mandated closed captioning for both new and old programs airing on broadcast stations (Federal Communications Commission 1996). Having access to the evening news and other television programs has enabled people who are deaf and hard of hearing to stay just as informed about current events and popular culture as the general population (Harkins and Strauss 2009). Today, closed captioning is available on every television; is used widely in noisy environments, such as airports, bars, and sports arenas; and is used in places where it is desirable to maintain a low background noise level, such as hospitals.

Figure 12–1: Ray Kurzweil and Stevie Wonder. The photo shows Ray Kurzweil standing next to Stevie Wonder as he plays the Kurzweil 250 piano.
Source: Image courtesy of Kurzweil Technologies, Inc.

ARPANET, one of the first prototypes of e-mail and Internet communications, was developed in part by Ken Harrenstien, a man who is deaf. Harrenstien, who became deaf when he was five, also worked on developing DEAFNET, a system that allows the deaf and hard of hearing to communicate. Vincent Cerf is one of the co-developers of some basic Internet technologies and the inventor of commercial e-mail. Not only did Cerf have his own hearing impairment, but he also married a woman who was deaf. Thus, Cerf was extremely motivated to create communication technologies that leveled the playing field for people who are deaf or who have difficulty hearing. According to Cerf, linking e-mail to the Internet was very important "because so much of the communication on the Internet is in written form, by preference, people with hearing loss are often placed on completely equal status with those of normal hearing" (Chertok 2009, p. 3). For people with hearing impairments, this dynamic platform for communication has proven invaluable.

Assistive Technology

As the world population continues to grow, so will the population of people with disabilities. AT will continue enabling these individuals to live independently. However, many pressing challenges in the field hinder its progress; these problems include high cost, a technological lag with mainstream products, and a high rate of abandonment.

Higher Cost

AT is an ideal proving ground for innovative enabling technologies because the benefits to people with disabilities are significant enough to justify the initially high cost of producing innovative products. Developing products that work for very specific needs force AT designers to create new proprietary technologies and concepts in order stay competitive in the marketplace (Silva 2008; Vanderheiden 1998). High costs are also attributed to the unstable relationship among public policy, funding, and disability. For example, funding to subsidize purchase of AT from related federal programs such as vocational rehabilitation, special education, and Medicaid, is limited because AT is not the primary focus of these programs (Galvin, Ross, and Phillips 1990). Many people who need AT cannot get funding from third-party payers or private sources, so they live without it, reducing demand (LaPlante, Hendershot, and Moss 1992). Without a dedicated source of funding and higher demand, AT manufacturers cannot safely invest in strategies that reduce costs through economies of scale or advanced manufacturing technology.

Technological Lag

Many AT products are not completely refined before they are introduced into the market. The increased level of human performance that AT provides justifies early market entry. For example, an unreliable speech recognition system is better than not being able to control a computer at all, so the higher risk of product failure is more tolerable to a person with a disability than it would be for the general consumer. AT products are produced in small production runs, then refined and improved frequently over time as feedback is obtained from early users. In the early stages of commercialization, these products often require more extensive customer service, which also leads to higher prices. If the product has the potential to be introduced into the larger consumer market, it will attract the interest of larger companies with the resources to develop more reliable and less expensive versions.

Because AT has been a somewhat limited market, progress in mainstream technology often advances beyond that used in AT, especially in high technology areas such as information technology (Vanderheiden 1998). Many AT producers rely on adapting existing mainstream products which can become obsolete before the next generation of the AT product is available. Software especially has a short life span, creating compatibility problems with rapidly changing mainstream products (e.g., new operating systems). This approach results in missed opportunities to develop broader solutions integrated with the product development cycle of the "host" products (Vanderheiden 1998).

Abandonment

Although AT products provide great benefits by supporting independence, many studies have found high rates of abandonment by unsatisfied end users (Johnston and Evans 2005). Common reasons for abandonment include "lack of consideration of user opinion, poor device procurement, poor device performance, and change in the user needs or priorities" (Philips and Zhao 1993). Other factors are related to the appearance of using AT products—fears about acceptance, embarrassment, or attracting unwanted attention (Hocking 1999). A third set of reasons for abandonment are social, including lack of attention to contextual issues such as space in the home and lack of training for family members on how to set up and use the technology (Ebner 2004). For older adults, the stigma associated with use of AT, high cost, lack of knowledge about available AT products, and barriers in the environment, such as steep ramps, broken, and blocked sidewalks that prevent use of walkers, wheelchairs, and scooters, all contribute to abandonment (Gitlin 1995).

The 1978 film *The Deer Hunter* illustrates an example of product abandonment. One of the characters returns from military service in Vietnam with both legs amputated, requiring him to use a wheelchair for mobility. Unable to adjust, he abandons his family and retreats to the local veterans' hospital because of the stigma associated with using a wheelchair at the time. Today, the stigma associated with wheelchair use has decreased, and wheelchair aesthetics and mechanics have improved significantly. Some chairs are designed and marketed more as high-performance products, like racing bicycles, rather than as medical products. The best designs create "positive associations with mobility, fitness, and ability" (Pullin 2009, p. 49). Furthermore, implementation of government regulations related to access for all in the built environment has increased the public's familiarity with and acceptance of wheelchairs.

The AT industry isn't a new field; however, it has yet to find a place in the larger context of consumer products. The industry needs to explore new directions that will provide it the resources to realize its full potential. Practicing universal design is emerging as an opportunity. AT companies have the knowledge to address usability needs for a wide range of individuals, knowledge that can be applied in universal design. However, to be effective, the overall quality of product design must improve. Creating mediocre products would only "result in people being further stigmatized by the very products that are intended to remove barriers for them" (Pullin 2009, p. 64). It would also continue to lead to high rates of abandonment. Without improving design quality, costs will remain high and may become unaffordable for those who really need AT. Designers need to tackle these challenges and look for ways in which their designs can appeal to larger markets and be more sustainable. By evaluating product potential in the early stages of development using new product development principles, the chances of the product appealing to its users will increase, resulting in a greater potential for success in the marketplace. History demonstrates that good AT products and knowledge developed by serving specialized markets can be introduced successfully to the mainstream.

Knowledge Translation Problem

Despite the problems identified above, the industry has an important knowledge base that can benefit universal design. The following examples demonstrate the potential benefits of this knowledge base. Human joints sometimes respond together or separately as external and internal forces are applied to them (DiBrezzo and Fort 2005). Opening a glass jar, swinging a golf club, or walking all generate forces on joints. Research on the impact of repetitive motion on shoulder function due to manual wheelchair use has been used to improve designs for wheelchair push rims and identify the best location for the wheel axles (Cooper, Teodorski, Sporner, and Collins 2011). Could this knowledge also be applied to mainstream applications, such as the design of bicycles, shopping carts, lawn mowers, hand tools, or other consumer products? Occupational therapists and AT developers have devised numerous methods to improve gripping performance for people with limited use of hands and fingers. Could that knowledge be applied to designs for packaging, container caps, and shoes? Although a wide range of research data and practical knowledge are available, designers either do not know the data exists or the form of the data does not match the needs of product designers (Carse, Thomson, and Stansfield 2010).

Figure 12-2: Age Gain Now Empathy System (AGNES) simulation suit. A researcher wears the AGNES suit, which has been calibrated to approximate older age and multiple chronic conditions using elastic bands and other devices that restrict movement and dexterity, thereby allowing a younger researcher to simulate the effects of aging and selected diseases, e.g., arthritis.
Source: Image courtesy of Nathan Fried-Lipski/MIT AgeLab

One limitation in knowledge translation from AT to mainstream design is that most AT activities are focused on a very small population group. They are usually optimized for the disability that they are intended to assist, such as people with hearing impairments or people who have no functional vision. AT developers do not always incorporate a cross-disability perspective into their designs. Additionally, products often are not designed well in terms of emotional design for a broader population. Thus, many AT products will not appeal to a mass market without significant adjustments. Mainstream product development teams often shy away from adopting AT ideas because of these emotional design issues. They do not realize the potential of knowledge translation. To obtain the broader knowledge AT experts should participate in knowledge translation with mainstream developers. Innovative methods need to be developed to package and translate this knowledge for mainstream consumer product design.

One promising method of knowledge translation is simulation. Several simulations of limitations in human performance have been developed. The best known are the empathic model (Shore 1976), the Third Age Suit ("A Day in the Life" 2010), and the MIT AgeLab's Age Gain Now Empathy System* (AGNES) (Figure 12-2). These simulation models are intended for use by product developers. They help provide an experience that simulates the aging experience and allow designers to test products during development stages. The goal is to give designers insights to incorporate "greater accessibility and usability for this market segment" (Erlandson 2008, p. 73).

---

*The Age Lab website for the project provides an overview of the system: http://agelab.mit.edu/agnes-age-gain-now-empathy-system.

While well intentioned, to be effective, these simulations should be calibrated properly to make sure that they provide accurate experiences. The AT and rehabilitation science community could help test such simulations, validate them, and produce more effective versions. Simulations can serve as a focus for knowledge translation, incorporating research information to build the model and then using the model as a design tool.

The experientially based approach to knowledge utilization incorporated in simulations is very compatible with the intuitive and creative method used by commercial product designers. An important limitation of simulations, however, is that emotional responses and social factors cannot be simulated (see Chapter 5). For this, it is still important to engage end users in product development activities through observational and ethnographic research, focus groups, and prototype evaluations (Field and Jette 2007). Advocates of user-centered design in the consumer product industry engage actively with end users to gather insights that drive design from the earliest stages of product and service development, right through the design process." (Black 2006). User-centered design techniques are used in development of dynamic websites, computer programs, appliances, input devices, kiosks, and mobile phones. Usability plays an important role in product effectiveness in these fields. Since the industry is very volatile and competitive, interaction designers must create user experiences that deliver information efficiently without frustrating end users, and that are also emotionally appealing. Otherwise, customers will quickly abandon the product. Additionally, interaction designers need to make sure the information is accessible and compliant with federal accessibility regulations. Thus, throughout the product development cycle, good designers involve potential users, individually or in focus groups, in identifying product requirements, evaluating design strategies, and testing prototypes. This process is consistent with established principles in the new product development process (Lane and Flagg 2010).

Simulation and other user-centered design approaches can be used together. The Center for Inclusive Design and Environmental Access (IDeA) has collected performance data related to the reaching and turning capabilities of wheelchair users for over ten years (Steinfeld et al. 2010). Initially, this research program focused on developing a basic database of structural and functional anthropometry. The center is now studying how the data can be used to improve small-scale spaces, such as bus interiors (Figure 12–3). The photo shows a simulated bus in the IDeA Center laboratory. The research participant is simulating use of the bus to help identify necessary design improvements and to compare different seating arrangements. Through interviews, consumer ratings and observations, researchers collect a wealth of information that can be used for developing new guidelines, standards, and product ideas. This study has already generated data to begin improving the design of buses.

While the AT community contributes important research knowledge to design more efficient products, knowledge from research fields that study human performance, and knowledge about design for health and social participation is also very valuable in the development of universally designed products. Synthesizing this knowledge into design tools, such as virtual simulations, databases, and design guidelines, will help to improve knowledge utilization. However, direct interaction with end users is also critical, especially during the early design process. Universal design challenges developers of AT products to "stop redeveloping new generations of assistive devices that refer to the situation as it appears today, and to start thinking about the future and develop innovative approaches" that allow people of all abilities to live more independently (Emiliani 2003, p. 22). The industry itself can benefit from access to broader knowledge bases and could serve as a facilitator for synthesis and application of this knowledge.

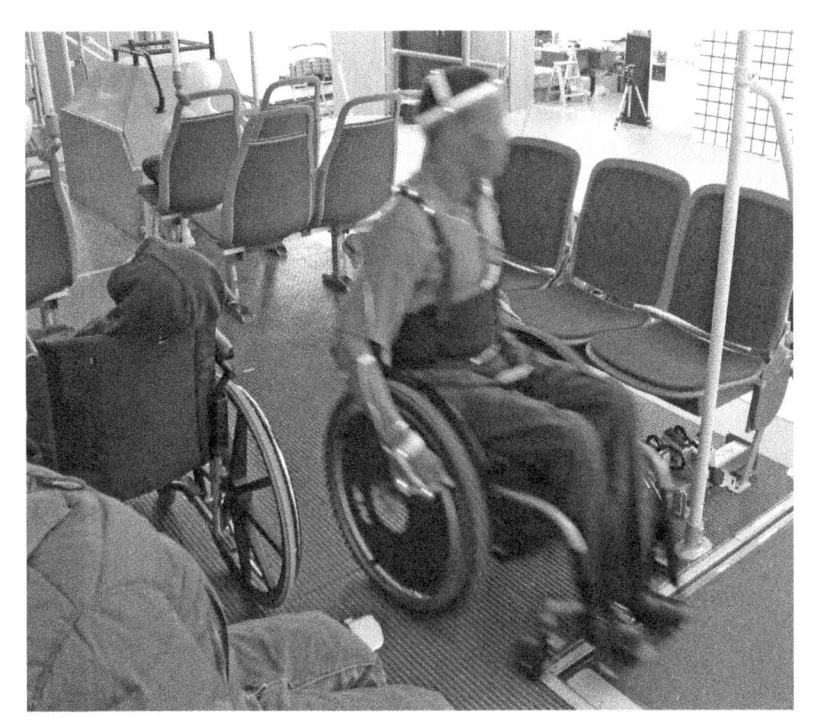

Figure 12–3: Full-scale bus simulation, IDeA Center, Buffalo, NY. Photo of simulated bus being used in a research study, including motion capture of all movements in the "bus."

The AT industry stands to gain as much as universal design practitioners by establishing a partnership. Each will develop new understandings and knowledge. "Finding appropriate devices that are truly assistive for a [person with a disability] remains an arduous task, because there has been difficulty in assessing and evaluating an individual's needs" (Ahasan et al. 2001, p. 188). New universally designed products can make the task of finding appropriate assistive devices easier. Not only can knowledge from AT be valuable to the development of new universally designed products, but a universal design perspective can benefit the practice of AT as well. AT designers traditionally have looked at what they design as intended for clients or patients rather than users or consumers (Newell 2003). Thus, AT products often look medical and awkward. In fact, the companies that market many AT products are part of the durable medical equipment industry, where an appearance that appeals to healthcare bureaucrats who approve these products for reimbursement seems to be the norm (white, chrome, no frills or decoration). The idea seems to be that anything paid for with public money has to look bad. Designers of both mainstream consumer products and AT must look beyond the medical model for solutions that appeal to users. Designs should promote opportunities for social participation and integration in the everyday lives of all people.

As an example of how the AT industry could learn from universal design, consider canes and hearing aids, two devices often abandoned by initial users. Universal design features of a cane would include handles that fit comfortably for a variety of hand sizes and grip types, a means to prevent a cane from falling out of reach, be adjustable in size to fit people of very different heights, and utilize lightweight and stylish materials and finishes. Just like eyeglasses, canes could appeal to a broad population. Consider that canes were once a fashion statement as much as they were assistive technologies. The appearance of hearing aids has changed significantly. Many are almost invisible, but users still complain about the impact of background noise on hearing quality and other problems. If hearing aids were more useful in amplifying sound and could also be used to listen to digital music and answer a mobile phone, perhaps they would be popular with the wider consumer product market. Why can't people who do not have limitations in hearing use them? Perhaps today's hearing aid can be perceived as a precursor of cyborg-like devices that allow everyone to have enhanced hearing abilities like superheroes?

Changing Marketplace

Universally designed products are marketable because they appeal to a diverse group of people. They would not be as successful if only people with disabilities used them, but to be successful in the broader marketplace they must appeal to a broader population, as the examples earlier in this chapter demonstrate. For example, consider the built-up handles commonly used by occupational therapists to adapt silverware and utensils for people who have gripping limitations. It was not until OXO applied this concept to a mass-marketed product so well that other companies in the utensil industry began to include built-up handles on their products too. The availability of inexpensive utensils with large, easy-to-grip handles in the local discount store and supermarket radically increased the availability and lowered the cost of this feature for everyone (see Figure 4–4). The OXO Good Grips products eventually eliminated the stigma associated with built-up handles and made them an element of style on their own. This is an example of universal design as assistive technology for the masses.

The growing elderly population is receiving significantly more attention from the mass-market consumer industries. Universally designed products appeal to older adults who are an increasing influence on the general market. In addition to utensils with larger nonslip handles, there are large-format books, audio books, automated can and jar openers (Figure 12–4a), lightweight garden tools (see Figure 4–7), and laundry appliances with front-loading doors that are raised on pedestals (Figure 12–4b). For each industry sector, the degree of adoption of universal design varies significantly. In the writing implement industry, for example, universal design has been adopted extensively. Most companies produce a line of pens with large grips. Extensive adoption has also occurred in the kitchen utensil industries, as noted above. However, in other industries, such as consumer electronics and automobiles, adoption of universal design has been limited. To leverage this market and increase the adoption rate, products need to be designed with the understanding that many users already have or will develop performance limitations in hearing, seeing, memory, dexterity, and/or mobility (Etchell and Yelding 2004).

In some product industries, design trends actually have hindered usability by older people. For example, the mobile telephone industry continues to make phones that are more complex in ever-smaller sizes, which results in functions that are difficult for older people to understand, very small keys, and cramped key spacing. Although voice activation features can reduce the need for using a keypad, they do not work well in noisy environments and require a greater understanding of the system to program properly. In Japan, older people were having so many problems with usability of mobile telephones that one company introduced a larger telephone with fewer features, designed specifically for the older consumer. However, Japanese experts in universal design report that this telephone was quickly labeled as an "old person's phone" and was not successful in the broader market. A similar effort is now under way in the United States and

Figure 12–4: Examples of universal design in products: (a) Automatic can and jar opener. (b) Elevated front-loaded washers and dryers that reduce bending and lifting.

Source: (a) Image courtesy of OneTouch Products, Limited. (b) Image courtesy of Whirlpool.

Europe, where cell phones are being created and advertised specifically for seniors. The Jitterbug, Doro PhoneEasy, and EmporialLife are examples marketed in the United States and Europe (Figure 12–5). All three phones are very simple in design. They have preprogrammed emergency buttons and a well-spaced numeric keypad and have eliminated cameras and games. Of the three phones, Jitterbug is being marketed as a phone that users of all abilities can use, extending the perception of benefits to more people than seniors.

In the home electronics industry, automation is simplifying control systems. Everyday frustration and confusion are common when having to learn how to operate too many devices (Norman 2011). Innovations such as the universal remote for controlling multiple devices, including a television, DVD player, and stereo receiver, drastically reduce the cognitive load of learning and remembering many different types of operations. The NevoLS, for example, is a unique control that combines both a physical and a digital interface. The physical properties of the remote provide comfortable griping for both small and large hands. Although the touch screen interface increases the complexity of the remote, the physical buttons increase product flexibility by making it possible to use with the traditional buttons or the more sophisticated interface (Wasser 2005).

Touch interfaces offer the potential to control other devices and equipment in homes, such as light and temperature, without adding more complexity. Control systems can be "layered" and easily accessed with a gesture. Currently such gadgets are expensive; however, it is only a matter of time before they become affordable. The stand-alone remote control actually may become

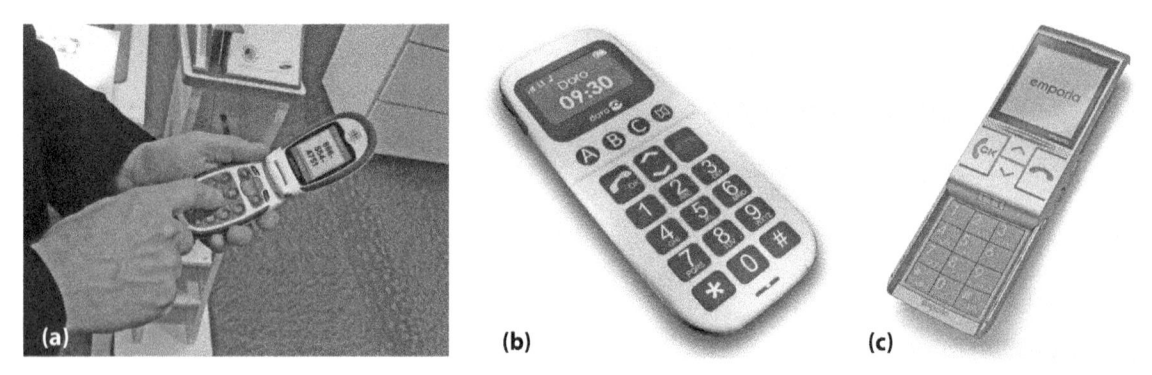

Figure 12–5: Mobile phones with universal design features: (a) Jitterbug Phone, a clamshell model; (b) DoroPhoneEasy 345 Phone, a conventional rectangular model; (c) EmporialLifePlus© Phone 2011, a slider model.
Source: (c) Image courtesy of Chris Bignell

obsolete soon. Applications on smart phones and small tablet computers are now available that control many electronic devices in the home (Etherington 2010). Thus, a remote control for a television or DVD player may simply become another application to download.

It should be noted that universal design could also be misused as a marketing gimmick, without much substance. For example, car manufacturers have promoted their increased attention to design features for older buyers (Paukert 2005). However, these efforts have focused on relatively minor concerns, such as easier-to-grasp controls, high-priced options, or luxury cars. Two key features of automobile design that could dramatically improve use by older people are improving the usability and comfort of seat belts and developing entry systems that make it easier to get in and out of the vehicle. However, there has been practically no innovation in these two areas. The conventional seat belt is extremely difficult to buckle for people with limited range of reach or arthritic hands. Many people who have recently had surgery in the front of their torso (e.g., breast or heart surgery, etc.) also find them very uncomfortable. Current fashions continue to emphasize the sport utility vehicles (although downsized) and sporty sedans that have a low profile, basic platforms that are difficult for older people to use. The former requires climbing up into the vehicle, and the latter requires significant bending at the trunk and flexing at the hips and knees to get in and out (Steinfeld, Tomita, Mann, and Deglopper 1999). Many of the new smaller "crossover" vehicles actually combine the worst elements of both.

Information technology and telecommunications are two industries where universal design is making significant inroads. Information transaction machines (e.g., automated teller machines) are now required by law to meet accessibility requirements that include many universal design features, including audible instructions and simplified and standardized protocols. Ever since the election controversy surrounding Florida ballots in 2000, an effort has been under way to simplify the voting process, including the adoption of electronic voting machines that can adapt to the user's preferences and abilities (Vanderheiden 2004). The telecommunications industry has been gradually introducing additional accessibility features. Title IV of the Americans with Disabilities Act passed in 1990 and required all states to establish a toll-free relay system for communicating with people who are deaf. More recent efforts have been focused on developing improved access to mobile phones by making them compatible with teletypewriters and hearing aids (Federal Communications Commission n.d.). On the high end of the market, video phones provide many inclusive benefits, such as audio, voice-to-text display, and sign and face communication (Figure 12–6). For elders living independently in their homes, video phones provide an added benefit of social participation through face-to-face interaction with friends and family. Joseph F. Coughlin, director of the AgeLab at the Massachusetts Institute of Technology, suggests that older adults will increasingly use 'virtual reality' to stay connected in society (Clifford 2009). Over the past few years, the presence of older adults on online social networks such as Facebook, Twitter, and Skype have all increased "with 39 million people currently aged 65 and older—and an estimated 55 million by 2020" (Zafar 2011).

Computers have become more physically compact and portable. Although the software components have increased in complexity, interfaces are becoming much simpler and more intuitive to use than in earlier generations. Computers have become a tool to increase productivity in work, to communicate with friends and family, for civic engagement, and for shopping. The availability of online participation and connectivity, in particular, has opened up new leisure-time pursuits for older adults. For example, applications like Apple's Face Time, which operates on the iPhone, the iPad, and the Mac computer platforms using identical interfaces, are extremely attractive to elders for keeping in touch with their families, particularly grandchildren. These devices allow grandparents to participate in daily events, such as a first bicycle ride, with virtually no effort. The availability of inexpensive devices for video communication is likely to make products like the videophone in Figure 12–6 obsolete very quickly.

Figure 12–6: Video phone. The photo shows a grandmother reading to her grandchild using the video display feature on the ACN Video Phone.
Source: Property of ACN, Inc. © 2011.

The most recent U.S. population survey reported that more than 68.7 percent of all households had Internet access and 52.2 percent of households headed by a person 55 years or older had Internet access in 2009 (U.S. Census Bureau 2009). Older adults now are the segment of the population with the fastest adoption rate of computer use (Wagner, Hassanein, and Head 2010). This trend can be interpreted in four ways:

1. Many companies see a market opportunity by making their products more user friendly to the older market, a market segment with more potential growth than others.
2. Trends in improved usability have reached a point where the older population is no longer intimidated by the learning curve.
3. Middle-aged adults are growing older and already have the skills necessary to use advanced technology.
4. The ubiquity of computers and other interactive devices forces older adults to learn to use them.

Computers and the Internet also support independent living. Information technology allows older adults to keep in touch with families who might live far away. All computers now come with preinstalled accessibility software that benefits individuals with visual impairments and hearing loss. Screen magnifiers, readers, speech recognition software, and text communication software such as instant messaging are now the norm on any desktop or laptop computer. These features provide aids not only for people with visual and hearing impairments but also for elders. Many technologies that were initially developed for those with severe impairments now benefit wider audiences (Tugend 2008). Even many younger people use accessibility features such as high contrast and larger type (www.apple.com/accessibility) particularly when ambient environmental conditions, such as low light levels or glare, create temporary limitations.

Internet accessibility has allowed people who are blind and visually impaired to obtain the same benefits of the web as sighted individuals using screen-reading software that converts text to speech. The Web Accessibility Initiative (www.w3.org/WAI/) also has paid attention to developing guidelines that address improved websites for people with limitations of vision, simplification of navigation, and reduction in hand movements. These developments, while focused on a specific demographic, benefit the other population sectors by making online navigation less burdensome. Many people who need accessible technology to use computers are aware of the available tools; however, others do not know that such technology exists and continue to use older versions or stand-alone tools. These users may not be aware of updates for existing tools or bypass them because they still continue to function.

As products continue to improve, so should the packages in which they are delivered. Designers must think about both the user opening the package and the graphics and type displayed on the outside of the package. For example, individuals with arthritis have trouble opening many different types of packages. Of course, there are many packaging designs that everyone has a problem with. Consider the compact disc package wrapper, which is now thankfully becoming obsolete due to online music distribution methods.

The ClearRX medication bottle for the Target Corporation is an example of innovative design in product packaging (Figure 12–7). Many people have a difficult time comprehending information displayed on medication containers, opening them, and accessing the contents. The ClearRX drastically reduces the stress related to fear of making a mistake that comes with performing all these tasks through larger text, color codes, hierarchical information, and affordance.

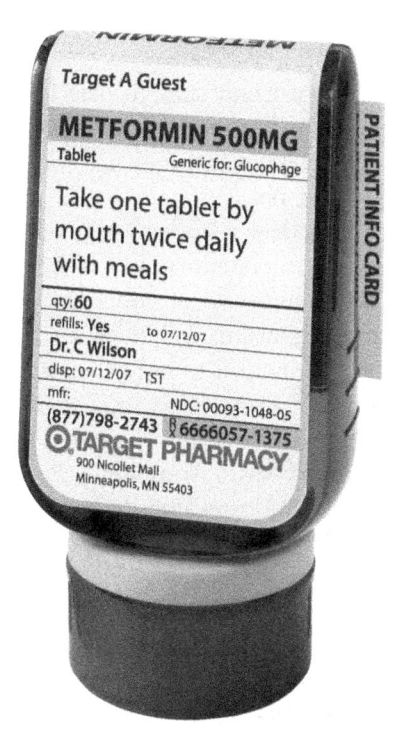

Figure 12–7: Target's ClearRX medication bottle. The bottle features large-type on labels and a color-coded ring to identify the type of medication.
Source: Image courtesy of Target.

Another example is the Duracell hearing aid battery package. The miniature batteries presented real usability problems for older people with limited dexterity. Realizing that existing batteries and packaging were causing significant problems for consumers, Duracell conducted a series of studies to find out how to assist consumers with taking the batteries out of the package and inserting them into hearing aids. The solution was an innovative package with tabs attached to the batteries themselves. The tab system allows for easy removal, gripping, and placing of the battery into the hearing aid, not only for older adults but for users of all abilities (Bix, Fuente, and Lockhart 2004).

Smarter Products

The intelligence built into products is increasing rapidly. The "smart" era in products has emerged as continuous Internet access, enriched geographic databases, and embedded sensors become ubiquitous. Even water filter pitchers, garbage cans, and door locks now are available with embedded electronics. Smart products are poised to make a significant impact in many industries. These conditions are providing opportunities to develop new generations of universally designed products.

The first industries to experience a major impact are the telephone, home appliance, healthcare, and automotive industries.

Telephones

Mobile telephones have been in common use only since the late 1990s, but already they are having a transformative effect on society and culture. For several years now, the ubiquity of mobile technology has enabled people to stay connected to colleagues, family, and friends everywhere they go. It has transformed society from a physical, geographic community to a virtual electronic community. We are now connected not only to our own immediate social networks but to the world. For underdeveloped countries, the mobile phone is even more important because it overcomes the lack of fixed-line infrastructure (James and Versteeg 2007). In developed countries, there are signs that many households are relying more on mobile use than traditional fixed phone lines. For example, in the United States, landline use has dropped from 97 percent in 2001 to 74 percent in 2010 (Taylor and Wang 2010).

The mobile phone not only has made a significant impact on communications, but with the introduction of so-called "smart phones," it is being adapted as a tool for many other tasks. A smart phone is like a twenty-first-century Swiss Army knife. Features on most smart phones include the ability to pay bills remotely, built-in cameras that allow users to scan a product and get additional information about it, and GPS navigation for wayfinding. They can be used to pay transit fares and even control lights, window shades, and entertainment centers in the home. A few years ago, automating these tasks required a specific tool for each. Today, paying our bills is as simple as a few touches of the finger on an interface no bigger than the size of a hand. Although mobile phones are continuing to revolutionize the way we work, study, and play, their designers need to be mindful of the diverse population of users, comprised of people with various physical, sensory, and cognitive abilities and skills (Czaja and Barr 1989).

The market today is saturated with smart phones. Thus, companies now are competing for market share by adding new features, including additional physical keys, new control types, increased screen size, new software applications, and gesture-based and voice-based interaction. Users may be overwhelmed, dissatisfied, and get "feature fatigue" if these changes aren't introduced in ways that can beused intuitively (Thompson, Hamilton, and Rust 2005). Smart phones can be a challenge for older adults and people with sensory, cognitive, and motor limitations in particular. Lack of universal design in smart phone design could have a significant impact on social participation, particularly within families, work groups, and social networks. For example, a work group using texting or video to communicate with each other could exclude members who cannot access the technology, a kind of social segregation. Yet there are good examples of how universal design features can help to facilitate social integration.

Smart phones with touch screens that use gesture-based interaction are easier to use than conventional keyboards and have the advantage of being popular with young people. Thus, there is no stigma attached to buying these products just because they are easier to use. They also have the "cool factor." Smart phones have many features that are compatible with social role of grandparents—video chat, games, and entertainment apps that can be used to interact with grandchildren. Furthermore, the screens of these phones are much larger than conventional mobile phones and thus easier to use with aging eyes and fingers. The iPhone, in particular, with its seamless integration with personal computers and the App Store, provide more functionality than a simple phone (Figure 12–8). Perhaps the touch-screen smart phone heralds a new era of user-centered design in the mobile phone market. In particular, the iPhone demonstrates how innovative interactive design can make a complex device simple and intuitive for users of all abilities. An Apple-supplied application called VoiceOver allows visually impaired people to use the touch interface. The latest version of the iPhone (iPhone 4S) includes two new features: Assistive Touch, an innovative feature which allows those with

Figure 12–8: Apple iPhone. The iPhone demonstrates how a complex device can be made simple and intuitive, given a well-designed user interface.

limited dexterity to easily control the physical buttons on the screen, and Siri, a voice recognition virtual assistant, which allows users to easily create reminders or find places. Siri's simplified voice recognition interface holds tremendous benefits for the older generation in particular.

Home Automation

More and more consumer electronics products are being connected using wireless networks—consider desktop and laptop computers, printers, and fax machines in the home. At one time, the concept of a smart home was based on a wired home infrastructure. Wireless technologies have made that nearly obsolete. Now any home can become smarter using "connected appliances." For instance, Microsoft Windows 7 has preinstalled software that allows users to easily set up a network that links all external technology devices in the home. Televisions can be used to browse the Internet, stream music, and download movies. The infrastructure for more advanced networking capabilities is coming online, with personal computers or wireless servers operating as a hub for all communications and media use within the home.

As technology progresses in the wireless era, homes evolve ever more into automated systems in which appliances, home security, mechanical systems, lighting, and entertainment are all networked seamlessly. This transformation will provide many benefits. Currently, it is still a cumbersome task to learn how to use all the separate systems that can be connected. The thermostat, mechanical system, lighting, security, and entertainment systems all have specific setup and control interfaces. Having control of all these systems under one interface will provide benefits not only to the general consumer market, but "to people with physical, sensory, and mental disabilities, allowing them to live more independently" (Salerno 2010).

The touch tablet is the first generation of interfaces that developers are using to create integrated controls for multiple devices within the domestic setting. Tablets are already being used as platforms by companies that see the market appeal of wireless products with centralized controls. The LG ThinQ is a noteworthy example of a centralized control that allows users to monitor appliances. The ThinQ currently connects with a vacuum, refrigerator, oven, and washer/dryer. All these appliances can be monitored at home or remotely through a smart phone, computer, or touch tablet (Figure 12–9) (O'Brien 2011).

Many other companies have developed applications for the iPad, Android tablets, and other touch tablets that control lighting, temperature, entertainment, garage openers, and doors locks. Although many of these applications are ad hoc and require connecting additional hardware to the controlled device to create seamless integration, they are steps in the right direction. The future in home automation likely will see more appliance companies incorporating wireless control interfaces in their products and developing software applications that can be downloaded onto a home computer, touch tablet, or mobile phone. The connected home of the future is starting to take shape and will prove to benefit many individuals of many abilities. This technology may seem out of reach for low-income consumers, but the plug-and-play concept allows individual households to build on a core by adding more devices incrementally. Even inexpensive video game systems could become the core through which households build a connected home.

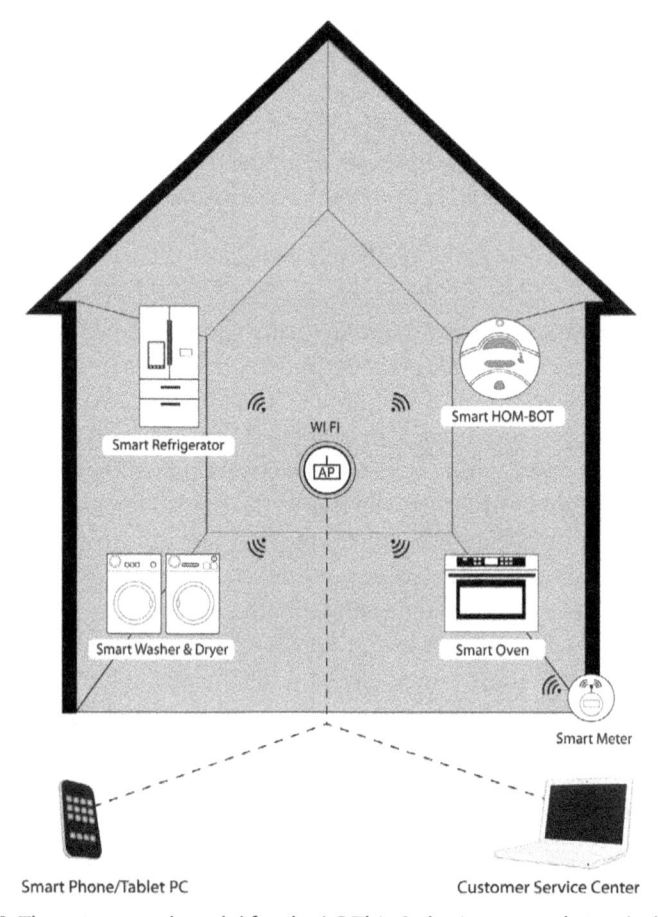

Figure 12–9: LG ThinQ. The conceptual model for the LG ThinQ depicts many household appliances, smart phones, computers, and customer support all connected wirelessly within and outside of the home.

Healthcare

Smart products are appearing rapidly in the medical industry. One of the most promising sectors is tele-care, which provides remote checkups and monitoring of patients. The increase in chronic diseases, a shortage of physicians, and the high cost of facility-based care will drive demand for tele-care (Moore 2009). These systems enable elders and those with impairments to age in place longer and live healthier lives by offering remote health services and care through communication technology. Rest Assured is a web-based tele-care service available on the market that connects patients to caregivers (Figure 12–10). This system targets elders and those with impairments but could be more broadly used, especially by households in rural areas or inner cities poorly served by health care providers (Vaught 2009).

Software that processes data gathered through sensors like smoke detectors, carbon monoxide detectors, natural gas detectors, and motion detectors can automatically identify problems in the home and alert both home owners and external parties, such as family and friends, fire departments or ambulance services, of emergency events. The sensor technologies in these devices are already ubiquitous (Stowe and Harding 2010). Additionally, products activated by users to communicate with a remote attendant in an emergency are also widely available. Remote sensing technology is being used in more complex systems that collect and analyze data about the individual and the home (Stowe and Harding 2010). These systems identify unusual activities that may not trigger emergency notifications, for example, changes in eating habits or increased levels of sugar in urine. Furthermore, personalized health monitoring devices, such as watches, wristbands, and even clothing, are gradually being introduced. Recently unveiled by Under Armor at the 2011 National Football League Combine, an event where players drafted from college showcase their abilities, the UA E39 vest monitors an athlete's biometric data, including

Figure 12–10: Rest Assured Tele-Care System. A woman in a wheelchair uses this system to talk to a caregiver remotely through a web camera and computer.

Source: Image courtesy of Dustin Wright, RestAssured

heart rate, breathing rate, skin surface temperature, and body position.* Eventually people with physical and cognitive health conditions, who today cannot live independently, may be able to use similar smart clothing to reduce reliance on services and caregivers.

Although tele-care services offer great promise, many serious ethical and privacy issues need to be addressed. Those who provide the services have the potential to abuse the system. People with cognitive impairments, especially, may be vulnerable to abuse by unscrupulous providers or hackers. Individuals whose behavior is monitored, or their guardians, should have control over such systems and the ability to shut them down at any time. Data collected must be secure, and access must be controlled by the individual or caregivers. The use of cameras has been particularly controversial. Thus, during implementation, it is important for providers to explain the privacy implications and obtain informed consent to collect information (Stowe and Harding 2010). As tele-care becomes more widely used, additional issues, now unforeseen, will no doubt be raised that have to be addressed.

Automobiles

The automobile has been a central aspect of life in North America for nearly a century. Recent surveys demonstrate that 90 percent of Americans use their personal automobile to get to destinations, and drivers spend an average of 87 minutes a day in automobiles (Langer 2005). Increasing time spent in vehicles along with an ever-escalating number of drivers on the road is stimulating the development of smart technologies in automotive design. One of the biggest problems drivers face is in-vehicle distractions, such as using entertainment systems and interacting with mobile devices (Steinfeld 2011). To prevent such distractions, advances in wireless technology, such as Bluetooth, allow drivers to use mobile devices through the vehicle's sound system. Voice recognition systems are a popular upgrade and are becoming standard features in many vehicles. Rear-facing cameras allow drivers with limited movement in the neck or torso to more easily park and drive in reverse (Steinfeld 2011). For wayfinding, audible navigation systems are now standard features in many vehicles. Parking assistant systems are available on many models from most manufacturers.

Population increases and traffic congestion will lead to new methods of regulating driving to optimize space on the roadway. Automating driving will allow more cars on the roads by maximizing the use of space. However, they also have the potential to reduce the physical skills and abilities needed to drive by automating many driving tasks such as hazard avoidance and speed control. One example of what the future may bring is the EN V, a small, two-person vehicle under development by GM and Segway (Figure 12–11). It communicates with other vehicles, senses changes in the environment, and automatically reacts as necessary to avoid accidents. Small personal vehicles like the EN V prototype could provide more independence and convenience in travel for those with mobility limitations than public transportation (Motavalli 2010). Google recently began testing a fleet of autonomous vehicles that even steer themselves. A single vehicle is equipped with sensors that collect road activity, such as distances of other vehicles around it, and reacts as a human driver would. Additionally, the vehicle generates a real-time map of its environment, recognizes stop signs and lights, and uses cameras to identify and track moving objects and obstacles (Markoff 2010).

---

*"Under Armour® Training Innovations," www.underarmour.com/shop/us/en/e39.

Figure 12–11: General Motors' EN V. This is a small two-person autonomous prototype vehicle.
Source: Image courtesy of saebaryo.

Although smart vehicles offer great potential to make driving safer and more convenient for people of all abilities, there are significant problems to overcome. Interaction with digital devices in cars is very different than with analog devices. New control systems will have to be developed. This could create a learning curve for many drivers, especially the use of digital control interfaces. For example, pressing a physical button is very different from pressing a button on a screen. The simple task of turning on a device may require time to learn because there is "no physical presence or spatial relationship to the device itself" (Norman 1993, p.79). Lack of "tangibility" can reduce the feeling of control, and too much automation can create a false sense of security and reduce vigilance (Norman 2007). Furthermore, smart products can make us so dependent on technology that, when they fail, disasters ensue (Norman 2007).

Case Studies

This section provides several in-depth examples of universal design in products to illustrate the points made earlier in the chapter in an integrated way. Each product is evaluated using the Goals of Universal Design, introduced earlier in Chapter 4.

Example: OXO Good Grips Measuring Cup

Founded by Sam Farber, OXO International developed several kitchen utensils that addressed the needs of people who have arthritic hands and have difficulty gripping. Farber, who had retired from leading a company with decades of experience manufacturing and marketing kitchen utensils, saw a gap in the market (Story and Mueller 2011). He teamed up with Smart Design, Inc., which studied the use of products and how to reduce difficulty in twisting, turning, pushing, pulling, and squeezing. The result was a new line of products with oversize handles with a rubberized surface that provided a comfortable, nonslip grip. The OXO Good Grips product line is now a benchmark for universal design. What makes Good Grips stand out from other comparable products is its sensitivity to user needs combined with a focus on emotional appeal. The product line appeals to able-bodied individuals of all ages because the utensils reduce effort and increase usability and comfort for everyone while enabling those with limited strength, dexterity, and sensory abilities to perform tasks they could once do only with assistive devices.[1] OXO also created a new aesthetic trend by combining a high-tech look with the visceral emotional appeal of curved forms, timeless colors (black and white), and the introduction of new methods of use that are both intuitive and fun. The measuring cup is a good example of the product line as a whole (Figure 12–12).

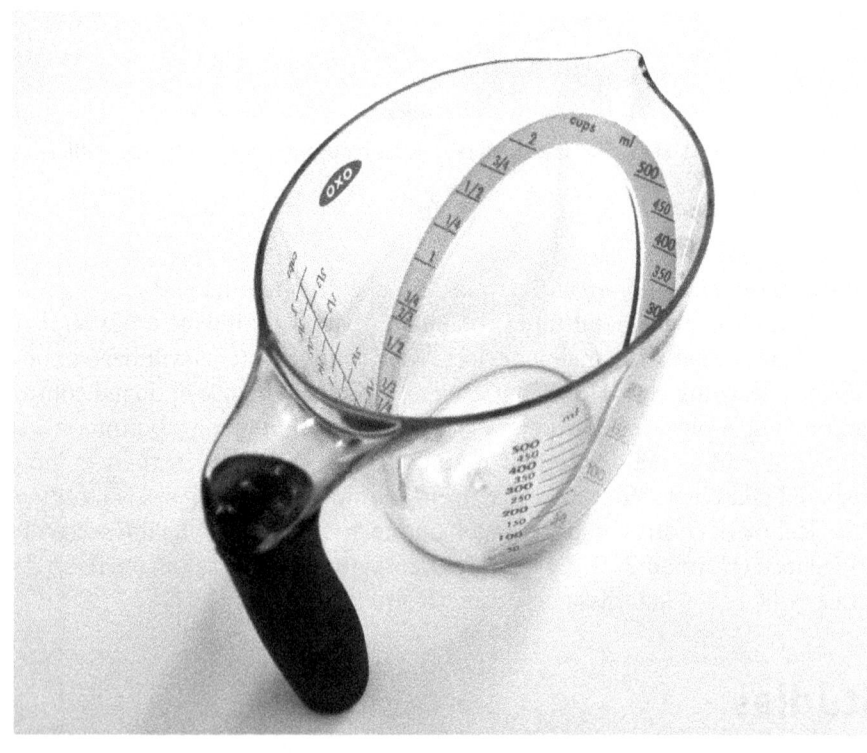

Figure 12–12: OXO Good Grips measuring cup. This product has a comfortable nonslip grip and measurements marked on both the outside of the cup and along an angled shelf inside, allowing the user to read the measurement without bending over or lifting the cup.

Goals of Universal Design

Body fit. The handle is oversized to make grasping easier. A user who has difficulty forming a grip can fit their entire hand in the gap between the handle and cup.

Comfort. The handle shape and nonslip surface facilitates gripping, even with wet slippery hands. The unique labeling system allows users to know exactly how much content is in the cup while it is at rest and during pouring without bending the body or lifting the cup.

Awareness. The angled placement of the measuring rule provides more accuracy in measurement of portions. The contrasting colors of the handle and the measuring rule makes it easy to find and use, even for users with poor vision.

Understanding. The conventional shape of the cup conveys the method of pouring through a well-known conceptual model. The use of the innovative measuring device inside the cup is intuitive.

Wellness. The nonslip grip eliminates risks in pouring hot liquids and the angled measuring rule reduces accident risk further by reducing the need to lift the cup when full. The design of the spout reduces spills.

Social integration. The ease of use of the product helps to reduce errors, accidents, and effort, enabling independent food preparation for a larger population for a longer period of time during the life span, at both younger and older ages.

Personalization. The availability of different size cups accommodates a wide range of needs. The combination of features allows this product to accommodate users of varying body sizes, postures, and functional abilities.

Cultural appropriateness. The labeling system is in both metric and standard measurement values, providing worldwide usability. By reducing the potential for accidents, it contributes to self image and competence.

[1] Smart Design media kit, www.smartdesignworldwide.com/pdf/SmartDesign_NDA_MediaKit.pdf.

Example: Humanscale Freedom Chair

The Freedom Chair is an iconic product in the office seating industry. Conceptualized and designed by Niels Diffrient and manufactured and marketed by Humanscale, the Freedom Chair is both functional and attractive (Figure 12–13). Most furniture designers tend to focus on looks rather than actual functionality and hope that visual cues will appeal to users and translate into sales. The Freedom Chair provides users with total body support by offering comfort in every adjustable setting. Each component of the chair was carefully articulated to fit the targeted body section, demonstrating the relationship between design and the body. Diffrient dedicated his time to each individual component, sometimes spending over a year

Figure 12–13: Freedom Chair. This chair is designed to help all users maintain good posture. It adapts automatically to changes in position and has few controls that are easy to reach and operate.
Source: Image courtesy of Humanscale.

on a specific part. The time and effort resulted in a piece of furniture that provides "absence of stress, absence of pressure, absence of anything that concentrates undesirable forces, psychological or physiological" (Zumstein 2006, p. 4).

Goals of Universal Design

Body fit. The headrest, armrests, and seat height are all adjustable to accommodate people with a wide range of statures.

Comfort. The chair affords good body posture through the shape of the different elements that interact with the body. It automatically supports the user as he or she shifts or reclines positions.

Awareness. The large, easy-to-locate levers and controls provide users with the means to adjust the chair effortlessly to fit their bodies.

Understanding. The chair responds automatically to users' movements. It has only two controls and each has only one adjustment motion. The shape of the controls provide affordances that communicate the way they should be used. Tactile markings and distinctive shapes allow use of the controls without looking. Limitations in range of control prevent users from making unnecessary adjustments.

Wellness. The chair is designed to ensure good seating posture and prevent back injury from long periods of seated work. It adjusts automatically to support users in different positions, encouraging frequent postural changes conducive to injury prevention. When not in use, the chair will not incline, reducing the potential for a fall if someone leans on the seat back.

Social integration. By helping to reduce back injuries and provide improved postural support for people who already have such injuries, the chair supports continued participation in work and reduces absenteeism and lost income.

Personalization. Rollers and lightweight material provide ease of movement. Automatic adjustment supports individual preferences in posture with no effort. Different versions are available with different types of upholstery to address different tastes.

Cultural appropriateness. The design uses hi-tech materials and functional shapes based on technology in a way that also recalls more traditional designs. Thus, it has continuity with the past and conveys a futuristic aesthetic at the same time.

Example: Apple iPhone

Launched in 2007, the Apple iPhone (see Figure 12–8) has become one of the most recognizable products of all time. Both the physical and the digital interfaces emphasize simplicity and functionality. The device fits easily into an adult hand. Simple touches, gestures, and voice commands are used for interaction, reducing the precision needed for small keyboards but also creating pleasing tactile feedback. Graphic icons are intuitive and provide users with a very simple and uniform navigation experience. The constraint of the colorful square icons and identifiable graphics of each icon create the appearance of a box of candy or a lacquered Japanese lunchbox (*bento*). The iPhone includes preinstalled accessibility software with screen magnification, Voiceover, Assistive Touch, and Siri, a voice recognition interface. A screen-access technology that was originally incorporated for blind and visually impaired users but is useful for all users. The iPhone is more than a phone; it is a tool used for many other purposes, including wayfinding, comparison shopping research, bill and fare payment, ticket purchases, coupon redemption, remote control, garage door opener, and much more. The innovative software system of free and inexpensive "apps," or applications, that can be easily downloaded and installed on the device provides unlimited customization opportunities. It allows users to cram literally hundreds of tools into a small package that can assist them with almost everything they do.

Goals of Universal Design

Body fit. The physical shape is sized for easy grip and fits well in pockets due to its thin profile. The large touch screen interface provides ample room for fingers of all sizes. App icons are larger targets than the keys on most telephone keypads and are spaced apart enough even for large fingers. The zoom feature allows links to be increased in size quickly with one intuitive gesture. The physical controls can be used without worrying about accuracy and great precision.

Comfort. The size of the device fits in the palm of a young adult's hand yet is not too small for large hands. The smooth case allows the phone to slip into storage pockets without difficulty.

Awareness. The interface of the iPhone is customizable for different types of users. The icons are recognizable and large enough for easy perception. The preinstalled Voiceover software allows blind and visually impaired individuals to use the phone effectively.

Understanding. Controls are minimized reducing complexity. The power adapter, power button, and volume controls are designed and placed intuitively on the phone and provide affordances for orientation. The rectangular shape and use of the full display size allows the applications icons to be formatted in a grid layout, making a large number visible at one time.

Wellness. Many applications on the iPhone promote health and wellness. For example, barcode scanner apps allow users to scan items in the grocery store in order to find out nutritional information, price, and expiration dates. The introduction of Siri, a voice recognition program, in the G4S version allows hands free use, reducing the potential for accidents and facilitating emergency communications.

Social integration. The usability and adaptability of the device made it a favorite of all ages, breaking down barriers between generations. The FaceTime application allows very easy video chat setup for everyone and provides a powerful means for multisensory social communications. The availability of many games provides an attractive intergenerational experience.

Personalization. Users can customize the interface by choosing their favorite apps to display on the main screen. The simple shape facilitates the production of third-party cases to customize the grip, durability, and appearance of the device. Assistive Touch allows the user to customize gestures to their abilities and preferences. Siri provides voice control for users who cannot use their hands or whose hands are busy at the time.

Cultural appropriateness. The rectangular shape allows users to select casings that promote identification with differnt cultural backgrounds and social worlds. The design of the app screen recalls very positive associations in both eastern and western cultures, the bento box and the candy box.

Example: Touch Graphics Interactive Touch Model

The interactive touch model is a device that incorporates a touch interface in a three-dimensional object. It is an example of a product that was originally designed as AT but will, after refinement in that market, be introduced as a mainstream commercial product. Developed initially as an AT company, Touch Graphics is now exploring universal design applications. The first use of the interface technology was in an exhibit on rockets at the New York Hall of Science. The second application was a talking kiosk designed to provide passengers at the Whitehall Ferry Terminal in Lower Manhattan with wayfinding and orientation information. This concept was then refined through another wayfinding application, called the Interactive Touch Model (Figure 12–14). The interactive model is a three-dimensional

Figure 12–14: Interactive Touch Model. This map of a campus provides tactile and audible feedback as the user touches different buildings and streets.

representation of the Carroll Center for the Blind Campus in Newton, Massachusetts. Three-dimensional interactive wayfinding systems promote better comprehension of relatively unfamiliar outdoor environments when compared to simple tactile maps. Blind students who are learning to navigate the campus use the model by exploring it with touch; as they do, a computer senses their touches and offers helpful audible descriptions and wayfinding information for each building and landscape feature. A formal learning protocol can be integrated into the software to teach students what they need to know about the school in a systematic way. Touches are detected by embedded electrodes connected to a multichannel sensor. Additional information can be provided using display screens or digital projectors. Two new prototypes using both audible and visual information displays are being tested at the Lighthouse in Chicago. The new prototype includes multisensory outputs, including tactile and audio information for blind and visually impaired users, visual and tactile information for deaf users, and information in all three modalities for all users. The production system can be applied easily to other environments. The digital fabrication approach makes it possible to economically produce unique models for each unique site.

Goals of Universal Design

Body fit. The sizes are scaled to ensure that the smallest components are perceptible through touch exploration. The latest prototype provides knee clearance for wheelchair users and is mounted at a height that is also comfortable for standing users. The depth of the model is within reaching ability of people with small stature.

Comfort. The mounting height reduces the need for bending by all but the tallest individuals and simultaneously puts all parts of the device within reach of wheelchair users. Control buttons can be operated with very little effort.

Awareness. Color and texture are used to improve understanding of different features in the model. In the latest model, color can be controlled and adjusted through the projection of a computer image from above. The illuminated model stands out strongly from its background. The touch sensitivity of the objects provides instant feedback to the user. Important features can be exaggerated in size and highlighted through overhead projection to make them more perceptible. Audible information can be adjusted in volume or accessed through headphones. A refreshable Braille display can also be used as an output device.

Understanding. The three-dimensional model provides a close simulation of the actual environment that is more understandable by the public than a two-dimensional representation. The simple three-button interface is based on the familiar remote control cursor as a conceptual model. It allows blind users to navigate through information in a database easily. The audio is easily discernible to users, providing necessary cues to a particular object for blind people. Earphones can be used in noisy environments or to reduce background noise from the model itself.

Wellness. The enclosure is designed to be perceptible to cane users, and the edges are rounded and free from hazards. Use of the device for improved orientation will help individuals understand and access health and wellness resources in their environment.

Social integration. Everyone can use the same models to access wayfinding information and increase knowledge of a building or campus. The models can also be used to find people and thus enhance social networking.

Personalization. Three types of outputs are available: text projection onto the model or a screen, audible voice synthesis, and refreshable Braille.

Cultural appropriateness. The models are designed to provide information on the local physical environment, making local resources more accessible to the public. Any information can be conveyed through the various modalities, allowing fit with local needs and desires.

Summary

Universal design as it applies to products demonstrates that the concept can be applied to any scale of the built environment. Today, there are many opportunities for introducing universal design in the new product development cycle. The aesthetics, interaction methods, form factors, technologies, and materials used in consumer products are rapidly changing, demanding innovation in most industries. New markets are creating opportunities for innovation to address specific needs but also are providing new opportunities for mass customization. The advancement of smart technology has enabled the development of products that can simplify many everyday tasks through improved access to information from one platform such as smart phones or tablet computers. Smart technology continuously collects data, analyzes surroundings and adjusts systems, and automatically provides augmented perception, improved situational awareness, and enhanced control.

In the consumer product industries, the conventional approach to diversity has been to let small companies serve niche markets whose customers depart from "average" abilities, such as people with disabilities (Emiliani 2003). However, universal design is starting to change this mind-set. Industries that serve special markets like the space program, people with disabilities, sports and healthcare, provide a proving ground to explore new enabling technologies and create better products through the incorporation of universal design features. The AT community, in particular, has an excellent opportunity to bring its knowledge about design for diversity and customization to bear in the mainstream market. The AT community can also benefit from studying how mainstream companies are successfully applying universal design ideas to address the increasing diversity of the population.

Review Topics

1. What are the limitations of assistive technology for people with disabilities? What is the relationship of such products to universal design?
2. Describe the knowledge translation problem and ways to overcome it.
3. How has the introduction of "smart" products affected product design? Give specific examples.

References

Ahasan, R., D. Campbell, A. Salmoni, A., and J. Lewko. 2001. "HFs/Ergonomics of Assistive Technology." *Journal of Physiological Anthropology and Applied Human Science* 20 (3): 187–197.

"Athletic Shoes." 2008. In P. J. Bungert and A. J. Darnay (eds.), *Encyclopedia of Products and Industries: Manufacturing,* vol. 1, pp. 21–30. Detroit, MI: Gale.

Bix, L., J. Fuente and H. Lockhart. 2004. "Packaging with Universal Appeal." *Packaging World Magazine* 79, http://www.packworld.com/article-17357.

Black, A. 2006. "User-centred Design: The Basics of User-Centred Design," www.creative-net.co.uk/About-Design/Design-Techniques/User-centred-design-/.

Byrd, D. and C. Yavelow. 1986. "The Kurzweil 250 Digital Synthesizer." *Computer Music Journal* 10 (1): 64–86.

Carse, B., A. Thomson, and B. Stansfield. 2010. "Use of Biomechanical Data in the Inclusive Design Process: Packaging Design and the Older Adult." *Journal of Engineering Design* 21 (2): pp. 289–303.

Chertok, B. L. 2009. "Internet Man, Renaissance Woman: An Interview with Vinton and Sigrid Cerf," www.hearingloss.org/magazine/2009MayJune/Cerf_Interview_MayJune2009_HLM.pdf.

Clifford, S. 2009. "Online, 'A Reason to Keep on Going'." *The New York Times*, June 1, www.nytimes.com/2009/06/02/health/02face.html.

Cooper, R. A., E. E. Teodorski, M. L. Sporner, and D. M. Collins. 2011. "Manual Wheelchair Propulsion over Cross-Sloped Surfaces: A Literature Review." *Assistive Technology* 23 (1): 42–51.

Crabb, N. 2009. "Assistive Technology and Adaptive Devices." In S. Burch (ed.), *Encyclopedia of American Disability History,* pp. 69–72. Library of American History. New York: Facts On File.

Czaja, S. J. and R. A. Barr. 1989. "Technology and the Everyday Life of Older Adults." *Annals of the American Academy of Political and Social Science* 503: 177–137.

"A Day in the Life . . . ." 2010. *The View* (Spring/Summer), www.lboro.ac.uk/research/theview/archive/ss10/articles/restricted-mobility/#article.

DiBrezzo, R. and I. Fort. 2005. "Biomechanics." In K. Christensen and D. Levinson (eds.), *Berkshire Encyclopedia of World Sport*, vol. 1, pp. 195–199. Great Barrington, MA: Berkshire.

Ebner, I. 2004. *Abandonment of Assistive Technology.* St Johns, MI: Michigan's Assistive Technology Resource, Michigan Department of Education.

Emiliani, P. L. 2003. "Information Technology, Telecommunications, New Media and Disability: Future Trends." In G. Craddock, L. P. McCormack, R. B. Reilly and H.T.P. Knops (eds.), *Assistive Technology-Shaping the Future,* pp. 83–88. Amsterdam: IOS Press.

Erlandson, R. F. 2008. *Universal and Accessible Design for Products, Services, and Processes.* Boca Raton, FL: CRC Press.

Etchell, L. and D. Yelding. 2004. "Inclusive Design: Products for All Consumers." *Consumer Policy Review* 14 (6): 186–189.

Etherington, D. (2010). "iPhone Becomes a Universal Remote This February."(January 4, 2010), http://gigaom.com/apple/iphone-becomes-a-universal-remote-this-february/.

Federal Communications Commission. n.d. "What Are the FCC's Requirements for Hearing Aid Compatibility for Digital Wireless Telephones?" www.fcc.gov/guides/hearing-aid-compatibility-wireless-telephones.

Federal Communications Commission. 1996. "Video Programming Accessibility," http://transition.fcc.gov/Bureaus/Cable/Orders/1996_TXT/fcc96071.txt.

Field, M. J. and A. M. Jette (eds.). 2007. *Assistive and Mainstream Technologies for People with Disabilities: The Future of Disability in America.* Washington, DC: National Academies Press.

Galvin, J., D. Ross, and B. Phillips. 1990. *Meeting User Needs through Assistive Technology.* Washington, DC: Request Rehabilitation Engineering Center, National Rehabilitation Hospital.

Gitlin, L. 1995. "Why Older People Accept or Reject Assistive Technology." *Generations* (Spring): 41–46.

Greenwald, B. H. 2009. "Bell, Alexander Graham (1847–1922)." In S. Burch (ed.), *Encyclopedia of American Disability History,* pp. 99–102. Library of American History. New York: Facts On File.

Harkins, J. and K. P. Strauss. 2009. "Telecommunications Act." In S. Burch (ed.), *Encyclopedia of American Disability History,* pp. 885–886. Library of American History. New York: Facts On File.

Hocking, C. 1999. "Function or Feelings: Factors in Abandonment of Assistive Devices." *Technology and Disability* 11 (1/2): 4.

James, J. and M. Versteeg. 2007. "Mobile Phones in Africa: How Much Do We Really Know?" *Social Indicators Research* 84 (1): 117–126.

Johnston, S. S. and J. Evans. 2005. "Considering Response Efficiency as a Strategy to Prevent Assistive Technology Abandonment." *Journal of Special Education Technology* 20 (3): 45–50.

Kumar, S. and K. B. Moore. 2002. "The Evolution of Global Positioning System (GPS) Technology." *Journal of Science Education and Technology* 11 (1): 59–80.

Lane, J. P. and J. L. Flagg. 2010. "Translating Three States of Knowledge—Discovery, Invention, and Innovation." *Implementation Science* 5 (9): 1–14.

Langer, G. 2005. "Traffic in the United States: A Look Under the Hood of a Nation on Wheels." ABC News poll, February 13, 2005, http://abcnews.go.com/Technology/Traffic/Story?id=485098&page=1.

LaPlante, M. P., G. E. Hendershot, and A. J. Moss. 1992. "Assistive Technology Devices and Home Accessibility Features: Prevalence, Payment, Need and Trends." *Advance Data* 217 (September 16): 1–12.

Markoff, J. 2010. "Google Cars Drive Themselves, in Traffic." *New York Times*, October 9.

Mihm, S. 2002. "A Limb which Shall be Presentable in Polite Society: Prosthetic Technologies in the Nineteeth Century." In K. Ott (ed.), *Artificial Parts, Practical Lives: Modern Histories of Prosthetics,* pp. 282–299. New York: New York University Press.

Moore, R. 2009. "Telehealth Connected Care." *Health Management Technology* 30 (3): 40.

Morris, J., J. Mueller, and M. Jones. 2010. "Tomorrow's Elders with Disabilities: What the Wireless Industry Needs to Know." *Journal of Engineering Design* 21 (2–3): 131–146.

Morrissey, P. A. and R. Silverstein. 1989. "The Technology-Related Assistance for Individuals with Disabilities Act of 1988," http://findarticles.com/p/articles/mi_m0842/is_n2_v15/ai_8200899/.

Motavalli, J. 2010. "G.M. EN-V: Sharpening the Focus of Future Urban Mobility." *New York Times.*

Newell, A. F. 2003. "Inclusive Design or Assistive Technology." In J. Clackson, R. Coleman, S. Keates and C. Lebbon (eds.), *Inclusive Design—Design for the Whole Population,* pp. 172–181. York, UK: Springer.

Norman, D. A. 1993. *Things that Make Us Smart: Defending Human Attributes in the Age of the Machine.* Reading, MA: Addison-Wesley.

Norman, D. A. 2007. *The Design of Future Things.* New York: Basic Books.

———. 2011. *Living with Complexity.* Cambridge, MA: MIT Press.

O'Brien, T. 2011. "LG Thinq Appliances Let You Remotely Burn Lasagna, Start the Dryer" (January), www.switched.com/2011/01/04/lg-thinq-control-home-appliances-smartphone/.

Paukert, C. 2005. "Aging Boomers Changing Face of Automobile Design." (December 20), www.autoblog.com/2005/12/20/aging-boomers-changing-face-of-automobile-design/.

Philips, B. and H. Zhao. 1993. "Predictors of Assistive Technology Abandonment." *Assistive Technology* 5 (1): 36–45.

Pullin, G. 2009. *Design Meets Disability.* Cambridge, MA: MIT Press.

Reuters. 1990. "Georges de Mestral, 82, Inventor Who Developed Velcro." *New York Times,* February 12.

Salerno, M. 2010. "New Devices Can Make Life Easier." *Toronto Sun.* June 28, 2010, www.torontosun.com/resalehomes/2010/06/28/14543381.html.

Serlin, D. 2010. "Prosthetics." In S. Burch (ed.), *Encyclopedia of American Disability History* (p. 743). Library of American History. New York: Facts On File.

Shore, H. 1976. "Designing a Training Program for Understanding Sensory Losses in Aging." *Gerontologist* 16 (2): 157–165.

Silva, J. 2008. "Rethinking the Cost of Assistive Technology Adaptive Technology Resource Centre, University of Toronto," http://inclusiveworkshop.ca/index.php?page=the-high-cost-of-at.

Steinfeld, A. 2011. "Universal Design of Automobiles." In W. F. E. Preiser and K. H. Smith (eds.), *Universal Design Handbook,* (2nd ed.) pp. 31.1-31.9. New York: McGraw-Hill.

Steinfeld, E., V. Paquet, C. D'Souza, C. Joseph, and J. Maisel. 2010. "Anthropometry of Wheeled Mobility Project: Final Report." Buffalo, NY: Prepared for U.S. Access Board by the IDeA Center.

Steinfeld, E., M. Tomita, W. C. Mann, and W. Deglopper. 1999. "Use of Passenger Vehicles by Older People with Disabilities." *OTJR: Occupation, Participation and Health* 19: 155–186.

Stephens, T. 2007. "How a Swiss Invention Hooked the World" (January 4), www.swissinfo.ch/eng/Home/Archive/How_a_Swiss_invention_hooked_the_world.html?cid=5653568.

Story, M. F. and J. L. Mueller. 2011. "Universal Design of Products." In W.F.E. Preiser and K. H. Smith (eds.), *Universal Design Handbook* (2nd ed.), pp. 32.1–32.11 New York: McGraw-Hill.

Stowe, S. and S. Harding. 2010. "Telecare, Telehealth and Telemedicine." *European Geriatric Medicine* 1 (3). pp. 193–197.

Taylor, P. and W. Wang. 2010. *The Fading Glory of the Television and Telephone.* Washington, DC: Pew Research Center

Thompson, D. V., R. W. Hamilton, and R. T. Rust. 2005. "Feature Fatigue: When Product Capabilities Become Too Much of a Good Thing." *Journal of Marketing Research* J431 (17): 431–442.

Tugend, A. 2008. "At a Certain Age, Simplicity Sells in High-Tech Gadgets." *New York Times*. April 12, 2008.

U.S. Census Bureau. 2009. "Internet Use in the United States: October 2009," www.census.gov/hhes/computer/publications/2009.html.

Vanderheiden, G. C. 1998. "Universal Design and Assistive Technology in Communication and Information Technologies: Alternatives or Complements?" *Assistive Technology* 10 (1): 29–36.

———. 2004. "Using Extended and Enhanced Usability (EEU) to Provide Access to Mainstream Electronic Voting Machines." *Information Technology and Disabilities* 10 (2), http://trace.wisc.edu/docs/2005-EEU-voting/.

———. 2006. "Design for People with Functional Limitations." In G. Salvendy (ed.), *Handbook of Human Factors and Ergonomics* (pp. 1,387–1,417). Hoboken, NJ: John Wiley and Sons.

Vaught, J. 2009. "In-Home Telecare Empowers Elderly." *Policy and Practice* 67 (5): 64–64.

Wagner, N., K. Hassanein, and M. Head. 2010. "Computer Use by Older Adults: A Multi-Disciplinary Review." *Computers in Human Behavior* 26: 870–882.

Wasser, S. 2005. "Universal Electronics' NevoSL WiFi-Equipped Touchscreen Remote," www.hemagazine.com/node/Universal_Electronicss_NevoSL_WiFi-equipped_touchscreen_remote.

Zafar, A. 2011. "Facebook for Centenarians: Senior Citizens Learn Social Media." *The Atlantic*, August 31, www.theatlantic.com/technology/archive/2011/08/facebook-for-centenarians-senior-citizens-learn-social-media/244357/?single_page=true.

Zumstein, K. 2006. "Niels Diffrient Has the Human Factor." *Onoffice* 2 (December): 32–38.

13

Public Transportation and Universal Design

Introduction

Public transportation plays an important role in creating an inclusive society. All passengers in a mass transportation system stand to benefit from universal design by improving resources used to plan trips and access to the system and reducing barriers and stress during trips. In fact, universal design also benefits the transportation providers by reducing workload, increasing rider self-sufficiency, reducing operating and maintenance costs, and increasing ridership. Thus, everyone shares in the investment.

A convenient, easy-to-use, safe, and effective public transportation system contributes substantially to the long-term health of a city by supporting environmental and social sustainability. Universal design of transportation benefits not only citizens of the community but also visitors. From an economic perspective, it encourages trade and tourism and can play an important role in business location decisions. In this chapter, we present ideas and real-world examples to demonstrate how universal design can be achieved simply and without the need for extraordinary capital investments if it becomes a goal that is integrated into capital projects and long-range improvement programs.

The advantages of universal design are notably evident in the design of public transportation systems. Thus, in this chapter, the last in the book, we devote a great deal of attention to details to demonstrate how all the aspects of universal design come together and benefit all citizens.

Background

Many countries have adopted policies to promote ridership in mass transport systems in order to reduce pressure on highway systems. New mass transit projects are conceived of regularly as part of showcase urban developments such as in Barcelona, Spain; Sydney, Australia; and Beijing,

China, prior to the Olympics. Rapidly expanding cities, such as Bogotá, Colombia; Ahmedabad, India; and Shanghai, China, have invested in major upgrades to public transportation systems. They seek to reduce not only congestion but also air pollution caused by overreliance on automoblies. Historically, public transportation has been a key factor in maintaining quality of life in European cities. Although the U.S. transportation market is dominated by investment in highways, in many U.S. cities, including New York City; Boston, Massachusetts; Washington, DC; and the Bay Area of northern California, public transit already plays a significant role in the overall urban transportation domain. Multimodal transportation hubs, often located at major rail terminals, and public transportation links to airports are being constructed to improve the continuity of the overall urban transportation system. Older transit lines also are being upgraded to improve service and address safety and convenience.

Both the development of completely new systems and strategic improvements in infrastructure are opportunities to introduce universal design. This chapter demonstrates how universal design can improve public transportation in a way that will serve the full range of citizens. Topics covered include the design of mass transportation terminals, vehicles, fare payment systems, and related information systems. In one chapter, there is not enough room to do justice to all the details of technology, architecture, operations, and planning that need to be addressed. Thus, we focus on some key issues and several examples of how to address the Goals of Universal Design.

Access to Public Transportation

In a mobile, global culture, full social participation hinges on accessibility of transportation systems, both at the community and the intercity scale. Transportation systems provide access to many social roles, especially employment. One of the main barriers to social participation is simply access to service. This takes three forms: lack of any public transportation in one's neighborhood, lack of ability to pay for service, and the presence of barriers that prohibit use of existing systems. In highly developed countries, one of the most underserved groups is people with disabilities. In the United States, more than half a million people with disabilities cannot leave their homes because of transportation barriers (Bureau of Transportation Statistics 2003). Even when they are able to leave their home, one-third of people with disabilities have *inadequate* access to transportation (National Organization on Disability 2004). Consequently, four times as many people with disabilities as people with no disabilities lack suitable transportation options to meet their daily mobility needs (National Council on Disability 2005).

Public transportation problems are the worst in rural areas. Even in the United States, one of the most urbanized countries in the world, approximately 20 percent of Americans, or about 60 million people, reside in rural communities ("Tackling Transportation Problems" 2000). Rural transportation infrastructure and service are often insufficient or ill equipped to meet residents' needs. The rural population has higher percentages of people living in poverty (11.8 percent), elders (13.8 percent), and people with disabilities (21.5 percent) than the population living in urban areas (Brown 2004). Approximately 7 percent of households in rural America do not have a vehicle, a percentage that rises to 45 percent for rural elderly persons and 57 percent for rural poor persons. Despite the obvious need, 38 percent of all rural residents live in areas without public transportation service (Dabson, Johnson, and Fluharty 2011). It is therefore not surprising that a lack of access to transportation is one of the most frequently cited problems for rural residents (Department for Transport 1999).

Poor transportation access limits individuals' ability to participate in community life and ultimately results in lower rates of life satisfaction. For example, according to the 2004 National Organization on Disability/Harris Survey of Community Participation, 34 percent of people with disabilities, compared to 61 percent of people without disabilities, reported feeling very satisfied with their life (National Organization on Disability 2004). A majority of those surveyed said that lack of a full social life was a reason for this dissatisfaction. For example, people with disabilities were about half as likely to have heard live music, gone to a movie, or attended a sporting event or concert over a one-year period (National Organization on Disability 2004).

The most significant barriers to transportation access can be found in low-income regions of the world, especially in rural villages, where public authorities have little ability to finance public transportation. In these locations, few people can afford their own vehicles, and most address mobility needs through walking, bicycles, motorcycles, and scooters. However, the need to reach distant services and employment still creates a demand for mass transportation services. Entrepreneurs respond through an informal service delivery system using small vans, used buses (e.g., old school buses purchased from high-income countries), many kinds of taxis, and pedicycles. In most cases, this informal system of individual operators provides limited and relatively expensive service. It can be uncomfortable and unsafe and has many barriers to people with mobility limitations, children, and elders; nevertheless, service is often more personalized and adjustable than formal public transportation systems. As development levels improve, government often seeks to regulate the informal systems in some way, including regulating vehicles to ensure availability of accessible features (Steinfeld and Seelman 2011). Informal operators can often create barriers to development of government-sponsored public transit because they fear losing income and control. Engaging such operators in the development of more effective systems and giving them a role in service delivery can increase their cooperation (Lomme 2010).

For affluent countries and regions, the two main challenges for transportation planners are to solve the "last mile problem" and get people to switch modes from driving their own cars to using mass transit. The "last mile problem" refers to the trip from origin to the entry point of a fixed route transportation system, and may actually be less than a mile in length. For people with disabilities, being able to negotiate the "last mile" is often the key to reducing reliance on special transport (or paratransit). Even in affluent communities, lack of service within convenient walking distance is a major barrier to using public transportation. Other "last mile" barriers include safety problems on pedestrian routes, like lack of sidewalks and pedestrian crossing controls, and poor security along the route and near stations. North Americans, especially, depend on private transportation more than public transportation. Other countries, such as Australia and New Zealand, also are heavily dependent on private vehicle transportation. Mode shift can reduce air pollution and congestion on highways, and it can increase ridership to a point where systems are economically sustainable and provide decent service. Although most public transit does not operate at a profit, even with high ridership levels, it is of note that governments heavily subsidizes highway construction and maintenance through taxes on gasoline and tolls. Increasing ridership through mode switch provides not only more revenue for transit operators but also greater political support for shifting public investment priorities more toward public transportation.

We may be entering a new era in public transportation due to economic conditions and disabling congestion. The American Public Transportation Association regularly releases national data on ridership in the United States. It recently revealed that Americans took 10.1 billion trips on public transportation in 2007, a 31 percent increase since 1995 (APTA 2007). The growth in the older population may increase demand further. In the United States, 62 percent of adults 50-plus have limited their daily driving due to higher gas prices (AARP 2005; Litman 2006). Driving is not a viable option for many older persons. Nearly 7 million persons 65 and older do not drive, due to either health or financial deterrents. Older adults with lower incomes are particularly affected by barriers in public transportation systems because they rely on public transportation more regularly (Houser 2005). One of seven non-drivers age 75 and older uses public transportation as his or her primary mode of transportation (Ritter, Straight, and Evans 2002).

In locations where ridership is low for public transportation, schedules and routes focus on the ride to work and do not adequately serve the places older people and other populations with special needs desire to go. Even using public transportation for the trip to work can be daunting. A recent study in the United States found that typical urban residents could reach only 30 percent of the jobs in their metropolitan area by transit within 90 minutes (Tomer et al. 2011). A common problem is a route structure that requires transfers from one route to another that extend the length of the trip and make it unpleasant or unfeasible. One rural community in the United States, Wenatchee, Washington, was faced with the decision to eliminate its public transportation system, which was losing money heavily due to low ridership. In one last try to save the system, Link Transit, the transit agency, redesigned routes to create one large loop through the community that connected all the main commercial destinations in the town. The community concentrated larger buses on this loop route. The agency purchased smaller vehicles, repurposed airport shuttles, to provide feeder service to the loop route, put only accessible buses in service, and provided accessibility at all the stops. Major businesses agreed to allow the agency to locate stops in their shopping plazas to provide more convenient access. Ridership trends have turned around and reached levels that are more viable. The agency is now planning on improving services rather than closing down (DeRock 2011).

Another approach is to improve the effectiveness of existing transportation resources. Lands Community Services, a community transportation program in Australia, provides transportation options for people underserved by conventional systems (www.lands.org.au/). The company owns some vehicles, but its main service is providing logistical support to fill the gaps in regular service. It schedules people into a variety of options, including rides by volunteer drivers, conventional bus transportation in the community, and other transport services the company operates. The objective is to match available resources with individual needs and reduce the demand on paratransit, which is the most expensive mode. As it operates several different types of vehicles, the company reduces costs by providing service with the lowest-cost option that still meets riders' needs. The company emphasizes training drivers to accommodate a wider range of riders, including people who have mental health conditions, who tend to pose significant challenges to drivers.

Components of Public Transportation Systems

To use a public transportation system effectively, riders need to search for the route to desired destinations and scheduling information; find, reach, and use stops and terminals; navigate toward the destination; and know when they have arrived at the correct destination. During the entire journey, riders need to perceive and understand information and often make decisions quickly without assistance. Most trips are related to scheduled events, such as the start of work. Riders must work within vehicle arrival and departure schedules. Transportation delays and mistakes create stress. Thus, providing support for situational awareness is a key human performance issue.

In intercity travel, there are many sources of stress, especially when a trip involves using airports. For example, stressful conditions are often encountered when obtaining boarding passes, checking baggage, clearing security, changing planes, and finding gates. These tasks usually are completed in places with high levels of noise and other sources of sensory overload. In railway and bus terminals, the check-in process is less complex but still stressful. Furthermore, destination verification—that is, knowing when one has arrived at the desired stop or station—is often more difficult, especially in crowded vehicles and when traveling in places where the native language is different from one's own. Large and fast-moving crowds and multimodal transfers present challenges, particularly for first-time or infrequent users.

Design for physical accessibility to transportation facilities is similar to accessibility design for public buildings in general. Thus, in this section, we focus only on the unique physical, perceptual, and cognitive challenges of transportation environments.

Terminals

The complexity and size of large terminals, especially airports and large multimodal stations, can create a significant physical burden on many travelers. A terminal plan with a shallow spatial syntax can reduce the physical effort expended between entry and departure or arrival gate as long as the links are not too long. The number of gates, particularly at airports, is the determining factor in travel distances within the terminal. When the number of gates requires new wings or separate satellite terminals, travel distances often become excessive. Automated transportation options, such as moving walkways and internal transit loops, are valuable features of contemporary terminals. Systems that accommodate wider ranges of passengers will require less special transport, such as people movers, carts, and transport wheelchairs. People movers and carts that share space with pedestrians complicate the terminal environment, increase the noise level, and often create safety hazards.

Most travelers understand the common spatial syntax of terminals: entry area, ticketing area, main circulation halls, departure gate areas, arrival gate areas, baggage claim (in airports), and exits. Terminal floor plans generally channel travelers through the terminals especially at security checkpoints, but in large terminals, often there are many choices to make on either side of security checkpoints. A shallow spatial syntax will reduce the number of decision points and thus reduce errors in wayfinding. This is especially important for travelers rushing to reach connecting flights.

In a treelike terminal syntax, travelers encounter a series of decision points as they proceed deeper into the building. At each point, they must make a decision on which way to go. If they make a mistake, they have to retrace their steps back down the "tree" and take another branch. In a treelike plan, changing vehicles while carrying baggage also requires a lot of effort, particularly if the arrival and departure gates are at the far ends of different branches. Although the overall system is easy to comprehend on a diagram, in actual use the plan is not as easy to comprehend due to limited visual access in the branches (Steinfeld 2001). In contrast, an "island" design has a much shallower spatial syntax. All the gates in each section are relatively close to one another and visible to travelers from a central space. Transit links, such as moving walkways, people movers, subways, or monorails, can connect the islands. Connecting terminals in a multi-building complex where security is available at each terminal with public transit connections to the regional transportation system help to reduce the depth of the spatial syntax and reduces the number of transfer points and bottlenecks.

Information for Orientation

All travelers need good information in terminals for general orientation; to find the locations of gates, platforms, stations and stops; to know where and when specific vehicles are arriving or departing; and to find amenities, such as restrooms and food services. Information needs in public transit are extensive, including route maps, fares, and schedules. This information is often voluminous and complex with many subtle variations that, if not perceived or understood, can cause transit patrons to miss connections or wind up on the wrong vehicle. Late-breaking news on schedule changes, pages, and other time-sensitive announcements often are provided. The ability to use all these information resources effectively is critical for travelers.

The two most common sources of information in terminals are you-are-here maps and staffed information desks. Neither is truly a universal design solution. The maps exclude people with visual impairments, and the latter exclude those who cannot speak the local languages. Thus, both information sources make some groups dependent on other people for personal assistance in using these buildings, unless they are extremely familiar with the environment. A ferry terminal in New York City successfully deployed a "talking kiosk." It provides both visual and audible information on the terminal building as well as schedule information (Figure 13–1). The multisensory interactive models described in Chapter 12 can extend the functions of the talking kiosk to provide tactile representations as well and more intuitive search processes.

Information is needed in terminals to identify and direct people to key locations, such as ticketing counters, security checkpoints, information services, amenities, and gates. Static visual signs typically provide this information. Key design criteria for visual signs include:

- Fonts large enough to be seen at the distance where people first encounter them
- High contrast between text and background
- Distinctive color for signs in contrast to the general terminal color scheme
- Overhead location (the most visible position)

Dynamic signs using electronic displays are replacing static signs in all types of terminals because they provide more useful and specific information than a simple static gate number. These signs provide information on routes served, destinations, and scheduled departures and arrivals. They can also provide estimated time of arrivals. Dynamic displays should be protected from glare, have a resolution that is high enough for the distance from which they are viewed, and be free from color distortion and flickering. They should present new information at a rate within the abilities of people with sensory and cognitive limitations to perceive and process. These issues must be investigated during building design because unexpected ambient conditions can make it difficult, if not impossible, to read electronic displays. In buildings with a lot of natural light, designers must anticipate daily, seasonal, and weather-related variations in light quantity and quality.

In public buildings, accessibility codes in the United States and some other countries require that signs identifying rooms and spaces must be both tactile and visual. However, in transportation terminals, the effectiveness of tactile signs for identification is questionable. Not

Figure 13–1: Information kiosk at a New York City ferry terminal. This kiosk provides information by both visual and audible means.

Source: Photograph courtesy of Steve Landau

only would such signs be difficult to find in large congested spaces, but searching for them would pose significant risk at boarding platforms. Use of internationally recognized ideograms for signs to identify important features or amenities—for example, restrooms, exits, and information—is a major aid to the travelers who cannot read the local languages; they also reduce the amount of information that needs to be displayed by condensing words into symbols, thereby simplifying displays and making them more legible. Tactile guide paths are useful for helping people with visual impairments find important destinations (Christophersen 2002). These devices can be designed to benefit all travelers. They should be limited to providing guides to key destinations, such as platforms and restrooms. Too many guide strips can become very confusing, and discriminating among many types of tactile codes used for different destinations may be extremely difficult if not impractical, especially within the busy environment of a transportation terminal.

Ideally, a Global Positioning System (GPS) orientation and wayfinding system could provide assistance in navigation through terminals, using both audible instructions and visual displays. However, GPS does not work indoors and is not accurate enough to find gates or even boarding areas in terminals. Relying on GPS systems near a boarding platform could be disastrous due to this lack of accuracy. Remote Infrared Audible Signs (RIAS) or "Talking Signs®" are useful technologies that overcome these problems (Crandall et al. 1999; Golledge, Marston, and

Costanzo 1998). These devices include transmitters at destinations that send out an infrared (IR) signal and receivers, which individuals hold to scan for the device location. If users deviate from the path, they lose the signal. As users get closer to the destination, the RIAS can provide more detail to guide them very precisely. The conceptual model used in the device is much simpler than a GPS navigation system. It is like a homing beacon where the signal gets stronger as one gets closer, providing continuous feedback to help stay on the route. However, in crowds, it may be difficult for the device to pick up IR signals, which depends on line of sight, unless they are spaced close together and the ceiling is high enough to afford good coverage of the approaching paths. The most important limitations of RIAS are that special receivers are needed to use them, each signal must be hardwired and maintained, and RIAS does not provide dynamic information, such as that provided on LCD (liquid crystal display) panels unless they are connected to a database and can be updated remotely. Other accessible technologies now under development in research labs will provide navigation assistance indoors.

System-wide Information

Four types of information are needed when using transportation systems:

1. Orientation information, such as system maps and schedules
2. Navigation information, such as instructions, route maps, and fare payment options
3. Information on the status of the system at any one time, such as elevator breakdowns or construction projects
4. Destination information, such as station signs and notification of one's stop

Different riders need different levels of content. First-time users of a system need more information of every type, and someone with a cognitive impairment may need more destination information than other people need. The information needs must be addressed in the right place. For example, before riders leave, they need to know some general information about the system. When on a crowded bus or train, they need to know the relative location of the desired stop.

In transportation environments, particularly those that serve foreign visitors, signs and other information should be provided in more than one language. This practice acknowledges that tourists and business travelers from other countries are using public transportation. It also helps to create a positive emotional response for visitors because of the feeling of security that comes from understanding basic information about a place. In large and complex transportation terminals, information clerks can provide personalized information on gates and schedules. Where the small size of a terminal does not justify clerks, or at times when it is not cost effective to have clerks present, telephone hotlines with direct connections to a central information service or automated systems are a good alternative. Some subway systems have free telephones that provide schedule information at each transit station. The Japan Tourist Office offers a toll free hotline in foreign languages that is available 24/7 from any location in Japan. Another option is an automated information kiosk. All these approaches can provide very useful assistance for all travelers but particularly people with visual impairments who cannot use conventional or dynamic signs.

The traditional form of information provided for navigation is a route map and schedule. This information is often hard to understand and use. It may be effective for regular riders, but often it is confusing for infrequent riders. For example, due to the need to make maps easier to use and carry, map content is often condensed by providing information only on key stops. In some systems, operating policies can become very complex. For example, New York City has express and local trains. The express trains stop infrequently, but riders on an express train need to know where to get off and transfer to reach a station served only by local trains. To make things more complex, some stops may not be served on Sundays and others are served only during rush hours. Fare policies can complicate decision making. In some systems, two stops only a few blocks apart may have radically different fares from certain destinations. Thus, creative graphic design is required for maps and schedules with an emphasis on helping riders perceive important information and understand the route and schedule complexities with minimum difficulty. A key problem with printed information is the difficulty disseminating short-term disruptions in service or changes in schedules.

The Internet and smart phones have radically changed the way transit information can be provided. In particular, the old static forms of information are no longer the most important. Many transit agencies now provide interactive maps. Transit information is also available from major map resources on the Internet, such as Google Maps and MapQuest. For some cities, these sources also have scheduling and estimated arrival time information. The most desirable type of information also includes information from transit agencies on construction projects, elevator breakdowns, scheduling changes, and the like. Such information may be available only through the agency's own sites. The websites of transit agencies, such as the Bay Area Rapid Transport (BART) in the San Francisco Bay Area in California and the Washington (DC) Metropolitan Transit Agency (WMTA) provide trip planners that address unusual events and even suggest alternative routes. However, ultimately, this information should be available through smart phones wherever riders are located.

Notification applications for smart phones are now available that provide information on the estimated arrival times at terminals and local stops throughout a transportation system. Some even provide notification of current service limitations. Other key sources of information are public address announcements, message boards, and other electronic displays. These systems often create barriers for people with sensory impairments. For example, public address systems and electronic displays in the same location do not always provide the same late-breaking information. People with hearing impairments may miss information broadcast by public address systems, such as reasons for delays and track or gate changes. This is a particular problem when people are using restrooms and waiting at gates in airports where flight information is not made available in both visual and auditory modes. In many contemporary systems, access to scheduling and route information by smart phones may be available, but it is difficult and frustrating to use, often requiring much searching and waiting for screens to refresh to get the information desired.

Digital technologies have enhanced in-vehicle information and increased the availability of information on estimated arrival times at stops. New systems provide information on upcoming stops prior to arrival on an electronic display board mounted at the front of the passenger compartment, as well as through audible announcements. These systems can utilize GPS technology to ensure that the right message will be broadcast. If all vehicles are equipped with GPS technology and the transit system provides access to the data on vehicle location, real-time information on expected arrival time at a stop can be obtained through the Internet or smart phones while waiting at stations or even at homes or offices. Third-party apps like Google Maps utilize this data to deliver this information to the user. A promising new approach to providing real-time data is a crowdsourcing application called Tiramisu developed by the Robotics Institute at Carnegie Mellon University (Steinfeld et al. 2011). This system does not require vehicles to have GPS installed or for an agency to provide access to GPS databases, eliminating any cost to the transit operator. Riders or drivers with the Tiramisu app on their smart phones continuously send information, including their real-time location and the available seats on a bus to a server, from which other Tiramisu users can obtain up to date scheduling information. If someone using Tiramisu is on a particular bus, other users waiting for a bus on that route can get real time data on time to arrival and seats available. If there is nobody with the app on a bus, but the trip has been recorded several times in the past, predicted arrival time is based on a historical estimate. And, if neither is available, they get data on scheduled arrival times (www.tiramisutransit.com/). Tiramisu even allows users to report problems they encounter and communicate them to other riders or the transit agency via a public website. This creates accountability for the agency to address problems. Tiramisu has been developed with accessibility built in so that it is usable by people with a wide range of disabilities.

Real-time captioning of announcements at gates, platforms, and bus stops is a less advanced technology and still one that is not yet implemented in terminals, except in isolated places. The disadvantage of real-time captioning in terminals, compared to texting or other broadcasts to riders, is that it does not reach individuals who are out of sight of the information when it is needed (e.g., in the restroom).

Vehicle Loading

Level changes are difficult for many passengers to negotiate, but they are often necessary in large terminals to efficiently process arriving and departing passengers and their baggage, especially where rail lines pass over or under one another. At local stops, they are necessary to reach elevated and underground lines and at stops where passengers must cross rail lines to reach the other side. As in any multilevel structure, elevators, ramps, and stairs are used to accommodate level changes Where there are no boarding platforms, getting from grade level to a vehicle is the most significant access problem for people with mobility limitations, including those who can walk but have limited strength, limited range of motion in lower extremities, or low stamina. Other passengers who are using wheeled mobility devices, such as people pushing strollers, shopping carts, or luggage, and parents with small children, encounter similar barriers. People who have visual impairments are at risk due to inherent safety issues with level changes.

No adult who is capable of independent function in a transportation system should be forced to rely on assistance to negotiate changes in level. Barriers to people with mobility impairments result in inconvenience, embarrassment, anger, and exposure to injury by poorly trained attendants (Kawauchi 1999). When people who have mobility impairments must use an entirely different circulation path from other travelers, they often expose themselves to security risks and encounter delays, in addition to the social segregation that results. In new construction, providing convenient access to vehicles should be a primary consideration in the early stages of building design, in order to reduce the need for duplicate elevators or ramps (Steinfeld 2010). From the perspective of management, universal design reduces the need for special training, reduces occupational injuries related to lifting, and improves productivity because workers do not have to leave their posts as often to assist individual travelers.

Accommodating level changes to board and exit a vehicle is one of the most difficult issues in universal design of transportation systems. Three basic strategies can be implemented: raise the level of the boarding platform, lower the floor level of the vehicle, and equip the vehicle with a mechanical device to overcome the vertical gap. Any of these methods can be used together or separately. Another design issue for vehicle loading is reducing accidents to passengers, especially people with visual impairments. For both accessibility and safety, the use of standardized approaches throughout a system eliminates surprises for travelers. Standardization significantly benefits people with visual impairments.

Rail Systems

Loading platforms for rail lines should be at the same level as the vehicle floor. For engineering reasons, there must be a horizontal gap between the rail cars and loading platform. The gap is necessary to accommodate the lateral tolerances of rolling stock, including differences in the width of vehicles that operate on the same line. This gap should be as small as possible to keep the front wheels of wheelchairs, walking aids, and people from falling into the gap. The horizontal gap can trap the front casters of wheelchairs and can be hazardous for users of walking aids and people with visual impairments (Kanbayashi 1999).

There are several approaches to reducing or eliminating the horizontal gap. A bridge plate, a small plate that extends over the gap, can be used to overcome small horizontal differences. Bridge plates can be manual or automatic. Automatic systems are clearly desirable, but in rapid transit, bridge plates have to deploy very quickly and be extremely reliable to avoid lengthening boarding times, and there is a risk of injury during vehicle loading and unloading, especially at peak travel times. Fixed thermoplastic "gap reducers" can be attached to vehicles or to the edge of a platform to reduce the gap. Reducers of different widths can be used to accommodate trains with several different widths running on the same track. Platform installation is used for bus systems. In these applications, resilient materials are used to cushion the impact of a bus as it docks at the platform. Gap reducers on train cars do not eliminate the gap entirely because there must be some tolerance to allow for vehicle sway.

In existing systems where there may be inconsistencies in platform heights, vehicles will have to be fitted with lifts or small ramps. Small ramps are preferable since all passengers can use them, and they take less time to deploy than lifts. Where there are great differences in platform heights on an existing line, lifts may be needed because ramps would be either too long to fit on the platforms or too steep to negotiate. In new systems, it is critical that platforms at stations be level and straight to keep the vertical and horizontal gaps uniform at every door.

One major obstacle to ensuring continuity in the travel chain in rail transport is the need to coordinate across different companies. In Europe, where crossing international borders is common, a high level of coordination is required to ensure compatibility of systems (Steinfeld 2001).

Street-Level Transit

Many systems, especially local transit and shuttle buses, but also streetcars and many light rail cars, usually unload on streets. Several technologies are available to reduce or compensate for the level change between vehicle and street/walkway surface: a "kneeling suspension," a "low-floor" vehicle, the folding or telescoping ramp, and the platform lift. The "kneeling suspension" is essentially a hydraulic feature built into the suspension system that brings the floor level closer to the ground when activated. A "low-floor" vehicle has a lower floor level than conventional vehicles and often is equipped with a kneeling suspension as well. Together, these two features eliminate all but one step up. Such vehicles reduce the difficulty of entering and exiting significantly for everyone. A folding or telescoping ramp added to a low-floor vehicle eliminates all steps. These three features together help children, parents with children, older people, and people with limitations in mobility. They also help people with visual impairments because the lack of stairs reduces the complexity of entering and exiting a strange vehicle. A wide doorway and handholds add additional levels of convenience. All these features reduce "dwell time," the time at which a vehicle will be at rest. Dwell time is a critical variable in transit operations. Small reductions in dwell time, aggregated across thousands of stops, can save operators millions of dollars.

Even with the kneeling feature and low floor, ramps can be quite steep when deployed to the street surface. U.S. regulations currently allow a 1:4 maximum slope, which is much too steep, but there are ramps available that can reduce that to 1:6. Debate about the safety of ramps' slopes is taking place and research is under way on this topic at the IDeA Center (D'Souza et al. 2010; Steinfeld, D'Souza, and Maisel 2010). Preliminary results indicate that even a 1:6 slope is not safe. The current state-of the-art technology can achieve a 1:8 slope to a sidewalk curb or slightly raised waiting pad, which is preferable to boarding from the road. Thus, perhaps more effort should be invested in making curb deployment possible and increasing the availability of pads in places where there are no sidewalks. The width of the vehicle is a major limitation to reducing the slope of ramps because width limits how long a ramp can be stowed in the vehicle with current technologies.

Other than platform boarding level with the vehicle floor, the only viable solution to the level change problem in high-floor vehicles is the wheelchair lift. Lifts can be installed at the front or rear doors. One type, the "telescoping" lift, slides out from under the bus floor. Another is integrated into the stairs of a bus and folds out when needed. Intercity and commuting buses designed for high-speed travel are very high off the ground. To make these accessible, a "cartridge lift" usually is installed in the baggage compartment. It telescopes out from the compartment when in operation. It is important to note that, as designed today, lifts benefit wheelchair users only, and they have four negative characteristics:

1. A long operation cycle that adds to "dwell time"
2. Higher maintenance cost
3. More frequent breakdowns
4. The need to load and unload wheelchair users separately, usually after other passengers

The extra time required for loading or unloading someone with the lift and the spectacle created while other passengers watch is particularly important from a social participation perspective because it reinforces the stigma associated with disability. With a low-floor vehicle equipped with an automated ramp or bridge plate, however, all passengers enter the same way when the device is deployed. No one becomes a spectacle, and deployment is thus faster. Where a ramp can be extended onto a raised sidewalk or pad, there is even greater convenience for all passengers.

Low-floor buses have become the standard in most urban bus systems. However, they also have some limitations. Lowering the floor level reduces the clearance between wheel wells, which makes entry and exit at the front difficult for wheelchair users. The sloping surface of the ramp can make it difficult for wheelchair users to pay their fare at the front of a bus. The wheel wells in a low floor bus take up more space and thus reduce capacity. The high-floor bus, by contrast, has more seats for the same length and better maneuverability where topography is steep. Combined with platform loading, it can be a good choice for high-capacity express bus routes. With a lift, the high-floor bus may be a good solution for rural areas and other routes where drivers may only need to deploy the lift infrequently.

Platform Boarding

In high-capacity urban transportation systems and intercity train transportation, eliminating all stairs is a good universal design solution because it significantly increases the speed of boarding and disembarking. A no-step system can be created by designing stations with graded or ramped entries and boarding platforms that are level with vehicle floors. This strategy not only benefits the operator by reducing dwell times, but it also benefits all riders by increasing safety and convenience and improving service response. High enough platforms can also improve security since entries to stations and platforms can be controlled easily when there are few of them. Although rail systems traditionally have used platform loading, bus systems can also benefit from the use of this strategy.

Some transit systems use mini-platforms instead of full platforms to provide access to light rail and commuter rail systems. Mini-platforms have a small raised platform level with the vehicle floor and are equipped with a ramp or lift. However, to keep platform length to a minimum, the platform serves only one car in a train. This approach, while less expensive, is not effective because if one car is full, people who cannot walk stairs have to wait for the next train or the operator has to reposition the train for access to another car. Doing this may not be feasible in some stations and certainly is time consuming. Moreover, the operator has to dock the train so the car door lines up precisely at the platform; unless the train is automated, this is not easy to do.

In Curitiba, Brazil, all express bus terminals and stops are raised off the ground and are accessible by ramp or lift as well as stairs (See Example). High-floor buses and raised platforms reduce the need for negotiating level changes. The stations and terminals all have accessible entries. Once riders enter a station, they stay at the higher level and never have to use stairs or any other vertical circulation until they leave the system. All vehicles are loaded with great ease from the platform. Bridge plates automatically extend from the buses when they dock at terminals to eliminate the gap.

The major safety concern at loading platforms is avoiding falls, especially for people with visual impairments. Several methods can protect people from falling. A full-height barrier with sliding doors is by far the safest strategy. A major constraint of this system is that the vehicle has to stop so that its doors are precisely lined up with the doors in the barrier when the train or bus stops at the platform. Partial-height barriers with gates have also been used. A major disadvantage of partial-height barriers is that they do not reduce noise as much as the full-height type. Barrier systems require complex control systems. Trains need to be computer controlled to stop precisely in the right place and when train length (number of cars) may vary over the course of a week or a day, the control system must ensure that the doors beyond the end of the shorter trains remain closed.

In lieu of barriers, multisensory warnings can heighten awareness of the platform edge. They can include lights embedded in the platform edge combined with tactile warnings on floor surfaces. Flashing warning signals and audio announcements provide advance notification that vehicles are about to arrive at the platform. Platform edges can be marked with a contrasting color and change in texture. Transit authorities have used many different textures, including rough concrete or stone and applied resilient plastic materials.

A tactile warning is a textured surface that contrasts enough with its background to provide reliable detection by people with visual impairments and their guide dogs. Laboratory research has demonstrated that tactile warnings with a distinctive pattern of small domes, truncated to provide a flat surface on the top, can be detectable to visually impaired travelers and are not barriers to people who have mobility impairments (Bentzen et al. 1994, Hauger et al. 1996). However, research has not been conducted to determine if these tactile warnings work effectively in actual transportation environments where there are large crowds and they may be approached at an angle rather than from a true perpendicular direction. The research has been limited to controlled studies that focused on detectability of the signals without distraction rather than on discrimination of the signals in real-world conditions, where the signal to noise ratio is likely to be lower (Steinfeld and Richmond 1999).

Some professionals question the relative reliability and safety of contemporary tactile warning signals) (Richmond and Steinfeld 1999; Steinfeld 2001). The textures may have to be very obtrusive to work with a high degree of reliability. However, exaggerated textures could cause tripping hazards for pedestrians. An important consideration in utilizing tactile tiles is to ensure that people with visual impairments can distinguish between an edge warning and a guide path. Guide paths on platforms should keep travelers away from the dangerous part of platforms, but they can be confused with tactile warnings at platform edges and put people at risk when they believe that the tactile warning is the guide path. Kanbayashi (1999) points out that tactile guide paths on a busy platform are not very useful as a navigation aid because people and luggage on the platform create obstacles to their use. He also reports that people with visual impairments still fall onto the tracks despite the presence of these tiles at platform edges. Another related problem is that trains have gaps between cars that appear, to users of white mobility canes, to be vehicle entries. Thus, clarifying the edge of the platform is not sufficient. The location of vehicle entries needs to be identified as well. One accident in Washington, DC, where tactile warnings were employed, was captured on video and distributed on YouTube; the graphic video demonstrates that protecting people from falls on open platforms is a problem that may not yet be solved (Weir 2009).

Figure 13–2 shows a guide strip on a subway platform in Barcelona, Spain. The traveler following the path is kept away from the platform edge. By keeping the path separate from the edge strip, the nonvisual traveler maintains a safe distance from the edge. Another tactile strip marks the edge of the platform. The path also acts as an affordance for the visual traveler, helping to reinforce safe use of the platform. The photos in Figure 13–3 show a subway platform in the Washington, DC, Metro system. It has an edge of gray granite with embedded lighting units along its entire length. The lenses of the fixtures are flush with the granite surface. When a train is about to arrive, the lights flash red. Set back from the granite is a strip of truncated domes. This strip is a dark red color to provide contrast with the granite and the main platform surface of red tiles. The strip was installed years after the original station was built. A color that was easy to discriminate from pavement backgrounds like yellow was not desirable due to the aesthetic impact. There are questions about the effectiveness of truncated domes, but, the combination of domes, flashing lights, and granite edge, should certainly provide greater safety than one system alone.

Figure 13–4 shows a full-height glazed enclosure with automated sliding doors in a monorail station serving JFK International Airport in New York City. Not only do such barriers protect people with visual impairments, but they also protect the general population from being pushed off the platform when there are large crowds, and they prevent people from committing suicide by jumping in front of a train. Although automated docking of vehicles makes this design feature feasible, all trains must be equipped with automated control systems. The trains are computer controlled and stop with their doors in front of the barrier doors. The monorail link to the airport

Figure 13-2: Multisensory guide path. This guide path in the Barcelona, Spain, subway is constructed from directional tactile tiles set into the platform surface.
Source: Photograph courtesy of Daniel Bishop

is a self-contained system using a radically different technology from the rest of the New York City transit system. One reason a monorail system was adopted was to reduce the visual impact of the new line in the residential community through which it passes. To fit with the existing station where the monorail connects to other transit lines required a complicated transfer at the station but, the monorail has greatly improved access to JFK.

Figure 13-3: Enhanced warning strip. This warning strip in the Washington, DC, subway includes truncated domes but also has flashing lights that provide an additional level of awareness. (a) View of strip along platform edge. (b) Close-up view of domes and lights with train at platform.

Figure 13-4: Full-height glazed platform barriers. Barriers like the ones installed at the JFK International Airport (NY) monorail are being used by many new systems to further increase platform safety.

In older systems, protective barriers may not be feasible without renovations to all stations on a line and new or renovated trains, which is not always possible. For example, a new line is being constructed in New York City. The transit agency wants existing trains to be compatible with all stations in the system to provide flexibility in deployment of rolling stock. In addition, when trains vary in length, as they do in New York, the system must be "smart" enough to know which doors should be open and which should be left closed for any train. This introduces increased costs and potential for error that, without a history of performance, could be a major limitation to the use of barriers on the platform in a system as busy and complicated as New York's. So the transit system decided not to include protective barriers on the new line.

Access to Airplanes and Boats

Since most airports in major cities have direct ramp access to large airplanes, access to large aircraft is not a major problem today. However, access to smaller planes, which often are boarded from the ground, is still problematic. Mobile ramps and scissor lifts are used in some airports to assist people who cannot manage stairs in boarding and disembarking. Such systems are awkward and difficult to deploy, especially in bad weather. Since the smaller planes are becoming more common to serve hub-and-spoke routes, airports are building enclosed boarding ramps for smaller planes to overcome these problems and generally to make trips more convenient and comfortable. Wherever boarding takes place from the ground, elevators are needed at the gates unless the gates serving the smaller planes are at ground level.

Providing access to ferries designed to carry automobiles and trucks is relatively easy to accomplish since the automobiles need an accessible entry also. However, if the passenger-seating compartment is on a different level from the automobile garage area, the boat must have an

Figure 13-5: Dock and ramp system. This floating dock and ramp system provides access to boat decks of different heights and accommodates tides.

elevator to provide full access. Boarding for passenger ferries and sightseeing boats from docks can be provided with ramp systems. Two factors complicate the design of ramps serving boats:

1. Many docks serve several different kinds of boats with different entry conditions and deck levels.
2. Tidal action results in the need to have an adjustable system that accommodates differences in the water height (Steinfeld 2001).

Floating docks with ramps are the most widely used approach to solve these problems. The bottom ramp landing is supported by the floating dock that moves up and down as the tides change. The ramp is hinged at the top and rolls free on the floating dock to accommodate level changes. More than one landing and ramp may be needed to serve multiple decks and accommodate wide differences in the sizes of the boats.

In Boston, Massachusetts, a set of floating docks connects to ramps that provide access to different types of boats (Figure 13–5). A hinged ramp provides access to the lowest landing. The landing floats and the wheels at the bottom allow the ramp slide along it to accommodate differences in water level due to tides. The length of the ramp is based on the lowest expected water level. Another ramp connects to a high landing, which is used to board upper decks of a boat or boats with higher decks than can be served by the lower ramp. The floating dock also supports the high landing so that it too adjusts to the tide.

Vehicle Design

Transportation systems use many kinds of vehicles. These include smaller vehicles for use in on-demand service, such as special transport vans and taxis to carry individuals with severe disabilities who cannot use fixed route transportation, to serve destinations fixed route transit does not reach, and to transport people from their home to a fixed route system. However, it is important to note that special transport serves people with cognitive impairments and mental health conditions who often do not need wheelchair-accessible vehicles. To reduce the cost of special transport and to supplement transit service, some localities require a taxi fleet to have some accessible vehicles. Others are requiring greater accessibility in each fleet. In Sweden, taxis are used for paratransit as well as regular on-demand service. Taxis can be made accessible with such features as wider and higher doors, hand grips to aid transfer in and out, increased legroom, telescoping ramps, and swivel seats (Short 1999). Some cities are moving toward fully accessible taxi fleets. London is a pioneering city in the provision of accessible taxis. It is estimated that almost 50 percent of the fleet is now accessible (Steinfeld and Seelman 2010).

One of the gaps in the provision of accessibility in transportation is shuttle bus service, such as those that connect hotels with air terminals. The use of low-floor buses for shuttle service is increasing, improving comfort and convenience for all riders. Low-floor buses even reduce the need for drivers to help passengers load luggage, but many shuttle buses are not yet equipped with ramps or lifts.

One of the most difficult design challenges in transportation is making the interiors of vehicles accessible and safe for wheelchair users. People using wheelchairs need an accessible path of travel from the entry to the wheelchair seating area. The aisles in buses, trains, and airplanes with forward-facing rows of seats are not wide enough for wheelchair access. Wider aisles in buses and trains can be provided in two ways: Perimeter or longitudinal seating can be used, or some of the seats near the entry doors can be removed. Both strategies also provide more space for standing passengers during rush hours, thus increasing overall system capacity. The extra space can also be used for luggage, bicycles, strollers, and large packages (Nelson\Nygaard Consulting Associates 2008). Another approach is to provide convertible seats that can be folded up against the wall when a person who uses a wheelchair needs the space.

It is important to note that wheelchair users are not the only passengers who need accommodations while in the passenger compartment. Frail older people, people with disabilities who do not use wheelchairs, pregnant women, and others who need to sit should have access to priority seating. This seating should be near a door of the vehicle and well marked.

Too much space can be a problem for other passengers. For example, in Curitiba, Brazil (see Example below), express buses have very few seats in order to maximize capacity during rush hours. The interiors are very convenient for wheelchair access but present problems for older riders and others if the limited priority seating for people with disabilities and elders is fully occupied. More convertible seating would provide a solution.

Safety in Transit

Securement systems prevent injury to both the wheelchair users and other passengers if a vehicle has to make an emergency stop. Train mass is so large that deceleration forces are not as great as in airplanes and buses. Thus, no securement systems are required on rail systems, as they are on buses. Tie-down devices are required on buses in the United States, but securing passengers with these systems requires considerable effort and time on the part of drivers, who often do not secure passengers properly. Passengers often refuse to be secured for comfort reasons or because they do not want to take the time. Research on wheelchair transportation safety demonstrates that many wheelchairs cannot withstand the structural load during a crash (Karg et al. 2009).

In other countries, wheelchair securement on buses is provided in three-sided compartments in which riders face backward. There are no tie-downs, and riders can access the securement area on their own. Reports from people who use wheelchairs, however, indicate that other passengers often stand in securement areas. Research and development activities are underway to develop devices to provide more effective securement. It is a difficult problem since there are so many different types of wheelchairs. Some question why wheelchairs must be secured while strollers, bicycles, shopping carts, and other large objects are not. Securement of wheelchairs represents just one of the many issues that present challenges for the universal design of safety systems.

The most difficult problem of wheelchair seating is on airplanes. A wheelchair that is a safe seating system for airplane travel probably would be unsuitable for regular use due to the structural forces that need to be resisted to provide crash protection on an airplane. Thus, wheelchair users need to be transferred out of their chairs and the chairs stowed for transport in the baggage compartment. Currently, airlines provide wheelchair access at least to the entry of the plane or the entry to the rampway; from there, passengers are then assisted to their seats in "transport" or "boarding" chairs." These are small chairs with seats that are narrow enough to fit between the aisles on a plane and that require an attendant to operate. The passenger must be belted in for safety. Many wheelchair users and their advocates consider the current strategies to be demeaning, dangerous, and fraught with inconvenience and difficulty for passengers. It makes passengers completely dependent on the airline staff. It is important that airlines carry these chairs in the aircraft so that people who cannot walk can be assisted to the lavatory en route (now a requirement in the United States). Many people who use wheelchairs complain that their chairs are often damaged during airline trips. Clearly, innovative design solutions are needed to address the problem of traveling with a wheelchair. The problem will become a more serious as the population ages.

Onboard Toilet Facilities

Access to toilet facilities has been successfully accommodated in many long-distance transportation systems. To conserve space, toilet facilities on vehicles can be designed so that turning a wheelchair around inside the toilet compartment is not necessary as long as the individual can back in or enter forward, reach all the fixtures and equipment, and open and close the door. The most difficult problem in using such a system is closing and locking the door to obtain privacy. An automated door and lock can solve this problem and is not cost prohibitive on an expensive vehicle. Larger airplanes are now providing toilet compartments that support wheelchair access. In smaller planes, toilet compartments can be designed to allow assisted transfers from the aisle to the toilet before the door is closed. This method requires curtains in the aisle to provide adequate privacy.

Ticketing and Fare Payment

Some transit systems offer the incentive of free access to people with disabilities who qualify for special transport services. These services typically are designed to provide door-to-door service for people who have difficulty using fixed-route systems. These services must be scheduled ahead of time and are very expensive for the transit agency. Thus, operators often require that riders pay the regular transit fare, reserve a ride at least a day before travel, and prove that they cannot use the fixed-route service through a qualifying process. Providing free fares on fixed-route services is an effective way to reduce demand for special transport service. Universal design improves the success of these incentive programs because improving usability and safety beyond minimal accessibility supports a wider range of disabilities and people with more severe disabilities than minimum code compliance does.

Ticketing and fare payment can be complex and difficult tasks for all riders, especially for first-time or infrequent users. People who have visual or cognitive impairments or those who speak a language that is not supported by the provider can have significant difficulty with these tasks. Each system usually has unique local policies and procedures and even methods of fare payment. Additional complications are caused when different service providers operate within the same metropolitan area. For example, a rider might take a commuter rail line into a city from a suburb but then have to take a bus to a destination. If the two lines are operated by different companies, each may require different tickets and use different fare payment procedures. Ticket prices may vary based on the length of the trip and time of day and are sometimes difficult to determine without prior experience with the system. When riders must purchase a ticket or token and then use it in a fare gate, they must use two different machines and sometimes wait in two queues, doubling the level of effort and time required to access the system. All these potential factors may be in play at the same time. Thus, designing business practices to reduce unnecessary complexity could be a very valuable contribution to the usability of transit systems.

There are several other causes of complexity related to ticketing and fare payment. Many systems require some type of eligibility check for reduced fares due to disability or aging. This determination of eligibility may involve making a special trip to obtain approval before utilizing the reduced fare programs. Screening methods that can be accomplished remotely or at any station could eliminate this burden. For example, in some locations, local businesses can sell transit passes; they can verify age or disability before selling reduced fare tickets. A related problem is a complex structure of reduced fares where many different groups have different rates. Consolidating all fare reduction programs into one rate can reduce the complexity of buying tickets. In systems where the cost of a ride is related to distance traveled, integrating destinations in the ticket purchase task can not only eliminate this problem for riders but also make it easier to purchase the right ticket. Reducing the number of payments needed is another way to reduce the complexity and stress of using transportation systems. In particular, coordination among local providers to accept one ticket reduces rider stress, delays, and administrative burden. Universal design clearly can help to reduce the stress and increase convenience for all riders by simplifying business practices. This is a good example of how universal design extends beyond the design of equipment and buildings to policies and procedures as well.

Strong affordances and intuitive methods of operation can be utilized in fare machines and ticketing gates. In particular, the steps for using these machines can be conveyed without complicated instructions and with illustrations to overcome language and literacy limitations. By guiding riders through a logical decision-making process, the machines can reduce errors, time delays, and confusion. To be usable by people with visual impairments, fare and ticketing machines should be standardized in design and include tactile or audible cues to their operation. Simplifying the task of purchasing tickets is a key to usability for everyone. Reducing the number of machines that need to be used is another good strategy. For example, rather than having a change machine, the ticketing machine can provide change. Smart cards are now used widely in transit systems. They make it possible to reduce to a minimum the number of times users actually have to pay and simplify the task of using a fare gate to a simply wave of the card. Smart cards also make it easier to use the same card for many different operators in a metropolitan area. Some systems can read smart cards that are in the pocket of the traveler.

Paying fares at the fare gate with credit or debit cards can simplify payment even more because doing so eliminates the need to buy a smart card. Charge cards or debit cards can be used to get access and even can be used in systems where distance traveled or time elapsed determines the fare. Such systems are already available for parking garages. Another new technology application is the use of smart phones for payment using wireless protocols or radiofrequency identification (RFID) tag readers in the phone. Phone-based systems are already in widespread use for purchasing tickets in Asia. These strategies eliminate the need for low-income people to spend the minimum sum often required to purchase a smart card, but they are not usable by people who are not eligible for credit or do not use banks that issue debit cards. Thus, the option of conventional tickets or payment in cash may be still necessary to provide an inclusive approach. In bus and streetcar systems, paying for tickets outside the vehicle is another way to reduce stress and complexity. Fare machines located at stops can be larger than on the bus and thus can be designed to accept many different types of payment. The user gets a paper receipt that they show the driver, eliminating the dwell time devoted to paying fares.

Turnstiles are impossible to negotiate with a wheelchair, a baby carriage, or baggage. They generally have been replaced by more usable systems, such as retracting or hinged gates. The use of alternate gates that must be operated and supervised by station staff increases the difficulty of providing accessibility. Many systems have only one accessible gate among many. The fare gate in Figure 13–6 was designed to be wider to accommodate wheeled mobility users. Similar fare gates next to the accessible gate are narrower. All the fare gates have smart card readers and accept individual tickets. The gate panels open like swinging doors when the fare is paid. The accessible gate has the International Symbol of Access (ISA) on the fare gate panels as well as near the ticket

Figure 13–6: Fare gates in a transit system. The wider "accessible" fare gate proved very popular with all riders.

slot. The panels also have the words "Reduced Fare," meaning that people who are entitled to reduced fares have to use that gate. The transit system installed these gates through a system-wide upgrade at great cost. However, the accessible fare gates broke down more than twice as much as other fare gates. An investigation discovered that they were used twice as often, but they were engineered to support 50 percent less traffic than the regular gates since the designers believed that fewer people would use them. These gates proved to be much more popular than the narrower gates. The extra width and "Reduced Fare" sign evidently attracted riders to these gates. Problems like this can be avoided if all gates are accessible and all accept reduced fare tickets.

Example: Curitiba's Integrated Transportation System

Curitiba, Brazil, a rapidly growing city, has a worldwide reputation for its accessible urban transit system (Figures 13-7a, 13-7b, 13-7c, 13-7d). Starting in the mid 1960s, the city planned and implemented a modern system that was designed from the ground up to replace a system of many poorly coordinated private bus lines. Today Curitiba has a population of 3.2 million and the transit system serves 2.3 million riders a day. By comparison, the London Tube serves 2.9 million passengers daily. The operation of the system is self sufficient; it has never had any public subsidy (International Transport Forum 2011). A main planning goal was to provide public transportation that would be so effective that citizens would find little need for private transportation, thereby creating more concentrated growth, protecting the environment, and reducing congestion and urban sprawl in the future. This goal has been realized spectacularly.

The system was designed to provide full accessibility for people with disabilities, but in addition, the planners perceived similar benefits for elderly persons, children, and others with limitations in mobility and improved efficiency for the general population. The design combined low implementation cost with a high level of performance and accessibility for all. The components of the system include express "busways" with dedicated rights-of-way on radial routes into the city core (BRT), conventional local bus routes that join each other or the busways at key terminals, interline connector buses that circumnavigate the city, and paratransit vans for door-to-terminal service for those who require it.

All transportation terminals and stops are fully accessible. There are three basic types: the first is an on-grade local terminal where transferring passengers cross from one loading area to another at grade. Buses with lifts provide accessibility at these terminals. The second type is the multimodal terminal where local buses deliver passengers to the stops on the express busway system. The third is the "tube station" at smaller intermediate stops along the busway. Sometimes tubes are linked together to construct larger stations at heavily used destinations. Busway vehicles are large "bus-trains," consisting of two- to three-unit articulated buses carrying 250 people each.

The bus-trains load and unload directly to raised platforms. This allows safe and rapid movement of passengers as well as full accessibility, as in a subway. All express bus terminals and stops have ramps and/or lifts. The tube stations are constructed of large prefabricated plastic and steel tubes with lifts at one end. By clever planning of circulation, transfers take place entirely within the secure areas of terminals, avoiding the necessity of multiple fare collections and transfer tickets at mode changes.

The planning, design, and construction of the system and rolling stock were coordinated by a new agency, Urbanização de Curitiba (URBS), set up for this purpose. This agency centralized purchasing and coordinated standards so that all the pieces of the system would work together. However, management of each district of the system is contracted to the existing private bus lines, which also purchase the vehicles. Private individuals operate "parataxi" vans. Originally they were designed specifically to provide people with disabilities home-to-station access, but experience demonstrated that there were not enough customers among the population of people with disabilities to maintain such a system on fares alone. These vehicles are now available for all riders as a taxi service.

Figure 13–7: Bus rapid transit system. The city of Curitiba, Brazil, integrated universal design goals throughout its transit system. (a) Accessible entry to the station. (b) View of station and platforms. (c) View of station with bus loading passengers. (d) People exiting the bus to the station platform.

Terminals and tube stations were constructed of low-cost prefabricated systems. The small size of the prefabricated structural components reduced construction costs significantly by allowing fabrication without expensive equipment and hand labor that is inexpensive in Brazil. The rolling stock was designed and bid out to specifications that included accessibility features and environmentally conscious power systems. Volvo, the winning bidder, established a production facility in Curitiba and invested their own money in the R&D. The company is now a major employer in the city, exporting buses to other Latin American cities. A surface bus system was chosen because it reduced the cost of developing a modern mass transit system significantly and provided, using the BRT concept, the same capacity as a fixed rail system.

The system is a good example of universal design. It provides a high level of access, especially for a bus system. The tube stations and platform loading create great convenience for all riders. A surface system is generally more pleasant to ride than a subway and facilitates wayfinding. Moreover, the integrated system of local routes, interline routes, and express routes with a single fare purchase provides a seamless experience with great convenience.

The vehicles for each type of line are color-coded, which makes understanding the type of service provided at each stop easy, even for riders who do not read. Moreover, the protection of platform edges on the express lines by the tube station design removes the safety hazard for visually impaired travelers. As of this author's visit in 1994, all the route information provided was in visual mode; thus, users with visual impairments did not have full access to information about the routes. Not all the express stations used the tube station construction, thus platform edge protection was not provided everywhere. Moreover, all stations had a human fare collector so that automation of fare collection was not an issue. Curitiba is an excellent model for developing economies and anywhere urbanizing areas are seeking to improve their mass transportation systems without investing in a fixed rail system (Steinfeld 2001).

Progress around the World

Access to public transportation varies greatly around the world. Western Europe has some of the best examples of accessible public transportation, but serious problems remain in the region, especially in Eastern Europe (International Disability Rights Monitor 2007). One primary problem is the lack of effective policies that address the needs of seniors and people with disabilities. In London, studies revealed that only 10 percent of trains and 29 percent of buses met access standards (Kuneida and Roberts 2006). Even where laws exist, there is limited compliance, especially in the developing world, where a regulatory framework and funding are rarely put into place to implement legislation (Kuneida and Roberts 2006; Roberts and Babinard 2005). Because the benefits of universal design features are not well understood, many policy initiatives that could benefit all riders as well as transit system performance are not incorporated; for example, raised boarding platforms that reduce the need for stairs to access buses and reduce overall boarding times for all riders (Roberts and Babinard 2005).

Unlike in urbanized and developed countries, low-income countries have very limited levels of accessibility in public transportation. The International Disability Rights Monitor (2004) reports that, in the Americas, only 20 percent of the countries in a survey had an accessible bus transportation system, although the United States and Canada reported accessible systems in all cities. Many transit providers, particularly in developing countries, have implemented accessibility only partially, providing a limited number of vehicles equipped with lifts or ramps on each route, improving only key stations, or providing access only on new lines. While a laudable start, these efforts are not sufficient. To utilize a transportation system effectively, people need to have access to all vehicles and the full service area as well as the pedestrian environment (Iwarsson, Jensen, and Ståhl 2000). Strategic planning is needed to establish a long-range planning process for improving accessibility throughout a system, including the pedestrian access to systems.

In new construction projects, the use of bus rapid transit (BRT) is a major trend globally and especially in developing countries of Latin America and Asia because the first cost is much lower than subways and elevated railways and these systems can be built much faster. A BRT system (Curitiba's express bus system was the first) is a high-capacity bus system with limited stops. Local routes feed riders to BRT stations and terminals. In high-level BRT systems, large articulated buses run on dedicated busways with a limited number of stops. To gain the most advantage in speed and capacity, raised platforms are used to load large numbers of riders quickly to avoid the increased dwell times caused by using ramps or lifts. In low-level systems, BRT buses run in mixed traffic roads and load to curbs or slightly raised pads (curb height). Low-floor buses with ramps can be used to provide access in these systems. In mixed-traffic roads, BRT can run on dedicated lanes, but it also can share lanes with other traffic. In the latter case, electronic systems can allow BRT vehicles to have priority at signaled intersections so that the traffic signals are always green when a BRT vehicle approaches. Besides Curitiba, notable accessible BRT systems have been constructed in Bogotá, Colombia; Quito, Equador; Ahmedabad, India; Shanghai, China; Brisbane, Australia; Calgary, Canada; and Los Angeles, California, in the United States.

Summary

Universal design in transportation systems is emerging as an important means to increase convenience and safety, attributes that improve utilization of public transportation. Universal design strategies are being adopted in bus and rail transit operations all over the world because they improve the quality of transit for all riders and can help encourage mode shift from automobiles to public transit (Burkhardt 2007; Wrestrand, Danielson, and Wretstrand 2007). They are also being used in taxi and other "on-demand" systems to solve the "last mile problem."

Although many of the lessons learned in the general design of accessible buildings are applicable to transportation terminals, stations, and stops, there are many unique concerns for access to vehicles, design of rolling stock, and access to information that require different treatment. For example, current mandatory accessibility standards do not provide much guidance on improvement of information services and fare systems, and selection of vehicles. Moreover, they mandate only minimum levels of access. A large transit system should be implementing strategies to constantly improve service, attract riders from special service transport to fixed-route service, and in particular, encourage mode shift from private vehicles to public transit. This will support a sustainable system that has long-term benefits to the community and public.

The most important universal design innovation in transit is the low-floor transit vehicle, which is now available on heavy rail, light rail, streetcars, and buses. These vehicles provide almost-level access from platforms and short-ramp access from curbs and street levels, although technological improvements to reduce the slope and improve safety of ramps are still needed. Other examples include electronic signs with real-time information on waiting times and equipment breakdowns, smart cards and pre-boarding fare payment for simplified and more convenient fare collection, and full-height safety barriers along platforms. Strategies for improving information resources include RIAS signs to help people with visual impairments find gates and identify buses and Internet/smart phone access to real-time information on accessible route selection, elevator breakdowns, route closures, and other temporary conditions that affect access.

The use of evidence-based practice in accessible transportation is limited, partly because there is little funding for research in this field. Yet the cost of not implementing universal design in transportation is potentially huge. If people with disabilities cannot use existing fixed-route systems, they will have to rely on special transport, and, as the population ages, the burden of this service will become unsustainable. Not implementing universal design today will have even more serious economic consequences 30 years from now. The knowledge of human performance and social participation issues in accessible transportation is still quite limited, but research on accessible transportation has identified accessibility problems with overall system design, the design of vehicles, information systems, and business practices. Key areas that need research attention include securement in buses, safety of boarding and unloading, protecting platform edges in existing systems, solving the information needs of people with sensory impairments, the last mile problem, and accessibility in the interior of vehicles.

It is very important that design practitioners, operating agencies, and researchers communicate more effectively to identify priorities for research and engage diverse user groups in the identification of barriers and solutions. In particular, since most research has focused on the needs of wheeled mobility users and people with visual impairments, it is important to discover the priorities of other groups. It is also important to identify best practices and to document the benefits of universal design. The value of including universal design features in transportation systems will be increased if research can demonstrate their widespread value to all travelers (Steinfeld 2001). For example, do low-floor buses benefit all other travelers as much as they benefit people with mobility impairments? Do they help to improve attitudes toward public transportation? If universal design strategies have such extended benefits, their value is far higher than simply meeting laws and regulations. Such research findings could be used to strengthen the business case for universal design. The impact of introducing universal design in Curitiba on a citywide basis is one example. There are other examples of good accessible systems, and many newer ones that have features that improve on some of the features in Curitiba. Nevertheless, the full integration of accessibility clearly made the system more desirable for all riders and has helped the city avoid the congestion and pollution seen by other rapidly growing cities that have not invested in making public transportation usable, safe, and convenient for all.

Review Topics

1. How have the Internet and smart phones radically changed the way transit information can be provided?
2. Accommodating level changes to board and exit a vehicle is one of the most difficult issues in universal design of transportation systems. Describe three basic strategies that can be implemented to overcome the vertical gap.
3. Describe how and why the Curitiba BRT is a good example of universal design.

References

AARP. 2005. "High Gas Prices Cause 50+ to Modify Lifestyle." Washington, DC: AARP Public Policy Institute.

American Public Transportation Association. 2007, December 4. "Public Transportation Ridership Continues to Grow: Nearly 50 Million More Trips Taken in Third Quarter 2007." Press release, www.apta.com/mediacenter/pressreleases/2007/Pages/071204_ridership.aspx.

Bentzen, B. L., T. L. Nolin, R. D. Easton, L. Desmarais, and P. A. Mitchell. 1994, September. "Detectable Warning Surfaces: Detectability by Individuals with Visual Impairments, and Safety and Negotiability for Individuals with Physical Impairments." Final Report DOT-VNTSC-FTA-94–4 and FTA-MA-06–0201–94–2. Washington, DC: U. S. Department of Transportation, Federal Transit Administration, Volpe National Transportation Systems Center, and Project ACTION, National Easter Seal Society.

Brown, D. 2004. *Public Transportation on the Move in Rural America*. http://www.nal.usda.gov/ric/ricpubs/publictrans.htm.

Bureau of Transportation Statistics. 2003. "Transportation Difficulties Keep over Half a Million Disabled at Home." *BTS Issue Brief* (3), www.bts.gov/publications/special_reports_and_issue_briefs/issue_briefs/number_03/pdf/entire.pdf.

Burkhardt, J. E. (2007). "High Quality Transportation Services for Seniors." Paper presented at the 11th International Conference on Mobility and Transport for Elderly and Disabled Persons, June 18–21, 2007, Montreal, Quebec.

Christophersen, J. (ed.). 2002. *Universal Design: 17 Ways of Thinking and Teaching*. Oslo, Norway: Husbanken.

Crandall, W., J. Brabyn, B. L. Bentzen, and L. Myers. 1999. "Remote Infrared Signage Evaluation for Transit Stations and Intersections." *Journal of Rehabilitation Research and Development* 36 (4): 341–55.

D'Souza, C., E. Steinfeld, V. Paquet, and D. Feathers. 2010. "Space Requirements for Wheeled Mobility Devices in Public Transportation: An Analysis of Clear Floor Space Requirements." Paper presented at the 89th Annual Meeting of the Transportation Research Board, January 10–14, 2010, Washington, DC.

Dabson, B., T. G. Johnson, C. W. Fluharty. 2011. "Rethinking Federal Investments in Rural Transportation: Rural Considerations Regarding Reauthorization of the Surface Transportation Act." A Rural Policy Research Brief, www.rupri.org/Forms/RUPRI_Transportation_April2011.pdf.

Department for Transport. 1999. "Low Floor Bus Trials in a Rural Area." http://webarchive.nationalarchives.gov.uk/+/http://www.dft.gov.uk/transportforyou/access/buses/pubs/research/lfbt/.

DeRock, R. A. 2011. "Cost-Effective Accessibility Improvements in Small Urban and Rural Environment." Paper presented at the Transportation Research Board, January 23–27, 2011, Washington, DC.

Golledge, R. G., J. R. Marston, and C. M. Costanzo. 1998. "Assistive Devices and Services for the Disabled: Auditory Signage and the Accessible City for Blind or Vision Impaired Travelers." Working Paper UCB-ITS-PWP-98-18. Berkeley: PATH Program, Institute for Transportation Studies, University of California, Berkeley.

Hauger, J., J. Rigby, M., Safewright, and W. McAuley. 1996. "Detectable Warning Surfaces at Curb Ramps." *Journal of Visual Impairments and Blindness* 90: 512–525.

Houser, A. 2005. *Community Mobility Options: The Older Person's Interest*. Washington, DC: AARP Public Policy Institute.

International Disability Rights Monitor. 2004. *IDRM: Regional Report of the Americas 2004*. Chicago: Center for International Rehabilitation.

International Disability Rights Monitor. 2007. *IDRM: Regional Report of Europe 2007.* Chicago: Center for International Rehabilitation.

International Transport Forum. 2011. "Listen to the Feedback." *Mobile* Issue 01.

Iwarsson, S., G. Jensen, and A. Ståhl. 2000. "Travel Chain Enabler: Development of a Pilot Instrument for Assessment of Urban Public Bus Transport Accessibility." *Technology and Disability* 12 (1): 3–12.

Kanbayashi, A. 1999. "Accessibility for the Disabled." *Japan Railway and Transport Review* (20): 22–24.

Karg, P., M. E. Buning, G. Bertocci, S. Fuhrman, D. Hobson, M. Manary, L. Schneider, and L. van Roosmalen. 2009. "State of the Science Workshop on Wheelchair Safety," *Assistive Technology* 21(3): 115–60.

Kawauchi, Y. 1999. "Railway Stations and the Right to Equality." *Japan Railway and Transport Review* (20).

Kuneida, M. and P. Roberts. 2006. *Inclusive Access and Mobility in Developing Countries.* Washington, DC: World Bank.

Litman, T. 2006. *Responses to "A Desire Named Streetcar."* Vancouver, BC: Victoria Transport Policy Institute.

Lomme, R. 2010. "Reforming Public Transport by Integrating Small and Informal Operators." Paper presented at the Sub-Saharan Africa Transport Policy (SSATP) Annual Meeting, Lilongwe, Malwai, October 20–23, 2009.

National Council on Disability. 2005. *The Current State of Transportation for People with dIsabilities in the United States.* Washington, DC: National Council on Disability.

National Organization on Disability. 2004. "N.O.D./Harris Survey of Americans with Disabilities," http://nod.org/what_we_do/research/surveys/harris/.

Nelson\Nygaard Consulting Associates. 2008. "Status Report on the Use of Wheelchairs and Other Mobility Devices on Public and Private Transportation." Washington, DC: Easter Seals Project ACTION, http://projectaction.easterseals.com/site/DocServer/Wheelchair.pdf?docID=71783.

Norman, D. 2002. *The Design of Everyday Things.* New York: Basic Books.

Ritter, A., A. Straight, and E. Evans. 2002. *Understanding Senior Transportation.* Washington, DC: AARP Public Policy Institute.

Roberts, P. and J. Babinard. 2005. *Transport Strategy to Improve Accessibility in Developing Countries.* Washington, DC: World Bank.

Short, J. 1999. "Transport Accessibility." *Japan Railway and Transport Review* (20): 4–8.

Steinfeld, A., J. Zimmerman, A. Tomasic, A. Yoo, and R. Aziz. 2011. "Mobile Transit Rider Information via Universal Design and Crowdsourcing." Paper presented at the Transportation Research Board 2011 Annual Meeting, January 23–27, 2011,Washington, DC.

Steinfeld, E. 2001. "Universal Design in Mass Transportation." In W. Preiser and E. Ostroff (eds.), *Universal Design Handbook,* pp. 23–25. New York: McGraw-Hill.

———. 2010. "Advancing Universal Design." In J. Maisel (ed.), *The State of the Science in Universal Design: Emerging Research and Developments,* pp. 1–19Y. Oak Park, IL: Bentham Sciences Publishers.

Steinfeld, E., C. D'Souza, and J. Maisel. 2010. "Clear Floor Space for Contemporary Wheeled Mobility Users." Paper presented at the 12th International Conference on Mobility and Transport for Elderly and Disabled Persons, June 2–4, 2010, Hong Kong.

Steinfeld, E. and G. Richmond. 1999. "Detection and Discrimination of Tactile Warning Signals in Field Conditions." In E. Steinfeld and G. S. Danford (eds.), *Enabling Environments: Measuring the Impact of Environment on Disability and Rehabilitation,* pp. 233–250. New York: Kluwer Science/Plenum.

Steinfeld, E., and K. Seelman. 2011. "Enabling Environments." In *World Report on Disability.* Geneva: World Health Organization.

"Tackling Transportation Problems in Rural America, New Technologies Address Needs of Smaller Cities and Towns." 2000. *Nation's Cities Weekly* 23 (5), www.highbeam.com/doc/1G1-63715357.html.

Tomer, A., E. Kneebone, R. Puentes, and A. Berube. 2011. *Missed Opportunity: Transit and Jobs in Metropolitan America*. Washington, DC: Brookings Institution.

Weir, K. 2009, Dec. 29. "Blind Man Falls onto Metro Tracks, Isn't the First to Slip." *Washington Examiner.* http://washingtonexaminer.com/local/blind-man-falls-metro-tracks-isn039t-first-slip.

Wrestrand, A., H. Danielson, and K. Wretstrand. 2007. "Integrated Organization of Public Transportation: Accessible Systems for All Passengers." Paper presented at the International Conference on Mobility and Transport for Elderly and Disabled Persons, June 18–21, 2007, Montreal, Quebec.

Wright, L. 2004. *Planning Guide: Bus Rapid Transit*. Eschborn, Germany: Deutsche Gesellschaft fur Technische Zusammernarbeit (GTZ).

Index

Note: Page numbers in *italics* indicate figures, illustrations, photos, and tables.

A
A117.1 (ICC/ANSI), 227
AARP, 265
abandonment, product design and, 311–312
Abledata.org, 309
abused people, limitations of, 52
"Accessibility for All" (Norway), 81
accessible design
   access to resources, 167–172, *168, 169, 171*
   communication about, 73
   Enabler concept, 50, *50*
   history of, 187, 192–195
   purpose of, 188–190
   universal design *vs.*, 23, 68, *69*
   See also public accommodation
acoustics
   hearing loss and, 279–281, 309–310, *310*, 315–316, 321
   interior design, 279–281
   perception of, 110, 116, 117–118
   product design, 309–310, *310*
   social participation and, 165–166
Active Symbol of Accessibility (ISA), 15, *16*
active transportation, 143–145, *144*

activities of daily living (ADL)
   defined, 248
   simplifying, 249
   See also home modification
ADA Accessibility Guidelines (ADAAG) (U.S. Access Board), 192
adaptable housing, 227–229, *229*
aesthetic expression, 30–31
affordances, 120–123, *121*, 126–127
African Americans. *See* race
Age Gain Now Empathy System (AGNES) (AgeLab, Massachusetts Institute of Technology), 313, *313*, 319
aging
   ageism, 61
   Aging, Demographics, and Memory Study (ADAMS), 149–150
   aging in place, 38, *38*
   demographics and, 46, 53, 54–55, 58–60
   Enabler concept, 50, *50*
   housing policy and, 224
   lifespan housing design, 232–235, *235*
   lighting and vision, 282–283
   product design and marketability, 316–321, *317, 318, 319, 321*
   public transportation and, 342

369

aging (*continued*)
  social participation and, 162, 166
  social participation and elder cohousing, 178
  target populations for home modification, 246–247 (*See also* home modification)
  See also demographics; interior design
airplanes, access to, 354–355
airports, 210, *210,* 343–344, 351–352
air quality, 146, 151
Alliance for Biking and Walking, 143
American Community Survey (2007–2008), 61
American Institute of Architects, 35
American Journal of Health Promotion, 139
American National Standards Institute (ANSI), 190–192, 227, 230
American Public Transportation Association, 341–342
Americans with Disabilities Act (1990), 27, 191–192, 211, 227, 318–319
anthropometry
  accommodation for average users, 101–102
  break with precedent, 102–103
  for choice, 100–101, *101*
  defined, 95, 96–99
  for extremes, 99–100
  furnishings and, 292
  key dimensions, *99*
Apple
  iPhone, 322–323, *323,* 331–332
  Stores, 130–132, *131*
Archea, J., 124
architects, career development of, 48
Architectura, De (Vitruvius), 30
Architectural and Transportation Barriers Compliance Board (U.S. Access Board), 191–192
Architectural Barriers Act (1968), 27
architecture. *See* design; housing; interior design; public transportation; streetscape design
ARPANET, 310
art, barriers and, 4–6, *5, 6*
artificial light, 283–284
assessments, home, 261–263
assistive technology (AT), 308, 310–316, *313, 315*
asthma, 146
athletic equipment, 308
"at risk" populations, 51
Austin (Texas), visitable housing in, 231, *232*
Australia
  home modification, 265–266
  housing, 233
  public accommodation, 204, *204*
  public transportation, 342
  universal design practice, 81
automobiles
  car safety and demographics, 55
  dependency on, 34
  housing and neighborhood context, 239
  product design, 326–327, *327*
  truck drivers and anthropometry, 98
  See also streetscape design; transportation
ax, evolution of, 1–3, *2*

B
Baby Boomers, 45–46, *47,* 58–60. *See also* aging
"back-door access," 17, *18*
back injuries, 104
balance, 108
bamboo flooring, 301
Barcelona (Spain), public transportation, 352, *353*
barriers, 1–25
  demographics and, 59
  design as evolution, 1–3, *2*
  to home modification, 263–265
  increasing adoption and, 70
  in intellectual life, 4–8, *5, 6*
  origins of universal design, 15–24, *16, 17, 18, 19, 20, 22, 23*
  perception and, 109–110
  social function of space, 8–12, *9*
  sociospatial order, *12,* 12–14, *14*
  as universal experience, 3–4
bathrooms. *See* restrooms
Bay Area Rapid Transport (BART) (San Francisco, California), 347
beds, 297–298, *298*
behavior setting, 124
Bell, Alexander Graham, 309
benchmarking, 82, 88
Bentham, Jeremy, *14*
best practices, identifying, 85–86. *See also* universal design practices
bicycling
  active transportation, 143–145, *144*
  demographics and, 60
biomechanics
  balance, 108
  defined, 95, 103–105
  energy expenditure, 107
  lifting effort, 107–108
  movement reduction, 105–106, *106*
boats, access to, 354–355

body shape/stature
　body fit, 96–99 (*See also* anthropometry)
　limitation and, 51
　target populations for home modification, 247 (*See also* home modification)
Boston, public transportation, 355
Brawley, Elizabeth, 285
"breaking down barriers," 13–14
business practices, public accommodation, 211–212, *212*. *See also individual names of businesses*
bus rapid transit (BRT), 363
busways, 360, *361*

C

cabinetry
　human factors and ergonomics (HFE), 108, 120
　interior design, 295–297, *297*
　modification to, 260 (*See also* home modification; housing)
Canada Mortgage and Housing Corporation, 266
canes, 315–316
capacity building, need for, 252–254
career development, demography and, 48
caregivers
　demographics of, 59
　health and wellness of, 150
　home modification and, 249
　limitation of, 51
Carnegie Mellon University, 205, *206*, 347–348
carpet, 299–300
Castle, The (Kafka), 7
Center for Building Technology (CBT), National Bureau of Standards, 35
Center for Inclusive Design and Environmental Access, 314
Centers for Disease Control and Prevention (CDC), 61, 147, 247
Centraal Museum (Utrecht, Netherlands), 216–219, *218*
Cerf, Vincent, 310
certification programs, 86–87
"character," 30–31
Chase, Clyde, 12–13
Chase, Marion, 12–13
Chemical Sensitivity Foundation, 151
Chicago (Illinois), visitable housing in, 234–235, *235*
children
　health and wellness of, 143–145, *144*, 146, 151
　housing policy and, 224
　lavatory sink design for, 71
　obesity rates of, 55
　product design for, 308–309
　social participation and human rights, 159
Cincinnati (Ohio) airport, 210, *210*
Civil Rights Act of 1964, 15
class action lawsuits, 193–194
ClearRX (Target Corporation), 320, *321*
click wheels, 123
closed captioning, 309
closure, law of, 113, *113*
clustering, 172–176, *173, 174*
coding, 128–129
cognition
　affordances, 120–123, *121*, 126–127
　cognitive load, 120
　conceptual models, 120–123, *122*, 127
　defined, 96, 119–120
　emotional response, 124–126, 129
　mental maps, 121–122, 128–129
cohort, defined, 47
cohousing movement, 35, 177–181, *178, 179*
color
　cognition and, 126
　color rendering index (CRI), 287, 290, *291*
　color vision deficiency (CVD), 291–292
　interior design and, 287–292, *288, 289, 291, 292*
community-based rehabilitation housing, 236–238
Community Building (Roskilde, Denmark), *178*
Community Design Center movement, 34
community gardens, 146
community residence concept, 176
community-supported agriculture (CSA), 145–146
companion restrooms, 21, 209–210, *210*
Complete Streets, 144–145
Comprehensive Assessment and Solution Process for Aging Residents (CASPAR), 262, *263*
computers, product design and, 319–320, 323–324, *324*
conceptual models, 120–123, *122*, 127
Concrete Change, 230
Connell, B. R., 72, 87–88, 89, 149
"conspicuous consumption," 31
consumer demand. *See* demographics; home modification; product design
continuity, law of, 113, *113*
Convention on the Rights of People with Disabilities (UN), 159–160, 167
Conventions on Human Rights (UN), 159–160
Cooper Hewitt Design Museum (New York), 76

Corbusier, Le, 32, 34
cork flooring, 301, *302*
Correlated Color Temperature (CCT) chart, 290, *291*
Coughlin, Joseph E., 319
crime
   crime scene tape, 4
   Panopticon and, 13, *14*
cubicle farms, 4
cultural factors
   demographics and, 52, 55–56
   designing for wellness guidelines, 153
   social participation and, 163–167
   See also economic factors; gender equity; race
Curitiba (Brazil), public transportation, 351, 360–362, *361*

D
Danford, G. S., 81, 189
daylighting, 284–285
DEAFNET, 310
de Chirico, Giorgio, 5, *6*
Deer Hunter, The (film), 312
deinstitutionalization, 175–176
Delf University (Netherlands), 17, *18*
dementia, 149–150, 226
de Mestral, Georges, 308
demographics, 45–65
   aging as example of, 58–60
   basic approaches to using, 60–62
   beneficiaries of universal design, 49–58, *50*, *52*, *53*, *54*, *55*, *57*
   demography for universal design, 45–48, *47*
   use of, in design, 48–49
   See also individual names of demographic groups
Denmark
   public accommodation, 207–208, *208*
   public transportation, 21, *22*
   social participation, 177–181, *178*, *179*
dependence, architecture of, 21
depression, 150
depth, spatial organization and, 172, *173*, *174*
Design for All Foundation (Europe), 23, 28-29, 214
deuteranopia, 291–292
Die Hard (films), 7–8
Diffrient, Niels, 329
digital sound synthesizers, 309
disability
   demographics and, 46, *52*, 52–53, 54–55
   disability rights movement, 15
   disablement, 137–138

disasters, health and wellness in, 150–151
disease prevention, 142–147, *144*, 151–152
disposable income, demographics and, 46–47, *47*. *See also* economic factors
distance, barriers and, 10
doors/doorways
   as barriers, 4, 8
   door handles, as affordances, 120–121, *121*, 126–127
   home modification, 257–258
   public accommodation, 189, 200, *202*, 202–204, *203*
   See also ramps
Doro PhoneEasy, 317, *318*
dryers, 100, *101*
Duncan, J. S., 162
Duracell, 321
dwell time, 350

E
Easter Seals Society, 36, 190, 191
ecological psychology, 124
economic factors
   affordability and designing for wellness guidelines, 152
   demographics and, 46–47, 59, 60
   health and wellness in low-resource settings, 147–149 (*See also* health and wellness)
   home modification, 264
   income as barrier, 11, 20
   product design, 311
   public accommodation, 195–197, *196*
   public transportation, 340–342
   social participation and design participation, 177–181, *178*, *179*
education
   about universal design, 48, 74–75
   acoustics in schools, 281
   social participation and, 170
Educational Facilities Laboratory, Ford Foundation, 35
Education for All Handicapped Children Act (1975), 308–309
Eileen Fisher Store (New York City), 200, *202*
elevators, residential, 258–259
emergencies
   cognition and, 124–125
   housing for, 148
Emotional Design, 125–126, 129
employee workstations, 102–103

EmporialLife, 317, *318*
Enabler concept, 50, *50*
energy expenditure, reducing, 107
entryways. *See* doors/doorways
EN V (General Motors, Segway), 326–327, *327*
Environmental Design Research Association (EDRA), 35
ergonomics. *See* human factors and ergonomics (HFE)
Erickson Retirement Living, 304
Europe. *See individual countries; individual names of countries*
Everson Museum (Syracuse, New York), 17, *17*
evidence-based design, designing for wellness guidelines, 153
exclusion, architecture of, 21
exercise, active transportation and, 143–145, *144*. *See also* health and wellness
exhibitions, about universal design, 76–78
Extended Home Living Services, 263
extreme events, limitation and, 52
eyeglasses, 308

F
Fair Housing Act
   Accessibility Guidelines (FHAAG), 228
   Amendments (1988), 27, 72, 246
   home modification, 245, 246
falls, reducing, 108, 249, 299, 351–354, *353, 354*. *See also* home modification; public transportation
familiarity, mental health and, 149–150
family restrooms, 21, 209–210, *210*
Fange, A., 262
Farber, Sam, 78–79, 328
fare payment, public transportation, 357–360, *359*
faucets
   as conceptual model, 122, *122*
   home modification for, 260
Federal Housing Administration (FHA), 223
figure-ground relationship, 111
figure-ground reversal, 124–125
film, barriers and, 7–8
Fiskars, 84, *84*, 128
Flag of Towns and Cities for All Program, 214
FlexHousing (Canada), 266
floor coverings, 299–302, *302*
fluorescent light, 284
Fokus Society (Sweden), 227
Food and Agriculture Organization (United Nations), 145
food deserts, 145
food security, 145–146
food stamps, 145
force, applying, 107
Ford Foundation, 35
"form follows function," 31
Freedom Chair (Humanscale), 329–331, *330*
full-height glazed enclosures, 352–353, *354*
functional proximity, 167–172, *168, 169, 171*
furnishings
   interior design, 292–298, *294, 295, 297, 298*
   social participation and sensory access, 165
future demand, predicting, 48

G
"gap reducers," 349
Gates Building, Carnegie Mellon University, 205, *206*
gender equity
   barriers and, 13
   demographics of, 59
   social participation and human rights, 159
   social participation and privacy, 170
   See also social participation
General Accounting Office, 190
General Electric
   Real Life Design (GE Appliances), 82
   Real Life Kitchen, 76–77
General Motors, 326–327, *327*
German Allergy and Asthma Association, 300
Germany, home modification policy, 266
Gerontological Society, 35
Gestalt Laws, 111–117, *112, 113, 114, 115*
Gitlin, L. N., 263, 269
glare, reducing, 286, *289*
Global Positioning System (GPS), 123–124, 307, 345
Global Universal Design Commission, Inc. (GUDC), 177, 213
Goals of Universal Design
   about, 90, *90*
   human factors and ergonomics (HFE), 95, 100, 102
   product design case studies and, 327, 329, 330–332, 333–334
   on social participation, 162–163
grab bars, 247, *251*, 260
Green Building Council, 189–190

Green House® Project, 176
gripping ability, 105, 107, 126–127
grouping, 111, *112*
Guggenheim Museum (New York City), *23*, 23–24
guidelines, designing for wellness, 152–153
Guterson, David, 6–7

H
Hall, E. T., 164–165
Hall, P., 28, 29
Hall of Remembrance, U.S. Holocaust Memorial Museum (Washington, DC), 18–20, *19*, 194
halogen light, 284
handicap parking permits, 21
handles, as affordances, 120–121, *121*, 126–127
Hanson, J., *171*, 171–172, *173*, *174*
Harrenstein, Ken, 310
Harrison, Marc, 295
health and wellness, 137–158
　defined, 139
　designing for wellness guidelines, 152–153
　disablement and, 137–138
　disease prevention, 142–147, *144*, 151–152
　health impact assessments, 152
　indoor air quality, 151
　injury protection, 140–142, *142*
　in low-resource settings, 147–149
　in major disasters, 150–151
　Maslow's Hierarchy of Needs, *138*, 138–139
　mental health, 149–150
　multiple chemical sensitivity (MCS), 151
　water-related diseases, 151–152
healthcare
　evidence-based design, 36–37, *37*
　healthcare-associated infections (HAIs), 147
　product design for, *325*, 325–326
health impact assessments, 152
health promotion, 39, *39*
hearing
　aids, 315–316, 321
　loss, 279–281, 309–310, *310*
　See also acoustics
Herman Miller Aeron Chair, *83*, 83–84
heterogeneity, of population, 53–54, *54*
Hettler, Bill, 139
Hierarchy of Needs (Maslow), *138*, 138–139
high-intensity discharge (HID) light, 283–284
Hiller, B., *171*, 171–172, *173*, *174*
Hippo Water Roller, *40*
Hispanic population, demographics and, 62

historic black colleges and universities (HBCU), 75–76
home automation, 260–261, *324*, *324*
Home Environmental Assessment Protocol (HEAP), 262, *263*
homelessness, 40, *40*
home modification, 245–273
　barriers to service delivery, 263–265
　common needs and solutions, 253–261, *254*, *255*, *256*, *257*
　defined, 248
　goals for, 248–250
　home assessments, 261–263
　knowledge needs, 268–269
　need for, 245–246
　policy, 265–268, *267*, *268*
　target populations of, 246–247
　universal design through home improvement, 250–253, *251*, *252*, *253*
　See also housing
Home Modification and Maintenance Services (Australia), 265–266
hotlines, for public transportation, 346
housing, 223–244
　adaptable housing, 227–229, *229*
　adoption of universal design practices and, 72
　barriers to, 11
　community-based rehabilitation and special-purpose housing, 236–238
　demographics and, 60
　health and wellness, in emergencies, 148
　human-centered design, 34–36
　lifespan design, 232–235, *235*
　as mass-marketed product, 33
　neighborhood context, 238–241, *242*
　practicing universal design and, 77–78, *78*, *81*
　residential location and limitation, 52
　set-aside approach, 223–227, *225*
　social housing, 34
　social participation and, 167–172, *168*, *169*, *171*, *175*, 177–181, *178*, *179*
　visitability, 229–232, *232*
　See also home modification; interior design
Housing Enabler (HE), 262–263
hue, 290
human factors and ergonomics (HFE), 35, 95–136
　anthropometry, 95, 96–103, *99*, *101*
　biomechanics, 95, 103–108, *106*
　cognition, 96, 119–129, *121*, *122*

perception, 96, 108–119, *112, 113, 114, 115, 118*
stairways as integrative approach, 130–132, *131*
See also interior design
human rights, 159–160, 167. *See also* social participation
Humanscale, 329–331, *330*
Hunter, S., 86

I
IDeA Center
  housing and, 234
  product design, 314, *315*
  public transportation, 350
  universal design practices, 75–76, 81, 86–87
identity behavior, 10–12
IKEA, 211–212, *212*
Illuminating Engineering Society of North America (IESNA), 282, 286
illusion, color and, *287*, 287–288
Imrie, R., 28, 29
incandescent light, 283–284
inclined stair platform lift, 258
Inclusive Design Guidelines (City of New York), 81
inclusive design (United Kingdom), 23, 29
Independent Living Movement, 18
India, public accommodation, 195–197, *196*
indoor air quality, 151
industrialization, 32
information systems, for public transportation, 344–348, *345*
information technology, product design and, 318–319
injury protection, 140–142, *142*
innovation diffusion, 67–70, *69, 74,* 82. *See also* universal design practices
Institute of Human Centered Design, 75
institutional life, barriers and, 17–18
instrumental activities of daily living (IADL), 248
integration, 82–87
intellectual life barriers, 4–8, *5, 6*
Interactive Touch Model (Touch Graphics), 332–334, *333*
interior design, 275–306
  acoustics, 279–281
  anthropometry for, 98
  biomechanics for, 104–108
  case studies, 303, *303,* 304
  cognition and, 127
  color, 287–292, *288, 289, 291, 292*
  floor coverings, 299–302, *302*
  furnishings, 292–298, *294, 295, 297, 298*
  importance of, 275
  lighting, 282–287
  public accommodation and building codes, 188–190 (*See also* public accommodation)
  wayfinding, 276–279, *278*
interior vertical circulation, 259–260
International Association of Universal Design (Japan), 73
International Classification of Functioning, Disability, and Health (ICF) (WHO), 137, 245
International Code Council (ICC), 192, 227, 230
International Cushion Products (ICP)/Whitespa, 79–81, *80*
International Disability Rights Monitor (2004), 362–363
International Standard (ISO), 279
International Symbol of Accessibility (ISA), 15, *16*
Internet
  product design, 310, 320
  public transportation, 347
interpersonal interaction, 163–167
Interstate Highway System, 239
intimate space, 164–165
iPhone (Apple), 322–323, *323,* 331–332
Irwin, Robert, 214
Iwarsson, Susan, 262–263
IWAY Standard (IKEA), 212

J
J. Paul Getty Museum (Los Angeles), 214, *215*
Jacob Javits Federal Building (New York City), 5
Jacobs, Jane, 34, 35
Japan
  product design and marketability, 316
  public accommodation, 219, *219*
  public transportation, 346
  social participation, 164
  universal design in, 73
JAWS Screen Reading Software, 309
Jette, A. M., 248
JFK International Airport, 351–352
Jitterbug J, 317, *318*
Johnson, Alison, 151

K
Kafka, Franz, 7
Kanbayashi, A., 352
Kansei Engineering, 125–126, 129
keyboarding, 105–106, *106*
Keyhold Garden concept, 146

kitchens
    home modification for, 267, 267–268, 268
    housing policy and, 228
    interior design, 295–297, 297
    Universal Kitchen, 295
kneeling suspension, 349–350
knowledge translation
    demographics, 48
    home modification, 268–269
    innovation, 69–70
    practicing universal design, 89
    product design and assistive technology (AT), 312–316, 313, 315
Kurzweil, Ray, 309, 310

L
Lands Community Services (Australia), 342
"last mile problem," 341
Laszlo, C. A., 280
lavatory sinks, 71
Law, C., 85–86
lawsuits, 193–194
Lawton, M. P., 248–249
Leadership in Energy and Environmental Design (LEED) (Green Building Council), 189–190, 213–214
legibility, color and, 289, 289
Lethal Weapon (films), 7–8
Levine, D., 81
LG ThinQ, 324, 324
LifeHouse™, 234–235, 235
Lifemark Initiative (New Zealand), 233
lifespan
    about, 46
    lifespan housing design, 232–235, 235
    See also aging
lifestyle, demographics and, 54–56, 55
Lifetime Homes (LTH) program, 233
lifting effort, reducing, 107–108
lifts
    home modification, 256–257, 257, 259–260
    public transportation, 350
lighting
    health and wellness, 150
    home modification for, 260
    interior design, 282–287
    interior design and color, 287–292, 288, 289, 291, 292
    light-emitting diode (LED) light, 283–284
    social participation and, 165–166, 166

Lighting Research Institute, 285
Link Transit (Wenatchee, Washington), 342
linoleum, 301
literature, about barriers, 6–7
Livable Housing Design (Australia), 233
London (England), public transportation, 356, 360
Louisiana, public accommodation and building codes, 188
"low-floor" vehicles, 349–350
low-resource settings, health and wellness in, 147–149
Lusher, Ruth Hall, 27
Lynch, Kevin, 276

M
Mace, Ron, 23, 27, 29, 45
marketing, 82–87
Maslow, Abraham, 138, 138–139
Massachusetts Institute of Technology (MIT), 313, 313, 319
mattresses, 297–298, 298
Mautz, R. K., 118
Mayor's Office for People with Disabilities (New York), 81
Medicaid Home and Community Based Waiver Program, 264
Melancholy and Mystery of a Street (de Chirico), 5, 6
mental health
    community-based rehabilitation housing and, 236–238
    design for health and wellness, 149–150
mental maps, 121–122, 128–129
Merrill, T., 118
MESI Science Museum (Tokyo, Japan), 219, 219
methicillin-resistant *Staphylococcus aureus* (MRSA), 147
Metropolitan Transit Authority (New York City), 303
Mizner Park (Boca Raton, Florida), 39, 169, 169–170
mobile phones. *See* telephones
modernist style
    barriers and, 12
    criticism of, 33–34
    modernism *vs.*, 31–33
monorail systems, 352–353
Morris Arboretum (Philadelphia), 214–215, 216
movement, reducing, 105–106, 106
multiple chemical sensitivity (MCS), 151
multisensory information, 116, 118, 118–119
Museum of Modern Art (New York), 76
Musician's Village (New Orleans, Louisiana), 41

N

Nahemow, L., 248–249
National Aeronautics and Space Administration (NASA), 307
National Architectural Accrediting Board, 74
National Association of Home Builders, 76–77
National Association of Minority Architects, 76
National Bureau of Standards, 35
National Dialogue on Universal Design (Australia), 81
National Endowment for the Arts (NEA), 15, 75–76. *See also* IDeA Center
National Football League Combine (2011), 325–326
National Household Travel Survey (2009), 146
National Institute for Mental Health, 35
National Institute for Occupational Safety and Health, 140–141
National Institute of Deafness and Other Communication Disorders, 280
National Institutes of Health, 61
National Organization on Disability/Harris Survey of Community Participation (2004), 341
National Wellness Institute (NWI), 139
natural light, 284–285
neighborhoods, housing and, 238–241, *242*
Neptuna (Malmo, Sweden), 241, *242*
New American Homes, 234
New York City
 public transportation, 303, *303*, 347, 351–352, 354
 on universal design, 81
 See also individual names of museums and buildings
New Zealand
 housing, 233
 streetscape design, *199*
nodes, 128, 276
noise. *See* acoustics
Noorda and Vignelli, 303
normalization theory, 237–238
Norman, D., 86, 125–126
Norway, universal design in, 81

O

obesity
 active transportation, 143–145, *144*
 demographics, 54–56, *55*
 home modification, 247
offices. *See* workplace design
Olmstead Law, 175
organic foods, 145–146

Ostroff, E., 68, 75
OXO Good Grips, 68, 78–79, *79*, 80–81, 83–84, 316, 328, *328*

P

packaging design, 320
Panopticon, 13, *14*
Paralyzed Veterans of America, 15
Paris, Texas (film), 8
parking, public accommodation and, 201–202. *See also* streetscape design; transportation
Pastalan, L. A., 118
pedestrians
 active transportation, 143–145, *144*
 public accommodation, 197–207, *199, 201, 202, 203, 204, 206, 208*
 safety and design, 141–142, *142*
perception
 appropriate stimulation for setting, 119
 clarity for, 117
 defined, 96, 108–111
 Gestalt Laws, 111–117, *112, 113, 114, 115*
 multisensory information for, *118*, 118–119
 reducing noise for, 117–118
 social participation and sensory access, 165
 See also interior design
performance. *See* human factors and ergonomics (HFE)
physical proximity, 167–172, *168, 169, 171*
piano nobile, 10
picnic area (example), 20, *20*
Pittsburgh Children's Museum (Pittsburgh), 215–216, *217*
platform boarding, 351–354, *353, 354*
pollution
 indoor air quality, 151
 reducing, 146
power, barriers and, 13–14
Preiser, W., 68
President's Committee for Employment of the Handicapped, 36, 190, 191
"Principles of Universal Design, The" (Connell, B. R.), 72, 87–88, 89, 149
privacy behavior
 barriers, 10–12
 social participation, 170
product design, 307–338
 assistive technology (AT), 308, 310–312
 assistive technology (AT) and knowledge translation, 312–316, *313, 315*

product design, (*continued*)
  biomechanics for, 104–108
  case studies, 327–334, *328, 330, 333*
  cognition and, 119–129
  demography in, 48
  Gestalt Laws in, *114,* 114–117, *115*
  historical perspective, 307–310, *310*
  human-centered approach, 34–36
  marketability and, 316–321, *317, 318, 319, 321*
  practicing universal design and, 82–87, *84, 87* (*See also* universal design practices)
  product development cycle, 32–33
  "smart" products, 321–327, *323, 324, 325, 327*
  social participation and, 180
protonopia, 291–292
proximity, law of, 112, *112*
psychosocial conditions, limitation and, 51
public accommodation, 187–221
  accessible design history and, 187, 192–195
  accessible design purpose and, 188–190
  business practices, 211–212, *212*
  case studies, 214–220, *215, 216, 217, 218, 219*
  economic factors, 195–197, *196*
  future of, 213–214
  pedestrian safety, 197–207, *199, 201, 202, 203, 204, 206, 208*
  restrooms, 209–210, *210*
  strategies, 197–198
  U.S. legislation, 27–28, 190–192
    (*See also individual names of laws*)
  See also public transportation
Public Broadcasting System, 309
public transportation, 339–367
  access to, 340–342
  background, 339–340
  case study, 360–362, *361*
  component types, 342–343
  elevators, 21, 22
  information for passengers, 344–348, *345*
  onboard restrooms, 357
  progress, worldwide, 362–363
  securement systems, 356–357
  terminals, 343–344
  ticketing and fare payment, 357–360, *359*
  vehicle design, 355–356
  vehicle loading, 348–355, *353, 354, 355*
  See also public accommodation
Pynoos, J., 265

R
race
  demographics and, 59
  education about universal design and, 75–76
  racial segregation, 15
  social participation and human rights, 159 (*See also* social participation)
radiofrequency identification (RFID), 359
Raheja, G., 195
rail systems. *See* public transportation
rambla, 170
ramps
  home modification, *251,* 252, *252,* 253, 253–257, *254, 255, 256*
  public accommodation, 205–207, *206*
  public transportation, 349, 354, 355
Real Life Design (GE Appliances), 82
"Real Life Kitchen" (GE), 76–77
real-time captioning, 348
redundant cueing, 118
Rehabilitation Act of 1973
  Section 503, 190–191
  Section 504, 27, 191, 223
Rehabilitation Engineering Research Center on Technology Transfer, 85
Rehabilitation International, 15
Remote Infrared Audible Signs (RIAS), 345–346
rental housing, modification to, 246
residents, visitors *vs.,* 172
resilient flooring, 301, *302*
Rest Assured Tele-Care System, 325, *325*
restrooms
  anthropometry for, 100–101, *102*
  companion restrooms, 21, 209–210, *210*
  grab bars, 247
  health and wellness, 148
  home modification, 259–260
  housing policy, 225, 228
  public accommodation, 190, 195–197, *196,* 209–210, *210*
  public transportation, 357
  sinks, 71
  social participation, 163
  social participation and privacy, 170
  toilet height, 102, 260
  waterless urinals, 36, 37
retirement, 46–47. *See also* aging
Rhode Island School of Design, 295
rights-of-way, public accommodation and, 197–198
ringlike spatial organization, *171,* 171–172, *173, 174*

Robotics Institute (Carnegie Mellon University), 347–348
Rogers, Everett, 69
roll-in showers, 259–260
Royal Danish Library (Copenhagen, Denmark), 207–208, *208*
rural communities, public transportation in, 340–342
Ryhl, C., 109

S
safety codes, 71
San Francisco, public transportation, 347
sanitation, 148–149
SAR group (Netherlands), 35
saturation, of color, 290
Scandinavia
  anthropometry used in, 101
  home modification policy, 266
  social participation and housing and, 180
  See also individual names of countries
Schindler, Pauline, 12–13
Schindler, Rudolf, 12–13
Schindler house, *12*, 12–13
Schon, D. A., 89
seasonal affective disorders (SAD), 285
seating, 294, *295*
segregation, 172–176, *173*, *174*
Segway, 326–327, *327*
self, symbolic interactionism (SI) theory and, 161
senses. *See* acoustics; perception; vision
sensorineural (SNHL) hearing loss, 279–281
Serra, Richard, 4–5, *5*
set-aside housing approach, 223–227, *225*
showers, roll-in, 259–260
signage, 118, *118*, 277–278, *278*, 303, 344–345
signal detection task (SDT), 110–111
similarity, law of, 111, *112*
single-family housing, visitability and, 229–232, *232*. *See also* housing
sinks, 71
situational awareness
  cognition and, 124
  health and wellness, 150
  perception and, 109
"Six Dimensions of Wellness" (Hettler), 139
slip resistance, 142
slope, calculating for ramps, 252, *252*
"smart" cards, 358–359
"smart" phones, 347, 359

"smart" product design, 321–327, 322–324, *323*, *324*, *325*, *327*
S.M.A.R.T.™ (Safe, Mixed-Income, Accessible, Reasonably-priced, Transit-oriented), 231, *232*
Smith, Eleanor, 230
Smithsonian Institution (Washington, D.C.), 203, *203*
Snow Falling on Cedars (Guterson), 6–7
social construction theory, 160–163, 188
social groups
  adaptation by, 1–3
  social function of space, 8–12, *9*
  sociospatial order, *12*, 12–14, *14*
  See also barriers
social housing programs, 223–227, *225*
social justice
  barriers to, 17
  universal design and, 40–41, *41*
social media
  networking Web sites as barriers, 10
  product design, 319
  social participation, 166–167
social participation, 159–186
  access to resources, 167–172, *168*, *169*, *171*
  architecture of, 21
  design participation, 177–181, *178*, *179*
  home modification and, 250
  housing policy and, 226
  human rights and, 159–160
  interpersonal interaction, 163–167
  segregation and clustering, 172–176, *173*, *174*
  social construction theory, 160–163, 188
social responsibility, human-centered design and, 34–36
social valuation, 237
sociopetal/sociofugal furniture arrangement, 165
sociospatial order, *12*, 12–14, *14*
"Soft Bathtub" (International Cushion Products/Whitespa), 79–81, *80*
space
  barriers and social function of space, 8–12, *9*
  social participation and interpersonal distance, 164–165
  social participation and spatial proximity, 167–172, *168*, *169*, *171*
  social participation and spatial syntax, *171*, 171–172, *173*, *174*
  space planning and public accommodation, 205
  spatial organization and barriers, 10
special-purpose housing, 236–238

spoiled identity, 11–12, 17
stairways
   alternatives to, and home modification, 256–257, *257,* 259–260
   human factors and ergonomics (HFE), 130–132, *131*
   public accommodation, 204, *204,* 205–207, *206*
   safety and design, 140–141
staph infections, 147
Starbucks, 9
Steinfeld, E., 29, 50, *50,* 72, 97, 189
stigma, 11–12, 17
stimuli. *See* perception
storage systems, 295–297, *297*
street-level transit, 349–350
street networks, 128
streetscape design
   health and wellness, 141–142, *142*
   public accommodation, 197–207, *199, 201, 202, 203, 204, 206*
   social participation, *169,* 169–170
substance abuse, limitation and, 52
Suburban Cohousing Community (Atlanta, Georgia), *179*
subway station (Copenhagen, Denmark), 21, *22*
Sullivan, Louis, 31
sustainability, 36, *37*
Sweden
   adaptable housing, 227
   home modification policy, 266
   housing and neighborhood context, 241, *242*
   marketplace example, *9*
Sydney Harbor (Australia), 114, *115*
symbolic interactionism (SI) theory, 160–163
symmetry, law of, 113, *113*

T

tablet computers, 323–324, *324*
"talking kiosks," 344, *344*
"Talking Signs," 345–346
TAMU Water Project, 152
Target Corporation, 320, 321
target value, 110, 114, 117
Tauke, B., 29, 81
taxis, 356
technology
   adaptation, 1–3
   assistive technology (AT), 308, 310–316, *313, 315*
   computers, 319–320, 323–324, *324*
   home automation, 260–261, 324, *324*
   information systems in public transportation, 344–348, *345*
   information technology, 318–319
   modernist style and, 31–33
   social participation and, 170–171, 180
   using conceptual models for, 127
   See also home modification; product design; public transportation; telephones
Technology Assistance for Individuals Act of 1988 (TECH Act of 1988), 309
tele-care services, *325,* 325–326
Telecommunications Act of 1996, 309
telephones
   mobile phones, product design, 316–317, *318,* 322–324, *323*
   mobile phones as barriers, 8
   mobile phones for public transportation, 331–332
   public, 71–72
   "smart" phones, 347
   video phones, 319, *319*
telescoping lifts, 350
Templer, J., 140
terminals, public transportation, 343–344
territorial behavior
   as barrier, 8–12, *9*
   social participation and, 168–169
Theory of the Leisure Class (Veblen), 31
Third Age Suit, 313
ticketing, public transportation, 357–360, *359*
tile flooring, 301
Tilted Arc (Serra), 4–5, *5*
Tiramisu (Robotics Institute, Carnegie Mellon University), 347–348
toilet height, 102, 260
toll roads, as barriers, 8
touch, perception of, 109, 116, 119
Touch Graphics, 332–334, *333*
touch interfaces, 317–318
touch screens, 127, 322–324, *323, 324*
Traditional Neighborhood Development (TND), 239–240
transportation
   active, 143–145, *144*
   demographics and, 46–47, 59–60
   health and wellness, reducing pollution, 146
   housing and neighborhood context, 239
   Interstate Highway System, 239
   street networks, 128

toll roads as barriers, 8
  See also automobiles; public transportation
treelike spatial organization, *171,* 171–172, *173, 174,* 343–344
Trenton (New Jersey), obesity rates in, 55
truck drivers, 98
turnstiles, *359,* 359–360
two-dimensional art, barriers and, 5
Type A/Type B housing units, 230

U
Under Armour, 325–326
Uniform Federal Accessibility Standards, 191
unisex accessible restrooms, 21, 209–210, *210*
United Kingdom
  building code, 72
  housing policy, 230, 233
  inclusive design, 23, 29
United Nations
  Convention on the Rights of People with Disabilities, 159–160, 167
  Conventions on Human Rights, 159–160
  Food and Agriculture Organization, 145
universal design, 27–44
  accessible design *vs.,* 23, 68, *69*
  barriers as universal experience, 3–4
  defined, 28–30, 68
  demography for, 45–48, *47* (*See also* demographics)
  goals of, 189 (*See also* public accommodation)
  health and wellness as universal benefit of, 137 (*See also* health and wellness)
  human-centered design, 34–36
  modernism and modernist style, 31–34
  origins of, 15–24, *16, 17, 18, 19, 20, 22, 23,* 27–28, 30–31
  related fields, 36–42, *37, 38, 39, 40, 41*
  target populations for, 56–57, *57*
  through home improvement, 250–253, *251, 252, 253* (*See also* home modification)
  "universal," 30, 56
  "universal designing," 29
  See also housing; human factors and ergonomics (HFE); interior design; product design; public transportation; transportation; universal design practices
Universal Design Education Project (UDEP), 75
Universal Design Handbook (Preiser, Ostroff), 68
Universal Design Identity Program (UD-id), 86–87, *87*
Universal Design New York (Danford, Tauke), 81

Universal Design New York 2 (Levine), 81
universal design practices, 67–93
  adoption, 70–72
  adoption and communicability, 70, 72, 73–78, *74, 77,* 87–90
  adoption and decision-making strategy, 70, 78–82, *79, 80*
  Goals of Universal Design, 90, *90*
  identifying best practices, 85–86
  improving communicability of universal design, 87–90, *90*
  introducing universal design, 82–87, *83, 84, 87*
  universal design as innovation, 67–70, *69*
Universal Kitchen, 295
universal remotes, 317
University at Buffalo, State University of New York, 75, *77*
"Unlimited by Design" (exhibition), 76, *77*
urban design
  cognition and, 121
  demographics and, 59–60
  urban cohousing (Boston, Massachusetts), *179*
  "urban renewal," 32
  See also housing; public transportation; transportation
Urbanização de Curitiba (URBS), 361, *362*
urinals, waterless, 36, *37*
U.S. Architectural Barriers Act (ABA), 223
U.S. Census Bureau, 61, 277
U.S. Department of Defense, 35
U.S. Department of Health, Education, and Welfare, 309
U.S. Department of Housing and Urban Development, 191, 264
U.S. Department of Veterans Affairs, 223, 264
U.S. Holocaust Memorial Museum (Washington, DC), 18–20, *19,* 194
usability
  barriers to, 3
  practicing universal design and, 80
  product design and, 314
Utterback, J. M., 70

V
value, of color, 290
Veblen, Thorstein, 31
vehicle miles traveled, 146
vehicles. *See* public transportation; transportation
Velcro, 308
Verbrugge, L. M., 248

vernacular design, 30–31
video phones, 319, *319*
Villages, The (Florida), 181
Ville Radieuse (Pessac, France), 32, 34
vinyl composite tiles (VCT), 301
virtual environments, 97, 166–167
vision
    interior design and lighting, 282–287
    interior design and wayfinding, 277–278, *278*
    perception of, 119
    product design for, 308, 309, 320
    social participation and, 165–166
visitability, 229–232, *232*
visitors, residents *vs.*, 172
Vitruvius, 30
voluntary clustering, 175
voting machines, 318–319

W

walking
    active transportation, 143–145, *144*
    demographics and, 56–57, 59–60
    housing and neighborhood context, 239–240
walk-up housing, 228–229, *229*
Washington (DC) Metropolitan Transit Agency (WMTA), 347, 352, *353*
water fountains, 100
waterless urinals, 36, *37*
water-related diseases, 151–152
water sanitation, 148–149, 151–152
wayfinding
    human factors and ergonomics (HFE), 118, *118*
    public transportation, 344–346
    universal design, 276–279, *278*, 303, *303*, 304
wellness, defined, 139. *See also* health and wellness
Wenatchee (Washington), public transportation, 342
wheelchairs
    product design, 314, *315*
    public transportation and, 356–357
    space for maneuvering, 97 (*See also* human factors and ergonomics (HFE))
    See also home modification; public transportation
Williamsville (New York), housing in, *225, 229*
Wolfensberger, W., 237, 238
Wonder, Stevie, 309, *310*
wood flooring, 300–301
workplace design
    acoustics, 281
    biomechanics for, 104–108
    demographics and, 59
World Health Organization (WHO), 58, 137, 245, 277
Wright, Frank Lloyd, *23*, 23–24
Wylde, M. A., 86

Y

"you-are-here" maps, 344